DISCARD

Managerial Decision Making

History of Management Thought

Series Editor:
Derek S. Pugh

Titles in the Series:

Contingency Theory
Lex Donaldson

Management Science
Samuel Eilon

Complex Organizations
Richard H. Hall

Managerial Decision Making
David J. Hickson

Administrative and Management Theory
John B. Miner

Human Relations
Lyman W. Porter & Gregory A. Bigley

Post-Modern Management Theory
Linda Smircich & Marta Calás

Managerial Decision Making

Edited by

David J. Hickson

Research Professor of International Management and Organization
Bradford Management Centre

Dartmouth
Aldershot • Brookfield USA • Singapore • Sydney

Published by
Dartmouth Publishing Company Limited
Gower House
Croft Road
Aldershot
Hants GU11 3HR
England

Dartmouth Publishing Company
Old Post Road
Brookfield
Vermont 05036
USA

British Library Cataloguing in Publication Data
Managerial Decision Making. - (History of
Management Thought Series)
  I. Hickson, David J. II. Series
  658.403

Library of Congress Cataloging-in-Publication Data
Managerial decision making / edited by David J. Hickson.
        p. cm.— (History of management thought)
    Includes bibliographical references.
    ISBN 1-85521-415-6 : $129.95 (est.)
    1. Decision-making. I. Hickson, David John. II. Series: History
of management thought (Aldershot, England)
HD30.23.M363 1994
658. 4'03—dc20
                                  94–5606
                                  CIP

Printed in Great Britain at the University Press, Cambridge

ISBN 1 85521 415 6

Contents

Acknowledgements

The editor and publishers wish to thank the following for permission to use copyright material.

Academy of Management for the essay: Barry M. Staw (1981), 'The Escalation of Commitment to a Course of Action', *Academy of Management Review*, **6,** pp. 577–87.

Administrative Science Quarterly for the essays: Henry Mintzberg, Duru Raisinghani and André Théorêt (1976), 'The Structure of "Unstructured" Decision Processes', *Administrative Science Quarterly*, **21,** pp. 246–75; Michael D. Cohen, James G. March and Johan P. Olsen (1972), 'A Garbage Can Model of Organizational Choice', *Administrative Science Quarterly*, **17,** pp. 1–25; Paul C. Nutt (1984), 'Types of Organizational Decision Processes', *Administrative Science Quarterly*, **29,** pp. 414–50; Paul A. Anderson (1983), 'Decision Making by Objection and the Cuban Missile Crisis', *Administrative Science Quarterly*, **28,** pp. 201–22; D.J. Hickson, C.R. Hinings, C.A. Lee, R.E. Schneck and J.M. Pennings (1971), 'A Strategic Contingencies' Theory of Intraorganizational Power', *Administrative Science Quarterly*, **16,** pp. 216–29.

American Political Science Association for the essays: Peter Bachrach and Morton S. Baratz (1962), 'Two Faces of Power', *The American Political Science Review*, **56,** pp. 947–52; Graham T. Allison (1969), 'Conceptual Models and the Cuban Missile Crisis', *The American Political Science Review*, **63,** pp. 689–718.

Blackwell Publishers for the essays: Charles E. Lindblom (1959), 'The Science of "Muddling Through"', *Public Administration Review*, **XIX,** pp. 79–88; David J. Hickson, Richard J. Butler, David Cray, Geoffrey R. Mallory and David C. Wilson (1989), 'Decision and Organization – Processes of Strategic Decision Making and their Explanation', *Public Administration*, **67,** pp. 373–90; Geoffrey R. Mallory, Richard J. Butler, David Cray, David J. Hickson and David C. Wilson (1983), 'Implanted Decision-Making; American Owned Firms in Britain', *Journal of Management Studies*, **20,** pp. 191–211.

Stewart R. Clegg (1989), 'Radical Revisions: Power, Discipline and Organizations', *Organization Studies*, **10,** pp. 97–115. Copyright © S.R. Clegg.

James G. March (1971), 'The Technology of Foolishness', *Civiløkonomen*, **18.** Reprinted in J. G. March (1988), *Decisions and Organizations*, pp. 253–65. Copyright © J. G. March.

H. Mintzberg, J. Waters, A.M. Pettigrew and R. Butler (1990), 'Studying Deciding: An Exchange of Views Between Mintzberg and Waters, Pettigrew, and Butler', *Organization Studies*, **11,** pp. 1–16. Copyright © H. Mintzberg, J.A. Waters, A.M. Pettigrew and R.J. Butler.

Series Preface

The *History of Management Thought* is based on the assumption that a knowledge of the intellectual history of an academic field is vital for a present day understanding of it. In the past scholars of management as a discipline have tended to ignore or underrate the historical development of their subject. This ignorance has encouraged the 'reinventing the wheel' and 'old wine in new bottles' phenomena which have plagued the subject of management since its birth. The insight that those who ignore history are condemned to repeat it, is surely most true about the development of ideas.

This indifference now appears to be beginning to change, and the history of management and management thought is attracting greater interest. The *History of Management Thought* builds on this development by presenting a number of volumes which cover the intellectual history of the subject. It makes available to a wide range of academics contributions to management thought that have been influential over the years. The volume topics range across the whole field of management studies from early management thought through to post-modern management theory.

Each volume in the *History of Management Thought* is edited by a leading international scholar who gives an introductory analytical historical review of the development of the subject, and then presents a selection of key articles. Many of these articles have previously only been published in journals, often in early volumes which are not generally available. They are now conveniently presented in book form, with each chosen article reproduced in full. They offer an important resource for use by academics and advanced students in the field for increasing their knowledge and understanding of the historical development of the disciplines of management.

DEREK S. PUGH
General Editor
History of Management Thought
Open University Business School, UK

Introduction

Organizations are 'indeterminate and faced with uncertainty' (Thompson 1967). Which is another way of saying that no-one knows what tomorrow may bring. Not even managers. Organizations are changing all the time, and the environments in which they function are changing all the time. New proposals, or new objections to proposals, may arise within the organization. Equipment may break down. There may even be fires or explosions. From without may come takeover bids, innovations by rivals, price wars, changes in government regulations or subsidies, political upheavals. The examples are infinite.

In this milieu, decisions have to be made about what should be done. Should large sums be invested in new equipment? Should a takeover bid be welcomed or resisted? Should marketing efforts be switched to Eastern Europe? Should new premises be built? Should departments be reorganized?

This level of decision is not routine. Even though there may be similar precedents to compare with and some experience to draw on, the circumstances this time are not the same as last time. Quite often, nothing remotely like it has ever happened before. Probably there will have to be reports or appraisals by different departments, such as (in industry) sales or finance or research and development, giving estimates or comments from their points of view. There may be talks with banks or customers or with corporate headquarters (if the organization is a subsidiary in a larger group). There will usually be much discussion around office desks, in committees and task groups, in the boardroom. Eventually a formal decision is reached. The board, or equivalent body that is empowered to make decisions of this kind and magnitude, approves action (or, sometimes, inaction) one way or the other. It authorizes implementation.

These, then, are the major decisions for which there are no rules. There may be rules as to how to make cost estimates or how to conduct meetings leading up to such a decision, but not for the decision making itself. It is what has been called 'nonprogrammed' (Simon 1960), 'unstructured' (Mintzberg et al. 1976) and 'strategic' (Hickson et al. 1986). Essentially it rests with a very few senior executives at the top, in a small organization perhaps only three or four, perhaps a dozen or so in a larger organization, but never very many. These are the oligarchy in whose hands is the power to shape the future course of the organization, insofar as they can do that given the uncertainties with which they have to deal, and the limits to their power set by the power of others such as departmental interests, owners, suppliers, customers, governments, and so on.

This level of decision is the very essence of management. It occurs in all forms of organizations: in private firms, in large public companies with shares on the stock exchange, in local government, in hospitals, in universities, in whatever the organization may be. Each form of organization has its particular characteristics in terms of managerial decision making, though management in each is likely to go about a decision on the same kind of matter in a similar manner (Hickson et al. 1986).

Two contrasting examples from a medium-sized industrial firm in Britain may help to illustrate the sort of thing that happens. These are taken from research by Hickson et al. 1986 and Miller, Wilson and Hickson 1993.

The New Marketing Function

Jacobite Manufacturers Ltd had long held a premier position in supplying a particular kind of precision metal component to a few big industrial buyers who assembled them into mass market products with household names. Being producer-goods manufacturers for a comparatively small number of customer companies, they knew their customers' needs well. A small sales office kept them continually in touch.

Jacobite were owned by an American group, which usually left them very much to their own devices. However, market trends in the United States caused the American corporation to set up a central Marketing Division. This found that there was no exactly equivalent activity at this British subsidiary, and so no-one to provide them with the market analyses that they were requiring from all subsidiaries. In their eyes, the nod and wink, word in your ear, close personal touch – by which Jacobite had a feel for what was happening – was insufficient. A more professional approach was needed to open up new markets. So they pressed Jacobite's management to appoint a Marketing Manager and establish a Marketing Department.

Jacobite's Chairman and Managing Director talked the matter over with his experienced Sales Director. They let the Works Director and Financial Director and other senior managers know what was afoot, but essentially the ultimate decision lay with just the two of them. It was chancy, incalculable, a bigger risk than it appeared at first sight. For if it went wrong and, far from expanding sales opportunities, weakened links with existing customers, that would be serious. In a firm which was successfully selling by well-tried methods in a well-known market, it risked disturbing existing tried and tested practices on which the whole future of the firm depended. Internally it could be divisive, alienating the existing sales staff whose commitment was vital. They were naturally resisting the whole idea, seeing it as setting up a rival to themselves that was quite unnecessary. Externally, inexperienced new marketing people using untried methods could in unforeseeable ways cut across vital relationships with customers and damage goodwill.

On balance, the MD and Sales Director decided to give it a try. The process was a quick one. It took only a few months to decide and to set up the rudiments of a new department and appoint a Marketing Manager. When he then embarked on market research and the possibility of fresh product designs, he actually did so in a sensitive way that won the cooperation of everyone concerned.

Then the American owners created a European regional headquarters in London, and he moved to it. However, when this new central management did not succeed, he declined to return to Jacobite itself. So their decision to yield to pressure to experiment in marketing, which had caused doubts, suspicions and costs in time and distraction, now lapsed. No successor was appointed by Jacobite, where selling continued as if nothing at all had happened.

The New Factory Buildings

Sales were rising. Jacobite's floor space was not enough to take the extra machinery required to meet the anticipated output volume. Top management considered different ways of utilizing existing space, such as extending buildings, even renting additional premises. A variety of costings and designs were looked at. Many more interests were involved than in the marketing decision just discussed. Banks were consulted about their terms for increased loans. Major customers were asked about their likely future orders. Equipment suppliers indicated what they could provide. There was a lot of discussion extending over several months between the senior people in production, planning, engineering, sales and finance, both day by day and in arranged meetings, led by the strong personality of the Chairman and MD who was deeply involved. A decision was taken to build new factory premises on an adjacent site.

Relative to the size of the company, this was a big commitment, incurring substantial indebtedness to pay for it, far bigger financially than the marketing decision. Formally it required the approval of the American owners, but as they did not have to provide the capital because it could be borrowed from banks, they readily rubber-stamped the decision after a presentation to their board by Jacobite's Chairman. Unlike the dissension over the marketing question, this time everyone at Jacobite itself was firmly in favour, for this meant further expansion and sustained a feeling of confidence in the future.

A decade later, economic recession forced drastic cost cutting. The bulk of the older premises were sold and all manufacturing was moved into the new buildings. In this respect, the decision had been a good one, for the new buildings could accommodate new equipment and new methods of work. On the other hand, perhaps new buildings and financial indebtedness had been unnecessary just to cope with a comparatively brief need for greater space. In retrospect, the old buildings might have sufficed after all.

These two examples show how different decision making can be on different matters, even in the same firm under the same ownership with the same managers. In the decision about marketing, the risks had to be weighed intuitively from experience, weighing as well the even more incalculable costs of going against the wishes of the owner firm to which Jacobite was a subsidiary. There was no half-way stage. The decision had to be yes or no – a new marketing function alongside the existing sales department or no such function. Once decided, implementation was straightforward. The company Chairman and the Sales Director carried the matter through between them.

Deciding on new buildings was an altogether more complex process. Although it was internally initiated, with no pressure from outside, every department had to be actively involved in forecasting future sales, estimating the capacity of machinery and personnel, and calculating costs. Information also had to be obtained externally. Not only was the process of deciding much more involved, but the decision itself was more complex. It was a matter of degree, of how much. Just how much space in what form would be best? How big a financial commitment should be made? Once this had been decided, implementation then required months of careful planning, so that the new premises would be built as intended and so machinery and people could be moved in with minimum loss of production time. Fortunately, general unanimity over the decision helped everything to go smoothly.

This book brings together the main ideas on how such decision making can be understood.

Reading the Readings

The readings are about decisions at this top level, not about lesser decisions lower down the hierarchies of organizations. Nor do they include the psychology of what takes place in the minds of decision makers. Specifically, they describe and theorize about the managerial process of making and implementing a decision, and the power that is therein exerted.

The chosen readings are specifically of work which has been published in learned journals. For a full appreciation of the study of decision making at the top, they should be read in conjunction with what has been published in books, inasmuch as some prominent thinkers have presented their most compelling ideas only in books, as is indicated below.

A Brief History of Research

The past can never be experienced again. That would require the re-running of some unimaginably comprehensive celestial video. Thus any look back at how research on managerial decision making has developed must be an extreme simplification and also a subjective one. Nonetheless, a backward glance may be helpful.

There is a sense in which the study of decision making began as soon as organization theory, or the sociology of organizations, began. Many would trace that to the German lawyer and sociologist Weber (see book dated 1947, or summary in Pugh and Hickson 1989 or 1993) who analysed how it is that people in organizations obey the decisions of others, accepting superior authority as legitimate. This authority to decide is wielded by top management, usually even more than by those who own an organization, if the managers are not also the owners (e.g. see the book by Burnham 1941, or the summary in Pugh and Hickson 1993).

The 1960s and just before saw the first research focused specifically on decision making. It produced a series of penetrating ideas about decisions themselves. It was argued that what could be decided was circumscribed by implicit givens, *'non decisions'*, which could be more important than the permissible decisions (Bachrach and Baratz 1962). Decisions taken overtly were more likely to be *'satisficing'* than optimum (see books by Simon 1945, 1960, or the summary in Pugh and Hickson 1989 or 1993), and to be merely *'incremental'* in a step-by-step process (Lindblom 1959). They could be 'computational', 'compromise', 'judgmental' or 'inspirational' in character (see book by Thompson 1967, or summary in Pugh and Hickson 1989 or 1993).

Then in the 1970s and 1980s attention turned to the *processes* of decision making. These were found to be *circuitous and repetitive* (Mintzberg *et al.* 1976). They could follow different patterns of movement through time, *'sporadic, fluid or constricted'* (Hickson *et al.* 1989, or see book 1986), progressing by 'logical incrementalism' (Quinn 1980). They might even correspond to a *'garbage can model'* of decision making (Cohen *et al.* 1972). Yet the managerial elite could mutually blinker one another from seeing alternative possibilities by 'groupthink' (see book by Janis 1982).

Throughout, there has been continual interest in the power that both circumscribes and is exercised within these processes. An organization can be regarded as a set of overlapping power plays, or an *'ensembles des jeux'* (see, for example, the book by Crozier and Friedberg 1980). Who holds the most influence in these power games depends on who best copes with *uncertainties* for the organization and who is most centrally and independently placed

(Hickson *et al.* 1971). Beneath these '*bureaucratic politics*' (Allison 1969) lie *hidden layers* of covert issues and interests which govern all that happens (see book by Lukes 1974).

Processes, Decisions and Power

The readings in this book are not arranged in the historical order just described, nor can they encompass all the authors mentioned. They are arranged according to whether they focus on the process of deciding (Part I), on the decision that is reached through that process (Part II), on the implementation of the decision (Part III), or on the power that is exerted (Part IV).

The readings are not so clear-cut as may be suggested by such an arrangement. Many of them deal with two or even with all of these aspects of decision making. They are arranged by what seems to be their main emphasis, in the hope that this is of some help to the reader and better than an undifferentiated list.

Part I: The Process

The first eight readings contribute to a view of how major decisions are made. In Chapter 1, Dutton discusses where they come from in the first place. How do issues arise and become matters for decision? She argues that what comes up depends on what is salient enough to attract attention, and on who 'sponsors' it. The issues that are current at any one time form the 'strategic agenda' for managerial decision makers.

Matters on such an agenda rarely race along to a decisive conclusion. So says Lindblom in Chapter 2 from the perspective of a political scientist long used to the processes of public administration, American government administration that is. He does not see decisions as bold strokes. There are too many possibilities and too many interests involved. Rather, decision makers proceed by '*successive limited comparisons*'. In other words, they compare this possibility against that, weigh this interest against that, a few at a time, inching forward from one comparison to the next. This '*strategy of disjointed incrementalism*' moves things along when otherwise the inherent complexities might seem too immense for any decisions to be made at all. To this extent 'the science of muddling through', as Lindblom calls it, is a practicable way of reaching decisions and may even be a desirable one.

Lindblom makes no clear distinction between the process of making a decision and the decision itself. Indeed, in reality they are not sharply separated: the one emerges within the other. To Lindblom, incremental decisions ensue from incremental processes.

There is very little evidence as to how far the incrementalism which Lindblom describes also occurs in other forms of organizations, especially private industry and commerce. Intuitively it must to some extent. In the third chapter, another very early classic in this field, Cyert, Simon and Trow tell the story of a 'business decision' which does seem to have proceeded little by little. The unanswered empirical question is 'how little or how big is an increment?' How swift and how great must a decision be for it *not* to be incremental?

Cyert *et al.* use the distinction made by Simon (referenced earlier) between *programmed* and *nonprogrammed* decisions to show that this process had elements of both.

Decision-making processes do not run a straight course. In 25 examples examined by Mintzberg *et al.* in Chapter 4, no less than seven kinds of processes, all twisting and turning, are discerned. These are simple impasse, political design, basic search, modified search, basic design, blocked design, and dynamic design processes. Whichever sort it was, decision making coiled back upon itself, *cycling and recycling*, and encountered all manner of interruptions. That is, the matter was discussed, information reassessed and alternatives reconsidered, over and over again.

A simpler classification into three patterns of process comes from Hickson *et al.* in Chapter 5. In the most extensive study to date, of 150 decisions (five each in 30 diverse organizations), the authors identified what they call *sporadic, or fluid, or constricted patterns of movement* towards a decision, as mentioned earlier. Sporadic processes are the most active and erratic; fluid processes smoother; constricted processes held within bounds. Which pattern occurs depends more on the characteristics of what is being decided than on the kind of organization in which it is being considered. Matters for decision which are to a similar extent complex and political in character are likely to proceed through a similar pattern of process even in different organizations. As Hickson *et al.* put it, '*the matter for decision matters most*'.

The breadth of coverage of this research exposes some particular features of decision-making processes which are encompassed within the three overall patterns. Strategic decisions are typically found to take between six and twelve months, though they can take up to four years. They are impeded and delayed, as Mintzberg *et al.* found, especially in the sporadic pattern. The number of main interests involved – from internal departments or divisions to external suppliers, customers, government agencies, etc. – ranges from a handful to 20 or more. These include both 'heavyweights' (notably production, sales and finance) which are both influential and often involved, and 'lightweights' (e.g. government departments and trades unions) which are less influential and less frequently involved (see the book by Hickson *et al.* 1986).

However, typifying entire processes as sporadic, fluid or constricted inherently obscures awareness of fluctuating phases within any one process. This had been shown some years earlier by Wilson who in Chapter 6 describes one of the decisions from the same research which, in effect, moved from a fluid phase into a conflict-riddent sporadic phase. Any one process may thus move through different sub-processes within its overall predominant pattern.

How far managers are in control of the processes in which they are engaged is challenged by the renowned '*garbage can model of organizational choice*' put forward by Cohen, March and Olsen (Chapter 7). According to this imaginative way of envisaging what transpires, streams of problems, solutions and participants pour into a potential decision-making situation – the organizational garbage can. What may happen is explicable less by logical causal sequence, where one thing leads to another (as is conventionally assumed), than by '*temporal order*'. In other words, when compatible problems, solutions and participants coincide (i.e. come together in time), then a decision can occur, almost by chance. The usual assumptions about what comes before what in the process are best forgotten. For solutions can come before problems, in the sense that participants can know what they want before a chance to achieve it drops into the can; and whether a decision occurs depends less on whether enough information has been gathered and more on who has time to attend to it.

The garbage can model may apply most aptly in '*organized anarchies*' such as public sector and (especially) educational organizations, where aims and what to do about them are least clear. But it could apply to decision making in any part of any organization part of the time.

In 'Studying Deciding', the final reading in Part I, Mintzberg and Waters, Pettigrew and Butler debate whether the very concept of a 'decision' is too definite, obstructing understanding of what are blurred and evolving processes.

Part II The Decision

The readings so far have dealt with overt decision making – recognizable situations where managers see themselves as endeavouring to make an identifiable decision. In an influential paper, 'The Two Faces of Power', Bachrach and Baratz (Chaper 9) contend that there is an unseen face which is just as important, if not more so. Beneath the decision making that takes place on the surface is *'nondecision making'*. This is the realm where entrenched power can prevent issues ever arising, ever getting on to what Dutton in Chapter 1 calls the 'strategic agenda'. No decision-making process, no decision. Just an unobserved nondecision.

This insight is reinforced by Hickson *et al.'s* (1986) finding that even in the overt processes studied by them, up to half were *'quasi–decision making'*. These were foregone conclusions, 'the making of a decision which some know has already all but been made'.

Most research has perforce to study what can be followed 'on the surface', so to speak; thus the three subsequent readings in Part II examine the manifest face of decisions.

Nutt (Chapter 10) classifies 73 decision-making processes in American health and health-related service organizations by the kind of solution being sought. Most are either *'historical'* (looking back to what was done elsewhere) or *'off-the-shelf'* (searching for the best ready-made solution). The other main types are *'appraisal'* (trying systematically to evaluate an idea), *'passive search'* (hoping for a fully workable idea but not knowing where to look for it), and *'nova'* (aiming at innovation).

To Anderson (Chapter 11) decisions are those alternatives that are least objectionable. Analysing the public records of American political decisions during the Cuban missile crisis in 1962, when the Soviet Union and the US confronted one another eye to eye (a favourite case for decision analysts), he found *'decision making by objection'*. Possible alternatives were objected to one by one until one remained that was not so much a positive choice but the least objectionable. March then asks in characteristically lively style whether decision makers should not suspend reasoned intelligence from time to time and try being more flexible – even foolish and 'playful' – when handling such difficult problems.

Conspicuous by their absence from Part II are Herbert Simon and James Thompson, whose penetrating ideas were published in books but never in journal pages and so could not be included here. Simon pioneered thinking about decision making with his concepts of 'programmed and nonprogrammed decisions' (1960) and of 'satisficing' (1945), both already mentioned. The first heightened awareness of the great range of nonprogrammed decisions, so generating the field of enquiry that brings this book into existence. The second concept, satisficing, reveals how decision makers do not seek the perfect optimum solution, but one that will do. Up to a point, it is just 'satisfactory' and it will 'suffice' (two words from which Simon coins satisficing). As he says, decision making is not about finding the sharpest needle in a haystack but one just sharp enough to sew with.

Also already mentioned, Thompson (1967) contributes a means of comparing one decision with another – as either computational, a compromise, judgmental or inspirational (summaries of the work of both Simon and Thompson appear in Pugh and Hickson 1989 and 1993).

Part III Implementing the Decision

Taking a decision is only part of the managerial problem. What happens then? How will it be carried out? How can managers ensure that it is implemented?

According to Nutt, managers tend to use one or other of four tactics: *intervention, participation, persuasion* or *edict* (Chapter 13). Again studying the non-business sector (i.e. health service and non-profit organizations in the US and Canada), he finds that managers most often used persuasion. In almost half the cases of planning and implementation that he studied, managers delegated the development of ideas to people with pertinent expertise, who then had to persuade the manager that their proposals were the right ones. This worked quite well, though the intervention tactic worked better. Here a manager was more continuously involved both in creating a need for change in the minds of key people and in demonstrating what had to be done.

How far should managers persist with implementation when it is not going well? If more time, more money and more effort might turn a situation around, should they continue to escalate their commitment rather than take another decision? Staw examines this problem in Chapter 14, getting *'knee-deep in the big muddy'* as he once described it.

Part IV Power in Decision Making

The many interests involved in decision making have been referred to. There are differing viewpoints on and differing stakes in a decision. In a classic analysis reprinted as Chapter 15, Allison looks at the same Cuban missile crisis decision made by the US government that Anderson examined, from three complementary points of view. He considers it in terms of a carefully calculating 'rational policy' model, an information filtering 'organizational process' model, and, most significantly here, a *'bureaucratic politics'* model. This third model portrays decision making as the outcome of bargaining between those in positions of power, a view as pertinent to other organizations as to government. Pettigrew underlines this with his account in Chapter 16 of how the control of information was used to exert influence in reaching a decision in private business in England.

The influence exerted by each of the parties to a decision, and by each of the parties implicated on the way to a decision, stems from their positioning in an organization, or their links with it. For those within management, Hickson *et al.'s* widely cited *'strategic contingencies' theory of intraorganizational power'* (Chapter 17) offers an explanation of their influence (and thereby shows what must be done to obtain it). Primarily, it is crucial to be able to 'cope with uncertainty'. In other words, to be able to do something about the main uncertainty or uncertainties that face an organization, as when a marketing department actively counters market fluctuations by novel selling methods or astute advertising. This enables the others in the organization to work undisturbed on a stable flow of orders. But the ability to cope with uncertainty confers strong influence only if those who cope are also not substitutable (no-one else can do what they do) and are centrally placed in the flows of work around the organization (so that many others depend upon what they do).

Clegg argues in Chapter 18 that this kind of theory takes a certain division of labour as its starting point. It assumes an organization with a set of specialist departments, and with layers of hierarchy in which those higher up have greater power than those lower down. It is therefore explaining a level of influence that is merely consequent upon the real power struggle. The real struggle is over who does what and who controls whom; over what is socially acceptable and meaningful. It is this that determines the basic power structure of an organization, from which the possibility of making and influencing decisions arises.

This pungent comment reinforces what was said earlier – that decision making only surfaces within a space ringed by latent interests and nondecision making (Bachrach and Baratz 1962), and even then it may be no more than quasi-decision making (Hickson *et al.* 1986).

The final reading in Part IV is an example of unseen influence from afar. Decision making in firms in Britain is likely to be faster and more informal if they are American owned, according to Mallory *et al.* (1983). This exposes one of three gaps in research on managerial decision making at the top, gaps where much less has been done.

The first hiatus concerns the origin of decision-making processes. How and why do they begin? In this book, only the opening chapter by Dutton deals directly with this question, which reflects the paucity of research on the front end, so to speak, of decision making. Most research has been on overt decision-making processes once they get under way, as the number of readings in Part I shows. The second gap is at the far end of decision making, the putting into effect of an officially authorized decision. Only two readings about implementation have been included in Part III.

Third, and most importantly, the Mallory *et al.* reading draws attention to the potential significance of societal culture. If, as they infer, a faster-moving more informal culture can (unawares) so markedly influence overseas managers under its aegis to behave likewise, then decision making everywhere must embody culture. Decision making in societies with differing cultures must itself differ.

In a general way this is recognized, of course. Differences in the regard for and use of authority are widely known, and the economic rise of Japan has provoked much Western research on the more consensual and slower Japanese approach, including their 'ringi' method of making decisions. Yet there is hardly any research specifically comparing high-level managerial decision making in different societies. Further, every author included here is from an Anglo culture (American, British or Canadian), with the solitary exception of Johan Olsen in Chapter 7 who is Norwegian. How great is the unknown bias in research so dominated by Anglo Westerners and published in English-language research journals?

References

*Allison, G.T. (1969), 'Conceptual Models and the Cuban Missile Crisis', *American Political Science Review*, **63** (3), 689–718.
*Bachrach, P. and M.S. Baratz (1962), 'The Two Faces of Power', *American Political Science Review*, **56**, 947–52.

Burnham, James (1941), *The Managerial Revolution*, Peter Smith.

*Cohen, M.D., J.G. March and J.P. Olsen (1972), 'A Garbage Can Model of Organizational Choice', *Administrative Science Quarterly*, **17** (1), 1–25.

Crozier, Michel and Erhard Friedberg (1980), *Actors and Systems*, University of Chicago Press.

Hickson, David J., Richard J. Butler, David Cray, Geoffrey R. Mallory and David C. Wilson (1986), *Top Decisions*, Blackwell and Jossey-Bass.

*Hickson, D.J., R.J. Butler, D. Cray, G.R. Mallory and D.C. Wilson (1989), 'Decision and Organization – Processes of Strategic Decision Making and their Explanation', *Public Administration*, **67** (4), Winter, 373–90.

*Hickson, D.J. C. R. Hinings, C.R. Lee, R.E. Schneck and J.M. Pennings (1971), 'A Strategic Contingencies Theory of Intraorganizational Power', *Administrative Science Quarterly*, **16** (2), 216–29.

Janis, Irving (1982), *Groupthink: Psychological Studies of Policy Decisions and Fiascoes*, Houghton Mifflin.

*Lindblom, C. (1959), 'The Science of Muddling Through', *Public Administration Review*, **XIX** (2), 79–88.

Lukes, Stephen (1974), *Power: A Radical View*, Macmillan.

Miller, Susan J., David C. Wilson and David J. Hickson (1993), 'Expansive Gestures: Fancies and Follies in Strategic Decision Making', Paper presented at 11th Colloquium of the European Group for Organizational Studies, Paris.

*Mintzberg, H., D. Raisinghani and A. Theoret (1976), 'The Structure of "Unstructured" Decision Processes', *Administrative Science Quarterly*, **21** (2), 246–75.

Pugh, Derek S. and David J. Hickson (1989), *Writers on Organizations*, Penguin (4th edition).

Pugh, Derek S. and David J. Hickson (1993), *Great Writers on Organizations: The Omnibus Edition*, Dartmouth.

Quinn, J.B. (1980), *Strategies for Change: Logical Incrementalism*, Irwin.

Simon, Herbert A. (1945), *Administrative Behavior*, Free Press (3rd edition 1976).

Simon Herbert A. (1960), *The New Science of Management Decision*, Harper and Row (2nd edition 1977).

Thompson, James D. (1967), *Organizations in Action*, McGraw-Hill.

Weber, Max (1947), *The Theory of Social and Economic Organization*, Free Press.

* Reprinted in this volume

Part I
The Process of Deciding

[1]

Understanding Strategic Agenda Building and Its Implications for Managing Change*

Jane E. Dutton

This article develops a model of strategic agenda building describing the conditions under which strategic issues are likely to receive collective organizational attention. The model depicts how the issue and organizational contexts determine the issues that reach the agenda. Within the issue context, the salience of an issue (i.e., its perceived magnitude, its abstractness, simplicity and immediacy) and the level of issue sponsorship (i.e., issue attachment and strategic location) determine the force behind an issue and the likelihood that it will be placed on the strategic agenda. However, the effect of issue salience and sponsorship on an issue's force is moderated by the size and variety of issues already under consideration (i.e., the agenda structure). The article concludes with consideration of the theoretical and practical implications of this dynamic, process-oriented approach to strategic issue identification and legitimation.

Three questions motivate the model presented in this article: (1) Why in an organization do some strategic issues (i.e., emerging developments, trends or concerns perceived as affecting achievement of the organization's objectives (Ansoff, 1980; King, 1982) receive attention, while others do not? (2) What makes different organizations attend to different strategic issues? (3) What are the implications of the answers to these questions for managing organizational change? Attention to strategic issues is the first step in the interpretive process through which action-initiatives are launched (Daft & Weick, 1984; Keisler & Sproull, 1983). Thus by understanding how issues gain attention in organizations new insights emerge about organizational change.

The process of attention allocation to strategic issues is conceptualized as an agenda building process. By understanding this process and its likely outcomes, individuals can manage it to their advantage. For example, facilitating or constraining issues from reaching an organization's agenda is a powerful tactic for initiating or preventing certain change initiatives. Thus, by understanding agenda building one can manage the ambiguity of problem setting in organizations (Metcalfe, 1981).

Agenda building refers to the process through which strategic issues gain decision makers' attention and are legitimated in the organization. Through a series of agenda building episodes, a *strategic agenda* is built. The strategic agenda or issue portfolio (Huff & Pondy, 1983) refers to the

* The author thanks Susan J. Ashford, Arthur Briel, Roger Dunbar, John Dutton, Jan Katz, Lance Sandelands, Jerry Waldron, Jim Walsh, Eric Walton and three anonymous reviewers for comments on earlier drafts of this article.

JANE E. DUTTON

set of strategic issues receiving collective attention in the organization. Collective attention is defined as the allocation of information processing capacity and resources to an issue (Simon, 1971). Evidence that allocation has occurred include: the naming of the issue, a commitment of managerial time, collection of information about the issue, etc. An agenda issue is collective in the sense that individuals are able to converse about the issue, i.e., there is some consensus about its existence.

This article present a model of agenda building based on the conditions influencing attention allocation to strategic issues. The term agenda building is used instead of agenda setting to highlight that the agenda is not dictated by top level decision makers. Instead, the agenda is the product of forces at multiple levels of the organization that consciously or sub-consciously work to make an issue consensual, legitimate and resource consuming. In this way the agenda building process is consistent with models of strategic change emphasizing its multi-level character (Bower, 1972; Burgelman, 1983).

Strategic issues are ambiguous, complex and potentially important (Dutton, Fahey & Narayanan, 1983) distinguishing them, in a relative sense, from more specific, less consequential, operational issues. The issues are strategic in the sense of being perceived by decision makers as potentially related, in some way to organizational goals and resource allocations necessary to achieve these goals (Chandler, 1982). So, for example, concerns such as "what should be done about political developments in South Africa?" are strategic issues for organizations that are currently doing or considering business in this region.

Although the agenda building model can be readily adapted to describe functional and business level agendas, the focus in this article is on the corporate level. The model is consistent with a strategic choice view of organizations depicting top level decision makers as consequential in determining organizational action (Child, 1972). This perspective supports recent arguments that a relatively small number of persons at top levels of organizations play a major role in interpretation processes and organizational action (Daft & Weick, 1984; Hambrick & Mason, 1984).

Agenda Building and the Allocation of Attention

The agenda building view builds on insights from theoretical treatments of attention allocation to issues generated from a diverse set of literatures. For example, economists have argued that attention, in the form of allocation of information processing capacity and resources to an issue (March &

Olsen, 1976; Simon, 1971), is determined by the costliness of the issue (Radner, 1975; Radner & Rothschild, 1975; Winter, 1981). However, this literature is limited as the most extensive research has been done on optimizing decisions once attention has been allocated.

In contrast, psychologists have adopted a view of attention allocation which considers characteristics of the perceiver (e.g., their schema in memory: Taylor & Crocker, 1980) and characteristics of the stimulus (e.g., an issue's vividness) in determining individual attention allocation. In the words of one psychologist, the allocation of attention is seen as a joint product of both theory-driven (i.e. perceiver) and data-driven forces (i.e. perceived, Norman, 1976).

Decision making theorists have also considered attention allocation to issues, although typically this phase of the decision process has been ignored (Mintzberg, Raisinghini & Theoret, 1976). While recent work has explored issue formulation and diagnosis (Dutton et al. 1983; Lyles & Mitroff, 1980), these models do not treat the question of how issues first gain decision makers' attention. With the exception of advocates of the garbage can model of decision making (Cohen, March & Olsen, 1972; March & Olsen, 1976), decision making theorists, like economists, have generally assumed that rational criteria such as issue cost determine attention allocation.

The agenda building view departs from these conceptions through its recognition that some issues are more socially acceptable to attend to than others i.e., there are legitimacy forces which constrain attention allocation to some issues. Norms and beliefs in organizations include and exclude some issues from public consideration and support, making the process a social and political as well as a psychological event.

Further, the agenda building view highlights the interdependence that exists between attentional events. Attention to one issue is related to others through both cognitive and political links. These ties are expressed in the model by arguing that inclusion of any strategic issue on the agenda is affected by the set of issues already under consideration.

Together these two points pave the way for a distinctive and more encompassing view of attention allocation to strategic issues. The model is built and explored in three steps. Part I describes the issue-specific context and its relationship to whether or not a strategic issue becomes an agenda item. This discussion provides answers to the first question i.e., what is it about particular strategic issues that captures decision makers' attention? Part II attempts to answer the second question concerning how different organizations respond to the same strategic issue. This question is answered by de-

JANE E. DUTTON

scribing how the organization-context systematically influences the issue-specific context. Part III addresses the third question in a discussion of the practical implications of an agenda building view. Particular attention is paid to the tactics decision makers can employ to manage the ambiguity of problem setting by manipulating the issue-specific context.

An Agenda Building Model

The agenda building process highlights the effort and resources that individuals expend to have an issue made a strategic agenda item. This process of agenda building may be formalized i.e., some organizations employ strategic issue management systems to identify and legitimate a subset of potential strategic issues for further consideration (Brown, 1981). In other organizations, the process may be informal and implicit — with no clearly identifiable system for generating the set of strategic agenda issues. However, whether the organization employs a formal or informal agenda building process, the assumption of this article is that all organizations attend to a limited issue set. This set of issues is the agenda — a structure that limits and orders an array of issues for top level decision makers in organizations. By focusing on the process by which this issue set is created, new insights on the process of strategy formulation and change are gained.

The agenda building model proceeds from the fundamental proposition that an issue is placed on the strategic agenda when individuals are aware of the issue (Issue Exposure) and/or those persons who are aware of the issue are involved with the issue (Issue Interest). Involvement in an issue is indicated by the amount of personal resources (e.g., time or effort) a single or multiple individuals are willing to expend on an issue. In essence, this proposition suggests that there is a relationship between the forces behind an issue (Exposure X Interest) and the probability of agenda placement. Rationale for this proposition is based on the view of decision makers as active mediators of what issues in organizations receive attention.

A political view depicts top level decision makers as continually striving to maximize their legitimate power. It assumes, as recent theorists have argued (e.g. Pfeffer, 1981; Smircich & Morgan, 1982), that decision makers must create an image of effectiveness to maintain legitimate power. Thus, decision makers attend to issues which create and preserve this image of effectiveness in the eyes of their "followers".

It is the high exposure, interest-consuming issues that have the greatest potential for demonstrating that top level decision makers are active and effective. Bold successful actions on wide exposure issues can reap great rewards in the form of heightened awareness of a decision maker and increased confidence in his or her abilities. However, it is also in dealing with these types of issues when decision makers undertake the greatest risk of legitimacy loss if they do not act effectively. The joint potential for great gains and losses in high exposure, high interest issues induces decision makers to encourage allocationg attention to these issues by their inclusion on the strategic agenda. Strategic agenda status can be manifest in a variety of ways such as placement on formal committee or departmental agendas, public statements about the issue, etc. The question that emerges from this discussion is: what conditions increase or decrease levels of issue interest and exposure?

This question can be answered by examining the influence of factors specific to an issue i.e. the issue context and factors specific to the organizational context. The model proposes that the organizational context influences agenda placement *through* its effect on the issue context. In this way, any episode of agenda building is an-issue-in-an-organization event (Downs & Mohr, 1976), and any outcomes (i.e. agenda placement or not) are related to forces operating at both the issue and organizational level.

The Issue-Specific Context

The model of agenda building is presented in Figure 1. As the Figure implies, a strategic issue gains force (i.e. interest and exposure) through the combined effect of perceived attributes of an issue (Issue Salience) and the political foundation of an issue (Issue Sponsorship), while the size and variety of items already on the issue agenda (Agenda Structure) moderate whether or not these factors translate into awareness and interest in the issue. The probability that any particular issue will be placed on the strategic agenda depends on the condition of these three factors at any one point in time. Although these three factors are interactive, for the purposes of describing the model and deriving hypotheses, each element is discussed separately below.

Issue Characteristics

Not all issues attract the decision makers attention equally. Differences in an issue's salience (Bauer, 1968; Cobb & Elder, 1972) draw different levels of interest and exposure to an issue, resulting in the admission of some issues on to the strategic agenda and the denial of others. An issue's salience is related to a variety of issue characteristics. In particular, it is proposed that the magnitude, abstractness, simplicity, and immediacy of an issue affect levels of issue exposure and interest.

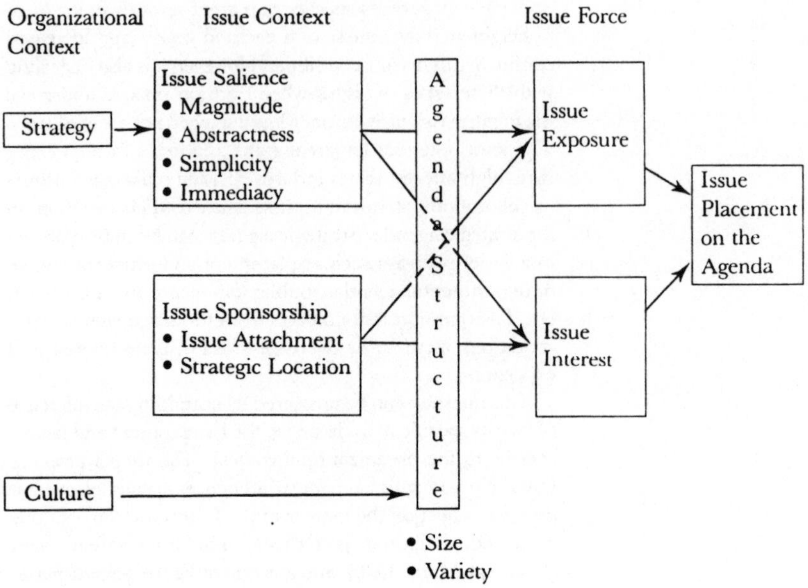

JANE E. DUTTON

Organizational   Issue Context   Issue Force
Context

Figure 1. Elements in the issue context and their effect on agenda building.

Issues vary in their magnitude or size of perceived impact on the organization's strategic goals. Some issues such as concerns over the advertising strategy of a major competitor or a competitor's patent infraction may be perceived as minor in terms of their potential to disrupt the organization's activities. Other issues, such as a competitor's pricing strategy or a potential product liability suit may be perceived as far more consequential. Even the same issue — e.g., a technological development that modifies the sequencing for a product's construction — may be perceived as minor in one firm and major in another, depending upon the firm's investment in the old sequence, the percentage of output represented by the product and other considerations of strategic impact.

Decision makers face a range of issues in terms of how abstractly or concretely they are defined (Cobb & Elder, 1972; Edelman, 1964). In the arena of public policy, Cobb and Elder (1972) argue that the more abstract a political issue is perceived to be, the wider its potential visibility to the public and the more probable its inclusion on the congressional agenda. When applied to an organizational context, the abstractness of a strategic issue is hypothesized to increase exposure and interest by determining the range of potential

AGENDA BUILDING

issue supporters. If an issue is very concrete, i.e., specific in its applicability, a narrow range of issue advocates or dissenters is activated, decreasing levels of issue interest and exposure. However, an issue may be defined too abstractly to convince proponents of its potential relevance. Issues representing future opportunities such as "How can we capitalize on changes in new markets?" are often too abstractly defined to capture the interest of decision makers (Dutton, 1983). In these cases it is difficult to incite interest as potential sponsors see the issue as irrelevant or unresolvable.

Strategic issues that are too complex may suffer the same fate as issues that are too abstract. The simplicity of an issue — the number of different concerns embedded in an issue and their level of technical sophistication — contributes to how easily an issue can be understood. For example, if an issue is very technically defined, organizational members may find it difficult to comprehend. Where understanding is a necessary precondition for interest, issue complexity may mar the chances of agenda inclusion.

Finally, the time pressure associated with an issue increases the level of issue interest. While time pressure or immediacy restricts the opportunity for gaining wide issue exposure as decision makers are compelled to take action quickly on these issue types (Bolland, 1979), the issue's immediacy intensifies any one person's willingness to expend resources on the issue. So, for example, an immediate crisis such as a labor strike in a single plant of a multiplant company is more likely to gain agenda status than a demographic shift in the population that threatens an organization's long-term labor supply. Although the latter issue is potentially more consequential for an organization's long run viability, it is likely to consume less collective attention than the more immediate strike issue. This hypothesis gains further support from studies of organizational and group responses to crisis. Consistently these studies have shown that the perception of time pressure is critical for inferring an event is a crisis (e.g. Billings, Milburn & Schaalman, 1980; Hermann, 1963).

Any particular issue varies in how important, abstract, simple and immediate it is perceived to be. Perceptions of issue characteristics change as new information and new interests define the issue in a different light, making it appear more or less appropriate for agenda inclusion. The subjective nature of issue characteristics contribute to the fluidity of an issue's definition over time. In other words, one would expect the meaning and significance of issues to change over time. The subjectivity of issue dimensions suggests that the definition of an issue becomes the target for debate and manipulation by organizational decision makers.

JANE E. DUTTON

> "Control over how the issues of conflict are defined means control over the choice of battlefields upon which conflict will take place. A group will always select a battlefield that gives it an advantage in terms of potential support" (Cobb & Elder, 1972, p. 102).

The activation of interests over the definition of a strategic issue politicizes the process of strategic agenda building.

Control over an issue's definition is important to issue sponsors — individuals who take a personal stake in making a strategic issue an agenda item. Sponsors play a major role in building the organization's agenda. Whether acting autonomously or as members of a coalition, they latch onto issues (March & Olsen, 1976) and mobilize interest and spread awareness about an issue. In the words of Walker (1977) certain individuals become "skillful entrepeneurs" in orchestrating an issue's agenda status. Cobb and Elder (1972) have applied the label "guardians of the formal agenda" to individuals who play this same role. Their role is not unlike the role of innovation champions who advocate the adoption of new technologies (Chakrabarti, 1974). The key point from the perspective of agenda building is to understand that certain individuals become attached to strategic issues. These sponsors help to intensify interest or to gain issue exposure, translating a concern into action by its placement on the agenda. Several researchers (e.g., Bower, 1972; Burgelman, 1983; Mazzolini, 1981; Quinn, 1980) have documented the role of sponsors in initiating the strategy reformulation process. The importance of issue sponsors to the agenda building process explicitly recognizes the political underpinnings of the change process.

Issue Sponsors

Issue sponsors vary in their degree of attachment to an issue. Some persons become committed to "pet issues" which they advocate for consideration. Where an individual is strongly personally committed to an issue, the issue stands a higher chance of agenda entry merely because the individual works harder to increase awareness of the issue's existence. These efforts, however, are likely to be more successful if the sponsor is strategically located and has personal credibility.

Issue sponsors are more effective when their strategic location gives them clout to influence decision makers' opinions about an issue. Individuals gain greater power when they are central, non-substitutable and cope with uncertainty for the organization in some way (Hickson, Hining, Lee, Schenk & Pennings, 1971). Individuals with this type of power are likely to be more successful in generating consensus that an issue is a broadly recognized and of high interest, i.e., a legitimate concern. A successful sponsor of an agenda item capitalizes on an opportunity created by some triggering event (e.g., an unanticipated event in the environment, a change in availability of key resources, Cobb & Elder, 1972) and catapults an issue to the agenda.

Success in doing this task is enhanced a by sponsor's credibility (Lyles & Mitroff, 1980) and authority in the organization (Pounds, 1969). Credibility and authority are usually associated with the strategic position of an issue sponsor. They enhance the sponsor's jurisdiction over an issue domain and increase the successful promotion of an issue on to or off the strategic agenda (McCall, Kaplan & Gerlach, 1982). In addition, the strategic location of an issue sponsor gives this person heightened visibility. Where the sponsor and his/her coalition have greater visibility, the issue gains exposure (Stevenson, Pearce & Porter, 1984) and has a higher probability of agenda status (Kingdon, 1984).

Issue Sponsorship and Issue Salience, although treated independently for discussion purposes, are in reality, likely to be closely related to one another. So, for example, one would expect issues that are strongly promoted through active sponsorship to be viewed as higher in magnitude, more abstract, simpler and more immediate. The mere act of issue sponsorship is likely to alter decision makers' perceptions of issue characteristics. Similarly, one might argue that issues with certain perceived characteristics (i.e., ones that are obviously of great magnitude and immediacy) may attract issue sponsors more readily than less consequential, less urgent issues. Potential issue sponsors are attracted to these sorts of issues as they know their chances of successfully drawing attention i.e., resources to these issue types are higher. Thus, issue sponsorship and issue salience jointly and interactively determine the level of interest and exposure directed toward an issue. However, both of these effects are dependent on the number and variety of issues currently receiving attention in the organization i.e., the agenda structure.

Agenda Structure

The entry of a new issue onto the strategic agenda is facilitated or constrained by the form or structure of the organization's agenda at the time an issue is being initiated. One can conceptualize the agenda as an issue array containing a limited number and variety of issues at any one point in time (Dutton & Duncan, 1987). For some organizations this array is very large, containing a wide range of distinctly different types of strategic issues. In other organizations the set of legitimate strategic issues may be very narrow with only limited diversity.

The size of the strategic agenda represents its capacity limits. If the agenda is large — e.g., many items are consid-

JANE E. DUTTON

ered legitimate items of concern — then the introduction of
a new issue is unlikely to exceed the agenda's capacity limits.
If, however, the agenda is restricted in size — i.e., decision
makers consider only a limited array of issues as legitimate
concerns — then the introduction of any one new item is
potentially very significant. With a smaller size agenda, the
level of interest and exposure must be higher (than with a
large agenda) to warrant the allocation of scarce attentional
resources. As a result, new strategic issues are scrutinized
more closely, reducing the probability of agenda placement.

The same argument applies to understanding how a
varied strategic agenda is more permeable than an agenda
with limited variety. If a varied agenda exists, any new
agenda item has an easier time gaining exposure or interest.
Issues which are similiar to issues encountered in the past
gain broader exposure and deeper interest within a shorter
period of time as they are easier to understand. Where an
organization has devoted resources to a wide range of issues
in the past, for any new potential issue, there are multiple
bases for understanding it, increasing the possibility of
agenda entry. This argument gains support from studies of
agenda building in Congress. Researchers have documented
how the simple inclusion of one item on the agenda, e.g., a
safety and health issue, increases the probability that other
safety-related issues will be considered in the future (Walker,
1977).

Any time a new issue reaches the agenda it modifies the
agenda structure operating during the next agenda building
episode. Suppose an organization legitimates concern over a
new industry entrant through its inclusion on the strategic
agenda. As part of the new agenda structure this issue will
influence the probability of agenda placement for the next
issue. Thus the process of agenda building is dynamic over
time, making each new episode contingent on the past. This
means that by altering the agenda structure an issue sponsor
can play a major role in the attention top decision makers
allocate to future strategic issues. By advocating a significantly novel strategic issue and gaining exposure and interest sufficient for agenda inclusion, an issue sponsor can
alter an agenda's variety. Consequently, any new issue will be
affected by the new agenda structure — extending a sponsor's
impact far beyond the issue he or she originally promoted.

The structure of the strategic agenda and the constraining
or facilitating role it plays in the admission of new items,
emphasizes that incorporation of a new issue cannot be
understood apart from the array of concerns that the organization has already faced. Old agenda items limit or extend
the agenda's capacity and bases for understanding, thus

playing a critical role in the incorporation of new items.

An agenda building episode builds issue interest and exposure, resulting in its inclusion or exclusion from the strategic agenda. The arguments linking the perceived characteristics of the issue, sponsorship and agenda structure to agenda placement are summarized in hypothesis form in Table 1.

(1) The greater the perceived magnitude of a strategic issue, the greater probability of agenda placement.

(2) The greater the abstractness of an issue, the greater the probability of agenda placement.

(3) The less perceived complexity of an issue, the greater the probability of agenda placement.

(4) The greater the immediacy of an issue, the greater the probability of agenda placement.

(5) The greater the power of an issue sponsor, the greater the probability of agenda placement.

(6) The greater the sponsor's personal attachment to an issue, the greater the probability of agenda placement.

(7) The greater the size of the agenda, the greater the probability of agenda placement.

(8) The greater the variety of issues on the agenda, the greater the probability of agenda placement.

Table 1. Hypotheses linking the issue context to agenda placement.

All of these hypotheses focus on issue-specific characteristics and events, allowing one to predict how in the same organization, different strategic issues command differing amounts of attentional resources. However, to predict organizational differences in issue attention, one must consider the organizational context in which agenda building takes place.

The Organizational Context

Each agenda building episode takes place in a larger organizational context consisting of unique patterns of beliefs, values, resources, roles, etc. It is proposed that these patterns influence agenda building through their impact on the issue

JANE E. DUTTON

context i.e., an issue's salience, issue interest and the agenda
structure. The effects of the organizational context are man-
ifold and complex. For illustrative purposes, two organizational characteristics will be discussed in terms of their implications for agenda building: the organization's strategy and
its culture.

An organization possesses a strategic frame (Huff, 1982) or   *Strategy*
strategic umbrella by defining some issues as major, imme-
diate, and simple while defining others as minor, long term
and complex. The organization's strategy poses a strategic
requirement (Hambrick, 1981) making some issues easier to
concentrate on and others easier to ignore. For example, an
organization pursuing a differentiation strategy (Porter,
1980) is likely to devote systematic attention to issues concerning maintenance of a brand image, customer service etc.,
as these issues are perceived as more important, immediate
and simple. The greater exposure and interest aroused with
these issue types makes them more probable candidates for
agenda inclusion than issues more compatible with alternative generic strategies (Porter, 1980). Thus an organization's
strategy exerts influence on agenda placement through its
effect on issue salience.

The rebirth of practical (e.g., Deal & Kennedy, 1982) and   *Organizational Culture*
academic interest (e.g., September 1983 edition of *Administra-
tive Science Quarterly*) in organizational culture compels one to
consider its relevance for agenda building. As applied here,
culture is defined as the set of shared beliefs and values of
organizational members (Smircich, 1983).

Both the content and consensus over organizational beliefs
and values vary across organizations. Where there is a high
level of consensus, a "strong culture" exists (Peters & Waterman, 1982), serving to clarify the meaning and interpretation
of actions in an organization. However, where a "weak"
culture exists there is less consensus. Beliefs and values are
more varied and diffuse, making actions more difficult to
interpret.

Translated into the context of agenda building, an organization's culture plays a role in determining the variety of
issues included in the strategic agenda at any one point in
time. Where the culture is strong, i.e., high consensus exists
over the domain of organizational inquiry (Shrivastava &
Schneider, 1984), the agenda structure is likely to be less
varied. There is a consensus about the key strategic issues but
the issues represent a limited range of concerns. As a result,
any new strategic issue which is encountered gains rapid
agenda status if it is consistent with dominant concerns of the
organization's culture, but has a much poorer chance of
inclusion if it departs from the dominant shared view. Thus,

AGENDA BUILDING

unlike the organization's strategy which affected agenda building through its relationship to issue salience, organizational culture has influence through its role in determining a high or low variety agenda.

Implications of an Agenda Building View

The view of attention allocation to strategic issues as captured in the model of agenda building has both theoretical and practical implications. As a theoretical level, the notion of strategic agenda building provides a fresh perspective for understanding the early stages of strategic decision making — where potential issues are recognized and diagnosed by decision makers (Keisler & Sproull, 1983; Lyles & Mitroff, 1980; Mintzberg et al., 1976). While previous researchers have treated this process on an issue-by-issue-basis (e.g. Dutton et al., 1983; Lyles, 1981), considering the recognition and diagnosis of each new problem or opportunity as an independent event — an agenda perspective provides a different view. An agenda building perspective implicitly assumes that each new strategic issue is dependent, in part, upon the set of issues that have already gained decision makers' attention. Thus researchers must understand the portfolio of issues (Huff & Pondy, 1983) confronting decision makers to understand interpretation (Daft & Weick, 1984) or action.

The agenda building perspective helps to explain the bias towards incremental change in organizations by uncovering the forces at work in problem setting (Metcalfe, 1981). It argues that the agenda structure acts as a conservative influence by keeping organizations most responsive to issues similar to those encountered in the past. In rare cases, actions occur such as the succession of top level executives that serve to break this cycle of incremental change (e.g. Starbuck, Greve & Hedberg, 1978). When new and powerful individuals enter the organization, they are equipped to change the variety and a number of issues considered, opening the door for more radical change.

The agenda building perspective implies that theoretical treatments of adaptation and change must consider how organizational and environmental pressures translate into a particular issue context. Just as researchers studying the adoption of innovations in organizations have concluded, one must consider the issue-in-an-organization as the relevant unit of analysis (Downs & Mohr, 1976). Thus, to understand why organizations initiate unique responses to the "same" strategic issue e.g., why various petroleum-dependent firms responded differently to the 1973 oil embargo, one must consider how the salience of the issue, issue sponsorship, and

JANE E. DUTTON

agenda structure interacted to enhance or diminish attention to this environmental event.

The components of the agenda building model reflect the political and cognitive forces at work in shaping strategic processes. In this way, the model is consistent with recent attempts to wed these two forces to explain organizational change processes (e.g. Lawrence & Dyer, 1983; Norman, 1983; Quinn, 1980).

Implications for Managing Change

The model of agenda building provides a basis for understanding why certain issues become agenda items, while others fail to even be recognized in an organization. This understanding forms the basis for identifying a range of tactics that members of an organization can use to influence the content of the strategic agenda. While these tactics do not assure that the "right" strategic issues have been identified, they have the potential for increasing a member's influence over which issues receive collective attention. This potential is important as it provides a logic for managing decision makers' ambiguity about which issues should be allocated resources. This ambiguity is reduced by knowing which issues are likely to gain agenda status.

The tactics for managing agenda building rely upon actions that influence the three factors that determine an issue's force: an issue's salience, an issue's sponsorship, and agenda structure. By influencing any one of these factors, the theory suggests that one can alter the likelihood that a particular issue or set of issues will gain agenda status. Where "making the agenda" represents the first in strategic decision processes or action commitments, these strategies can have a profound influence on the strategic direction of an organization.

The tactics for managing the strategic agenda can be looked at in two ways. First the tactics can be used to increase the probability than an issue will receive collective attention. These tactics rely on increasing an issue's salience, its sponsorship or increasing the variety and size of the organization's agenda. Alternatively, a reversal of these tactics could be used to decrease the probability of agenda inclusion for an issue by decreasing its issue force, thus helping to preserve the status quo (Bachrach & Baratz, 1962). Tactics that fall into this category are ones that try to minimize an issue's salience, decrease its base of sponsorship, or limit the size and variety of the agenda. In the discussion of tactics provided below, only the former alternative will be considered, i.e., avenues for increasing an issue's probability of agenda placement.

AGENDA BUILDING

However, one should keep in mind that the tactics could be employed in reverse to accomplish the opposite objective.

One set of tactics for influencing what issues comprise the strategic agenda focuses on manipulating an issue's salience, and in particular, on an issue's magnitude, abstractness, simplicity and immediacy. These tactics are probably the most frequently used when compared with the other tactics, as they are the least costly in terms of how much effort must be expended to affect an issue's inclusion on the agenda.

Tactics for altering an issue's salience represent attempts to manage an issue's meaning for other organizational members. The management of an issue's meaning is possible because issues are largely ambiguous events or developments as opposed to hard, concrete facts (Dutton et al., 1983). Where the attributes of issues are based largely on subjective impressions as opposed to indelible charateristics, they are vulnerable to manipulation. In cases where decision makers are aware that impressions of issue characteristics affect attention devoted to an issue, attempts can be made to orchestrate these impressions. Listed below are a number of possible tactics for increasing an issue's salience by altering its perceived characteristics.

Perceived issue magnitude: The perceived impact of an issue is often difficult to assess. For example, issues of social responsibility such as "lifelining" or competitive issues such as "deregulation" could be insignificant or very consequental to firms in the banking industry. Decision makers in these firms could intensify the level of interest and exposure to these issues by altering perceptions of the issues' perceived impact.

For example, issues can be described as directly relevant to the firm's profitability or to other goals that are central to the organization's assessment of its performance. Estimates of the issue's impact on the firm's operations could convey that the magnitude of the issue's effect is very large. Statements such as "this issue could be devastating" or "this issue is a critical one" convey a sense that the magnitude of the issue is very great, and failure to pay attention to the issue would be harmful to the organization.

Perceived issue abstractness: An issue's abstractness is important for determining the range of potential issue supporters as well as for affecting the perceived feasibility of resolving of an issue. Where decision makers want to increase the probability of agenda placement for an issue, they must walk the fine line between making an issue too abstract or too concrete.

If a decision maker wishes to make the issue more abstract, well-known tactics such as "clouding an issue" can translate very specific issues into more generalizable, abstract ones. Advocates of various causes have frequently used this ploy to

JANE E. DUTTON

expand the base of support for their issues. For example,
issues of child abuse have been labeled more abstractly as
issues of "human equality" (Nelson, 1979). More currently,
proponents of women's rights have re-labeled their cause as
one of "human rights" in efforts to expand levels of support
and interest in the issue.

As opposite tactic is one that tries to narrow an issue's
support base by decreasing the issue's abstractness. Familiar
phrases such as "grounding an issue" communicate that an
issue's relevance to a potential support base may be enhanced
if it is made less abstract. Thus, issues such as "human
rights" as mentioned above may be viewed as too abstract to
incite the interest of potential support groups. The level of
issue abstractness helps to define the boundaries and intensity of interest of issue advocates.

Perceived issue simplicity: In a similar way, the perceived simplicity of an issue helps to define an issue's support base by
affecting its level of comprehendability. If an issue is defined
very simply, a broader base of interest may be activated as
advocates are able to understand an issue's relevance or
impact. For example, proponents of the "right to life" issue
have won more supporters by simplifying the issue of abor-
tion into a basic human right of being. These proponents
would probably have far less support if the issue was defined
in more complex terms, involving definitions of when a fetus
becomes "a person".

Perceived issue immediacy: Finally, decision makers may chose
to try to manipulate the perceived time pressure associated
with an issue to push its inclusion on to an organization's
agenda. In fact researchers who have studied the perception
of crisis have found that immediacy is a critical attribute in
spurring action in the wake of crisis (e.g., Hermann, 1963).
Thus, "putting the heat on" or "making an issue pressing"
are commonly used tactics for increasing percieved issue
immediacy, and correspondingly, enhancing the probability
that the issue will command organizational attention.

Tactic 2: Modifying Issue Sponsorship

The opportunity to attach individuals to issues (and vice
versa) provides a potent lever to influence the agenda building process. When one wants to increase the probability that
an issue will gain agenda status, the object is to attach a
powerful person with high commitment to the issue candidate. The bases of power and personal commitment of an
issue sponsor permit and encourage the expenditure of
resources on an issue. In addition, a powerful and committed
issue sponsor bestows the issue with a degree of momentum
that perseveres even after the issue-sponsor attachment has
ceased.

There are several tactics available for influencing an issue

AGENDA BUILDING

sponsor's success. One tactic involves taking measures to expand the bases of power of an individual who is promoting consideration of an issue. Actions such as giving a lofty title to an issue sponsor, or increasing his/her opportunities to form friendships with influential others are examples of power-related tactics.

Measures could also be employed to increase the level of commitment of an individual to an issue. A participatory process could be used to surface and raise issues, increasing the probability that an individual will become committed to an issue. Public declaration of an individual's involvement with an issue or providing an opportunity to chose which issue to advocate provide additional avenues to enhance issue commitment (Salancik, 1977).

Tactic 3: Modifying the Agenda Structure

The agenda structure sets information and political constraints which foster or foreclose new issue entry. The size of the strategic agenda determines the capacity limits that, when exceeded, stop additional issue entry. In contrast, the variety in the agenda determines the bases for potential political support for any new item approaching agenda status. There are several measures that can be taken to directly and indirectly influence the agenda structure, and hence, the probability of new issue inclusion.

Strategic agendas appear in organizations in many forms. Organizations that utilize strategic issue management (SIM) systems (King, 1982) employ rather explicit strategic agendas through the formal identification and labeling of a subset of strategic issues designated as *the* key "strategic issues".

For organizations that do not employ SIM systems, the measures taken to affect the agenda structure will be more indirect in terms of their impact. For example, formal committees used in strategy making could be designed to include a diverse range of interests. The heterogeneity of interests in committees increases the likelihood that divergent and varied developments are raised as potential strategic issues. Metcalfe (1981) has made a similar recommendation in his own design for adaptive organizational systems. The logic for the use of a heterogeneous committee structure is that it ensures divergent views are available for problem solving as well as problem setting (Metcalfe, 1981). The agenda structure could also be indirectly altered by expanding the information processing capacity of the organization. Thus Galbraith (1973) has elaborated on a wide range of design options intended to increase an organization's capacity for information processing — and in particular, vertical integration and the creation of lateral relations.

At a practical level, the agenda building framework has identified multiple tactics for affecting strategic change and

JANE E. DUTTON

managing ambiguity *through* their influence on the Issue
Context. On the one hand, individuals can take actions to
prevent an issue from making the agenda, thus helping to
preserve the status quo (Bachrach & Baratz, 1962). On the
other hand, they can take actions to encourage change by increasing the probability of new issue entry. The range of
available tactics are summarized in Table 2.

Issue Salience	*Issue Sponsorship*	*Agenda Structure*
Alter perceived issue characteristics:	Alter strategic location of issue sponsor	Alter agenda size
*Magnitude ("magnify the issue" vs. "minimize the issue")	e.g. — expand bases of power — form friendships with powerful people	Alter agenda variety e.g. committee membership
*Abstractness ("cloud the issue" vs. "narrow down the issue")	Alter issue attachment e.g. build personal commitment by:	
*Simplicity ("go to the heart of the issue" vs. "tie the issue to other concerns")	— participative issue surfacing — providing choice in issue selection — public attachment	
*Immediacy ("make the issue pressing" vs. "play down the issue")		

Table 2. Tactics for managing agenda building.

The agenda building perspective, although rich in its
theoretical and practical implications, presents new challenges for researchers. One challenge involves operationalizing the constructs of agenda and agenda structure. New
research questions must be addressed including how individual and organizational agendas are interrelated. Recent
research reveals that effective mangers are astute agenda
builders. (Kotter, 1982; Huff, 1982). This finding suggests
that future research should try to determine how individual
agendas become linked to the strategic agenda. This type of
research would highlight the dynamic processes which weave
together individual and organizational action. Further, it
may be that individuals who are most successful at controlling the strategic agenda are those that yield the greatest

AGENDA BUILDING

influence. The point is captured by Walker (1977) in his own conclusion about the legislative agenda:

> "Those who manage to shape the legislative agenda, in other words are able to magnify their influence many times over by determining the focus of attention and the energy in the entire political system". (p. 445).

Thus agenda building becomes a useful framework for exploring the political dynamics underlying the process of organizational change.

JANE E. DUTTON

References

Ansoff, H.L.
1980 "Strategic issue management." *Strategic Management Journal*, 1:131—148.

Bachrach, P., and B. Baratz
1962 "Two faces of power." *American Political Science Review*, 56:947—952.

Bauer, R.
1968 "The policy process." In R. Bauer and K. Gergen (eds.), *The Study of Policy Formulation.* New York: Free Press.

Billings, R.S., T.W. Milburn, and M. Schaalman
1980 "A model of crisis perception: A theoretical and empirical analysis." *Administrative Science Quarterly*, 25:300—316.

Bolland, J.M.
1979 *Conflict and Consensus in American Communities: Agenda Setting as a Prelude to Social Change.* Unpublished Ph.D. dissertation, Ohio State University.

Bower, J.L.
1972 *Managing the Resource Allocation Process Study of Corporate Planning and Investment.* Boston: Harvard University Press.

Brown, J.K.
1981 *Guidelines for Managing Corporate Issues Programs,* New York: Conference Board.

Burgelman, R.A.
1983 "A process model of internal corporate ventures in the diversified major firm." *Administrative Science Quarterly*, 28: 223—244.

Chakrabardi, A.K.
1974 "The role of champion in product innovation." *California Management Review*, 58—62.

Chandler, A.D.
1962 *Strategy and Structure.* Cambridge: Mass, M.I.T. Press.

Child, J.
1972 "Organizational structure, environment and performance: The role of strategic choice." *Sociology*, 6:2—22.

Cobb, R.W., and C.D. Elder
1972 *Participation in American Politics. The Dynamics of Agenda Building.* Boston: Allyn and Bacon, Inc.

Cohen, M., J. March, and J. Olsen
1972 "A garbage can model of organizational choice." *Administrative Science Quarterly*, 17:1—25.

Daft, R.L., and K.E. Weick
1984 "Toward a model of organizations as interpretation systems." *Academy of Management Review*, 9:284—296.

Deal, T.E., and A.A. Kennedy
1982 *Corporate Cultures.* Reading MA: Addison Wesley.

Downs, G.W., and L.B. Mohr
1976 "Conceptual issues in the study of innovation." *Administrative Science Quarterly*, 21:700—714.

Dutton J.E.
1983 *The Process of Strategic Issue Resolution.* Unpublished Ph.D. Dissertation. Northwestern University.

Dutton, J.E., and R.B. Duncan
1987 "The influence of the strategic planning process on strategic change." *Strategic Mangement Journal*, forthcoming.

Dutton, J.E., L. Fahey, and V.K. Narayanan
1983 "Toward understanding strategic issue diagnosis." *Strategic Management Journal*, 4:307—323.

Edelman, M.
1964 *The Symbol Uses of Politics.* Urbana: University of Illinois Press.

Galbraith, J.
1977 *Organization Design.* Reading. MA: Addison-Wesley.

Hambrick, D.C.
1981 "Environment, strategy and power within top management teams." *Administrative Science Quarterly*, 26:253—275.

Hermann, C.F.
1963 "Some consequences of crisis which limit the viability of organization." *Administrative Science Quarterly*, 8:343—388.

Hickson, D.J., C.R. Hining, C.A. Lee, R.E. Schneck, and J.M. Pennings
1972 "A strategic contingencies theory of intra-organizational power." *Administrative Science Quarterly*, 16:216—222.

Huff, A.S.
1982 "Industry influences on strategic reformulation." *Strategic Management Journal*, 119—131.

Huff. A.S.. and L.R. Pondy
1983   *Issue Management by School Superintendents*. Final
       Report to National Institute of Education,
       Part 1.

Keisler. S.. and L. Sproull
1982   "Managerial response to changing
       environment: Perspectives in problem setting
       from social cognition." *Administrative Science
       Quarterly* 27. 4:548—570.

King. W.R.
1982   "Using strategic issue analysis." *Long Range
       Planning*. 15:45—49.

Kingdon. John W.
1984   *Agendas. Alternatives. and Public Policies*. Boston:
       Little. Brown and Company.

Kotter. J.P.
1982   *The General Managers*. New York: Free Press.

Lawrence. P.R.. and D. Dyer
1983   *Renewing American Industry*. New York: Free
       Press.

Lyles. M.A.
1981   "Formulating strategic problems: Empirical
       analysis and model development." *Strategic
       Management Journal*. 2:61—75.

Lyles. M.A.. and I. Mitroff
1980   "Organizational problem formulation: An
       empirical study." *Administrative Science Quarterly*,
       25:102—120.

March. J.G.
1981   "Decision making perspectives." In A.H. Van
       De Ven and W.F. Joyce (eds.), *Perspectives in
       Organization Design and Behavior*: 205—244, New
       York: Wiley-Interscience.

March. J.G.. and J.P. Olsen
1976   *Ambiguity and Choice in Organizations*. Bergen:
       Universitetsforlaget.

Mazzolini. R.
1981   "How strategic decisions are made." *Long
       Range Planning*. 14:85—96.

McCall. M.. R.E. Kaplan. and M.L. Gerlach
1982   *Caught in the Act: Decision Makers at Work*.
       Technical Report No. 20. Center for Creative
       Leadership.

Metcalfe. L.
1981   "Designing precarious partnerships." In P.
       Nystrom and W. Starbuck (eds.). *Handbook of
       Organization Design*, New York: Oxford
       University Press. 2:503—530.

Mintzberg, H., Raisinghini, and A. Theoret
1976   "The structure of unstructured decision
       processes." *Administrative Science Quarterly*,
       21:246—275.

Nelson, B.
1979   "Setting the public agenda: The case of child
       abuse." In A. Wildavsky, *The Policy Cycle*,
       Beverly Hills: Sage Publications.

Norman, D.A.
1976   *Memory and Attention* (2nd Ed.), New York:
       Wiley.

Normann, R.
1985   "Developing capabilities for organizational
       learning." In J.M. Pennings (ed.).
       Organizational Strategy and Change, 217—248, San
       Francisco: Jossey-Bass.

Peters, T.J., and R.H. Waterman
1982   *In Search of Excellence*. New York: Harper and
       Row.

Pfeffer, J.
1981   *Power in Organizations*. Marshfield, MA: Pitman
       Publishers, Inc.

Porter, M.
1980   *Competitive Strategy: Techniques for Analyzing
       Industries and Competitors*, New York: Free Press.

Pounds, W.F.
1969   "Processes of problem finding." *Industrial
       Management Review*, 11:1—19.

Quinn, J.B.
1980   *Strategies for Change*. Homewood, IL: Richard
       D. Irwin.

Radner, R.
1975   "Satisfying." *Journal of Mathematical Economics*,
       2:25—262.

Radner, R., and M. Rothchild
1975   "On the allocation of effort." *Journal of
       Economic Theory*, 10:358—376.

Salancik, Gerald
1977   "Commitment and the control of
       organizational behavior and belief." In B.
       Staw and G. Salancik (eds.), *New Directions in
       Organization Behavior*, Chicago: Sinclair-Press.

Shrivastava, P., and S. Schneider
1984   "Organizational frames of reference." *Human
       Relations*, 37, 10:795—809.

JANE E. DUTTON

References

Simon, H.
1971   "Designing organizations for an information
        rich world." In Martin Greenberger (ed.),
        Computers, Communication and the Public Interest.
        Baltimore: John Hopkins Press.

Smircich, L.E., and G. Morgan
1982   "Leadership: The management of meaning."
        Journal of Applied Behavioral Science, 18:257—273.

Starbuck, W.H., A. Greve, and B.T. Hedberg
1978   "Responding to crisis." In C.F. Smart and
        W.T. Standbury (eds.), *Studies in Crisis
        Management,* 111—137, Montreal: Butterworth
        and co., Ltd.

Stevenson, W.B., J.L. Pearce, and L.W. Porter
1985   "The concept of 'coalition' in organization
        theory and research." *Academy of Management
        Review.*

Taylor, S.E., and J.C. Crocker
1980   "Schematic bases of social information
        processing." In E.T. Higgins, P. Hermann and
        M.P. Zanna (eds.), *The Ontario Symposium on
        Personality and Social Psychology,* 89—134,
        Hillsdale, NJ: Erlbaum.

Walker, J.L.
1977   "Selling the agenda in the U.S. senate: A
        theory of problem selection." *British Journal of
        Political Science,* 7:423—445.

Winter, S.
1981   "Attention allocation and input proportions."
        Journal of Economic Behavior, 2:31—46.

[2]

The Science of "Muddling Through"

By CHARLES E. LINDBLOM

Associate Professor of Economics
Yale University

❯ Short courses, books, and articles exhort administrators to make decisions more methodically, but there has been little analysis of the decision-making process now used by public administrators. The usual process is investigated here—and generally defended against proposals for more "scientific" methods.

Decisions of individual administrators, of course, must be integrated with decisions of others to form the mosaic of public policy. This integration of individual decisions has become the major concern of organization theory, and the way individuals make decisions necessarily affects the way those decisions are best meshed with others'. In addition, decision-making method relates to allocation of decision-making responsibility—who should make what decision.

More "scientific" decision-making also is discussed in this issue: "Tools for Decision-Making in Resources Planning."

SUPPOSE an administrator is given responsibility for formulating policy with respect to inflation. He might start by trying to list all related values in order of importance, e.g., full employment, reasonable business profit, protection of small savings, prevention of a stock market crash. Then all possible policy outcomes could be rated as more or less efficient in attaining a maximum of these values. This would of course require a prodigious inquiry into values held by members of society and an equally prodigious set of calculations on how much of each value is equal to how much of each other value. He could then proceed to outline all possible policy alternatives. In a third step, he would undertake systematic comparison of his multitude of alternatives to determine which attains the greatest amount of values.

In comparing policies, he would take advantage of any theory available that generalized about classes of policies. In considering inflation, for example, he would compare all policies in the light of the theory of prices. Since no alternatives are beyond his investigation, he would consider strict central control and the abolition of all prices and markets on the one hand and elimination of all public controls with reliance completely on the free market on the other, both in the light of whatever theoretical generalizations he could find on such hypothetical economies.

Finally, he would try to make the choice that would in fact maximize his values.

An alternative line of attack would be to set as his principal objective, either explicitly or without conscious thought, the relatively simple goal of keeping prices level. This objective might be compromised or complicated by only a few other goals, such as full employment. He would in fact disregard most other social values as beyond his present interest, and he would for the moment not even attempt to rank the few values that he regarded as immediately relevant. Were he pressed, he would quickly admit that he was ignoring many related values and many possible important consequences of his policies.

As a second step, he would outline those relatively few policy alternatives that occurred to him. He would then compare them. In comparing his limited number of alternatives, most of them familiar from past controversies, he would not ordinarily find a body of theory precise enough to carry him through a comparison of their respective consequences. Instead he would rely heavily on the record of past experience with small policy steps to predict the consequences of similar steps extended into the future.

Moreover, he would find that the policy alternatives combined objectives or values in different ways. For example, one policy might offer price level stability at the cost of some risk of unemployment; another might offer less price stability but also less risk of unemployment. Hence, the next step in his approach—the final selection—would combine into one the choice among values and the choice among instruments for reaching values. It would not, as in the first method of policy-making, approximate a more mechanical process of choosing the means that best satisfied goals that were previously clarified and ranked. Because practitioners of the second approach expect to achieve their goals only partially, they would expect to repeat endlessly the sequence just described, as conditions and aspirations changed and as accuracy of prediction improved.

By Root or by Branch

For complex problems, the first of these two approaches is of course impossible. Although such an approach can be described, it cannot be practiced except for relatively simple problems and even then only in a somewhat modified form. It assumes intellectual capacities and sources of information that men simply do not possess, and it is even more absurd as an approach to policy when the time and money that can be allocated to a policy problem is limited, as is always the case. Of particular importance to public administrators is the fact that public agencies are in effect usually instructed not to practice the first method. That is to say, their prescribed functions and constraints—the politically or legally possible—restrict their attention to relatively few values and relatively few alternative policies among the countless alternatives that might be imagined. It is the second method that is practiced.

Curiously, however, the literatures of decision-making, policy formulation, planning, and public administration formalize the first approach rather than the second, leaving public administrators who handle complex decisions in the position of practicing what few preach. For emphasis I run some risk of overstatement. True enough, the literature is well aware of limits on man's capacities and of the inevitability that policies will be approached in some such style as the second. But attempts to formalize rational policy formulation—to lay out explicitly the necessary steps in the

process—usually describe the first approach and not the second.[1]

The common tendency to describe policy formulation even for complex problems as though it followed the first approach has been strengthened by the attention given to, and successes enjoyed by, operations research, statistical decision theory, and systems analysis. The hallmarks of these procedures, typical of the first approach, are clarity of objective, explicitness of evaluation, a high degree of comprehensiveness of overview, and, wherever possible, quantification of values for mathematical analysis. But these advanced procedures remain largely the appropriate techniques of relatively small-scale problem-solving where the total number of variables to be considered is small and value problems restricted. Charles Hitch, head of the Economics Division of RAND Corporation, one of the leading centers for application of these techniques, has written:

I would make the empirical generalization from my experience at RAND and elsewhere that operations research is the art of sub-optimizing, i.e., of solving some lower-level problems, and that difficulties increase and our special competence diminishes by an order of magnitude with every level of decision making we attempt to ascend. The sort of simple explicit model which operations researchers are so proficient in using can certainly reflect most of the significant factors influencing traffic control on the George Washington Bridge, but the proportion of the relevant reality which we can represent by any such model or models in studying, say, a major foreign-policy decision, appears to be almost trivial.[2]

Accordingly, I propose in this paper to clarify and formalize the second method,

[1] James G. March and Herbert A. Simon similarly characterize the literature. They also take some important steps, as have Simon's recent articles, to describe a less heroic model of policy-making. See *Organizations* (John Wiley and Sons, 1958), p. 137.

[2] "Operations Research and National Planning—A Dissent," 5 *Operations Research* 718 (October, 1957). Hitch's dissent is from particular points made in the article to which his paper is a reply; his claim that operations research is for low-level problems is widely accepted.

For examples of the kind of problems to which operations research is applied, see C. W. Churchman, R. L. Ackoff and E. L. Arnoff, *Introduction to Operations Research* (John Wiley and Sons, 1957); and J. F. McCloskey and J. M. Coppinger (eds.), *Operations Research for Management*, Vol. II, (The Johns Hopkins Press, 1956).

THE SCIENCE OF "MUDDLING THROUGH" 81

much neglected in the literature. This might be described as the method of *successive limited comparisons*. I will contrast it with the first approach, which might be called the rational-comprehensive method.[3] More impressionistically and briefly—and therefore generally used in this article—they could be characterized as the branch method and root method, the former continually building out from the current situation, step-by-step and by small degrees; the latter starting from fundamentals anew each time, building on the past only as experience is embodied in a theory, and always prepared to start completely from the ground up.

Let us put the characteristics of the two methods side by side in simplest terms.

ited comparisons is to see how the root method often breaks down in *its* handling of values or objectives. The idea that values should be clarified, and in advance of the examination of alternative policies, is appealing. But what happens when we attempt it for complex social problems? The first difficulty is that on many critical values or objectives, citizens disagree, congressmen disagree, and public administrators disagree. Even where a fairly specific objective is prescribed for the administrator, there remains considerable room for disagreement on sub-objectives. Consider, for example, the conflict with respect to locating public housing, described in Meyerson and Banfield's study of the Chi-

Rational-Comprehensive (Root)	Successive Limited Comparisons (Branch)
1a. Clarification of values or objectives distinct from and usually prerequisite to empirical analysis of alternative policies.	1b. Selection of value goals and empirical analysis of the needed action are not distinct from one another but are closely intertwined.
2a. Policy-formulation is therefore approached through means-end analysis: First the ends are isolated, then the means to achieve them are sought.	2b. Since means and ends are not distinct, means-end analysis is often inappropriate or limited.
3a. The test of a "good" policy is that it can be shown to be the most appropriate means to desired ends.	3b. The test of a "good" policy is typically that various analysts find themselves directly agreeing on a policy (without their agreeing that it is the most appropriate means to an agreed objective).
4a. Analysis is comprehensive; every important relevant factor is taken into account.	4b. Analysis is drastically limited: i) Important possible outcomes are neglected. ii) Important alternative potential policies are neglected. iii) Important affected values are neglected.
5a. Theory is often heavily relied upon.	5b. A succession of comparisons greatly reduces or eliminates reliance on theory.

Assuming that the root method is familiar and understandable, we proceed directly to clarification of its alternative by contrast. In explaining the second, we shall be describing how most administrators do in fact approach complex questions, for the root method, the "best" way as a blueprint or model, is in fact not workable for complex policy questions, and administrators are forced to use the method of successive limited comparisons.

Intertwining Evaluation and Empirical Analysis (1b)

The quickest way to understand how values are handled in the method of successive lim-

cago Housing Authority[4]—disagreement which occurred despite the clear objective of providing a certain number of public housing units in the city. Similarly conflicting are objectives in highway location, traffic control, minimum wage administration, development of tourist facilities in national parks, or insect control.

Administrators cannot escape these conflicts by ascertaining the majority's preference, for preferences have not been registered on most issues; indeed, there often *are* no preferences in the absence of public discussion sufficient to bring an issue to the attention of the electorate. Furthermore, there is a question

---

[3] I am assuming that administrators often make policy and advise in the making of policy and am treating decision-making and policy-making as synonymous for purposes of this paper.

[4] Martin Meyerson and Edward C. Banfield, *Politics, Planning and the Public Interest* (The Free Press, 1955).

of whether intensity of feeling should be considered as well as the number of persons preferring each alternative. By the impossibility of doing otherwise, administrators often are reduced to deciding policy without clarifying objectives first.

Even when an administrator resolves to follow his own values as a criterion for decisions, he often will not know how to rank them when they conflict with one another, as they usually do. Suppose, for example, that an administrator must relocate tenants living in tenements scheduled for destruction. One objective is to empty the buildings fairly promptly, another is to find suitable accommodation for persons displaced, another is to avoid friction with residents in other areas in which a large influx would be unwelcome, another is to deal with all concerned through persuasion if possible, and so on.

How does one state even to himself the relative importance of these partially conflicting values? A simple ranking of them is not enough; one needs ideally to know how much of one value is worth sacrificing for some of another value. The answer is that typically the administrator chooses—and must choose—directly among policies in which these values, are combined in different ways. He cannot first clarify his values and then choose among policies.

A more subtle third point underlies both the first two. Social objectives do not always have the same relative values. One objective may be highly prized in one circumstance, another in another circumstance. If, for example, an administrator values highly both the dispatch with which his agency can carry through its projects *and* good public relations, it matters little which of the two possibly conflicting values he favors in some abstract or general sense. Policy questions arise in forms which put to administrators such a question as: Given the degree to which we are or are not already achieving the values of dispatch and the values of good public relations, is it worth sacrificing a little speed for a happier clientele, or is it better to risk offending the clientele so that we can get on with our work? The answer to such a question varies with circumstances.

The value problem is, as the example shows, always a problem of adjustments at a margin. But there is no practicable way to state marginal objectives or values except in terms of particular policies. That one value is preferred to another in one decision situation does not mean that it will be preferred in another decision situation in which it can be had only at great sacrifice of another value. Attempts to rank or order values in general and abstract terms so that they do not shift from decision to decision end up by ignoring the relevant marginal preferences. The significance of this third point thus goes very far. Even if all administrators had at hand an agreed set of values, objectives, and constraints, and an agreed ranking of these values, objectives, and constraints, their marginal values in actual choice situations would be impossible to formulate.

Unable consequently to formulate the relevant values first and then choose among policies to achieve them, administrators must choose directly among alternative policies that offer different marginal combinations of values. Somewhat paradoxically, the only practicable way to disclose one's relevant marginal values even to oneself is to describe the policy one chooses to achieve them. Except roughly and vaguely, I know of no way to describe—or even to understand—what my relative evaluations are for, say, freedom and security, speed and accuracy in governmental decisions, or low taxes and better schools than to describe my preferences among specific policy choices that might be made between the alternatives in each of the pairs.

In summary, two aspects of the process by which values are actually handled can be distinguished. The first is clear: evaluation and empirical analysis are intertwined; that is, one chooses among values and among policies at one and the same time. Put a little more elaborately, one simultaneously chooses a policy to attain certain objectives and chooses the objectives themselves. The second aspect is related but distinct: the administrator focuses his attention on marginal or incremental values. Whether he is aware of it or not, he does not find general formulations of objectives very helpful and in fact makes specific marginal or incremental comparisons. Two policies, X and Y, confront him. Both promise the same degree of attainment of objectives a, b, c, d, and e. But X promises him somewhat more of f than does Y, while Y promises him somewhat more of g than does

X. In choosing between them, he is in fact offered the alternative of a marginal or incremental amount of f at the expense of a marginal or incremental amount of g. The only values that are relevant to his choice are these increments by which the two policies differ; and, when he finally chooses between the two marginal values, he does so by making a choice between policies.[5]

As to whether the attempt to clarify objectives in advance of policy selection is more or less rational than the close intertwining of marginal evaluation and empirical analysis, the principal difference established is that for complex problems the first is impossible and irrelevant, and the second is both possible and relevant. The second is possible because the administrator need not try to analyze any values except the values by which alternative policies differ and need not be concerned with them except as they differ marginally. His need for information on values or objectives is drastically reduced as compared with the root method; and his capacity for grasping, comprehending, and relating values to one another is not strained beyond the breaking point.

Relations Between Means and Ends (2b)

Decision-making is ordinarily formalized as a means-ends relationship: means are conceived to be evaluated and chosen in the light of ends finally selected independently of and prior to the choice of means. This is the means-ends relationship of the root method. But it follows from all that has just been said that such a means-ends relationship is possible only to the extent that values are agreed upon, are reconcilable, and are stable at the margin. Typically, therefore, such a means-ends relationship is absent from the branch method, where means and ends are simultaneously chosen.

Yet any departure from the means-ends relationship of the root method will strike some readers as inconceivable. For it will appear to them that only in such a relationship is it possible to determine whether one policy choice is better or worse than another. How can an administrator know whether he has made a

---

[5] The line of argument is, of course, an extension of the theory of market choice, especially the theory of consumer choice, to public policy choices.

wise or foolish decision if he is without prior values or objectives by which to judge his decisions? The answer to this question calls up the third distinctive difference between root and branch methods: how to decide the best policy.

The Test of "Good" Policy (3b)

In the root method, a decision is "correct," "good," or "rational" if it can be shown to attain some specified objective, where the objective can be specified without simply describing the decision itself. Where objectives are defined only through the marginal or incremental approach to values described above, it is still sometimes possible to test whether a policy does in fact attain the desired objectives; but a precise statement of the objectives takes the form of a description of the policy chosen or some alternative to it. To show that a policy is mistaken one cannot offer an abstract argument that important objectives are not achieved; one must instead argue that another policy is more to be preferred.

So far, the departure from customary ways of looking at problem-solving is not troublesome, for many administrators will be quick to agree that the most effective discussion of the correctness of policy does take the form of comparison with other policies that might have been chosen. But what of the situation in which administrators cannot agree on values or objectives, either abstractly or in marginal terms? What then is the test of "good" policy? For the root method, there is no test. Agreement on objectives failing, there is no standard of "correctness." For the method of successive limited comparisons, the test is agreement on policy itself, which remains possible even when agreement on values is not.

It has been suggested that continuing agreement in Congress on the desirability of extending old age insurance stems from liberal desires to strengthen the welfare programs of the federal government and from conservative desires to reduce union demands for private pension plans. If so, this is an excellent demonstration of the ease with which individuals of different ideologies often can agree on concrete policy. Labor mediators report a similar phenomenon: the contestants cannot agree on criteria for settling their disputes but can agree on specific proposals. Similarly, when one administrator's objective turns out to be another's means, they often can agree on policy.

Agreement on policy thus becomes the only practicable test of the policy's correctness. And for one administrator to seek to win the other over to agreement on ends as well would accomplish nothing and create quite unnecessary controversy.

If agreement directly on policy as a test for "best" policy seems a poor substitute for testing the policy against its objectives, it ought to be remembered that objectives themselves have no ultimate validity other than they are agreed upon. Hence agreement is the test of "best" policy in both methods. But where the root method requires agreement on what elements in the decision constitute objectives and on which of these objectives should be sought, the branch method falls back on agreement wherever it can be found.

In an important sense, therefore, it is not irrational for an administrator to defend a policy as good without being able to specify what it is good for.

Non-Comprehensive Analysis (4b)

Ideally, rational-comprehensive analysis leaves out nothing important. But it is impossible to take everything important into consideration unless "important" is so narrowly defined that analysis is in fact quite limited. Limits on human intellectual capacities and on available information set definite limits to man's capacity to be comprehensive. In actual fact, therefore, no one can practice the rational-comprehensive method for really complex problems, and every administrator faced with a sufficiently complex problem must find ways drastically to simplify.

An administrator assisting in the formulation of agricultural economic policy cannot in the first place be competent on all possible policies. He cannot even comprehend one policy entirely. In planning a soil bank program, he cannot successfully anticipate the impact of higher or lower farm income on, say, urbanization—the possible consequent loosening of family ties, possible consequent eventual need for revisions in social security and further implications for tax problems arising out of new federal responsibilities for social security and municipal responsibilities for ur-

ban services. Nor, to follow another line of repercussions, can he work through the soil bank program's effects on prices for agricultural products in foreign markets and consequent implications for foreign relations, including those arising out of economic rivalry between the United States and the U.S.S.R.

In the method of successive limited comparisons, simplification is systematically achieved in two principal ways. First, it is achieved through limitation of policy comparisons to those policies that differ in relatively small degree from policies presently in effect. Such a limitation immediately reduces the number of alternatives to be investigated and also drastically simplifies the character of the investigation of each. For it is not necessary to undertake fundamental inquiry into an alternative and its consequences; it is necessary only to study those respects in which the proposed alternative and its consequences differ from the status quo. The empirical comparison of marginal differences among alternative policies that differ only marginally is, of course, a counterpart to the incremental or marginal comparison of values discussed above.[6]

Relevance as Well as Realism

It is a matter of common observation that in Western democracies public administrators and policy analysts in general do largely limit their analyses to incremental or marginal differences in policies that are chosen to differ only incrementally. They do not do so, however, solely because they desperately need some way to simplify their problems; they also do so in order to be relevant. Democracies change their policies almost entirely through incremental adjustments. Policy does not move in leaps and bounds.

The incremental character of political change in the United States has often been remarked. The two major political parties agree on fundamentals; they offer alternative policies to the voters only on relatively small points of difference. Both parties favor full employment, but they define it somewhat differently; both favor the development of

[6] A more precise definition of incremental policies and a discussion of whether a change that appears "small" to one observer might be seen differently by another is to be found in my "Policy Analysis," 48 *American Economic Review* 298 (June, 1958).

water power resources, but in slightly different ways; and both favor unemployment compensation, but not the same level of benefits. Similarly, shifts of policy within a party take place largely through a series of relatively small changes, as can be seen in their only gradual acceptance of the idea of governmental responsibility for support of the unemployed, a change in party positions beginning in the early 30's and culminating in a sense in the Employment Act of 1946.

Party behavior is in turn rooted in public attitudes, and political theorists cannot conceive of democracy's surviving in the United States in the absence of fundamental agreement on potentially disruptive issues, with consequent limitation of policy debates to relatively small differences in policy.

Since the policies ignored by the administrator are politically impossible and so irrelevant, the simplification of analysis achieved by concentrating on policies that differ only incrementally is not a capricious kind of simplification. In addition, it can be argued that, given the limits on knowledge within which policy-makers are confined, simplifying by limiting the focus to small variations from present policy makes the most of available knowledge. Because policies being considered are like present and past policies, the administrator can obtain information and claim some insight. Non-incremental policy proposals are therefore typically not only politically irrelevant but also unpredictable in their consequences.

The second method of simplification of analysis is the practice of ignoring important possible consequences of possible policies, as well as the values attached to the neglected consequences. If this appears to disclose a shocking shortcoming of successive limited comparisons, it can be replied that, even if the exclusions are random, policies may nevertheless be more intelligently formulated than through futile attempts to achieve a comprehensiveness beyond human capacity. Actually, however, the exclusions, seeming arbitrary or random from one point of view, need be neither.

Achieving a Degree of Comprehensiveness

Suppose that each value neglected by one policy-making agency were a major concern of at least one other agency. In that case, a helpful division of labor would be achieved, and no agency need find its task beyond its capacities. The shortcomings of such a system would be that one agency might destroy a value either before another agency could be activated to safeguard it or in spite of another agency's efforts. But the possibility that important values may be lost is present in any form of organization, even where agencies attempt to comprehend in planning more than is humanly possible.

The virtue of such a hypothetical division of labor is that every important interest or value has its watchdog. And these watchdogs can protect the interests in their jurisdiction in two quite different ways: first, by redressing damages done by other agencies; and, second, by anticipating and heading off injury before it occurs.

In a society like that of the United States in which individuals are free to combine to pursue almost any possible common interest they might have and in which government agencies are sensitive to the pressures of these groups, the system described is approximated. Almost every interest has its watchdog. Without claiming that every interest has a sufficiently powerful watchdog, it can be argued that our system often can assure a more comprehensive regard for the values of the whole society than any attempt at intellectual comprehensiveness.

In the United States, for example, no part of government attempts a comprehensive overview of policy on income distribution. A policy nevertheless evolves, and one responding to a wide variety of interests. A process of mutual adjustment among farm groups, labor unions, municipalities and school boards, tax authorities, and government agencies with responsibilities in the fields of housing, health, highways, national parks, fire, and police accomplishes a distribution of income in which particular income problems neglected at one point in the decision processes become central at another point.

Mutual adjustment is more pervasive than the explicit forms it takes in negotiation between groups; it persists through the mutual impacts of groups upon each other even where they are not in communication. For all the imperfections and latent dangers in this ubiquitous process of mutual adjustment, it will often accomplish an adaptation of policies to a wider range of interests than could be done by one group centrally.

Note, too, how the incremental pattern of policy-making fits with the multiple pressure pattern. For when decisions are only incremental—closely related to known policies, it is easier for one group to anticipate the kind of moves another might make and easier too for it to make correction for injury already accomplished.[7]

Even partisanship and narrowness, to use pejorative terms, will sometimes be assets to rational decision-making, for they can doubly insure that what one agency neglects, another will not; they specialize personnel to distinct points of view. The claim is valid that effective rational coordination of the federal administration, if possible to achieve at all, would require an agreed set of values[8]—if "rational" is defined as the practice of the root method of decision-making. But a high degree of administrative coordination occurs as each agency adjusts its policies to the concerns of the other agencies in the process of fragmented decision-making I have just described.

For all the apparent shortcomings of the incremental approach to policy alternatives with its arbitrary exclusion coupled with fragmentation, when compared to the root method, the branch method often looks far superior. In the root method, the inevitable exclusion of factors is accidental, unsystematic, and not defensible by any argument so far developed, while in the branch method the exclusions are deliberate, systematic, and defensible. Ideally, of course, the root method does not exclude; in practice it must.

Nor does the branch method necessarily neglect long-run considerations and objectives. It is clear that important values must be omitted in considering policy, and sometimes the only way long-run objectives can be given adequate attention is through the neglect of short-run considerations. But the values omitted can be either long-run or short-run.

[7] The link between the practice of the method of successive limited comparisons and mutual adjustment of interests in a highly fragmented decision-making process adds a new facet to pluralist theories of government and administration.

[8] Herbert Simon, Donald W. Smithburg, and Victor A. Thompson, *Public Administration* (Alfred A. Knopf, 1950), p. 434.

Succession of Comparisons (5b)

The final distinctive element in the branch method is that the comparisons, together with the policy choice, proceed in a chronological series. Policy is not made once and for all; it is made and re-made endlessly. Policy-making is a process of successive approximation to some desired objectives in which what is desired itself continues to change under reconsideration.

Making policy is at best a very rough process. Neither social scientists, nor politicians, nor public administrators yet know enough about the social world to avoid repeated error in predicting the consequences of policy moves. A wise policy-maker consequently expects that his policies will achieve only part of what he hopes and at the same time will produce unanticipated consequences he would have preferred to avoid. If he proceeds through a *succession* of incremental changes, he avoids serious lasting mistakes in several ways.

In the first place, past sequences of policy steps have given him knowledge about the probable consequences of further similar steps. Second, he need not attempt big jumps toward his goals that would require predictions beyond his or anyone else's knowledge, because he never expects his policy to be a final resolution of a problem. His decision is only one step, one that if successful can quickly be followed by another. Third, he is in effect able to test his previous predictions as he moves on to each further step. Lastly, he often can remedy a past error fairly quickly—more quickly than if policy proceeded through more distinct steps widely spaced in time.

Compare this comparative analysis of incremental changes with the aspiration to employ theory in the root method. Man cannot think without classifying, without subsuming one experience under a more general category of experiences. The attempt to push categorization as far as possible and to find general propositions which can be applied to specific situations is what I refer to with the word "theory." Where root analysis often leans heavily on theory in this sense, the branch method does not.

The assumption of root analysts is that theory is the most systematic and economical way to bring relevant knowledge to bear on a

THE SCIENCE OF "MUDDLING THROUGH"

specific problem. Granting the assumption, an unhappy fact is that we do not have adequate theory to apply to problems in any policy area, although theory is more adequate in some areas—monetary policy, for example—than in others. Comparative analysis, as in the branch method, is sometimes a systematic alternative to theory.

Suppose an administrator must choose among a small group of policies that differ only incrementally from each other and from present policy. He might aspire to "understand" each of the alternatives—for example, to know all the consequences of each aspect of each policy. If so, he would indeed require theory. In fact, however, he would usually decide that, *for policy-making purposes,* he need know, as explained above, only the consequences of each of those aspects of the policies in which they differed from one another. For this much more modest aspiration, he requires no theory (although it might be helpful, if available), for he can proceed to isolate probable differences by examing the differences in consequences associated with past differences in policies, a feasible program because he can take his observations from a long sequence of incremental changes.

For example, without a more comprehensive social theory about juvenile delinquency than scholars have yet produced, one cannot possibly understand the ways in which a variety of public policies—say on education, housing, recreation, employment, race relations, and policing—might encourage or discourage delinquency. And one needs such an understanding if he undertakes the comprehensive óverview of the problem prescribed in the models of the root method. If, however, one merely wants to mobilize knowledge sufficient to assist in a choice among a small group of similar policies—alternative policies on juvenile court procedures, for example—he can do so by comparative analysis of the results of similar past policy moves.

Theorists and Practitioners

This difference explains—in some cases at least—why the administrator often feels that the outside expert or academic problem-solver is sometimes not helpful and why they in turn often urge more theory on him. And it explains why an administrator often feels more confident when "flying by the seat of his

pants" than when following the advice of theorists. Theorists often ask the administrator to go the long way round to the solution of his problems, in effect ask him to follow the best canons of the scientific method, when the administrator knows that the best available theory will work less well than more modest incremental comparisons. Theorists do not realize that the administrator is often in fact practicing a systematic method. It would be foolish to push this explanation too far, for sometimes practical decision-makers are pursuing neither a theoretical approach nor successive comparisons, nor any other systematic method.

It may be worth emphasizing that theory is sometimes of extremely limited helpfulness in policy-making for at least two rather different reasons. It is greedy for facts; it can be constructed only through a great collection of observations. And it is typically insufficiently precise for application to a policy process that moves through small changes. In contrast, the comparative method both economizes on the need for facts and directs the analyst's attention to just those facts that are relevant to the fine choices faced by the decision-maker.

With respect to precision of theory, economic theory serves as an example. It predicts that an economy without money or prices would in certain specified ways misallocate resources, but this finding pertains to an alternative far removed from the kind of policies on which administrators need help. On the other hand, it is not precise enough to predict the consequences of policies restricting business mergers, and this is the kind of issue on which the administrators need help. Only in relatively restricted areas does economic theory achieve sufficient precision to go far in resolving policy questions; its helpfulness in policy-making is always so limited that it requires supplementation through comparative analysis.

Successive Comparison as a System

Successive limited comparisons is, then, indeed a method or system; it is not a failure of method for which administrators ought to apologize. None the less, its imperfections, which have not been explored in this paper, are many. For example, the method is without a built-in safeguard for all relevant values, and it also may lead the decision-maker to overlook excellent policies for no other reason than that they are not suggested by the chain of successive policy steps leading up to the present. Hence, it ought to be said that under this method, as well as under some of the most sophisticated variants of the root method—operations research, for example—policies will continue to be as foolish as they are wise.

Why then bother to describe the method in all the above detail? Because it is in fact a common method of policy formulation, and is, for complex problems, the principal reliance of administrators as well as of other policy analysts.[9] And because it will be superior to any other decision-making method available for complex problems in many circumstances, certainly superior to a futile attempt at superhuman comprehensiveness. The reaction of the public administrator to the exposition of method doubtless will be less a discovery of a new method than a better acquaintance with an old. But by becoming more conscious of their practice of this method, administrators might practice it with more skill and know when to extend or constrict its use. (That they sometimes practice it effectively and sometimes not may explain the extremes of opinion on "muddling through," which is both praised as a highly sophisticated form of problem-solving and denounced as no method at all. For I suspect that in so far as there is a system in what is known as "muddling through," this method is it.)

One of the noteworthy incidental conse-quences of clarification of the method is the light it throws on the suspicion an administrator sometimes entertains that a consultant or adviser is not speaking relevantly and responsibly when in fact by all ordinary objective evidence he is. The trouble lies in the fact that most of us approach policy problems within a framework given by our view of a chain of successive policy choices made up to the present. One's thinking about appropriate policies with respect, say, to urban traffic control is greatly influenced by one's knowledge of the incremental steps taken up to the present. An administrator enjoys an intimate knowledge of his past sequences that "outsiders" do not share, and his thinking and that of the "outsider" will consequently be different in ways that may puzzle both. Both may appear to be talking intelligently, yet each may find the other unsatisfactory. The relevance of the policy chain of succession is even more clear when an American tries to discuss, say, antitrust policy with a Swiss, for the chains of policy in the two countries are strikingly different and the two individuals consequently have organized their knowledge in quite different ways.

If this phenomenon is a barrier to communication, an understanding of it promises an enrichment of intellectual interaction in policy formulation. Once the source of difference is understood, it will sometimes be stimulating for an administrator to seek out a policy analyst whose recent experience is with a policy chain different from his own.

This raises again a question only briefly discussed above on the merits of like-mindedness among government administrators. While much of organization theory argues the virtues of common values and agreed organizational objectives, for complex problems in which the root method is inapplicable, agencies will want among their own personnel two types of diversification: administrators whose thinking is organized by reference to policy chains other than those familiar to most members of the organization and, even more commonly, administrators whose professional or personal values or interests create diversity of view (perhaps coming from different specialties, social classes, geographical areas) so that, even within a single agency, decision-making can be fragmented and parts of the agency can serve as watchdogs for other parts.

---

[9] Elsewhere I have explored this same method of policy formulation as practiced by academic analysts of policy ("Policy Analysis," 48 *American Economic Review* 298 [June, 1958]). Although it has been here presented as a method for public administrators, it is no less necessary to analysts more removed from immediate policy questions, despite their tendencies to describe their own analytical efforts as though they were the rational-comprehensive method with an especially heavy use of theory. Similarly, this same method is inevitably resorted to in personal problem-solving, where means and ends are sometimes impossible to separate, where aspirations or objectives undergo constant development, and where drastic simplification of the complexity of the real world is urgent if problems are to be solved in the time that can be given to them. To an economist accustomed to dealing with the marginal or incremental concept in market processes, the central idea in the method is that both evaluation and empirical analysis are incremental. Accordingly I have referred to the method elsewhere as "the incremental method."

[3]

OBSERVATION OF A BUSINESS DECISION

RICHARD M. CYERT, HERBERT A. SIMON, AND DONALD B. TROW*

DECISION-MAKING — choosing one course of action rather than another, finding an appropriate solution to a new problem posed by a changing world—is commonly asserted to be the heart of executive activity in business. If this is so, a realistic description and theory of the decision-making process are of central importance to business administration and organization theory. Moreover, it is extremely doubtful whether the only considerable body of decision-making theory that has been available in the past—that provided by economics—does in fact provide a realistic account of decision-making in large organizations operating in a complex world.

In economics and statistics the rational choice process is described somewhat as follows:

1. An individual is confronted with a number of different, specified alternative courses of action.

2. To each of these alternatives is attached a set of consequences that will ensue if that alternative is chosen.

3. The individual has a system of preferences or "utilities" that permit him to rank all sets of consequences according to preference and to chose that alternative that has the preferred consequences. In the case of business decisions the criteri-

* Graduate School of Industrial Administration, Carnegie Institute of Technology. This is a preliminary report on research carried out under a grant from the Ford Foundation for studies in organization and decision-making. The authors are grateful to the Foundation for its support, to the executives of the company that opened its doors to them, and to colleagues and graduate students who have assisted at various stages of data collection and analysis.

on for ranking is generally assumed to be profit.

If we try to use this framework to describe how real human beings go about making choices in a real world, we soon recognize that we need to incorporate in our description of the choice process several elements that are missing from the economic model:

1. The alternatives are not usually "given" but must be sought, and hence it is necessary to include the search for alternatives as an important part of the process.

2. The information as to what consequences are attached to which alternatives is seldom a "given," but, instead, the search for consequences is another important segment of the decision-making task.

3. The comparisons among alternatives are not usually made in terms of simple, single criterion like profit. One reason is that there are often important consequences that are so intangible as to make an evaluation in terms of profit difficult or impossible. In place of searching for the "best" alternative, the decision-maker is usually concerned with finding a *satisfactory* alternative—one that will attain a specified goal and at the same time satisfy a number of auxiliary conditions.

4. Often, in the real world, the problem itself is not a "given," but, instead, searching for significant problems to which organizational attention should be turned becomes an important organizational task.

Decisions in organizations vary widely

with respect to the extent to which the decision-making process is *programmed*. At one extreme we have repetitive, well-defined problems (e.g., quality control or production lot-size problems) involving tangible considerations, to which the economic models that call for finding the best among a set of pre-established alternatives can be applied rather literally. In contrast to these highly programmed and usually rather detailed decisions are problems of a non-repetitive sort, often involving basic long-range questions about the whole strategy of the firm or some part of it, arising initially in a highly unstructured form and requiring a great deal of the kinds of search processes listed above. In this whole continuum, from great specificity and repetition to extreme vagueness and uniqueness, we will call decisions that lie toward the former extreme *programmed*, and those lying toward the latter end *non-programmed*. This simple dichotomy is just a shorthand for the range of possibilities we have indicated.

It is our aim in the present paper to illustrate the distinctions we have introduced between the traditional theory of decision, which appears applicable only to highly programmed decision problems, and a revised theory, which will have to take account of the search processes and other information processes that are so prominent in and characteristic of non-programmed decision-making. We shall do this by recounting the stages through which an actual problem proceeded in an actual company and then commenting upon the significance of various items in this narrative for future decision-making theory.

The decision was captured and recorded by securing the company's permission to have a member of the research team present as an observer in the company's offices on substantially a full-time basis during the most active phases of the decision process. The observer spent most of his time with the executive who had been assigned the principal responsibility for handling this particular problem. In addition, he had full access to the files for information about events that preceded his period of observation and also interviewed all the participants who were involved to a major degree in the decision.

THE ELECTRONIC DATA-PROCESSING DECISION

The decision process to be described here concerns the feasibility of using electronic data-processing equipment in a medium size corporation that engages both in manufacturing and in selling through its own widely scattered outlets. In July, 1952, the company's controller assigned to Ronald Middleton, an assistant who was handling several special studies in the accounting department, the task of keeping abreast of electronic developments. The controller, and other accounting executives, thought that some of the current developments in electronic equipment might have application to the company's accounting processes. He gave Middleton the task of investigation, because the latter had a good background for understanding the technical aspects of computers.

Middleton used three procedures to obtain information: letters to persons in established computer firms, discussions with computer salesmen, and discussions with persons in other companies that were experimenting with the use of electronic equipment in accounting. He also read the current journal literature about computer developments. He informed the controller about these matters principally through memorandums that de-

OBSERVATION OF A BUSINESS DECISION   239

scribed the current status of equipment and some of the procedures that would be necessary for an applications study in the company. Memorandums were written in November, 1952, October, 1953, and January, 1954. In them, in addition to summarizing developments, he recommended that two computer companies be asked to propose possible installations in the company and that the company begin to adapt its accounting procedures to future electronic processing.

In the spring of 1954 a computer company representative took the initiative to propose and make a brief equipment application study. In August he submitted a report to the company recommending an installation, but this was not acted upon—doubt as to the adequacy of the computer company's experience and knowledge in application being a major factor in the decision. A similar approach was made by another computer company in September, 1954, but terminated at an early stage without positive action. These experiences convinced Middleton and other executives, including the controller, that outside help was needed to develop and evaluate possible applications of electronic equipment.

Middleton drew up a list of potential consultants and, by checking outside sources and using his own information, selected Alpha as the most suitable. After preliminary meetings in October and November, 1954, between representatives of Alpha and the company accounting executives, Alpha was asked to develop a plan for a study of the application of electronic data-processing to sales accounting. Additional meetings between Alpha and company personnel were held in February, 1955, and the proposal for the study was submitted to the controller in March.

Although the proposal seemed com-petent and the price reasonable, it was felt that proposals should be obtained from another consulting firm as a double check. The controller agreed to this and himself selected Beta from Middleton's list. Subsequently representatives of Beta met with Middleton and other department executives. Middleton, in a memorandum to the controller, listed criteria for choosing between the two consultants. On the assumption that the written report from Beta was similar to the oral proposal made, the comparison indicated several advantages for Beta over Alpha.

After the written report was received, on May 2, the company's management committee authorized a consulting agreement with Beta, and work began in July, 1955. The controller established a committee, headed by Middleton, to work on the project. Middleton was to devote full time to the assignment; the other two committee members, one from sales accounting and one from auditing, were to devote one-third time.

The consulting firm assigned two staff members, Drs. Able and Baker, to the study. Their initial meetings with Middleton served the purpose of outlining a general approach to the problem and planning the first few steps. Twenty-three information-gathering studies were defined, which Middleton agreed to carry out, and it was also decided that the consultants would spend some time in field observation of the actual activities that the computer might replace.

During July, Middleton devoted most of his time to the twenty-three studies on volume of transactions and information flow, obtaining data from the sales department and from the field staffs of the other two committee members. Simultaneously, steps were taken to secure the co-operation of the field personnel who would be visited by the consultants early in August.

On July 22 Middleton submitted a progress report to the controller, describing the data-gathering studies, estimating completion dates, and summarizing the program's objectives. On July 25 the consultants met with Middleton and discussed a method of approach to the design of the data-processing system. The field trip took place early in August. The consultants obtained from field personnel information as to how accounting tasks were actually handled and as to the use actually made of information generated by the existing system.

On August 8 Middleton submitted another progress report, giving the status of the data-gathering studies and recording some ideas originating in the field trip for possible changes in the existing information-processing system. On August 10 he arranged with the assistant controller to obtain clerical assistance on the data-gathering studies, so that the consultants would not be held up by lack of this information, and on August 17 this work was completed.

On the following day the consultants met with the company committee to review the results of the twenty-three studies. They then listed the outputs, files, and inputs required by any sales accounting system the company might adopt and drew a diagram showing the flow of the accounting information. The group also met with the assistant controller and with the controller. The latter took the opportunity to emphasize his basic decentralization philosophy.

Upon returning from his vacation early in September, Middleton discussed the flow diagram in greater detail with Able and Baker, and revisions were made on the basis of information Middleton supplied about the present accounting system. Baker pointed out that all the alternative systems available to the company could be defined by the location of seven principal functions and records. Further analysis reduced this number to three: stock records, pricing of orders, and accounts receivable. The possible combinations of locations of these gave eighteen basic alternative systems, of which eight that were obviously undesirable were eliminated. Middleton was to make a cost analysis of the existing system and the most decentralized of the proposed systems, while the consultants were to begin costing the most centralized system.

Middleton reviewed these tentative decisions with the other members of the company committee, and the group divided up the work of costing. Middleton also reported to the controller on the conference, and the latter expressed his attitudes about the location of the various functions and the resulting implications for the development of executive responsibility.

During the next week, in addition to working on his current assignments, Middleton gave an equipment salesman a preliminary overview of the probable requirements of a new system. Next, there was a two-day meeting of the consultants and the company's committee to discuss the form and implications of a centralized electronic system. The consultants presented a method of organizing the records for electronic processing and together with the committee calculated the requirements which this organization and company's volume of transactions would impose on a computer. The group then discussed several problems raised by the system, including the auditing problems, and then met with the assistant controller to review the areas they had discussed.

On the following day, Middleton summarized progress to date for the controller, emphasizing particularly the work that had been done on the centralized system. The controller expressed satisfaction with several new procedures that would be made possible by an electronic computer. During the next several days the committee members continued to gather the information necessary to determine the cost of the present system. Middleton also checked with the assistant controller on the proposed solutions for certain problems that the consultants had indicated could not be handled readily by a computer and relayed his reactions to the consultants.

A week later the consultants returned for another series of meetings. They discussed changes that might be necessary in current practices to make centralized electronic processing possible and the way in which they would compare the centralized and decentralized proposals. The comparison presented some difficulties, since the data provided by the two systems would not be identical. A general form for a preliminary report was cleared with the assistant controller, and a date was set for its submission. The processing, outputs, and costs for the two alternatives would be described, so that additional information required for a final report could be determined.

During the next week Middleton continued collecting cost data. He phoned to the consultants to provide them with important new figures and to inform them of the controller's favorable reaction to certain proposed changes in the system that had implications for the company's policies.

On October 17 Baker met with Middleton to review the content of the accounting reports that would be produced by the centralized system, to discuss plans for the preliminary report, and to discuss the relative advantages and disadvantages of the centralized and decentralized systems. On the next day, Middleton checked on their decisions relative to the report with the controller and assistant controller and raised the possibility of an outside expert being retained by the company to review the final report submitted by Beta. During the last days of this week, Middleton attended the national meeting of a management society, where he obtained information about the availability of computers and computer personnel and the existence of other installations comparable to that contemplated for the company.

Work continued on the planning and costing of the two systems—Middleton worked primarily on the decentralized plan, and the consultants on the centralized. On October 27 the two consultants met with Middleton and they informed each other of the status of their work. Baker discussed methods for evaluating system reliability. Plans for the preliminary report were discussed with the company committee and the assistant controller. Since the controller strongly favored decentralization of authority, the question was raised of the compatibility of this with electronic processing in general and with the centralized system in particular. The groups concluded, however, that centralization of purely clerical data-processing operations was compatible with decentralization of responsibility and authority.

After several meetings between the committee and the consultants to iron out details, the preliminary report was presented to the company committee, the controller, and the assistant controller on November 3. The report was devoted primarily to the centralized system. The following points were made in the oral presentation: (1) that both the centralized and decentralized proposals would yield substantial and roughly equivalent savings but that the centralized system would provide more and better accounting data; (2) that the alternatives had been costed conservatively; (3) that the centralized system involved centralization of paper work, not of management; (4) that not all problems raised by the centralized system had been worked out in detail but that these did not appear insurmountable; (5) that the centralized system would facilitate improved inventory control; and (6) that its installation would require nine to twelve months at a specified cost. At this meeting the group decided that in the final report only the two systems already considered would be costed, that the final report would be submitted on December 1, and that investigation of other accounting applications of the system would be postponed.

In informal conversations after the meeting the controller told Middleton he had the impression that the consultants strongly favored the centralized system and that he believed the cost considerations were relatively minor compared with the impact the system would have on executives' operating philosophies. The assistant controller told Middleton he thought the preliminary report did not adequately support the conclusions. The committee then reviewed with the assistant controller the reasons for analyzing in detail only the two extreme systems: the others either produced less information or were more costly.

The next day the committee met with the controller and assistant controller to determine what additional information should be requested for the final report. The controller outlined certain questions of practicability that the final report should answer and expressed the view that the report should contain a section summarizing the specific changes that the system would bring about at various levels of the organization. He thought the comparison between systems in the preliminary report had emphasized equivalence of savings, without detailing other less tangible benefits of the centralized system.

Middleton reported these discussions to the consultants and with them developed flow charts and organization charts for inclusion in the final report, settled on some intermediate deadlines, and worked up an outline of the report. Within the company he discussed with the controller and assistant controller the personnel and organizational requirements for installation of an electronic system and for operation after installation. Discussion focused on the general character and organizational location of the eventual electronic-data-processing group, its relation to the sales accounting division, and long-term relations with manufacturing accounting and with a possible operations research group.

On November 14 the controller, on recommendation of Middleton, attended a conference on automation for company senior executives. There he expressed the view that three to five years would be required for full installation of a centralized electronic system but that the fear of obsolescence of equipment should not deter the company in making the investment. He also concluded that a computer installation would not reverse his long-range program for decentralizing information and responsibility.

Middleton, his suggestion being accepted, made tentative arrangements with an independent expert and with two large computer companies for the review of the consultants' report. Middleton presented to the controller and assistant controller a memorandum he had prepared at the latter's request, establishing a new comparison of the centralized and a modified decentralized system. The modification made the two systems more nearly comparable in data-processing capacity, hence clarified the cost comparison, which was now in favor of the centralized system. Consideration of the possibility of starting with a partially electronic decentralized system as a step toward a completely electronic system led to the decision that this procedure had no special advantages. The controller reported that conversations with the sales manager and the president had secured agreement with the concept of removal of stock record-keeping from field locations—an aspect of the plan to which it had been assumed there would be sales department opposition. The group discussed several other specific topics and reaffirmed that the final report should discuss more fully the relative advantages and disadvantages of centralized and decentralized systems.

Toward the end of November there was further consultation on the report, and final arrangements for its review were made with the two equipment companies and the independent expert. Each equipment company was expected to determine the method for setting up the proposed system on its computer and to check the consultants' estimates of computer capacity. During this week the controller informed the company's management committee that the report from the consultants would be submitted shortly and would recommend a rather radical change to electronic data-processing.

The final report, which recommended installation of the centralized system, was submitted on December 1. The report consisted of a summary of recommendations, general description of the centralized system, a discussion of the

installation program, and six appendixes: (1) statistics on volume of transactions (the twenty-three studies); (2) costs of the present system; (3) the requirements of a fully centralized system; (4) changes in allocation of functions required by the system; (5) an outline of the alternative decentralized system; and (6) a description of the existing system in verbal and flow-chart form. When the report was received and reviewed initially, the company's committee members and the consultants made some further computations on installation costs.

At a meeting the following Monday the assistant controller proposed an action program: send copies of the report to equipment companies, send copies to the sales department, and await the report of the independent expert. The controller decided that the second and third steps should be taken before giving the report to the machine companies, and the assistant controller indicated to Middleton some points requiring further clarification and elaboration.

By January 7 Middleton had prepared an outline for a presentation of the report to the sales department. This was revised on the basis of a meeting with the other interested accounting executives. A final outline was agreed upon after two more revisions and three more meetings. The report was presented on January 28 to the president and to six of the top executives of the sales department. The presentation discussed large-scale computers briefly, described with flow charts the proposed system, emphasized the completeness and accuracy of the information produced, discussed costs and savings, and mentioned the current trend in other companies toward electronic data-processing.

At Middleton's recommendation the same presentation was made subsequently to top members of the accounting department and still later to a group from the manufacturing department. At the same time the preliminary report of the independent expert was received, agreeing that the electronic installation seemed justifiable and stating that there might not be any cost savings but that it would make possible numerous other profitable applications of the computer. The consultants' report was then distributed to the computer companies, and Middleton began more detailed planning of the installation.

Middleton, the assistant controller, and the controller now met with the independent expert, who reported his conclusions: the feasibility study was excellent, the estimates of processing time were probably optimistic, the installation program should provide for an early test run, and the two principal available computers were highly competitive. Independent confirmation had been obtained on the last two points from another outside source. Middleton now proposed that the company proceed with its planning while awaiting the final written report from the independent expert and the proposals of the equipment companies. The assistant controller preferred to wait until these reports were actually in hand.

During the next week the equipment companies proceeded with their analysis, meeting several times with Middleton. Baker sent a memorandum on his estimates of processing time to meet the criticism of the independent expert. Middleton prepared two charts, one proposing a schedule and the staffing requirements for the installation phase, the other proposing organizational arrangements for the computer center. Middleton and the assistant controller presented these to the controller at the beginning of February, discussion centering responsibility for accuracy of input information.

Middleton and the assistant controller also had a meeting with sales executives who reported that on the basis of their own internal departmental discussions of the consultants' report they were in general agreement with the program. Middleton and one of the other committee members then spent two days inspecting computer installations in two other companies.

In the middle of February the two equipment companies presented their reports, each bringing a team of three or four men to present their recommendations orally. The two recommendations were substantially alike (except for the brand of the machine recommended!), but one report emphasized the availability of its personnel to give help during the installation planning stage.

Discussions were held in the accounting department and with consultant Baker about these reports and the next steps to be taken. The question was debated whether a commitment should be made to one equipment company or whether a small group should continue planning the system in detail, postponing the equipment decision until fall. Most of the group preferred the former alternative.

On February 15 the controller, in conference with the assistant controller and Middleton, dictated a letter to the company's president summarizing the conclusions and recommendations of the study and requesting that the accounting department be authorized to proceed with the electronics program.

On the following day the controller read the letter to the management committee. The letter reviewed briefly the history of the project and summarized the conclusions contained in the consultants' report: that there was ample justification for an electronic-data-processing installation; that the installation would warrant use of the largest computers; and that it would produce savings, many intangible benefits, and excess computer capacity for other applications. The letter quoted the consultants' estimate of the cost of the installation and their recommendation that the company proceed at once to make such a conversion and to acquire the necessary equipment. It then cited the various cross-checks that had been made of the consultants' report and concluded with a repetition of the conclusions of the report—but estimating more conservatively the operating and installation costs—and a request for favorable management committee action. Supplementary information presented included a comparison of consultant and equipment company cost estimates and a list of present and proposed computer installations in other companies. After a few questions and brief discussion, the management committee voted favorably on the recommendation, and the controller informed Middleton of the decision when the meeting ended.

THE ANATOMY OF THE DECISION

From this narrative, or more specifically from the actual data on which the narrative is based, one can list chronologically the various activities of which the decision process is composed. If we wish to describe a program for making a decision of this kind, each of these activities might be taken as one of the steps of the program. If the rules that determined when action would switch from one program step to another were specified, and if the program steps were described in enough detail, it would be possible to replicate the decision process.

The program steps taken together define in retrospect, then, a program for an originally unprogrammed decision. The program would be an inefficient one because it would contain all the false starts and blind alleys of the original process, and some of these could presumably be avoided if the process were repeated. However, describing the process that took place in terms of such a program is a useful way of organizing the data for purposes of analysis.

In order to make very specific what is meant here by a "program," Chart I has been prepared to show the broad outlines of the actual program for the first stages of the decision process (through the first seven paragraphs of the narrative).

CHART I
PROGRAM STEPS FROM INCEPTION OF THE PROBLEM TO SELECTION OF A CONSULTANT

KEEPING-UP PROGRAM (paragraphs 1 and 2 of narrative):
Search for and correspond with experts;
Discuss with salesmen and with equipment users;
Search for and read journals;

PROCUREMENT PROGRAM (paragraph 3):
Discuss applications study with salesmen who propose it;
Choice: accept or reject proposed study;
(If accepted) transfer control to salesmen;
Choice: accept or reject applications proposal;
(If rejected) switch to consultant program;

CONSULTANT PROGRAM (paragraphs 4 through 7):
Search for consultants;
Choice: best consultant of several;
Transfer control to chosen consultant;
Choice: accept or reject proposal;
(If accepted): begin double-check routine;
Request expenditure of funds;
(If authorized) transfer control to consultants;
And so on.

Subprograms.—The various program steps of the decision process fall into several subprograms, some of which have been indicated in Chart I. These subprograms are ways of organizing the activities *post factum*, and in Chart I the organizing principle is the method of approach taken by the company to the total problem. It remains a question as to whether this organizing principle will be useful in all cases. As in the present example, these subprograms may sometimes be false starts, but these must be regarded as parts of the total program, for they may contribute information for later use, and their outcomes determine the switching of activity to new subprograms.

In this particular case the reasons for switching from one subprogram to another were either the proved inadequacy of the first one or a redefinition of the problem. Other reasons for switching can be imagined, and a complete theory of the decision process will have to specify the conditions under which the switch from one line of attack to another will occur.

Common processes.—In the whole decision-making program there are certain steps or "routines" that recur within several of the subprograms; they represent the basic activities of which the whole decision process is composed. For purposes of discussion we have classified these common processes in two categories: the first comprises processes relating to the communication requirements of the organization; the second comprises processes relating directly to the solution of the decisional problem.

Communication processes.—Organizational decision-making requires a variety of communication activities that are absent when a decision is made in a single human head. If we had written out the program steps in greater detail, many more instances of contacts among different members of the organization would be recorded than are now explicit in the narrative. The contacts may be oral or written. Oral contacts are used for such purposes as giving orders, transmitting information, obtaining approval or criticism of proposed action; written communications generally take the form of memorandums having the purpose of transmitting information or proposing action.

The information-transmitting function is crucial to organizational decision-making, for it almost always involves acts of selection or "filtering" by the information source. In the present instance, which is rather typical in this respect, the consultants and subordinate executives are principal information sources; and the controller and other top executives must depend upon them for most of their technical information. Hence, the subordinate acts as an information filter and in this way secures a large influence over the decisions the superior can and does reach.

The influence of the information source over communications is partly controlled by checking processes—for example, retaining an independent expert to check consultants—which give the recipient an independent information source. This reduces, but by no means eliminates, filtering. The great differences in the amounts and kinds of information available to the various participants in the decision process described here emphasize the significance of filtering. It will be important to determine the relationship of the characteristics of the information to the resultant information change and to explore the effects of personal relations between people on the filtering process and hence upon the transmission of information.

Problem-solving processes.—Alongside the organizational communication processes, we find in the narrative a number of important processes directed toward the decision problem itself. One of the most prominent of these is the search for alternative courses of action. The first activities recounted in the narrative—writing letters, reading journals, and so on—were attempts to discover possible action alternatives. At subsequent points in the process searches were conducted to obtain lists of qualified consultants and experts. In addition to these, there were numerous searches—most of them only implicit in the condensed narrative—to find action alternatives that would overcome specific difficulties that emerged as detail was added to the broader alternatives.

The data support strongly the assertion made in the introduction that searches for alternative courses of action constitute a significant part of non-programmed decision-making—a part that is neglected by the classical theory of rational choice. In the present case the only alternatives that became available to the company without the expenditure of time and effort were the systems proposals made early in the process by representatives of two equipment companies, and these were both rejected. An important reason for the prominent role of search in the decision process is that the "problem" to be solved was in fact a whole series of "nested" problems, each alternative solution to a problem at one level leading to a new set of problems at the next level. In addition, the process of solving the substantive problems created many procedural problems for the organization: allocating time and work, planning agendas and report presentations, and so on.

Examination of the narrative shows that there is a rich variety of search processes. Many questions remain to be answered as to what determines the particular character of the search at a particular stage in the decision process: the possible differences between searches for procedural alternatives, on the one hand, and for substantive alternatives, on the other; the factors that determine how many alternatives will be sought before a choice is made; the conditions under which an alternative that has tentatively been chosen will be subjected to further check; the general types of search strategies.

The neglect of the search for alternatives in the classical theory of decision would be inconsequential if the search were so extensive that most of the alternatives available "in principle" were generally discovered and considered. In that case the search process would have no influence upon the alternative finally selected for action. The narrative suggests that this is very far from the truth —that, in fact, the search for alternatives terminates when a satisfactory solution has been discovered even though the field of possibilities has not been exhausted. Hence, we have reason to suppose that changes in the search process or its outcome will actually have major effects on the final decision.

A second class of common processes encompasses information-gathering and similar activity aimed at determining the consequences of each of several alternatives. In many decisions, certainly in the one we observed, these activities account for the largest share of man-hours, and it is through them that subproblems are discovered. The narrative suggests that there is an inverse relation between the cost or difficulty of this investigational task and the number of alternative courses of action that are examined carefully. Further work will be needed to determine if this relation holds up in a broader range of situations. The record also raises numerous questions about the *kinds* of consequences that are examined most closely or at all and about the conditions under which selection of criteria for choice is prior to, or subsequent to, the examination of consequences.

Another set of common processes are those concerned with the choices among alternatives. Such processes appear at many points in the narrative: the selection of a particular consulting firm from a list, the choice between centralized and decentralized electronic-data-processing systems, as well as numerous more detailed choices. These are the processes most closely allied to the classical theory of choice, but even here it is notable that traditional kinds of "maximizing" procedures appear only rarely.

In some situations the choice is between competing alternatives, but in many others it is one of acceptance or rejection of a single course of action— really a choice between doing *something* at this time and doing nothing. The first such occasion was the decision by the controller to assign Middleton to the task of watching developments in electronics, a decision that initiated the whole sequence of later choices. In decisions of this type the consequences of the single alternative are judged against some kind of explicit or implicit "level of aspiration"—perhaps expressed in terms of an amount of improvement over the existing situation—while in the multiple-alternative situations, the consequences of the several alternatives are compared with each other. This observation raises a host of new questions relating to the circumstances under which the decision will be formulated in terms of the one or the other of these frameworks and the personal and organizational factors that determine the aspiration levels that will be applied in the one-alternative case.

Another observation derivable from our data—though it is not obvious from the condensed narrative given here—is that comparability and non-comparability of the criteria of choice affects the decision processes in significant ways. For one thing, the criteria are not the same from one choice to another: one choice may be made on the basis of relative costs and savings, while the next may be based entirely on non-monetary criteria. Further, few, if any, of the choices were based on a single criterion. Middleton and the others recognized and struggled with this problem of comparing consequences that were sometimes measured in different, and incomparable, units, and even more often involved completely intangible considerations. The narrative raises, but does not answer, the question of how choices are made in the face of these incommensurabilities and the degree to which tangible considerations are overemphasized or underemphasized as compared with intangibles as a result.

CONCLUSION

We do not wish to try to transform one swallow into a summer by generalizing too far from a single example of a decision process. We have tried to illustrate, however, using a large relatively non-programmed decision in a business firm, some of the processes that are involved in business decision-making and to indicate the sort of theory of the choice mechanism that is needed to accommodate these processes. Our illustration suggests that search processes and information-gathering processes constitute significant parts of decision-making and must be incorporated in a theory of decision if it is to be adequate. While the framework employed here—and particularly the analysis of a decision in terms of a hierarchical structure of *programs*— is far from a complete or finished theory, it appears to provide a useful technique of analysis for researchers interested in the theory of decision as well as for business executives who may wish to review the decision-making procedures of their own companies.

[4]

The Structure of "Unstructured" Decision Processes

Henry Mintzberg, Duru Raisinghani, and André Théorêt

A field study of 25 strategic decision processes, together with a review of the related empirical literature, suggests that a basic structure underlies these "unstructured" processes. This structure is described in terms of 12 elements: 3 central phases, 3 sets of supporting routines, and 6 sets of dynamic factors. This paper discusses each of these elements in turn, and then proposes a general model to describe the interrelationships among them. The 25 strategic decision processes studied are then shown to fall into 7 types of path configurations through the model.•

How do organizations go about making "unstructured," "strategic" decisions? Researchers of administrative processes have paid little attention to such decisions, preferring instead to concentrate on routine operating decisions, those more accessible to precise description and quantitative analysis. As a result, the normative models of management science have had a significant influence on the routine work of the lower and middle levels of organizations and almost no influence on the higher levels. But it is at the top levels of organizations where better decision-making methods are most needed; excessive attention by management scientists to operating decisions may well cause organizations to pursue inappropriate courses of action more efficiently.

Although there is a body of normative literature on techniques for strategic decision making, for example, strategy planning, models of the firm, cost-benefit analysis, the evidence from empirical studies of their application indicates that all too often these techniques have made little real difference in the decisional behavior of organizations (Grinyer and Norburn, 1975; Hall, 1973; Whitehead, 1967). These techniques have been unable to cope with the complexity of the processes found at the strategy level, about which little is known.

This paper defines a *decision* as a specific commitment to action (usually a commitment of resources) and a *decision process* as a set of actions and dynamic factors that begins with the identification of a stimulus for action and ends with the specific commitment to action. *Unstructured* refers to decision processes that have not been encountered in quite the same form and for which no predetermined and explicit set of ordered responses exists in the organization. And *strategic* simply means important, in terms of the actions taken, the resources committed, or the precedents set. This paper uses empirical research to suggest a basic framework that describes unstructured, strategic decision processes. The suggested framework embodies the results of our own study of 25 such decision processes, as well as evidence from published empirical studies.

I. INTRODUCTION TO STRATEGIC DECISION MAKING

Published Research on Decision Processes

Most of the empirical literature can be neatly classified into three groups: research by cognitive psychologists on individual decision making in game situations, research by social psychologists on group decision making in the laboratory, and

•
The authors wish to express their appreciation to Richard Cyert for a number of helpful comments he made as discussant for an earlier version of this paper presented at the TIMS XX International Meeting, and to Danny Miller for his help in data analysis and his many useful suggestions.

June 1976, volume 21

Decision Processes

research by management theorists and political scientists on organizational decision making in the field.

The research on individual decision making, perhaps best represented by the Newell and Simon book *Human Problem Solving* (1972), relies largely on eliciting the verbalizations of decision makers' thought processes as they try to solve simplified, fabricated problems, such as in cryptarithmetic or chess. These are then analyzed to develop simulations of their decision processes. This research indicates that, when faced with a complex, unprogrammed situation, the decision maker seeks to reduce the decision into subdecisions to which he applies general purpose, interchangeable sets of procedures or routines. In other words, the decision maker deals with unstructured situations by factoring them into familiar, structurable elements. Furthermore, the individual decision maker uses a number of problem solving shortcuts—"satisficing" instead of maximizing, not looking too far ahead, reducing a complex environment to a series of simplified conceptual "models."

Thus, we can conclude from the studies of individual decision making that decision processes are programmable even if they are not in fact programmed: although the processes used are not predetermined and explicit, there is strong evidence that a basic logic or structure underlies what the decision maker does and that this structure can be described by systematic study of his behavior.

Much of the large body of research on group decision making, carried out primarily in the social psychology laboratory, is of little use to us here, for two reasons. First, it is concerned not with the structure of the decision process so much as with the interactions among the participants. Second, because the structure of the strategic decision process is determined by its very complexity, oversimplification in the laboratory removes the very element on which the research should be focused.

In field research on organizational decision making, an early study of an unstructured business decision process by Cyert, Simon, and Trow (1956) at Carnegie-Mellon University stimulated some follow-up studies that have produced a number of insights. Cyert and March (1963) reported on 4 decision processes; 2 were further analyses of parts of the EDP equipment decision process described in the Cyert, Simon, and Trow study, while 2 were new studies. Carter (1971a and 1971b) analyzed 3 decision processes related to computer equipment and 3 related to acquisitions, all in one firm. In Australia, Dufty and Taylor (1962) studied in detail the decision process of a transportation company that had to transfer certain employees after a merger; while in West Germany, Witte (1972) analyzed the documentary evidence from 233 decision processes involving the acquisition of data processing equipment.

In the public arena, Gore (1956) analyzed the processes of 33 decisions made by federal field offices in the state of Washington, while Snyder and Paige (1959) examined "the U.S. decision to resist aggression in Korea." Finally, Pfiffner (1960) reported on the study of Nicolaidis (1960) of 332 "policy" decision processes in the public sector. A ninth study

(Soelberg, 1967), not strictly organizational but nonetheless important in its results, analyzed how a group of candidates for master's degrees decided what job to take after graduation.

Research on 25 Strategic Decision Processes

This paper reports on empirical evidence collected over the span of five years by more than 50 teams of four to five students taking courses in management policy at the master's degree level. Each team studied an organization for three to six months. One assignment was to isolate one strategic decision made by the organization, describe the decision process in narrative form, and then "program" it. The assignment read in part: "By 'program,' the instructor means describe the steps included in the decision in enough detail so that you can represent the decision in flow chart form as you would a computer program." The groups were given a list of guiding questions, which eventually numbered 21, to encourage them to view the decision process comprehensively. Typical questions were: What was the source of the initial stimulus? Were stimuli frequent and/or intense? Were specific constraints and objectives established early? Where did management seek solutions? Were many alternative solutions proposed or did management "satisfice" by taking and testing alternatives one at a time? To what extent was each step or subroutine programmed?

Students were also exposed to some of the field literature cited above, but were encouraged to reject or extend the theory as they saw fit. Many chose to do so. The teams typically conducted structured interviews based on the guiding questions, with a number of the decision makers and other people involved in the process; the interviews took place either after the decision was made or near the termination of the process. Some groups also analyzed documentation when available. At the conclusion of the series of interviews, the teams reconstructed the decision processes and drew general conclusions vis-à-vis the theory. A typical report comprised 2,500 words plus figures, although many were far longer.

How reliable is such a data base for research? The strategic decision process may be researched by observation, by study of organizational records, and by interview or questionnaire. Investigation of records is often impossible because strategic decision processes seldom leave reliable traces in the files of the organization.[1] As Barnard (1966: 192–193) noted:

Not the least of the difficulties of appraising the executive functions or the relative merits of executives lies in the fact that there is little direct opportunity to observe the essential operations of decision. It is a perplexing fact that most executive decisions produce no direct evidence of themselves and that knowledge of them can only be derived from the cumulation of indirect evidence. They must largely be inferred from general results in which they are merely one factor, and from symptomatic indications of roundabout character.

Observation is certainly a powerful and reliable method, but extremely demanding of research resources because strategic decision processes typically span periods of years; often forced to study the process after completion, therefore, the researcher is obliged to rely heavily on interviewing. The best trace of the completed process remains in the minds of those people who carried it out.

[1]
The studies by Snyder and Paige (1958) and Witte (1972) are interesting exceptions.

Decision Processes

Table 1

25 Decision Processes Studied

Decision	Duration Years	Type of Organization	Type of Decision Process			Number of Steps Reported							
			By Stimulus	By Solution	By Process	Rec.	Diag.	Search	Design	Eval. Choice	Auth.	Interrupts	Branches and (re)cycles
1 Change of retirement age policy in small electronic firm	>4	Mfg.	Problem	Given	Simple Interrupt	3	1	–	–	1	–	2	1
2 Acquisition of distribution agency by marketing board	<1	Inst.	Problem	Given	Simple Interrupt	1	1	–	–	3	1	2	1
3 Institution of new form of treatment in hospital	>4	Inst.	Problem-Crisis	Given	Political Design	1	1	–	5	3	–	6	5
4 Purchase of seat on stock exchange	>4	Serv.	Opportunity	Modified	Political Design	1	–	1	3	5	4	3	8
5 Firing of radio announcer	<1	Serv.	Problem	Given	Basic Sr.	1	1	1	–	3	–	–	1
6 Merger of consulting firm	<1	Serv.	Crisis	Ready-Made	Basic Sr.	1	–	2	–	3	–	–	2
7 Acquisition of jet aircraft for regional airline	1–2	Serv.	Problem	Ready-Made	Basic Sr.	1	–	3	–	3	–	2	4
8 Purchase of new radiology equipment for hospital	1–2	Inst.	Problem	Modified	Modified Search	1	1	1	2	1	5	–	6
9 Purchase of new switching equipment for telecommunication co.	?	Govt.	Opp.-Prob.	Modified	Modified Search	1	–	2	2	2	3	–	3
10 Purchase of new DP system for municipality	1–2	Govt.	Opp.-Prob.	Modified	Modified Search	1	1	–	3	5	3	1	7
11 Purchase of new DP system for firm	1–2	Serv.	Problem	Modified	Modified Search	1	1	4	2	2	2	–	6
12 Development of new TV program	<1	Serv.	Problem	Custom-Made	Basic Design	1	–	–	2	2	–	–	1
13 Development of new beer for brewery	1–2	Mfg.	Opportunity	Custom-Made	Basic Design	1	–	1	2	3	1	1	2
14 Development of bid in new industrial market	<1	Mfg.	Opportunity	Custom-Made	Basic Design	1	1	1	3	4	–	–	3
15 Development of new electronics product	1–2	Mfg.	Opp.-Prob.	Custom-Made	Basic Design	1	1	1	3	3	–	–	3
16 Development of promotional program for racetrack	<1	Serv.	Problem	Custom-Made	Basic Design	1	1	–	4	3	–	1	3
17 Development of new supper club in hotel	<1	Serv.	Opportunity	Custom-Made	Basic Design	1	–	–	3	2	3	–	3
18 Development of new container terminal in port	?	Govt.	Opp.-Prob.	Custom-Made	Basic Design	1	1	1	3	6	1	1	3
19 Development of new market for deodorant	<1	Mfg.	Opportunity	Custom-Made	Basic Design	1	2	–	2	7	1	–	6
20 Development of urban renewal program	>4	Govt.	Opp.-Prob.	Custom-Made	Imp. Des.	1	1	–	2	2	–	1	1
21 Development of new runway for airport	2–4	Govt.	Opp.-Prob.	Custom-Made	Imp. Des.	1	–	–	4	1	4	4	5
22 Development of new building for new college program	1–2	Inst.	Problem Crisis	Custom-Made	Dynamic Design	1	–	3	3	5	–	2	4
23 Development of new laboratory for university	2–4	Inst.	Problem	Custom-Made	Dynamic Design	2	1	–	4	2	3	3	5
24 Development of new plant for small firm	>4	Mfg.	Problem Crisis	Custom-Made	Dynamic Design	1	–	4	4	6	1	3	6
25 Development of new headquarters building for bank	>4	Serv.	Problem Crisis	Custom-Made	Dynamic Design	1	–	–	7	6	–	4	6
Totals						28	15	25	63	83	33	36	95

Tapping the memories of the decision makers could introduce two forms of error, distortion and memory failure. There is no reason to suspect any systematic distortion in this study, and we feel that the possibility of random distortion was reduced in many cases by multiple interviewing. As for memory failure, there is no doubt that some information on false starts or unsuccessful steps during the decision processes went unreported. However, it should be noted that the decision processes chosen for study were typically recently completed ones; they were selected because they were interesting to the managers involved and the later parts, at least, remained fresh in the managers' minds. In general, this research proceeded on the premise that what the student teams captured really happened, but that not all that happened was necessarily captured by the student teams.

Our own analysis of the data of these student reports proceeded iteratively, in three steps. The first involved 28 decision processes and sought to determine the basic structure of the strategic decision process. The second focused on 20 other decision processes reported by student teams in later courses, typically in more detail. Here the initial structure was elaborated and a number of hypotheses were tested. The final step examined more intensively 25 decision processes of the first two studies, 9 from the first and 16 from the second. Two researchers independently reduced each decision process to a sequence of routines and dynamic factors, and data were generated that supported a number of the hypotheses advanced in this paper. The criteria for including a decision process in the final study were clear indications that the outcome was perceived as strategic, that is, important, by the organization that produced it and that the description was sufficiently complete and detailed for the purpose of the study.

Characteristics of Strategic Decision Making

Certain characteristics of strategic decision making are indicated by analyzing the 25 decision processes. Table 1 shows these decisions categorized in various ways. Six were made in manufacturing firms, 9 in service firms, 5 in quasi-government institutions, and 5 in government agencies. Typically, the processes spanned long time periods—8 lasted less than one year, 7 one to two years, 2 two to four years, and 6 greater than four years; time data could not be inferred accurately from two reports. The decisions varied widely: an airline choosing new jet aircraft, a radio station firing a star announcer, a consulting firm negotiating a merger after losing its major client, a hospital instituting a new form of treatment after intense political activity, and so on. Most decisions involved some kind of new equipment or facility or a venture into a new market, product, or service.

These 25 descriptions suggest that a strategic decision process is characterized by novelty, complexity, and open-endedness, by the fact that the organization usually begins with little understanding of the decision situation it faces or the route to its solution, and only a vague idea of what that solution might be and how it will be evaluated when it is developed. Only by groping through a recursive, discontinu-

Decision Processes

ous process involving many difficult steps and a host of dynamic factors over a considerable period of time is a final choice made. This is not the decision making under *uncertainty* of the textbook, where alternatives are given even if their consequences are not, but decision making under *ambiguity*, where almost nothing is given or easily determined.

Decisions Categorized by Process, Solution, or Stimulus

The decisions studied here were categorized (a) by the stimuli that evoked them, (b) by their solutions, and (c) by the process used to arrive at them. All three proved to be important for this study.

Decisions may be categorized by the stimuli that evoked them along a continuum. At one extreme are *opportunity* decisions, those initiated on a purely voluntary basis, to improve an already secure situation, such as the introduction of a new product to enlarge an already secure market share. At the other extreme are *crisis* decisions, where organizations respond to intense pressures. Here a severe situation demands immediate action, for instance, seeking a merger to stave off bankruptcy. Thus, opportunity and crisis decisions may be considered to form the two ends of the continuum. *Problem* decisions may then be defined as those that fall in between, evoked by milder pressures than crises.[2] The 25 decisions were categorized as follows: 1 crisis decision, 5 opportunity decisions, and 9 problem decisions; 4 decisions were categorized as problem-crises and 6 as opportunity-problems. During the development of a solution, a given decision process can shift along the continuum because of a delay or a managerial action: an ignored opportunity can later emerge as a problem or even a crisis, and a manager may convert a crisis to a problem by seeking a temporary solution, or he may use a crisis or problem situation as an opportunity to innovate.

Decisions may be classified by solution in four ways. First, the solutions may be *given* fully-developed at the start of the process. Second, they may be found *ready-made*, that is, fully-developed, in the environment during the process, as in the case of purchasing jet aircraft. Third, *custom-made* solutions may be developed especially for the decision, for example, construction of a new headquarter's building. Finally, the solution may combine ready-made and custom-made features—ready-made solutions are *modified* to fit particular situations, such as adapting equipment for special-purpose application. The 25 decisions included 4 given, 2 ready-made, 14 custom-made, and 5 modified solutions.

The third method of categorizing decisions is by the process used to arrive at them. A categorizing scheme of process is discussed at length in the final section of the paper.

The Phases of Decision Making

A number of frameworks have been put forward to describe the phases of decision making. In 1910, John Dewey suggested five phases of reflective thought: (1) suggestion, wherein the mind leaps to a possible solution; (2) intellectualization of the felt difficulty into a problem or question; (3) development of hypotheses; (4) reasoning or mental elabora-

2
One decision can be evoked by another, for example a new building must be found to house a new project. Such derivative decisions may be thought of as problem decisions by our definition.

tion of these; and (5) testing of the hypotheses (Dewey, 1933: 107). Using this as a cue, various other frameworks have been proposed, with the number of phases ranging from three to eight or more. Perhaps most well known is Simon's intelligence-design-choice trichotomy (Simon, 1965: 54).

In his research, Witte (1972) addressed the issue of the "phase theorem," seeking to discover whether distinct phases do exist and whether they follow a simple sequence as suggested in most of the literature. He found that the 233 decision processes dealing with data processing equipment did indeed "consist of a number of different operations that occur at different points in time" (p. 166), with an average of 38 and a maximum of 452. The sequence of five phases, however, problem recognition to gathering of information to development of alternatives to evaluation of alternatives to choice, was not supported for his whole sample or even for the subsample of the most efficient decisions. Witte found that the decision process consisted of a plurality of sub-decisions, and when he tested the phase theorem in terms of the subdecisions, he again found no support for the sequence.

Witte carried out his tests by dividing the decision processes into 10 equal time intervals and then noting the level and type of activity in each. He did not test problem recognition which by definition started the process. He found that communication activity dominated every time interval and that the total level of activity peaked at the beginning and end of the whole process, but was lower in the middle periods. He also found that the number of choices peaked at the end. Witte concluded (p. 180):

> We believe that human beings cannot gather information without in some way simultaneously developing alternatives. They cannot avoid evaluating these alternatives immediately, and in doing this they are forced to a decision. This is a package of operations and the succession of these packages over time constitutes the total decision-making process.

The framework used in this paper agrees with Witte's basic conclusions. We find logic in delineating distinct phases of the strategic decision process, but not in postulating a simple sequential relationship between them. Our central framework resembles the Simon trichotomy, although we define the phases differently, using the terms *identification, development,* and *selection.* We describe these three phases in terms of seven central "routines." In addition, we note the existence of three sets of routines that support the central phases, *decision control, communication,* and *political,* as well as six sets of dynamic factors that help to explain the relationship among the central and supporting routines. Together, these constitute the 12 basic elements of the strategic decision process. Each is discussed below together with its treatment in the literature, the data yielded in our study, as well as some hypotheses generated and some anecdotal material for illustration.

II. ELEMENTS OF THE STRATEGIC DECISION PROCESS

The Identification Phase in Strategic Decision Making

The identification phase of decision making comprises two routines in the framework of this paper: *decision recognition,* in which opportunities, problems, and crises are recognized

Decision Processes

and evoke decisional activity, and *diagnosis,* in which management seeks to comprehend the evoking stimuli and determine cause-effect relationships for the decision situation.

Decision Recognition Routine

Most strategic decisions do not present themselves to the decision maker in convenient ways; problems and opportunities in particular must be identified in the streams of ambiguous, largely verbal data that decision makers receive (Sayles, 1964: 163; Mintzberg, 1973: 67–71). The need for a decision is identified as a difference between information on some actual situation and some expected standard. In a study of these differences, Pounds (1969) found that these standards were based on past trends, projected trends, standards in some comparable organization, the expectations of other people, and theoretical models.

In at least 18 of the 25 cases in the present study, the decision processes were evoked by many stimuli, originating both inside and outside the organization. In many cases, low amplitude stimuli were collected, cumulated, and stored over a period of years—in one case, 25 years—before a more intensive signal finally evoked action.

Problem, opportunity, and crisis decisions are most clearly distinguished in the recognition routine. The opportunity decision is often evoked by an idea, perhaps a single stimulus, although it may remain dormant in the mind of an individual until he is in a position to act on it. There were 6 clear cases of this in the 25 decision processes. Crisis decisions are typically triggered by single stimuli. They present themselves suddenly and unequivocally, and require immediate attention, as in the cases, for example, of a fire or a bankruptcy. Problem decisions typically require multiple stimuli. Decision makers, presumably, wish to read the situation before taking action.

An interesting phenomenon in recognition is that of matching. A decision maker may be reluctant to act on a problem for which he sees no apparent solution; similarly he may hesitate to use a new idea that does not deal with a difficulty. But when an opportunity is matched with a problem, a manager is more likely to initiate decision making action.

What exactly determines the moment of action? The determining factor may be viewed as the relationship between the cumulative amplitude of stimuli and an action threshold. The amplitude of each stimulus depends on a number of factors, including the influence of its source, the interest of the decision maker in it, the perceived payoff of taking action, the uncertainty associated with it, and the perceived probability of successful termination of the decision. When stimuli are cumulated, we would expect their combined amplitude to be a function of the amplitude of each, as well as their pattern and frequency of occurrence. We can hypothesize that the perceived amplitude of an unattended stimulus decays over time; that quick reinforcement of one stimulus by another magnifies their perceived combined amplitudes; and that the greater the frequency, clarity, or consistency of related stimuli, the greater their perceived combined amplitude.

Our study reveals little about threshold levels, but Radomsky (1967) found that a manager's threshold level shifts continuously according to his workload and the number and type of decision processes in his active inventory. A manager faced with a number of crises presumably does not look for problems, while one faced with only a few mild problems is likely to search actively for opportunities. Thus, there is the need to reassess the increasingly popular point of view in the descriptive literature that organizations tend to react to problems and avoid uncertainty rather than seek risky opportunities (Cyert and March, 1963; Braybrooke and Lindblom, 1963). Based on our evidence, a more balanced and supportable conclusion would be that strategic decision making comprises both the exploitation of opportunities and the reaction to problems and crises, perhaps with the latter behavior more prevalent. Of 25 decisions chosen for study, 5 could be termed pure opportunities, and 6 opportunity-problems. The remaining 14 were categorized as problems, crises, or problem-crises.

Diagnosis Routine

Once a cumulation of stimuli reaches a threshold level, a decision process is initiated, and resources are mobilized to deal with it. At this point, the decision maker is faced with an array of partially ordered data and a novel situation. No strategic decision situation comes to him preformulated. We hypothesize that the first step following recognition is the tapping of existing information channels and the opening of new ones to clarify and define the issues. This behavior is prevalent in our study, with evidence reported for 18 of the 25 decision processes. Such behavior represents a first step in the diagnosis routine.

It is difficult to imagine strategic decision making without some form of diagnosis. Nevertheless, substantive discussion of this routine is almost totally absent in both the descriptive and normative literature. Two exceptions in the normative literature are Bonge (1972) and Emory and Niland (1966: 50, 66). Also, Drucker (1971) argues that a careful attention to diagnosis is one factor that distinguishes Japanese from American decision makers.

Diagnosis need not be a formal, explicit routine. We find evidence of a formal diagnostic step, for example, the creation of an investigating committee or task force or the request that consultants analyze a new issue, in 14 of the 25 decision processes. In the remaining 11 cases, diagnosis was presumably an informal or implicit activity, simply not reported. There is some evidence from our study that formal diagnosis is most common in the mild problem range of the opportunity-problem-crisis continuum. An explicit diagnostic step is reported in the case of 2 out of 5 opportunity decision processes, 4 out of 6 opportunity-problems, 7 out of 9 problems, 1 out of 4 problem-crises, and 0 out of 1 crises. Perhaps opportunities do not require much investigation—there is nothing to correct, only something to improve—while intense problems and crises may produce time and cognitive pressures that discourage the use of formal diagnosis.

Decision Processes

The Development Phase

The heart of the decision-making process is the set of activities that leads to the development of one or more solutions to a problem or crisis or to the elaboration of an opportunity. Our evidence supports the hypothesis that the
greatest amount of decision-making resources are consumed
in the development phase of the strategic decision process.
In 22 of the 25 cases, there was considerable development
activity, and this activity appeared to dominate the other two
phases in 21 of the decision processes studied. In only 3
cases did the organizations begin with fully-developed solutions, and in one of these, the organization was drawn into
development activity—redesign of its structure—to effect acceptance of its proposed solution.

Development may be described in terms of two basic
routines, search and design. Search is evoked to find ready-
made solutions; design is used to develop custom-made
solutions or to modify ready-made ones. This distinction is
fundamental—the difference between what psychologists call
convergent and divergent thinking. It is one thing to find a
needle in a haystack, quite another to write a fugue (Reitman,
1964).

Search Routine

Evidence of search is found in 13 of the 25 decisions, with a
total occurrence of 25. Based on evidence of this study and
that in the literature, four types of search behaviors can be
isolated. (1) Memory search is the scanning of the organization's existing memory, human or paper. (2) Passive search is
waiting for unsolicited alternatives to appear. Cyert and March
(1963: 80) note that "not only are organizations looking for
alternatives; alternatives are also looking for organizations."
(3) Trap search involves the activation of "search generators"
to produce alternatives, such as letting suppliers know that
the firm is looking for certain equipment (Soelberg, 1967). (4)
Active search is the direct seeking of alternatives, either
through scanning a wide area or focusing on a narrow one.[3]

There is considerable support for the contention that search is
a hierarchical, stepwise process. In general, one would expect the decision maker to begin with memory and passive
search, and some convenient forms of trap search as well.
Cyert and March (1963: 120–122) hypothesize that search
begins in local or immediately accessible areas, with familiar
sources. Numerous examples of this appeared in our study.
Initial failure in search leads presumably to use of more active
search procedures and to search in more remote and less
familiar areas. There is clear evidence of this in 8 of the 25
cases. Finally, it seems reasonable to hypothesize that faced
with repeated failure in search for an acceptable ready-made
solution, the organization turns where possible to design of a
custom-made solution.

[3]
Newell and Simon (1972) discuss a
number of combinations of scanning and
focusing, including "scan-search,"
"depth first," "breadth first," and "prog-
ressive deepening."

Design Routine

Use of the design routine is reported in 20 of the 25 decision
processes. These decisions fall into two groups: those with

custom-made solutions and those with modified solutions, where search was used to narrow down the available ready-made alternatives and then design was used to modify these for special application.

The results of this study suggest that the design of a custom-made solution is a complex, iterative procedure, which proceeds as follows: the designers may begin with a vague image of some ideal solution. They factor their decision into a sequence of nested design and search cycles, essentially working their way through a decision tree, with the decisions at each node more narrow and focused than the last. Failure at any node can lead to cycling back to an earlier node. Thus a solution crystallizes, as the designers grope along, building their solution brick by brick without really knowing what it will look like until it is completed.[4]

Sixty-three instances of design activities, many of these themselves nested, are reported in the 20 cases where some design was present. For decision processes with custom-made solutions, design is reported an average of just over three times, while for those with modified solutions the average is 2.4.

The hypothesis with the strongest support in our study is that the organization designs only one fully-developed custom-made solution. For all 14 decision processes that led to custom-made solutions, although choices from among competing alternatives were sometimes made at single nodes, in every case only one decision tree was followed to its ultimate conclusion. That is, only one solution emerged from the design process. Snyder and Paige (1958: 320) support this finding, noting that "the decision makers were confronted [in this case at major nodes] with single sets of proposed courses of action rather than conflicting alternatives." In contrast, organizations that chose ready-made solutions typically selected them from among a number of alternatives and in the five cases of modified solutions, that is, search followed by design, two organizations produced only one fully-developed solution. In the other three cases, all their decisions involving modifications to standard electronic equipment, developed two full solutions. Apparently, because design of custom-made solutions is expensive and time consuming, organizations are unwilling to spend the resources on more than one alternative. In contrast, the cost of generating extra alternatives during the search routine is small, and when relatively little design is involved, as in modified solutions, organizations are prepared to fully develop a second solution to compare it with the first. (Soelberg (1967) discusses the notion of a "confirmation candidate.")

The Selection Phase

Selection is logically considered to be the last step in the decision process: however, because the development phase frequently involves factoring one decision into a series of subdecisions, each requiring at least one selection step, one decision process could involve a great number of selection steps, many of these intricately bound up with the development phase. Witte (1972) found an average of 6, and a maximum of 51 distinct choices in the decision processes he studied. These were distributed throughout the 10 equal time

[4]
Reitman (1964), Klein (1962), and Manheim (1966) discuss design in terms similar to these. Unfortunately, however, there has been almost no attention to the design routine in the literature of administration.

Decision Processes

periods, although they occurred more frequently in the last period.

The normative literature describes the selection phase in terms of three sequential routines: determination of criteria for choice, evaluation of the consequences of alternatives in terms of the criteria, and the making of a choice. In reality, selection seldom allows a neat delineation of these three routines, and our study suggests that it is more appropriate to describe it in terms of screen, evaluation-choice, and authorization.

Our study and those in the empirical literature suggest that selection is typically a multistage, iterative process, involving progressively deepening investigation of alternatives. Multistage selection appears in virtually everyone of the 20 cases of our study where selection was described in some detail. Two multistage patterns of the three routines occur in our study. First, the selection routines are applied sequentially to a single choice. Screening is used first to reduce a large number of ready-made alternatives to a few feasible ones; evaluation-choice is then used to investigate the feasible alternatives and to select a course of action; finally, authorization is used to ratify the chosen course of action at a higher level in the organizational hierarchy. In the second pattern, a single selection step is itself multistage or nested. An alternative may be evaluated in a general way, then in succeedingly more intense ways, or one choice can be subjected to authorization at successively higher levels in the organization.

In the 25 decision processes, evaluation-choice activity is noted in 83 instances, and authorization in 33. Hence, each decision process averaged almost 5 selection steps, 4.8 for custom-made solutions, 6.4 for modified solutions (more than half of these authorization), 2 for ready-made solutions, and 2.8 for given solutions.

Screen Routine

The screen routine is evoked when search is expected to generate more ready-made alternatives than can be intensively evaluated. Screening is discussed in the literature by Cyert and March (1963: 80), Cyert and MacCrimmon (1968: 580), and Soelberg (1967). It is a superficial routine, more concerned with eliminating what is infeasible than with determining what is appropriate. Screening appears to challenge the appropriateness of alternatives that have never been used before and to reduce the alternatives to a number that can be stored and later handled by time-constrained decision makers. The 25 cases report little evidence of screening, in all likelihood not because there was an absence of screening but because it was an implicit part of search: as ready-made alternatives appeared, they were quickly screened and either rejected immediately or stored.

Evaluation-Choice Routine

By far the largest part of the literature on the strategic decision process has focused on the evaluation-choice routine. This is rather curious since this routine seems to be far less significant in many of the decision processes we studied than diagnosis or design. Particularly in the case of the custom-made solution, evaluation-choice often appeared to be a kind of trimming on the process, a ratification of the solution that was determined explicitly during design and in part implicitly during diagnosis as well.

The evaluation-choice routine may be considered to use three modes: judgment, bargaining, and analysis.[5] In judgment, one individual makes a choice in his own mind with procedures that he does not, perhaps cannot, explain; in bargaining, selection is made by a group of decision makers with conflicting goal systems, each exercising judgment; and in analysis, as described above, factual evaluation is carried out, generally by technocrats, followed by managerial choice by judgment or bargaining.

Our study reveals a number of interesting findings about these three modes. Judgment seems to be the favored mode of selection, perhaps because it is the fastest, most convenient, and least stressful of the three; it is especially suited to the kinds of data found in strategic decision making. Bargaining appears in more than half of the decision processes—typically where there was some kind of outside control or extensive participation within the organization and the issues were contentious.

The normative literature emphasizes the analytic mode, clearly distinguishing fact and value in the selection phase. It postulates that alternatives are carefully and objectively evaluated, their factual consequences explicitly determined along various goal, or value, dimensions and then combined according to some predetermined utility function—a choice finally made to maximize utility. A more pragmatic rendition of this view sees the analyst presenting his factual analyses of the consequences of various alternatives to the manager who determines the value trade-offs in his head and thereby makes a choice.

Our study reveals very little use of such an analytic approach, a surprising finding given the importance of the decision processes studied. Of the 83 instances of evaluation-choice activity, in only 18 could evaluation be distinguished from choice. (These cases occurred typically in large business organizations and concerned technical decisions; surprisingly, analysis was not more prevalent in the opportunity range.) In the typical situation, therefore, evaluation and choice are inextricably intertwined. The raw data, presumably facts and values, indistinguishably are plugged into a mind or a meeting, and a choice later emerges.

The other empirical studies also provide little evidence to support the prevailing normative views of decision making. Those who have addressed the issue of utility functions, notably Soelberg (1967) and Carter (1971a and 1971b) find no evidence to support their existence. These two researchers, as well as Cyert, Simon, and Trow (1956), note rather that the criteria used in decision processes are multiple and noncomparable. No study finds that even weightings on individual goal dimensions are established in advance of making choices; rather the weights are determined implicitly, in the context of making choices. Soelberg goes one step further and describes a confirmation period before the announcement of a decision during which the decision maker rationalizes to himself his implicit choice as well as the goals

[5]
This represents a modification of frameworks presented by March and Simon (1958: 213) and by Thompson and Truden (1964).

Decision Processes

it represents. Here the determination of criteria in effect follows the making of the choice.

Virtually every student of actual selection procedures agrees
that the selection of strategic alternatives requires consideration of a great number of factors, most of them "soft," or
nonquantitative; as a result they find that the evaluation-
choice routine is in practice a crude one. A plethora of value
and factual issues, few of them concrete, many involving
emotions, politics, power, and personality must be considered. This is further complicated by dynamic factors and uncertainty. Thus, the evaluation-choice routine gets distorted,
both by cognitive limitations, that is, by information overload,
and by unintended as well as intended biases. This has been
found to apply to all the modes of selection, including
analysis. (See Snyder and Paige, 1958; Pfiffner, 1960; Cyert
and March, 1963; Feldman and Kanter, 1965; Soelberg,
1967; Whitehead, 1967; Stagner, 1969; Carter, 1971a and
1971b; Kakar, 1971–72; and Newell and Simon, 1972.)

How do decision makers cope with the cognitive strain of
selection? A number of researchers suggest various proxy
means of choice, such as using imitation or tradition (Pfiffner,
1960: 130) or assessing the sponsor of an alternative instead
of the alternative itself (Carter, 1971b; Mintzberg, 1973: 89).
Both Soelberg (1967) and Carter (1971a and 1971b) propose
elaborate schemes to describe how strategic choices are
actually made. Soelberg, for example, distinguishes primary
goals and secondary constraints in a theory that combines the
notions of maximizing and satisficing. Soelberg believes that
scaling is essentially disjoint: each alternative is evaluated
independently along independent goal dimensions. On some
criteria, the decision maker seeks merely satisfactory performance. On others, usually one, never more than three in
Soelberg's view, he seeks to get as much as possible. In
screening, the secondary constraints are used to reject alternatives. The alternatives that remain are then rated as acceptable, unacceptable, or marginal in terms of the primary goal's
dimensions. The acceptable ones enter into an "active ros-
ter" where they are later compared with each other, unless
an "outstanding" alternative is found, in which case search is
terminated. In making this comparison, the decision maker
prefers a dominant alternative, one that is best along all the
primary goal dimensions. If none can be found, he uses crude
internal scales such as "significantly better" and "a little
better," to compare alternatives.

Authorization Routine

Decisions are authorized when the individual making the
choice does not have the authority to commit the organization
to a course of action. The decision must follow a tiered route
of approval up the hierarchy and perhaps also out to parties in
the environment that have the power to block it. Typically,
authorization is sought for a completed solution, after final
evaluation-choice; but, we also found instances of the seeking
of authorization to proceed with a decision process, either at
the outset or during development.

Authorization is common in strategic decision making; it is
reported in 14 of the 25 cases under study, for a total of 33

instances. Of the 11 cases where authorization is not reported, 6 were business decisions made in autonomous organizations by the chief executive, and 4 were local decisions involving small resource commitments made by the top management of subsidiary organizations; the remaining case, decision 20, almost certainly involved authorization although it is not reported. In those cases where authorization took place and is reported, it involved the approval either of top management, in 12 instances; the board of directors, in 6 instances; a parent firm or owner, in 4 instances; a higher level of government, in 6 instances; and outside agencies, in 5 instances. Authorization was most common in government and institutions, appearing in 8 of 10 cases for a total of 21 instances; it is reported in only 6 of 15 manufacturing and service organizations, with a total of 12 instances.

Authorization appears to be a typically binary process, acceptance or rejection of the whole solution. Acceptance leads to presentation of the solution to the next highest level if necessary; rejection leads to its abandonment or redevelopment. In a few cases, conditional acceptance occurred, leading to a recycling of the solution through the development phase with every attempt made to overcome the objections without altering the essential features of the solution.

The authorization routine experiences difficulties beyond all of those found in evaluation-choice. The time for it is typically limited; at this level the decision must be considered in the light of other strategic decisions and overall resource constraints; outside political forces are often brought to bear on the decision at the point of authorization; and the authorizers generally lack the in-depth knowledge that the developers of the solution have. In capital budgeting as well as in less formal types of authorization, a major problem is presented by the fact that the choices are made by people who often do not fully comprehend the proposals presented to them. Thus, in authorization the comparative ignorance of the manager is coupled with the inherent bias of the sponsor (Carter, 1971a and 1971b; Pettigrew, 1972). This explains why empirical studies of capital budgeting have shown it to be a somewhat distorted, political process, far less analytical than the normative literature suggests (Carter, 1971a and 1971b; Bower, 1970).

Three Sets of Supporting Routines

Studies of strategic decision processes suggest that three sets of routines support the three central phases. Decision control routines guide the decision process itself; communication routines provide the input and output information necessary to maintain decision making; and political routines enable the decision maker to work his way to a solution in an environment of influencing and sometimes hostile, forces.

Decision Control Routines

Faced with a decision situation, not only does the decision maker execute the steps leading to a solution, but he also plans his approach and allocates the organizational resources to get there. This metadecision making, decision making about the decision process itself, is analogous to program control in a time-shared computer system.

Decision Processes

Decision control activities are difficult to study because they
tend to be implicit and informal, taking place in the mind of
the decision maker, and to leave little trace of themselves.
Nevertheless, a number of researchers note their existence,
including Newell and Simon, who refer to problem planning
"to guide action in exploring a problem space" (1972: 82),
and Cyert, Simon, and Trow (1956: 247). We consider decision control to comprise two basic routines—*decision planning* and *switching.*

In a few of the cases in our study, explicit reference is made
to decision planning or to the existence of informal decision
plans. When faced with a new decision situation, the decision
maker presumably attempts to establish some preliminary
bounds on the decision space. He may determine a rough
schedule for solution, a development strategy, and an estimate of the resources he is prepared to commit to developing
the solution; he may establish some preliminary constraints
and perhaps develop an image of an ideal solution as well
(Soelberg, 1967: 210). But like so much else in strategic
decision making, these decision plans typically appear to be
informal and flexible, modified and clarified as the decision
process progresses.

Broad planning has to be converted into specific action. In the
switching routine, the decision maker directs his attention to
the next step, to choosing the appropriate routine such as
diagnosis or search, to determining what resources to commit to it, and to evoking the actual routine. Subsequently, he
monitors the results to update his decision plan.

Decision Communication Routines

We have already seen evidence of an active stream of communication throughout the decision process: scanning the
environment for stimuli, searching intensively for diagnostic
information and for information about alternatives and their
consequences, transmitting information up the hierarchy to
facilitate authorization, and monitoring the progress of the
decision process itself. Witte (1972) found that communication activities dominated every phase of unstructured decision
making.

Three communication routines can be delineated. The *exploration* routine involves the general scanning for information
and the passive review of what comes unsolicited. It is likely
used to identify decision situations, to build conceptual models, and to develop a general data base for decision making.
The *investigation* routine involves the focused search and
research for special-purpose information. Investigation appears to be used to find or confirm information during diagnosis, search, and evaluation-choice activities. There is evidence that investigation in strategic decision processes relies
largely on informal, verbal channels of communication (Aguilar, 1967; Snyder and Paige, 1958: 373; Mintzberg, 1973:
38–44, 70). We hypothesize that investigation is most active
during diagnosis and the earlier stages of development, and
again during the early stages of evaluation-choice. In 15 of our
cases, information collection appeared to be most active during development, and in a further 5.5 cases, during diagnosis.
In 1.5 cases it appeared most active during selection. (In

some cases, two phases appeared to be equal, and in 3, we could draw no obvious conclusion from the data.) Cyert, Simon, and Trow (1956: 247) found that the largest share of manhours in the decision process they studied was devoted to gathering information to determine the consequences of alternatives, and Witte (1972) found that communication followed a U-shaped curve, most active toward the beginning and end of the decision processes.

The third communication routine is *dissemination*. We find evidence that the greater the number of persons involved or interested in the outcome of the decision, the more time the decision makers spend disseminating information about its progress. This relationship was especially evident in six cases in our study where many individuals were involved, notably where authorization was a significant part of the selection phase rather than a formality. We also find anecdotal evidence that the further along the decision process, the greater the dissemination of information about it. In effect, the clearer the solution becomes and the more committed to it is the decision maker, the greater is his propensity to communicate information about it to ensure its eventual acceptance.

Political Routines

There is considerable evidence that political activities are a key element in strategic decision making: Pettigrew (1972), Carter (1971a and 1971b), and Bower (1970: 68) emphasize the internal political activities for strategic decisions in business organizations while Gore (1964: 290–291) and others point out the sources of internal and external political pressures in public organizations. Political activities reflect the influence of individuals who seek to satisfy their personal and institutional needs by the decisions made in an organization. These individuals may be inside or outside the organization; what ties them to the decision process is their belief that they will be affected by the outcome. Their political activities serve to clarify the power relationships in the organization; they can also help to bring about consensus and to mobilize the forces for the implementation of decisions. We find eight cases in our study that involved intense political activity and a number of others involving such activity of a less intense nature. Our study suggests a relationship between such activity and the duration of the decision process. By conservative estimates, assuming the decisions lasting longer than 4.0 years averaged 5.0 years and those of less than 1.0 year averaged .8 years, these eight decisions averaged 3.6 years whereas the others averaged 1.6 years.

Political activity generally manifests itself in the use of the *bargaining* routine among those who have some control over choices.[6] We found two cases where bargaining occurred early in the decision process, when principals within the organizations disputed the need to recognize the issue in the first place. One of these cases led to long delays until the issue was resolved and the other led to a rearrangement of the power structure by the chief executive to eliminate the sources of resistance, in effect a political design activity. In two other cases, intensive bargaining among insiders took place during development and selection; in four cases, bargaining took place between the organization and outsiders

6
Another form of bargaining takes place in decision making, between the organization and its suppliers, and concerns the price and arrangements for inputs. Such bargaining—perhaps it should be called *negotiating* to distinguish it—is not inherently political in nature.

Decision Processes

when the latter confronted and temporarily blocked proposed
decisions late in the final selection phase. Apparently, when
concerned centers of power are disregarded during development, they are likely to confront the organization late in the
selection phase. In three cases, such confrontation resulted in
renewed development activity intended to modify the solutions in line with the objections, while in the fourth case, the
organization directly resisted the pressures to change its solution.

Organizations sometimes try to preempt this resistance late
in the selection phase by disseminating information about the
solution during the development and early selection phases or
by inviting the potential dissidents to participate in the development phase. Gore (1964), Carter (1971a and 1971b),
Bower (1970), and Pfiffner (1960) refer to one or both of
these behaviors, which we call, respectively, the *persuasion*
and the *coöptation* routines. In general, we may conclude that
the more important and contentious the outcome of a decision and the more the influence over choice rests outside the
organization, the greater the emphasis on selection and
communication processes in general and the bargaining and
persuasion routines in particular.

Dynamic Factors

The delineation of steps in almost any strategic decision process shows that there is not a steady, undisturbed progression from one routine to another; rather, the process is
dynamic, operating in an open system where it is subjected
to interferences, feedback loops, dead ends, and other factors. "One gets the picture of everything chasing after everything else, trying to adjust to it . . ." (Diesing, 1967: 186).
These dynamic factors are perhaps the most characteristic
and distinguishing features of decision processes that are
strategic. It is therefore surprising that they are hardly mentioned in the literature.

We find in our study that dynamic factors influence the
strategic decision process in a number of ways. They delay it,
stop it, restart it. They cause it to speed up, to branch to a
new phase, to cycle within one or between two phases, and
to recycle back to an earlier point in the process. We shall
discuss six groups of dynamic factors: *interrupts,* which
are caused by environmental forces, *scheduling delays* and
timing delays and speedups, which are effected by the decision maker, and *feedback delays, comprehension cycles,* and
failure recycles, which are largely inherent in the decision
process itself.

Interrupts. Of the 25 decision processes, 15 are reported
to have experienced a total of 36 sudden events that inter-
rupted them and caused changes in pace or direction. In 7 of
the cases, unexpected constraints were met, typically late in
the selection phase, causing delays and usually forcing the
organizations to cycle back to the development phase. One
firm, for example, met a capital requirement difficulty and had
to rework its capital structure, while another faced the sudden expropriation of the plant that it had just bought.

In 16 cases, the decision processes encountered political
impasses that caused temporary delays. Typically, these took

place late in the decision process when inside or outside groups blocked proposals in the selection phase. In one case, civic groups used legal actions and government legislation to block a new airport runway, while in another, a conservative staff group in a hospital repeatedly blocked acceptance of a new form of treatment. In a number of these cases, the decision makers cycled back to development to modify the solution, to find another, or to engage in political design activity to remove the dissidents from positions of power. In other cases, bargaining took place, or the decision makers simply delayed until the blocking forces disappeared.

In six cases, decision processes encountered unexpected new options, proposals that stimulated new development or selection activity. Thus, some new options caused delays, by interrupting a process nearing termination, while others caused speedups, because the new option appeared to be so good that design was terminated and final evaluation-choice begun. In four cases, new options were accepted in place of those under consideration; in the remaining two cases, the new options were developed but not ultimately selected.

Finally, there were seven cases where interrupts resulted in a speedup of the decision process. Five of these came in response to the delaying interrupts discussed above: two removed unexpected constraints and three responded to political impasses. The two other cases, one involving a strike and the other the discovery of a competitor action, resulted in a speedup in the selection of proposals.

A number of interrupts we have described led to other interrupts; in effect, one interrupt specifically evoked another. Thus, we find 36 interrupts in 15 decision processes, an average of 2.4 each, and we hypothesize that interrupts beget interrupts.

Interrupts appear to be most common in high pressure environments. We find them in 4 of the 5 problem-crisis and crisis decision processes, a total of 15 times, but in only 11 of the 20 opportunity and problem decision processes, a total of 21 times. They were also more common in the public or quasi-public organizations, appearing in 8 of the 10 government and institutional organizations, a total of 20 times, compared with 7 of the 15 business organizations, a total of 16 times.

Here again we find a strong relationship with duration: decision processes without interrupts averaged 1.3 years, while those with delaying interrupts averaged 3.6 years. This is presumably related to the earlier finding that duration and political activity are related, since delaying interrupts and political activity are often found together. Hence we hypothesize that interrupts of a political nature significantly delay strategy decision processes.

Scheduling delays. Because managers are severely time-constrained, they factor complex decisions into manageable steps; this enables them to introduce scheduling delays so that they can attend to the multiplicity of tasks that always await their attention (Mintzberg, 1973: 31–35, 80–81). Hence, every step of the strategic decision process is separated by

Decision Processes

significant time delays; presumably as a result, only 8 of 23 decision processes had a reported duration of less than one year.

Feedback delays. During a feedback delay, the decision maker awaits the results of the previous action taken. Each step in the strategic decision process involves a certain time-consuming activity; in addition, many steps require reaction. And in creative design processes, there may be a period of incubation before insight occurs (Lonergan, 1967). Thus, we would expect especially complex decision processes involving outsiders to span long time periods.

Timing delays and speedups. Timing is apparently a major factor in strategic decision making, yet it has hardly been studied, perhaps because it is almost always effected in one manager's mind. Hardwick and Landuyt (1966: 283), for example, surveyed 183 books in the area of administration and found only 10 that even mentioned timing or surprise. Managers may purposely speed up or delay a decision process to take advantage of special circumstances, to await support or better conditions, to synchronize action with another activity, to effect surprise, or to gain time. In general, managers try to time the initiation of decision steps to facilitate their smooth execution. In competitive and hostile environments, where the issues are contentious, we would expect to find a greater incidence of timing speedups and delays. In our study we find examples of speedups to beat a competitor to a market and delays to wait for resistance to subside. In the study of crisis decision processes, Schwartzman (1971) found that managers sought delays that would reduce the pressures; they tried to "buy time" by stalling, bluffing, or finding temporary solutions.

Comprehension cycles. Throughout this paper, strategic decision making has been described as a groping, cyclical process. Inherent in it are factors causing the decision process to cycle back to earlier phases. Pfiffner noted that "the decision-making process is not linear but more circular; it resembles 'the process of fermentation in biochemistry rather than the industrial assembly line' . . ." (1960: 129). By cycling within one routine or between two routines, the decision maker gradually comes to comprehend a complex issue. He may cycle within identification to recognize the issue; during design, he may cycle through a maze of nested design and search activities to develop a solution; during evaluation, he may cycle to understand the consequences of alternatives; he may cycle between development and investigation to understand the problem he is solving (Diesing, 1967: 187); he may cycle between selection and development to reconcile goals with alternatives, ends with means. The most complex and novel strategic decisions seem to involve the greatest incidence of comprehension cycles. We found specific evidence of cycling and recycling in all 25 decision processes, with a total of 95 occurrences. Two took place within the identification phase, 14 within development, and 25 within selection. In 1 case, there was recycling from development back to identification, in 50 cases from selection back to development, and in 3 cases from selection all the way back to identification.

Failure recycles. Decision processes are sometimes blocked for want of an acceptable solution. Solutions may be rejected in evaluation-choice as having too low a payoff; they may meet constraints they cannot satisfy; they may simply not appeal to those expected to authorize them. Faced with no acceptable solution, the decision maker may simply delay until one appears or he may change his criteria so that a solution previously rendered unacceptable becomes acceptable. A more typical finding in our study, however, is that organizations faced with failure in finding or designing an acceptable solution cycle back to the development phase. We find 13 cases where the decision processes either entered a special design branch to remove a constraint, or developed a new solution or modified an existing one by following a new path from an earlier node of the decision tree. In some cases, a previously rejected alternative was reintroduced under the new conditions. Given the failure of a solution, it would appear that the decision maker first tries to branch to remove a constraint and thereby make the solution acceptable; if that is infeasible, he tries to recycle to the development phase to modify the solution; if that is not possible, he tries to develop a whole new solution; finally, if resources will not permit this or if he meets with continued failure, the decision maker will accept a previously unacceptable solution.

III. A GENERAL MODEL OF THE STRATEGIC DECISION PROCESS

The elements of the strategic decision process can now be brought to a common base. We have developed a general model of the process shown in Figure 1, that comprises the seven basic routines, as well as some of the dynamic factors discussed in this paper. We believe this model can be used to illustrate the structure of each of the 25 decision processes studied.

The "main line" through the center of the model shows the two routines that must be a part of any decision process, recognition of the situation and the evaluation-choice of a solution. The three modes of the evaluation-choice program are shown at X_3. In theory, therefore, the most basic decision process involves simply the recognizing of a given solution and then the evaluation and choice of it. Needless to say, we encountered no case quite that simple.

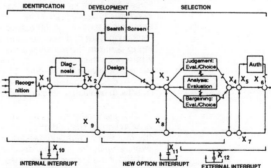

Figure 1. A general model of the strategic decision process.

Decision Processes

Most decision processes involve development activity after recognition. Hence, at X_2, there is a branch off the main line into the search (and screen) routine to find a ready-made solution or into the design routine to develop a custom-made solution. In virtually all cases, in fact, development was a nested activity; hence, at X_4 the model contains a branch from the evaluation-choice routine back to the development phase at X_9 to initiate another search or design cycle. Modified solutions, as noted earlier, first follow one or more search cycles to find a ready-made solution, and then a series of design cycles, to modify it. In addition to nested development, nested selection also occurred frequently; hence at X_4 and X_8 there is a loop from the evaluation-choice routine back to itself.

Any decision process may or may not involve formal diagnosis or authorization. Hence, the model shows branches at X_1 and X_5 which take the process off the main line and later return it there when completed. In addition, authorization may be tiered, hence the loop at X_6 and X_7, and authorization to proceed may be sought after recognition or during development, resulting in a branch from the authorization routine at X_6 back to development at X_9. And there is evidence that the decision process may branch from selection at X_4 or X_6 all the way back to diagnosis to allow for reconsideration of the whole decision situation. All of these branches also represent the comprehension cycles for example, cycling within evaluation-choice at X_4 and X_8 and the failure recycles, from the evaluation-choice routines at X_4 or the authorization routine at X_6 back to redevelopment at X_9 to modify an unacceptable solution or develop a new one, or back to the evaluation-choice routine at X_8 to modify criteria.

Many strategic decision processes involve interrupts of one kind or another. The three most common ones are shown in the model. At X_{10} are *internal* or political interrupts in the identification phase, where there is disagreement on the need to make a strategic decision. Such interrupts come from within the organization and may lead either to cycling in the recognition routine, to resolve the disagreement by bargaining or persuasion, to delays, until the resistance subsides, or to political design activity, to remove the resistance. At X_{12} are *external* interrupts during the selection phase, where outside forces block the selection of a fully-developed solution. These interrupts typically lead either to modification in the design to bring it in line with the difficulty encountered, to complete redevelopment of a new solution if necessary, or to bargaining to confront the resistance directly. At X_{11} are *new option* interrupts, which typically occur late in development or during the evaluation-choice routine. These lead the process either back to design, to elaborate or modify the new option, or directly to evaluation-choice to select or reject it immediately.

Finally, the model shows an inherent delay, in the form of a broken line, at the end of each of the routines. This reflects the fact that scheduling, feedback, and timing delays separate every step in the strategic decision process. This model does not show the supporting routines, except for bargaining as a mode of selection; but decision control, communication, and political routines can occur together with any of the routines shown in the model.

Our final analysis led us to describe the 25 decision processes in terms of this model. Each was translated into a sequence of events, consisting of the central routines, interrupts, branches, and cycles. (Decision control and communication routines as well as scheduling and feedback delays were excluded as these occurred almost regularly. Timing speedups and delays were difficult to report on.) Because the narratives were not always consistently specific and because of some difficulties in interpretation (for example, is any deep probe to be called diagnosis?), such description was at times difficult. However, two researchers so described each process independently and we then assured ourselves that the two descriptions agreed in basic form and shape, even if not in every detail.

We found that all 25 decision processes could be represented in terms of the basic model, with minor additions which do not appear to be common.[7] We found further that decision processes fell into seven groupings according to the path configurations through the model. These appeared to depend in large part on the type of solution and the nature of the dynamic factors encountered. Interestingly, four of these seven types reflect the specific nature of the decision outcome (for example, all decisions of Type 4 involved new equipment). The seven path configurations are discussed below, more or less in order of complexity.

Type 1. Simple impasse decision processes. Decision processes 1 and 2 were the simplest of the study and the closest to the main line of the model. They involved no development activity at all. Both, however, met interrupts which complicated the flow of events.

Decision process 1 is shown in Figure 2. Here, a small manufacturing firm three times considered instituting a policy of mandatory retirement at age 65; twice the proposal was blocked in debate at the senior executive level, and a third time 10 years later in a period of recession, it was accepted.

Type 2. Political design decision processes. Decision processes 3 and 4 were similar to those of type 1 in that they were evoked by given solutions, but different in that the impasses were more difficult ones, and in both cases the

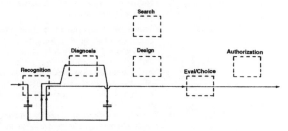

7
There is one consistent difference between the reports and the model. In some cases, development activity was reported without selection activity following it. We assumed this to be an omission in the reports, and in the examples below, we always show development activity followed by evaluation-choice activity, unless there was an interrupt.

Figure 2. A simple impasse decision process—retirement at age 65 (decision process 1).

Decision Processes

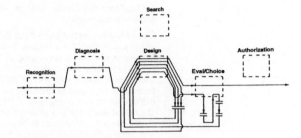

Figure 3. A political design decision process—a new hospital treatment (decision process 3).

organizations found it necessary to branch into extensive political design activity. Together, these two decision processes encountered 9 interrupts and involved 9 development and 12 selection steps.

Decision process 3 is shown in Figure 3. In this case, a preeminent hospital finally accepted a new form of treatment, involving a major shift in its philosophy after much political activity. The decision process began when a new director was appointed. He recognized the need for the new treatment and investigated it (diagnosis). However, after repeatedly meeting resistance from a group of conservative doctors, he engaged in a series of political design activities. First, he hired four doctors experienced with the new treatment, but was again blocked (interrupt). Subsequently, the head of nursing was replaced (political design) and other pressures built up, including an accusation of malpractice from a medical association (interrupt). A report on implementation was then prepared (design) and agreement was reached to implement the treatment in one public ward (evaluation-choice). Eighteen months later, there was a strike (interrupt) and because the new treatment was more effective under conditions of reduced staff, it was allowed in a second public ward (evaluation-choice). With increasing numbers of the new staff favoring the treatment, there was a sudden demand for full implementation and a threat to resign by one highly respected member of staff (two interrupts). Two doctors sympathetic to the treatment were then promoted to senior executive positions (political design) and the treatment was finally accepted in the private wards (final evaluation-choice).

There are a number of intriguing features about this decision process. First, all the design activities except one were political, initiated to change the power structure. Second, it is difficult to distinguish evaluation-choice and recognition activity in this decision process. Was debate over the desirability of instituting a new form of treatment the recognition of the need to make a decision or was it the evaluation of a solution? (We took the point of view of the director, who recognized the need early, and accordingly, we treated the debate as evaluation-choice activity). Third, should this be treated as an opportunity, problem, or crisis decision process? Here especially we can see that opportunities, problems, and crises are to some extent in the eyes of the beholder. One group felt a threat to the hospital's reputation; the other saw no need for a questionable opportunity. Fourth, despite one's perception of the stimuli, it is clear that over time the pressures increased, forcing the issue from the opportunity toward the crisis end of the continuum.

Type 3. Basic search decision processes. In decision processes 5, 6, and 7 the organizations were able to establish relatively clear guidelines for solution at the outset, and development consisted simply of finding, in one or two nested search steps, the best available ready-made solution.[8] These were relatively straight-forward processes, involving only two interrupts, six search steps, and nine selection steps. Two of the processes lasted less than one year, and the other between one and two years.

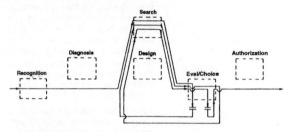

Figure 4. A basic search decision process—new jets for regional airline (decision process 7).

Decision process 7, shown in Figure 4, is the most interesting of the three. A regional airline, having expanded into charter service, was forced to consider the acquisition of jet aircraft. Search was conducted, and a choice was made. But the board, out of concern over the choice made, brought in a new chief executive. He quickly cancelled the contract (interrupt), and began active search again. At the same time, he was approached by salesmen. A number of alternatives were rejected (screen). The remaining alternatives were investigated more intensively for performance and possible financing (evaluation), and for the availability of used aircraft of the preferred model types (search). There remained three feasible alternatives for new aircraft, and negotiations for financing now began. Suddenly, a foreign airline went into receivership, and two used aircraft of the desired type became available at a good price with attractive financing (new option interrupt). The president acted quickly to purchase them (evaluation-choice).

Type 4. Modified search decision processes (equipment). Four of the 25 decision processes were characterized by development activity in which ready-made alternatives were modified through limited design activity. Interestingly, all 4 dealt with the purchase of systems of sophisticated technological equipment.[9] All 4 processes entailed extensive cycling in development, between 3 and 5 instances, and together they had 7 search and 9 design steps. All 4 required the authorization, for a total of 13 instances.

8
The decisions studied by Soelberg (1967) of the students' choice of job fit into this category.

9
The decision processes studied by Witte (1972) and by Cyert, Simon, and Trow (1956) fit into this grouping as well.

Decision Processes

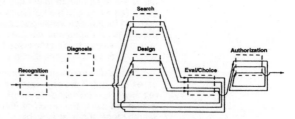

Figure 5. A modified search decision process (equipment) new electric switching equipment (decision process 9).

In decision process 9, shown in Figure 5, a telecommunication organization found it necessary to automate one of its switching functions. Requirements were drawn up (design), and two broad options were considered, electromechanical and computerized (search). Fifteen manufacturers were then contacted (search) and 13 were eliminated (screen). The 2 remaining manufacturers then developed specific systems and bids (nested design), and 1 was selected (evaluation-choice). The decision was then authorized at three successive levels of the hierarchy.

Type 5. Basic design decision processes (marketing). The most common processes, found in eight cases, involved extensive design activity, which typically led to complex and innovative custom-made solutions. There is little evidence of interrupts, only three instances, or of political activity. All processes were evoked by opportunities or relatively mild problems, and all were of relatively short duration. Most interesting, every case dealt with a marketing issue: four new products or services, three new markets, and a new promotional program. Seven of the eight organizations were private firms, while the eighth involved a container terminal built by a government-owned port authority. Clearly these were commercial decisions taken by business, or business-like, organizations, and measurable factors of profit clearly outweighed any political considerations.

Decision process 17, one of the simplest cases, is shown in Figure 6. A hotel found itself with a large, vacant room in the evenings. Because kitchen staff had to be maintained for another restaurant, it was decided to do something with the

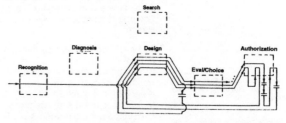

Figure 6. A basic design decision process (marketing) a new supper club for a hotel (decision process 17).

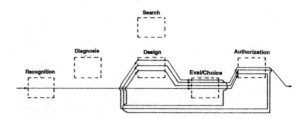

Figure 7. A blocked design decision process (public works) a new airport runway (decision process 21).

room. This proposal was authorized by the owner of the hotel. One executive of the hotel decided that a supper club should be opened (design). Another executive favored a British pub, but the supper club idea prevailed (evaluation-choice). The decision process then involved a series of nested design cycles, many followed by authorization by the owner.

Type 6. Blocked design decision processes (public works). Two processes were identical to type 5 decision processes until they entered the final stages of the selection process. Then both proposed solutions met strong resistance from outside groups. Both were public works projects developed by government agencies, and both were resisted by groups of citizens who protested the disruptions these projects would cause.

Decision process 20 involved resistance to a neighborhood redevelopment plan, and decision process 21, resistance to an extended airport runway. In decision process 21, shown in Figure 7, the runway extension was necessary if the airport was to maintain its status. The announcement of the completed design was the signal for a series of attacks on the organization and its proposal. First a civic group proposed an alternative plan, but that was found unacceptable. Then, bills were introduced in the legislature to block the original proposal. Finally, law suits were instituted to render the proposal illegal on a technicality. The organization chose to meet most of these threats through direct confrontation bargaining. (At the time of the study, the decision process was not yet completed.)

Type 7. Dynamic design decision processes (facilities). The dynamic design decision processes are the most complex of the decision processes encountered. Processes 22 to 25 followed a basic design or modified search pattern, but all four encountered multiple interrupts with the result that the flow of activities became very complicated. None took less than a year, and two took more than four years. One was categorized as a problem and three as problem-crises. Again, most interestingly, all four cases involved the same type of output, new facilities: a new plant, new college building, new university laboratory, and bank headquarters building. We conclude that the dynamic nature of these facilities decisions reflects (a) the relatively large investment needed, (b) the complex design activity involved in such facilities, and, paradoxically, (c) the likelihood of new option interrupts because of the availability of ready-made structures.

Decision Processes

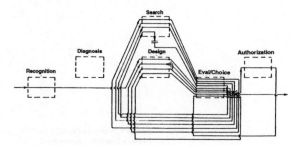

Figure 8. A dynamic design decision process (facilities) a new plant for a small firm (decision process 24).

Decision process 24 is diagrammed in Figure 8. Here a small manufacturing firm was faced with a series of pressures that indicated that its plant was obsolete. A proposal to sell the building was developed (design), and a real estate agent then contacted (search), but no buyers were found. It was then realized that the city might expropriate the land (interrupt), and an agent was hired to negotiate a good price should that occur. Meanwhile, a neighboring firm moved out, and their adjoining parking lot was acquired to provide room for expansion or to increase the expropriation value of the property (evaluation-choice). At the same time, the firm employed architects to investigate two alternatives, but rejected both proposals as too expensive (evaluation-choice). At the same time, the firm employed architects to investigate two alternatives, but rejected both proposals as too expensive (evaluation-choice), and attention was then focused on moving. Three alternative sites were found (search), and employees were polled and road networks investigated (evaluation). One area proved to be the most desirable, and when an existing facility was found there at a good price (search), it was identified as a favorite candidate and purchased (evaluation-choice). The company planned the modification of the building (design), and commenced the alteration. Two months later, however, the provincial government expropriated at the same time both the old plant and the new and gave the firm a short time to vacate (interrupt). Now the firm faced a crisis. It did, however, have a considerable source of funds from the expropriation and could consider buying land and building a new plant. Only one area was investigated, and a suitable site was located (search). The firm obtained rezoning sanctions from the municipal government, a mortgage from the bank (design), and the assurance that this property would not be expropriated (authorization). The site was purchased (evaluation-choice), and the engineering department, in consultation with the architect, prepared building plans, (design); the plans were quickly finalized (evaluation-choice). To summarize, what started as a basic design decision process, type 5, reverted to a dynamic design process, type 7, because of a governmental interrupt.

CONCLUSION

In this paper we have tried to show at the same time that

strategic decision processes are immensely complex and dynamic and yet that they are amenable to conceptual structuring. We believe we have been able to capture some of the flavor of their structure in our study of 25 of these processes. In making this statement, we are encouraged by the facts that one model describes much of what we observed, that the decision processes fall into distinct groupings within the model, and that the decisions of each of four of these seven groupings involved similar outcomes.

We have, however, barely scratched the surface of organizational decision making. Little is known about the most important routines, notably diagnosis, design, and bargaining. Diagnosis is probably the single most important routine, since it determines in large part, however implicitly, the subsequent course of action. Yet researchers have paid almost no attention to diagnosis, preferring instead to focus on the selection routines, which often appear to be just a trimming on the overall decision process. Furthermore, while we have addressed ourselves to the question of how organizations make single strategic decisions, we have not looked at the interrelationships among such decisions over time in the same organization, in effect the process of strategy formulation. The empirical study of strategy formulation has also been neglected in the literature. Another major gap in the literature is the relationship between decision process and structure. The literature still lacks a single acceptable theory to describe how decision processes flow through organizational structures. In fact, it does not even provide a helpful typology of the kinds of decisions made in organizations, especially of those decisions that are found between the operating decisions of the bottom of the hierarchy and the strategic decisions of the top. All of these gaps in the literature seriously block us from achieving even an elementary understanding of how organizations function; all are greatly in need of empirical research.

Henry Mintzberg is a professor of Management Policy in the Faculty of Management, McGill University, Montreal; Duru Raisinghani is an organization analyst in the Planning Branch of the Treasury Board Secretariat, Government of Canada, Ottawa; and André Théorêt is an associate professor, Faculté d'Administration, Université de Sherbrooke, Sherbrooke, Quebec.

REFERENCES

Aguilar, Francis J.
1967   Scanning the Business Environment. New York: Macmillan.

Barnard, Chester I.
1966   The Functions of the Executive. Cambridge, Mass.: Harvard University Press.

Bonge J. W.
1972   "Problem recognition and diagnosis: basic inputs to business policy." Journal of Business Policy: 45–53.

Bower, Joseph L.
1970   Managing the Resource Allocation Process. Cambridge, Mass.: Harvard University, Graduate School of Business Administration, Division of Research.

Braybrooke, David, and Charles E. Lindblom
1963   A Strategy of Decision. New York: Free Press.

Carter, E. Eugene
1971a   "Project evaluations and firm decisions." The Journal of Management Studies: 253–279.
1971b   "The behavioral theory of the firm and top level corporate decisions." Administrative Science Quarterly: 413–428.

Cyert, Richard M., and Kenneth B. MacCrimmon
1968   "Organizations." In E. Aronson and G. Lindzey, (eds.), The Handbook of Social Psychology, 2nd ed. Reading, Mass.: Addison-Wesley.

Decision Processes

Cyert, Richard M., and James G. March
1963 A Behavioral Theory of the Firm. Englewood Cliffs, N.J.: Prentice-Hall.

Cyert, Richard M., Herbert A. Simon, and Donald B. Trow
1956 "Observation of a business decision." Journal of Business: 237–248.

Dewey, John
1933 How We Think, new ed. Boston: D.C. Heath.

Deising, Paul
1967 "Noneconomic Decision-Making." In M. Alexis and C. Z. Wilson, (eds.), Organizational Decision-Making: 185–200. Englewood Cliffs, N.J.: Prentice-Hall.

Drucker, Peter F.
1971 "What we can learn from Japanese management." Harvard Business Review (March-April): 110–122.

Dufty, N. F., and P. M. Taylor
1962 "The implementation of a decision." Administrative Science Quarterly: 110–119.

Emory, C. William, and Powell Niland
1968 Making Management Decisions. Boston: Houghton Mifflin.

Feldman, Julian, and Herschel E. Kanter
1965 "Organizational decision making." In James G. March, (ed.), Handbook of Organizations, (chapter 14). Chicago: Rand McNally.

Gore, William J.
1956 "Administrative decision making in federal field offices." Public Administration Review: 281–291.

Gore, William J.
1964 Administrative Decision-Making: A Heuristic Model. New York: John Wiley.

Grinyer, Peter H., and David Norburn
1975 "Planning for existing markets: perception of executives and financial performances." The Journal of the Royal Statistical Society, Series A: 70-97.

Hall, William K.
1973 "Strategic planning models: are top managers really finding them useful?" Journal of Business Policy: 33–42.

Hardwick, C. T. and B. F. Landuyt
1966 "Timing and surprise." In Administrative Strategy and Decision Making. Cincinnati, Ohio: South Western Publishing Company, Second Edition (chapter 1).

Kakar, S.
1971–"Rationality and irrationality
1972 in business leadership." Journal of Business Policy: 39–44.

Klein, Burton H.
1962 "The decision making problem in development." In The Rate and Direction of Innovative Activity: 477–508. Princeton, N.J.: Princeton University Press.

Lonergan, Bernard J. F.
1967 Insight: a Study of Human Understanding. New York: Philosophical Library.

Manheim, Marvin L.
1966 Hierarchical Structure: A Model of Design and Planning Processes. Cambridge, Mass.: M.I.T. Press.

March, James G., and Herbert A. Simon
1958 Organizations. New York: John Wiley.

Mintzberg, Henry
1973 The Nature of Managerial Work. New York: Harper and Row.

Newell, Allen, and Herbert A. Simon
1972 Human Problem Solving. Englewood Cliffs, N.J.: Prentice-Hall.

Nicolaidis, Nicholas George
1960 Policy Decision and Organization Theory. D.P.A. thesis, University of Southern California.

Pettigrew, Andrew M.
1972 "Information control as a power resource." Sociology: 187–204.

Pfiffner, John M.
1960 "Administrative rationality." Public Administration Review: 125–132.

Pounds, William F.
1969 "The process of problem finding." Industrial Management Review (Fall): 1–19.

Radomsky, John
1967 The Problem of Choosing a Problem. M.S. thesis, Sloan School of Management, Massachusetts Institute of Technology.

Reitman, William R.
1964 "Heuristic decision procedures, open constraints, and the structure of ill-defined problems." In M. W. Shelley and G. L. Bryan, (eds.), Human Judgments and Optimality: 282–315. New York: John Wiley.

Sayles, Leonard R.
1964 Managerial Behavior: Administration in Complex Organizations. New York: McGraw-Hill.

Schwartzman, Ruben
1971 Crisis Decision Making. MBA thesis, McGill University, Montreal.

Simon, Hebert A.
1965 The Shape of Automation. New York: Harper and Row.

Snyder, Richard C., and Glenn D. Paige
1958 "The United States decision to resist aggression in Korea: the application of an analytical scheme." Administrative Science Quarterly: 341–378.

Soelberg, Peer O.
1967 "Unprogrammed decision making." Industrial Management Review (Spring): 19–29.

Stagner, Ross
1969 "Corporate decision making: an empirical study." Journal of Applied Psychology: 1–13.

Thompson, James D., and A. Truden
1964 "Strategies, structures, and processes of organizational decision." In H. J. Leavitt and R. Pondy, (eds.), Reading in Managerial Psychology. Chicago: University of Chicago Press.

Whitehead, Clay Thomas
1968 Uses and Limitations of Systems Analysis. Ph.D. dissertation, Sloan School of Management, Massachusetts Institute of Technology.

Witte, Eberhard
1972 "Field research on complex decision-making processes—the phase theorem." International Studies of Management and Organization: 156–182.

[5]

DECISION AND ORGANIZATION – PROCESSES OF STRATEGIC DECISION MAKING AND THEIR EXPLANATION

DAVID J. HICKSON, RICHARD J. BUTLER, DAVID CRAY, GEOFFREY R. MALLORY AND DAVID C. WILSON

Strategic decisions shape the course taken by an organization, whether it be in the public sector or the private sector. An analysis is reported of 150 cases of the making of such decisions in both publicly and privately owned organizations. Three types of decision-making process are identified, *sporadic*, *fluid*, and *constricted*. Differences due to the nature of the subject matter under decision, and to the nature of the organization, are examined. Differences in the propensity to sporadic decision-making processes in the administration of publicly owned organizations are described.

Decision making is at the heart of what administrators and managers do. It is not something they do individually when it concerns major strategic matters, they do it as part of a social process with many others that may become drawn out over a long period. It is not something that always succeeds in achieving what was intended, and it is not always clear what was intended, but nevertheless strategic decisions are milestones in the fortunes of organizations. This paper explores 150 cases of such decisions in 30 public and private organizations in Britain, how they were arrived at, and why they tend to be arrived at in one way rather than another.

TOPICS OF DECISION

What are the strategic decisions that shape the course of an organization? How many kinds of these decisions are there which, in total across all organizations, private sector and public sector, shape the course of a society? The Bradford studies of strategic decision making in British organizations (a full description appears in Hickson et al. 1986) classified 150 decisions by their subject matter into ten categories of topic. These categories are listed in Table 1 together with examples of the subject matter covered.

It can be seen that almost anything can loom up and take on significance for

David J. Hickson is Research Professor of International Management and Organization at the University of Bradford Management Centre. For co-authors' affiliations see p. 390.

Public Administration Vol. 67 Winter 1989 (373–390)
© 1989 Royal Institute of Public Administration ISSN 0033–3298 $3.00

TABLE 1   Topics of decision

Topic Category	n	Examples
1. Technologies	23	Equipment and/or premises, e.g. whether to invest in new machinery and buildings, buy 'new generation' aircraft, close geriatric ward.
2. Reorganizations	22	Internal re-structurings, e.g. whether to insert regional level between branches and headquarters, merge departments, change overseas branches into subsidiaries ('domestication' in host nations).
3. Controls	19	Planning, budgeting, and requisite data processing, e.g. what the five year 'strategic plan' or annual 'business plan' are to be, whether to purchase computer.
4. Domains	18	Marketing and distribution, e.g. whether to bypass wholesalers and distribute direct, introduce 'no-charge' banking, standardize name for all branches of the company.
5. Services	16	New, expanded, or reduced services, e.g. whether to launch novel form of interdisciplinary university degree, to increase municipal housing, to decrease European air services.
6. Products	12	New products, e.g. whether to launch a new beer, a new glass-impregnated cement, or to generate electricity.
7. Personnels	12	Job assessment, training, unions, e.g. whether to make a first productivity agreement, to use consultants to re-grade all staff, to resist unionization.
8. Boundaries	11	Purchases of and mergings with other organizations e.g. whether to buy subsidiary company, to merge colleges.
9. Inputs	9	Finance and other supplies e.g. whether to raise funds by a share issue, or (local government) by a lottery, or to change the sources of supply of components.
10. Locations	8	Site and sites dispersal, e.g. whether to build new plant abroad, to move company's principal offices, to reduce dispersal (by closing branches).
Total	150	

organizations in the eyes of those at the top, not just the computer installations or product launches or investments that have attracted most attention from journalists and researchers. Most frequent were decisions to re-equip, rebuild, or reorganize, the 23 'technologies' topics and the 22 'reorganizations'. Next came the making of plans, the fixing of budgets, and commitments on the requisite electronic data-processing, all 'controls' topics, and 'domain' or market-type decisions on price, distribution and image. New 'services' and 'products' decisions were not such a high proportion as might have been supposed, together rather less than a fifth of the total. From the varied 'personnel' topics, for example complete staff regrading or unionization, the numbers drop through 'boundary' topics on takeover bids and similar moves, to 'inputs' of money or materials and finally to the eight decisions on 'locations' of major plants or corporation headquarters. Decisions on location do not happen often since most organizations stay put most of the time.

Therefore, it is not just an organization's external world and outputs to that world which are strategic for that organization, but also internal questions such as reorganization or personnel problems. Moreover, these ten kinds of topic are strategic for all kinds of organizations. What is strategic in one form of organization tends to be so in others, too. There are no clear differences in frequency of topic between, say, larger or smaller organizations, nor public and private organizations (though sampling may have reduced the chances of some differences showing up). The only detected difference was a tendency for there to be proportionately more reorganization decisions in service organizations. Their élites decide to add (or remove) a level in the hierarchy, such as a regional level between local offices and headquarters, or to merge or add departments, more often than do their counterparts in manufacturing. This is both in private services such as finance or transport, and in public services such as education, health or utilities. Hence the élites in service organizations appear to think that the services provided can be bettered by continually reshuffling the organization that provides them, whereas manufacturers keep their eyes on the product and are less inclined to look behind them at their organization itself.

But as Table 1 has shown, all managers and administrators are most often concerned with decisions on the equipment and/or premises which are their organization's technology. If they are in manufacturing they are repeatedly concerned with the possibility of re-equipping or rebuilding, if they are in air transport they are concerned with possible new aircraft, if they are in health services they are concerned with expensive body-scanners and the like, and so on.

THE SETTINGS FOR DECISION

These decisions are arrived at through processes which involve numbers of senior administrators and managers, and at various points either political representatives in the public sector or non-executive external directors in the private sector, often over long periods. The matters arising for decision, which arouse these decision-making processes at the top, can be thought of as having two inherent components (Figure 1). They raise *problems* and they implicate *interests*.

FIGURE 1 *Model of decision making (adapted from Hickson et al., 1986)*

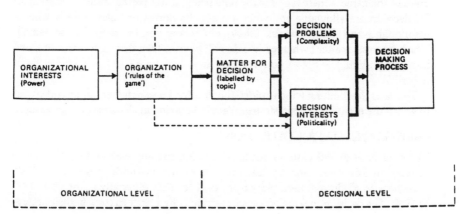

376   HICKSON, BUTLER, CRAY, MALLORY AND WILSON

The problems raised vary in complexity, being sometimes less so, sometimes
more so. For example, in the private sector the possible alternatives for even the
largest share issue can be weighed up in the precise language of capitalization,
financial ratios, trends in yields, and the like. There are risks, of course, but those
concerned know what has to be considered and only the finance department and
finance sub-committee of the board are closely involved, together with external
financial advisers and banks. Calculations can be made and compared. So in a
giant multinational insurance conglomerate which was studied, even a then un-
precedentedly large share issue could be decided upon quite straightforwardly.

Much more complexity has to be faced when a substantial reorganization is
under discussion. The obstacles to this or that course of action are not so readily
anticipated. Everyone whose work and prospects may be directly affected is deeply
concerned, and so are many others who anticipate they may be indirectly affected
sooner or later. But it is difficult for those of any point of view to present convincing
evidence, clear to the others, for their case. There are too many imponderables,
and no firm figures. This was the difficulty when a decision was being taken in
a municipality to merge departments.

Figure 1 depicts decision-making processes ensuing from the *degree of complexity*
of decision problems, and also from the *degree of politicality* of decision interests.
That is, processes differ both because of the problems being dealt with and because
different interests have to be accommodated. The interests implicated by one topic
differ from those drawn in by another. It hardly needs saying that some matters
are much more political, in the generalized non-party-political sense, than others.

So whilst a major share issue directly implicates only a limited set of interests
among financial and legal directors, plus external advisers and sources of capital,
a possible reorganization can encounter a welter of diverse interests among the
many departments, levels in the hierarchy, and associated outside organizations
affected, which give it a much higher politicality.

The kinds of problems raised and the kinds of interests implicated will be shaped
by the *organizational setting*, as Figure 1 suggests. The ultimate framework of power
differs as between public and private sectors, for instance, and it determines the
'rules of the game'. These fix – for the time being, if not permanently – what topics
for decision are allowable and what are not. Its norms or 'rules' govern what is
mentionable and unmentionable ('they won't stand you bringing that up again'),
which interests matter ('whatever we do will have to take them into account'), and
how things should be done ('you won't get anywhere with it unless X knows about
it first').

This was the thinking which guided the Bradford research team in its endeavour
to widen the perspective upon strategic decision making in all forms of organization.

SAMPLE AND DATA COLLECTION

The data base of 150 cases of strategic decision making was obtained by interviewing in 144 cases, and by intensive case-study methods in six cases. Data
collection, in all Britain, took place from 1974 to 1980, especially in the years 1977
to 1980. The decision-making processes described often reached back in their origins,

and most were concluded by the time of the data collection, so that they occurred over periods from the mid-1960's to the early 1980's.

Organizations were first approached by a letter to the chief executive, supplemented by telephone calls as necessary. Of those approached, two-thirds, that is 30 organizations, cooperated. They range in size from 100 to over 50,000 employees; there are 17 privately owned (manufacturers, financial institutions, road transport, etc.), and 13 publicly (state) owned (health service districts, universities, utilities, etc.); there are 11 manufacturing (metal components, glass, chemicals, breweries) and 19 service (banking, insurance, airways, local government, etc.). Most were relatively prominent, a large proportion being national or international leaders in the private or public sectors and household names, which prevents publication of some details in case histories. They were taken from published directories with the aim of getting as even a coverage as possible over a selection matrix which offset private and public ownership categories against manufacturing and service categories, to reflect as far as practicable the diversity of contemporary organizations. However, the resulting set of organizations depended upon personal managerial collaboration because those at the top who were centrally involved in cases of decision making had to be willing to give considerable information about decisions that to them were still important and had occurred sufficiently recently to be readily recalled. They also had to be willing and able to give time to researchers. As in all this sort of research, any biases introduced by self-selection are beyond knowing.

In an initial interview the chief executive reviewed the history of the organization, its outputs and basic structure, and external relationships. He was asked to nominate major decisions involving more than just one department or section and with widespread effects, five of which were chosen to include when possible one each concerning inputs, outputs, core technology, personnel and reorganization, but there was no hard and fast sticking to these categories.

Centrally involved 'eye-witness' informants were then interviewed about each case, for example managing directors and function directors in firms, vice-chancellors and deans in universities, management team members in health districts, and chief officers in local government. Since what was wanted was information about *processes* of decision making which take place at top managerial levels, middle management or lower employees or unions were not approached as they would know nothing first hand of the inner workings at this level. Interviewees were informants giving information about events, not respondents talking about themselves; each was interviewed at length, often more than once.

Each interview began with an historical narrative of the sequence of events as they unfolded. This was followed by numerous open-ended questions about particular aspects of the story which led the informant to elaborate on certain features of what had happened, seven of which were then in addition rated on five-point scales (for example, of influence and of prevalence of delays). These ratings provided precise summings up, whilst the narrative notes gave them meaning.

In each of three organizations, a public utility, a university, and a private manufacturer, two cases were studied in far greater depth by intensive methods. Three were followed concurrently as they happened, and three were traced historically, by interviews, casual discussions, lunchtime contacts, and document searches throughout management across departments by a researcher who spent hours or days weekly in the organizations over two to three years. These six case studies are fully reported by Wilson (1980, 1982).

THREE TYPES OF DECISION-MAKING PROCESS

How are these many kinds of decisions, on such a variety of topics, arrived at? Three main ways are suggested by the data. These three ways of making decisions are about how a topic passes through the many hands in an organizational, or social, process at the level of top management or administration. Whilst each is a sketch, rather than a drawing complete in every detail, the outlines are clearly there.

They are outlines of *sporadic processes, fluid processes,* and *constricted processes.* The three types are derived from analysis of 136 processes on which data in the required form was complete. A larger number of process variables was reduced to ten for the final analysis.

The first three all concern information. 'Expertise' is the number of internal and external sources, from staff experts to consultants or other organizations in the same field, from which information comes; 'disparity' is the variability in the quality of that information, as indicated by the differing confidence that management had in its sources; and 'effort' is how information was acquired, from merely having it on hand in people's personal experience and knowledge, to having it accessible in records, to research to collect it, to creating it by meetings or other means that synthesized it from disparate sources. In addition to formal and informal interaction (meetings versus more casual contacts), a feature of the content of the interaction, 'negotiation scope', is represented by a scale of seven ordered categories running from the decision not being open to negotiation at all, for example, when a chief executive forces a conclusion and leaves little room for negotiation among the others interested, to so much negotiation that a decision is made when negotiation is still inconclusive and dissent persists. Then there are the 'disruptions' of the process by delays, and the impediments encountered, the latter being indicated on a nine point scale running from least impedance, the matter for decision in effect having to wait in a queue of items demanding attention, through impediments in the form of search and problem-solving activities, to most impedance, resistance from a source external to the organization.

Process time, the period of decision making that was studied, runs from the first recalled action that started movement towards a decision to the decision itself. Finally, there is the 'authority level' within or above the organization where the process ends in an authorized decision, following which implementation can legitimately proceed. The lowest level at which such a decision was authorized was the semi-autonomous division; the highest was at national or international headquarters, and in between were the chief executive and board levels or equivalent.

It had been apparent from personal familiarity with the case histories that some decisions were made in a more fluent way than others, but analysis beyond this general intuition was required to sort through this large number of cases, each described by a large number of process characteristics, to see whether a pattern could be discerned. Hierarchical statistical cluster analysis was used to work out a three-fold clustering or grouping of cases (by progressively minimizing the error sum of squares within clusters), in which the cases in each group have more similarities than they have with those in the other groups and, most vitally, each is a *meaningful* type (Anderberg 1973, p. 183; Everitt 1974, p. 59). Each denotes something substantial about processes, and together the three are a balanced representation, for the cases divide evenly between them into clusters of 53, 42, and 41 processes. About a third of all strategic decisions are made in each way.

Sporadic processes

The first of the three ways in which a strategic decision may be made is through a *sporadic* type of process. A summary of the characteristics of this and the other two types appears in Figure 2. By comparison with decisions reached by fluid or constricted processes, a decision made in a sporadic way is likely to have run into

FIGURE 2   *Three ways of making decisions (names of variables in italics)*

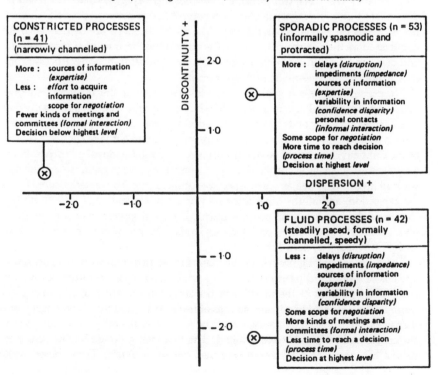

more disrupting delays, due to all kinds of impediments from having to await a report to meeting resistance. The information that came in will have been of more uneven quality, for in some of it there was confidence and in some of it there was little or none, and it will have come from a wider range of sources. There will have been some scope for negotiation during a great deal of informal contact and discussion on and off. It will have taken longer to get a decision, and this eventually will have been made at the highest level. That is, in terms of the variables summarized in Figure 2, the process will have probably shown higher impedance, higher disruption, more sources of expertise, between which there are greater differences in the confidence placed in their information and views, more informal interaction, some negotiation, longer process time, and final authorization at a high level.

This means that in a full third of the occasions when top managers or administrators enter upon a decision, they are likely to have begun on a twisting trail that will not end for a year or two, or even longer. As they make their way along it they will come up against all sorts of obstacles that delay direct movement towards a conclusion. They will have to turn aside whilst staff experts prepare fresh estimates or reassess capacity, they will have to pause until the time is judged right to move on, they will have to take time to negotiate among themselves and with outsiders such as banks or customers. They will find that not all the information they get can be relied upon, so they and their staff will have to sift out what they feel they can place confidence in, and what is better ignored. They will be drawn into bursts of activity in corridors and offices, in between the delays, when the matter is on everyone's mind and answers to questions are demanded there and then, until the excitement dies down as other things become even more pressing and demand attention. *In brief, a sporadic type of decision-making process is one that is informally spasmodic and protracted.*

For example, it was a sporadic process that brought the management of a nationalized industrial firm to a decision to buy a one-third share in a company that was a large purchaser of its products. This decision was an attempt to ensure future sales in a situation where either, other interested parties might take complete control of the company, or it might go out of business. Two multinational oil corporations, a multinational chemical corporation, and another very large nationalized industry were all involved as well as the prospective subsidiary which wanted assured funds for expansion, and all the other interests wanted to expand or at least to protect the firm's demand for their own products. The local government, on the other hand, resisted expansion on ecological grounds. The prospective subsidiary itself wished to ensure its own future.

The decision-making process in this nationalized firm moved in fits and starts. Spasms of work by departmental staff to produce forecasts of future output and costs, and estimates of the investment the subsidiary might make in new plant if capital were injected into it, and spasms of hectic to-ing and fro-ing amongst senior managers, were broken by pauses whilst the reaction of the other powerful interests to reports and proposals were awaited. The financial grounds for injecting new capital by means of a takeover were very much in doubt. Time passed while successive reports and proposals were tossed backwards and forwards between the organizations concerned, and renegotiated to suit their differing interests, until after eighteen months an agreement was reached. The board of the nationalized industry made a commitment to take a one-third share in its customer firm, along with one of the oil corporations and the other state-owned industry, each of which also took one-third. A difficult uneven process came to an end.

Fluid processes

Quite the opposite to sporadic processes in most ways are *fluid* processes. Although they, too, leave scope for negotiation, there is not nearly so much informal activity along the corridors of decision in the executive suite or administrative block, for more is handled in the relatively formal setting of meetings. More of the discussion is channelled through pre-arranged project groups, working parties, sub-committees, boards and the like, and there is less hubbub between whiles. Impediments and delays are less likely. Fewer sources of expertise are called upon, and there is a comparatively uniform degree of confidence in their information and views. Though the decision is likely to be taken at a similarly high level, it will be reached much more quickly, in months rather than years. In terms of the variables summarized in Figure 2, a fluid process, therefore, is probably comparatively less disrupted, less impeded, has fewer sources of expertise with less of a gap between them in the confidence placed in them, passes through more kinds of committees, sees some negotiation, and in a shorter time reaches an outcome at a high level of authorization.

This means that almost a third of strategic decisions at the top flow along fairly fluently to quite a quick decision. In this type of process, managers and administrators attend a greater number of committees and kindred bodies, but far from getting in the way these formally arranged proceedings seem to facilitate a conclusion comparatively rapidly. Whilst any one meeting may be frustratingly fruitless, the arranging of meetings makes sure that things move along, if not during the meetings then in between them in anticipation of them. In these processes, there are fewer occasions when it is necessary to wait for the timing to be right, or for reports to be compiled, or for opposition to be reconciled. It is possible to move ahead comparatively steadily with at least a clear degree of confidence in the information gleaned, even if the level of confidence is less than desirable, and despite there being some scope for negotiation over the possible decision. *In brief, a fluid type of decision-making process is one that is steadily paced, formally channelled and speedy.*

One fluidly processed decision was in a metropolitan municipality to venture into the realms of chance by launching a lottery to augment the normal funds from local tax payers and the national government. In not much more than a month, following the return of the leader of the council from a holiday, the proposal for a lottery was manoeuvred through a local government committee structure that was not prepared for it.

Another fluid process carried the management of a savings bank to the conclusion that they would try to upgrade it to the status of a cheque issuing bank, competing

382   HICKSON, BUTLER, CRAY, MALLORY AND WILSON

with the established national banks across the full range of services, by applying
for membership of the big banks' 'Clearing House'. This forms the basis of the
cheque system, and therefore of credit banking, by clearing cheques between banks
to arrive at the net balances owing from one to another. Essentially, the process
of reaching the decision was very simple. It revolved around the deliberations of
a special working committee of senior managers set up to consider the matter.
This met constantly, steadily collating information with which to assess the cost
of admission to the Clearing House and of competing in the wider and tougher
market that would be opened up, and sounding out competitor banks and the Bank
of England on the chances of admission. In about a year the main board had
accepted the committee's recommendations to make this radical move which, if
successful, would transform the business. Here again this was a smooth committee-
focused process ending at the highest level.

The contrast between fluid processes and sporadic processes shares something
with that frequently made between 'rational' and 'political' decision making, the
rational flowing more evenly and the political more turbulently (Miles, 1980).
Likewise, the types of processes put forward by Mintzberg *et al.* (1976) range from
comparatively uninterrupted 'search' and 'design' kinds to those that are more
'blocked' and 'political'. We would resist any implication that sporadic processes
are not guided by rationalities but, this having been said, the sporadic-fluid distinction fits a broad difference in the nature of decision making that has often been
intuitively assumed and alluded to.

Constricted processes

At first sight, the third type of process, *constricted*, seems sharply different from
the fluid type and more akin to the sporadic. A constricted process can share some
of the delays that sporadics encounter, more so than the fluids at any rate, and
also like the sporadics it draws on numerous sources for information and views, and
is not so committee-focused. However, a second look at the summary in Figure 2
shows that it is as different from the sporadic type as it is from the fluid. It allows
less scope for negotiation about the decision, and that decision is made at a level
below the highest point – though still high in the hierarchy, of course, since it
is a strategic decision. Thus it is a process less fluid than the fluids and less sporadic
than the sporadics.

The unique character of a constricted process is that it tends to be more held
in, more restrained, than either of the other two types. Although it draws on the
information and views of quite a few departmental and external experts, what is
needed is readily available and requires no great effort to obtain it. No special
investigations are undertaken outside the organization itself, and internally there
are no undue difficulties in reconciling and synthesizing disparate material. The
process is neither so informally active as sporadic processes tend to be, nor so
formally active within meetings and committees as fluid processes tend to be. It
ends with a decision that does not have to be made by a higher headquarters or
board, but can probably be made by the chief executive without higher recourse.
In the wording of the variables underlined in Figure 1, it probably brings in expertise

that can provide information and views with no great effort, it does not give much scope for negotiation nor figure much on the agendas of formal committees and the like, and it can be made at a chief executive or similar level.

This means that almost another third of strategic decisions are likely to be arrived at in a way that does not stir up so much activity as the other types of processes do. The pertinent facts and figures are already in being or can be easily put together, and to get hold of them it is only necessary to pick up the phone and ask whoever has them at his or her fingertips, or could calculate them more or less routinely. There is not much in this to negotiate over, and the matter does not generate much coming and going between offices, nor is there any reason to set up a special project team or working party or sub-committee. It does not concern all the committees, anyway, but can go through with just the approval of a local board or whatever. Many of those in management are not closely involved, and the process moves in well-worn channels under the control of the chief executive, who takes the final decision. *In brief, a constricted type of decision-making process is one that is narrowly channelled.*

A decision to modernize an insurance company was made in this way. On the surface it was merely a commitment to updating and centralizing the data processing for the main line of business, vehicle insurance, but as with a number of the other cases its significance for those concerned was in a wider context. The company had been taken over by a larger firm, and despite assurances, there was a risk of its business being absorbed into that of the parent and the company being obliterated as a working organization. They realized that the best defence was for the parent's management to see its subsidiary as a profit earner too good to be disturbed. The company was already in a leading position in its sector of the market, so that the range of insurances offered and the sales approach were felt to be as good as possible. Any move to ensure continued profitability and, equally important, to sustain an image as a vigorous up-to-the-minute enterprise had therefore to be in the direction of improving administration and organization.

The decision process circled around the chief executive within whose purview it legitimately came, never far out of his hands. There was no committee work, not even a special task force or group to work out details. Approval from the board of directors sitting as a board was not needed, though individual directors knew what was in the wind. The motor insurance department, the claims department, and other departments where appropriate, produced analyses of the existing system and what would be required of any new system. Externally, IBM were quick to offer their sales and advisory services, the insurance industry trade association was contacted about experience elsewhere, and some of the larger brokers who handled business for the company confided what competitors were doing. In just a few months, with no real delays, it was decided that a reorganization of the administration based on centralized micro-film records ought both to raise earnings by improving the premium-to-expenses ratio, and improve efficiency in the field by speeding up the calculations of premiums and cover sent out to sales agents. This it was felt would go as far as anything else could to ensure company autonomy, as indeed it has done.

384   HICKSON, BUTLER, CRAY, MALLORY AND WILSON

A constricted process may always be a possibility when there is a good base of information to start with, or at least one can be assembled without too much effort. A corporate plan, for example, does not have to start from scratch but can begin where the previous one left off. It can proceed from the principal estimates on which the previous plan was constructed, projecting them forwards. Departments can simply be asked to update their forecasts, which they are well used to doing.

WHICH WAY WILL A DECISION MOVE?

When the élite at the head of an organization start the ball rolling, so to speak, and begin upon a process of deciding what will culminate in a decision to do – or not to do – something, which way will the ball roll? How will they move it towards their goal – sporadically, fluidly or constrictedly?

Some of the categories of topic do show distinct propensities to go one way rather than another, insofar as this sample of processes is a guide. Or, rather, they show propensities *not* to follow one or other kind of process. Decisions on whether to launch a new product, for example, are *non-fluid*. Of ten such decisions in the fully analysed sample, none followed a fluid type of process. It seems they cannot be got through smoothly in this evenly paced, formally channelled manner. Perhaps that is what might be expected. The consequences of launching a product are far too serious. They reverberate through the organization. Success will carry the organization forward, failure will hold it back. Reputations will be made or unmade. Everyone's interests are at stake and the decision is a political 'hot potato'. The effects, good or bad, will be felt for years afterwards. Parameters will be set for subsequent decisions about markets and supplies and investment, and the management's overall strategy will have taken another step, wittingly or unwittingly. So such a momentous decision must undergo either the intense oscillating activity of a sporadic process, or if everyone is used to new product launches and 'knows the score', then be held 'closer to the chest' of a top executive within the more routine channels of a constricted process that people are familiar with.

On the other hand, decisions on whether to reorganize tend to be *non-constricted*. Of twenty such decisions in the fully analysed sample, only four followed a constricted type of process. It seems that they cannnot be held within known bounds. They are far too novel to follow accustomed channels. A decision of quite this nature has rarely occurred before.

Strategic reorganization decisions are much less definable than new products decisions. How the decision should be processed, who will become involved, who may be influential, what the consequences may be, are relatively ambiguous. Typical instances were a financial institution establishing its worldwide branches as legally distinct subsidiaries, a municipal authority merging departments, and a public sector manufacturer reforming itself on divisional lines. With this sort of decision, often the only thing people feel sure of is that whatever the effects may be they will be living with those effects for a long time. Of all topics, reorganizations were felt to have the most indefinite consequences which would endure as long as anyone cared to foresee (on average twelve years, which really denotes infinity). More than most, these decisions are a step into the unknown, a political gamble.

But new product launches and major reorganizations are just two of the variety of topics that are the subject of decisions. The search for explanation why one type of process occurs rather than another has to extend across all topics. When it does, the beginnings of explanation can be discerned.

In brief, the primary reasons why one type of process is more probable than another are the *complexity* and *politicality* inherent in the matter for decision. The nature of what is under decision, in these terms, is more important even than the kind of organization in which the decision making takes place. Whether the matter in hand is highly complex or relatively straightforward, and is highly political, or relatively disturbing, makes a great deal of difference.

Thus if a matter is *highly complex*, that is involving a diversity of participants and having potentially very serious consequences, *and* if it is also *highly political*, that is contentious and influenced by external as well as internal interests, then it is most likely to be processed in a *sporadic* way.

If it is *less complex*, that is with less diversity among participants and somewhat less serious consequences (though these consequences may be diffuse, and it may be quite novel), and if it is *least political* compared to other strategic decisions, that is not contentious and with an even spread of influence, then it is most likely to be processed in a *fluid* way.

Finally, if a matter is *least complex*, being comparatively familiar and with comparatively limited consequences, and *less political*, decisively influenced by internal 'heavyweight' interests and pushed along to a conclusion, then it is most likely to be processed in a *constricted* way.

The likelihood in all cases is approximately two to one that the predicted type of process will occur.

This means for any variety of decision that the type of route it follows depends mainly upon how complex and how political it is. It probably will move erratically and unsteadily towards a conclusion, with many impediments along the way, in a sporadic process, *if* for instance it is a controversial and exceptionally large investment in new plant and premises; that is, highly complex and political. It probably will move along much more smoothly, through a framework of recognized committees, in a fluid process, *if* for instance it is a decision on new equipment which although substantial and vital for the future is plainly seen to be needed, by all concerned, and does not bring a clash of interests; that is, less complex and least political. It probably will follow acknowledged channels on a constricted process *if* it is a well-recognized improvement in facilities of a sort that has taken place before and is supported by the principal departmental interests; that is, least complex and less political.

DIFFERENCES BETWEEN ORGANIZATIONS

So far decision-making processes have been considered as if they were nowhere in particular. Yet they are somewhere. They take place within the managements of organizations, and these organizations make very different settings for these processes. What kinds of processes occur in what kinds of organizations? In other words, can the nature of organizations add anything more to the explanation why one type of process occurs rather than another?

In the 30 organizations studied, two factors appeared which seem to affect what happens. They are *ownership*, whether public (ownership by the state) or private, and *purpose*, in the crude sense of whether the organization is manufacturing or service. Taking just the proportion of decision making which is sporadic in character, 47 per cent of the processes analysed in publicly owned organizations were of the sporadic type, and 49 per cent of those in manufacturing – almost half in each case: a disproportionate number (Table 2).

TABLE 2   Organization differences

	SPORADIC Processes
MANUFACTURING:	49%
PUBLICLY (state) OWNED:	47%

n=136 decs.		SPORADIC		FLUID		CONSTRICTED	
Orgs.	Decs.	Decs.	%	Decs.	%	Decs.	%
Public Manufacturing	2	9	7	78	0	0	2	22
Private Manufacturing	8	36	15	42	7	19	14	40
Public Services	11	53	22	41	17	32	14	26
Private Services	8	38	9	24	18	47	11	29

Nevertheless, that of itself would not be very persuasive. Fortunately, it is possible to go further and test these apparent effects of public ownership and of being in manufacturing by manipulating each factor in turn within the organizations covered. This can be done by working down the column for sporadic processes in Table 2 (which shows data for 29 organizations, some data being incomplete for this purpose on one organization).

Looking first at *publicly owned manufacturers*, no less than 78 per cent of the processes studied were sporadic. Here are organizations subjected to the effects *both* of public ownership and of manufacturing. The combined effect is pronounced. However, there are only two such organizations, and this is 78 per cent of merely nine processes in them. It is hardly a statistic that could stand alone.

But suppose that the effects of one factor at a time are now removed, successively exposing the effects of the other. This can be done in Table 2 by looking next at the *private* manufacturers. That is, by removing public ownership. In private industry, the proportion of sporadic processes drops sharply, to 42 per cent. Trying it the other way around, restoring public ownership but removing manufacturing, the proportion in public *services* is 41 per cent, virtually the same. This strongly suggests that either public ownership or manufacturing raise the proportion of sporadic cases, and that both factors together may even double the proportion compared to what it might be with either factor alone.

This interpretation is again strongly supported by removing both factors, as it were, and looking at *private services*, neither public nor manufacturing. Only 24 per cent of their processes fall into the sporadic grouping.

So the organizational rules of the game in *manufacturing* seem to give rise to greater hurly burly. The prevalence of sporadic-type processes means that decisions are more often felt to be very serious, with the future of the enterprise at stake. The division of labour into typical manufacturing functions such as production, sales, finance, personnel and so forth, creates the potential for contention over objectives, whereas decision making in service organizations such as insurance or credit companies, or utilities, or transport, does not face this level of complexity and politicality so frequently. It can more often proceed fluidly with less excitation.

The rules of the game in *state-owned* organizations give rise to sporadic processes probably because of public accountability. Public interest and public scrutiny bring government departments and agencies into decision making more often, complicating it with extra external involvements. Decisions tend to become both serious and contentious. However, some caution is necessary in not taking this interpretation too far. The public sector organizations included universities, poly-technics, health service districts, and a local authority, all relatively fragmented and relatively loosely coordinated professional forms of organization which have 'politicking' tendencies built into their structures. It is not possible here clearly to disentangle the effects of public ownership from those of this kind of structure and personnel.

Even so, since the more directly publicly accountable of these organizations have the most sporadic processes, the evidence does point to ownership as the main reason for sporadic processes. Comparing the municipality, two districts of the national health service, two polytechnics, and two universities, there are propor-tionately most sporadic-type processes in the decision making of the municipality, less in the NHS districts, much the least in the universities. This progression is in line with differences in the directness of public accountability in the four forms of organization. Sporadic processes occur most in the political-party-controlled, directly publicly accountable municipality, and least in the politically independent and less directly publicly accountable universities. Although the cases of decision making took place in the 1970s or early 1980s, and since then both local govern-ments and universities have been brought under greater and more direct national government control, their relative differences in propensity to sporadic decision-making processes will have remained the same.

The way in which sporadic processes are more likely over politically charged matters – high politicality – can be readily seen in the making of a decision on housing in the municipality. This local authority covered a sprawling semi-industrialized area in Northern England. Its decision-making processes had to wend their way through the typical array of departments and committees and sub-committees, in the hands of a complicated mixture of appointed officials and elected councillors.

388   HICKSON, BUTLER, CRAY, MALLORY AND WILSON

Since there was direct and instant accountability to the public through the elected council, political party contention as well as interdepartmental politics shaped decision making.

This particular decision was precipitated by national politics, when government abandoned a scheme to buy land itself, and offered an already acquired, relatively huge area within a municipality's territory to the council. It was accepted, and scheduled for private housing. A consortium of builders was formed to negotiate with the council: work commenced on roads and services. Before anything further could be decided, the 1974 reorganization of local government intervened to halt everything. When a fresh form of the municipality emerged, as a metropolitan district, the majority political party changed and the question was reopened. The Housing Committee now decided on public housing of a greater density. The builders' consortium disbanded. But resistance arose from an adjacent village whose residents feared losing their identity and environment. Months passed in protests, until elections approached. The process now accelerated as the controlling party attempted to get the matter through all committees and finally settled, so that the decision could not be overturned by a change in party control. It failed in this. The election reversed control. Eventually a compromise was reached under which some housing of each type was to be built. The decision had taken two years of intense but spasmodic activity on which direct political accountability had made a greater impact.

By contrast, a much larger proportion of decision making in the universities was fluid in character, 'steadily paced, formally channelled, and speedy'. Such processes do not take long to describe. A university's budget, for example, was agreed smoothly in three months without interruption, even though it included a shift in priorities towards a new arts faculty and hence away from other faculties. It moved steadily via the development committee, a meeting of all department heads, the finance committee, and finally the Council. Even a much more novel decision to establish a formal 'joint venture' in teaching with a larger university in another city, unusual since universities are inclined each to guard their independence and self-sufficiency, went through quite fluidly in much the same time.

Quite how this may be is very much a question of interpretation. However, it seems significant that the universities, per decision, had more kinds of committees, more standing committees, and more people on the committees, than any of the other forms of organization studied. That is, university decision making is extremely committ*eed* – more of them, more routinely, with more members. It is arguable that this practice has evolved to cope with the unique multiplicity of departments in universities. Because of their mutual independence, since rarely does the teaching and research of one depend much upon another, and each is in a position to advance the claims of their own 'product line' of teaching and research irrespective of the others, a means has to be found of expressing these many interests, and yet of moving matters for decision towards a conclusion. Hence the committee system.

It may come as a relief to those who administer universities that major decisions get through this system in no more time than is taken in other organizations. Of course, it is a labour intensive system, costly in manpower and womanpower, loathed by those whose time is taken up on hot, boring, afternoons, but it does not – on average – slow down decision making. Major decisions get through university hierarchies in hardly more than the time taken in, say, private industry. Indeed, over 150 cases in all the organizations studied there is no relationship between number of committees and total time to arrive at a conclusion. Committees help as much as they hinder.

In the municipality, too, a great deal of what occurred took place in and around its extensive committee system, but here the necessity of including political party representation, and responding directly to political pressures, meant that the system did not work as smoothly as in the universities. Since it was subject to even greater strains, it might be held to have worked even better in containing them, but it could not avoid the numerous external eventualities which held up the process in the case of the housing decision.

IN CONCLUSION

We have tried to demonstrate that it is possible not only to study small numbers of strategic decisions in great detail, but also to describe in sufficient detail the wider panorama of decisions in any one organization and in all organizations. In order to compare different kinds of decisions in different kinds of organizations, concepts were needed with which to describe and contrast them. From these, we derived three broad characterizations of decision-making processes, termed sporadic, fluid, and constricted.

Fortunately, the designing of the study to include more than one decision in each organization enabled us to begin to disentangle how far the type of process may be due to the features of the matter under decision as against those of the organization in which it is being dealt with. Overall, it is possible to conclude that the form of organization is not the primary factor affecting how decisions are made. It is of secondary importance. More important are the complexity and the political-ity of the matter under decision. 'The matter for decision matters most' (Hickson *et al.*, 1986, p. 248). So to account for, or to predict, what happens in a particular industry, or in the public sector as against the private sector, it is not the features of its organizations as organizations that should first be looked to. The charac-teristics of what is under decision should be considered. Their differences within any one organization are likely to outweigh differences between organizations. A corporate plan is a corporate plan, a new investment is a new investment, a takeover is a takeover, a reorganization is a reorganization, and so on, whatever the form of organization in which such a matter for decision arises. What happens when a particular matter is being decided in public administration will have a great deal in common with the process of deciding upon the same sort of matter in private industry or commerce, more in common than the differences, which are obvious at first sight, may lead one to believe.

390   HICKSON, BUTLER, CRAY, MALLORY AND WILSON

REFERENCES
Anderberg, Michael R. 1973. *Cluster analysis for applications* New York: Academic Press.
Astley, W. Graham, Runo Axelsson, Richard J. Butler, David J. Hickson and David C. Wilson. 1982.
    'Complexity and cleavage: dual explanations of strategic decision making'. *Journal of Management Studies* 19, 4, 357–75.
Everitt, Brian. 1974. *Cluster analysis* London: Heinemann.
Hage, Jerald. 1980. *Theories of organization: form, process and transformation* New York: Wiley.
Hickson, David J., Richard J. Butler, David Cray, Geoffrey R. Mallory and David C. Wilson. 1985.
    'Comparing one hundred and fifty decision processes' in J. M. Pennings (ed.), *Organizational strategy and change*. San Francisco: Jossey-Bass.
—. 1986. *Top decisions: strategic decision making in organizations* Oxford: Blackwell; San Francisco: Jossey-Bass.
Miles, Robert H. 1980. *Macro-organizational behavior* California: Goodyear.
Mintzberg, Henry, D. Raisinghani and A. Theoret. 1976. 'The structure of 'unstructured' decision processes' *Administrative Science Quarterly* 21, 246–75.

Co-authors' affiliations:
Richard J. Butler is Reader in Organizational Behaviour at the University of Bradford Management Centre; David Cray and Geoffrey R. Mallory are Associate Professors, Decision Analysis Laboratory, School of Business, Carleton University, Ottawa; and David C. Wilson is Lecturer in Organizational Behaviour, University of Warwick Business School.

[6]

Electricity and Resistance: A Case Study of Innovation and Politics*

David C. Wilson[1]

Abstract

David C. Wilson
Organizational
Analysis Research
Unit,
University of Bradford
Management Centre,
Bradford, England

This article presents a case study of decision making in a British chemical organization. The initial problem is one of whether the generation of electricity is a feasible proposition in addition to the production of chemicals. This issue acts as a platform for protracted political debate as soon as questions of career succession and career interests are aroused. The focus shifts from economic criteria to those of career aspirations. The decision spans four years, from 1964 to 1968, and data for the case study were collected over a three-year period, from 1976 to 1979. Existing notions of decision making are examined for their adequacy in explaining the events that took place and modifications to these concepts are explored in the analysis of the case study. It is found that both the effects of the organization and the specific individuals within it, combine simultaneously to produce the events of this decision. The article begins with a short introduction of existing decision making theories, follows with an account of the case study, and concludes with an analysis of its decisional characteristics.

Functional and Political Criteria in Organizational Decision Making

One account of decision making portrays organizations as managerially contrived, subsuming a logic of managerial effectiveness which encompasses decision making in the dictates of technical criteria derived from immutable algorithmic precepts. Hence, decision making is flavoured with 'techniques' (Ellul 1964), and evokes planned responses to all possible contingencies (Luce and Raiffa 1957; Baumol 1959; Moore and Thomas 1976). Decisional criteria governing the choice of one alternative from a set of multiple alternatives are based upon utility maximization, relying on the rational choice processes of economic theory.

Despite Simon's attempt to finally seal the demise of rational economic man (Simon 1947), subsequent concepts of decision making still adhere to economic principles, displaying a modified economic rationality. As Astley et al. (1981) point out, the rationality which is applied in decision making is in fact severely bounded, whereby search procedures are truncated long before theoretically optimal alternatives can be identified. The result is incremental decision making with solutions typically close to existing routines (Lindblom 1959), and satisficing decision making, where what is felt to be adequate for the circumstances results in satisfactory rather than optimal solutions (March and Simon 1958). However imperfect its execution, decision making is still seen as an

Organization Studies
1982, 3/2:119–140
© 1982 EGOS
0170-8406/82/
0003-0007 $1.00

intendedly rational process purposefully directed towards the solution of problems.

Beyond the conventional wisdom of this rationality there is an alternative account of organizational decision making. This view portrays decision making less as product of organizational functioning and more as the result of power exertion which serves localized interests, often at the expense of other conflicting interests (Cyert and March 1963; Axelrod 1970; Abell 1975; Allison 1969). Case studies such as those of Pettigrew (1973) and those in Bachrach and Baratz (1970) provide colourful illustrations of the way in which political purpose facilitates access to information by two actors but excludes a third, or where preferential location in a communication network enables the selective filtering of what constitutes 'relevant' information (Leavitt 1972).

Similarly, March and Olsen (1976) de-emphasize goal-directed rationality in favour of an image of spontaneous and purposeless decision making, wherein political activity has primacy and goals are discovered through it. Outcomes are not always devised congruent with specific problems. Indeed, a solution may exist prior to the problem arising. Cohen et al. (1972:2) thus depict an organization as a collection of 'choices looking for problems'.

The focus for this article is provided by these two mutually exclusive perspectives on decision making. On what occasions does decision making subscribe to a goal-directed, utility-maximizing economic rationality — albeit a modified rationality — and when is decision making beset with interest, ambition, and political intrigue? The following section develops an account of a new product decision in Toxicem, a leading British chemical producer.

Methodology and Access

The data for the study were collected over a three-year period from 1976 to 1979, during which the author was a member of the Organizational Analysis Research Unit at the University of Bradford. Initial access was gained by discussions with the Chief Executive. The author was working as a researcher involved in a wider comparative study of decision making (see Butler et al. 1981 for the details of this research). An opportunity to conduct extended research came fortuitously. Toxicem was acting as 'host' to a senior manager from a large banking concern. It was intended that he should get a bird's eye view of how Toxicem functioned as a chemical company and, at my request, I was allowed to accompany the banker for the following week.

Virtually all senior and middle managers were observed and interviewed during this time and through this I discovered that Toxicem was just about to decide whether or not to launch a new product. I asked the Chief Executive whether I could follow this new product through its decision process and he agreed to let me have access to all senior and middle managers and all documentary evidence. During the ensuing extended contact time with Toxicem, the Chief Executive developed an interest in the research itself and, over lunch, we identified four major areas that had, in his opinion, contributed significantly to the overall strategy of Toxicem. After talking through each of these areas I decided upon the decision to generate electricity as the best documented topic with ready access to verbal information from those who had participated in the decision-making process.

As Toxicem had a relatively small number of functional departments, and as the decision topic invoked readily identifiable sides for and against the generation of electricity, it was a relatively simple task to unravel who were the key decisional participants. These are shown in Figure 1. Identification of participants was a process of chain reactions. Those members of the organization who were obviously involved directly in the decision were interviewed in the first instance. Their accounts of the events of the decision process led to the identification of other members who were less directly involved in the decision. Subsequent discussions with these informants led to the identification of further participants and thus extended the gradually increasing number of informants.

Figure 1
The Key Participants in
the Case Study

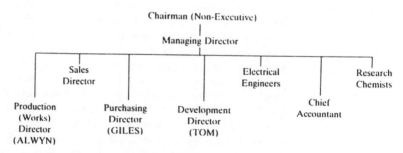

Interviews with each informant were open-ended and multiple, usually occurring once per week. As Dalton (1958:275–277) experienced, the formalities of interviewing lessened with the passing of time. Many of the informants subsequently became friends and acquaintances as a result of the extended contact time. One significant consequence of such relationships was that information about the topic, the people in the organization, and about the organization itself, was readily available and was culled from a wide variety of settings. Often, lunchtimes in the managers' dining room proved useful sources of information as did lunch in the staff social club. In addition, the creation of informal relations meant that many 'casual' conversations were possible, taking place in corridors, foyers, or reception rooms. Indeed, the experience of the present study concurs with Dunn and Swierezck (1977:142) whereby 're-search data properly described as "anecdotes" are important sources of information'.

In addition, minutes of meetings, memoranda, personal letters, and other documents were scrutinized at length. Not only did this activity help to identify

key participants in the decision, but also it highlighted specific points of
ambiguity or vagueness that served as useful cues for discussion with informants. Like many case study analysts, I soon developed my own shorthand which
enabled almost verbatim statements to be recorded either at the time of their
occurrence, or shortly afterwards (see, for example, the developing of 'inti-
mates' and the writing of accounts, in Dalton 1958:273–285).

The present case study was conducted alongside five other extended cases of
decision making in other organizations (Wilson 1980). In an attempt to allevi-
ate some of the criticisms of researcher bias and subjectivity in case study
methods (Weick 1969:18–21; Campbell and Stanley 1966:6–12; McClintock et
al. 1979:627), these five other cases were resubmitted to key respondents in an
early draft form. The result was that no change of stories or events was
requested by any of the key respondents beyond small alterations in numerical
data such as costs or estimates. These were duly altered in the final reconstruction of the decision. In the present case, however, it was not possible to
resubmit the case study for the same process of 'validation' as the present
Managing Director (Alwyn) had figured strongly as a political figure in the
decision. Over lunch, towards the end of the research he told me how he felt he
had been extremely tolerant in allowing extended research in Toxicem, but
now felt that 'I was overdoing things to the point of becoming a political
embarrassment'. Bitterness over his appointment as Managing Director
(which stemmed from the outcome of the present decision) was still quite
marked among some other directors. This was especially true of Giles, the
Purchasing Director, and as my continued presence in the organization would
bring me into contact with Giles and others who were sympathetic to his views,
Alwyn argued that I would only re-open what were comparatively recent
wounds and exacerbate an already delicate situation. I was asked to leave, with
which I duly complied, fortunately having collected sufficient data for the
compilation of the present case study. Resubmission, under the circumstances, would have been undesirable, but it was felt that as the present case
had been conducted in a similar method to the five other 'validated' cases, the
likelihood of subjective bias significantly distorting the portrayal of events was
substantially reduced.

Background to the Case Study

Prior to 1960, Toxicem was using a single, low pressure boiler in order to supply
steam for various chemical processes at pressures of 80 to 150 pounds per
square inch (psi). The rapid rise of steam demand in Toxicem necessitated the
purchase of a new and larger boiler. Although there were a few dissenters, the
majority of those concerned favoured the purchase of a boiler capable of
operating at 400 psi. Higher pressure boilers were generally thought to be
required to cope with the steady increase in demand experienced by the British
chemical industry.

The higher pressure boiler was duly purchased in 1962 and, although capable of operating at 400 psi, most of the usage of the boiler was in producing low pressure steam at 80 psi. The demand for high pressure steam had not accelerated as quickly as had been predicted. In order to get a pressure of 80 psi, this boiler first had to be fuelled to raise 400 psi. The loss caused by having to reduce pressure from 400 to 80 psi meant little at the time in financial terms, but it stimulated the idea in some of the engineers' minds that this spare pressure capacity could be used in a productive way, particularly to facilitate the generation of electrical power.

Early Days: The Germ of an Idea

A suggestion to use the spare pressure capacity began to crystallize around the idea of electrical power generation. The chemists and engineers in Toxicem started to experiment with the notion of using steam pressure to drive a turbine and alternator which could theoretically provide Toxicem with enough electricity to supply their own requirements. Many informal discussions were held between the people interested in the concept of electricity generation. Small-scale experiments and hypothetical calculations were worked out, often on the backs of envelopes and scrap paper. Gradually, a small group of chemists, electricians, and engineers were coming to thinking that not only was electricity generation a feasible proposition, but also that it should be given priority in the policy of Toxicem.

The main problem at this time was that Toxicem had little spare money available for such projects. Thus, although the idea of electricity generation became more and more fixed in the minds of its proponents, it had to remain a hypothetical project. The Capital Control Committee, a standing committee which makes decisions on expensive projects such as this, would never have entertained the idea of spending some £150,000 on generation equipment.

However, encouraged by Alwyn, the energetic Welsh Works Director, the proponents of electricity generation invited the National Industrial Fuel Efficiency Service (N.I.F.E.) to conduct a general survey of efficiency in Toxicem. This visit was a standard procedure in Toxicem and occurred every two or three years, but on this occasion Alwyn was determined to ask their opinion on the question of electricity generation, in order to add weight to his argument. The report came back to Alwyn, suggesting that N.I.F.E. considered that savings of up to £39,000 per annum could be saved by Toxicem generating their own electricity. Alwyn submitted an informal report to his colleagues who were in favour of the project. It read as follows:

'1) We are large consumers of steam, and so the steam required for power generation has already been raised. The cost of giving it the extra energy to 600 psi to put it through a turbo-alternator is relatively small. The steam passes out from the turbo-alternator at the pressure of 85 psi which we use for most of our plants, and we are able to use all the

remaining energy in the steam, including its latent heat. The fuel efficiency of a
back-pressure generator set such as ours would be 75%. The efficiency of modern power
stations is of the order of 35%, and the average efficiency of all power stations is 28%.
2) Our electrical power demand, and the amount of power our steam usage enables us to
generate, correspond quite closely. We shall need to continue to purchase a small
portion of electricity requirements.
3) The Central Electricity Generating Board is required to earn sufficient profit on its
sales of electricity to finance new power stations. We would prefer to retain this money
to finance our own expansion.
The average cost per unit of electricity purchased from the Local Electricity Board over
the last 12 months (i.e. before the new increases take effect on October 1st) has been
1.2d. The fuel, labour and maintenance cost of the electricity we can generate ourselves
will be 0.2d. per unit, so the margin left for overheads and profit is considerable.'

There was, however, still little chance of such a project being allowed to come
to fruition. There were still problems of economics to sort out leaving little
spare money for projects of this nature.

The Purchase of a Boiler

Despite Toxicem's lack of funds, it was clearly evident that a second boiler
would have to be purchased. The demand for steam had risen steadily throughout the previous three or four years and number one boiler was being used to its
capacity. The question of the purchase of this second boiler was to be taken at
Board level due to its high capital cost. The Board asked for information about
the requirements for steam and about the various available boilers from the
Works Director, the Purchasing Director, and the Development Director. It
was here that Alwyn saw a glimmer of hope:

'Obviously it was not possible to tackle the question of electricity generation head on.
This second boiler was important for us, however. If generation was to become a reality
then the purchase of this boiler was critical. Here was an opportunity to take a step in the
right direction.'

In order to run a turbo-alternator it is necessary to have a boiler capable of
raising steam to a pressure of 600 psi. Anything less than this is useless as far as
driving a turbine is concerned. Alwyn realized that the number two boiler to be
purchased must have this 600 psi capability. He could then consider his next
move with the knowledge that electricity generation was technologically possible.
Alwyn gathered his supporters together and informed them of the intended
purchase of a new boiler and its necessary high pressure capability. They began
to search for information about the projected requirement for steam usage,
plus the various boilers that were on the market at the time, determined to
secure the purchase of a high pressure boiler. Although the projected demand
for steam over the next few years was sufficient to warrant a high pressure

boiler, the price of the boiler was not. They were substantially more expensive than the lower pressure boilers. The additional cost of a high pressure 70,000 lbs. per hour Water Tube Boiler was in the region of £15,000. There seemed no solution to this problem, so Alwyn and the engineers could move no further. They sat back and waited.

Meanwhile, Giles, the Purchasing Director, had also been gathering information about the specification of new boilers. Giles had the reputation as something of a 'whizz-kid' in Toxicem. He had reached his directorship comparatively rapidly through his apparently infallible ability to secure favourable and successful contracts with major suppliers and he was well respected in Toxicem as well as in the chemical industry as a whole. Giles was not a man to play about with ideas such as electricity generation.

'I really thought that this project was ludicrous. No-one could give any facts and figures which supported electricity generation. Nobody knew enough about the problems and the technology of electricity production to be able to say anything worthwhile.'

He considered such ideas wasted time and effort, at the expense of hard facts and figures. Consequently he favoured the purchase of the cheaper, low pressure boiler on economic grounds, although he did admit that the higher pressure boiler was probably a better investment in the long term. 'It was just too expensive'.

At this time, purely by coincidence, the National Coal Board circulated an information sheet around manufacturing industries which used coal as a source of energy. In this document they stated that they had large stocks of pulverized, low quality coal stockpiled in a local pit. They could supply such fuel at a very low cost for at least the next ten years. Giles was not one to miss such an opportunity, and arranged a meeting of himself, Alwyn, and the Managing Director with the National Coal Board. The calorific value of this fuel was very low (8750) and most boilers would not be able to raise steam with such coal. However, this fuel could be used to fire a Water Tube Boiler using superheated steam, raising its pressure capability to 600 psi.

On financial criteria, it was more economical for Toxicem to purchase a higher pressure boiler using this new found cheap fuel, than it was to buy a low pressure boiler which needed higher quality coal. In December 1964 Toxicem bought a high pressure boiler, on Giles' recommendation. Alwyn and his engineers were overjoyed: 'This boiler was certainly capable of eventually producing electrical power with the addition of an alternator. The idea was, at least, a feasible reality in the future.'

They had kept very quiet about the possibility of generating electricity, never mentioning the fact in the meeting with the National Coal Board. They appeared to fully support the purchase of the high pressure boiler on economic criteria only. The boiler was duly installed and began working at 400 psi (reduced to 80 psi) to supply Toxicem's steam requirements.

The Case for Higher Pressures

The new boiler worked without problems for a year. However, as a result of Toxicem's continued expansion in the production of chemicals, it was being used to its full capacity by early 1966. It was now that Alwyn and his supporters made their move. Alwyn argued:

'Obviously, by increasing the pressure of the boiler the total output of steam could be substantially increased. But it seemed a waste to reduce this high pressure steam to the required 80 psi for the chemical plant. It was like boiling a kettle when you only wanted lukewarm water. The spare steam capacity could be used to drive a turbine and thus generate electricity.'

Armed with the information from N.I.F.E., Alwyn and his supporters submitted their proposals to the Managing Director. These proposals were circulated around top and middle managers and they immediately brought protests from Giles and from Tom, the Development Director, who were both totally opposed to the idea of electricity generation. The Managing Director proposed that debate on this issue should take place in the Capital Control Committee in order to provide a forum for all interested parties to present their case. In March 1966, Tom and Giles submitted a short report to the Committee in which they spelled out their objections to the concept of electricity generation. These were three-fold:

'1) that Toxicem's proper business was manufacturing chemicals, and that they should leave generating electricity to bodies like the Central Electricity Generating Board which were set up to do so;
2) that technical staff would not be competent to run the system, and that breakdowns in the boiler plant or generation house would lead to costly shut-downs;
3) that in order to raise sufficient high pressure steam on the 70,000 lbs/hr coal fired boiler to run the Generator, Toxicem would have to purchase a better and more expensive grade of coal.'

Alwyn, the engineers and chemists immediately countered these three objections by arguing that Toxicem could, in fact:

'produce electricity more economically than the Central Electricity Generating Board. In any case, existing staff were more than competent, and the existing supplies of low quality coal were not going to last forever and alternative sources would have to be found even at 400 psi pressures.'

The Capital Control Committee met a further three times in April, May, and June 1966, but no progress was made on this issue. The Chairman and the Managing Director suggested that deadlock had been reached because of lack of specific information about the technological and economic aspects of electricity generation. They suggested that both the opponents and proponents of the debate should clarify in more specific detail their positions. Accordingly, Alwyn and the proponents and Giles and Tom (with full support from their respective departments) went out to seek information to substantiate their cases. Giles and Tom approached the Accountancy Department to try and work through their figures, confirm their calculations and thus lend support to their view. However, Accountancy was noncommittal, also suggesting that further figures were necessary in order to present a convincing case. Alwyn and his supporters attempted the same strategy with the same result. It was clear that Accountancy had no real interest either way in the outcome of this argument.

The Diseconomies of Electricity Generation

Both Giles and Tom realized that if Toxicem was to produce their own electricity, then this would mean negotiating with the Electricity Supply Industry which presently supplied them. There would need to be arrangements about release from the national grid and about any standby arrangements with the local Electricity Board, should any failures or breakdowns occur in the boiler or the turbo-alternator. In particular Tom, who had dealt with the Electricity Supply Industries in the past, felt that they would be totally against private electricity generation in industry:

'I knew from experience that the electricity boards were hostile to any firm which attempted to become independent of the national grid. I knew of a couple of firms which had tried it and gone back to the national grid within a year because of all the problems they had with generators breaking down and intermittent supply of electricity ruining their production processes.'

Giles contacted the Industrial Section of the Electricity Council for their opinion on private generation. Tom was correct in his assumptions. The Electricity Council were most certainly not in favour of the private generation of electricity by organizations. Basically, the Electricity Council's attitude was that an organization's finances could be better directed than towards private generation, that it would prove a costly exercise and that the job of supplying electricity should be left to the specialists, that is, the local Electricity Boards.

In particular, Giles and Tom emphasized the point that standby charges for reconnection to the national grid in the event of the failure of the private system would be expensive. They wrote to the local Electricity Board asking for a specific figure for standby charges if Toxicem was to embark upon private generation. The local Electricity Board was hostile to the whole idea. At first they refused any information at all, suggesting that reconnection to the national grid would be impossible anyway for various technical reasons and that no precise figures could be given. They also refused to meet with Toxicem representatives to discuss the issue of private generation.

Alwyn was now beginning to fear that he had lost the battle in the light of both the Electricity Council's and the Electricity Board's hostile attitude to private generation. Even so, he had contacted two suppliers of turbo-alternators in order to find out how much they would cost to buy, install, and run.

In order to produce a realistic purchase price these suppliers needed to know the cost of standby charges from the Electricity Board, which they duly contacted. They received a curt reply stating that standby charges would be £5 per kVa per annum. This figure was then submitted along with the price of the turbo-alternator to Toxicem. Giles was more than satisfied: 'I knew that, given standby charges of this magnitude, the Capital Control Committee would never consider the purchase of a turbo-alternator.' The figures were submitted, and were rejected by the Committee as Giles predicted. Despondently, Alwyn retreated to consider his next move.

A Re-awakening: Career Issues and Interests

The Managing Director of Toxicem announced his impending retirement. It was clear that, within the organization itself, Giles and Alwyn would be prime candidates for the vacated directorship. More important, however, was that from Alwyn's point of view Giles had in a sense 'won' the battle over the issue of electricity generation. This would put Giles in an advantageous position in the promotions stakes especially combined with his 'whizz-kid' image. Energetic though Alwyn might be, charisma he did not have.

It was felt, especially by Giles and Alwyn, that success in gaining the managing directorship would be primarily determined by the track record of each candidate in the debate about private electricity generation. Although this was never expressly stated by the outgoing Managing Director, it was commonly thought among senior managers to originate from him.

Alwyn was well aware of his so-called failure. He thus set out to scrutinize all the memoranda, mathematics, and documents that the debate had produced. In a month he had found an important error in the figures given to Toxicem by the turbo-alternator suppliers concerning standby charges. Alwyn asked Toxicem's electrical engineers for their advice on a charge of £5 per kVA for standby supplies. They told him that such a charge was ridiculously high and was obviously an error that had not previously been identified by anyone. In the light of the Electricity Board's policy of noncooperation on this issue, Alwyn was not convinced that this mistake for standby charges was as innocent as it seemed.

Alwyn first informed the Capital Control Committee of the errors and, second, wrote to the Federation of British Industries concerning the excessive standby charges. Informing the Capital Control Committee had the effect of re-opening the debate on the issue and also cast doubts over the information given by the electricity supply organizations in general. Alwyn also received the following reply from the Federation of British Industries:

'I cannot understand how the £5 per kVa per annum has arisen. I attach a copy of a reply to my enquiry to the Electricity Board concerning the Board's charges for stand-by and parallel-running supplies. From this you will note that the annual charge for standby supplies is £1.5.0d per k Va for high voltage supplies or £1.15.0d per kVA for low voltage supplies. Supplies actually taken are charged for at more or less standard rates.

If it should appear that the Board are attempting to impose charges otherwise than those stated in the attached copy letter, I would be very pleased to hear the details from you.'

The debate was re-opened. Giles felt the ground shifting beneath his feet. The figures upon which he had based his case had been proved to be more than a little erroneous. The whole argument against private generation was now open to question.

Months of Conflict

There followed nearly a year of disputes between Alwyn and his supporters and Giles and Tom and their supporters. These disputes concerned the economics of electricity generation, but because the majority of figures and calculations were computed on hypothetical measures of steam pressure, generator output and so on, no agreement about the 'real' cost of private generation could be reached on either side. The only firm figure that could be obtained during this period was the cost of standby charges from the Electricity Board.

Feuding between the proponents and opponents of electricity generation became bitter, reflected in heated discussions in the dining room every lunch-time and in the sheer volume of memoranda produced stating the cases for or against. Giles also realized:

'that the original plan of getting standby facilities only once per year was inadequate. We should have to have standby facilities during all holiday periods in case any breakdowns occurred.'

The following two months were spent negotiating such terms of standby with the Electricity Board. By January 1968, these charges had been agreed on all sides. Giles and Tom circulated a memorandum to the Capital Control Committee in which they stated all their objections to the private generation issue.

In this document they listed and expanded old arguments but introduced a new argument concerning the practice of other chemical companies on electricity generation. According to Giles, this document was the definitive statement about the pitfalls of electrictiy generation and showed the folly of embarking upon such an enterprise. A very long and involved document, it may be crystallized into the following points:

1) At least six well-known British chemical manufacturers had tried and rejected private generation.

2) The projected forecast of electricity usage in 1969 for XLtd was too high.

3) The Electricity Board has the right to radically increase the negotiated standby charges should the generator be unable to supply electricity for more than five days.

4) Steam pressure variation would radically affect electricity output. In order to minimize such variation, a higher quality coal would have to be purchased from the National Coal Board. Additional costs could therefore be as much as £12,000 for this item alone.

5) The turbo-alternator manufacturers would not accept liability if their machine was not supplied with clean steam. Toxicem could not guarantee such clean steam. In addition, this would mean an increase on chemical control or supervision on water supply and boiler conditions.

6) The cost of increasing the boiler operating pressure from 400 to 600 psi was too high, and would also reduce boiler reliability.

7) Existing maintenance staff was unable and unqualified to look after the proposed high pressure set-up.

Cases For and Against Generation Are Sharpened

Alwyn and his supporters from engineering and electrical services countered each of these arguments in turn. These counterarguments were also contained in a detailed memorandum which was submitted to the Capital Control Committee. In effect, each of the points made by Giles was refuted in this document in an equally convincing manner.

Alwyn's main argument was that private generation was an economic proposition and that Toxicem stood to make a substantial profit in the generation of its own electricity. He submitted a breakdown of estimated costs to the Capital Control Committee showing that by August 1969 the total cost would be £135,000 (less than half the figure estimated by Giles and Tom). Each of the major arguments against private generation were shown in fact to be economic according to Alwyn. The only argument he accepted was that maintenance staff would involve an extra cost due to the need for increased supervision. Alwyn, however, emphasized that Giles' figure of £250 for this extra cost was ridiculously low, and consequently allowed £800 for this item. This report increased the antagonism between the proponents and the opponents of private generation. Giles explained:

'I saw the allowance of extra money for maintenance staff as a personal insult. It implied that Alwyn had no faith in Tom's and my calculations. He was trying to make us look incompetent in the eyes of the Capital Control Committee.'

These assumptions were correct.

Alwyn and his supporters never missed an opportunity to be derogatory to their opponents on this issue, the main occasion for mutual insults being lunchtime in the dining room. Missing such lunchtime 'debates' was considered an admission of failure or defeat and consequently no-one missed any of these sessions. Fired by the competition for the upcoming managing directorship, the arguments became increasingly personal. Controversy still raged concerning the accuracy of financial calculations and projected estimated costs for private generation. The Managing Director called another meeting of the Capital Control Committee. In this meeting he informed the Committee that since it was apparent that no decision or even compromise could be achieved on this issue, then a vote would be taken among all the senior managers to finally resolve the debate one way or the other. Giles comments: 'This played straight into Alwyn's hands. We knew that he had very strong support from the engineers and the electricians.' Giles and Tom had no determined support from other areas of the organization apart from themselves. As a result, Alwyn's case won the vote by using the extra muscle, and the case was finally presented by the Capital Control Committee to the Board of the company in September 1968.

As was the norm in Toxicem, the Board merely acted in a rubber stamping capacity, and the decision to purchase a turbine was approved. The first turbine was purchased exactly one year later in August 1969.

The Aftermath

The turbine was proving very successful in its operations. Very few of the problems posed by Giles and Tom appeared in practice. In the six-month period since its purchase, the turbine was estimated to be saving Toxicem some £60,000 per year. Just over a year later Alwyn was promoted to the position of Managing Director.

Over the next three years, the turbine operated at a steady profit, having effectively paid for its capital cost in two years. There had been problems of the turbine blades becoming salted and the necessity of having research chemists on night shifts in order to look after the purification of water, but overall such problems had been minimal in contrast to the apparently substantial financial saving. Giles and Tom were not, however, to be silenced so easily. Giles in particular was very bitter at not securing the managing directorship, and he continued to oppose private generation. Although a financial profit was undoubtedly being achieved, he argued that it was not really the result of any foresight or expertise on the part of Alwyn:

'Since 1969, the price of electricity purchased from the Electricity Boards has risen dramatically and, coupled with the effects of economic inflation, the turbine only appears to be making a profit. If it hadn't have been for inflation, then the success of the project would have been questionable.'

The Case for Another Boiler

The demand for electricity and process steam had risen in Toxicem to a level where a third boiler was certainly required. In view of a recent strike by the coal miners it was decided to purchase a new gas-fired boiler.

When estimates for the new boiler and attached turbine and alternator were submitted to the Capital Control Committee, the purchase of all items was automatic. The Board accepted the figures without question and the new boiler and turbo-alternator set were acquired in July 1974. Alwyn, as Managing Director, submitted the case to the Committee and to the Board, which, in the light of his previous participation in the issue, authorized the purchase without question.

Yet, Giles had had some success in persuading previous supporters of electricity generation that perhaps it was only due to the effects of inflation that the project had been seen to be so successful. Had a vote been taken, as in the purchase of the first turbo-alternator, it was possible that the vote would have gone against the purchase of a second turbine. Giles' influence, however, came too late. Both boilers and number two turbo-alternator were working successfully. The first turbo-alternator was now used as a standby. The following extract from one of Alwyn's memoranda indicates the profitability of private generation:

'1) What the total costs of electricity, including purchased fuel will be this year (turbo-alternator No. 2 now in use).
The figure comes to £80,452. It includes the cost of standby charges to the Electricity Board.
2) What the total costs of meeting our electrical demand this year would have been, had we never embarked on power generation.
The figure would have been £325,135.
3) What the total costs would have been had we not invested in a second turbo-alternator, but continued using the first one, supplemented by substantial purchase from the Electricity Board.
The figure would have been £198,358.
It will be seen from the above that the financial savings from generating power ourselves are amounting to some £245,000 per annum. The first turbo-alternator is currently in "moth-balls" and will be brought into service again when the demand for electricity has grown beyond the capacity of Unit No. 2.'

Yet when last in touch with Toxicem the issue was still contested. The feeling among the 'losers' (Giles and Tom) was still that the so-called profitability of electricity generation was solely due to subsequent information and the rising price of electricity rather than to any strategic foresight on the part of Alwyn and his supporters. Some months later, Tom had suffered a mild heart attack and now only worked part-time as Development Director. Giles was still actively opposed to private generation and was waiting for the time when the demand for steam and electricity dropped, so that he can again point to the folly of private electricity generation which is no part of a chemical company's business.

Analysis: The Electricity Generation

The Issue as a Strategic Decision

Following Mintzberg et al. (1976) and Normann (1971), strategic decisions are those which are considered important to the organization, are novel to the organization, and consequently incur a large degree of uncertainty for decision makers.

Much of the literature concerning strategic decisions focuses on new product decisions as the more important issues of organizational decision making. Pettigrew (1973), for example, shows how the new computer issue assumes a critical level of importance in the Brian Michael organization, and Normann (1971) argues that new product decisions are invariably uncertain and trouble-some.

The danger here is that, as Normann (1971:205) points out, not all new product decisions in all organizations represent uncertain and important issues. Indeed, new product decisions were the most numerous types of topics occurring in Toxicem between 1960 and 1978 (Wilson 1980:262). In this way, the new product decisions become 'programmed' and the organization develops spec-ific, institutionalized procedures for handling these routine decisions (Simon 1947). The justification for treating the electricity generation issue as a strategic decision lies in its novelty to Toxicem.

As Walker (1969:881) argues, a strategic decision is one which is 'new to the organization adopting it, no matter how old the program or policy may be or how many other organizations may have adopted it'. Strategic decisions are thus made about issues previously unencountered or unexplored in an organ-ization. Such is the case with the present study; from this perspective, the electricity generation issue becomes a strategic decision for Toxicem.

The Case as an Incremental and Satisficing Decision

The most striking aspect of the electricity generation issue is that the decision-making process cannot be described as *wholly* incremental or satisficing. It is possible to depict the decision-making process as comprising two distinctly different 'phases' (Mintzberg et al. 1976). Figure 2 summarizes the two stages and their more important constituent events.

Stage 1 of the decision represents the antithesis of either satisficing or in-crementalism. Here, decision making is portrayed as founded upon a basis of 'technical rationality' (Thompson 1967:14). Although there are disagreements between Alwyn, Tom, and Giles concerning electricity generation, each course of action is fully scrutinized by the interested parties. Each decisional partici-pant attempts to gain support for their point of view by enumerating the full range of alternatives, clearly defining objectives, and attempting to achieve the maximization of utility functions in the consideration of the alternative ways of producing electricity from turbines and alternators. The decision represents almost a stereotype of the 'synoptic' mode of decision making described by Lindblom (1959) and Braybrooke and Lindblom (1963:37) and is flavoured with little of the 'satisficing' activities proposed by March and Simon (1958:140).

Figure 2
The Generation of
Electrical Power in
Toxicem Figurative
Representation

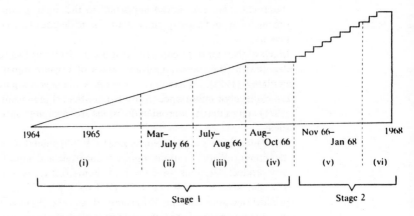

Stage 1 (smooth line)
(i) Initial thoughts of electricity generation
(ii) Formal proposals and objections to electricity generation
(iii) Scrutiny of facts and figures concerning private generation. Approaches made to the Electricity Board.
(iv) Figures produced. Rejected by Capital Control Committee. Toxicem decides *not* to generate its own electrical power.

Stage 2 (stepped line)
(v) The Managing Director announces his impending retirement. The debate on private generation is re-opened. Some 15 months of debate and negotiation ensue.
(vi) In the face of a deadlock situation, a vote is taken. On the strength of this result, Toxicem decides to *go ahead* and generate its own electrical power.

Stage 1 of the decision-making process (see Figure 2) is characterized by an extremely detailed search for an optimal solution, with Alwyn and Giles each indulging in the detailed scrutiny of the decisional implications such as the cost of an alternator and its upkeep, the types of fuel that would be required, and the possible action of the Electricity Board, the nationally owned monopoly supplier of British electricity. Between March and August 1966, the decision-making process displays none of the inadequacies described by March and Simon (1958:140–144) but instead is marked by an energetic search for information. Indeed, in March 1966 the Chairman and the Managing Director suggested that deadlock in the debate had been reached because of the lack of specific information and suggested that the opponents and proponents of the issue should clarify and justify in greater detail their respective positions.

However, in October 1966, the decision-making process becomes subject to delays as in Stage 2 (Figure 2) and functional criteria make way for the political manoeuvrings of localized interests. The conflicts of interest are not concerned with the primary issue of electricity generation, but focus instead upon career succession and the winning of the recently vacated Managing Directorship. Decision making becomes protracted and circuitous as political negotiations ensue (Abell 1975; Mintzberg et al. 1976; Pettigrew 1973). Information becomes employed as a political lever in an attempt to provide ready-made solutions to the problems being confronted (March and Olsen 1976; Jamous and Peloille 1970:149). Political activity gains primacy, the decision-making process loses its previously sharp goal-directed focus, and seemingly purposeless and irrelevant events occur between the proponents and the opponents of the electricity generation issue (Cohen et al. 1972). Consequently, the decision-making process becomes fragmented and incremental with the concommitant rise in political activity (Braybrooke and Lindblom 1963; Mintzberg et al. 1976; Butler et al. 1981). Some 15 months of debate and negotiation ensue (see Figure 2), resulting in the eventual purchase of a first turbine in August 1969.

This interpretation of the case study decision as neither wholly an incremental nor a satisficing decision has some implications for theories of decision making. The one decision-making process displays *both* characteristics of incremental and synoptic decision making. Beginning as a synoptic decision the case study decision develops into a hesitant, discontinuous, and incremental mode for a further two years. The decision-making process is only emergently incremental. In a similar vein, the satisficing behaviour of Alwyn and Giles, who restrict their scrutiny to information which will fully support their career interests but perhaps merely adequately support the issue of electricity generation, only emerges in the later stages of the decision. This behaviour is additionally facilitated by the relative lack of any concrete information on likely costs, in addition to the passive roles of the Accountancy Department and of the former Managing Director. As Astley et al. (1981) point out, the notions of satisficing and incremental decision making are, in themselves, inadequate concepts by which the characteristics of a decision-making process may be described. They explain only a partial aspect of part of a complex process (Butler et al. 1981).

Moreover, Lindblom's concept of incrementalism also appears to confuse the degree of change at the *outcome* of the decision-making process and the *piecemeal process* by which the outcome may be reached. The purchase of electricity generating equipment was a big step, or a large change from the status quo. It was the first time any such project had occurred in the organization and it represented a radical departure from the primary tasks of chemical production. Nonetheless, this nonincremental outcome (as defined by Lindblom 1959) was reached by an incremental, discontinuous decision-making process. It is suggested, therefore, that processual incrementalism be distinguished from outcome incrementalism (Wilson 1980). The degree of change from previous conditions may vary independently of the piecemeal quality of the decision-making process itself (Astley et al. 1981).

Power, Institution, and the Individual in Decision Making

One of the striking features of the case study is the role of Alwyn as an individual, superimposed against the fabric of Toxicem, as a political actor in the decision, and as a successful contender for career succession. His dominant presence, like that of Debré in the reform of the medical profession in France (Jamous and Peloille 1970:144), merits some discussion.

In Toxicem, one of the overriding institutional norms was one of quick action on highly quantifiable, accurate data:

'We pride ourselves on generating quantifiable data and making fast decisions on the basis of this information. When we go for something we all go together from the Managing Director right down to the gardener.' (Managing Director, Toxicem, in Wilson 1980)

The organization becomes a decisional system, developing repertoires of activities such as standard procedures, formal rules, and clearly established routines for handling decision-making processes (Pugh et al. 1968, 1969; Normann 1971; Simon 1947; Thompson 1967). Thus, faced with any problem, an organization will submit decisions to these predefined mechanisms for their solution.

Following Clegg (1979), power itself becomes institutionalized within the organizational structure, and as Crozier (1973:214) concurs: 'from a structural point of view, no power relationship can be dissociated from the institutional system or systems within which it develops'. Viewing the organization as a decisional system attempts to show how every power relationship is mediated by a whole array of structured conditions and constraints within the organization (Hickson et al. 1971). Indeed, Giddens (1976) points to the neglect of such 'structuration' in the conceptualization of power by Wrong (1968) and White (1971), who argue that power may be separated from the relationships within and the composition of the organization. Toxicem is clearly aware that it is substitutable in the production of chemicals, and consequently takes steps to ensure that it is innovative (creating uncertainty for others in the same business) and central (what it does immediately affects other chemical companies). Hickson et al. (1971) present dynamic models of such contingent power, concentrating upon the nature of power structures. However, it is in the *activation* of this power structure that the individual may take precedence over institutionalization (Pettigrew 1973:265).

'Strategies are formulated on the basis of perceptions. Accuracy here is critical. Those who correctly understand how a structure operates are in a much better position to make it work to their advantage.'

It is this activation of a power structure that reflects an individual's 'persona' (De Waele and Harré 1976:192).

'The powers of human beings are both actively exercised, often monitored, and always potentially under the control of a person through the organized structure of his cognitive and other resources, his nature, and so on are both variable and modifiable by self-intervention. They cannot therefore be traits.'

The term persona is used to distinguish it from personality characteristics. For example, entrepreneurial personality is invariably described as a trait, where the powerful leader takes adventurous, perhaps risky, decisions towards his vision of the organization's future (Collins and Moore 1970; Mintzberg 1978). The entrepreneurial personality pervades all decisions from new product to personnel topics. Persona, on the other hand, describes the variable characteristics of behaviours by individuals whereby the same individual may display one type of behaviour at one time, and another type of behaviour at a different time.

In the case study, Alwyn in the early stages displays little of the individualistic intervention that comes to the fore in the later stages of the decision. He develops a different persona as soon as career succession becomes the primary issue. His aspirations set on the managing directorship, Alwyn intervenes in the decision by finding an apparent mistake in some critical calculations. He does this in the knowledge that the debate will be re-opened. By questioning the competence of Giles and the Purchasing Department, he undermines their credibility in coping with uncertainty for Toxicem's supply of raw materials. Alwyn effectively undermines the delicate interdepartmental balance of power.

Toxicem's decisional system fails to accommodate the new issues and interests that arise from Alwyn's intervention. Individual activities come to the fore and the institutionalized Capital Control Committee is unable to function as a forum for debate between the various departments. The arousal of Alwyn's persona acts as the spark which forces a surfacing of awareness in other organizational members of how the system of decision making functions. It lays bare the balance of power between organizational departments. Personae are entities, called forth by the recognition of situations, whereby individuals have the capacity to endow the world with meaning and so negotiate with others who hold conflicting interpretations. From a Machiavellian perspective, the creation of such a situation may be a deliberate and conscious act (Secord and Backman 1961; Jamous and Peloille 1970; De Waele and Harré 1976). Although Alwyn himself may not necessarily be endowed with such Machiavellianism, the situation created by the passive role of the old Managing Director certainly is. His behaviour is to play off his two possible successors against each other in a situation where specific information was scarce and a decision one way or another was consequently difficult.

138   David C. Wilson

Summary

The analysis of the case study has led to the following speculations. First, notions of satisficing and incrementalism fail to adequately describe the essential features of this strategic decision. Distinctions are required between the particular characteristics of both decision-making processes and decision-making outcomes. Second, the case study gives evidence of the effect of institutionalization upon decision-making activities which simultaneously makes decision making predictable and yet facilitates the political manoeuvrings of Alwyn, resulting in a highly negotiable and protracted decision. The case is, therefore, argued for future theories of decision making to accommodate the organizational effects of institutionalized procedures with the individualistic manoeuvrings that such procedures may invoke.

Although this study is based upon a single case study and runs the risk of the accusation of 'making so much of so little' (Weick 1969:18), it has served to illustrate that existing notions of decision making can only partially describe the characteristics of this particular decision. Broader and more detailed concepts are required (Hage 1980), which can be applied across a large sample of organizations (Astley et al. 1981), and future work already well under way (Butler et al. 1981) should serve to confirm or modify the present interpretation of strategic decision making in Toxicem.

Notes   * In accordance with O.S. policy that the Editor-in-Chief should not influence decisions upon manuscripts with which he has a personal concern, Cornelis Lammers of the Editorial Board acted in his stead taking responsibility for the reviewing process and acceptance of this article because of the Editor-in-Chief's close working relationship with the author.

1. Acknowledgements are due to the following members of the Organizational Analysis Research Unit in Bradford for their comments and criticisms on this and earlier drafts of the paper. Richard J. Butler and David J. Hickson are, respectively, Research Lecturer and Professor and David Cray and Geoff Mallory are Research Fellows in the Unit. This research was supported by the Social Science Research Council, England.

References

Abell, P.
1975 *Organizations as bargaining and influence systems*. London: Heinemann.

Allison, G. T.
1969 'Conceptual models and the Cuban missile crisis'. *American Political Science Review*, September.

Astley, W. G., R. Axelsson, R. J. Butler, D. J. Hickson, and D. C. Wilson
1981 'Decision making: theory III'. Working paper, Organizational Analysis Research Unit, Bradford.

Axelrod, R.
1970 *Conflict of interests: a theory of divergent goals with applications to politics*. Chicago: Markham.

Bachrach, P., and M. S. Baratz
1970 *Power and poverty: theory and practice*. Oxford: Oxford University Press.

Baumol, W. J.
1959 *Business behaviour, value and growth*. New York: Macmillan.

Braybrooke, D., and C. E. Lindblom
1963 *A strategy of decision*. New York: Free Press.

Butler, R. J., D. Cray, D. J. Hickson, G. R. Mallory, and D. C. Wilson
1981 'Complexity and cleavage in decision making: an empirical investigation'. Working paper, Organizational Analysis Research Unit, Bradford.

Campbell, D. T., and J. C. Stanley
1966 *Experimental and quasi-experimental designs for research.* Chicago: Rand McNally.

Clegg, S.
1979 *The theory of power and organization.* London: Routledge and Kegan Paul.

Cohen, D. M., J. G. March, and J. P. Olsen
1972 'A garbage can model of organizational choice'. *Administrative Science Quarterly* 17/1:1–25.

Collins, O., and D. G. Moore
1970 *The organization makers.* New York: Appleton–Century–Crofts.

Crozier, M.
1973 'The problems of power'. *Social Research* 41/2:211–228.

Cyert, R., and J. G. March
1963 *A behavioral theory of the firm.* Englewood Cliffs, N.J.: Prentice–Hall.

Dalton, M.
1958 *Men who manage.* New York: Wiley.

De Waele, J.-P., and R. Harré
1976 'The personality of individuals' in *Personality.* R. Harré (ed). London: Basil Blackwell.

Dunn, W. N., and F. W. Swierczek
1977 'Planned organizational change: towards a grounded theory'. *Journal of Applied Behavioural Science* 13/2:135–157.

Ellul, J.
1964 *The technological society.* New York: Knopf.

Giddens, A.
1976 *New rules of sociological method.* London: Hutchinson.

Hage, J.
1980 *Theories of organizations: form, process and transformation.* New York: Wiley.

Hickson, D. J., C. R. Hinings, C. A. Lee, R. E. Schneck, and J. M. Pennings
1971 'A strategic contingencies theory of intra-organizational power'. *Administrative Science Quarterly* 16/2:216–229.

Jamous, H., and B. Peloille
1970 'Professions or self-perpetuating systems? Changes in the French university-hospital system' in *Professions and professionalization.* J. A. Jackson (ed). Cambridge: Cambridge University Press.

Leavitt, H. J.
1972 *Managerial psychology* (3rd edition). Chicago: University of Chicago Press.

Lindblom, C. E.
1959 'The science of "muddling through"'. *Public Administration Review* 19:79–88.

Luce, D. R., and H. Raiffa
1957 *Games and decisions: introduction and critical survey.* New York: Wiley.

March, J. G., and H. A. Simon
1958 *Organizations.* New York: Wiley.

March, J. G., and J. P. Olsen
1976 *Ambiguity and choice in organizations.* Oslo: Universitet Sforlaget.

McClintock, C. C., D. Brannon, and S. Maynard-Moody
1979 'Applying the logic of sample surveys to qualitative case studies: the case cluster method'. *Administrative Science Quarterly* 24/4:612–629.

Mintzberg, H., D. Raisinghani, and A. Theoret
1976 'The structure of "unstructured" decision processes'. *Administrative Science Quarterly* 21/2:246–275.

Mintzberg, H.
1978 'Patterns in strategy formation'. *Management Science* 24/9:934–948.

Moore, P. G., and H. Thomas
1976 *The anatomy of decisions.* Harmondsworth: Penguin.

Normann, R.
1971 'Organizational innovativeness: product variation and reorientation'. *Administrative Science Quarterly* 16/2:203–215.

Pettigrew, A.
1973 *The politics of organizational decision making*. London: Tavistock.

Pugh, D. S., D. J. Hickson, C. R. Hinings, and C. Turner
1968 'Dimensions of organization structure'. *Administrative Science Quarterly* 13/1:65–105.

Pugh, D. C., D. J. Hickson, C. R. Hinings, and C. Turner
1969 'The context of organization structures'. *Administrative Science Quarterly* 14:91–114.

Secord, P. F., and C. Backman
1961 'Personality theory and the problem of stability and change in individual behaviour: an interpersonal approach'. *Psychological Review* 68:21–32.

Simon, H. A.
1947 *Administrative behavior*. New York: Free Press.

Thompson, J. D.
1967 *Organizations in action*. New York: McGraw Hill.

Walker, J.
1969 'The diffusion of innovation among the American States'. *American Political Science Review* LXIII:879–893.

Weick, K.
1969 *The social psychology of organizing*. Reading, Mass: Addison–Wesley.

White, D. M.
1971 'The problem of power'. *British Journal of Political Science* 2:479–490.

Wilson, D. C.
1980 Organizational strategy. Ph.D. thesis. University of Bradford.

Wrong, D. H.
1968 'Some problems of defining social powers'. *American Journal of Sociology* 79/5:673–681.

[7]

*Michael D. Cohen, James G. March, and
Johan P. Olsen*

A Garbage Can Model of Organizational Choice

*Organized anarchies are organizations characterized by problematic preferences,
unclear technology, and fluid participation. Recent studies of universities, a familiar form of organized anarchy, suggest that such organizations can be viewed for
some purposes as collections of choices looking for problems, issues and feelings
looking for decision situations in which they might be aired, solutions looking for
issues to which they might be an answer, and decision makers looking for work.
These ideas are translated into an explicit computer simulation model of a garbage can decision process. The general implications of such a model are described
in terms of five major measures on the process. Possible applications of the model
to more narrow predictions are illustrated by an examination of the model's predictions with respect to the effect of adversity on university decision making.*

Consider organized anarchies. These are
organizations—or decision situations—characterized by three general properties.[1] The
first is problematic preferences. In the organization it is difficult to impute a set of preferences to the decision situation that satisfies
the standard consistency requirements for a
theory of choice. The organization operates
on the basis of a variety of inconsistent and
ill-defined preferences. It can be described
better as a loose collection of ideas than as a
coherent structure; it discovers preferences
through action more than it acts on the basis
of preferences.

The second property is unclear technology.
Although the organization manages to survive and even produce, its own processes are
not understood by its members. It operates
on the basis of simple trial-and-error procedures, the residue of learning from the acci-
dents of past experience, and pragmatic in-

[1] We are indebted to Nancy Block, Hilary Cohen,
and James Glenn for computational, editorial, and
intellectual help; to the Institute of Sociology, University of Bergen, and the Institute of Organization
and Industrial Sociology, Copenhagen School of Economics, for institutional hospitality and useful discussions of organizational behavior; and to the Ford
Foundation for the financial support that made our
collaboration feasible. We also wish to acknowledge
the helpful comments and suggestions of Søren
Christensen, James S. Coleman, Harald Enderud,
Kåre Rommetveit, and William H. Starbuck.

ventions of necessity. The third property is
fluid participation. Participants vary in the
amount of time and effort they devote to
different domains; involvement varies from
one time to another. As a result, the boundaries of the organization are uncertain and
changing; the audiences and decision makers
for any particular kind of choice change
capriciously.

These properties of organized anarchy
have been identified often in studies of organizations. They are characteristic of any organization in part—part of the time. They are
particularly conspicuous in public, educational, and illegitimate organizations. A
theory of organized anarchy will describe a
portion of almost any organization's activities,
but will not describe all of them.

To build on current behavioral theories of
organizations in order to accomodate the concept of organized anarchy, two major phenomena critical to an understanding of anarchy must be investigated. The first is the
manner in which organizations make choices
without consistent, shared goals. Situations
of decision making under goal ambiguity are
common in complex organizations. Often
problems are resolved without recourse to
explicit bargaining or to an explicit price system market—two common processes for decision making in the absence of consensus.
The second phenomenon is the way members

1

of an organization are activated. This entails the question of how occasional members become active and how attention is directed toward, or away from, a decision. It is important to understand the attention patterns within an organization, since not everyone is attending to everything all of the time.

Additional concepts are also needed in a normative theory of organizations dealing with organized anarchies. First, a normative theory of intelligent decision making under ambiguous circumstances (namely, in situations in which goals are unclear or unknown) should be developed. Can we provide some meaning for intelligence which does not depend on relating current action to known goals? Second, a normative theory of attention is needed. Participants within an organization are constrained by the amount of time they can devote to the various things demanding attention. Since variations in behavior in organized anarchies are due largely to questions of who is attending to what, decisions concerning the allocation of attention are prime ones. Third, organized anarchies require a revised theory of management. Significant parts of contemporary theories of management introduce mechanisms for control and coordination which assume the existence of well-defined goals and a well-defined technology, as well as substantial participant involvement in the affairs of the organization. Where goals and technology are hazy and participation is fluid, many of the axioms and standard procedures of management collapse.

This article is directed to a behavioral theory of organized anarchy. On the basis of several recent studies, some elaborations and modifications of existing theories of choice are proposed. A model for describing decision making within organized anarchies is developed, and the impact of some aspects of organizational structure on the process of choice within such a model is examined.

THE BASIC IDEAS

Decision opportunities are fundamentally ambiguous stimuli. This theme runs through several recent studies of organizational choice.[2] Although organizations can often be

viewed conveniently as vehicles for solving well-defined problems or structures within which conflict is resolved through bargaining, they also provide sets of procedures through which participants arrive at an interpretation of what they are doing and what they have done while in the process of doing it. From this point of view, an organization is a collection of choices looking for problems, issues and feelings looking for decision situations in which they might be aired, solutions looking for issues to which they might be the answer, and decision makers looking for work.

Such a view of organizational choice focuses attention on the way the meaning of a choice changes over time. It calls attention to the strategic effects of timing, through the introduction of choices and problems, the time pattern of available energy, and the impact of organizational structure.

To understand processes within organizations, one can view a choice opportunity as a garbage can into which various kinds of problems and solutions are dumped by participants as they are generated. The mix of garbage in a single can depends on the mix of cans available, on the labels attached to the alternative cans, on what garbage is currently being produced, and on the speed with which garbage is collected and removed from the scene.

Such a theory of organizational decision making must concern itself with a relatively complicated interplay among the generation of problems in an organization, the deployment of personnel, the production of solutions, and the opportunities for choice. Although it may be convenient to imagine that choice opportunities lead first to the generation of decision alternatives, then to an examination of their consequences, then to an evaluation of those consequences in terms of objectives, and finally to a decision, this type of model is often a poor description of what actually happens. In the garbage can model, on the other hand, a decision is an outcome

---

[2] We have based the model heavily on seven recent studies of universities: Christensen (1971), Cohen and March (1972), Enderud (1971), Mood

(1971), Olsen (1970, 1971), and Rommetveit (1971). The ideas, however, have a broader parentage. In particular, they obviously owe a debt to Allison (1969), Coleman (1957), Cyert and March (1963), Lindblom (1965), Long (1958), March and Simon (1958), Schilling (1968), Thompson (1967), and Vickers (1965).

or interpretation of several relatively independent streams within an organization.

Attention is limited here to interrelations among four such streams.

Problems. Problems are the concern of people inside and outside the organization. They might arise over issues of lifestyle; family; frustrations of work; careers; group relations within the organization; distribution of status, jobs, and money; ideology; or current crises of mankind as interpreted by the mass media or the nextdoor neighbor. All of these require attention.

Solutions. A solution is somebody's product. A computer is not just a solution to a problem in payroll management, discovered when needed. It is an answer actively looking for a question. The creation of need is not a curiosity of the market in consumer products; it is a general phenomenon of processes of choice. Despite the dictum that you cannot find the answer until you have formulated the question well, you often do not know what the question is in organizational problem solving until you know the answer.

Participants. Participants come and go. Since every entrance is an exit somewhere else, the distribution of "entrances" depends on the attributes of the choice being left as much as it does on the attributes of the new choice. Substantial variation in participation stems from other demands on the participants' time (rather than from features of the decision under study).

Choice opportunities. These are occasions when an organization is expected to produce behavior that can be called a decision. Opportunities arise regularly and any organization has ways of declaring an occasion for choice. Contracts must be signed; people hired, promoted, or fired; money spent; and responsibilities allocated.

Although not completely independent of each other, each of the streams can be viewed as independent and exogenous to the system. Attention will be concentrated here on examining the consequences of different rates and patterns of flows in each of the streams and different procedures for relating them.

THE GARBAGE CAN

A simple simulation model can be specified in terms of the four streams and a set of garbage processing assumptions.

Four basic variables are considered; each is a function of time.

A stream of choices. Some fixed number, m, of choices is assumed. Each choice is characterized by (a) an entry time, the calendar time at which that choice is activated for decision, and (b) a decision structure, a list of participants eligible to participate in making that choice.

A stream of problems. Some number, w, of problems is assumed. Each problem is characterized by (a) an entry time, the calendar time at which the problem becomes visible, (b) an energy requirement, the energy required to resolve a choice to which the problem is attached (if the solution stream is as high as possible), and (c) an access structure, a list of choices to which the problem has access.

A rate of flow of solutions. The verbal theory assumes a stream of solutions and a matching of specific solutions with specific problems and choices. A simpler set of assumptions is made and focus is on the rate at which solutions are flowing into the system. It is assumed that either because of variations in the stream of solutions or because of variations in the efficiency of search procedures within the organization, different energies are required to solve the same problem at different times. It is further assumed that these variations are consistent for different problems. Thus, a solution coefficient, ranging between 0 and 1, which operates on the potential decision energies to determine the problem solving output (effective energy) actually realized during any given time period is specified.

A stream of energy from participants. It is assumed that there is some number, v, of participants. Each participant is characterized by a time series of energy available for organizational decision making. Thus, in each time period, each participant can provide some specified amount of potential energy to the organization.

Two varieties of organizational segmentation are reflected in the model. The first is the mapping of choices onto decision makers, the decision structure. The decision structure of the organization is described by D, a v-by-m array in which d_{ij} is 1 if the ith participant is eligible to participate in the making of the jth choice. Otherwise, d_{ij} is 0. The second is the mapping of problems onto choices, the access structure. The access structure of the organization is described by A, a w-by-m array in which a_{ij} is 1 if the jth choice is accessible to the ith problem. Otherwise, a_{ij} is 0.

In order to connect these variables, three key behavioral assumptions are specified. The first is an assumption about the additivity of energy requirements, the second specifies the way in which energy is allocated to choices, and the third describes the way in which problems are attached to choices.

Energy additivity assumption. In order to be made, each choice requires as much effective energy as the sum of all requirements of the several problems attached to it. The effective energy devoted to a choice is the sum of the energies of decision makers attached to that choice, deflated, in each time period, by the solution coefficient. As soon as the total effective energy that has been expended on a choice equals or exceeds the requirements at a particular point in time, a decision is made.

Energy allocation assumption. The energy of each participant is allocated to no more than one choice during each time period. Each participant allocates his energy among the choices for which he is eligible to the one closest to decision, that is the one with the smallest energy deficit at the end of the previous time period in terms of the energies contributed by other participants.

Problem allocation assumption. Each problem is attached to no more than one choice each time period, choosing from among those accessible by calculating the apparent energy deficits (in terms of the energy requirements of other problems) at the end of the previous time period and selecting the choice closest to decision. Except to the extent that priorities enter in the organizational structure, there is no priority ranking of problems.

These assumptions capture key features of the processes observed. They might be modified in a number of ways without doing violence to the empirical observations on which they are based. The consequences of these modifications, however, are not pursued here. Rather, attention is focused on the implications of the simple version described. The interaction of organizational structure and a garbage can form of choice will be examined.

ORGANIZATIONAL STRUCTURE

Elements of organizational structure influence outcomes of a garbage can decision process (a) by affecting the time pattern of the arrival of problems choices, solutions, or decision makers, (b) by determining the allocation of energy by potential participants in the decision, and (c) by establishing linkages among the various streams.

The organizational factors to be considered are some that have real-world interpretations and implications and are applicable to the theory of organized anarchy. They are familiar features of organizations, resulting from a mixture of deliberate managerial planning, individual and collective learning, and imitation. Organizational structure changes as a response to such factors as market demand for personnel and the heterogeneity of values, which are external to the model presented here. Attention will be limited to the comparative statics of the model, rather than to the dynamics produced by organizational learning.

To exercise the model, the following are specified: (a) a set of fixed parameters which do not change from one variation to another, (b) the entry times for choices, (c) the entry times for problems, (d) the net energy load on the organization, (e) the access structure of the organization, (f) the decision structure of the organization, and (g) the energy distribution among decision makers in the organization.

Some relatively pure structural variations will be identified in each and examples of how variations in such structures might be related systematically to key exogenous variables will be given. It will then be shown how such factors of organizational structure affect important characteristics of the decisions in a garbage can decision process.

Fixed Parameters

Within the variations reported, the following are fixed: (a) number of time periods—twenty, (b) number of choice opportunities—ten, (c) number of decision makers—ten, (d) number of problems—twenty, and (e) the solution coefficients for the 20 time periods—0.6 for each period.[3]

Entry Times

Two different randomly generated sequences of entry times for choices are considered. It is assumed that one choice enters per time period over the first ten time periods in one of the following orders: (a) 10, 7, 9, 5, 2, 3, 4, 1, 6, 8, or (b) 6, 5, 2, 10, 8, 9, 7, 4, 1, 3.

Similarly, two different randomly generated sequences of entry times for problems are considered. It is assumed that two problems enter per time period over the first ten time periods in one of the following orders: (a) 8, 20, 14, 16, 6, 7, 15, 17, 2, 13, 11, 19, 4, 9, 3, 12, 1, 10, 5, 18, or (b) 4, 14, 11, 20, 3, 5, 2, 12, 1, 6, 8, 19, 7, 15, 16, 17, 10, 18, 9, 13.

Net Energy Load

The total energy available to the organization in each time period is 5.5 units. Thus, the total energy available over twenty time periods is $20 \times 5.5 = 110$. This is reduced by the solution coefficients to 66. These figures hold across all other variations of the model. The net energy load on the organization is defined as the difference between the total energy required to solve all problems and the total effective energy available to the organization over all time periods. When this is negative, there is, in principle, enough energy available. Since the total effective energy available is fixed at 66, the net load is varied by varying the total energy requirements for problems. It is assumed that each problem has the same energy requirement under a given load. Three different energy load situations are considered.

Net energy load 0: light load. Under this condition the energy required to make a choice is 1.1 times the number of problems attached to that choice. That is, the energy required for each problem is 1.1. Thus, the minimum total effective energy required to

[3] The model has also been exercised under conditions of a set of solution coefficients that varies over the time periods. Specifically, the following series has been used: 1, 0.9, 0.7, 0.3, 0.1, 0.1, 0.3, 0.7, 0.9, 1, 0.6, 0.6, 0.6, 0.6, 0.6, 0.6, 0.6, 0.6, 0.6, 0.6. This simulation, using only one combination of choice and problem entry times, gives results consistent with all of the conclusions reported in the present article.

resolve all problems is 22, and the net energy load is $22 - 66 = -44$.

Net energy load 1: moderate load. Under this condition, the energy required for each problem is 2.2. Thus, the energy required to make a choice is 2.2 times the number of problems attached to that choice, and the minimum effective energy required to resolve all problems is 44. The net energy load is $44 - 66 = -22$.

Net energy load 2: heavy load. Under this condition, each problem requires energy of 3.3. The energy required to make a choice is 3.3 times the number of problems attached to that choice. The minimum effective energy required to resolve all problems is 66, and the net energy load is $66 - 66 = 0$.

Although it is possible from the total energy point of view for all problems to be resolved in any load condition, the difficulty of accomplishing that result where the net energy load is zero—a heavy load—is obviously substantial.

Access Structure

Three pure types of organizational arrangements are considered in the access structure (the relation between problems and choices).

Access structure 0: unsegmented access. This structure is represented by an access array in which any active problem has access to any active choice.

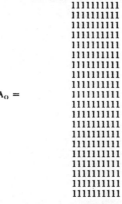

$$A_0 =$$

```
1111111111
1111111111
1111111111
1111111111
1111111111
1111111111
1111111111
1111111111
1111111111
1111111111
1111111111
1111111111
1111111111
1111111111
1111111111
1111111111
1111111111
1111111111
1111111111
1111111111
```

Access structure 1: hierarchical access. In this structure both choices and problems are arranged in a hierarchy such that important problems—those with relatively low numbers—have access to many choices, and important choices—those with relatively low numbers—are accessible only to important problems. The structure is represented by the following access array:

$$A_1 = \begin{array}{l} 1111111111 \\ 1111111111 \\ 0111111111 \\ 0111111111 \\ 0011111111 \\ 0011111111 \\ 0001111111 \\ 0001111111 \\ 0000111111 \\ 0000111111 \\ 0000011111 \\ 0000011111 \\ 0000001111 \\ 0000001111 \\ 0000000111 \\ 0000000111 \\ 0000000011 \\ 0000000011 \\ 0000000001 \\ 0000000001 \end{array}$$

Access structure 2: specialized access. In this structure each problem has access to only one choice and each choice is accessible to only two problems, that is, choices specialize in the kinds of problems that can be associated to them. The structure is represented by the following access array:

$$A_2 = \begin{array}{l} 1000000000 \\ 1000000000 \\ 0100000000 \\ 0100000000 \\ 0010000000 \\ 0010000000 \\ 0001000000 \\ 0001000000 \\ 0000100000 \\ 0000100000 \\ 0000010000 \\ 0000010000 \\ 0000001000 \\ 0000001000 \\ 0000000100 \\ 0000000100 \\ 0000000010 \\ 0000000010 \\ 0000000001 \\ 0000000001 \end{array}$$

Actual organizations will exhibit a more complex mix of access rules. Any such combination could be represented by an appropriate access array. The three pure structures considered here represent three classic alternative approaches to the problem of organizing the legitimate access of problems to decision situations.

Decision Structure

Three similar pure types are considered in the decision structure (the relation between decision makers and choices).

Decision structure 0: unsegmented decisions. In this structure any decision maker can participate in any active choice opportunity. Thus, the structure is represented by the following array:

$$D_0 = \begin{array}{l} 1111111111 \\ 1111111111 \\ 1111111111 \\ 1111111111 \\ 1111111111 \\ 1111111111 \\ 1111111111 \\ 1111111111 \\ 1111111111 \\ 1111111111 \end{array}$$

Decision structure 1: hierarchical decisions. In this structure both decision makers and choices are arranged in a hierarchy such that important choices—low numbered choices—must be made by important decision makers—low numbered decision makers—and important decision makers can participate in many choices. The structure is represented by the following array:

$$D_1 = \begin{array}{l} 1111111111 \\ 0111111111 \\ 0011111111 \\ 0001111111 \\ 0000111111 \\ 0000011111 \\ 0000001111 \\ 0000000111 \\ 0000000011 \\ 0000000001 \end{array}$$

Decision structure 2: specialized decisions. In this structure each decision maker is associated with a single choice and each choice has a single decision maker. Decision makers specialize in the choices to which they attend. Thus, we have the following array:

$$D_2 = \begin{matrix} 1000000000 \\ 0100000000 \\ 0010000000 \\ 0001000000 \\ 0000100000 \\ 0000010000 \\ 0000001000 \\ 0000000100 \\ 0000000010 \\ 0000000001 \end{matrix}$$

As in the case of the access structure, actual decision structures will require a more complicated array. Most organizations have a mix of rules for defining the legitimacy of participation in decisions. The three pure cases are, however, familiar models of such rules and can be used to understand some consequences of decision structure for decision processes.

Energy Distribution

The distribution of energy among decision makers reflects possible variations in the amount of time spent on organizational problems by different decision makers. The solution coefficients and variations in the energy requirement for problems affect the overall relation between energy available and energy required. Three different variations in the distribution of energy are considered.

Energy distribution 0: important people— less energy. In this distribution important people, that is people defined as important in a hierarchial decision structure, have less energy. This might reflect variations in the combination of outside demands and motivation to participate within the organization. The specific energy distribution is indicated as follows:

Decision maker	Energy	
1	0.1	
2	0.2	
3	0.3	
4	0.4	
5	0.5	$= E_0$
6	0.6	
7	0.7	
8	0.8	
9	0.9	
10	1.0	

The total energy available to the organization each time period (before deflation by the solution coefficients) is 5.5.

Energy distribution 1: equal energy. In this distribution there is no internal differentiation among decision makers with respect to energy. Each decision maker has the same energy (0.55) each time period. Thus, there is the following distribution:

Decision maker	Energy	
1	0.55	
2	0.55	
3	0.55	
4	0.55	
5	0.55	$= E_1$
6	0.55	
7	0.55	
8	0.55	
9	0.55	
10	0.55	

The total energy available to the organization each time period (before deflation by the solution coefficients) is 5.5.

Energy distribution 2: important people— more energy. In this distribution energy is distributed unequally but in a direction opposite to that in E_0. Here the people defined as important by the hierarchical decision structure have more energy. The distribution is indicated by the following:

Decision maker	Energy	
1	1.0	
2	0.9	
3	0.8	
4	0.7	
5	0.6	$= E_2$
6	0.5	
7	0.4	
8	0.3	
9	0.2	
10	0.1	

As in the previous organizations, the total energy available to the organization each time period (before deflation by the solution coefficients) is 5.5.

Where the organization has a hierarchical decision structure, the distinction between important and unimportant decision makers is clear. Where the decision structure is unsegmented or specialized, the variations in energy distribution are defined in terms of the same numbered decision makers (lower numbers are more important than higher numbers) to reflect possible status differences which are not necessarily captured by the decision structure.

Simulation Design

The simulation design is simple. A Fortran version of the garbage can model is given in the appendix, along with documentation and an explanation. The $3^4 = 81$ types of organizational situations obtained by taking the possible combinations of the values of the four dimensions of an organization (access structure, decision structure, energy distribution, and net energy load) are studied here under the four combinations of choice and problem entry times. The result is 324 simulation situations.

SUMMARY STATISTICS

The garbage can model operates under each of the possible organizational structures to assign problems and decision makers to choices, to determine the energy required and effective energy applied to choices, to make such choices and resolve such problems as the assignments and energies indicate are feasible. It does this for each of the twenty time periods in a twenty-period simulation of organizational decision making.

For each of the 324 situations, some set of simple summary statistics on the process is required. These are limited to five.

Decision Style

Within the kind of organization postulated, decisions are made in three different ways.

By resolution. Some choices resolve problems after some period of working on them. The length of time may vary, depending on the number of problems. This is the familiar case that is implicit in most discussions of choice within organizations.

By oversight. If a choice is activated when problems are attached to other choices and if there is energy available to make the new choice quickly, it will be made without any attention to existing problems and with a minimum of time and energy.

By flight. In some cases choices are associated with problems (unsuccessfully) for some time until a choice more attractive to the problems comes along. The problems leave the choice, and thus it is now possible to make the decision. The decision resolves

no problems; they having now attached themselves to a new choice.

Some choices involve both flight and resolution—some problems leave, the remainder are solved. These have been defined as resolution, thus slightly exaggerating the importance of that style. As a result of that convention, the three styles are mutually exclusive and exhaustive with respect to any one choice. The same organization, however, may use any one of them in different choices. Thus, the decision style of any particular variation of the model can be described by specifying the proportion of completed choices which are made in each of these three ways.

Problem Activity

Any measure of the degree to which problems are active within the organization should reflect the degree of conflict within the organization or the degree of articulation of problems. Three closely related statistics of problem activity are considered. The first is the total number of problems not solved at the end of the twenty time periods; the second is the total number of times that any problem shifts from one choice to another, while the third is the total number of time periods that a problem is active and attached to some choice, summed over all problems. These measures are strongly correlated with each other. The third is used as the measure of problem activity primarily because it has a relatively large variance; essentially the same results would have been obtained with either of the other two measures.

Problem Latency

A problem may be active, but not attached to any choice. The situation is one in which a problem is recognized and accepted by some part of the organization, but is not considered germane to any available choice. Presumably, an organization with relatively high problem latency will exhibit somewhat different symptoms from one with low latency. Problem latency has been measured by the total number of periods a problem is active, but not attached to a choice, summed over all problems.

Decision Maker Activity

To measure the degree of decision maker activity in the system, some measure which reflects decision maker energy expenditure, movement, and persistence is required. Four are considered: (a) the total number of time periods a decision maker is attached to a choice, summed over all decision makers, (b) the total number of times that any decision maker shifts from one choice to another, (c) the total amount of effective energy available and used, and (d) the total effective energy used on choices in excess of that required to make them at the time they are made. These four measures are highly intercorrelated. The second was used primarily because of its relatively large variance; any of the others would have served as well.

Decision Difficulty

Because of the way in which decisions can be made in the system, decision difficulty is not the same as the level of problem activity. Two alternative measures are considered: the total number of choices not made by the end of the twenty time periods and the total number of periods that a choice is active, summed over all choices. These are highly correlated. The second is used, primarily because of its higher variance; the conclusions would be unchanged if the first were used.

IMPLICATIONS OF THE MODEL

An analysis of the individual histories of the simulations shows eight major properties of garbage can decision processes.

First, resolution of problems as a style for making decisions is not the most common style, except under conditions where flight is severely restricted (for instance, specialized access) or a few conditions under light load. Decision making by flight and oversight is

a major feature of the process in general. In each of the simulation trials there were twenty problems and ten choices. Although the mean number of choices not made was 1.0, the mean number of problems not solved was 12.3. The results are detailed in Table 1. The behavioral and normative implications of a decision process which appears to make choices in large part by flight or by oversight must be examined. A possible explanation of the behavior of organizations that seem to make decisions without apparently making progress in resolving the problems that appear to be related to the decisions may be emerging.

Second, the process is quite thoroughly and quite generally sensitive to variations in load. As Table 2 shows, an increase in the net energy load on the system generally increases problem activity, decision maker activity, decision difficulty, and the uses of flight and oversight. Problems are less likely to be solved, decision makers are likely to shift from one problem to another more frequently, choices are likely to take longer to make and are less likely to resolve problems. Although it is possible to specify an organization that is relatively stable with changes in load, it is not possible to have an organization that is stable in behavior and also has other desirable attributes. As load changes, an organization that has an unsegmented access structure with a specialized decision structure stays quite stable. It exhibits relatively low decision difficulty and decision maker activity, very low problem latency, and maximum problem activity. It makes virtually all decisions placed before it, uses little energy from decision makers, and solves virtually no problems.

Third, a typical feature of the model is the tendency of decision makers and prob-

TABLE 1. PROPORTION OF CHOICES THAT RESOLVE PROBLEMS UNDER FOUR CONDITIONS OF CHOICE AND PROBLEM ENTRY TIMES, BY LOAD AND ACCESS STRUCTURE

		Access structure			
		All	Unsegmented	Hierarchical	Specialized
Load	Light	0.55	0.38	0.61	0.65
	Moderate	0.30	0.04	0.27	0.60
	Heavy	0.36	0.35	0.23	0.50
	All	0.40	0.26	0.37	0.58

TABLE 2. EFFECTS OF VARIATIONS IN LOAD UNDER FOUR CONDITIONS
OF CHOICE AND PROBLEM ENTRY TIMES

		Mean problem activity	Mean decision maker activity	Mean decision difficulty	Proportion of choices by flight or oversight
Load	Light	114.9	60.9	19.5	.45
	Moderate	204.3	63.8	32.9	.70
	Heavy	211.1	76.6	46.1	.64

lems to track each other through choices. Subject to structural restrictions on the tracking, decision makers work on active problems in connection with active choices; both decision makers and problems tend to move together from choice to choice. Thus, one would expect decision makers who have a feeling that they are always working on the same problems in somewhat different contexts, mostly without results. Problems, in a similar fashion, meet the same people wherever they go with the same result.

Fourth, there are some important interconnections among three key aspects of the efficiency of the decision processes specified. The first is problem activity, the amount of time unresolved problems are actively attached to choice situations. Problem activity is a rough measure of the potential for decision conflict in the organization. The second aspect is problem latency, the amount of time problems spend activated but not linked to choices. The third aspect is decision time, the persistence of choices. Presumably, a good organizational structure would keep both problem activity and problem latency low through rapid problem solution in its choices. In the garbage can process such a result was never observed. Segmentation of the access structure tends to reduce the number of unresolved problems active in the organization but at the cost of increasing the latency period of problems and, in most cases the time devoted to reaching decisions. On the other hand, segmentation of the decision structure tends to result in decreasing problem latency, but at the cost of increasing problem activity and decision time.

Fifth, the process is frequently sharply interactive. Although some phenomena associated with the garbage can are regular and flow through nearly all of the cases, for ex-

ample, the effect of overall load, other phenomena are much more dependent on the particular combination of structures involved. Although high segmentation of access structure generally produces slow decision time, for instance, a specialized access structure, in combination with an unsegmented decision structure, produces quick decisions.

Sixth, important problems are more likely to be solved than unimportant ones. Problems which appear early are more likely to be resolved than later ones. Considering only those cases involving access hierarchy where importance is defined for problems, the relation between problem importance and order of arrival is shown in Table 3. The system, in

TABLE 3. PROPORTION OF PROBLEMS RESOLVED UNDER FOUR CONDITIONS OF CHOICE AND PROBLEM ENTRY TIMES, BY IMPORTANCE OF PROBLEM AND ORDER OF ARRIVAL OF PROBLEM (FOR HIERARCHICAL ACCESS)

		Time of arrival of problem	
		Early, first 10	Late, last 10
Importance of problem	High, first 10	0.46	0.44
	Low, last 10	0.48	0.25

effect, produces a queue of problems in terms of their importance, to the disadvantage of late-arriving, relatively unimportant problems, and particularly so when load is heavy. This queue is the result of the operation of the model. It was not imposed as a direct assumption.

Seventh, important choices are less likely to resolve problems than unimportant choices. Important choices are made by oversight and flight. Unimportant choices are made by resolution. These differences are observed under both of the choice entry sequences but are sharpest where important choices enter relatively early. Table 4 shows

TABLE 4. PROPORTION OF CHOICES THAT ARE MADE BY FLIGHT OR OVERSIGHT UNDER FOUR CONDITIONS OF CHOICE AND PROBLEM ENTRY TIMES, BY TIME OF ARRIVAL AND IMPORTANCE OF CHOICE (FOR HIERARCHICAL ACCESS OR DECISION STRUCTURE)

		Time of arrival of choice	
		Early, first 5	Late, last 5
Importance of choice	High, first 5	0.86	0.65
	Low, last 5	0.54	0.60

the results. This property of important choices in a garbage can decision process can be naturally and directly related to the phenomenon in complex organizations of important choices which often appear to just happen.

Eighth, although a large proportion of the choices are made, the choice failures that do occur are concentrated among the most important and least important choices. Choices of intermediate importance are virtually always made. The proportion of choice failures, under conditions of hierarchical access or decision structures is as follows:

Three most important choices 0.14
Four middle choices 0.05
Three least important choices 0.12

In a broad sense, these features of the process provide some clues to how organizations survive when they do not know what they are doing. Much of the process violates standard notions of how decisions ought to be made. But most of those notions are built on assumptions which cannot be met under the conditions specified. When objectives and technologies are unclear, organizations are charged to discover some alternative decision procedures which permit them to proceed without doing extraordinary violence to the domains of participants or to their model of

what an organization should be. It is a hard charge, to which the process described is a partial response.

At the same time, the details of the outcomes clearly depend on features of the organizational structure. The same garbage can operation results in different behavioral symptoms under different levels of load on the system or different designs of the structure of the organization. Such differences raise the possibility of predicting variations in decision behavior in different organizations. One possible example of such use remains to be considered.

GARBAGE CANS AND UNIVERSITIES

One class of organization which faces decision situations involving unclear goals, unclear technology, and fluid participants is the modern college or university. If the implications of the model are applicable anywhere, they are applicable to a university. Although there is great variation among colleges and universities, both between countries and within any country, the model has general relevance to decision making in higher education.

General Implications

University decision making frequently does not resolve problems. Choices are often made by flight or oversight. University decision processes are sensitive to increases in load. Active decision makers and problems track one another through a series of choices without appreciable progress in solving problems. Important choices are not likely to solve problems.

Decisions whose interpretations continually change during the process of resolution appear both in the model and in actual observations of universities. Problems, choices, and decision makers arrange and rearrange themselves. In the course of these arrangements the meaning of a choice can change several times, if this meaning is understood as the mix of problems discussed in the context of that choice.

Problems are often solved, but rarely by the choice to which they are first attached. A choice that might, under some circumstances, be made with little effort becomes an arena for many problems. The choice becomes almost impossible to make, until the problems drift off to another arena. The matching of problems, choices, and decision makers is partly controlled by attributes of content, relevance, and competence; but it is also quite sensitive to attributes of timing, the particular combinations of current garbage cans, and the overall load on the system.

Universities and Adversity

In establishing connections between the hypothetical attributes of organizational structure in the model and some features of contemporary universities, the more detailed implications of the model can be used to explore features of university decision making. In particular, the model can examine the events associated with one kind of adversity within organizations, the reduction of organizational slack.

Slack is the difference between the resources of the organization and the combination of demands made on it. Thus, it is sensitive to two major factors: (a) money and other resources provided to the organization by the external environment, and (b) the internal consistency of the demands made on the organization by participants. It is commonly believed that organizational slack has been reduced substantially within American colleges and universities over the past few years. The consequences of slack reduction in a garbage can decision process can be shown by establishing possible relations between changes in organizational slack and the key structural variables within the model.

Net energy load. The net energy load is the difference between the energy required within an organization and the effective energy available. It is affected by anything that alters either the amount of energy available to the organization or the amount required to find or generate problem solutions. The energy available to the organization is partly a function of the overall strength of exit opportunities for decision makers. For example, when there is a shortage of faculty, administrators, or students in the market for participants, the net energy load on a university is heavier than it would be when there is no shortage. The energy required to find solutions depends on the flow of possible problem solutions. For example, when the environment of the organization is relatively rich,

solutions are easier to find and the net energy is reduced. Finally, the comparative attractiveness and permeability of the organization to problems affects the energy demands on it. The more attractive, the more demands. The more permeable, the more demands. Universities with slack and with relatively easy access, compared to other alternative arenas for problem carriers, will attract a relatively large number of problems.

Access structure. The access structure in an organization would be expected to be affected by deliberate efforts to derive the advantages of delegation and specialization. Those efforts, in turn, depend on some general characteristics of the organizational situation, task, and personnel. For example, the access structure would be expected to be systematically related to two features of the organization: (a) the degree of technical and value heterogeneity, and (b) the amount of organizational slack. Slack, by providing resource buffers between parts of the organization, is essentially a substitute for technical and value homogeneity. As heterogeneity increases, holding slack constant, the access structure shifts from an unsegmented to a specialized to a hierarchical structure. Similarly, as slack decreases, holding heterogeneity constant, the access structure shifts from an unsegmented to a specialized to a hierarchical structure. The combined picture is shown in Figure 1.

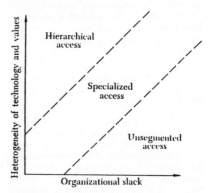

FIGURE 1. HYPOTHESIZED RELATIONSHIP BETWEEN SLACK, HETEROGENEITY, AND THE ACCESS STRUCTURE OF AN ORGANIZATION

Decision structure. Like the access structure, the decision structure is partly a planned system for the organization and partly a result of learning and negotiation within the organization. It could be expected to be systematically related to the technology, to attributes of participants and problems, and to the external conditions under which the organization operates. For example, there are joint effects of two factors: (a) relative administrative power within the system, the extent to which the formal administrators are conceded substantial authority, and (b) the average degree of perceived interrelation among problems. It is assumed that high administrative power or high interrelation of problems will lead to hierarchical decision structure, that moderate power and low interrelation of problems leads to specialized decision structures, and that relatively low administrative power, combined with moderate problem interrelation, leads to unsegmented decision structures. The hypothetical relations are shown in Figure 2.

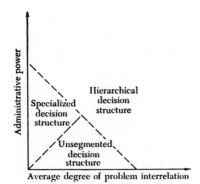

FIGURE 2. HYPOTHESIZED RELATIONSHIP BE-TWEEN ADMINISTRATIVE POWER, INTERRELA-TION OF PROBLEMS, AND THE DECISION STRUC-TURE OF AN ORGANIZATION

Energy distribution. Some of the key factors affecting the energy distribution within an organization are associated with the alternative opportunities decision makers have for investing their time. The extent to which there is an active external demand for attention affects the extent to which decision makers will have energy available for use within the organization. The stronger the relative outside demand on important people in the organization, the less time they will spend within the organization relative to others. Note that the energy distribution refers only to the relation between the energy available from important people and less important people. Thus, the energy distribution variable is a function of the relative strength of the outside demand for different people, as shown in Figure 3.

FIGURE 3. HYPOTHESIZED RELATIONSHIP BE-TWEEN EXIT OPPORTUNITIES AND THE DISTRIBU-TION OF ENERGY WITHIN AN ORGANIZATION

Within a university setting it is not hard to imagine circumstances in which exit opportunities are different for different decision makers. Tenure, for example, strengthens the exit opportunities for older faculty members. Money strengthens the exit opportunities for students and faculty members, though more for the former than the latter. A rapidly changing technology tends to strengthen the exit opportunities for young faculty members.

Against this background four types of colleges and universities are considered: (a) large, rich universities, (b) large, poor universities, (c) small, rich colleges, and (d) small, poor colleges.

Important variations in the organizational variables among these schools can be expected. Much of that variation is likely to be within-class variation. Assumptions about these variables, however, can be used to generate some assumptions about the predominant attributes of the four classes, under conditions of prosperity.

Under such conditions a relatively rich school would be expected to have a light energy load, a relatively poor school a moderate energy load. With respect to access structure, decision structure, and the internal distribution of energy, the appropriate position of each of the four types of schools is marked with a circular symbol on Figures 4, 5, and 6. The result is the pattern of variations indicated below:

and unimportant people. The expected results of these shifts are shown by the positions of the square symbols in Figure 6.

At the same time, adversity affects both access structure and decision structure. Adversity can be expected to bring a reduction in slack and an increase in the average interrelation among problems. The resulting hypothesized shifts in access and decision structures are shown in Figures 4 and 5.

Table 5 shows the effects of adversity on the four types of schools according to the previous assumptions and the garbage can model. By examining the first stage of adversity, some possible reasons for discontent among presidents of large, rich schools can be seen. In relation to other schools they are not seriously disadvantaged. The large, rich

	Load	Access structure	Decision structure	Energy distribution
Large, rich	Light 0	Specialized 2	Unsegmented 0	Less 0
Large, poor	Moderate 1	Hierarchical 1	Hierarchical 1	More 2
Small, rich	Light 0	Unsegmented 0	Unsegmented 0	More 2
Small, poor	Moderate 1	Specialized 2	Specialized 2	Equal 1

With this specification, the garbage can model can be used to predict the differences expected among the several types of school. The results are found in Table 5. They suggest that under conditions of prosperity, overt conflict (problem activity) will be substantially higher in poor schools than in rich ones, and decision time will be substantially longer. Large, rich schools will be characterized by a high degree of problem latency. Most decisions will resolve some problems.

What happens to this group of schools under conditions of adversity—when slack is reduced? According to earlier arguments, slack could be expected to affect each of the organizational variables. It first increases net energy load, as resources become shorter and thus problems require a larger share of available energy to solve, but this effect is later compensated by the reduction in market demand for personnel and in the relative attractiveness of the school as an arena for problems. The market effects also reduce the differences in market demand for important

schools have a moderate level of problem activity, a moderate level of decision by resolution. In relation to their earlier state, however, large, rich schools are certainly deprived. Problem activity and decision time have increased greatly; the proportion of decisions which resolve problems has decreased from 68 percent to 21 percent; administrators are less able to move around from one decision to another. In all these terms, the relative deprivation of the presidents of large, rich schools is much greater, in the early stages of adversity, than that of administrators in other schools.

The large, poor schools are in the worst absolute position under adversity. They have a high level of problem activity, a substantial decision time, a low level of decision maker mobility, and a low proportion of decisions being made by resolution. But along most of these dimensions, the change has been less for them.

The small rich schools experience a large increase in problem activity, an increase in

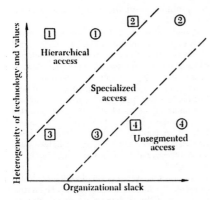

① Large, poor school, good times
② Large, rich school, good times
③ Small, poor school, good times
④ Small, rich school, good times

1 Large, poor school, bad times
2 Large, rich school, bad times
3 Small, poor school, bad times
4 Small, rich school, bad times

FIGURE 4. HYPOTHESIZED LOCATION OF DIF-
FERENT SCHOOLS IN TERMS OF SLACK AND HET-
EROGENEITY

decision time, and a decrease in the proportion of decisions by resolution as adversity
begins. The small, poor schools seem to move
in a direction counter to the trends in the
other three groups. Decision style is little affected by the onset of slack reduction, problem activity, and decision time decline, and
decision-maker mobility increases. Presidents
of such organizations might feel a sense of
success in their efforts to tighten up the organization in response to resource contraction.

The application of the model to this particular situation among American colleges
and universities clearly depends upon a large
number of assumptions. Other assumptions
would lead to other interpretations of the impact of adversity within a garbage can decision process. Nevertheless, the derivations

from the model have some face validity as a
description of some aspects of recent life in
American higher education.

The model also makes some predictions of
future developments. As adversity continues,
the model predicts that all schools, and particularly rich schools, will experience improvement in their position. Among large,
rich schools decision by resolution triples,
problem activity is cut by almost three-
fourths, and decision time is cut more than
one-half. If the model has validity, a series of
articles in the magazines of the next decade
detailing how President X assumed the presidency of large, rich university Y and guided
it to "peace" and "progress" (short decision
time, decisions without problems, low problem activity) can be expected.

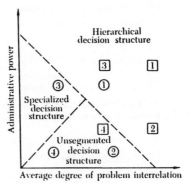

① Large, poor school, good times
② Large, rich school, good times
③ Small, poor school, good times
④ Small, rich school, good times

1 Large, poor school, bad times
2 Large, rich school, bad times
3 Small, poor school, bad times
4 Small, rich school, bad times

FIGURE 5. HYPOTHESIZED LOCATION OF DIF-
FERENT SCHOOLS IN TERMS OF ADMINISTRATIVE
POWER AND PERCEIVED INTERRELATION OF
PROBLEMS

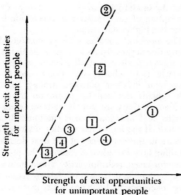

Strength of exit opportunities
for unimportant people

① Large, poor school, good times
② Large, rich school, good times
③ Small, poor school, good times
④ Small, rich school, good times

① Large, poor school, bad times
② Large, rich school, bad times
③ Small, poor school, bad times
④ Small, rich school, bad times

FIGURE 6. HYPOTHESIZED LOCATION OF DIF-
FERENT SCHOOLS IN TERMS OF EXIT OPPORTUNI-
TIES

CONCLUSION

A set of observations made in the study of some university organizations has been translated into a model of decision making in organized anarchies, that is, in situations which do not meet the conditions for more classical models of decision making in some or all of three important ways: preferences are problematic, technology is unclear, or participation is fluid. The garbage can process is one in which problems, solutions, and participants move from one choice opportunity to another in such a way that the nature of the choice, the time it takes, and the problems it solves all depend on a relatively complicated intermeshing of elements. These include the mix of choices available at any one time, the mix of problems that have access to the organization, the mix of solutions looking for problems, and the outside demands on the decision makers.

A major feature of the garbage can process is the partial uncoupling of problems and choices. Although decision making is thought of as a process for solving problems, that is often not what happens. Problems are worked upon in the context of some choice, but choices are made only when the shifting combinations of problems, solutions, and decision makers happen to make action possible. Quite commonly this is after problems have left a given choice arena or before they have discovered it (decisions by flight or oversight).

Four factors were specified which could be expected to have substantial effects on the operation of the garbage can process: the organization's net energy load and energy distribution, its decision structure, and problem access structure. Though the specifications are quite simple their interaction is extremely complex, so that investigation of the probable behavior of a system fully characterized by the garbage can process and previous specifications requires computer simulation. No real system can be fully characterized in this way. Nonetheless, the simulated organization exhibits behaviors which can be observed some of the time in almost all organizations and frequently in some, such as universities. The garbage can model is a first step toward seeing the systematic interrelatedness of organizational phenomena which are familiar, even common, but which have previously been regarded as isolated and pathological. Measured against a conventional normative model of rational choice, the garbage can process does appear pathological, but such standards are not really appropriate. The process occurs precisely when the preconditions of more normal rational models are not met.

It is clear that the garbage can process does not resolve problems well. But it does enable choices to be made and problems resolved, even when the organization is plagued with goal ambiguity and conflict, with poorly understood problems that wander in and out of the system, with a variable environment, and with decision makers who may have other things on their minds.

There is a large class of significant situa-

TABLE 5. EFFECT OF ADVERSITY ON FOUR TYPES OF COLLEGES AND
UNIVERSITIES OPERATING WITHIN A GARBAGE CAN DECISION PROCESS

Type of school/ type of situation	Outcome					
	Organi- zational type	Deci- sion style propor- tion resolu- tion	Problem activity	Problem latency	Deci- sion maker activity	Deci- sion time
Large, rich universities						
Good times	0200	0.68	0	154	100	0
Bad times, early	1110	0.21	210	23	58	34
Bad times, late	0111	0.65	57	60	66	14
Large, poor universities						
Good times	1112	0.38	210	25	66	31
Bad times, early	2112	0.24	248	32	55	38
Bad times, late	1111	0.31	200	30	58	28
Small, rich colleges						
Good times	0002	1.0	0	0	100	0
Bad times, early	1002	0	310	0	90	20
Bad times, late	0001	1.0	0	0	100	0
Small, poor colleges						
Good times	1221	0.54	158	127	15	83
Bad times, early	2211	0.61	101	148	73	52
Bad times, late	1211	0.62	78	151	76	39

tions in which the preconditions of the garbage can process cannot be eliminated. In some, such as pure research, or the family, they should not be eliminated. The great advantage of trying to see garbage can phenomena together as a process is the possibility that that process can be understood, that organizational design and decision making can take account of its existence and that, to some extent, it can be managed.

APPENDIX

Version five of the Fortran program for the garbage can model reads in entry times for choices, solution coefficients, entry times for problems, and two control variables, NA and IO. NA controls various combinations of freedom of movement for decision makers and problems. All results are based on runs in which NA is 1. Comment cards included in the program describe other possibilities. The latter variable, IO, controls output. At the value 1, only summary statistics are printed. At the value 2, full histories of the decision process are printed for each organizational variant.

The following are ten summary statistics:

1. (KT) Problem persistence, the total number of time periods a problem is activated and attached to a choice, summed over all problems.

2. (KU) Problem latency, the total number of time periods a problem is activated, but not attached to a choice, summed over all problems.

3. (KV) Problem velocity, the total number of times any problem shifts from one choice to another.

4. (KW) Problem failures, the total number of problems not solved at the end of the twenty time periods.

5. (KX) Decision maker velocity, the total number of times any decision maker shifts from one choice to another.

6. (KS) Decision maker inactivity, the total number of time periods a decision maker is not attached to a choice, summed over all decision makers.

7. (KY) Choice persistence, the total number of time periods a choice is activated, summed over all choices.

8. (KZ) Choice failures, the total number of choices not made by the end of the twenty time periods.

9. (XR) Energy reserve, the total amount of effective energy available to the system but not used because decision makers are not attached to any choice.

10. (XS) Energy wastage, the total effective energy used on choices in excess of that required to make them at the time they are made.

In its current form the program generates both the problem access structure and the decision structure internally. In order to examine the performance of the model under other structures, modification of the code or its elimination in favor of Read statements to take the structures from cards will be necessary.

Under $IO = 2$, total output will be about ninety pages. Running time is about two minutes under a Watfor compiler.

APPENDIX TABLE: FORTRAN PROGRAM FOR GARBAGE CAN MODEL, VERSION FIVE

```
C       THE GARBAGE CAN MODEL. VERSION 5
C       ***
C       IO IS 1 FOR SUMMARY STATISTICS ONLY
C       IO IS 2 FOR SUMMARY STATISTICS PLUS HISTORIES
C       ***
C       NA IS 1 WHEN PROBS AND DMKRS BOTH MOVE
C       NA IS 2 WHEN DMKRS ONLY MOVE
C       NA IS 3 WHEN PROBS ONLY MOVE
C       NA IS 4 WHEN NEITHER PROBS NOR DMKRS MOVE
C       ***
C       IL IS A FACTOR DETERMINING PROB ENERGY REQ
C       ***
C       VARIABLES
C          ***
C          NUMBERS
C             COUNTERS   UPPER LIMITS       NAME
C                ***
C                I           NCH           CHOICES
C                J           NPR           PROBLEM
C                K           NDM           DECMKRS
C                LT          NTP           TIME
C          ***
C          ARRAYS
C             CODE          DIMEN          NAME
C             ***
C             ICH           NCH            CHOICE ENTRY TIME
C             ICS           NCH            CHOICE STATUS
C             JET           NPR            PROB. ENTRY TIME
C             JF            NPR            PROB. ATT. CHOICE
C             JFF           NPR            WORKING COPY JF
C             JPS           NPR            PROB. STATUS
C             KDC           NDM            DMKR. ATT. CHOICE
C             KDCW          NDM            WORKING COPY KDC
C             XEF           MCH            ENERGY EXPENDED
C             XERC          NCH            CHOICE EN. REQT.
C             XERP          NPR            PROB. EN. REQT.
C             XSC           NTP            SOLUTION COEFFICIENT
C          ***
C          2-DIMENSIONAL ARRAYS
C             ***
C             CODE          DIMEN          NAME
C             ***
C             IKA           NCH,NDM        DECISION STRUCTURE
C             JIA           NPR,NCH        ACCESS STRUCTURE
C             XEA           NDM,NTP        ENERGY MATRIX
C          ***
C          ***
C          ***
C       ***
C       SUMMARY STATISTICS FOR EACH VARIANT
C             COL 1: KZ: TOTAL DECISIONS NOT MADE
C             COL 2: KY: TOTAL NUMBER ACTIVE CHOICE PERIODS
C             COL 3: KX: TOTAL NUMBER CHANGES BY DECISION MAKERS
C             COL 4: KW: TOTAL PROBLEMS NOT SOLVED
C             COL 5: KV: TOTAL NUMBER CHANGES BY PROBLEMS
C             COL 6: KU: TOTAL NUMBER LATENT PROBLEM PERIODS
C             COL 7: KT: TOTAL NUMBER ATTACHED PROBLEM PERIODS
C             COL 8: KS: TOTAL NUMBER PERIODS DMKRS RESTING
C             COL 9: XR: TOTAL AMOUNT OF UNUSED ENERGY
```

Continued overleaf

```
C              COL 10:XS: TOTAL AMOUNT OF WASTED ENERGY
C         ***
C         INPUT BLOCK. READ-IN AND INITIALIZATIONS.
          DIMENSION ICH(20),JF(20),XERC(20),XEE(20),XSC(20),JFF(20),XERP(20
         *),JET(20),JPS(20),ICS(20),KDC(20),KDCW(20),JIA(20,20),IKA(20,20),
          CXEA(20,20),KABC(20,20),KBBC(20,20),KCBC(20,20)
1001    FORMAT(5(I3,1X))
1002    FORMAT(10(I3,1X))
1003    FORMAT(25(I1,1X))
1004    FORMAT(10F4.2)
          NTP=20
          NCH=10
          NPR=20
          NDM=10
8       READ(5,1002)(ICH(I),I=1,NCH)
          READ(5,1004)(XSC(LT),LT=1,NTP)
          READ(5,1002)(JET(J),J=1,NPR)
          READ(5,1003) NA,IO
          WRITE(6,1050) NA
1050    FORMAT('1        DEC.MAKER MOVEMENT CONDITION (NA) IS  ',I1/)
          DO 998 IL=1,3
          IB=IL-1
          DO 997 JAB=1,3
          JA=JAB-1
          DO 996 JDB=1,3
          JD=JDB-1
          DO 995 JEB=1,3
          JE=JEB-1
          XR=0.0
          XS=0.0
          KS=0
          DO 10 I=1,NCH
          XERC(I)=1.1
          XEE(I)=0.0
10      ICS(I)=0
          DO 20 K=1,NDM
          KDC(K)=0
20      KDCW(K)=KDC(K)
          DO 40 J=1,NPR
          XERP(J)=IL+1.1
          JF(J)=0
          JFF(J)=0
40      JPS(J)=0
C         SETTING UP THE DECISION MAKERS ACCESS TO CHOICES.
          DO 520 I=1,NCH
          DO 510 J=1,NDM
          IKA(I,J)=1
          IF(JD.EQ.1) GO TO 502
          IF(JD.EQ.2) GO TO 504
          GO TO 510
502     IF(I.GE.J) GO TO 510
          IKA(I,J)=0
          GO TO 510
504     IF(J.EQ.1) GO TO 510
          IKA(I,J)=0
510     CONTINUE
520     CONTINUE
C         SETTING UP THE PROBLEMS ACCESS TO CHOICES.
          DO 560 I=1,NPR
          DO 550 J=1,NCH
```

```
         JIA(I,J)=0
         IF(JA.EQ.1) GO TO 532
         IF(JA.EQ.2) GO TO 534
         JIA(I,J)=1
         GO TO 550
   532   IF ((I-J).GT.(I/2)) GO TO 550
         JIA(I,J)=1
         GO TO 550
   534   IF(I.NE.(2*J))  GO TO 550
         JIA(I,J)=1
         JIA(I-1,J)=1
   550   CONTINUE
   560   CONTINUE
         DO 590 I=1,NDM
         DO 580 J=1,NTP
         XEA(I,J)=0.55
         IF(JF.EQ.1)GO TO 580
         XXA=I
         IF(JE.EQ.0)GO TO 570
         XEA(I,J)=(11.0-XXA)/10.0
         GO TO 580
   570   XEA(I,J)=XXA/10.0
   580   CONTINUE
   590   CONTINUE
C        *** FINISH READ   INITIALIZATION
         DO 994 LT=1,NTP
  1006   FORMAT(2X,6HCHOICE,2X,I3,2X,6HACTIVE )
C        CHOICE ACTIVATION
         DO 101  I=1,NCH
         IF(ICH(I).NE.LT)GO TO 101
         ICS(I)=1
   101   CONTINUE
C        PROB. ACTIVATION
         DO 110 J=1,NPR
         IF(JET(J).NE.LT)GO TO 110
         JPS(J)=1
   110   CONTINUE
C        FIND MOST ATTRACTIVE CHOICE FOR PROBLEM J
         DO 120 J=1,NPR
         IF (JPS(J).NE.1) GO TO 120
         IF(NA.EQ.2)GO TO 125
         IF(NA.EQ.4)GO TO 125
         GO TO 126
   125   IF(JF(J).NE.0)GO TO 127
   126   S=1000000
         DO 121 I=1,NCH
         IF (ICS(I).NE.1) GO TO 121
         IF(JIA(J,I).EQ.0)GO TO 121
         IF(JF(J).EQ.0)GO TO 122
         IF(JF(J).EQ.1)GO TO 122
         IF((XERP(J)+XERC(I)-XEE(I)).GE.S)GO TO 121
         GO TO 123
   122   IF((XERC(I)-XEE(I)).GE.S)GO TO 121
         S=XERC(I)-XEE(I)
         GO TO 124
   123   S=XERP(J)+XERC(I)-XEE(I)
   124   JFF(J)=I
   121   CONTINUE
         GO TO 120
   127   JFF(J)=JF(J)
```

Continued overleaf

```
120     CONTINUE
        DO 130 J=1,NPR
131     JF(J)=JFF(J)
130     JFF(J)=0
        LTT=LT-1
        IF(LT.EQ.1)LTT=1
C       FIND MOST ATTRACTIVE CHOICE FOR DMKR K
        DO 140 K=1,NDM
        IF(NA.EQ.3)GO TO 145
        IF(NA.EQ.4) GO TO 145
        GO TO 146
145     IF(KDC(K).NE.0)GO TO 147
146     S=1000000
        DO 141 I=1,NCH
        IF (ICS(I).NE.1) GO TO 141
        IF(IKA(I,K).EQ.0)GO TO 141
        IF(KDC(K).EQ.0)GO TO 142
        IF(KDC(K).EQ.1)GO TO 142
148     IF((XFRC(I)-XEE(I)-(XEA(K,LTT)*XSC(LTT))).GE.S)GO TO 141
        GO TO 143
142     IF((XERC(I)-XEE(I)).GE.S)GO TO 141
        S=XERC(I)-XEE(I)
        GO TO 144
143     S=XERC(I)-XEE(I)-XEA(K,LTT)*XSC(LTT)
144     KDCW(K)=I
141     CONTINUE
        GO TO 140
147     KDCW(K)=KDC(K)
140     CONTINUF
        DO 150 K=1,NDM
151     KDC(K)=KDCW(K)
        IF(KDC(K).NE.0)GO TO 150
        XR=XR+(XEA(K,LT)*XSC(LT))
        KS=KS+1
150     KDCW(K)=0
C       ESTABLISHING THE ENERGY REQUIRED TO MAKE EACH CHOICE.
        DO 199 I=1,NCH
        IF(ICS(I).EQ.0)GO TO 199
        XERC(I)=0.0
        DO 160 J=1,NPR
        IF (JPS(J).NE.1) GO TO 160
        IF( JF(J).NE.1)GO TO 160
        XERC(I)=XERC(I)+XERP(J)
160     CONTINUE
        DO 170 K=1,NDM
        IF(IKA(I,K).EQ.0)GO TO 170
        IF(KDC(K).NE.1)GO TO 170
        XEE(I)=XEE(I)+XSC(LT)*XEA(K,LT)
170     CONTINUE
199     CONTINUE
C       MAKING DECISIONS
        DO 299 I=1,NCH
        IF (ICS(I).NE.1) GO TO 299
        IF(XERC(I).GT.XEE(I))GO TO 299
        XS=XS+XEE(I)-XERC(I)
        ICS(I)=2
        DO 250 J=1,NPR
        IF(JF(J).NE.1)GO TO 250
        JPS(J)=2
250     CONTINUE
```

```
        IF(NA.EQ.3)GO TO 261
        IF(NA.EQ.4)GO TO 261
        GO TO 299
  261   DO 262 K=1,NDM
        IF(KDC(K).NE.1)GO TO 262
        KDCW(K)=1
  262   CONTINUE
  299   CONTINUE
        DO 200 I=1,NCH
  200   KABC(LT,I)=ICS(I)
        DO 210 K=1,NDM
        KBBC(LT,K)=KDC(K)
        IF(KDCW(K).EQ.0)GO TO 210
        KDC(K)=0
  210   KDCW(K)=0
        DO 220 J=1,NPR
        KCBC(LT,J)=JF(J)
        IF(JPS(J).EQ.0) GO TO 230
        IF(JPS(J).EQ.1) GO TO 220
        KCBC(LT,J)=1000
        GO TO 220
  230   KCBC(LT,J)=-1
  220   CONTINUE
  994   CONTINUE
C       FINISH TIME PERIOD LOOP. BEGIN ACCUMULATION OF 10 SUMMARY STATISTICS.
        KZ=0
        KY=0
        KX=0
        KW=0
        KV=0
        KU=0
        KT=0
        DO 310 I=1,NTP
        DO 320 J=1,NCH
        IF(KABC(I,J).NE.1)GO TO 320
        KY=KY+1
        IF(I.NE.NTP)GO TO 320
        KZ=KZ+1
  320   CONTINUE
  310   CONTINUE
        DO 330 I=2,NTP
        DO 340 J=1,NDM
        IF(KBBC(I,J).EQ.KBBC(I-1,J))GO TO 340
        KX=KX+1
  340   CONTINUE
  330   CONTINUE
        DO 350 I=1,NTP
        DO 360 J=1,NPR
        IF(KCBC(I,J).EQ.0)GO TO 351
        IF(KCBC(I,J).EQ.-1) GO TO 360
        IF(KCBC(I,J).EQ.1000) GO TO 352
        KT=KT+1
        GO TO 360
  351   KU=KU+1
        GO TO 360
  352   IF(I.NE.NTP)GO TO 360
        KW=KW+1
  360   CONTINUE
  350   CONTINUE
        KW=NPR-KW
```

Continued overleaf

```
      DO 370 I=2,NTP
      DO 380 J=1,NPR
      IF(KCBC(I,J).EQ.KCBC(I-1,J))GO TO 380
      KV=KV+1
 380  CONTINUE
 370  CONTINUE
C     BEGIN WRITEOUT OF MATERIALS FOR THIS ORGANIZATIONAL VARIANT.
1000  FORMAT(1H1)
1019  FORMAT(2X,'LOAD=',I1,' PR.ACC.=',I1,' DEC.STR.=',I1,' EN.DIST.=',
     BI1,2X,'STATS 1-10',3X,8I5,1X,2F6.2/)
      WRITE(6,1019)IB,JA,JD,JE,KZ,KY,KX,KW,KV,KU,KT,KS,XR,XS
      IF(IO.EQ.1) GO TO 995
2000  FORMAT(' CHOICE ACTIVATION HISTORY',34X,'DEC.MAKER ACTIVITY HISTOR
     BY'/' 20 TIME PERIODS,10 CHOICES',33X,'20 TIME PERIODS,10 DEC. MAKE
     CRS'/' 0=INACTIVE,1=ACTIVE,2=MADE',33X,'0=INACTIVE,X=WORKING ON CHO
     DICE X'//9X,'  1 2 3 4 5 6 7 8 9 10',30X,'1 2 3 4 5 6 7 8 9 10'/)
      WRITE(6,2000)
2001  FORMAT( 5X,I2,3X,10I2,25X,I2,3X,10I2)
      WRITE(6,2001)(LT,(KABC(LT,J),J=1,NCH),LT,( KBBC(LT,J),J=1,NDM),
     B LT=1,NTP  )
2002  FORMAT(/' PROBLEM HISTORY:ROWS=TIME,COLS=PROBS.. -1=NOT ENTERED..
     BO=UNATTACHED,X=ATT.TO CH.X,**=SOLVED'/10X,
     C'  1   2   3   4   5   6   7   8  9 10 11 12 13 14 15 16 17 18 19 20'/)
      WRITE(6,2002)
2003  FORMAT(20(5X,I2,3X,20(1X,I2)/))
      WRITE(6,2003)(LT,(KCBC(LT,J),J=1,NPR),LT=1,NTP)
      WRITE(6,1000)
 995  CONTINUE
 996  CONTINUE
 997  CONTINUE
 998  CONTINUE
      STOP
      END

*******   DATA AS FOLLOWS  (AFTER GUIDE CARDS)   ***********


        1          2          3          4          5          6          7          8
     5678901234567890123456789012345678901234567890123456789012345678901234567890

      5.006.007.004.009.002.010.003.001
      00.700.300.100.100.300.700.901.00
      00.600.600.600.600.600.600.600.60
       008.007.010.003.003.001.007.009
       005.002.004.002.004.010.006.001


        250
```

Michael D. Cohen is an NSF-SSRC post-doctoral fellow at Stanford University; James G. March is David Jacks Professor of Higher Education, Political Science, and Sociology at Stanford University; and Johan P. Olsen is an assistant professor of Political Science at the University of Bergen.

BIBLIOGRAPHY

Allison, Graham T.
  1969 "Conceptual models and the Cuban missile crises." American Political Science Review, 63: 689–718.

Christensen, Søren
  1971 Institut og laboratorieorganisation på Danmarks tekniske Højskole. Copenhagen: Copenhagen School of Economics.

Cohen, Michael D., and James G. March
  1972 The American College President. New York: McGraw-Hill, Carnegie Commission on the Future of Higher Education.

Coleman, James S.
  1957 Community Conflict. Glencoe: Free Press.

Cyert, Richard M., and James G. March
  1963 Behavioral Theory of the Firm. Englewood Cliffs: Prentice-Hall.

Enderud, Harald
  1971 Rektoratet og den centrale administration på Danmarks tekniske Højskole. Copenhagen: Copenhagen School of Economics.

Lindblom, Charles E.
  1965 The Intelligence of Democracy. New York: Macmillan.

Long, Norton
  1958 "The local community as an ecology of games." American Journal of Sociology, 44: 251–261.

March, James G., and Herbert A. Simon
  1958 Organizations. New York: John Wiley.

Mood, Alexander (ed.)
  1971 More Scholars for the Dollar. New York: McGraw-Hill, Carnegie Commission on the Future of Higher Education.

Olsen, Johan P.
  1970 A Study of Choice in an Academic Organization. Bergen: University of Bergen.
  1971 The Reorganization of Authority in an Academic Organization. Bergen: University of Bergen.

Rommetveit, Kåre
  1971 Framveksten av det medisinske fakultet ved Universitetet i Tromsø. Bergen: University of Bergen.

Schilling, Warner R.
  1968 "The H-bomb decision: how to decide without actually choosing." In W. R. Nelson (ed.), The Politics of Science. London: Oxford University Press.

Thompson, James D.
  1967 Organizations in Action. New York: McGraw-Hill.

Vickers, Geoffrey
  1965 The Art of Judgment. New York: Basic Books.

[8]

Studying Deciding: An Exchange of Views Between Mintzberg and Waters, Pettigrew, and Butler

Preface

This exchange of views on the study of decisions and change in organizations was prompted by the question, 'Does decision get in the way?', which is asked in the opening piece by Henry Mintzberg and James Waters. They distrust the concept of decision itself; so does Richard Butler, but he tries to prevent any throwing out of the baby with the bathwater, arguing that existing theory can cope with this distrust. Andrew Pettigrew prefers to enlarge the scene so that the changing activity around the baby in the bath is not missed.

Sadly, Henry Mintzberg's colleague, Jim Waters, died suddenly before this exchange could be published. It has become a posthumous memorial to him and his work.

David Hickson
Editor-in-Chief

Does Decision Get in the Way?

Henry Mintzberg
Department of
Management,
McGill University,
Montreal, Canada

Jim Waters
Graduate School of
Management,
Boston College,
Chestnut Hill,
Mass., U.S.A.

Organization
Studies
1990, 11/1: 001-016
© 1990 EGOS
0170-8406/90
0011-0001 $1.00

'Decision' is one of the most widely and firmly accepted concepts in the field of organization theory. With the ambiguities that surround so many of the field's other concepts — decentralization, participation, planning, etc. — there tends to be a sense of security about decision. Everyone knows that it exists and what it is. True there may be some overlap with concepts such as 'problem'; debates may have continued over the extent to which organizations really can make choices; and much ambiguity certainly remains about how organizations make decisions. But *that* they make decisions which determine their actions is universally accepted. Even so strident a group of critics of conventional views of decision-making as March and his colleagues nonetheless seem to accept as given the assumption that organizations do make 'choices' and 'decisions' (see, e.g., March and Olsen 1976: 10–13).

For years, we studied the process of strategy formation based on the definition of (realized) strategy as 'a pattern in a stream of decisions' (e.g., Mintzberg 1972, 1978; Mintzberg and Waters 1982). Eventually it occurred to us that we were in fact not studying streams of decisions at all, but of actions, because those are the traces actually left behind in organizations (e.g., stores opened in a supermarket chain, projects started in an architectural firm). Decisions simply proved much more difficult to track down. As Barnard noted many years ago:

'Not the least of the difficulties of appraising the executive functions or the relative merits of executives lies in the fact that there is little direct opportunity to observe the essential operations of decision. It is a perplexing fact that most executive decisions produce no direct evidence of themselves and that knowledge of them can only be derived from the cumulation of indirect evidence. They must largely be inferred from general results in which they are merely one factor, and from symptomatic indications of roundabout character.' (1970:192–193)

If a decision is really a *commitment* to action (see Mintzberg, Raisinghani, and Théorêt 1976), then the trace it leaves behind in an organization can range from a clear statement of intent — as in the recorded minute of a meeting — to nothing.

To proceed with our research, based on the definition we were using, we made the implicit assumption that decisions inevitably preceded actions, that if an organization *did* something, then it must have previously *decided* to do so. As Barnard suggested, it was just a matter of tracking the decision down, but, on reflection, another interpretation is possible: that decisions are difficult to uncover because sometimes they don't exist, in other words, that the relationship between decision and action can be far more tenuous than almost all the literature of organization theory suggests (Weick 1979, being one notable exception). To quote Nicolaides in his rarely cited dissertation on decision-making:

'It is evident on the basis of [my] analysis that an organizational decision is in reality a constellation or a galaxy of numerous individual decisions. Some of these decisions are "registered" in the book of the organizational activities, while others remain hidden in the inner sanctum of the human psyche. When and where a decision begins and ends is not always clear.' (1960:173)

Let us consider some of the ambiguities associated with the concept of decision.

For one thing, action can occur without commitment to act — as when a doctor strikes one's knee. Even the law recognizes such a phenomenon. Section 214 of the Canadian Criminal Code states that 'Murder is first degree when it is planned and deliberate,' otherwise it is second degree. In other words, a person can murder without deciding. In a collective context, Swanson (1971) has described 'commensal heteronomy,' as a 'set of legitimated procedures for collective action' in which problems are informally talked over and talked around 'until a kind of common view emerges [which becomes] the basis for action':

'In some societies, all small in population and localized in residence, the whole people, or the men, or all adults, will gather informally, once a day, to gossip, socialize, and debate . . . There is no agenda, no machinery for making decisions, and no apparatus for the people's acting jointly to carry out a collective task or to authorize some participants to represent or enforce the common view. There is an informal "leader" whose position depends upon the respect his abilities warrant.

He periodically summarizes the drift of the discussion and continues to do so over whatever period of hours, days, or weeks it continues; this until there is no substantial dissent from his report.' (pp. 613–614)

For those who think this is a far cry from the behaviour of formal organizations, consider the comment by an executive of the largest corporation in the world, remarkably similar to Swanson's words above:

'We use an iterative process to make a series of tentative decisions on the way we think the market will go. As we get more data we modify these continuously. It is often difficult to say who decided something and when — or even who originated a decision . . . I frequently don't know when a decision is made in General Motors. I don't remember being in a committee meeting when things came to a vote. Usually someone will simply summarize a developing position. Everyone else either nods or states his particular terms of consensus.' (Quoted in Quinn 1980:134)

But social systems can act even without consensus. The story circulated in Europe several years ago that the top management of another large automobile firm had hired consultants to find out who in their company had 'decided' to introduce a major new model. Perhaps someone really did decide, in a clandestine manner; the consultants would then track him or her down. But conceivably no one did. Perhaps someone merely sketched a new speculative design, someone else picked up on that to see what a mockup would look like, and, like a rolling snowball, these activities developed their own momentum: thousands of 'decisions' and actions later — concerning bumpers and assembly lines and advertising campaigns — a new model appeared. In effect, 'decisions', like strategies, can emerge inadvertently.

To further complicate matters, the environment can sometimes 'decide' too, as we noted in our study of an architectural firm (Mintzberg et al. 1988). It was prepared to do a variety of projects, taking whatever work came along that was up to its standards. As it happens, what came along in disproportionate numbers, for a time, were performing art centres. The firm had received considerable publicity for the first one it did, and so the world of such centres beat a path to its door. In effect, the firm ceded those decisions to its clients, who chose for it by asking it to do this particular kind of work. From the firm's point of view, its actions reflected its performance more than its decisions.

One fundamental problem with decision is the difficulty of identifying commitment in the collective context of organization. Must there always be a clear *point* as well as a clear *place* of commitment? What, in effect, is commitment? Associating it with some specific document may simplify the problem of identification, but sometimes at the price of distortion.

Consider the example of a company that announces the 'decision' to build a new factory. Tracing back, one might find the minute of a meeting in which the decision was 'made', which really means recorded. But perhaps the real commitment preceded that minute by six months, when the president visited the site and made up his mind. Here, then, commitment (i.e., decision) has to be traced back to someone's mind, indeed perhaps even to that person's subconscious, and that can become rather problematic.

Shift this into the more complex organizational setting where the commitment must be collective, and the problem of identifying decision magnifies enormously. Given that an action was taken, and that broad support preceded it, we must find out when and where consensus emerged — for that must be the real 'point' of decision. Unfortunately, it may not be a point at all, but a gradually unfolding and subtle process, as the comment of the General Motors executive suggested earlier, and as Snyder and Paige (1958) noted about the United States decision in 1950 'to resist aggression in Korea'. The stages they identified in their research 'do not reveal and cannot reveal when the individual decision-makers made up their minds. What is revealed is the time when group opinion coalesced and was made official . . .' (p. 369). In essence, commitment — and, by direct implication, decision — is an elusive concept, at the limit no more than some presumed psychological state, individual or collective.

Another associated problem with decision in an organizational context is that it reinforces an undifferentiated, mechanistic image of one or few central decison-makers, thereby diverting attention from the fact that organizational actions do not always correspond directly to leadership intentions. For example, in a study of a film-making agency (Mintzberg and McHugh 1985), the formal decision was made to fund a short documentary film. But the film inadvertently ran long, and so had to be marketed as a feature. The organization 'acted' though the management never 'decided'. There are other instances when a central decision is consciously subverted by others in the organization, so there is decision but no action. To explain this, conventional management theory falls back on the convenience of 'implementation'. The 'organization' (meaning its top management) decided, but failed to implement its choice, but might it not be equally correct — indeed descriptively more illuminating — to say that the 'organization' (meaning the true collectivity) never really did 'decide'?

A focus on decision can also mask the ways in which general commitments are reshaped, elaborated, and defined over time through complex processes within and without organizations. For example, a company may announce a decision to diversity its related businesses, but, over the years, based on the firms available for acquisition (and their prices) and the company's own successes and failures with those it does buy, the result comes to look like conglomerate diversification. In effect, the pattern (the many actions, forming the *realized* strategy) subverted the original commitment (the single decision at the outset), indeed, ironically in this instance, probably at the management's own hand. Thus, preoccupation with *the* decision runs the risk of imputing a direct relationship between the abstraction of mental intention at the individual or small group level and the concreteness of realized action at the organizational level. A great deal of real-world behaviour can get lost in between.

As a result of all this, in our research we were drawn into defining strategy as 'a pattern in a stream of actions,' instead of decisions (Mintzberg and Waters 1985). For us, realized strategy came to mean consistent behaviour, whether or not decisional. (Indeed, and fully in the spirit of our own research, which set out to study behaviour and work back to intention, our actions reflected this before we became aware of what was happening and then 'decided' to change our formal definition!) It made more sense for us to study streams of actions, and then go back and investigate the role of decision, *if any*, in determining these actions.

The implications of this go well beyond our research on strategy, however. The important general conclusion is that the concept of 'decision' may sometimes serve to confuse things. In essence, decision, like so many other concepts in organization theory, can sometimes turn out to be an artificial construct, one that in this case imputes commitment to action. We have seen that, for individuals as well as for organizations, commitment need not precede action, or, perhaps more commonly, the commitment that does precede action can be vague and confusing. This view does for decision what the thrust of our research does for strategy: just as the *pattern* in behaviour (strategy) may or may not have been intended, so too the *single* behaviour may or may not have involved prior commitment (decision).

Of course, it is in one context in particular, the traditional machine-like bureaucracy, that decision is assumed to precede action. Administrators are supposed to decide on all things, and then have those decisions formally authorized at a higher level before others implement them down below. Likewise, in a bureaucratic society, citizens are expected to decide formally and receive approval before acting, whether it be to enlarge a house (get a building permit), to engage in work (get put on the payroll), sometimes even to propagate the species ('Even the decision to bear a child is usually made by the [Chinese work] unit; the married women within the group decide whose turn it is to become pregnant' [Mathews and Mathews 1983:19]). A research community intent on operationalizing its concepts falls into the same trap, forcing itself, however inadvertently, to restrict its study to the context of machine bureaucracy, and likewise ends up bureaucratizing its own procedures, for the sake of 'scientific rigor'.

Not all organizations or all society, not even all research, is fully bureaucratic (yet), and so we must apply our concepts with care. 'Decision' can sometimes get in the way of understanding behaviour.

References

Barnard, C. I.
1938 *The functions of the executive*. Cambridge, Mass.: Harvard University Press.

March, J. G., and J. P. Olsen
1976 *Ambiguity and choice in organizations*. Bergen, Norway: Universitetsforlaget.

Mathews, J., and L. Mathews
1983 *One billion: a China chronicle*. New York: Ballantine Books.

Mintzberg, H.
1972 'Research on strategy making'. *Proceedings of the 32nd annual meeting of the Academy of Management*. Minneapolis.

Mintzberg, H.
1978 'Patterns in strategy formation'. *Management Science* 24: 934–948.

Mintzberg, H., and A. McHugh
1985 'Strategy formation in an adhocracy'. *Administrative Science Quarterly* 30: 180–197.

Mintzberg, H., S. Otis, J. Shamsie, and J. A. Waters
1988 'Strategy of design: a study of architects in co-partnership' in *Strategy management frontiers*. J. Grant (ed.). Greenwich, CT.: JAI Press.

Mintzberg, H., D. Raisinghani, and A. Théorêt
1976 'The structure of "Unstructured" decision process'. *Administrative Science Quarterly* 25: 465–499.

Mintzberg, H., and J. A. Waters
1982 'Tracking strategy in an entrepreneurial firm'. *Academy of Management Journal* 25: 465–499.

Mintzberg, H., and J. A. Waters
1985 'Of strategies, deliberate and emergent'. *Strategic Management Journal* 6: 257–272.

Quinn, J. P.
1980 *Strategies for change: logical incrementalism.* Homewood, Ill.: Irwin.

Snyder, R. C., and G. D. Paige
1958 'The United States decision to resist aggression in Korea: the application of an analytical scheme'. *Administrative Science Quarterly* 3: 341–378.

Swanson, G. E.
1971 'An organizational analysis of collectivities'. *American Sociological Review* 36: 607–624.

Weick, K. E.
1979 *The social psychology of organizing*, 2nd ed. Reading, Mass.: Addison-Wesley.

Studying Strategic Choice and Strategic Change.
A Comment on Mintzberg and Waters: 'Does Decision Get in the Way?'

Andrew M. Pettigrew
Centre for Corporate Strategy and Change, University of Warwick, Coventry, U.K.

All academics are wordsmiths. Social Science academics are incorrigible wordsmiths. So does it matter beyond mere taste whether one describes choice behaviour in an organizational context as problem-solving, decision-making, or strategy formulation? No doubt the sociologist of knowledge would tell us that words rise and fall in potency depending on features of socio-political context. Thus in expressing his/her ideas the academic is not making free scholarly choices but is reflecting deeper contextual forces, some relating to broad societal consideration, and others to stages in the development of particular disciplines or fields of study.

In adding to the points raised by Mintzberg and Waters, and Butler, I will argue that words do matter. Beneath the words lie ontological and epistemological assumptions which open up and close down fields of inquiry. I agree with Richard Butler that a focus around organizational decision-making has been theoretically and empirically additive. I would also argue that recent advances in the field of business strategy and policy studies have benefited greatly from twenty years or more of scholarly activity on decision-making. But it is also clear that decision-making can close down wide areas of concern for organizational scholars and my current preference is to approach the study of strategy with a vocabulary that leans rather more heavily on change than choice.

I was first made aware of the strengths and limitations of the vocabularies of strategic choice and change at an international gathering of researchers interested in how strategic decisions are made and implemented. The proceedings of this 1983 conference were eventually published by Pennings (1985). Penning's introductory and concluding chapters to that volume still contain some of the most perceptive analytical comments about the literatures on strategic decision-making and change. Part of the difficulty of studying strategic decisions is the very nature of what is being studied. Thus Pennings accurately portrays such decisions as significant, unstructured, complex, collective and consequential. Strategic decisions can also be portrayed as a process, a structure, or an outcome. Furthermore, they can be analysed across a variety of levels of analysis, using concepts from a range of disciplines, and be discussed in a more or less prescriptive or descriptive mode. No wonder there is also multiplicity in the research strategies available to study strategic decisions. No surprise indeed that Mintzberg and Waters, and Butler should come to different conclusions about the analytical power of mobilizing empirical inquiry around 'decision making'.

An interesting re-labelling exercise took place as Pennings' conference moved from formulation to implementation. The focus in the pre-conference documentation moved from 'strategic decision-making in complex organizations' to a 1985 book of proceedings entitled *Organizational Strategy and Change*. Now the change of label could have been due to marketing consideration by the publishers, but an equally plausible explanation could be a noticeable move during the conference discussions towards change and away from choice as the prime mobilizing concept for the proceedings.

What are some of the limitations of 'decision' in organizational analysis and do they extend beyond the points made by Mintzberg and Waters?

Neither Mintzberg and Waters, nor Butler dwell on the levels of analysis problem, but this can be a critical analytical limitation for decision-making studies. Is the unit of analysis the decision episode? If the unit of analysis is the discrete decision event abstracted from the series of decisions and other actions of which it is a part, this can be a severe analytical and empirical limitation. Hardy (1985) in her work on the organizational closure of factories and hospitals was very clear to build antecedent conditions into her analysis. Thus she did not take the closure decision to mean the point when the management finally made the closure decision and announced it, but when initial moves were made to restrict investment and allow the factory to die on the vine. This decision not to invest preceded the final decision and announcement by around five years.

Equally well, a concern with the decision episode may also lead to a preoccupation with the front-end decision to-go-ahead stage and the consequent neglect of key implementation processes. Research on processes of choice and change in the NHS by Pettigrew, McKee and Ferlie (1988) reveals the clear gap that frequently exists between statements of strategic intent and operational implementation. A focus on front-end choice processes to the neglect of on-going choice and change processes would present a rather partial view of organizational life in the NHS. If the analytical choice is between the decision episode or event as the unit of analysis and decision-making as a continuous process in context, the latter must be the preferred option.

So the language of decision-making can be more powerful when decision-making is understood as a continuous process in context. Decision-making is also more attractive as a construct when it can include the front stage of visible decisions and the back stage of non-decision-making, Bachrach and Baratz (1962). Difficult as non-decision-making is to study, ideas such as the mobilization of bias do push the analyst of decision-making to features of the content and context of decisions which can crucially shape decision process.

Interestingly, although the Bradford studies of strategic decision-making (Hickson et al. 1986) can be criticized for treating the decision episode as the unit of analysis and for downplaying the significance of non-decision-making, the Bradford work more than most decision research does try to get to grips with how variability in the content and context of decisions shapes decision process. Hickson et al. (1986) prefer to call decision content, 'decision problem or decision topic,' but whatever the language, the message is clear. There are extensive differences in decision process, and why?; because 'the problem raised, and the interests implicated, by one decision are not the same as those encountered by the previous decision' (1986:240). 'To know the process, first know the complexity of the problems and the politicality of the interests' (1986:241).

What is the role and significance of context in shaping decision process? Does the nature of the decision problem and interests shape the process more than the organization context through which the process proceeds? Here again, Hickson et al. are clear 'it is the complexity and politicality of what is under decision which matters rather than the organization' (1986:247). Now this is an important empirical finding, and one entirely consistent with a preoccupation with the decision episode as the unit of analysis. Would the Bradford studies have produced this finding if they had taken a more dynamic view of decision-making (as a continuous process and not an episode) and placed the decision process in a context which includes not only the inner context, but also the outer context of the organization (Pettigrew 1985a, 1987)?

Penning's view in 1985 was that the more dynamic and contextual decision-making is seen to be, the less useful becomes the mobilizing construct of strategic decision-making. 'In fact, the Starbuck, Normann and others view of organisations . . . is so encompassing that they prefer to speak about strategic change and strategic development rather than specific socially and temporally bounded actions. They appear to hint at the futility of efforts to artificially lift a specific decision, however defined, out of its context because of the ubiquitous continuity of organizational behaviour', Pennings (1985:475).

This line of argument takes us back to some of the tensions evident in the

Mintzberg and Waters, and Butler exchange. Decision is the more exclusive and limiting concept. While decision can get in the way of understanding behaviour, it is also evident that scholars of decision-making have been the most active in developing alternative process theories of action and behaviour. I refer here to the well known and much used boundedly rational, incremental, political and garbage-can theories of choice. When the focus of explanation moves from a particular choice process to wider concerns with the strategy or strategic development of the organization, then the more inclusive vocabulary of continuity and change rapidly supersedes the language of the language of choice and strategic decision-making.

As I have argued in detail elsewhere (Pettigrew 1985b, 1989), research on strategic change should be context and process sensitive. Until recently, the change literature was blighted by the same ahistorical, aprocessual, and acontextual limitations evident from work on strategic decision-making. Thus there has been a tendency to treat the change episode as the unit of analysis and thus fall into the same methodological trap regarding the decision event or episode as the unit of analysis. Where the change project is treated as the unit of analysis, the focus is on a single event or a set of discrete episodes somehow separate from the immediate and more distant antecedents that give these events form, meaning, and substance. Such episodic views of change not only treat innovations as if they had a clear beginning and a clear end but also, where they limit themselves to snap-shot time-series data, fail to provide data on the mechanisms and processes through which changes are created. Studies of transformation are, therefore, often preoccupied with the intricacies of narrow changes rather than the holistic and dynamic analysis of changing.

The suggestion made here is that one way to respond to the above weaknesses in the literature on change is to encourage a form of research which is contextualist and processual in character (Pettigrew 1985b, 1989). A contextualist analysis of a process such as change draws on phenomena at vertical and horizontal levels of analysis and the inter-connections between those levels through time. The vertical level refers to the interdependencies between higher or lower levels of analysis upon phenomena to be explained at some further level; for example, the impact of a changing socioeconomic context on features of intraorganizational context and interest-group behaviour. The horizontal level refers to the sequential interconnectedness among phenomena in historical, present, and future time. An approach that offers both multilevel or vertical analysis and processual, or horizontal, analysis is said to be contextualist in character.

In summary, the key points to emphasize in analysing change in a contextualist mode are:

(i) The importance of interconnected levels of analysis
- target changes should be studied in the context of changes at other levels of analysis
- the search is for patterns of reciprocal connectivity between levels

- a source of change is the asymmetries between levels of context
- processes at different levels have their own momentum, rates, pace and trajectory
- some levels of context may impact more visibly and rapidly than others and thus, in the short term, sources of change may appear unidirectional rather than multidirectional.

(ii)   The interconnectedness of the past, present and future
- antecedent conditions shape the present and the emerging future. History is not an event in the past but is alive in the present
- history is about events and structures, acts and underlying logics
- there are no predetermined timetables; trajectories of change are probabilistic and uncertain because of changing contexts

(iii)   The importance of context and action
- it is not a question of nature *or* nurture, or context or action, but context *and* action
- context is not just a stimulus environment but a nested arrangement of structures and processes where the subjective interpretation of actors perceiving, comprehending, learning, and remembering helps shape process.

(iv)   The nature of causation about change
- causation is neither linear nor singular. Changes have multiple causes and are to be explained more by loops than lines. 'The shifting interconnectedness of fused strands' as Mancuso and Ceely (1980) put it.
- the directions of change follow multiple paths; there is no necessary path to development, the trajectory could involve growth, decline, decay, death or regeneration.

Thus contextualism offers an analytical mode to study change that is not tied to a particular theory of change. It provides an approach capable of drawing on concepts from a variety of disciplines and several levels of analysis. Featherman and Lerner (1985) conclude their review of what they call developmental contextualism by drawing attention to its intellectual pluralism. 'Different modes of analysis and causal explanation do not need reduction or integration into one over-arching theoretical paradigm: evidence from distinct paradigmatic approaches can accrue or co-exist to account for a complex phenomena' such as change. Featherman and Lerner (1985:672). Furthermore, contextualism offers a meta level approach capable of exploring several content areas of change in multifareous contexts through time. Thus reality can be caught in flight while, at the same time, there is a commitment to embeddedness as a principle of analysis.

References

Bachrach, P., and M. S. Baratz
1962   'The two faces of power'. *American Political Science Review* 56: 947–952.

Featherman, D. L., and R. M. Lerner
1985   'Ontogenesis and Sociogenesis: problematics for theory and research about development and socialisation across the lifespan'. *American Sociological Review* 50/5: 659–676.

Hardy, C.
1985 *The management of organizational closure*. Aldershot: Gower.

Hickson, D. J., R. J. Butler, D. Cray, G. R. Mallory, and D. C. Wilson
1986 *Top decisions: strategic decision making in organizations*. Oxford: Basil Blackwell.

Mancuso, J. C., and S. G. Ceely
1980 'The self as memory processing'. *Cognitive Therapy and Research* 4/1: 1–25.

Pennings, J. M.
1985 *Organizational strategy and change*. San Francisco: Jossey Bass.

Pettigrew, A. M.
1985a *The awakening giant: continuity and change in ICI*. Oxford: Basil Blackwell.

Pettigrew, A. M.
1985b 'Contextualist research: a natural way to link theory and practice' in *Doing research that is useful in theory and practice*. E. E. Lawler (ed.), 222–249. San Francisco: Jossey Bass.

Pettigrew, A. M.
1987 'Context and action in the transformation of the firm'. *Journal of Management Studies* 24/6: 649–670.

Pettigrew, A. M.
1989 'Longitudinal field research on change: theory and practice' in *New frontiers in management*, R. M. Mansfield (ed.), 21–49. London: Routledge.

Pettigrew, A. M., L. McKee, and E. Ferlic
1988 'Understanding change in the NHS'. *Public Administration* 66 (Autumn): 297–317.

Decision-making Research: Its Uses and Misuses.
A Comment on Mintzberg and Waters: 'Does Decision Get in the Way?'

Richard Butler
Management
Centre, University
of Bradford,
Bradford U.K.

There is no problem in agreeing with the final sentence of Mintzberg and Water's short 'think piece,' namely that ' "decision" can sometimes get in the way of understanding behavior' if this is taken to mean that over-concentration upon one concept in social theory can produce a distortion in the kind of understanding that is arrived at, but then, this problem applies to any concept used in social theory; organization, group, role, strategy and the like are all concepts which we find useful, but all are capable of misuse.

It is now half a century since Barnard (1938) put decision-making at the core of organization theory and the study of managerial work. At that time, there was a good reason for this since the predominant model of industrial and commercial organization was a mechanistic–bureaucratic model against which Barnard's insights represented a break from the principles of Scientific Management. Decision-making, with the attendant processes of communication and cooperation, gave a model of executive work which involved discretion, choice, delegation and the development of trust. Through these ideas theory was able to progress, especially through the work of Simon (1947), and Cyert and March (1963) who, in different ways, developed the image of an organization as a kind of satisficing coalition. Underlying this image was a model of man as intendedly rational but the extent to which that rationality could be achieved was limited by the complexity of the actual situation of decision-makers.

Later works by authors such as Allison (1971) and Pettigrew (1973) revived a more Machiavellian image of organizational decision-making by deliberately introducing an overt political dimension, an image that matched a wider societal interest in the processes of power. Mintzberg, Raisinghani and Théorêt (1976) were also able to make a distinct contribution to organizational decision-making research by pointing out that the way in which decisions are made in organizations (i.e., the decision processes) varies between decisions, but that it is possible to draw up patterns of these variations, showing that some decisions can, for instance, be made very smoothly while others experience considerable interruptions and disruptions. Hickson, Butler, Cray, Mallory and Wilson (1986) in the Bradford studies also explored this theme empirically over a sample of 150 decisions. An addition to theory from the Bradford research is that it provided an explanatory framework for the three predominant patterns they observed using, in particular, a set of variables capturing the dual notions of the complexity and the politicality of the decision issue or topic under consideration as major explanatory dimensions. Up to this time explanation had tended to be subordinated to description.

In this way it is possible to trace a history of decision-making research, as applicable to the field of organizations, which demonstrates a steady step by step accretion of theory. By any account, this is not a bad record, which demonstrates well the way in which programmatic research can build up our understanding of a concept and of its place in the wider field of organization theory. If Mintzberg and Waters now suggest a discarding, or at least a revision of the framework underlying this research, we can only assume that dissatisfaction with the usefulness of existing theories has grown to the point where we can no longer make accommodations in this programmatic way. If they are on the threshold of a new conceptual framework this would indeed be significant for an author who has already greatly contributed to the area; we need to sit up and take note.

Before inventing a new framework and concepts (and the field of organization and management is not short of these) perhaps we should see whether the problems raised by the authors can be accommodated within existing theory. Although I cannot guarantee to have captured every aspect of their argument, I found it useful to develop a series of maxims which attempt to capture the gist of their argument. Six such maxims, given below, seem to give adequate coverage to their ideas.

1. The connection between decision and action is problematic. If we accept that a decision is an intention to act, the extent to which action follows becomes, as Mintzberg and Waters suggest, a matter of implementation since the problem they raise is that some intentions get translated more perfectly into action than others. In other words, degree of implementation becomes a variable of decision-making, an important one that remains to be investigated in more detail. An interesting question here, and one of potentially great practical significance, is why some decisions achieve a greater degree of implementation than others. Two types of low decision implementation could be posited. The first is that the original intention was only weakly implemented; quoting Mintzberg and

Water's example, perhaps the new store that opened was smaller than intended, or that no store was opened after all. The second type of weak implementation would be when the implementation was of a completely different substance than the original intention; taking the new store example, this might mean that no store was opened but that the land was sold at a great profit for development as a leisure park. In short, there can be unintended outcomes from a decision, either beneficial or not. This is not a new idea since the notion of the unintended consequences of action have been well established in sociology at least since Merton (1968).

2. *In an organization, the locus of decision-making can be diffuse.*   Thompson (1967) points out that some decisions in an organization can be attributed to one person, an attribution that is more likely to hold under the condition of low or modest complexity. It is central to the research of Cyert and March (1963), March and Olsen (1976), Thompson (1967), Hickson et al. (1986), and others, that complexity, uncertainty or ambiguity (whichever term one wishes to use) concerning ends/means relations will tend to increase the diffuseness of decision-making as more specialists and interest units get involved as an organization attempts to resolve uncertainty. Concurrently, a large number of specialists also tends to increase the uncertainty over outcome preferences because there are more interests with a stake in the decision, and hence the chances of political behaviour increases. The precise terminology varies between the different authors but the direction of the argument does not. Under these conditions, the locus of the decision cannot be tied down to one point in the organization since it traces out a trajectory (Hage 1981) as the attention given by different interests shifts both horizontally and vertically in the organization.

It is by providing a mapping technique helping us to describe the nature of this trajectory as a decision goes through different phases that Mintzberg, Raisinghai and Théorêt (1976) made their particular contribution to organizational decision-making theory. The Bradford studies also produced decision profiles by subjecting the scores of their 150 decisions on a set of descriptive variables to cluster analysis; three dominant profiles emerged, the sporadic, the fluid and the constricted. The sporadic decision type comes nearest to describing the kind of process that Mintzberg and Waters are concerned with when they raise the problem of not being able to identify a single decision-making locus; a sporadic decision involves many interests, it tends to move both horizontally and vertically in the organization and exhibits stops and starts. Where is such a decision made? Not in any one place, but it is made, nevertheless, through a diffuse and complex organizational process.

Also related to this question is the distinction between ratification and the use of real power in the decision-making process. Sporadic decisions involve the highest levels in the organization, but the decision is not only made there. In some cases it is possible to see ratification more as a symbolic process, and indeed an interesting variable to investigate would be the extent to which ratification is symbolic and separated from the executive power. A constitutional monarchy is an example of almost complete separation between executive power and symbolic ratification, but one can sometimes see a similar symbolic role in some large complex organizations.

3. Action without a decision is possible. This maxim is the converse of number one above. Yes, quite true and in biological organisms this is known as reflex action. In social organization there is already a vocabulary to describe this, perhaps best known by March and Simon's (1958) notion of programmed decisions. Again, the question is containable within existing theory.

4. Action in an organization can occur without consensus. The coalition model of organization states quite clearly through the notion of quasi-resolution of conflict (see Cyert and March) that only sufficient consensus is needed for decisions to proceed. This point was further elaborated by Thompson through the notion domain consensus, a concept which never implied that everybody had to agree before anything could happen, but just that sufficient consensus had to be achieved. What is meant by 'sufficient' remains undefined; there is room for further research here but at present there is no reason to suppose that this question cannot be contained within the existing framework.

5. Exogenous events can trigger decisions. Mintzberg and Waters describe the case of client demand for designing performing arts centres pushing an architectural firm towards specializing in this kind of work. Sometimes decisions can be reactive, but in this particular example a decision still had to be made. From the description given, this would sound like what the Bradford group called a fluid decision: there were a number of new product or service decisions in their study that came into that category. Of course, the clients or customers get listened to in this type of decision but the essential point from a decision theory angle is how those preferences get taken into account in the decision-making process; it tends not to happen through direct involvement but through information gleaned from the environment. If, indeed, this was a fluid decision, it would tend to happen fairly quickly and be made upon the basis of summary, formalized information and to be decentralized. What we need to emphasize is that the nature of decision-making processes can vary according to the type of issue or topic under consideration.

6. Decisions are made within a context and help to influence the context for future decisions. Context is also set by a set of factors exogenous to a particular decision. The first part of this statement can be put into systems language if we say: the output from decision 1 forms part of the input for decision 2. This is an important point and one that needs further attention. The developing theory of institutionalization (Meyer and Scott 1983) is of some help here. Institutionalization theory attempts to explain the setting of the 'Rules of the game' under which decision-making takes place, how those rules get reinforced by successive decisions, and, more precariously, how a long-term performance gap between expected and actual performance might begin to force a change in these rules. Decision-making theory is just beginning to get to grips with this aspect but, again, to say that the existing theory is inadequate is not sufficient cause for abandoning the underlying framework; rather it should provide an impetus for further research until that framework has been demonstrated as inadequate.

Elaboration of the above points has been used to emphasize that the problems with regard to decision-making theory raised by Mintzberg and Waters can be attended to within the framework of theory, what I have in general terms called the satisficing coalitional model of organizational decision-making, that has evolved over the past 50 years or so. There is scope for development, but no overwhelming evidence of a need to invent a completely new vocabulary, if indeed this was what Mintzberg and Waters had in mind.

I should emphasize the doubt as to what they do have in mind, since we learn towards the end of their piece that it is not really decision-making that they wish to study, but strategy. Now the problem here might be that Mintzberg has allowed himself to be confounded by his own previous definition of strategy which he describes as 'a pattern in a stream of decisions'. This has never struck me as a particularly satisfactory view of strategy since, by definition, strategy must surely involve a degree of intention to act, a kind of plan which is to be put into effect. The word strategy belongs, after all, to a language borrowed from the study of military campaigns translated into the business arena. A military commander who, when asked to describe his strategy, had to say 'I can only tell you after the battle' could not really be said to have a strategy. Certainly, one can attempt to retrospectively reconstruct a strategy by looking at the kinds of decisions made and the actions taken by a general over time. If one did this, decision processes cease to be dependent variables and now become independent variables, that is, one might use a description of decision processes to attempt to work out whether there was a plan, or an intention, worked out beforehand; process would become an explanation of strategy.

In conclusion, I must say to Mintzberg and Waters that if they wish to go and study strategy, then go and study strategy; do not be constrained by feeling that they have to define all aspects of strategy in terms of decision-making processes. There are many factors that go to make up the strategy of an organization. Patterns in decision processes and of actions may be part of that explanation but to rely entirely on this would, indeed, be to allow decision to get in the way of understanding behaviour.

References

Allison, G. T.
1971   *The essence of decision: explaining the Cuban missile crisis*. Boston: Little-Brown.

Barnard, Chester I.
1938   *The functions of the executive*. Cambridge, Mass: Harvard University Press.

Cyert, R., and J. G. March
1963 *The behavioral theory of the firm.*
      Englewood-Cliffs, N.J.: Prentice-
      Hall.

Hage, J.
1981 *Theories of organizations: form, pro-
      cess and transformation.* New York:
      Wiley.

Hickson, D. R., R. J. Butler, D. Cray, G.
R. Mallory, and D. C. Wilson
1986 *Top decisions: strategic decision
      making in organizations.* San Fran-
      cisco: Jossey Bass. Also Oxford:
      Basil Blackwell.

March, James G., and Johan P. Olsen
1976 *Ambiguity and choice in organiza-
      tions.* Bergen: Universitetsforlaget.

March, James G., and Herbert A. Simon
1958 *Organizations.* New York: Wiley.

Merton, Robert K.
1968 *Social theory and social structure.*
      New York: Free Press.

Meyer, John W., and W. Richard Scott
1983 *Organizational environments: ritual
      and rationality.* Beverly Hills: Sage.

Mintzberg, H., D. Raisinghani, and A.
Théorêt
1976 'The structure of "unstructured" de-
      cision processes'. *Administrative Sci-
      ence Quarterly* 21/2 (June): 246–275.

Pettigrew, A.
1973 *The politics of organizational deci-
      sion making.* London: Tavistock.

Simon, H. A.
1947 *Administrative behaviour.* New
      York: Free Press.

Thompson, James D.
1967 *Organizations in actions.* New York:
      McGraw-Hill.

Part II
The Decision

[9]

TWO FACES OF POWER[1]

PETER BACHRACH AND MORTON S. BARATZ

Bryn Mawr College

The concept of power remains elusive despite the recent and prolific outpourings of case studies on community power. Its elusiveness is dramatically demonstrated by the regularity of disagreement as to the locus of community power between the sociologists and the political scientists. Sociologically oriented researchers have consistently found that power is highly centralized, while scholars trained in political science have just as regularly concluded that in "their" communities power is widely diffused.[2] Presumably, this explains why the latter group styles itself "pluralist," its counterpart "elitist."

There seems no room for doubt that the sharply divergent findings of the two groups are the product, not of sheer coincidence, but of fundamental differences in both their underlying assumptions and research methodology. The political scientists have contended that these differences in findings can be explained by the faulty approach and presuppositions of the sociologists. We contend in this paper that the pluralists themselves have not grasped the whole truth of the matter; that while their criticisms of the elitists are sound, they, like the elitists, utilize an approach and assumptions

which predetermine their conclusions. Our argument is cast within the frame of our central thesis: that there are two faces of power, neither of which the sociologists see and only one of which the political scientists see.

I

Against the elitist approach to power several criticisms may be, and have been levelled.[3] One has to do with its basic premise that in every human institution there is an ordered system of power, a "power structure" which is an integral part and the mirror image of the organization's stratification. This postulate the pluralists emphatically—and, to our mind, correctly—reject, on the ground that

nothing categorical can be assumed about power in any community. . . . If anything, there seems to be an unspoken notion among pluralist researchers that at bottom *nobody* dominates in a town, so that their first question is not likely to be, "Who runs this community?," but rather, "Does anyone at all run this community?" The first query is somewhat like, "Have you stopped beating your wife?," in that virtually any response short of total unwillingness to answer will supply the researchers with a "power elite" along the lines presupposed by the stratification theory.[4]

Equally objectionable to the pluralists—and to us—is the sociologists' hypothesis that the power structure tends to be stable over time.

Pluralists hold that power may be tied to issues, and issues can be fleeting or persistent, provoking coalitions among interested groups and citizens, ranging in their duration from momentary to semi-permanent. . . . To presume that the set of coalitions which exists in the community at any given time is a timelessly stable aspect of social structure is to introduce systematic inaccuracies into one's description of social reality.[5]

A third criticism of the elitist model is that it wrongly equates reputed with actual power:

If a man's major life work is banking, the pluralist presumes he will spend his time at the bank, and not in manipulating community decisions. This presumption holds until the banker's activities and participations indicate otherwise. . . . If we

[1] This paper is an outgrowth of a seminar in Problems of Power in Contemporary Society, conducted jointly by the authors for graduate students and undergraduate majors in political science and economics.

[2] Compare, for example, the sociological studies of Floyd Hunter, *Community Power Structure* (Chapel Hill, 1953); Roland Pellegrini and Charles H. Coates, "Absentee-Owned Corporations and Community Power Structure," *American Journal of Sociology*, Vol. 61 (March 1956), pp. 413–19; and Robert O. Schulze, "Economic Dominants and Community Power Structure," *American Sociological Review*, Vol. 23 (February 1958), pp. 3–9; with political science studies of Wallace S. Sayre and Herbert Kaufman, *Governing New York City* (New York, 1960); Robert A. Dahl, *Who Governs?* (New Haven, 1961); and Norton E. Long and George Belknap, "A Research Program on Leadership and Decision-Making in Metropolitan Areas" (New York, Governmental Affairs Institute, 1956). See also Nelson W. Polsby, "How to Study Community Power: The Pluralist Alternative," *Journal of Politics*, Vol. 22 (August, 1960), pp. 474–84.

[3] See especially N. W. Polsby, *op. cit.*, p. 475f.

[4] *Ibid.*, pp. 476.

[5] *Ibid.*, pp. 478–79.

presume that the banker is "really" engaged in running the community, there is practically no way of disconfirming this notion, even if it is totally erroneous. On the other hand, it is easy to spot the banker who really *does* run community affairs when we presume he does not, because his activities will make this fact apparent.[6]

This is not an exhaustive bill of particulars; there are flaws other than these in the sociological model and methodology[7]—including some which the pluralists themselves have not noticed. But to go into this would not materially serve our current purposes. Suffice it simply to observe that whatever the merits of their own approach to power, the pluralists have effectively exposed the main weaknesses of the elitist model.

As the foregoing quotations make clear, the pluralists concentrate their attention, not upon the sources of power, but its exercise. Power to them means "participation in decision-making"[8] and can be analyzed only after "careful examination of a series of concrete decisions."[9] As a result, the pluralist researcher is uninterested in the reputedly powerful. His concerns instead are to (a) select for study a number of "key" as opposed to "routine" political decisions, (b) identify the people who took an active part in the decision-making process, (c) obtain a full account of their actual behavior while the policy conflict was being resolved, and (d) determine and analyze the specific outcome of the conflict.

The advantages of this approach, relative to the elitist alternative, need no further exposition. The same may not be said, however, about its defects—two of which seem to us to be of fundamental importance. One is that the model takes no account of the fact that power may be, and often is, exercised by confining the scope of decision-making to relatively "safe" issues. The other is that the model provides no *objective* criteria for distinguishing between "important" and "unimportant" issues arising in the political arena.

[6] *Ibid.*, pp. 480–81.
[7] See especially Robert A. Dahl, "A Critique of the Ruling-Elite Model," this REVIEW, Vol. 52 (June 1958), pp. 463–69; and Lawrence J. R. Herson, "In the Footsteps of Community Power," this REVIEW, Vol. 55 (December 1961), pp. 817–31.
[8] This definition originated with Harold D. Lasswell and Abraham Kaplan, *Power and Society* (New Haven, 1950), p. 75.
[9] Robert A. Dahl, "A Critique of the Ruling-Elite Model," *loc. cit.*, p. 466.

II

There is no gainsaying that an analysis grounded entirely upon what is specific and visible to the outside observer is more "scientific" than one based upon pure speculation. To put it another way,

If we can get our social life stated in terms of activity, and of nothing else, we have not indeed succeeded in measuring it, but we have at least reached a foundation upon which a coherent system of measurements can be built up. . . . We shall cease to be blocked by the intervention of unmeasurable elements, which claim to be themselves the real causes of all that is happening, and which by their spook-like arbitrariness make impossible any progress toward dependable knowledge.[10]

The question is, however, how can one be certain in any given situation that the "unmeasurable elements" are inconsequential, are not of decisive importance? Cast in slightly different terms, can a sound concept of power be predicated on the assumption that power is totally embodied and fully reflected in "concrete decisions" or in activity bearing directly upon their making?

We think not. Of course power is exercised when A participates in the making of decisions that affect B. But power is also exercised when A devotes his energies to creating or reinforcing social and political values and institutional practices that limit the scope of the political process to public consideration of only those issues which are comparatively innocuous to A. To the extent that A succeeds in doing this, B is prevented, for all practical purposes, from bringing to the fore any issues that might in their resolution be seriously detrimental to A's set of preferences.[11]

[10] Arthur Bentley, *The Process of Government* (Chicago, 1908), p. 202, quoted in Polsby, *op. cit.*, p. 481n.
[11] As is perhaps self-evident, there are similarities in both faces of power. In each, A participates in decisions and thereby adversely affects B. But there is an important difference between the two: in the one case, A openly participates; in the other, he participates only in the sense that he works to sustain those values and rules of procedure that help him keep certain issues out of the public domain. True enough, participation of the second kind may at times be overt; that is the case, for instance, in cloture fights in the Congress. But the point is that it need not be. In fact, when the maneuver is most successfully executed, it neither involves nor can be identified with decisions arrived at on specific issues.

Situations of this kind are common. Consider, for example, the case—surely not unfamiliar to this audience—of the discontented faculty member in an academic institution headed by a tradition-bound executive. Aggrieved about a long-standing policy around which a strong vested interest has developed, the professor resolves in the privacy of his office to launch an attack upon the policy at the next faculty meeting. But, when the moment of truth is at hand, he sits frozen in silence. Why? Among the many possible reasons, one or more of these could have been of crucial importance: (a) the professor was fearful that his intended action would be interpreted as an expression of his disloyalty to the institution; or (b) he decided that, given the beliefs and attitudes of his colleagues on the faculty, he would almost certainly constitute on this issue a minority of one; or (c) he concluded that, given the nature of the law-making process in the institution, his proposed remedies would be pigeonholed permanently. But whatever the case, the central point to be made is the same: to the extent that a person or group—consciously or unconsciously—creates or reinforces barriers to the public airing of policy conflicts, that person or group has power. Or, as Professor Schattschneider has so admirably put it:

All forms of political organization have a bias in favor of the exploitation of some kinds of conflict and the suppression of others because *organization is the mobilization of bias*. Some issues are organized into politics while others are organized out.[11]

Is such bias not relevant to the study of power? Should not the student be continuously alert to its possible existence in the human institution that he studies, and be ever prepared to examine the forces which brought it into being and sustain it? Can he safely ignore the possibility, for instance, that an individual or group in a community participates more vigorously in supporting the *nondecision-making* process than in participating in actual decisions within the process? Stated differently, can the researcher overlook the chance that some person or association could limit decision-making to relatively non-controversial matters, by influencing community values and political procedures and rituals, notwithstanding that there are in the community serious but latent power conflicts?[12] To do so is, in our judgment,

to overlook the less apparent, but nonetheless extremely important, face of power.

III

In his critique of the "ruling-elite model," Professor Dahl argues that "the hypothesis of the existence of a ruling elite can be strictly tested only if . . . [t] here is a fair sample of cases involving key political decisions in which the preferences of the hypothetical ruling elite run counter to those of any other likely group that might be suggested."[14] With this assertion we have two complaints. One we have already discussed, viz., in erroneously assuming that power is solely reflected in concrete decisions, Dahl thereby excludes the possibility that in the community in question there is a group capable of preventing contests from arising on issues of importance to it. Beyond that, however, by ignoring the less apparent face of power Dahl and those who accept his pluralist approach are unable adequately to differentiate between a "key" and a "routine" political decision.

Nelson Polsby, for example, proposes that "by pre-selecting as issues for study those which are generally agreed to be significant, pluralist researchers can test stratification theory."[15] He is silent, however, on how the researcher is to determine *what* issues are "generally agreed to be significant," and on how the researcher is to appraise the reliability of the agreement. In fact, Polsby is guilty here of the same fault he himself has found with elitist methodology: by presupposing that in any community there are significant issues in the political arena, he takes for granted the very question which is in doubt. He accepts as issues what are reputed to be issues. As a result, his findings are fore-ordained. For even if there is no "truly" significant issue in the community

society like ours a ruling elite might be so influential over ideas, attitudes, and opinions that a kind of false consensus will exist—not the phony consensus of a terroristic totalitarian dictatorship but the manipulated and superficially self-imposed adherence to the norms and goals of the elite by broad sections of a community. . . . This objection points to the need to be circumspect in interpreting the evidence." But that he largely misses our point is clear from the succeeding sentence: "Yet here, too, it seems to me that the hypothesis cannot be satisfactorily confirmed without something equivalent to the test I have proposed," and that is "by an examination of a series of concrete cases where key decisions are made. . . . "

[11] E. E. Schattschneider, *The Semi-Sovereign People* (New York, 1960), p. 71.

[12] Dahl *partially* concedes this point when he observes ("A Critique of the Ruling-Elite Model," pp. 468–69) that "one could argue that even in a

[14] *Op. cit.*, p. 466.

[15] *Op. cit.*, p. 478.

under study, there is every likelihood that Polsby (or any like-minded researcher) will find one or some and, after careful study, reach the appropriate pluralistic conclusions.[16]

Dahl's definition of "key political issues" in his essay on the ruling-elite model is open to the same criticism. He states that it is "a necessary although possibly not a sufficient condition that the [key] issue should involve actual disagreement in preferences among two or more groups."[17] In our view, this is an inadequate characterization of a "key political issue," simply because groups can have disagreements in preferences on unimportant as well as on important issues. Elite preferences which border on the indifferent are certainly not significant in determining whether a monolithic or polylithic distribution of power prevails in a given community. Using Dahl's definition of "key political issues," the researcher would have little difficulty in finding such in practically any community; and it would not be surprising then if he ultimately concluded that power in the community was widely diffused.

The distinction between important and unimportant issues, we believe, cannot be made intelligently in the absence of an analysis of the "mobilization of bias" in the community; of the dominant values and the political myths, rituals, and institutions which tend to favor the vested interests of one or more groups, relative to others. Armed with this knowledge, one could conclude that any challenge to the predominant values or to the established "rules of the game" would constitute an "important" issue; all else, unimportant. To be sure, judgments of this kind cannot be entirely objective. But to avoid making them in a study of power is both to neglect a highly significant aspect of power and thereby to undermine the only sound basis for discriminating between "key" and "routine" decisions. In effect, we contend, the pluralists have made each of these mistakes; that is to say, they have done just that for which Kaufman and Jones so severely taxed Floyd Hunter: they have begun "their structure at the mezzanine without showing us a lobby or foundation,"[18] *i.e.*, they have begun by studying the issues rather than the values and biases that are built into the political system and that, for the student of power, give real

meaning to those issues which do enter the political arena.

IV

There is no better fulcrum for our critique of the pluralist model than Dahl's recent study of power in New Haven.[19]

At the outset it may be observed that Dahl does not attempt in this work to define his concept, "key political decision." In asking whether the "Notables" of New Haven are "influential overtly or covertly in the making of government decisions," he simply states that he will examine "three different 'issue-areas' in which important public decisions are made: nominations by the two political parties, urban redevelopment, and public education." These choices are justified on the grounds that "nominations determine which persons will hold public office. The New Haven redevelopment program measured by its cost—present and potential—is the largest in the country. Public education, aside from its intrinsic importance, is the costliest item in the city's budget." Therefore, Dahl concludes, "It is reasonable to expect . . . that the relative influence over public officials wielded by the . . . Notables would be revealed by an examination of their participation in these three areas of activity."[20]

The difficulty with this latter statement is that it is evident from Dahl's own account that the Notables are in fact uninterested in two of the three "key" decisions he has chosen. In regard to the public school issue, for example, Dahl points out that many of the Notables live in the suburbs and that those who do live in New Haven choose in the main to send their children to private schools. "As a consequence," he writes, "their interest in the public schools is ordinarily rather slight."[21] Nominations by the two political parties as an important "issue-area," is somewhat analogous to the public schools, in that the apparent lack of interest among the Notables in this issue is partially accounted for by their suburban residence—because of which they are disqualified from holding public office in New Haven. Indeed, Dahl himself concedes that with respect to both these issues the Notables are largely indifferent: "Business leaders might ignore the public schools or the political parties without any sharp awareness that their indifference would hurt their pocketbooks . . ." He goes on, however, to say that

[16] As he points out, the expectations of the pluralist researchers "have seldom been disappointed." (*Ibid.*, p. 477).

[17] *Op. cit.*, p. 467.

[18] Herbert Kaufman and Victor Jones, "The Mystery of Power," *Public Administration Review*, Vol. 14 (Summer 1954), p. 207.

[19] Robert A. Dahl, *Who Governs?* (New Haven, 1961).

[20] *Ibid.*, p. 64.

[21] *Ibid.*, p. 70.

the prospect of profound changes [as a result of the urban-redevelopment program] in ownership, physical layout, and usage of property in the downtown area and the effects of these changes on the commercial and industrial prosperity of New Haven were all related in an obvious way to the daily concerns of businessmen.[22]

Thus, if one believes—as Professor Dahl did when he wrote his critique of the ruling-elite model—that an issue, to be considered as important, "should involve actual disagreement in preferences among two or more groups,"[23] then clearly he has now for all practical purposes written off public education and party nominations as key "issue-areas." But this point aside, it appears somewhat dubious at best that "the relative influence over public officials wielded by the Social Notables" can be revealed by an examination of their nonparticipation in areas in which they were not interested.

Furthermore, we would not rule out the possibility that even on those issues to which they appear indifferent, the Notables may have a significant degree of *indirect* influence. We would suggest, for example, that although they send their children to private schools, the Notables do recognize that public school expenditures have a direct bearing upon their own tax liabilities. This being so, and given their strong representation on the New Haven Board of Finance,[24] the expectation must be that it is in their direct interest to play an active role in fiscal policy-making, in the establishment of the educational budget in particular. But as to this, Dahl is silent: he inquires not at all into either the decisions made by the Board of Finance with respect to education nor into their impact upon the public schools.[25] Let it be

[22] *Ibid.*, p. 71.
[23] *Op. cit.*, p. 467.
[24] *Who Governs?*, p. 82. Dahl points out that "the main policy thrust of the Economic Notables is to oppose tax increases; this leads them to oppose expenditures for anything more than minimal traditional city services. In this effort their two most effective weapons ordinarily are the mayor and the Board of Finance. The policies of the Notables are most easily achieved under a strong mayor if his policies coincide with theirs or under a weak mayor if they have the support of the Board of Finance. . . . New Haven mayors have continued to find it expedient to create confidence in their financial policies among businessmen by appointing them to the Board." (pp. 81-2)
[25] Dahl does discuss in general terms (pp. 79-84) changes in the level of tax rates and assessments

understood clearly that in making these points we are not attempting to refute Dahl's contention that the Notables lack power in New Haven. What we *are* saying, however, is that this conclusion is not adequately supported by his analysis of the "issue-areas" of public education and party nominations.

The same may not be said of redevelopment. This issue is by any reasonable standard important for purposes of determining whether New Haven is ruled by "the hidden hand of an economic elite."[26] For the Economic Notables have taken an active interest in the program and, beyond that, the socio-economic implications of it are not necessarily in harmony with the basic interests and values of businesses and businessmen.

In an effort to assure that the redevelopment program would be acceptable to what he dubbed "the biggest muscles" in New Haven, Mayor Lee created the Citizens Action Commission (CAC) and appointed to it primarily representatives of the economic elite. It was given the function of overseeing the work of the mayor and other officials involved in redevelopment, and, as well, the responsibility for organizing and encouraging citizens' participation in the program through an extensive committee system.

In order to weigh the relative influence of the mayor, other key officials, and the members of the CAC, Dahl reconstructs "all the *important* decisions on redevelopment and renewal between 1950–58 . . . [to] determine which individuals most often initiated the proposals that were finally adopted or most often successfully vetoed the proposals of the others."[27] The results of this test indicate that the mayor and his development administrator were by far the most influential, and that the "muscles" on the Commission, excepting in a few trivial instances, "never directly initiated, opposed, vetoed, or altered any proposal brought before them. . . ."[28]

This finding is, in our view, unreliable, not so much because Dahl was compelled to make a

in past years, but not actual decisions of the Board of Finance or their effects on the public school system.
[26] *Ibid.*, p. 124.
[27] *Ibid.* "A rough test of a person's overt or covert influence," Dahl states in the first section of the book, "is the frequency with which he successfully initiates an important policy over the opposition of others, or vetoes policies initiated by others, or initiates a policy where no opposition appears." (*Ibid.*, p. 66)
[28] *Ibid.*, p. 131.

subjective selection of what constituted *important* decisions within what he felt to be an *important* "issue-area," as because the finding was based upon an excessively narrow test of influence. To measure relative influence solely in terms of the ability to initiate and veto proposals is to ignore the possible exercise of influence or power in limiting the scope of initiation. How, that is to say, can a judgment be made as to the relative influence of Mayor Lee and the CAC without knowing (through prior study of the political and social views of all concerned) the proposals that Lee did *not* make because he anticipated that they would provoke strenuous opposition and, perhaps, sanctions on the part of the CAC?[29]

In sum, since he does not recognize *both* faces of power, Dahl is in no position to evaluate the relative influence or power of the initiator and decision-maker, on the one hand, and of those persons, on the other, who may have been indirectly instrumental in preventing potentially dangerous issues from being raised.[30] As a re-

[29] Dahl is, of course, aware of the "law of anticipated reactions." In the case of the mayor's relationship with the CAC, Dahl notes that Lee was "particularly skillful in estimating what the CAC could be expected to support or reject." (p. 137). However, Dahl was not interested in analyzing or appraising to what extent the CAC limited Lee's freedom of action. Because of his restricted concept of power, Dahl did not consider that the CAC might in this respect have exercised power. That the CAC did not initiate or veto actual proposals by the mayor was to Dahl evidence enough that the CAC was virtually powerless; it might as plausibly be evidence that the CAC was (in itself or in what it represented) so powerful that Lee ventured nothing it would find worth quarreling with.

[30] The fact that the initiator of decisions also refrains—because he anticipates adverse reactions—from initiating other proposals does not obviously lessen the power of the agent who limited his initiative powers. Dahl missed this point: "It is," he writes, "all the more improbable, then, that a secret cabal of Notables dominates the public life of New Haven through means so clandestine that not one of the fifty prominent citizens interviewed in the course of this study—citizens who had participated extensively in various decisions—hinted at the existence of such a cabal. . . " (p. 185).

In conceiving of elite domination exclusively in the form of a conscious cabal exercising the power of decision-making and vetoing, he overlooks a more subtle form of domination; one in which those who actually dominate are not conscious of

sult, he unduly emphasizes the importance of initiating, deciding, and vetoing, and in the process casts the pluralist conclusions of his study into serious doubt.

V

We have contended in this paper that a fresh approach to the study of power is called for, an approach based upon a recognition of the two faces of power. Under this approach the researcher would begin—not, as does the sociologist who asks, "Who rules?" nor as does the pluralist who asks, "Does anyone have power?" —but by investigating the particular "mobilization of bias" in the institution under scrutiny. Then, having analyzed the dominant values, the myths and the established political procedures and rules of the game, he would make a careful inquiry into which persons or groups, if any, gain from the existing bias and which, if any, are handicapped by it. Next, he would investigate the dynamics of *nondecision-making*; that is, he would examine the extent to which and the manner in which the *status quo* oriented persons and groups influence those community values and those political institutions (as, *e.g.*, the unanimity "rule" of New York City's Board of Estimate[31]) which tend to limit the scope of actual decision-making to "safe" issues. Finally, using his knowledge of the restrictive face of power as a foundation for analysis and as a standard for distinguishing between "key" and "routine" political decisions, the researcher would, after the manner of the pluralists, analyze participation in decision-making of concrete issues.

We reject in advance as unimpressive the possible criticism that this approach to the study of power is likely to prove fruitless because it goes beyond an investigation of what is objectively measurable. In reacting against the subjective aspects of the sociological model of power, the pluralists have, we believe, made the mistake of discarding "unmeasurable elements" as unreal. It is ironical that, by so doing, they have exposed themselves to the same fundamental criticism they have so forcefully levelled against the elitists: their approach to and assumptions about power predetermine their findings and conclusions.

it themselves, simply because their position of dominance has never seriously been challenged.

[31] Sayre and Kaufman, *op. cit.*, p. 640. For perceptive study of the "mobilization of bias" in a rural American community, see Arthur Vidich and Joseph Bensman, *Small Town in Mass Society* (Princeton, 1958).

[10]

Types of Organizational
Decision Processes

Paul C. Nutt

Seventy-eight case studies of decision making were profiled
to identify the nature of the process. Analysis revealed
evaluative, historical model, off-the-shelf, search, and nova
process types. These processes differ in their approach to
idea generation, the guarantors applied, and process-
management rationale. Variations in each type are described to lay out the distinctions between the processes.
The study found that managers do not use the normative
methods prescribed by scholars for good decision making.
Most decision processes were found to be solution cen-
tered, which seemed to restrict innovation, limit the number
of alternatives considered, and perpetuate the use of questionable tactics.

INTRODUCTION

Considerable work in decision making has been directed toward
the development of normative processes (e.g., Steiner, 1969;
Nadler, 1970, 1981; Delbecq and Van de Ven, 1971; Gluick,
1976; Hofer and Schendel, 1978; Warfield, 1978; Churchman,
1979; Ackoff, 1981; Mason and Mitroff, 1981). Somewhat less
attention has been directed toward how managers go about
making decisions. A few key studies provide touchstones.

Soelberg (1967) divided the decision process into equal increments and studied the type of activity in each increment,
finding that most of the activity took place at the beginning and
at the end of the process. The Cyert and March (1963) studies
showed how managers imposed their views on the process.
Alternatives were pruned according to their conspicuousness
and the clout of their proponents, not according to expected
differences in performance. Mintzberg, Raisinghani, and
Théorêt (1976), who classified patterns found in decision
processes, called the key phases recognition, diagnosis, development (in the form of design or search), and selection (comprising choice procedures and authorization). The design and
search steps were used to create custom-made and modified
solutions, to identify a ready-made solution, and to sanction a
fully developed solution that was available when the process
began. The Mintzberg, Raisinghani, and Théorêt study made a
major contribution by identifying key phases of decision making
and external factors that influence the process. However, a
twenty-five-case data base was too limited to probe more
subtle characteristics such as subphases and tactics. As a
result, Mintzberg, Raisinghani, and Théorêt (1976) concluded by
noting that little is known about how managers engage in the
critically important activities of diagnosis and solution development. More studies, with larger data bases, that deal with a
new set of topics are needed to understand and appreciate the
decision processes used in organizations.

Using an empirically derived framework of the decision process
that identifies process types, this research seeks to refine our
understanding of how managers carry out a decision process.
Classification (McKelvey, 1978) was the first step in framing
hypotheses for this study. Careful descriptions of how managers go about decision making can determine if widely advocated
methods are used. For instance, is it true that normative models
have no influence in the middle and upper reaches of management, as Mintzberg, Raisinghani, and Théorêt (1976) have
claimed? Is it true, as March (1981) contended, that decision

© 1984 by Cornell University.
0001-8392/84/2903-0414/$1 00

makers make sense of their needs by determining what can be done from a review of available solutions? More precise descriptions of how organizations identify, refine, and select solutions to problems are needed to begin to answer this question. The use of normative methods calls for problems to be carefully defined (e.g., Pounds, 1969), specific goals to be set (Locke et al., 1981), the development of competing ideas in the form of alternatives (e.g., Mason and Mitroff, 1981), creativity in the identification and detailing of alternatives (e.g., Nadler, 1981), and the creation of a climate that eases implementation (e.g., Huse, 1975). Practice can be compared with these prescriptions to detect departures from recommended procedures that may have damaged results. Such a comparison helps to determine if the questionable benefits of normative methods recently discussed in the literature (e.g., Armstrong, 1982; Bresser and Bishop, 1983) are due to poor methods or poor practice, adding to our understanding of why formal methods fail.

The study describes decision processes used by organizations by attempting to enrich and broaden existing typologies and identify process types, variations, and themes within types that have particular significance in the understanding of organizational decision making.

IDENTIFYING DECISION PROCESSES

An approach called "process reconstruction" was used to identify process types (Nutt, 1983). Multiple case studies of projects were profiled using interviews that identify critical events, determine the sequence of these events, and fit the events and their sequence to a generic representation of activities thought to be essential in decision making. Common patterns in these cases were content analyzed to determine how decision making is conducted in organizations. This approach calls on the organizational researcher to collect data that tell stories about organizational processes and to look for patterns in these data (Daft, 1983). Stories in this research form the epistemology of decision-making practice.

A decision process is made up of a set of activities that begins with the identification of an issue and ends with action. To classify these activities, a framework can be imposed or patterns in the activities allowed to emerge from an examination and comparison of the cases. The emergent approach used by Soelberg (1967), Bower (1970), Witte (1972), Mintzberg, Raisinghani, and Théorêt (1976), and others examines the raw data (each case) and uses intuition to organize decision activities into patterns that describe the nature and sequence of key phases and within-phase steps. This approach becomes unwieldly, however, when large data bases must be assessed. The mass of detail makes it difficult to tease out patterns in the data that represent the practice variations. As a result, researchers using the emergent approach have been forced to examine a limited number of cases, which makes the generalizability of their conclusions suspect. However, imposing a framework to organize the data has the disadvantage of creating the appearance of orderliness in what may be a chaotic process. Decision procedures may not actually have the neat sequence of steps implied when this type of classification schema is used. The advantages of generalizability and organi-

Types of Decision Processes

zation, essential for a large data base, was thought to outweigh these disadvantages.

Morphology

Using a framework to classify decision activities is similar to using the classification procedure applied by linguists (Pike, 1967) who use notions of "etics and emics" (from phonetics and phonemics). An *emic* analysis is based on a minimal set of conceptual components that provide a referent that can be used to describe the object being analyzed (e.g., the decision process). Components of the thing being described (decision making) are used to identify elements in the classificatory framework. This frame allows the analyst to examine similarities and differences. The *etic* describes the process that uses a framework to profile an object (e.g., a project). It draws on the thing being classified (the project) as a point of reference. Such a classification is phyletic (McKelvey, 1978), because it attempts to identify and explain the origin of types of practice.

The framework (the emic) used in this research was derived from a synopsis of the recommended staging of activities required by normative methods reported in the literature. Normative methods were used to develop the classification frame so that departures of practice from recommended procedure could be detected. This approach has an action-making character instead of the action-taking character, or after-the-fact representation, prevalent in most decision-making research. Action making captures the steps taken to determine needs, develop an idea, and assess its merits.

To construct the framework, key activities were identified by comparing the purpose of stages and steps used by normative methods. The stages of formulation, concept development, detailing, evaluation, and implementation were distilled from this analysis (Nutt, 1984). Formulation (stage 1) is carried out to improve problem understanding and to set objectives by systematically examining needs and opportunities stipulated by an executive. Alternative ways to deal with the problem and meet the objective would be identified in concept development (stage 2). In detailing (stage 3), seemingly viable alternatives are refined to make their operating features clear, so they can be tested for workability. Stage 4, evaluation, is used to determine the merits (benefits, costs, and other features) of each alternative. Implementation (stage 5) is carried out to install the plan.

Search, synthesis, and analysis were steps often used in each process stage. The search step is used to gather information, such as by using a group process to stimulate the information sources of people. In the synthesis step, relationships are derived, such as by using morphology (Zwicky, 1968) to assemble ideas in a relational format. Analysis is used to prune or to prioritize ideas, objectives, problems, potential solutions, and the like.

Combining the steps and stages creates a morphology, like that shown in Figure 1, which is used to profile each project (the etic). Key project activities are located in an appropriate stage and step combination, or cell, of the morphology and are connected by an arrow to show the order in which these activities are carried out. The morphology is used to summarize each decision process for the purposes of classification and comparison.

Sample

The 78 participating organizations were active in a student intern program, and all were involved in service delivery (e g , hospitals, governmental agencies, insurance companies, and consulting firms), so the generalizability of the findings is limited to service organizations. The organizations were widely dispersed across the United States and Canada, so a broad representation of decision making was included in the study. All organizations that were contacted agreed to participate.

At each organization, the chief executive, operating, or financial officer (CEO, COO, or CFO, respectively) gave permission to profile a project that had been carried out by the organization. The author described the purpose of the study and its requirements, and the executive was asked to suggest a project. If several projects were suggested, the author selected one that broadened the data base. The contact person was asked to name two individuals, including the sponsor (the manager responsible for the project), who knew the most about the details of the decision process, so they could be interviewed in depth. Several interviews with each person were conducted and reconciled, so classifications would have less chance of error. As in Mintzberg and Waters' (1982) research, attempts were made to reconcile interview data with other sources of information, such as documents and reports.

Creating process profiles. Multiple interviews (with two executives from each project) were used to minimize distortion and memory failure, the two most common errors in the reconstruction of events (Mintzberg, Raisinghani, and Théorêt, 1976). The interviews were used to identify decision activities and their sequence. Questions were posed to identify all activities that were undertaken, and the interviewee was asked to describe the first activity, the second, and so on, until all key activities were laid out. This information was fit to the morphology categories by matching activities to the stage-step definitions. For example, activities were sorted to determine how need or the opportunity to act was discovered (search), reconciled (synthesis), and prioritized (analysis). The morphology was used to capture how (or if) each step in each stage was carried out and the order of these events. The morphologies developed from the interview with each executive were compared and differences were identified. An additional meeting with both executives was used to reconcile these differences; the executives were asked to modify the information contained in the morphology until a consensus emerged.

Data collection and data reduction averaged twenty hours per case. The data were collected and compiled over a period of six years. A morphology and a corresponding narrative were prepared for each case. One of the cases in the data base is described to illustrate the level of detail.

An illustrative process profile. The development of a renal dialysis center is profiled in Figure 1. The project was carried out at a large university hospital that had recently developed a new outpatient clinic. A renal dialysis unit had not originally been included because such a unit was thought to cut into the

Types of Decision Processes

income potential of the medical faculty and detract from the university's role as a referral center. Subsequently, a federal law was enacted that provided subsidies for much of the treatment cost for chronic renal disease, and the demand for dialysis greatly increased. The hospital had only a single four-station unit, and as demand grew, physicians began to refer patients to a proprietary unit that, during this same period, had opened in the city. Compared with the proprietary unit, the university hospital's dialysis unit lacked amenities, causing patients to prefer the proprietary center. Before long, the proprietary dialysis center was serving nearly all the self-paying and third-party patients, leaving the public assistance patients for the university. The result was not only the lost revenues from patients being treated elsewhere, but also unreimbursed cost. As shown in Figure 1, declining revenues triggered stage 1 of the process. Hospital executives' cursory analysis suggested that the capacity should be doubled and that the amenities should be provided to attract the insured patient. They proposed doubling the capacity, increasing the number of dialysis stations from four to eight.

Figure 1. The development of a renal dialysis center.

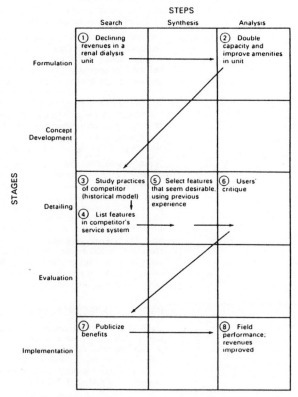

In stage 3, the practices of a competitor provided the sponsor with a template. A list of features that described the competitor's dialysis system were enumerated to guide solution development. A remodeling expert determined the physical changes needed to fit the competitor's approach to dialysis into the clinic's building. Nephrologists suggested types of dialysis equipment, and nurses working in the dialysis unit were asked about staffing requirements and operating policies. Information on issues such as staffing and policies and procedures were drawn from the staff's experiences with units in which they had been trained or knew about.

No formal evaluation was conducted. Users of the system were asked to verify that proposed changes were acceptable. Memoranda that publicized the expected benefits of the unit were used to promote implementation. Field performance was determined by monitoring dialysis revenue.

Classifying the Morphologies

A project was retained for the classification phase of the study if there was agreement about the process and sufficient detail to understand what was done. All but five of the 78 projects met these tests. In three cases, the follow-up interviews did not produce an agreement on key activities or their sequence. In two cases there was agreement about processes but too little detail to classify them. The 73 remaining projects were analyzed to detect process types.

Precise classification is a key step in multiple case study research (Yin, 1981). Considerable care was taken to insure that the categories identified were defensible. The morphologies for the 73 cases were sorted by the author until a set of groupings, or patterns, emerged that seemed mutually exclusive. Two criteria were used in classification: the stability and the clarity of the distinctions. A stable classification has within-category similarities and between-category differences that can be explicitly specified. The clarity criterion required that the distinctions among these categories have theoretical as well as practical significance (McKelvey, 1978).

A profile was deemed unique when the trace of the decision activities through the morphology had a distinct pattern of stages and steps (process). A category was selected for each process and noted on the back of the morphology for recall purposes. The morphologies were stored for a year. To get an indication of intrarater reliability, the sorting process was repeated by the author a year later without referring to the first sort. These two classifications were found to be perfectly matched. Interrater reliability was tested by having other researchers sort the morphologies. There was over 90 percent agreement about the classification, suggesting that the process categories are defensible.

PROCESS TYPES DISCOVERED

Each of the decision processes began with formulation and ended with implementation; the distinguishing feature of each process type proved to be the intermediate stages used. These processes are here called historical model, off-the-shelf, appraisal, search, and nova. Table 1 summarizes all the projects by stages, to highlight the patterns in these processes. The

Types of Decision Processes

themes in these patterns are summarized in Table 2. The decision processes were found to differ in terms of the origin of ideas, the guarantors (Churchman, 1971) used, and the rationale applied to manage the process.

Historical Model Processes

The historical model process activates the stages of formulation, detailing, and implementation. This process uses concepts drawn from the practices of others to guide solution development. The sponsor visits an organization or recalls an experience that offers a way to deal with the problem or further specify an opportunity. For example, the renal dialysis center project staff (Figure 1) sought ideas by visiting a successful competitor to identify desirable physical features. Policies, procedures, and staffing patterns were selected by having key staff recall practices in places where they had trained. The historical model process was used in 40 percent of the cases studied.

The historical model allows the sponsor to visualize actual operations, which demonstrates that action is feasible and puts solution development on a tangible basis at the outset. The guarantor applied is one of demonstrable workability. Because costs are modest and the process appears to be foolproof, sponsors thought this approach clever. The equivalent of a pilot project has been conducted that demonstrates workability. Stage 2 is skipped because the process is not used to provide ideas. The evaluation stage is also skipped. The plan functioned elsewhere, so it was assumed that it would work in the new setting.

Variations. Each of the archetypal processes had several variations that used the same sequence of stages but differed in the nature or intensity of key activities. The historical model process had three variations. The model was either provincial, enriched, or based on the pet idea of a key executive.

Provincial model. The historical model used was *provincial* when the practice or procedure of a single organization or work unit, thought to have high prestige, was used as a template for solution development. For example, in one of the cases, when the organization's material management system failed, an executive was hired who had installed a similar system in an organization thought to be highly prestigious. In this situation, the installed system becomes nearly a carbon copy of the practices used by the high-prestige organization. The provincial historical model occurred quite often, representing over half of the historical model cases and 20 percent of the total cases (Table 2).

Finer process distinctions were made by observing solution development tactics in the detailing stage. Five distinct tactics were identified by comparing the detailing activities shown in Table 1 that were used in provincial historical model development. These tactics could be summarized as: hiring a system, making site visits, using past experience, assessing outside requirements, and using the literature, as shown in Table 3. One-third of the provincial projects were carried out by hiring a key individual to install a program. For instance, in the materials management project (Table 1, case 5), the CEO hired away from a competitor a manager he knew to have a good track record. In

Table 1

Decision Activity by Stage and Process Type

Projects	Formulation	Conceptualization	Detailing	Evaluation	Implementation
Historical Model Processes					
Provincial 1. Family practice outpatient care	Deterioration of referral base due to hospital location suggests future decline in occupancy.	Not activated	Hire director of competitor's family practice to install same program.	Not activated	CEO reviews plan, details and authorizes funds.
2. Hospital home care	Increase community visibility through greater potential user contact in a home care service.	Not activated	Site visits to organizations offering home care services.	Not activated	Hire director to reproduce favored program.
3. Lost charges	Routine audit reveals charges for lab services, etc. not billed to patients; audit implies nursing units fail to keep proper records.	Not activated	Copy features of incentive program used in another hospital; prepare schedule of incentives proportional to increase in captured charges.	Not activated	Install budget plan and offer incentives to nursing units, using a memo.
4. Renal dialysis unit	For-profit dialysis unit syphoning off all but charity and Medicaid patients from university hospital.	Not activated	Copy features of for-profit unit, particularly amenities; hire architect to reproduce the facility.	Not activated	Publicize benefits of plan; demonstrate financial feasibility.
5. Materials management system	Stockouts seem too frequent.	Not activated	Hire new director to implement system used in previous organization.	Not activated	Demonstrate new system's prospects of overcoming the stockout problem.
6. CT scanner in osteopathic hospital	New scanner required to be competitive with allopathic hospitals and provide residency teaching equipment.	Not activated	Site visits to hospitals with CT scanner in operation; select manufacturer with best features.	Not activated	Demonstrate features of preferred equipment; contract with manufacturer for turnkey system.
7. Burn unit	Capacity inadequate but burn care costs are not fully reimbursed; Kellogg Foundation funds found that could be used to defray costs.	Not activated	Hire burn care specialist to reproduce the system used by the hospital where he had trained.	Not activated	Demonstrate financial feasibility using charges, grant funds, and resident training opportunities.
8. Cash flow management	Negative cash flow during hospital construction.	Not activated	Newly hired administrator demonstrated that cash flow need not fall during construction; administrator implements inventory reduction and purchasing controls program	Not activated	Report on cash flow changes to get continuing support for program and spread it throughout the hospital

Types of Decision Processes

9. Community Health Center	Source of funds for CHC in city offered by Robert Wood Johnson Foundation.	Not activated	Determine donations from RWJ requirements; mayor determines service providers' (e.g., MD's) objections to the requirements.	Not activated	Mayor negotiates with RWJ and providers to create compromise proposal, which RWJ funds.
10. EMS expansion	Opportunities to expand stemmed from new Federal EMS funds for cities to offer emergency services to rural areas.	Not activated	Federal guidelines used to develop a regionalized plan of emergency services; stipulations of city (retain control) built into decision mechanisms.	Not activated	Proposal rejected by HEW because the existing rural EMS programs ignored.
11. Mobile CT scanner	After CT scanner project is rejected, hospital forms consortium to get around regulation requirements.	Not activated	Mobile CT scanner copied from features of mobile x-ray unit. Scheduling, billing, and patient transport requirements worked out with consortium members.	Not activated	Regulator found project nonreviewable, consortium members budget project.
12. Chronic renal dialysis center for children	Loss of service due to pediatric nephrologist's resignation; board of trustees stipulate need to reacquire this service.	Not activated	Hire pediatric nephrologist who reproduces program developed at previous hospital; personnel from the hospital recruited.	Not activated	Hospital board of trustees were presented with program and its costs by pediatric nephrologist.
13. Development of regional perinatal center	Designation as a regional center determined need to upgrade OB department and improve its low morale, poor occupancy, and decaying facility.	Not activated	Perinatal center described in the literature used as a model; key user groups were asked to comment on plan as it evolved.	Not activated	Argue for plan adoption, using high-risk service needs that could be met.
14. Tiered pricing in an emergency department	Competition from small clinics suggests potential erosion of market share; projected admissions from ER set as objective.	Not activated	Site visits suggest billing categories used by others; adopt changes in pricing for minor injuries.	Not activated	Memo written dictating new charge rates to hospital personnel.
15. Medical chart recording system	Delinquent and slow chart completion caused JCHA accreditation bodies to issue notice of violation.	Not activated	Visit area hospitals and adopt scheme used by local university hospital; check feasibility.	Not activated	Modify by-laws to require 2-week record completion by medical staff, under penalty of loss of admitting privileges.
Enriched 16. Ambulatory surgery	Board of trustees identifies ambulatory surgery as a priority.	Not activated	Site visits to free standing ambulatory surgery center to determine building features and procedures; architect hired to duplicate favored option.	Not activated	Demonstration of plan's value to key groups (medical staff and trustees).

Continued overleaf

Table 1

Decision Activity by Stage and Process Type *(continued)*

Projects	Formulation	Conceptualization	Detailing	Evaluation	Implementation
17. Revamp organization structure for a congregation of sisters	Order wants to become less involved in day-to-day operations of its hospitals and other health and social service institutions.	Not activated	Site visits to multi-hospital systems; best features of four structures seen as feasible were amalgamated.	Not activated	Charter amended and quarterly reports monitored to measure progress.
18. Program evaluation data system in HHS-BCHS	Opportunity to use BCHS data base to evaluate federal initiatives (e.g., community health center, family planning centers).	Not activated	Contractor approach used; proposal features documented; modifications required of winner, based on good features of the other proposals.	Not activated	Funding made contingent on site visits, which insured that modifications were made.
19. Open-heart surgery	Medical staff demanded an open-heart program, approved by board of trustees.	Not activated	Visit other organizations with "successful" programs; document procedures using systems analysis; combine best attributes of each program into plan; test feasibility of plan.	Not activated	Site visit team sells plan to CEO and board of trustees to secure funding.
Pet-Idea 20. Outpatient registration system	Anecdotal failure to bill for service used to suggest need to change from decentralized to centralized registration.	Not activated	Proforma visits precede manager presenting his registration idea.	Not activated	Pilot program leads to partial adoption.
21. Primary nursing	Problems with training and retention of aides and patient care accountability suggested a need to change nursing care practices.	Not activated	Proforma literature search used to identify primary nursing idea (RN's have fewer patients but 24-hour responsibility).	Not activated	Change agent introduces program using unfreezing and refreezing tactics.
22. Preadmission testing	Hospital admission delays and high costs.	Not activated	CEO cites early testing as a way to reduce delay and cost; revise building to accommodate program.	Not activated	Announced program with memorandum to affected parties.
23. Community laboratory	Newspaper reports of low quality and high cost in commercial labs creates opportunity.	Not activated	CEO's longstanding plan to market his hospital for a community laboratory surfaced; plan reviewed by key people; pricing turnaround time set.	Not activated	Persuasion used to convince medical staff and board of trustees to market laboratory as commercial service.

Types of Decision Processes

24. Supply management cart system	Manager alleged charges were lost by departments not using recently implemented cart system.	Not activated	Modify the cart system's procedure to modify nonparticipants.	Not activated	Issue an edict requiring all departments to use cart system.
25. AMA and ANA joint practice	Need for collaborative MD and RN care led to joint practice concept.	Not activated	Elaborate specifics of joint practice (e.g., joint decision making and record review).	Not activated	Secure grant funding; let RFP test concept in variety of hospitals.
26. HMO development	Low Blue Cross market share and demands for cost reduction by state department of insurance.	Not activated	HMO generally believed to reduce cost and, therefore, has potential of increasing market share via its promotion.	Not activated	Select hospital participant and agree to billing schedule to operate HMO.
27. ER physician coverage	Audit shows slow response of contract MD's, failure to do treatment review, and failure to repay loans.	Not activated	RFP written that favors an ER service preferred by the CEO.	Not activated	Demonstrate superiority of new group to trustees; contract with the new ER physicians.
28. Revision of paid time-off policy	An executive identified excessive sick leave, suggesting need to reverse policy.	Not activated	Executive proposes plan developed by him in previous organization; compare sick time provisions to ensure costs will fall.	Not activated	Demonstrate value of new plan to CEO, memo written to specify new time-off options.
29. Development of child and adolescent hospital	Need for merging child and adolescent care linked to recent reports by newly elected state officials.	Not activated	CEO's child and adolescent concept developed by study of existing facilities providing each type of care.	Not activated	Presentation to university trustees, proposing funding.
30. Helicopter patient-transport system	Incidence of trauma patients in OR used by CEO to argue for fast transport by helicopter.	Not activated	Helicopter services known to CEO investigated; CEO's flight teacher hired to complete plan.	Not activated	Plan rejected by trustees as infeasible, but resurrected when competitor hospital announced plans to offer rapid transport services.
Off-the-Shelf					
Truncated Search					
31. Treatment planning simulator	Cancer center designation requires equipment.	Not activated	Location options explored (lead-shielding problems); RFP prepared.	RFP responses assessed using technological criteria.	Increased cost ($20/case) justified using benefits of center designation.
32. Labor and delivery service	Problems stemming from accreditation, market share decline, and consumer preferences.	Not activated	RFP used to locate architects with experience in birthing units to propose space configurations.	Size of facility for examining and birthing rooms and cost used to select among architect's proposals.	Encumber funds.

Continued overleaf

Table 1

Decision Activity by Stage and Process Type *(continued)*

Projects	Formulation	Conceptualization	Detailing	Evaluation	Implementation
33. Parking	Complaints about inadequate parking space.	Not activated	Consultant who served on board of directors retained to provide standard plan (parking ramp and walkway with temporary surface lot).	Parking habit survey used to forecast size of ramp and cost.	Property cost excessive, project abandoned.
34. Shared service in voluntary hospital consortium	Demonstrate to third parties the ability to act (e.g., regulators).	Not activated	RFP used to select proposals for a community-wide paging system.	Assess proposals using efficiency and service criteria.	Cost sharing and problems of selling idea to medical staff caused an abort.
35. Expanding hospital ancillary service space	Space requirements below that required for residency teaching certification.	Not activated	Architect used in past asked to offer space plan consistent with needs; financing plans prepared.	CEO makes changes that mollify powerful user groups and ensure certification.	Demonstration of project feasibility to trustees (e.g., tax-exempt-bond financing available and regulator views).
36. Total hospital information system	Trustees call for a demonstration of the value of subsidiary consulting firm.	Not activated	Consulting firm profiles information needs of each department and tailors them to their computerized information-system concepts.	Simulated comparisons to current manual systems and pilot tests.	Funds allocated by CEO for phased system installation.
37. Unregulated hospital expansion	Space shortages documented by comparing space to comparable hospitals.	Not activated	Hospital's architect asked to prepare plans; affected departments were interviewed to detail bed needs.	Revisions in plans to accommodate users.	Funds authorized by trustees after project supported by users.
38. Regulated hospital expansion	Trustees identify need to enlarge facility.	Not activated	Organization's consultant made space estimates and retained architect; architect interviewed users to prepare plans.	Cost and space need conflicts played out for trustees, who dictate compromises.	Regulatory approval to expand.
39. Hospital alcoholism detoxification unit	Census countdown and image in market area poor.	Not activated	RFP to solicit proposals for detox services.	Cost, sobriety indexes, and projected revenues used to select proposal.	Demonstrate potential of the increasing census count to trustees to secure funding authorization.
40. Hospital ancillary and bed expansion	Fears of lawsuits and physician dissatisfaction due to high occupancy that periodically forced beds into halls.	Not activated	Feasibility study that documented capital and space requirements done by hospital's auditor.	Made contingency plans, anticipating regulatory rejection or required modification.	Lawsuit filed; compromise with regulator, cutting proposed beds in half, secured an approval.

Types of Decision Processes

41. Computerized laboratory	Unrestricted donation to hospitals promotes search for a problem.	Not activated	Computerized laboratory solicited from acquaintance.	Vendor's system reviewed to document benefits.	Expenditures authorized by CEO.
42. Operating room remodeling	Traffic patterns in critical care units cause loss of accreditation.	Not activated	Changes in space allocation explored that meet accreditation requirements; architects asked to bid.	Proposals reviewed by medical and nursing staff and trustees.	Let contract to architect to complete plan.
43. Site selection for HMO	Site needs taken from plan for new HMO construction.	Not activated	Building envelope proposals reviewed to determine site requirements; hospital consultant tours city and inspects vacant lots; data collected on lots.	Site candidates' suitability explored (e.g. zoning and ownership).	Consultant describes merits of favored site to trustees.
44. Branch bank	Employees cash friends' checks and return with large sums of money, provoking fears of theft by management.	Not activated	RFPs sent to local banks for an automatic teller.	Attributes of proposals compared.	Contract with bank.
45. Revamping a university hospital's accounts payable	Delays in financial reports four times industry norms, due to university reviews; poor service from vendor results.	Not activated	Flow-chart review of procedures to identify audit traces; available software package (sole source) used to computerize entries to permit direct invoice payment.	Determine reduction in payment time, compare to norms.	Use evaluation information to demonstrate merit of by-passing campus review.
46. Laboratory consolidation	12 labs scattered through a children's hospital were thought to operate inefficiently.	Not activated	Architect hired (sole source) to consolidate labs; lab was sized, traffic patterns considered, procedures integrated into a detailed layout; layout reviewed and revised to reconcile space allocations among current labs.	Adjustments made to user assessments; costs traded off by administrators against service, with cost dominant.	Bids for construction and physical move to integrated lab.
47. University hospital relocation	Need for move to new facility caused by new hospital construction.	Not activated	Sole-source consultant inventoried departments to be transferred, to determine requirements.	PERT used to find best sequence of events.	Periodic updates with newsletter preceded actual move; dual operation before patient moves.
48. Data processing system for a city	Long delays in obtaining unit cost indicators (cost/ton garbage).	Not activated	Controller writes RFP to automate information acquisition for city.	Review RFP responses to write a more comprehensive RFP and return to detailing stage.	Demonstrate depth of EDP knowledge to city council in promoting favored option.
49. Computerized EKG interpretation	Computer aids can reduce cost of interpretation and increase precision.	Not activated	Site visits to prepare RFP; use specifics of past vendor proposals to rewrite RFP and ask	Determine effect on MD fees, cost, and time to	Concurrent operation of computerized and manual system to demonstrate benefits.

Continued overleaf

Table 1

Decision Activity by Stage and Process Type *(continued)*

Projects	Formulation	Conceptualization	Detailing	Evaluation	Implementation
50. Modifying telephone system	Bell system performance poor and cost increases of 300% in 10 years; unwillingness to work with a new building design.	Not activated	RFP written to select bids from other phone systems.	Cost and performance comparisons to Bell; user reviews past performance to determine if massive failures.	Assurances by favored new phone service company.
51. Storeroom expansion	Complaints about space shortages over several years.	Not activated	Search for sites periodically; acquire list of desirable features; old ice rink becomes available.	Ice rink cost much lower than previously explored options (transport costs ignored).	CEO authorizes funds for purchase.
52. Hospital MIS	Approval to move to a new facility provided an opportunity to computerize hospital information.	Not activated	Vendor search mounted to determine best system; features identified and the RFP recycled several times.	Review proposals and ask for more bids; on-line system selected over batch; criteria of cost and future growth used to select vendor.	Demonstration of features.
Appraisal Processes					
Covert					
53. Pharmacokinetic dosing service	Opportunity to exploit dosing developments to get Blue Cross reimbursement for pharmacist on a fee-for-service basis.	Not activated	Not activated	Document costs and benefits of dosing; develop arguments supporting fee for service to underwrite pharmacist dosing time.	Blue Cross accepts arguments; billing procedures set.
54. Patient origin information system	Inaccurate information on patients identified in routine audit (e.g., admitting physician, hospital transferring, etc.).	Not activated	Not activated	Compare hospital's and physicians' logs to measure error rates.	Physician format proposed as superior data-capturing approach.
55. Redesign of OB-GYN unit of university hospital	Unit built to house 15% high risk proved to have inadequate high-risk capacity; demand 25% more than expected; critics offer plan.	Not activated	Not activated	Assess the cost of modifying the unit to accommodate more high-risk patients, using a queuing model.	Problem identified and solution that resolves it sold to a university vice-president.

Types of Decision Processes

Overt 56. Aging programs under Title III	Secure federal funds to operate programs.	Not activated	Not activated	Public hearings to assess current and proposed services; guidelines (funds proportional to county aged population) user preferences, and past performance used to propose a bundle of programs.	Let contracts to provider organizations.
57. Health planning under PL93–641	Encumber federal funds to maintain planning organization.	Not activated	Not activated	Volunteer committees apply guidelines and criteria to identify needs; frame needs (e.g. cost of care, accessibility, etc.) as requirements around program areas (e.g., longterm care).	Federal funding provided.
Passive Search Processes					
Sequestered 58. Patient relations	Incident reports filed by patients suggest potential malpractice problems of unknown origin.	Not activated	Not activated	Not activated	Department head hired to install AHA's Patient Relations Department, discovered at an AHA conference.
59. Data processing	System at 100% capacity; need to prioritize computer uses, allocate time, or expand available options.	Not activated	Not activated	Not activated	Other CEO's were found to be successful in forcing priorities on users; memo written outlining processes to ask for computer access.
60. Mobile CT scanner	Regulator rejected hospital's scanner application, due to low projected use; medical staff pressured CEO to appeal because of legal implications of ER operation without a scanner.	Not activated	Not activated	Not activated	Appeals rejected, CEO found that a mobile scanner could subvert regulatory review; project manager hired to implement and to solicit use by other rural hospitals.
Open 61. Mobile decentralized pharmacy	Excessive time to dispense medications.	Not activated	Not activated	Not activated	Mobile system discovered in literature; pilot used to demonstrate feasibility.

Continued overleaf

Table 1

Decision Activity by Stage and Process Type *(continued)*

Projects	Formulation	Conceptualization	Detailing	Evaluation	Implementation
62. Outpatient surgery	Need to shut down unused beds to increase occupancy; put unused space to use.	Not activated	Not activated	Not activated	Look for fashionable service to fill low-use areas; OPS implemented by hiring staff.
Nova Processes					
Internal Staff Consultants					
63. Medical records system	Medical staff at clinic kept own records which were often lost in transit to clinic; university needed additional information on clinic patients.	Automate and centralize records.	CRT system with integrated billings, appointments, and storage capabilities designed; software developed.	Cost comparison to current system using a pilot in one department.	Install and modify as problems develop.
64. PBX staffing	PBX operators file frequent grievances over workload; objective to reduce grievances without cost increases.	Modify work schedule; delegate to operators.	Operators suggested schedule options.	Queuing model used to find options that kept costs at current level.	Operators requested supervisor to install new schedule.
65. Renovation of a nursing station in a children's hospital	A combined surgical and medical nursing station caused lack of privacy; discussions with parents faced with different concerns (e.g., death vs. rehabilitation) were compromised.	Split the nursing station; delegate to nurses.	Staff provided layouts to reallocate existing space.	Nurses prioritized the options.	Project budgeted.
66. Pride program	New CEO of a university hospital finds an image problem has caused low morale and low motivation; objective of improving hospital image set.	Physical facility redecoration and minor renovation selected for emphasis by CEO.	Clean-up ordered; "Pride" posters, pencils, buttons, and university hospital fact card used to call attention to hospital's national standing.	Employee views of changes were solicited through discussions at all levels.	Memos indicate requirements to wear pride buttons and distribute material when discussing the hospital with others.
67. Children's hospital marketing	Increased competition from other hospitals for specialized services believed related to falling occupancy.	Marketing hospital to demonstrate its special programs.	Lectures and discussion for area pediatricians, radio ads, newspaper articles, brochures were developed to increase awareness of hospital in catchment area.	CEO reviewed and modified marketing materials.	Programs budgeted and sold to key people among trustees and medical staff, who were solicited to make testimonials.
68. Pharmacy technician	Liability audit by insurance carrier found creates delays, low quality, poor control.	Decentralized drug	Flow charts used to document steps that satellites, partial and full decentralization options proposed.	Options compared in delivery time, training, and control to determine feasibility.	Cooptation by participation of users and by demonstration.

Types of Decision Processes

Outside Consultants				
69. Emergency department case processing	Complaints about excessive waiting time in emergency.	Delays due to communicating test results (e.g., lab or x-ray) to physicians.	Isolate communication delays; develop new SOP to order tests; set targets for turnaround by urgent, emergency, and convenience care categories.	Determine wait time under new and old system, using queuing model.	Establish a pilot program; demonstrations of performance used to argue for adoption.
70. Medical office building	15-year trend of declining occupancy; studies of medical staff revealed major admitters about to retire.	Office building proposed as way to attract new physicians; building location set near MD's who practice in suburbs.	Consultant prepares build-and-buy options; zoning approvals requested for the options.	Determine cost to hospital to set subsidy levels for options.	Offer space in building to prospective medical staff members with stipulation they must be admitters.
71. AV-TV service center	Fiscal solvency threatened by reduced federal funding at university; free service policy questioned.	Prioritize current AV-TV services and propose new ones.	Users surveyed to rank current and proposed services.	AV-TV director trimmed services that required additional investment.	Set rental rates for current service.
72. Hospital consolidation	Order of sisters operating two hospitals in a city question wisdom of two hospitals; hospital in financial crisis is located in a low-income area.	Develop special roles for each hospital and merge managements.	Options for service allocation developed.	Options assessed using public reaction, need, cost of remodeling, and role of the order.	Project budgeted; services transferred, shut down, or moved to new site.
73. Reference laboratory	Hospital Association found that 15 outside labs service a given hospital for special tests, creating inconsistent specimen requirements, complex contracts, and monitoring problems; cost seemed excessive and quality low.	Select a single (reference) lab for a given test on a bidding basis.	Solicit bids from laboratories on a per-test basis.	Measure turnaround time, service, commitments, price per test.	Write contract holding hospitals to a certain volume for each test at each lab.

the burn-unit project (case 7), a burn specialist was recruited from a military hospital known to have a high-quality burn care program, and in the chronic renal dialysis center for children (case 12), a specialist was recruited from a high-prestige medical center. These key individuals were hired on the basis of their credentials (e.g., where he or she had trained) rather than on the basis of knowledge of the individuals' abilities.

Table 2

Archetypal Processes and Variations

Process type and variations	Frequency*	Stages activated	Themes
Historical model	41%	1, 3, 5	Adopt the practices of others.
Provincial (20%)			Single sources.
Enriched (6%)			Multiple sources.
Pet idea (15%)			Preconceived idea.
Off-the-shelf	30%	1, 3, 4, 5	Aggressive and overt search.
Extended search (7%)			Evaluation criteria defined by attributes of the alternatives.
Truncated search (23%)			Generic criteria used.
Appraisal	7%	1, 4, 5	Seeking a rationale.
Covert (4%)			Deflecting criticism.
Overt (3%)			Shaping the plan's features.
Search	7%	1, 5	Passive and defensive search.
Sequestered (4%)			Sponsor conducted.
Open (3%)			Sponsor delegated.
Nova	15%	1, 2, 3, 4, 5	New Ideas sought.
Internal staffers (8%)			Carried out by organization's staff.
Outside consultants (7%)			Specialist from outside the organization used.

*Percentage of all cases.

Site visits were used in nearly 30 percent of the provincial cases. In each case, several visits were conducted to identify a program that fit with implicit and unstated criteria used by the sponsor. A subordinate was then asked to copy the features of the favored site. Equipment (CT scanner, case 6), contract program managers (home care, case 2), and program features (tiered ER pricing, case 14) were identified in this way.

Executives were also prone to copy a program that they knew about, without a site visit. A third of the provincial models used this approach, as previously described for the renal dialysis project (case 4). The guidelines of a funding agency were used to specify operating features in two cases. Only rarely (one case) was the idea drawn from the literature.

Enriched model. The historical model used was *enriched* when it drew on the practices of several organizations or work groups and attempted to cull out the best features from each. Before purchasing major equipment, such as CT or NMR scanners (diagnostic equipment that creates extraordinarily clear cross-sectional pictures of the body), staff members from some hospitals visited several sites of care to compare types of equipment and treatment procedures. The hospitals then used

Types of Decision Processes

an amalgamation of the practices and procedures from the sites visited. The enriched historical model was comparatively rare. It occurred in only 13 percent of the historical model cases and 6 percent of all cases.

Key solution development tactics for the enriched historical model projects stemmed from site visits or bids by contractors (Table 3). Site visits were used in most (80 percent) of these projects. For instance, hospital staff members visited institutions similar to their own to identify the best features of programs to carry out ambulatory surgery (case 16) and open-

Table 3

Tactics Used in Process Types

Process type	Process variations	Key stages	Tactics
Historical model	Provincial	Detailing	Recruiting; site visits; copying known system; using outside requirements; reviewing the literature
	Enriched	Detailing	Site visits; contractor bids
	Pet idea	Detailing and formulation	Justify the pet idea by: Selectively interpreting environments; identifying problems it solves; reviewing a similar system
Off-the-shelf	Truncated search	Detailing	RFP's; sole-source contracting
	Extended search	Detailing	RFP's; matching
Appraisal	Covert	Evaluation	Posturing; verification
	Overt	Evaluation	Public hearing; documentation
Search	Sequestered	Implementation	Peers; literature
	Open	Implementation	Peers; literature
Nova	Internal staff	Concept development	Problem-corrective; idea-driven (more common)
	Consultants	Concept development	Problem-corrective (more common); idea driven

heart surgery (case 19). Internal operations projects, such as an MIS, and organizational restructuring (case 17) were also done in this way.

The contractor-bidding approach (case 18) is similar to the procedure used by several federal agencies. Ideas are solicited by requesting multiple bids for each phase of a project. Contractors are compensated for their efforts, and the resulting ideas are used to rewrite the requirements (contract-end items) for the next phase of the project. This approach is much like visiting a site, because it solicits ideas for the purpose of synthesis. For instance, the Department of Defense uses this process when developing large projects, such as the B-1 Bomber.

Pet-idea model. The historical model process was also used to promote the *pet idea* of an executive. When the time seemed ripe, some executives in the cases identified a problem that justified his or her idea and initiated a project. This process was always self-serving and may or may not have been in the best interest of the organization. For instance, in one of the cases, the CEO of a nonprofit hospital had long hoped to compete with several physician-owned, for-profit laboratories in the community by reducing costs and improving quality. The CEO achieved considerable publicity (which is essential for the upwardly mobile hospital executive) when his hospital-based "community lab" concept became a reality. The pet-idea historical model was observed in one-third of the historical model cases and nearly 15 percent of all cases.

Pet-idea projects had an executive artfully steering the process used to carry out detailing. In these projects, the sponsor used three tactics to make his or her idea seem legitimate. Some pet-idea sponsors selectively interpreted environmental trends and other factors that made their preconceived idea seem like the response to an opportunity. Other sponsors identified as important problems that their idea could solve and marshalled support for this position. Still other sponsors carefully selected site visits or literature reviews that made their idea seem desirable.

The comparable-system-review tactic was used in nearly half of the pet-idea cases. For instance, executives steered subordinates toward helicopter-based emergency service (case 30) and a registration system (case 20) that were like those the executives would later propose and told subordinates to do a careful review of how the system operated. A literature review that supported or described a system similar to the pet idea was offered as an "interesting idea" in the primary nursing (case 21) and child and adolescent projects (case 29). In these cases, a subordinate was asked to do a careful review of this literature to see if the idea "meets our needs." Performance information was offered by the executive in about 20 percent of the cases. The executive justified these performance norms by citing previous experience in operating the same or a related program (e.g., preadmission testing, case 22). In about 40 percent of the pet-idea projects, the idea was offered as an answer to a need that had been previously articulated. In these cases, the proponent of the pet idea was instrumental in stipulating the performance gap that initiated this process. For example, in the community lab project (case 23), the executive planted reports that legitimized problems with commercial labs in the city. This made the commercialization of the hospital's lab seem like a response to an opportunity.

Linkage to the literature. The historical model process appears to be rooted in the behavior of people in organizations. For example, Pfiffner (1960) found that imitation and tradition were often used by managers to dictate what can be considered in a decision process. According to Cyert and March (1963), sponsors are prone to look to familiar sources for their ideas, which begins with their own experiences. Newell and Simon (1972) have demonstrated the same behavior experimentally, finding that people often use a "progressively deepening" approach. Only alternatives that keep the individual on familiar terrain

Types of Decision Processes

during problem solving are pursued. When past experience fails, the sponsor is moved to examine the practices of respected people or organizations. In each case, pragmatism, which stems from using proven ideas, appears to outweigh other considerations.

The problem-solving literature seems implicitly to endorse using the historical model approach. Copying the practices of others is not explicitly advocated, but the origin of ideas is treated as memory based. For example, Maier (1970) called for modifying known ideas to make them acceptable, which subordinates the creation of ideas to making the idea palatable. The theoretical arguments that lie behind the historical model find little use in stages 2 and 4.

Off-the-Shelf Processes

The off-the-shelf process activates the formulation, detailing, evaluation, and implementation stages. This process attempts to identify the best available ideas. The guarantor assumes that competition among ideas will produce a superior decision. Search is aggressive and overt. An off-the-shelf process was observed in 30 percent of the cases studied.

Search aids, such as a request for a proposal (RFP), were often used. In response to the needs stated in the RFP, vendors or consultants took one of their prepackaged solutions and tailored it to fit the organization's statement of need. A small-scale repeat of stage 3 was used to tailor and rationalize the prototype for its new user. The organization evaluated the programs submitted to select the one that seemed best suited to its situation. Evaluation is an important part of the off-the-shelf process as compared with the historical model process, in which this stage is not used. Stage 1 is used to write the RFP; stage 2 is skipped; stage 3 is used to shape the plan; and stage 4 is used to pick the best ideas from those submitted.

Variations. The key process variation was the scope of the search. Some projects *truncated* and others *extended* search. Search was extended when the sponsoring executive was unsure of potentials, and it was truncated when standards to judge a vendor's idea seemed clear. For example, if a CFO believed he or she had knowledge of the state of the art in financial analysis packages, a satisficing approach would be used when a package was identified that met his or her expectations. The more insecure CFO's would accumulate several competing packages and study them at length before making a choice.

Extended search. An extended search is used to extract criteria from the features of the competing ideas. This type of process was used when the controller in a city government patiently sought out proposals from a score of EDP manufacturers, in an attempt to learn what constituted an adequate system (Table 1, case 48). The extended search process occurred in a relatively small proportion of the cases (23 percent of the off-the-shelf cases and 7 percent of all cases).

Tactics used in the detailing stage of extended search projects were RFP's and matching, although most projects relied almost exclusively on RFP's. Projects included generating options for equipment (e.g., computerized EKG interpretation, case 49) and systems (e.g., an MIS, case 52). The one instance of search without an RFP involved knowing the requirements but not the options that could be matched to these requirements (case 51). When an option was uncovered it was rigorously evaluated to compare it with norms.

Truncated search. Generic criteria were used to select among vendor proposals in a truncated search process. This process was used to devise an obstetrics unit using a new concept called "birthing" (Table 1, case 32). Generic criteria were used to evaluate the birthing-unit ideas offered in consultants' off-the-shelf programs. A truncated search was carried out in most (77 percent) of the off-the-shelf cases and 24 percent of all cases.

Tactics used in the detailing stage of truncated search projects included RFP processes or sole-source contracting. Truncated search with a sole-source contractor was used in two-thirds of these projects. Apparently architects, auditors, and the like cultivate organizations until they achieve "consultant loyalty," much like the brand loyalty promoted by advertisers. Many executives seemed to overstate their ability to recognize a good system when they saw one. Using a sole-source consultant suggests that the scope of ideas considered is limited, creating some potential problems for organizations that apply satisficing criteria.

The remaining third of the truncated-search projects solicited competition among consultants and vendors. RFP's were used to solicit ideas or to find someone to carry out the project. For example, RFP's were sent to architects to initiate building renovations and to vendors to identify equipment options (e.g., the treatment planning simulator, case 31).

Linkage to the literature. The off-the-shelf solution is similar to what Mintzberg, Raisinghani, and Théorêt (1976) call ready-made. The process is used to identify available ideas and compare them. The vendor with a good-looking prototype is asked to shape it to fit the user's needs. Typically an RFP is written to identify vendors. The vendors use their prototype to sell the client on the merits of their stock solution. Mintzberg, Raisinghani, and Théorêt (1976) found, in the cases they studied, that jet aircraft purchases, equipment selection, data processing, and even mergers were carried out in this way. Twenty-eight percent of the Mintzberg, Raisinghani, and Théorêt cases were of this type, which is nearly identical to the proportion of off-the-shelf processes discovered in this research.

The diffusion-of-innovation literature describes organized attempts to coax potential users to adopt ideas like those devised by NASA that are nonclassified military discoveries (Lee and Bereano, 1981). Diffusion arises from the urge to share what appears to be a good idea. Typical examples are hardware (e.g., CT scanners or computers), systems (e.g., solar energy or information), and management tactics (e.g., executive compensation schemes). These innovations are often exploited by a consulting firm for their market potential.

Diffusion has been described as ideas in search of problems (Cyert and March, 1963). As a result, the problem is often shaped to fit available capabilities. Critics claim that the value of the diffused idea is often misrepresented as a result of under-

Types of Decision Processes

reporting of failures, assumptions of universal fit, after-the-fact rationalizations of benefits, and extensive problems in applying it (Waters, Salipante, and Notz, 1978). Because failures carry with them recriminations, they are quickly buried. User testimonials cited by the innovation diffuser tend to distort the prospect of success.

The setting itself can have powerful interactive effects. Even when the fit is good, the diffusion tends to be oversold. No one, client or vendor, has an incentive to be less than enthusiastic, and both tend to ignore the turmoil and chaos associated with making the change, say, from one EDP system to another. Finally, the ability to tailor can be oversold, leading to, for example, a data-processing system that cannot process the volume of inquiries or create the required number of reports.

Appraisal Processes

The appraisal process activates the formulation, evaluation, and implementation stages. This type of process begins with an idea that has an unknown or contentious value. A process that resembles the scientific method is used. The guarantor is similar to the norms of science.

Evaluation findings are used to win over the support needed to implement. For example, the chairman of the university pharmacy department sought to use a procedure for prescribing highly toxic drugs that predicted an ideal dosage based on the plasma concentration in its intended recipient (case 52). Because the procedure seemed likely to reduce hospitalization due to toxic reactions, it was proposed that Blue Cross reimburse the pharmacy for time spent in preparing the individualized doses. Blue Cross balked, because reimbursing a third party for pharmacy charges would set a precedent. Field trials were carried out to further document cost savings for various types of drugs and conditions that Blue Cross claimed limited the benefits of reduced hospitalization.

The appraisal process builds a strong motivation for action, but does so at the expense of fine tuning the idea, as in historical model and off-the-shelf planning processes. Detailing considers only issues that make an assessment feasible. All other detailing activities are assumed to be carried out on the job, during the shake-down period, as the idea is put into operation. Operators, department heads, and other management personnel often have to make procedural refinements to make the idea work. Appraisal processes were comparatively rare, occurring in less than 7 percent of the cases studied.

Variations. The appraisal can be covert, carried out to devise politically defensible arguments to support the idea, or overt, attempting to remove real uncertainty about the plan's value. A *covert* appraisal, as in the drug-dosing case, was carried out to develop politically effective arguments to justify implementation. The idea was modified to blunt the attacks of its adversaries. An *overt* appraisal is less defensive, more inquisitive, and more open to change. For example, the framework of benefits for government programs for the aging are fixed through legislative mandate and bureaucratic rule making, but programs from a cafeteria of options can be selected to meet local needs, revealed by an evaluation. The covert and overt variations of appraisal processes were found to occur with about equal frequency.

Further process distinctions can be made by examining the tactics used in the evaluation stage. Covert processes were used to verify the costs and benefits or to make current and proposed system comparisons. Some appraisals were used to structure arguments and gather support (Bower, 1970). Other appraisal efforts were postures, undertaken to placate key constituencies rather than to produce new information (Nutt, 1980). Still others were merely verifications, which produced just enough information to insure that current understandings were accurate (Nutt, 1979). For instance, initiators of the pharmacological dosing project (case 53) already knew the costs and benefits but did an evaluation to be doubly sure that the numbers were defensible. Defensive evaluations were undertaken in other cases when the costs or benefits were not clearly known. For instance, initiators in the OB-GYN project (case 55) determined the cost of modifying the unit to correct a forecasting error before they revealed the error.

Overt appraisals were carried out to document unknown benefits and, often, to assess through consumer input the reaction of potential users (e.g., cases 56 and 57). Public hearings were mounted to hear user views of proposed services. Such an approach is widely used in service organizations, such as public utilities commissions and power-sitting boards, which hear the views of interested citizens before granting rate increases or licenses to expand.

Linkage to the literature. Academics, bench scientists, and physicians are some of the individuals prone to use a research procedure. The most rational process imaginable to these individuals, the scientific method, is used as a model to identify the activities necessary for a project. There are at least two schools of thought that implicitly substitute analysis for synthesis: evaluation research and research on organizational effectiveness.

The rise in evaluation research in the public sector (e.g., Weiss, 1980, 1981) parallels the demise of federally sponsored planning in many social action programs. Evaluation is used to frame questions for the decision process, such that analytic inputs control the questions posed and the options considered. Analysis tends to take the place of idea creation.

Organizational effectiveness research (e.g., Goodman and Pennings, 1977) poses a similar dilemma for strategists and OD specialists. The score-card approach is better suited to private-sector organizations with capital intensive, single-product technologies, because goals are clear and comparatively easy to measure in such settings. However, researchers propose the approach for universal application, and quantifiable indices are used even when good proxies of organizational effectiveness are difficult, if not impossible, to identify. Bad proxies can create irrational organizational behavior, such as orphanages developing stringent placement criteria because their budget is census-based (Kerr, 1975).

Search Processes

The stages activated in a search process are formulation and implementation. A search process was used when a sponsor sensed a need but lacked a workable idea. Search differs from historical model and off-the-shelf processes in that the spon-

Types of Decision Processes

sor does not know where to look to find a viable idea. An RFP is not used, because needs are poorly understood. The sponsor mobilizes people he or she trusts, makes a stab at defining the needs, and waits for a reply. The sponsor and his or her colleagues carry out a search process that is passive and defensive to locate a viable idea that treats perceived symptoms. The search is expected to provide a full-blown idea that needs little, if any, detailing. Evaluation is not used. Once a workable idea was discovered, the sponsor saw no necessity to test it. The force of the idea was seen by the sponsor as sufficient rationale to promote adoption. Search processes were found to be used in 7 percent of the cases.

Variations. The search process seemed logical to use when the sponsor was faced with a need regarded as trivial, not meriting much of his or her attention, or a need that was ill-defined. An ill-defined need is threatening, because a sponsor's inability to define a need may raise questions about his or her competence. The two dimensions of search processes are the scope of involvement — whether only the sponsor is involved or subordinates are also involved — and need perception — whether needs are perceived as trivial or as ill-defined. The combinations of scope of involvement and need perception define four variations in the search process.

A sequestered search was carried out when the sponsor faced a need that was ill-defined and threatening. For instance, the CEO of a hospital became alarmed at the frequency of patient complaints and his inability to classify them (case 58). Fearing that the hospital's practices would lead to legal action, the CEO began a passive and defensive search. While attending a professional meeting, the CEO discovered that the functions of a model patient-relations department being proposed by the American Hospital Association seemed to match his needs, so he established a similar department. A sequestered search process occurred in 60 percent of the search cases.

An open search was used for needs seen as trivial, and subordinates were brought in to help. The sponsor defined the need in vague terms and asked his or her subordinates to seek a solution. For example, alleged excessive time to dispense medications caused a hospital executive to charge his subordinates with finding a new dispensing system (case 61). An open-search process was used in 40 percent of the open-search cases. The actual use of an open search may be considerably higher, however, because organizations are unlikely to report on projects they see as inconsequential.

A casual search would be mounted by the sponsor for a need seen as trivial, and *a bold search* would involve subordinates in a search for a solution to an ill-defined need. These possible search approaches were not observed. Decisions that result from a casual search may be seen by the executive as inconsequential, and thus not be reported, and decisions that stem from a bold search may be threatening (because the inability to define a problem raises questions about the executive's competence), so executives do not use this type of process.

The sequestered and open-search processes both used peers and the literature as tactics to seek out ideas. Peers seem to be an important source of passive-search ideas. For instance, when an organization developed data-processing bottlenecks (case 59), the CEO checked with colleagues to see what they had done when faced with a similar problem. The literature (practitioner journals and conferences) was the other major source of ideas. For instance, when turned down for a CT scanner by a regulatory agency, a hospital CEO read up on innovative scanner programs, looking for one that allowed him to skirt the regulatory process (case 60). He found that a mobile scanner, shared by several hospitals, was not reviewable under the regulatory agency's guidelines.

Linkage to the literature. A search-based process is related to the passive-search approach identified by Mintzberg, Raisinghani, and Théorêt (1976). A passive search occurs when an executive lets people know that he or she is looking for a way to deal with a need. The sponsor assesses ideas that emerge, comparing them to preset expectations. Aspirations put expectations in a state of flux when viable ideas are either easy or hard to find (March and Simon, 1958). A concept of workability emerges, making evaluation a perfunctory comparison to expectations. Mintzberg, Raisinghani, and Théorêt (1976) found that 16 percent of their cases were search based, nearly three times the proportion found in this study.

Both March and Simon (1958) and Etzioni (1964) advocate a search approach, stressing the notion of learning and the application of transient norms. Home purchasers and car buyers face similar dilemmas: the next house or car lot they visit may provide an option that has better features than the currently favored option. Churchman (1971) and others recognize that this type of search, carried to an extreme, leads to very high search costs. Researchers have proposed cut-off rules that limit search time, the number of options, and the like, as well as satisficing criteria (March and Simon, 1958). Search planning has both a normative and a behavioral root. It is both recommended (e.g., Etzioni, 1964; March and Simon, 1958) and found to be used in practice (Mintzberg, Raisinghani, and Théorêt, 1976).

Nova Processes

A nova process uses all stages — formulation, conceptualization, detailing, evaluation, and implementation — in an attempt to create an innovative plan. The guarantor of innovation is applied. New ideas are created to challenge approaches in use by organizations. These new ideas are sought without specific reference to the practices of others. Stage 2, in which options are identified and pursued in subsequent stages, is particularly important in a nova process. The nova process is the *only* process with activity in stage 2. Nova processes were observed in 15 percent of the cases studied.

Variations. Nova processes are supported by internal and outside consultants. The *internal consultant* is drawn from the organization's staff. The *outside consultant* is usually selected from among individuals or organizations known to the user, often on a sole-source basis. For example, the consultant was often drawn from the firm that provided auditing services, from an old-boy network of friends and former associates, or from organizations thought to be high in prestige. The process differs from the off-the-shelf process, because the consultant sells process, not a product, and because the sponsor asks for or tolerates innovation-seeking activities. A wide variety of

Types of Decision Processes

projects were carried out with these variations on the nova theme. The internal and external consultant nova process variations occurred about equally in the cases.

Nova processes exhibited systematic differences from other processes in their generation of alternatives. The tactics used by staff and consultants to identify solutions could be classified as problem-corrective or as idea-driven. The corrective tactic was to respond to complaints and propose a modification to overcome the identified malfunction. Outside consultants seem prone to be problem-reactive, perhaps fearing that they may offend a client by attempting to redefine the problem. For example, in the ER department project (case 69), the consultant never questioned the origin of the delays. As a result, a plan was quickly adopted that reduced the delays by changing hospital procedures. Eventually the CEO's use of on-call physicians was identified as the real cause of the delays, rendering the project trivial. Staff-managed projects had similar difficulties. Staff members were also reluctant to challenge the sponsor's definition of the problem and often limited their scope of inquiry to the immediate neighborhood of the problem symptoms (Newell and Simon, 1972). For example, in the medical record plan (case 63), no one questioned the feasibility of processing certain types of the medical staff's patient information. Eventually the medical record system was rejected because it failed to protect the confidentiality of patient records and, not incidentally, because it would have revealed the medical faculty's private-practice income.

Idea-driven projects were more than twice as common for internal staff consultants than for outside consultants. Apparently outside consultants feel more constrained than internal staff to offer ideas that depart from the traditional programs and policies used by the organization. For example, innovative ideas were solicited from the telephone operators in case 64, from the nursing staff in case 65, the administration in case 66, and the pharmacy staff in case 68. Only the hospital consolidation project (case 72) and the medical office building project (case 70) sought innovative ideas from outside consultants. This suggests that executives should be more attuned to the outside consultants' unwillingness to challenge stipulations of needs and should encourage them to offer new ideas.

Linkage to the literature. Churchman (1979), Simon (1969), and many others are advocates of nova approaches. The process is engaged to provide what Mintzberg, Raisinghani, and Théorêt (1976) call a "custom-made" solution. (Over 55 percent of the projects reported in their study developed custom-made solutions, compared to 15 percent of cases in this study.) Those who advocate custom-made solutions also call for innovation (e.g., Gordon, 1971). Typically, theorists contend that having multiple options, which are detailed and winnowed to select options that are then formally evaluated, leads to the best results. This permits a comparison among potentially viable courses of action, which often leads to a superior synthesis (Mason and Mitroff, 1981). But perceptions of time constraints and high costs drastically limit the number of alternatives developed by a nova process (Mintzberg, Raisinghani, and Théorêt, 1976), and multiple alternatives are therefore seldom developed. In other ways, however, the nova process is similar to the process recommended by theorists, in that all stages are activated and new ideas are sought.

PROCESS-EVOKING STIMULI

To determine when organizations use these processes, the process types were matched to the stimuli that appear to have provoked them. This matching depicts the type of situation that seems to initiate some processes and not others.

Decisions are recognized as arising from problems or opportunities (Mintzberg, 1973) or crisis (Smart and Vertinsky, 1977). A problem has multiple stimuli, an opportunity is evoked by an idea, and a crisis is precipitated by fewer stimuli, which demand immediate attention (Mintzberg, Raisinghani, and Théorêt, 1976). A crisis has importance and immediacy.

The evoking stimuli of projects in Table 1 were sorted into problem, opportunity, and crisis categories to relate the process types to stimuli. A review of activities in the formulation stage (Table 1) was used to determine if the project was initiated to deal with a problem or an opportunity. Crisis projects were identified following Billings, Milburn, and Schaalman (1980), who used resource demands and time pressure as proxies for crisis. In this study, executives filled out a questionnaire for each project in which they assessed time pressure (low, moderate, or high) and the resource demands (far below, below, same, above, or far above the typical project budget). When the project called for resources far above the typical project and time pressure was high, the project was classified as evoked by a crisis (Table 4).

The data in Table 4 relate each process to process-evoking stimuli. The frequency of use of the various processes suggests how organizations respond to situations perceived as problems, opportunities, or crises. Overall, crisis-evoked processes were found to occur comparatively infrequently (13 percent). Opportunities stimulated a process in one-quarter of the cases and problems in nearly two-thirds of the cases. Mintzberg, Raisinghani, and Théorêt (1976) found 44 percent of their projects to be opportunity-evoked, 36 percent problem-evoked, and 25 percent crisis-evoked. The frequency with which opportunity-evoked and crisis-evoked processes occurred in the Mintzberg, Raisinghani, and Théorêt study is nearly twice that reported in Table 4. This discrepancy could be due to the smaller data base in their study, to the way projects in the two studies were selected, or to other factors.

Crisis-Evoked Processes

Thirteen percent of the cases were termed crisis-evoked. In responding to a crisis, organizations used the provincial historical model in 30 percent of the cases, truncated off-the-shelf search in 30 percent, and a consultant-driven nova process in 20 percent of the cases. Open search, overt appraisal, and staff-driven nova processes were not used. Organizations may not view these processes as a useful way to deal with a crisis.

Crisis-evoked projects had no special label or category and often appeared suddenly when either dissatisfaction or complaints reached crisis proportions and precipitated the need for immediate action. For example, in the cash-flow management case (case 8, Table 1), the discovery of a cash-flow deficiency

Types of Decision Processes

and the size of potential losses called for immediate action. In another case, new certification requirements to maintain a residency teaching program identified space deficiencies that prompted construction (case 35). In case 36, the hospital's CEO had to demonstrate to a skeptical board of trustees the value of an investment in a subsidiary consulting firm.

Opportunity-Evoked Processes

Opportunities proved to be the key process-evoking stimuli in 25 percent of the cases studied. An opportunity was found to stimulate all variations of the historical model and off-the-shelf processes and proved to be the only stimulant for the overt-appraisal and open-search processes. Organizations examined the practices of others, sought expertise with an RFP, evaluated the opportunity, or looked to see how others responded to the opportunity. Key stimuli were technological innovations (e.g., computerized EKG's and CT scanners), new service possibilities (e.g., burn care and open heart surgery), internal operations (e.g., MIS), new discoveries (pharmacological dosing), and the sudden availability of new resources.

Table 4

Process Type by Stimulus

Process type and variations	Problem	Type of Stimulus Opportunity	Crisis
Historical model			
Provincial (N=15)	60%*	20%	20%
Enriched (N=4)	50%	50%	0%
Pet idea (N=11)	73%	27%	0%
Off-the-shelf			
Truncated search (N=17)	66%	17%	17%
Extended search (N=5)	60%	40%	0%
Appraisal			
Covert (N=3)	33%	33%	33%
Overt (N=2)	0%	100%	0%
Search			
Sequestered (N=3)	67%	0%	20%
Open (N=2)	0%	100%	0%
Nova			
Staff-driven (N=6)	100%	0%	0%
Consultant-driven (N=5)	60%	0%	40%
Totals (N=73)	62%	25%	13%

*Percentage of cases represented by the provincial historical model process variation.

Nova and the sequestered-search processes were not used to explore a perceived opportunity. The availability of ideas makes sequestered search appear silly. The opportunity may imply that an innovation-seeking process is unnecessary, because an innovation is available before the process begins.

Problem-Evoked Processes

Problems stimulated two-thirds of projects. Only the overt-appraisal and open-search processes were *not* used when the problem was stipulated. An overt appraisal cannot be carried out, because a problem, not a solution to be assessed, has been offered. Without an idea to assess, the estimation of merits would be an illogical way to proceed. Open searches were not undertaken, because ambiguity had been cleared away by a stipulation of the problem, rendering such a search illogical. Responding to the problem, even if this dealt with symptoms and surface concerns, was the only legitimate way for the organization to proceed. The most commonly used processes were the historical model, off-the-shelf, and nova processes, which were used in 87 percent of the problem-stimulated processes studied.

RECONCILING PROCESS DESCRIPTIONS WITH OTHER DECISION MODELS

In the garbage can model proposed by Cohen, March, and Olsen (1972), solutions are used to formulate problems, because, as Wildavsky (1969) pointed out, managers don't know what they want until they see what they can get. Past experiences and current discoveries produce alternatives that are used to identify problems and thereby specify needs. For the problem-evoked cases in this study (Table 4), this matching was found to be problem-to-solution, not solution-to-problem, as the garbage can model implies. Performance-gap information was often present at the outset and typically in a form that suggested that the gap could not have been a reconstruction. Needs were articulated and searches were conducted to find ways to fill these needs. RFP's, site visits, and nova processes were used to discover ways to deal with perceived performance gaps. The competition among alternatives often promoted a lively debate about the merits of a particular historical model or vendor proposal.

When opportunities stimulated decision making, however, the process resembled the garbage can model. The availability of a new technology or a good idea was the dominant force that drove the process of inquiry in these cases. Ideas were used to determine needs. For example, executives with pet ideas could be described as creating a process in which solutions were looking for problems in 16 percent of the cases studied. In 19 percent of the cases, the installation of a new system, such as computerized EKG interpretation, was preceded by a recognition that the technology was potentially valuable. Thus, a process similar to the garbage can model was used in a minority (35 percent) of the cases studied, but not to the degree that Cohen, March, and Olsen (1972) imply that it would be used. Furthermore, the rationale of the pet-idea and opportunity-driven processes seems clearer than that in the garbage can model. The opportunity-driven processes appear to have been motivated by a recognition that an idea was useful and the pet-idea processes by an executive's attempt at self-promotion. These decision processes were neither capricious nor whimsical, and each had a clear purpose. Executives were deliberate and manipulative in the pet-idea projects but were not impulsive. No sudden changes were noted in what was deemed important.

Possibilities for improved performance called for action when a new system was discovered. Solution seeking resembled Weick's (1979) notions of sense making in opportunity-driven projects. The sponsor seemed to require a tangible solution to discuss and through this discussion developed an understand-

Types of Decision Processes

ing of what *could* be done. The commitment to action appeared to flow from this sense-making process. The simulations used by Cohen, March, and Olsen (1972) may not have been able to identify motivations that provoke pet-idea and opportunity-driven processes.

March (1981) contended that organizational action taking can be related to rule, rational change model, learning, conflict, contagion, and regeneration processes. With the exception of rule following, which requires SOP's, all of March's processes have analogues in the process types identified in this research. None of the cases were routine, so SOP's were not observed. It is interesting to note, however, that the perspective offered by March (1981) failed to explain why nova and enriched historical processes occur. Such processes may represent a sophisticated understanding of idea development that goes beyond March's generative rules. Action taking with innovation-seeking attributes was found in nearly 21 percent of the cases studied.

Finally the processes discovered can be mapped to Thompson's (1967) computational, compromise, judgmental, and inspirational strategies. Decision makers in this study typically framed the decision by treating outcomes as clear. This act created a sense of security (possibly false) from which the process unfolded. Furthermore, many of the decision makers seemed to recognize limitations in understanding cause-and-effect relations. In most cases, the process was undertaken to clear away this ambiguity. As a result, most of the decisions that were studied could be classified as following Thompson's judgmental strategy. The nova, search, off-the-shelf, and historical model processes attempt to find a solution that can sweep away causal uncertainty. These processes represent 93 percent of the decision processes studied, suggesting that a judgmental approach may dominate the tactics used by organizations in decision making.

Compromise tactics call for the decision maker to treat outcome preferences as uncertain. This situation was seldom observed, suggesting that compromise tactics are seldom used. This may explain why bargaining (Thompson's compromise strategy) had so small a role in the cases. Only in the covert-appraisal cases, where a solution existed with contentious merits, did the decision makers frame the situation as having uncertain outcome preference and certain causality, which was observed in only 4 percent of the cases.

Computational tactics were used in the overt-appraisal process. Beliefs about causality were believed to be clear, because a solution existed that was thought to merit evaluation. These tactics represented only 3 percent of the cases, suggesting that few decisions are made with a computational approach, which may explain why Mintzberg, Raisinghani, and Théorêt (1976) found that normative methods are seldom used in decision making.

Inspirational action taking was not observed. Uncertainty seemed intolerable, causing responsible executives to assume it away. Causation or, more frequently, desired results were treated as clear and specifiable.

DISCUSSION AND CONCLUSIONS

This study had several limitations. First, the participating organizations were cooperative volunteers and predominately service organizations. As a result, the frequencies with which the processes, variations, and tactics were observed to be used must be regarded as preliminary estimates. Second, a frame was imposed on the data to make its collection and representation feasible. Such a frame may have created an artificial sense of order. The actual process may have been far more chaotic than that described, and the chaos may have had important messages that were lost. Third, only a few contextual factors were considered. For example, perceived uncertainty and the need for change were not formally determined. Anderson and Paine (1975) contend that these factors play important roles in strategic choice.

This research, however, adds to the store of knowledge about how organizations carry out the process of decision making. These findings bear on several issues, including the extent to which questionable tactics and normative methods are used by organizations. Departures from recommended procedure provide a commentary on how well organizations appear to deal with the identification, refinement, and selection of solutions and their implementation.

Use of Normative Models and Preferred Practices

The analysis of process provides a basis for observations about innovation and innovation-seeking processes, the value and use of normative processes and methods, and the solution-centered behavior noted in a majority of the cases.

Views of innovation. Nova processes are regarded by Churchman (1979) and others as ideal because the insights about needs and possible solutions developed in a nova process often lead to innovative ideas. Executives, however, seldom use nova processes. They prefer to copy the ideas of others or to search for ready-made solutions instead of seeking innovation.

Success seems related to a different approach, which Schön (1983) called "reflection in action." According to Schön, the successful executive accepts the uncertainty in perceived needs, reflects on the inherent confusion in these needs, and conducts the equivalent of an experiment that varies *both* means and ends. New theories or explanations are constructed that attempt to explain away the confusion and the uncertainty. The acceptance of uncertainty, the search for new theories and understandings (innovation), multiple means (several alternatives), and fluid assumptions about ends (avoiding dogmatic need stipulations) characterize the successful decision maker. Schön calls for what Thompson (1967) described as the inspirational strategy for decision making, used when both causal relations and ends are uncertain. The decision makers observed in this study often found uncertainty intolerable, which enticed them to create an artificial certainty: the inspirational strategy seems to be avoided. For example, an RFP rapidly produces tangible results but requires the sponsor to be explicit about needs, which are often far from clear early in the process. As a result, ends were often prematurely fixed and a single means quickly identified, setting in motion a process that stifled innovation.

Types of Decision Processes

Others take a different view of innovation. For instance, March (1981) calls innovation "foolishness," because being the first to experiment with or use a new idea can be deadly. Managers find that recriminations for failure have more important implications for their advancement than does the development of new ideas (Ritti and Funkhouser, 1979). Incentives, professionalism, and slack (Daft and Becker, 1978) help to promote innovation but cannot fully overcome this basic conservatism. Managers feel strongly about demonstrating workability before committing to a new idea. Such demonstrations are often impossible, suggesting that innovation will be rare in organizations (Cohen and March, 1974). Using this perspective, the frequency of innovation observed in this research (15 percent, nova processes), seems a more accurate measure than the 55 percent frequency reported by Mintzberg, Raisinghani, and Théorêt (1976).

Exceptions are found in executives who seek to set a new mood. Real changes as well as symbolic acts are used to convey this intention (Christensen, 1976). See, for example, the "Pride Program," case 66, in Table 1. Some risk taking is justified when a new leader arrives on the scene, to demonstrate that the organization is being revitalized, and this may be one of the few instances in which an organization willingly initiates an innovation-seeking process.

Normative methods. Nothing remotely resembling the normative methods described in the literature was carried out. Not even hybrid variations were observed. Either managers have little knowledge of these methods or find them naive. The sequence of problem definition, alternative generation, refinement, and selection, called for by nearly every theorist, seems rooted in rational arguments, not behavior. Executives do not use this process. Instead, ideas drive the process, which is used to rationalize and shape the idea or determine if it has value. The approach used to look for ideas has a dramatic effect on how the decision process unfolds, dictating the activities that are undertaken and their sequence. For example, some organizations have their computer operations tailor-made, others purchase a computer and modify its software, and still others install computers and software developed by vendors, with little, if any, changes.

Executives in this study seem to have had firm predispositions about how the process of looking for ideas should unfold. Bobbitt and Ford (1980) contend that these attitudes are influenced by the executive's belief structures and past experiences. This suggests that a decision process is used because it fits the executive's notions of pragmatism. These processes will be applied repeatedly if they appear to have produced acceptable results. Contingency models (Allison, 1971; Vroom and Yetton, 1973; Linestone et al., 1981; Nutt, 1982), which call for the executive to select a process that fits the situation, were not observed. Because of these belief structures, there may be significant barriers to overcome before a contingency approach to process selection is used by organizations.

Miles, Snow, and Pfeffer (1974) believe that an expanded range of search is one of the keys to success. However, Bobbitt and Ford (1980) contend that executives who have a low tolerance for ambiguity and a high need for structure will adopt a decision process that has a narrow zone of search. The frequency with which the provincial historical model and truncated off-the-shelf processes were used suggests that a restricted search occurs quite often, which limits the executive's range of discretion. The scanning for strategic ideas, called for by Child (1972) and others, is limited. The provincial and pet-idea-based historical model processes, the truncated off-the-shelf process, and the search processes, used in 65 percent of the cases studied, dramatically limit this discretionary range.

Solution centering. Executives initiate processes that create concrete ideas as soon as possible (Mintzberg, 1973). A solution-centered process, which quickly identified the features of the plan, was used in 84 percent of the cases studied. There was a clear preference and, indeed, often a demand for concrete ideas quite early in the process. This leads to the off-the-shelf, historical model, and evaluative processes, because each provides a tangible plan in the early stages of the process.

These processes may have several limitations. First, a solution-centered process may result in single-loop learning, which Argyris and Schön (1978) argue limits the scope of learning and thereby the insights that can be gained. The frequency with which organizations used these processes corresponds to the Argyris and Schön findings that most organizations are single-loop learners. Second, Maier (1970) found that a fixation on either problems or solutions is undesirable, suggesting that more problem centering in a decision process should improve results. Delbecq's (1967) contention that executives should stay problem-centered as they explore possibilities also supports this view. However, what seems to be a premature commitment to action is strongly rooted in the behavior of executives. This suggests that technically sound decision methods that also have strong behavioral underpinnings are needed. For example, techniques like stakeholder analysis (Mason and Mitroff, 1981), which offer a sponsor a way to consider the specifics of an idea but also explore intentions, may be particularly valuable in improving results. Such a technique reconciles behavioral and theoretical arguments.

The Paradox of Problem Definition

Executives are admonished to avoid solving the wrong problem (e.g., Mitroff, 1974). However, there are few tests that can be applied to determine if the "correct" problem has been selected. For example, consider an organization that has a cash-flow problem, in which their receivable and payable accounts become unbalanced. Should the cash-flow problem be attacked or should the problem be defined as one of needing to increase revenue? If one attacks the revenue-generation problem, a redesign of products or services might be considered, along with marketing efforts to identify new customers. If the cash-flow problem is attacked, the solution becomes a financial analysis of ways to balance the flow of funds within the organization. It is almost trivial to observe that these solutions are dramatically different, and yet organizations often accept problems that channel their energies and restrict their scope of inquiry, as this example illustrates.

Types of Decision Processes

Identifying the problem is one of the most fundamental of managerial paradoxes. Problems can be viewed in terms of the systems they imply, which have a hierarchial relationship. Every system can be thought of as a part of a larger system and, at the same time, containing many small systems. Thus, choosing the scope may be the key act in decision making, because the nature of the solution is dictated by this decision. Two tests can be used to select scope: control and salience. The executive may choose to restrict his or her purview to those systems over which he or she has control. The salience test is used to select a problem that stands out from other potential problem definitions. The prominence of some problems gives them a sense of urgency, as compared to others. To make the selection of an appropriate scope less arbitrary, system theorists call for the sponsor to compare systems that are one level up and one level down from the salient system.

The difficulties of problem definition relate to the role of options in a decision process. Virtually every theorist recommends that more than one option should be developed. Furthermore, empirical studies have shown that processes with multiple options outperform processes that lack them (Abernathy and Rosenbloom, 1969; Janis and Mann, 1977).

Several of the archetypal processes described in this paper generated options. For example, in an off-the-shelf process, an organization searches for vendors, who offer their prototypes. In the historical model process a variety of organizations may be visited, each of which becomes an option or has ideas that can be used to construct an option. This conception of an alternative can be described as one in which options are narrowly defined. Each option flows from a particular definition of a problem that specifies a particular scope of inquiry. Churchman (1971) pointed out that multiple alternatives or options are used to validate or guarantee that a decision process has produced a desirable result. The competition among ideas serves as a guarantor that the product has merit. The more limited the number of alternatives considered, the more limited the guarantee.

A new type of guarantor can be defined from the generation of broadly defined options, that is, a set of options for each of several levels of inquiry. For instance, options for balancing accounts receivable and accounts payable are dramatically different from options that compare account balancing with revenue generation. The comparison of broadly defined options may generate insights that are missing when a decision process deals with narrowly defined options. If so, a new guarantor for decision processes has been created. In addition, calling on a decision process to provide broadly defined options resolves some of the dilemmas in selecting an appropriate level for inquiry. Pragmatic tests can still be applied, such as limiting the scope of inquiry to the sponsor's purview. However, adding broadly defined options takes some of the pressure off the salience criteria, which reduces the prospect that the decision process will perpetually respond to symptoms.

The nature of organizational decision processes is still but dimly understood. More research is needed before a coherent statement can be made about how organizations make decisions. For instance, more study is needed to determine how problems are screened and selected as important. This suggests problem selection as a key topic for future inquiry. Nevertheless, the provisional conclusions about the failure to use normative methods, innovation, and solution-centered biases should offer fertile ground for future work on organizational decision processes.

REFERENCES

Abernathy, W. J., and R. S. Rosenbloom
1969 "Parallel strategies in developmental projects." Management Science, Vol. 15, No. 10.

Ackoff, Russell L.
1981 Creating the Corporate Future. New York: Wiley.

Allison, Graham T.
1971 Essence of a Decision: Explaining the Cuban Missile Crisis. Boston: Little, Brown.

Anderson, Carl R., and Frank T. Paine
1975 "Managerial perceptions and strategic behavior." Academy of Management Journal, 18: 811–823.

Argyris, Chris, and Donald A. Schön
1978 Organizational Learning: A Theory of Action Perspective. Reading, MA: Addison-Wesley.

Armstrong, J. Scott
1982 "The value of formal planning for strategic decisions: Review of empirical research." Strategic Management Journal, 3: 197–211.

Billings, Robert S., Thomas W. Milburn, and Mary Lou Schaalman
1980 "Crisis perception: A theoretical and empirical analysis." Administrative Science Quarterly, 25: 300–315.

Bobbitt, H. Randolph, and Jeffrey D. Ford
1980 "Decision maker choice as a determinant of organizational structure." Academy of Management Review, 15: 13–24.

Bower, Joseph L.
1970 Managing the Resource Allocation Process: A Study of Corporate Planning and Investment. Homewood, IL: Irwin.

Bresser, Rudi K., and Ronald C. Bishop
1983 "Dysfunctional effects of formal planning: Two theoretical explanations." Academy of Management Review, 8: 588–599.

Child, John
1972 "Organizational structure, environment and performance: The role of strategic choice." Sociology, 6: 1–22.

Christensen, S.
1976 "Decision making and socialization." In James G. March and Johan P. Olsen (eds.), Ambiguity and Choice in Organizations: 351–385. Bergen, Norway: Universitetsforlaget.

Churchman, C. West
1971 The Design of Inquiring Systems. New York: Basic Books.
1979 The Systems Approach, rev. ed. New York: Dell.

Cohen, Michael D., and James G. March
1974 Leadership and Ambiguity: The American College President. New York: McGraw-Hill.

Cohen, Michael D., James G. March, and Johan P. Olsen
1972 "A garbage can model of organizational choice." Administrative Science Quarterly, 17: 1–25.

Cyert, Richard M., and James G. March
1963 A Behavioral Theory of the Firm. Englewood Cliffs, NJ: Prentice-Hall.

Daft, Richard L.
1983 "Learning the craft of organizational research." Academy of Management Review, 8: 539–546.

Daft, Richard L., and Selwyn W. Becker
1978 The Innovative Organization. New York: Elsevier.

Delbecq, André
1967 "The management of decision making in the firm: Three strategies for the types of decision making." Academy of Management Journal, 10: 329–339.

Delbecq, André, and Andrew H. Van de Ven
1971 "A group process model for program planning and problem identification." Journal of Applied Behavioral Science, 7: 466–492.

Etzioni, Amitai
1964 Modern Organizations. Englewood Cliffs, NJ: Prentice-Hall.

Gluick, William
1976 Business Policy, Strategy Formation, and Management. New York: McGraw-Hill.

Goodman, Paul S., and Johannes M. Pennings
1977 New Perspectives on Organizational Effectiveness. San Francisco: Jossey-Bass.

Gordon, W. J.
1971 Synectics. New York: Harper & Row.

Hofer, Charles W., and Dan Schendel
1978 Strategic Management: Analytical Concepts. St. Paul, MN: West Publishing.

Huse, Edgar F.
1975 Organization Development and Change. St. Paul, MN: West Publishing.

Janis, Irving J., and Leon Mann
1977 Decision Making: A Psychological Analysis of Conflict, Choice, and Commitment. New York: Free Press.

Kerr, Steven
1975 "On the folly of rewarding A while hoping for B." Academy of Management Journal, 19: 769–783.

Lee, Alfred M., and Philip L. Bereano
1981 "Developing technology assessment methodology: Some insights and experiences." Technology Forecasting and Social Change, 19: 15–31.

Linstone, Harold, Arnold J. Meltsner, Marvin Adelson, Arnold Mysior, Linda Umbdenstock, Bruce Clary, Donna Wagner, and Jack Shuman
1981 "The multiple perspective concept: With applications to other decision areas." Technological Forecasting and Social Change, 20: 275–325.

Locke, Edwin A., K. N. Shaw, L. M. Saari, and G. P. Latham
1981 "Goal setting and task performance, 1969–1980." Psychological Bulletin, 90: 125–152.

Maier, Norma R. F. W.
1970 Problem Solving and Creativity: In Individuals and Groups. New York: Brooks/Cole.

Types of Decision Processes

March, James G.
1981 "Footnotes to organizational change." Administrative Science Quarterly, 26: 563–577.

March, James G., and Herbert A. Simon
1958 Organizations. New York: Wiley.

Mason, Richard O., and Ian L. Mitroff
1981 Challenging Strategic Planning Assumptions. New York: Wiley-Interscience.

McKelvey, Bill
1978 "Organizational systematics: Taxonomic lessons from biology." Management Science, 24: 1428–1440.

Miles, Raymond E., Charles C. Snow, and Jeffrey Pfeffer
1974 "Organization-environment: Concepts and issues." Industrial Relations, 13: 244–264.

Mintzberg, Henry
1973 The Nature of Managerial Work. New York: Harper & Row.

Mintzberg, Henry, Duru Raisinghani, and André Théorêt
1976 "The structure of 'unstructured' decision processes." Administrative Science Quarterly, 21: 246–275.

Mintzberg, Henry, and James A. Waters
1982 "Tracking strategy in an entrepreneurial firm." Academy of Management Journal, 25: 465–499.

Mitroff, Ian I.
1974 "On systematic problem solving and the error of the third kind." Behavioral Science, 9: 383–393.

Nadler, Gerald
1970 Work Design: A Systems Concept. Georgetown, Ontario: Irwin.
1981 The Planning and Design Approach. New York: Wiley.

Newell, Allen, and Herbert A. Simon
1972 Human Problem Solving. Englewood Cliffs, NJ: Prentice-Hall.

Nutt, Paul C.
1979 "Calling out and calling off the dogs: Managerial diagnosis in organizations." Academy of Management Review, 4: 203–214.
1980 "On managed evaluation processes." Technological Forecasting and Social Change, 17: 313–328.
1982 "Hybrid planning methods." Academy of Management Review, 7: 442–454.

1983 "Stage-based and process reconstruction paradigms for planning research." Paper presented at the Academy of Management National Meeting, Dallas, August.
1984 Planning Methods. New York: Wiley.

Pfiffner, John M.
1960 "Administrative rationality." Public Administration Review, 20: 125–132.

Pike, Richard L.
1967 Language in Relation to a Unified Theory of the Structure of Human Behavior. The Hague: Mouton.

Pounds, William
1969 "The process of problem finding." Industrial Management Review, Fall: 1–19.

Ritti, R. Richard, and G. Ray Funkhouser
1979 The Ropes to Skip and the Ropes to Know: Studies in Organizational Behavior, rev. ed. Columbus, OH: Grid Publishing.

Schön, Donald A.
1983 The Reflective Practitioner: How Professionals Think in Action. New York: Basic Books.

Simon, Herbert A.
1969 The Science of the Artificial. Cambridge, MA: MIT Press.
1977 The New Science of Management Decision, rev. ed. Englewood Cliffs, NJ: Prentice-Hall.

Smart, Carolyne, and Ilan Vertinsky
1977 "Designs for crisis decision units." Administrative Science Quarterly, 22: 640–657.

Soelberg, Peer O.
1967 "Unprogrammed decision making." Industrial Management Review, 8(2): 19–29.

Steiner, George
1969 Top Management Planning. New York: Macmillan.

Thompson, James D.
1967 Organizations in Action. New York: McGraw-Hill.

Vroom, Victor, and P. Yetton
1973 Leadership and Decision Making. Pittsburgh: The University of Pittsburgh Press.

Warfield, John N.
1978 Societal Systems. New York: Wiley.

Waters, James A., Paul F. Salipante, Jr., and William W. Notz
1978 "The experimenting organization: Using the results of behavioral science research." Academy of Management Review, 3: 483–492.

Weick, Karl E.
1979 The Social Psychology of Organizing, rev. ed. Reading, MA: Addison-Wesley.

Weiss, Carol H.
1980 "Knowledge creep and decision accretion." Knowledge, Creation, Diffusion, Utilization, 1: 381–404.
1981 "Use of social science research in organizations: The constrained repertoire theory." In H. Stein (ed.), Organization and Human Services: 180–204. Philadelphia: Temple University Press.

Wildavsky, Aaron
1969 "Rescuing policy analysis for PPBS." Public Administration Review, March/April: 189–202.

Witte, E.
1972 "Field research on complex decision making processes — The phase theory." International Studies of Management and Organization, Fall: 156–182.

Yin, Robert K.
1981 "The case study crisis: Some answers." Administrative Science Quarterly, 26: 58–65.

Zwicky, Franz
1968 Discovery, Invention, Research through the Morphological Approach. New York: Macmillan.

[11]

Decision Making by Objection and the Cuban Missile Crisis

Paul A. Anderson

The standard description of the task of making a decision — to identify goals, search for alternatives, predict the consequences, evaluate the alternatives, select the best course of action — has been roundly criticized both for overestimating the information-processing capacity of individuals and for misrepresenting the social nature of decisions in an organizational context. These critiques have been far more successful in refuting the standard description of making a decision than in proposing well-developed, empirically based alternative descriptions. A detailed analysis of archival documents from the Cuban missile crisis suggests that U.S. decision making displayed three notable characteristics: decision making during the missile crisis involved sequential choice over an array of noncompeting courses of action, the act of making decisions led to the discovery of goals, and decision makers were more concerned with avoiding failures than with achieving successes. These deviations from the standard task description are used to develop an alternative characterization of the decision-making task, decision making by objection, which emphasizes sequential choice, goal discovery, and the avoidance of failures.•

INTRODUCTION

In conventional terms, the task of making a decision can be decomposed into five subtasks: (1) identifying the relevant goals; (2) searching for alternative courses of action; (3) predicting the consequences of following each alternative; (4) evaluating each alternative in terms of its consequences for goal achievement; and (5) selecting the best alternative for achieving the goal. This description of the decision-making task has been subject to two varieties of criticism. The first challenges the task description from an information-processing perspective and argues that, because of limited information-processing capacity, individuals can at best only roughly approximate the rational computational ideal implied in the task description. If individuals are not up to the task, neither are organizations (though they should do somewhat better in certain respects). The path from goals to choice, moreover, is not a fixed sequence, but includes loops and cycles. These arguments are familiar; they need not be recounted (Simon, 1955, 1976; March and Simon, 1958; Mintzberg, Raisinghani, and Théorêt, 1976).

The second variety of criticism challenges the task description in a different and, in some senses, more fundamental way by questioning the adequacy of the task description itself, quite apart from the information-processing capacity of individuals. In this view, organizational action is not the result of the intellectual process implicit in the task description, but is a product of social interaction within the organization. The result is to deny the task description as a metaphor for why organizations act as they do (Allison, 1971; Cohen, March, and Olsen, 1972; March, 1972; Cohen and March, 1974; March and Olsen, 1976; Weick, 1976; Sproull, Weiner, and Wolf, 1978; Weick, 1979a; Feldman and March, 1981). This species of criticism might be termed "seeing-as" theory, in that we are asked to see organizational action as a product of something other than the standard decision-making task description. These arguments are also familiar and need not be recounted.

© 1983 by Cornell University.
0001-8392/83/2802-0201/$00.75
•
I would like to thank Lee Sproull, Greg Fischer, Sara Kiesler, David Zubrow, Richard Smith, Patrick Larkey, Zeev Maoz, and Alexander George for comments and reactions to the ideas presented here. The comments of the ASQ reviewers were most helpful in sharpening the argument. The CMU–Ford Motor Company Research Fund provided the resources to acquire the documents from the John F. Kennedy Library.

While either variety of criticism is adequate to refute the adequacy of the standard description, understanding organizational decision making (beyond the fact that the standard description is inadequate) requires integrating the behavioral aspects of individual information processing and decision making with the social and symbolic interaction views of organizations. If the standard characterization is inadequate because individuals do not have the information-processing capacity to perform the goals-to-choices task, and it is inadequate because the goals-to-choices sequence is not what decision makers do anyway, then what is it that decision makers do when they do whatever it is that they do? Or, put in the context of Cohen, March, and Olsen (1972), if organizations are collections of garbage cans, what happens in a garbage can? My purpose here is not to suggest a grand union between the two domains. It is, instead, a more modest attempt to use relatively fine-grained observation of foreign policy decision-making behavior to suggest elements of that union.

From the standpoint of the information-processing view, decision making is largely an intellectual task in which goals are identified, alternatives sought, consequences predicted, alternatives evaluated, and choices made. While there is no doubt that making a decision can present considerable intellectual challenge to an individual, making a decision for the organization is also a social act. Information and alternatives do not, as a general rule, come to decision makers in the form of private visions, and decisions not divulged to anyone hardly fall within the domain of organizational decisions (though they may, of course, influence organizational action). Gathering information, making choices, and communicating decisions are social acts. Managers spend the bulk of their time in short, face-to-face meetings (Mintzberg, 1973; Sproull, 1982), information comes to the president largely in the form of arguments supporting a course of action (Halperin, 1974), and decisions become signs and symbols to other members of the organization (Feldman and March, 1981). Organizational decision making, therefore, is not just a product of individual intellectual information processing, but also involves social information processing.

Although the intellectual information-processing aspects of decision making can be successfully studied in the laboratory, the controlled laboratory setting works against studying the social information-processing aspects of decision making. While laboratory subjects can be confronted with intellectual tasks that are as real as any facing an organizational member, the social elements of the setting — the signs, symbols, and meanings — are artificial. The social information-processing character of organizational decision making, therefore, can best be studied in natural decision settings. Unfortunately, high density observations of decisions in natural settings can generally be obtained only under the most unusual circumstances. There is, however, a rich source of detailed observations that have been underutilized: the detailed records foreign ministries and departments of state routinely produce as a normal by-product of the policy process. These rich archival records have been largely used by historians, who have a narrative style of analysis; they have rarely been exploited by analytically oriented social scientists.[1]

1

The Stanford Studies of the outbreak of WWI described by Holsti (1972) and Axelrod's (1977) cognitive mapping studies are notable exceptions.

Decision Making by Objection

The central question of this research is how the description of the decision-making process that emerges from the archival evidence differs from the standard description of the decision-making task. In the prototypic decision situation, decision makers confront a problem in need of some solution. They face an array of competing possible courses of action and their task is to select the alternative that will solve the problem and achieve their goals. The evidence discussed below suggests that during the Cuban missile crisis, decision making deviated from the prototype in three important respects. The standard description assumes that making a decision involves choosing one alternative from a set of competing courses of action. The evidence from the crisis suggests that instead of seeing competing alternatives, decision makers frequently face a series of yes-no choices over an array of noncompeting courses of action. Second, the standard description assumes that decision makers identify goals as a first step. This implies that decision making is goal-directed. The goals serve as the benchmark from which alternatives are sought and then evaluated. The evidence from the crisis, however, suggests that goals are discovered throughout the course of making a decision. Finally, the standard description assumes that the whole point of decision making is to solve a problem. The evidence from the crisis suggests that what decision makers are looking for is not a solution to a problem but a course of action that does not have a high probability of making matters worse. Whether the action will solve the problem is a secondary concern.

DATA

Given the scarcity of detailed analyses of the interactions of real decision-making groups, an important descriptive question needs to be answered as a step toward developing a fine-grained descriptive model of decision making as social information processing: In what ways does decision making deviate from the standard description of the task? One of the best known cases of group decision making in modern U.S. foreign policy is the conduct of the Executive Committee of the National Security Council (the ExCom) during the Cuban missile crisis of 1962. Decision making during the crisis has been studied extensively (Allison, 1971; George, Hall, and Simons, 1971; Chayes, 1974; Hafner, 1977; Bernstein, 1980) and is considered by some analysts to have been a paradigmatic instance in which the decision-making task was performed according to the standard description in a high-quality manner (Janis, 1972; George, 1980). Position papers, notes, minutes, and memoranda generated during the crisis were deposited in the John F. Kennedy Library and many have now been declassified. These rich and detailed by-products of the decision-making process provide an extraordinary opportunity for discovering in detail the nature of the task that confronted the decision makers. The archival records that provide the best opportunity to examine decision making as social information-processing are the summary records of the ExCom meetings. These records are essentially transcripts of the meetings written in the third person by the NSC staff. The records of the fifth through eighth meetings of the ExCom are currently open for research. The fifth and sixth meetings dealt with enforcing the blockade and maintaining pressure on the Soviet government. Khrushchev's conciliatory "Friday Letter" was received between the sixth and seventh meetings. The public hard-line Soviet proposal involving a trade of missiles in Turkey for missiles in Cuba was received during the seventh meeting. The records of the second, third, fourth, and ninth meetings are currently classified and closed to research, and detailed records only begin after the first meeting. The records open for research contain some sensitive material that has been excised, a process known as "sanitizing." The deleted material largely concerns intelligence sources and methods and does not amount to more than 10 percent of the material.

Although it is clear that the whole of the foreign policy decision-making process does not take place in groups where careful and detailed minutes are kept, groups are ideal settings in which to study decision making as social information processing. Obviously, the groups involve social interaction, but, more importantly, they involve social interaction within the context of shared standards of legitimacy, provided in part by organizational goals like the national interest. Whatever the disagreements among policy makers, there is the shared presumption that they ought to come to agreement when national security and the national interest are at stake. As Halperin (1974) has argued, whatever the private motives that lead individuals to support a proposal, they must be able to justify that position to others with an argument grounded in terms of the national interest. Second, advisory and decision-making groups involve *public* information processing. If advocates want to gain supporters, defeat opponents, and build a consensus, they must do so with public arguments and justifications. As a result, much of the process is exposed to observation by the need to influence others. It is possible, therefore, to think of the records of group discussions as a naturally occurring form of the "think-aloud protocol" like those used by Newell and Simon (1972) to study human problem solving.

METHOD

An inductive strategy was adopted for determining how decision making during the missile crisis deviated from the standard description. The records of the discussion in the ExCom were used as a form of think-aloud protocol. Analyzing protocols involves categorizing the interactions in terms relevant to the decision-making task and using the resulting trace to identify the characteristics of the underlying process. In addition to the coded interactions, documents generated as a by-product of the decision-making process, as well as existing analyses of the crisis, are used to identify the deviations from the standard description of the decision-making task.

Coding

The problem, of course, was to assign codes to text. The standard approach to coding is to develop a complex set of rules that specify the conditions under which a particular type of statement should be assigned a particular code. That approach requires investing considerable resources in training coders to understand the detailed nuances that govern the application of the rules. The approach adopted here was to develop a coding procedure that could be used by relatively untrained and inexperienced coders. The coding system is essentially a variation on the parlor game "20 Questions" where players attempt to

Decision Making by Objection

guess the identity of an object that the leader has chosen. The players ask a series of binary yes-no questions about the object (Is it bigger than a breadbox?) in an attempt to guess its identity. In coding the interactions, the coding scheme takes the role of the guesser and the coder answers binary yes-no questions about the piece of text to be coded. The coding categories, displayed in Table 1, reflect the initial descriptive orientation.

Table 1

Coding Categories

Task description	A description of a task facing the decision makers: For example, "A decision must be made by 2:00 AM this morning if we want to stop the ship outside Cuban territorial waters."
Task goal	A goal that refers to a task facing the decision makers: "He added that if there was any prospect of success in following a political track, we would have to keep heavy pressure on the Russians."
Outcome goal	A goal that refers to an external state of affairs: "Both General Taylor and Secretary Dillon pointed out that we could not permit Soviet technicians to go through the quarantine even though technicians are not on the embargo list."
Alternative	An explicit course of action that is capable of being performed: "Secretary McNamara recommended that the East German ship not be stopped because it might be necessary for us to shoot at it or to ram it."
Description, own	A description of behavior by the decision unit: "The destroyer *Pierce* is following the ship which is still outside the barrier."
Description, other	A description of the behavior of an external actor: "The Attorney General said that fifteen ships have turned back, which is an impressive action taken by the Russians."
Prediction	A statement of possible future action by an external actor: "We could expect a veto from the Russians in the Security Council."
Consequence, own	A description of the consequences of an action by the decision unit: "Director McCone agreed that such action would be effective because it would greatly reduce imports into Cuba and also take away from the Cubans their outgoing cargoes."
Consequence, other	A description of the consequences of an action by an external actor: "He said the Soviet weapons in Cuba were pointed at our heart and put us under great handicap in continuing to carry out our commitments to the free world."
Decision	An authoritative decision: "The President again said we should let the East German passenger ship go through."
Interpretation, own	An interpretation by the decision makers of the reasons for their action: "The purpose of these talks is to arrive at a solution of the crisis or, if no solution is possible, to provide a basis for later action, having been unable to negotiate a settlement."
Interpretation, other	An interpretation by the decision makers of the reasons for an action by an external actor: "He said he believed the Soviets had turned their ships around because they did not want us to see what was on them."

The design of the questions was guided by two principles. First, codes should be assigned to text in a relatively efficient way. In principle, one-half of the possible coding categories can be eliminated by the answer to each question, and n questions are sufficient to assign a piece of text to one of 2^n coding categories. What this means in practice is that the questions form a hierarchical, binary discrimination net that progressively narrows possibilities. The second principle was that the coder should be able to answer a question solely on the basis of the fragment of text, without knowledge of the coding scheme or of the categories. The practical application of this principle is that the questions must be narrowly focused, with clear yes-or-no answers. A fragment of the binary discrimination net for conditional sentences (explicit if-then assertions) is displayed in the figure.

The binary-discrimination-net coding scheme was used to design an interactive computer program to guide the coding of documents. The program read a fragment of text from a data file, displayed it to the coder, and began the game of 20

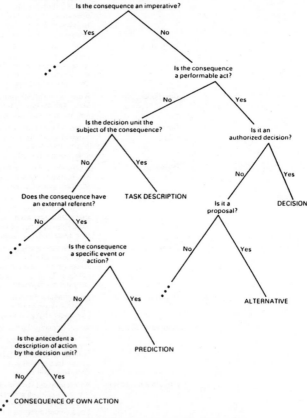

Figure. A partial binary discrimination net for conditional sentences.

Decision Making by Objection

questions. The responses by the coder determined the path the program took through the binary net. The program continued asking questions, going deeper in the net, until it reached a terminal point in the network and assigned a coding category. The binary net contains a total of 43 questions, and the program needed to ask about five to seven questions to code a fragment of text. This coding procedure can be used with any size fragment of text; the convention adopted here was to treat the sentence as the unit of analysis. The frequencies of the different kinds of interactions in the four meetings of the ExCom are displayed in Table 2.

Table 2

Frequency (in percent) of Interactions in the ExCom Meetings

Category	Meetings				
	#5	#6	#7	#8	All meetings
Task description	11	6	13	16	11
Task goal	13	11	9	9	11
Outcome goal	1	7	5	1	3
Alternative	17	22	23	25	21
Description, own	6	9	3	5	6
Description, other	11	2	8	1	6
Prediction	7	9	3	5	6
Consequence, own	10	3	3	4	5
Consequence, other	0	3	3	1	2
Decision	3	10	5	13	7
Interpretation, own	3	5	0	1	2
Interpretation, other	3	0	5	1	2
Unclassified	17	11	20	18	16
Total interactions	113	87	87	80	367

Once the program assigned a category to a fragment of text, the program imbedded the code in the text and rewrote the file. Maintaining the link between the original text and the code means that the context and content of the interactions are preserved, a particular advantage that allows for iterative analysis of the data in studying the details of interactions. The analytic coding procedure is a systematic way of annotating the raw description of the decision process.

STRUCTURE OF ALTERNATIVES

The conventional description assumes that decision makers face an array of competing alternative courses of action and that decision making involves choosing one course of action and rejecting the others. But that assumption probably owes more to the technical requirements of the theory of probability and decision theory than to the reality of decision making. Choices can be seen as coming in two varieties. Some sorts of choices involve selecting an alternative from a set of competing, mutually exclusive courses of action — to launch an airstrike or to impose a blockade. Other sorts of choices involve deciding whether to pursue a particular course of action — to trade or not to trade missiles in Turkey for missiles in Cuba. The records of the ExCom indicate that decision making during the missile crisis involved sequential choices over arrays of compatible, noncompeting courses of action more frequently than it did choices among competing alternatives.

During the early days of the crisis, the overriding objective of the ExCom was to force the removal of the Soviet missiles from Cuba. As portrayed in published accounts of the crisis (Sorensen, 1965; Abel, 1966; Allison, 1971; Detzer, 1979), the ExCom faced a choice between two competing alternatives: to impose a blockade or to launch an airstrike. This choice appears, however, to have been one of the few choices between competing alternatives decision makers confronted during the crisis.

The imposition of a blockade did not resolve the problem facing the ExCom, for with the blockade in place they faced the further problem of translating that initial show of determination into the removal of the missiles from Cuba. The prevailing opinion in the ExCom was that if the missiles were to be removed, additional pressure would have to be applied to the Cuban and Soviet governments; the blockade would not be sufficient. A wide range of political and military measures were available to the U.S. government to increase the pressure for the removal of the missiles. On the political front there was action in the UN.-Security Council and the U.S.-sponsored resolution condemning the Soviet action, and, in the likely event the Soviet government vetoed the resolution, the UN General Assembly offered a forum. If the action shifted to the General Assembly, the U.S. was prepared to support a Brazilian resolution calling for a nuclear-free zone in Latin America (Smith, 1962a). Moreover, the talks in New York between American and Soviet representatives, with Secretary-General U Thant as intermediary, provided a mechanism for pressing for a halt to construction on the missile sites. On the military side, "Secretary McNamara said there were many ways of increasing pressure on the Russians by military measures, i.e., quarantine, inspection at sea, surveillance, the addition of jet fuel on the list of products embargoed, and the holding of all petroleum tankers" (Smith, 1962a: 3). There was, in addition, the airstrike alternative which, although rejected as a first response, was a possible move if the missiles were not removed in a timely manner (Sorensen, 1965). In addition to these courses of action there were two other measures the U.S. could have used to block Cuban imports and exports. The exact nature of these alternatives is unclear because the descriptions of the alternatives are classified and have been excised from the records of the ExCom open for research.

The U.S. pursued a course of action that included political action in the UN Security Council and the OAS, the release of U-2 photographs of the missile sites, a selective blockade of Cuba, and surveillance flights. At no time, however, was that particular array of actions in competition with an alternative array of actions. The mix of means by which the U.S. applied pressure to the Soviet government was the product of a sequential choice process. What the ExCom faced was a series of choices of whether to pursue particular courses of action; the U.S. response was the sum of these choices.

Whether to increase the pressure for the removal of the missiles by adding petroleum, oil, and lubricants (POL) to the list of embargoed goods illustrates the process of sequential

Decision Making by Objection

choice. Although there was conflict and disagreement over the issue, it did not occur in the context of choosing one alternative over another. The issue of strengthening the blockade by including POL was treated by itself as a yes-no choice and not, as the standard task description would predict, in the context of a group of competing courses of action. The following excerpt from the record of the ExCom illustrates this (Smith, 1962b: 2):

Secretary McNamara read a list of Bloc ships and their locations and noted that there would be no intercepts at sea today. The tanker Graznyy is apparently moving but will not cross the line today. He suggested that shortly we should embargo fuel used by bombers and substances from which airplane fuel is made, i.e., petroleum products.

The President suggested that if we decide to embargo bomber fuel, we should also mention the fact we were embargoing fuel which was contributing to the operational capability of the strategic missiles.

Secretary Rusk asked that POL not be embargoed for at least twenty-four hours in order to avoid upsetting the U Thant talks now under way in New York.

Under Secretary Ball asked for agreement on the embargo of petroleum as the next step in the effort to increase pressures — the timing of the embargo to be decided in relation to the New York talks.

Secretary Dillon stated his reservations concerning this course of action. He said it ended up in stopping Soviet ships. Thus, a confrontation with the Russians would not be over the missiles, but over Soviet ships. He believed we should go for the missiles rather than force a confrontation with the USSR at sea.

A decision on adding petroleum to the embargo list was delayed until the political path was decided upon.

The records of the ExCom indicate that conflict and disagreement with respect to courses of action did not occur as a result of advocacy of competing alternatives but as a result of objections to pursuing a particular course of action. A surprisingly large number of alternatives were proposed during the meetings, and few of them were inconsistent with previous proposals. The coded summary records indicate that 13 alternatives were proposed in the fifth, 17 in the sixth, 18 in the seventh, and 16 in the eighth meeting of the ExCom. The frequency of alternatives inconsistent with previously suggested alternatives was very low: 2 in the fifth, 6 in the sixth, 2 in the seventh, and 3 in the eighth.[2] Moreover, when competing courses of action were proposed, they tended to be proposals not to follow a particular course of action rather than well-articulated alternative courses of action. For example, the 17 alternatives proposed during the sixth meeting of the ExCom on October 26 (Smith, 1962b) are listed in Table 3. The alternatives inconsistent with previously proposed courses of action are in italics. In every instance except two, the inconsistent alternative represented a proposal to continue the status quo or a simple objection to a proposed course of action. The two exceptions were Secretary of Defense McNamara's proposal to give prior warning to the Cubans and Russians of U.S. air reconnaissance activities, and Secretary Dillon's statement that it would be better to go for the missiles than to force a confrontation at sea. Thus, on the evidence of the detailed records of the meetings of the ExCom, decision making during the crisis frequently involved yes-no choices over an array of noncompeting alternative courses of action.[3]

2
The large number of alternatives discussed at each meeting appears, on the surface, to be inconsistent with the widely recognized limitations on human information-processing capabilities (Miller, 1956; Simon, 1974). However, because the alternatives were never considered together, but were examined sequentially in a yes-no fashion, the large number of alternatives is not inconsistent with limited information-processing capacities.

3
Axelrod's (1973) study of decision making in the U.S. Military Assistance Program, based on interviews with governmental officials, also found that decision makers did not conceptualize solutions to problems in terms of mutually exclusive alternatives. When he asked them to describe possible solutions to particular problems, he found that decision makers provided a list of courses of action that could be implemented in any combination. Decision makers did not conceptualize the various means at their disposal in terms of mutually exclusive courses of action.

Table 3

_____

Alternatives from the Sixth Meeting of the ExCom*

_____

1. Secretary McNamara suggested that shortly we should embargo fuel used by bombers and substances from which airplane fuel is made, i e , petroleum products.

2. The president suggested that if we decide to embargo bomber fuel, we should also mention the fact that we were embargoing fuel which was contributing to the operational capacity of the strategic missiles.

3. *Secretary Rusk asked that POL not be embargoed for at least twenty-four hours in order to avoid upsetting the U Thant talks now under way in New York.*

4   *Under Secretary Ball asked for agreement on the embargo of petroleum as the next step in the effort to increase pressures — the timing of the embargo to be decided later in relation to the New York talks.*

5. *Secretary Dillon believed we should go for the missiles rather than force a confrontation with the USSR at sea.*

6. Secretary McNamara asked that public announcement be made of our continuation of air surveillance.

7. Secretary McNamara recommended that daylight reconnaissance measures be flown today and a night mission tonight, including the dropping of flares.

8. *Secretary Rusk asked that the night mission not be flown because of the unfortunate effect which it might have on the U Thant negotiations in New York.*

9. *Secretary McNamara thought that one way of avoiding reaction to night reconnaissance was to inform the Cubans and the Russians in advance that we were initiating such flights.*

10. *Ambassador Stevenson opposed any public announcement of our surveillance activities.*

11. Acting USIA Director Wilson requested that better aerial pictures be made available to USIA for distribution.

12. Mr. McCloy stated that our quarantine was vital and should be kept in place until the Russians had accepted all of our conditions.

13. Secretary Rusk felt that it was better for us not to participate in such actions as would be necessary if it were done by an organization, i.e., the OAS, to which we belong.

14. The president asked whether we could commit ourselves not to invade Cuba.

15. As to the message to Castro, the president agreed in general, but wanted to have another look at it.

16. Ambassador Stevenson wanted to know whether he should seek a standstill on all Soviet arms or only offensive weapons.

17. In addition, Ambassador Stevenson needed to know whether in return we would be prepared to suspend the quarantine.

_____

*Alternatives inconsistent with previously proposed courses of action are in italics.

_____

When decision making involves sequential choice, the resulting pattern of activity does not represent an alternative chosen over other competing courses of action. Although it is possible to represent sequential choice over an array of noncompeting alternatives in terms of mutually exclusive alternatives, that is merely a technical solution. For example, three sequential, binary choices can be represented in terms of a decision tree with eight mutually exclusive alternatives. This sort of reconstruction does not, however, reflect decision-making behavior during the missile crisis. There is no evidence that the variety of possible actions was ever examined simultaneously. Moreover, once a decision was made, it was not reconsidered. Identifying

Decision Making by Objection

the actions during the missile crisis as a branch on a decision tree, therefore, does not represent one alternative chosen over another, so much as it does a path through a binary maze. The maze-like character of decision making suggests an alternate explanation for the frequent lack of coherence in governmental action. Standard explanations are based on the problems of coordination and control in organizations (March and Simon, 1958) or on bureaucratic politics (Allison, 1971). Sequential choice over an array of noncompeting alternatives suggests a third explanation. Governmental action may lack coherence because, even in tightly controlled foreign policy crises, it is the product of sequential choice.

DISCOVERY OF GOALS

A second major deviation from the standard task description of decision making has to do with goals. If the standard task description is to be believed, identifying goals is the first step in making a decision. On the basis of the records of the ExCom's deliberations, a more accurate description is that goals are discovered in the course of making a decision.

In order to talk sensibly about discovering goals in the course of making a decision, it is necessary to distinguish global goals from discovered goals. Global goals stimulate the decision process by identifying a situation as a problem. But defining something as a problem does not directly identify a solution. In the missile crisis, the problem posed by the missiles in Cuba and the goal of getting them removed stimulated the process without providing a precise definition of an acceptable resolution of the crisis. The problem of the missiles could have been resolved in any number of ways, including an invasion, a blockade, or a missile trade. The initial or global goal was not sufficient to identify uniquely the "best" course of action, because what the "best" was had yet to be determined. Goal discovery is a social process in which the causal texture (Weick, 1979b) links objectives, constraints, and imperatives with alternatives and their consequences through discussion and debate.

Several reasons, goals, or objectives have been proposed by observers and participants to explain the choice of a blockade (Sorensen, 1965; Abel, 1966; Allison, 1971): The blockade (1) demonstrated U.S. firmness and commitment to the removal of the missiles; (2) avoided the Pearl Harbor analogy that plagued a possible airstrike; (3) did not put extreme pressure on Khrushchev and gave him an opportunity to avoid attack; (4) was a middle course between inaction and attack; (5) placed the burden of the choice of the next step on Khrushchev; (6) took advantage of U.S. Naval superiority in the area; and (7) allowed the U.S. to exploit its advantage in worldwide naval forces. What is striking about the list is that only the first item, the necessity of removing the missiles from Cuba, was mentioned at the first meeting of the ExCom (Sorensen, 1962a, 1965). If these were the goals, then their absence in the first meeting is an anomaly in the context of the standard analysis of decision making. The argument in this section is that most of the goals on that list were discovered during the course of deliberations.

Robert Kennedy is widely credited with introducing a consideration into the deliberations that played an important role in moving the ExCom away from an airstrike and toward a blockade (Sorensen, 1965; Abel, 1966; Allison, 1971; Detzer, 1979). An airstrike represented, according to Robert Kennedy, "a surprise attack by a very large nation against a very small one. This, I said, could not be undertaken by the U.S. if we were to maintain our moral position at home and around the globe" (Kennedy, 1969: 16–17). The Pearl-Harbor-in-reverse analogy introduced consistency with moral traditions as a goal and caused at least one airstrike advocate, Treasury Secretary Douglas Dillon, to shift his position.

The Pearl Harbor analogy — i.e., consistency with U.S. moral traditions — appears on the list of goals and objectives used to explain the choice of a blockade and, like most of those items, was not part of the discussion during that first meeting. Robert Kennedy did not walk into the meeting and say that whatever the response, it had to be consistent with U.S. moral traditions. It was not a global goal, in that it did not stimulate the decision process. Robert Kennedy's concern with moral traditions was stimulated by his reaction to discussions of an airstrike. The first reference to his concern is a note he passed to the president during the first meeting commenting on the discussion of an airstrike: "I now know how Tojo felt when he was planning Pearl Harbor" (Kennedy, 1969: 9). He made his objection known to the other members of the ExCom two days later in a response to former Secretary of State Dean Acheson's advocacy of an airstrike (Kennedy, 1969: 16–17). From the evidence available, Robert Kennedy's concern was essentially a reaction to proposals for an airstrike; it occurred during discussions of the alternative and took the form of an objection that introduced a constraint on an acceptable alternative.

But in what sense was his reaction a discovery? Without penetrating too deeply into Robert Kennedy's psyche, it is plausible to suppose he did not walk into the first meeting with a conscious conviction of the necessity of maintaining the public image of American traditions. It is, however, conceivable he believed in its importance but did not or had no reason to make an immediate association between appropriate action and U.S. traditions in the same way that he might have associated Soviet missiles in Cuba and the necessity of removing their threat. It took a proposal for a surprise attack on the missile sites to stimulate the association. Douglas Dillon's shift from the airstrike to the blockade group can be given the same sort of interpretation, with Robert Kennedy's argument serving as the stimulus for the association:

What changed my mind was Bobby Kennedy's argument that we ought to be true to ourselves as Americans, that surprise attack was not in our tradition. Frankly, these considerations had not occurred to me until Bobby raised them so eloquently (Abel, 1966: 67).

There is no reason to suppose Kennedy's argument convinced Dillon of the importance of American traditions. The argument stimulated the association with Dillon's existing beliefs. Thus the goal of preserving the public perception of a U.S. tradition of fairness was a discovery in the sense that Kennedy's arguments caused Dillon to recognize an association with his existing beliefs.

Another of the goals on the list, a graduated response that preserved options, also occurred as a discovery in the context of arguing about alternatives (Abel, 1966: 67). Selecting a blockade

Decision Making by Objection

as a first step did not preclude more forceful options. An airstrike would have immediately removed options and threatened a spiral of escalation without graduation or convenient exit. This advantage of a blockade, as put forth by Robert Kennedy, Douglas Dillon, and Robert McNamara, convinced McGeorge Bundy to join the advocates of a blockade. The discovery of goals during the course of making a decision can be interpreted in the larger context of the role of argumentation in decision making. Axelrod (1977) suggested that novel arguments play an important role in the argumentation and debate process of decision making. From the perspective of goal discovery, novel arguments have an impact on decision making because they stimulate new associations among existing belief structures.

Given the available evidence, the goal discovery process can account for all the goals on the list with the exception of the last two: the advantage to the U.S. of a confrontation at sea in the Caribbean and the worldwide superiority of the U.S. Navy. Accounts of U.S. decision making (Sorensen, 1965; Abel, 1966; Hilsman, 1967; Allison, 1971; Schlesinger, 1978; Detzer, 1979) provide evidence that the others were discovered in the course of the process, i.e., they were put forth as arguments for a blockade and against an airstrike. There is no evidence in the records now available, however, for the discovery of the final two items. If the evidence for their discovery is not in the records closed to research, Weick's (1979a) "retrospective sense making" seems the most likely explanation for the discovery of the last two goals. While the blockade possessed the "missing" advantages, they were "discovered" after the choice had been made, in order to demonstrate the inevitability of the blockade as the only reasonable course of action. In this view, they played no role in determining the final selection, because the opportunity to discover them never arose.

Goal discovery did not stop with the decision to impose a naval blockade on Cuba. Throughout the meetings of the ExCom, goal statements were an important force in shaping the arguments and discussions. The interaction sequences in the ExCom reveal a relationship between goals and alternatives. A goal statement was followed by another goal statement 31 percent of the time and by an alternative 27 percent of the time. Moreover, 21 percent of the goals were preceded by alternatives. Thus, goals or alternatives preceded goals 52 percent of the time, and goals were followed by another goal or an alternative 58 percent of the time. Goals, therefore, tended to produce and be produced by alternatives and other goals.

Goals are discovered through argumentation and debate. In addition to playing a role in evaluating specific alternatives, goals can become devices for advocates to direct the attention of the group to constraints, objectives, and imperatives that define acceptable situations. In order to further examine the role of goals in the decision-making process, each goal statement from the ExCom meetings was classified into one of three groups: evaluative, attention directing, and modifying. Goals were classified as evaluative when they provided grounds for accepting or rejecting an alternative under active discussion; they were classified as modifiers when they served to modify or extend an existing alternative (i.e., "In commenting on the draft cable, Mr. Nitze called attention to the importance of

getting Soviet missiles out urgently."); they were classified as
attention directing when they were not directly related to
current alternatives but, instead, emphasized general characteristics of an acceptable resolution to the problem. As shown
in Table 4, 58 percent of the goal statements were attempts by
participants to call the attention of the group to criteria defining
an acceptable resolution of the crisis. Thus, goals were not
restricted to evaluating specific alternatives but were also used
to direct the attention of the decision makers to criteria that
should be used to define acceptable situations.

Table 4

Frequency (in percent) of Goal Functions

Goal type	Evaluative	Attention directing	Modifier
Task goal (N = 40)	44	55	3
Outcome goal (N = 12)	8	67	25
Combined (N = 52)	35	58	8

In the standard task description of decision making, identifying
goals is the first step in the process. From that point on, the
focus of the task is on alternatives, predictions, and evaluations.
The evidence from the missile crisis that goals are discovered in
the course of making a decision suggests that decision making
does not involve choosing alternatives so much as it involves
discovering goals. Once agreement on goals has been reached,
the alternative often follows as a matter of course.

Although the analysis of the missile crisis is generally consistent with the view of goals put forth by March (1972) and Weick
(1979a), two novel characteristics are worth noting. First,
March and Weick both argue that choices can precede goals
and that retrospective views of choices can be a way to
discover goals. While it is certainly true that goals can emerge
from previous choices, during the missile crisis the goals
discovered in the course of making the decision had the most
impact. Thus it was not retrospective discovery, but the near
simultaneous discovery of goals and choices. The second
characteristic that emerges is the emphasis of the role of
argumentation and debate in the goal discovery process, which
provides a more explicit description of the process of goal
discovery. Goals are discovered through a social process involving argumentation and debate in a setting where justification
and legitimacy play important roles. Not just any sort of goal will
be discovered; it will be one that is consistent with shared
organizational goals.

EVALUATION OF ALTERNATIVES

The third important difference from the standard task description concerns the evaluation of alternatives. Implicit in the task
description is the assumption that the whole purpose of making
a decision is to choose an alternative that will solve a problem.
What is striking is that decision makers frequently choose
alternatives that they do not expect will solve the problem.
Moreover, decision makers behave this way in the face of
important problems. During the Vietnam troop buildup, U.S.
policymakers had no illusion that their attempts to solve the

Decision Making by Objection

problem confronting them would be successful. They had, Gelb (1979) argued, reasonably accurate and generally pessimistic views of the likelihood of success. Similarly, President Kennedy accepted the Cuban blockade option even though he doubted it would force the Soviet government to withdraw its missiles from Cuba:

The President said we will get the Soviet strategic missiles out of Cuba only by invading Cuba or by trading. He doubted that the quarantine alone would produce a withdrawal of the weapons. (Smith, 1962b: 6).

Decision makers do not, of course, choose an alternative *because* it is likely to fail; it is simply that the "best" or "satisfactory" alternative often has a low probability of success. But even if alternatives with a high probability of success are rare, there is something paradoxical about a "good," "optimal," or "satisfactory" alternative with a low probability of success. The paradox is magnified by the fact that decision makers appear to hold that an alternative can be both unattractive, i.e., have a low probability of success, and satisfactory. It would be less of a paradox if they modified their beliefs in ways that equated satisfactoriness with attractiveness, i.e., inflated their subjective estimates of the probability of success. But they do not. Decision makers often choose an unattractive alternative as a satisfactory solution to a problem.

Evaluative terms often reflect an underlying two-valued logic: if not good, then bad; if not a success, then a failure; if not satisfactory, then unsatisfactory. But the duality of those terms is deceiving. Decision makers inhabit a world of complexity, uncertainty, and many-valued logics where the logical complement of success is not always failure and where the causal texture linking means to ends is equivocal (Weick, 1979b). March and Simon (1958: 113–114) implicitly recognized the inadequacy of two-valued, evaluative terms when they distinguished the probability that a choice will result in a "positively valued state of affairs" from the probability that a choice will result in a "negatively valued state of affairs." These two probabilities are independent in the sense that both can be low, one can be high and the other low, or both can be high. The result is a four-valued evaluation function:

1. A *good* alternative has high probability of producing a positively valued state of affairs and a low probability of producing a negatively valued state of affairs.

2. A *bland* alternative has low probabilities of producing either positively or negatively valued states of affairs.

3. A *mixed* alternative has high probabilities of producing positively or negatively valued states of affairs.

4. A *poor* alternative has a low probability of producing a positively valued state of affairs and a high probability of producing a negatively valued state of affairs.

Binary evaluations generally recognize only the first and fourth classes of alternatives; an alternative is either good or poor. Separating positive and negative outcomes recognizes two additional types. The result is that an alternative that is not "good" need not necessarily be "poor."

Only a perverse decision process would fail to select a readily available good alternative. But March and Simon (1958: 116) suggested that when a good alternative is not available, the search for new alternatives will be less vigorous if the set contains bland alternatives. This proposition implies that bland alternatives, those with low probabilities of either success or failure, will be acceptable when no good alternative is readily available. This conditional preference for bland alternatives would produce the following preference order over the types of alternatives: good > bland > mixed > poor.

The preference order over the four types of alternatives and the tendency to suspend search in the face of a bland alternative can be explained by assuming that, in the absence of a good alternative, decision makers attend to the probability of a negative outcome in evaluating alternatives. An alternative with an unacceptably high probability of producing a negatively valued outcome will always be less preferred than an alternative that does not. In this view, the probability that an alternative will produce a positively valued outcome is a secondary consideration. Research on individual decision making generally supports this view of evaluation (Payne and Braunstein, 1971; Kahneman and Tversky, 1979; Tversky and Kahneman, 1981).

This view of evaluation suggests that decision makers are looking for alternatives that do not have high probabilities of making the current situation worse. Thus, evaluations are not absolute, because "good" and "bad" are not fixed, but are anchored to the situation facing decision makers. Anchoring evaluations to the status quo is a property of prospect theory (Kahneman and Tversky, 1979) and has been supported by experimental evidence (Tversky and Kahneman, 1981). Thus, although evaluation is based on the conservative strategy of avoiding alternatives with high probabilities of undesirable outcomes, if the status quo is sufficiently intolerable, extreme alternatives may present low probabilities of making an intolerable situation worse.

The blockade during the Cuban missile crisis is a clear example of a bland alternative. Inaction, diplomacy, and an airstrike had high probabilities of producing undesirable states of affairs. Although the blockade did not have a high probability of forcing the withdrawal of the missiles, it also did not have a high probability of producing an immediate undesirable outcome (Sorensen, 1965). The standard task description assumes that the purpose of decision making is to solve a problem, but decision makers appear to operate with a very different perspective. Whether the action will solve the problem that motivated the process is less important than whether it has a high probability of making matters worse.

THE MODEL OF DECISION MAKING BY OBJECTION

Although the Cuban missile crisis shared some characteristics of Cohen, March, and Olsen's (1972) garbage can model, that model is not wholly appropriate for understanding the group decision-making process during the missile crisis. The missile crisis was in danger of becoming an organizational garbage can, but President Kennedy and his top advisers controlled the issues that they allowed to be attached to the crisis. For example, some wanted to use the crisis as an occasion to finally do what the Bay of Pigs had failed to do — get rid of Castro — and others attempted to use the proposal to remove the Jupiter missiles from Turkey and push for a pilot multilateral nuclear force in the Mediterranean (Finletter, 1962; Smith, 1962b;

Decision Making by Objection

Steinbruner, 1974). In both instances, the attempts were successfully blocked.

The crisis also shared characteristics of Weick's (1979a) enactment-selection-retention model. Decision makers devoted a surprising amount of time and effort to providing interpretations for their actions, and some went so far as to draw lessons from the crisis before it had even been resolved (Cleveland, 1979). Nevertheless, decision making during the crisis was far more directed and intentional than Weick's metaphor of organizational action would lead us to expect.

The findings of this study do not, however, suggest a wholesale denial of the standard concepts of decision making. Goals were still identified, there was search for alternatives, and consequences were evaluated. However, the way goals were identified, alternatives sought, and consequences evaluated was very different from what standard descriptions would predict. If what decision makers do when they make a decision is redescribed to take account of the deviations from standard descriptions of decision making, the new characterization is best termed "decision making by objection." In schematic form, decision making by objection proceeds as follows:

1. A problem is defined and a global goal is identified, which produces a rough description of an acceptable resolution of the problem.

2. A course of action is proposed. The alternative will be accompanied by an argument describing the positive outcomes associated with undertaking the action.

3. The proposed course of action will produce one of three responses: If there is general agreement on the desirability of following the course of action, it will be ratified. If there is no support and no formal opposition, the alternative will die for what amounts to the lack of a second — the fate of the majority of alternatives proposed during the missile crisis. The third and most interesting case is when there is an objection to the alternative. Objections are framed in terms of the negative or undesirable consequences of the alternative, and the effect is to propose constraints, beyond the global goal, that further define an acceptable resolution of the problem.

4. If there is disagreement over the newly introduced constraint, a secondary discussion on the merits of the new goal may ensue. Only if there is an imperative to act will a competing course of action be proposed.

5. In the absence of an imperative to act, the original alternative is generally discarded and a different independent course of action is proposed.

This description of the task of decision making is far less linear than standard descriptions propose. The iterative and self-defining character of the task is emphasized, rather than the stages of the task. Alternatives stimulate arguments that lead to the discovery of the goals, which then influence the choice of alternatives.

Consider, for example, the differences between a standard and a decision-making-by-objection reconstruction of the choice between a blockade and an airstrike. Standard accounts proceed along the following lines: The goal was to remove the threat to the United States posed by the strategic weapons in Cuba. The initial search produced two alternatives, an airstrike against the missiles and a policy of inaction. Neither alternative was wholly acceptable, and further search produced the blockade option. The ExCom split into blockade and airstrike advocates. The two groups argued, debated, and challenged each other's assumptions and predictions. The consequences of following each course of action were presented to President Kennedy and he made his choice.

A reconstruction of the choice using the decision-making-by-objection model as a basis would look something like this: The initial goal was to deal with the threat posed by the missiles in Cuba. The attention of the ExCom quickly focused on an airstrike against the missile sites. Even though the military insisted during the very first meeting that the airstrike could not be limited (Sorensen, 1962a), surgical versus large-scale airstrikes were not clearly delineated until much later. As part of an objection to the airstrike proposal, Secretary of Defense McNamara made his missile-is-a-missile argument. After a secondary discussion, which resulted in a rejection of McNamara's do-nothing proposal and the definition of the removal of the missiles as the only acceptable resolution of the problem, advocacy of an airstrike resumed. Bobby Kennedy objected to the airstrike proposal with his Pearl-Harbor-in-reverse argument, and in doing so proposed the additional constraint of consistency with tradition as part of the definition of an acceptable resolution of the crisis. More or less at the same time, McNamara objected to the surgical airstrike by arguing that it could not be limited and would entail a full-scale attack on Cuba, with the risk of a spasm military response by Khrushchev. McNamara's objection implicitly imposed the constraint of not placing Khrushchev in a position where a quick military response was likely. The Kennedy-McNamara objections provided a basis for renewing the blockade alternative, which had been proposed during the first meeting after the discovery of the missiles. The Kennedy-McNamara objections and the realization of the impossibility of the surgical airstrike left only two alternatives with any support: a general airstrike and a blockade. However, because the constraints on an acceptable resolution of the problem were inconsistent with born alternatives — the airstrike violated the constraint of maintaining traditions and avoiding a high probability of an initial military response by the Russians and the blockade violated the constraint of removing the missiles — the ExCom was unable to recommend either of the two alternatives to the president, who had to choose between them.[4]

Although there are no stark differences between the two reconstructions, the decision-making-by-objection narrative is better able to account for three characteristics of the decision-making process. First, the documentary evidence of the initial meetings of the ExCom suggests that the decision makers confronted an ambiguous, ever-changing set of options. On October 17 (the day after the discovery of the missiles), Sorensen prepared a memo for President Kennedy summarizing the ExCom's deliberations and listing four alternatives: political pressure followed by a military strike if satisfaction was not received; a military strike without prior warning; political pressure followed by a blockade; or a full-scale invasion of Cuba (Sorensen, 1962b). One day later, the alternatives were: a surgical airstrike with or without advance warning; a full airstrike with or without advance warning; a blockade with advance pressure and warning; an invasion, with advance warning; and a letter to Khrushchev, followed by a blockade or

[4]
This account is largely constructive and interpretive. The detailed records of the early deliberations of the ExCom are classified and are not currently available for research. The facts of the account are consistent with the available evidence, but the decision-making-by-objection interpretation goes beyond the available evidence. Thus the account resembles more of a prediction based on decision making by objection than a description of what actually took place.

Decision Making by Objection

an airstrike depending on his response (Sorensen, 1962c). Embedded in these alternatives was the further issue of the nature of the warning and political pressure. It was not until much later that the list of alternatives stabilized, and in the end, only two alternatives were presented to President Kennedy. Thus the standard list of alternatives: inaction, diplomatic pressures, a secret approach to Castro, invasion, surgical airstrike, and blockade (Allison, 1971), is a retrospective reconstruction that imposes order on an ambiguous set of alternatives. The sequential style and goal-discovery aspects of the process of decision making by objection would tend to produce the sort of ambiguity found in the deliberations of the ExCom.

Second, the decision-making-by-objection model captures the ambiguity and change in preferred courses of action. As new goals are discovered, preferences change, and as alternatives are proposed, individuals change the arguments they make. Existing accounts indicate that Secretary of Defense McNamara originally favored inaction, and after that was rejected, he became an early advocate of a blockade (Sorensen, 1965; Abel, 1966; Kennedy, 1969); yet on October 18 (the third day of the crisis), Sorensen indicated McNamara's first choice was a full airstrike, with a blockade as his probable second choice (Sorensen, 1962c). Sorensen's assessment of McNamara's preferences probably reflects McNamara's argument against a surgical airstrike rather than his preference for a full airstrike. The model of decision making by objection recognizes the ambiguity in advocacy that follows from the sequential choice style of decision making. Without a clear set of competing courses of action to provide a reference, relating preferences to arguments can be problematic.

Finally, the decision-making-by-objection model, with its emphasis on sequential choice and goal discovery, accounts for Dean Acheson's (1969) assessment of the ExCom's meetings as repetitive, leaderless, and a waste of time. Acheson's assessment appears to be "sour grapes" because his advice was not followed. But Acheson's preferred operating style as secretary of state (Halperin, 1974: 200) was to work out a solution to a problem, in consultation with the president, beforehand and to allow decision-making groups to comment on, not change, the course of action he advocated. This is not what happened during the missile crisis. The ExCom was not directed, but moved from topic to topic, from binary choice to binary choice without a firm hand to guide it and without the structure implied by the standard task description. Thus it was repetitive and leaderless, though probably not a waste of time.

Although one case does not establish that decision making by objection is the dominant mode of decision making in foreign affairs, the model does display several attributes that make it an interesting explanation of group decision making. The process of decision making by objection, with its emphasis on sequential evaluation of alternatives, produces binary choices as a default. It does not, however, exclude competing alternatives; competing alternatives will appear when (1) there are objections to the initial course of action, and (2) there is a shared recognition that some action is required. Decision making by objection is group decision making via argumentation and debate, and goal discovery will occur as a consequence of the interaction of advocates of opposing views. An alternative with a high probability of making matters worse will simultaneously produce objections that lessen the likelihood it will be chosen and stimulate the discovery of goals.

The model of decision making by objection also ties into a broader theoretical perspective. First, the decision-making-by-objection model is a behavioral description. Most alternatives to standard descriptions of decision making focus on what the actions of decision makers mean, not explicitly on what decision makers do. Although only a first approximation, the model of decision making by objection specifies an explicit, almost operational, decision-making process consistent with both the alternative metaphors for decision making posed by March (1972) and Weick (1979a) and with research demonstrating the limited information-processing capacities of individuals (March and Simon, 1958). Second, this study of decision making by objection is strongly empirical in that it draws on detailed primary-source information about decision making in a real setting. Because standard descriptions are closely tied to what we mean by the concept of decision, it is likely that it acts as a schema for recall and interpretation (Taylor and Crocker, 1980). As a result, analyses that rely on secondary-source reconstructions of the decision-making process may be biased in favor of the standard task descriptions. Although any analysis will be biased toward its prior organizing principles, this study of decision making does have an advantage in being drawn from primary-source material. Third, the model of decision making by objection preserves the social information-processing character of decision making in an organization. The standard approach, as March (1978) has noted, has been to use the same task description for decision making whether speaking of individuals, groups, or organizations. But decision making in an organization is not simply a bigger version of the intellectual task facing a solitary decision maker; making a decision in the name of the organization is a social act. According to the model of decision making by objection, making decisions is a process involving argumentation and debate in an explicitly social setting, a process constrained by the need to justify actions in terms of shared symbols, goals, and objectives.

The striking characteristics of the decision-making-by-objection process observed during the missile crisis represent neither blind variation nor random noise but sensible adaptations to the demands of the task environment of decision making. Organizations have a capacity for many simultaneous actions. In the face of a complex policy issue, decision makers will be presented with a diverse menu of alternatives reflecting the diverse capabilities of the organization. To do anything but make a series of binary choices would overwhelm the limited information-processing capacity of the decision makers. Discovering goals in the course of making a decision avoids the need to specify all goals at the outset and to resolve all goal conflict. Objections to pursuing proposed courses of action help define the characteristics of an acceptable resolution of the problem, introduce new goals into the process, and provide a mechanism for limited coordination and control. Avoiding alternatives with high probabilities of failure is an inexpensive screening procedure that exploits what little certainty exists, without requiring trade-offs between successes and failures. Although the direct empirical support in this study for the model

Decision Making by Objection

of decision making by objection was found in one organization facing a singular problem at one point in time, it clearly points to the need for more empirical and theoretical work to increase our understanding of how the complexities of the task environment affect the performance of the decision-making task. In understanding the ways that decision-making behavior reflects the task environment, we are in a better position to understand decision making in complex policy settings and to suggest improvements to the process of policymaking.

REFERENCES

Abel, Ellie
1966 The Missile Crisis. New York: Bantam.

Acheson, Dean
1969 "Dean Acheson's version of Robert Kennedy's version of the Cuban missile affair." Esquire, 71: 76, ff.

Allison, Graham T.
1971 Essence of Decision: Explaining the Cuban Missile Crisis. Boston: Little, Brown.

Axelrod, Robert
1973 "Bureaucratic decision making in the Military Assistance Program: Some empirical findings." In M. H. Halperin and A. Kanter (eds.), Readings in American Foreign Policy: A Bureaucratic Perspective: 154–171. Boston: Little, Brown.
1977 "Argumentation in foreign policy settings: Britain in 1918, Munich in 1938, and Japan in 1970." Journal of Conflict Resolution, 21: 727–756.

Bernstein, Barton J.
1980 "The Cuban missile crisis: Trading the Jupiters in Turkey?" Political Science Quarterly, 95: 97–125.

Chayes, Abram
1974 The Cuban Missile Crisis: International Crises and the Role of Law. New York: Oxford University Press.

Cleveland, Harlan
1979 "Public management research: The theory of practice and vice versa." In Proceedings of the Public Management Research Conference: Setting Public Management Research Agendas: Integrating the Sponsor, Producer, and User: 19–26. Washington, DC: U.S. Government Printing Office.

Cohen, Michael D., and James G. March
1974 Leadership and Ambiguity. New York: McGraw-Hill.

Cohen, Michael D., James G. March, and Johan P. Olsen
1972 "A garbage can model of organizational choice." Administrative Science Quarterly, 17: 1–26.

Detzer, David
1979 The Brink: Cuban Missile Crisis, 1962. New York: Thomas Y. Crowell.

Feldman, Martha S., and James G. March
1981 "Information in organizations as signal and symbol." Administrative Science Quarterly, 26: 171–186.

Finletter, Thomas K.
1962 "Telegram to the secretary of state," 25 October 1962. NATO, Weapons Cables — Turkey Folder. National Security Files, Papers of John F. Kennedy, John F. Kennedy Library.

Gelb, Leslie, with Richard K. Betts
1979 The Irony of Vietnam: The System Worked. Washington, DC: Brookings Institution.

George, Alexander L.
1980 Presidential Decisionmaking in Foreign Policy: The Effective Use of Information and Advice. Boulder, CO: Westview.

George, Alexander L., David K. Hall, and William R. Simons
1971 The Limits of Coercive Diplomacy: Laos, Cuba, Vietnam. Boston: Little, Brown.

Hafner, Donald L.
1977 "Bureaucratic politics and 'those frigging missiles': JFK, Cuba, and U.S. missiles in Turkey." Orbis, 21: 307–333.

Halperin, Morton H.
1974 Bureaucratic Politics and Foreign Policy. Washington, DC: Brookings Institution.

Hilsman, Roger
1967 To Move a Nation. Garden City, NY: Doubleday.

Holsti, Ole R.
1972 Crisis, Escalation, War. Montreal: McGill-Queen's University Press.

Janis, Irving L.
1972 Victims of Groupthink. Boston: Houghton Mifflin.

Kahneman, Daniel, and Amos Tversky
1979 "Prospect theory: An analysis of decision under risk." Econometrica, 47: 263–300.

Kennedy, Robert F.
1969 Thirteen Days: A Memoir of the Cuban Missile Crisis. New York: Norton.

March, James G.
1972 "Model bias in social action." Review of Educational Research, 42: 413–429.
1978 "Bounded rationality, ambiguity, and the engineering of choice." The Bell Journal of Economics, 9: 587–610.

March, James G., and Johan P. Olsen
1976 Ambiguity and Choice in Organizations. Bergen: Universitetsforlaget.

March, James G., and Herbert A. Simon
1958 Organizations. New York: Wiley.

Miller, George A.
1956 "The magic number seven, plus or minus two: Some limits on our capacity for processing information." Psychological Review, 63: 81–97.

Mintzberg, Henry
1973 The Nature of Managerial Work. New York: Harper and Row.

Mintzberg, Henry, Duru Raisinghani, and André Théorêt
1976 "The structure of 'unstructured' decision processes." Administrative Science Quarterly, 21: 246–275.

Newell, Allen, and Herbert Simon
1972 Human Problem Solving. Englewood Cliffs, NJ: Prentice-Hall.

Payne, John W., and Myron L. Braunstein
1971 "Preferences among gambles with equal underlying distributions." Journal of Experimental Psychology, 87: 13–18.

Schlesinger, Arthur M., Jr.
1978 Robert Kennedy and His Times. New York: Ballantine.

Simon, Herbert A.
1955 "A behavioral model of rational choice." Quarterly Journal of Economics, 69: 99–118.
1974 "How big is a chunk?" Science, 183: 482–488.
1976 Administrative Behavior. New York: Free Press.

Smith, Bromley
1962a "Summary record of NSC Executive Committee meeting #5," 25 October 1962. Executive Committee Meetings 1–5 10/23/62–10/26/62 Folder. National Security Files, Papers of John F. Kennedy, John F. Kennedy Library.
1962b "Summary record of NSC Executive Committee meeting #6," 26 October 1962. Executive Committee Meetings 6–10 10/26/62–10/28/62 Folder. National Security Files, Papers of John F. Kennedy, John F. Kennedy Library.

Sorensen, Theodore C.
1962a "TCS notes at 11:45 a.m. meeting on Cuban missile discovery," 16 October 1962. Cuba, General 1962 Folder. Papers of Theodore Sorensen, John F. Kennedy Library.
1962b "Memorandum," 17 October 1962. Cuba, General 10/17/62–10/27/62 Folder. Papers of Theodore Sorensen, John F. Kennedy Library.
1962c "Memorandum," 18 October 1962. Cuba, General 10/17/62–10/27/62 Folder. Papers of Theodore Sorensen, John F. Kennedy Library.
1965 Kennedy. New York: Harper and Row.

Sproull, Lee S.
1982 "The nature of managerial attention." Social Science Working Paper, Department of Social Sciences, Carnegie-Mellon University.

Sproull, Lee, Stephen Weiner, and David Wolf
1978 Organizing an Anarchy: Belief, Bureaucracy, and Politics in the National Institute of Education. Chicago: University of Chicago Press.

Steinbruner, John D.
1974 The Cybernetic Theory of Decision. Princeton, NJ: Princeton University Press.

Taylor, Shelley E., and Jennifer C. Crocker
1980 "Schematic bases of social information processing." In E. T. Higgins, P. Hermann, and M. P. Zanna (eds.), The Ontario Symposium on Personality and Social Psychology, 1: 89–134. Hillsdale, NJ: Lawrence Erlbaum.

Tversky, Amos, and Daniel Kahneman
1981 "The framing of decisions and the psychology of choice." Science, 211: 453–458.

Weick, Karl E.
1976 "Educational organizations as loosely-coupled systems." Administrative Science Quarterly, 21: 1–19.
1979a The Social Psychology of Organizing. Reading, MA: Addison-Wesley.
1979b "Cognitive processes in organizations." In B. M. Staw (ed.), Research in Organizational Behavior, 1: 41–74. Greenwich, CT: JAI Press.

[12]

12

The Technology of Foolishness

James G. March

Choice and Rationality

The concept of choice as a focus for interpreting and guiding human behavior has rarely had an easy time in the realm of ideas. It is beset by theological disputations over free will, by the dilemmas of absurdism, by the doubts of psychological behaviorism, by the claims of historical, economic, social, and demographic determinism. Nevertheless, the idea that humans make choices has proven robust enough to become a major matter of faith in important segments of contemporary Western civilization. It is a faith that is professed by virtually all theories of social policy-making.

The major tenets of this faith run something like this:

> Human beings make choices. If done properly, choices are made by evaluating alternatives in terms of goals on the basis of information currently available. The alternative that is most attractive in terms of the goals is chosen. The process of making choices can be improved by using the technology of choice. Through the paraphernalia of modern techniques, we can improve the quality of the search for alternatives, the quality of information, and the quality of the analysis used to evaluate alternatives. Although actual choice may fall short of this ideal in various ways, it is an attractive model of how choices should be made by individuals, organizations, and social systems.

These articles of faith have been built upon, and have stimulated, some scripture. It is the scripture of theories of decision-making. The scripture is

---

This chapter is based on a paper first published in *Civiløkonomen* (Copenhagen) 18 (1971).

254   Decision-making under ambiguity

partly a codification of received doctrine and partly a source for that
doctrine. As a result, our cultural ideas of intelligence and our theories
of choice bear some substantial resemblance. In particular, they share three
conspicuous interrelated ideas:

The first idea is the *pre-existence of purpose*. We find it natural to base an
interpretation of human-choice behavior on a presumption of human purpose.
We have, in fact, invented one of the most elaborate terminologies in the
professional literature: 'values', 'needs', 'wants', 'goods', 'tastes',
'preferences', 'utility', 'objectives', 'goals', 'aspirations', 'drives'. All of
these reflect a strong tendency to believe that a useful interpretation of
human behavior involves defining a set of objectives that (a) are prior
attributes of the system, and (b) make the observed behavior in some sense
intelligent *vis-á-vis* those objectives.

Whether we are talking about individuals or about organizations,
purpose is an obvious presumption of the discussion. An organization is
often defined in terms of its purpose. It is seen by some as the largest
collectivity directed by a purpose. Action within an organization is justified
(or criticized) in terms of the purpose. Individuals explain their own
behavior, as well as the behavior of others, in terms of a set of value
premises that are presumed to be antecedent to the behavior. Normative
theories of choice begin with an assumption of a pre-existent preference
ordering defined over the possible outcomes of a choice.

The second idea is the *necessity of consistency*. We have come to
recognize consistency both as an important property of human behavior
and as a prerequisite for normative models of choice. Dissonance theory,
balance theory, theories of congruency in attitudes, statuses, and
performances have all served to remind us of the possibilities for
interpreting human behavior in terms of the consistency requirements of
a limited capacity information-processing system.

At the same time, consistency is a cultural and theoretical virtue. Action
should be made consistent with belief. Actions taken by different parts
of an organization should be consistent with each other. Individual and
organizational activities are seen as connected with each other in terms
of their consequences for some consistent set of purposes. In an
organization, the structural manifestation of the dictum of consistency
is the hierarchy with its obligations of coordination and control. In the
individual, the structural manifestation is a set of values that generates
a consistent preference ordering.

The third idea is the *primacy of rationality*. By rationality I mean a
procedure for deciding what is correct behavior by relating consequences
systematically to objectives. By placing primary emphasis on rational
techniques, we implicitly have rejected – or seriously impaired – two other
procedures for choice: (a) the processes of intuition, by means of which

people may do things without fully understanding why; (b) the processes of tradition and faith, through which people do things because that is the way they are done.

Both within the theory and within the culture we insist on the ethic of rationality. We justify individual and organizational action in terms of an analysis of means and ends. Impulse, intuition, faith, and tradition are outside that system and viewed as antithetical to it. Faith may be seen as a possible source of values. Intuition may be seen as a possible source of ideas about alternatives. But the analysis and justification of action lie within the context of reason.

These ideas are obviously deeply imbedded in the culture. Their roots extend into ideas that have conditioned much of modern Western history and interpretations of that history. Their general acceptance is probably highly correlated with permeation of rationalism and individualism into the style of thinking within the culture. The ideas are even more obviously imbedded in modern theories of choice. It is fundamental to those theories that thinking should precede action; that action should serve a purpose; that purpose should be defined in terms of a consistent set of pre-existent goals; and that choice should be based on a consistent theory of the relation between action and its consequences.

Every tool of management decision that is currently a part of management science, operations research, or decision theory assumes the prior existence of a set of consistent goals. Almost the entire structure of microeconomic theory builds on the assumption that there exists a well-defined, stable, and consistent preference-ordering. Most theories of individual or organizational choice behavior accept the idea that goals exist and that (in some sense) an individual or organization acts on those goals, choosing from among some alternatives on the basis of available information. Discussions of educational policy, for example, with the emphasis on goal-setting, evaluation, and accountability, are directly in this tradition.

From the perspective of all of man's history, the ideas of purpose, consistency, and rationality are relatively new. Much of the technology currently available to implement them is extremely new. Over the past few centuries, and conspicuously over the past few decades, we have substantially improved man's capability for acting purposively, consistently, and rationally. We have substantially increased his propensity to think of himself as doing so. It is an impressive victory, won – where it has been won – by a happy combination of timing, performance, ideology, and persistence. It is a battle yet to be concluded, or even engaged, in many cultures of the world; but within most of the Western world, individuals and organizations see themselves as making choices.

256   Decision-making under ambiguity

The Problem of Goals

The tools of intelligence as they are fashioned in modern theories of choice are necessary to any reasonable behavior in contemporary society. It is difficult to see how we could, and inconceivable that we would, fail to continue their development, refinement, and extension. As might be expected, however, a theory and ideology of choice built on the ideas outlined above is deficient in some obvious, elementary ways, most conspicuously in the treatment of human goals.

Goals are thrust upon the intelligent man. We ask that he act in the name of goals. We ask that he keep his goals consistent. We ask that his actions be oriented to his goals. We ask that a social system amalgamate individual goals into a collective goal. But we do not concern ourselves with the origin of goals. Theories of individual organizational and social choice assume actors with pre-existent values.

Since it is obvious that goals change over time and that the character of those changes affects both the richness of personal and social development and the outcome of choice behavior, a theory of choice must somehow justify ignoring the phenomena. Although it is unreasonable to ask a theory of choice to solve all of the problems of man and his development, it is reasonable to ask how something as conspicuous as the fluidity and ambiguity of objectives can plausibly be ignored in a theory that is offered as a guide to human choice behavior.

There are three classic justifications. The first is that goal development and choice are independent processes, conceptually and behaviorally. The second is that the model of choice is never satisfied in fact that deviations from the model accommodate the problems of introducing change. The third is that the idea of changing goals is so intractable in a normative theory of choice that nothing can be said about it. Since I am unpersuaded of the first and second justifications, my optimism with respect to the third is somewhat greater than most of my fellows.

The argument that goal development and choice are independent behaviorally seems clearly false. It seems to me perfectly obvious that a description that assumes goals come first and action comes later is frequently radically wrong. Human choice behavior is at least as much a process for discovering goals as for acting on them. Although it is true enough that goals and decisions are 'conceptually' distinct, that is simply a statement of the theory. It is not defense of it. They are conceptually distinct if we choose to make them so.

The argument that the model is incomplete is more persuasive. There do appear to be some critical 'holes' in the system of intelligence as described by standard theories of choice. There is incomplete information, incomplete goal consistency, and a variety of external processes impinging on goal development – including tuition and tradition. What is somewhat disconcerting about the argument, however, is that it makes the efficacy of the concepts of intelligent choice dependent on their inadequacy. As we become more competent in the techniques of the model, and more committed to it, the 'holes' become smaller. As the model becomes more accepted, our obligation to modify it increases.

The final argument seems to me sensible as a general principle, but misleading here. Why are we more reluctant to ask how human beings might find 'good' goals than we are to ask how they might make 'good' decisions? The second question appears to be a relatively technical problem. The first seems more pretentious. It claims to say something about alternative virtues. The appearance of pretense, however, stems directly from the theory and the ideology associated with it.

In fact, the conscious introduction of goal discovery as a consideration in theories of human choice is not unknown to modern man. For example, we have two kinds of theories of choice behavior in human beings. One is a theory of children. The other is a theory of adults. In the theory of childhood, we emphasize choices as leading to experiences that develop the child's scope, his complexity, his awareness of the world. As parents, or psychologists, we try to lead the child to do things that are inconsistent with his present goals because we know (or believe) that he can only develop into an interesting person by coming to appreciate aspects of experience that he initially rejects.

In the theory of adulthood, we emphasize choices as a consequence of our intentions. As adults, or economists, we try to take actions that (within the limits of scarce resources) come as close as possible to achieving our goals. We try to find improved ways of making decisions consistent with our perceptions of what is valuable in the world.

The asymmetry in these models is conspicuous. Adults have constructed a model world in which adults know what is good for themselves, but children do not. It is hard to react positively to the conceit. The asymmetry has, in fact, stimulated a rather large number of ideologies and reforms designed to allow children the same moral prerogative granted to adults – the right to imagine that they know what they want. The efforts have cut deeply into traditional child-bearing, traditional educational policies, traditional politics, and traditional consumer economics.

In my judgment, the asymmetry between models of choice for adults and models of choice for children is awkward; but the solution we have adopted is precisely wrong-headed. Instead of trying to adapt the model of adults to children, we might better adapt the model of children to adults. For many purposes, our model of children is better. Of course, children know what they want. Everyone does. The critical question is whether they

258   Decision-making under ambiguity

are encouraged to develop more interesting 'wants'. Values change. People become more interesting as those values and the interconnections made among them change.

One of the most obvious things in the world turns out to be hard for us to accommodate in our theory of choice: A child of two will almost always have a less interesting set of values (yes, indeed, a *worse* set of values) than a child of twelve. The same is true of adults. Values develop through experience. Although one of the main natural arenas for the modification of human values is the area of choice, our theories of adult and organizational decision-making ignore the phenomenon entirely.

Introducing ambiguity and fluidity to the interpretation of individual, organizational, and societal goals, obviously has implications for behavioral theories of decision-making. The main point here, however, is not to consider how we might describe the behavior of systems that are discovering goals as they act. Rather it is to examine how we might improve the quality of that behavior, how we might aid the development of interesting goals.

We know how to advise a society, an organization, or an individual if we are first given a consistent set of preferences. Under some conditions, we can suggest how to make decisions if the preferences are only consistent up to the point of specifying a series of independent constraints on the choice. But what about a normative theory of goal-finding behavior? What do we say when our client tells us that he is not sure his present set of values is the set of values in terms of which he wants to act?

It is a question familiar to many aspects of ordinary life. It is a question that friends, associates, students, college presidents, business managers, voters, and children ask at least as frequently as they ask how they should act within a set consistent and stable values.

Within the context of the normative theory of choice as it exists, the answer we give is: First determine the values, then act. The advice is frequently useful. Moreover, we have developed ways in which we can use conventional techniques for decision analysis to help discover value premises and to expose value inconsistencies. These techniques involve testing the decision implications of some successive approximations to a set of preferences. The object is to find a consistent set of preferences with implications that are acceptable to the person or organization making the decisions. Variations on such techniques are used routinely in operations research, as well as in personal counseling and analysis.

The utility of such techniques, however, apparently depends on the assumption that a primary problem is the amalgamation or excavation of pre-existent values. The metaphors – 'finding oneself', 'goal clarification', 'self-discovery', 'social welfare function', 'revealed pre-reference' – are metaphors of search. If our value premises are to be 'constructed' rather than 'discovered', our standard procedures may be useful; but we have no *a priori* reason for assuming they will.

Perhaps we should explore a somewhat different approach to the normative question of how we ought to behave when our value premises are not yet (and never will be) fully determined. Suppose we treat action as a way of creating interesting goals at the same time as we treat goals as a way of justifying action. It is an intuitively plausible and simple idea, but one that is not immediately within the domain of standard normative theories of intelligent choice.

Interesting people and interesting organizations construct complicated theories of themselves. In order to do this, they need to supplement the technology of reason with a technology of foolishness. Individuals and organizations need ways of doing things for which they have no good reason. Not always. Not usually. But sometimes. They need to act before they think.

Sensible Foolishness

In order to use the act of intelligent choice as a planned occasion for discovering new goals, we apparently require some idea of sensible foolishness. Which of the many foolish things that we might do now will lead to attractive value consequences? The question is almost inconceivable. Not only does it ask us to predict the value consequences of action, it asks us to evaluate them. In what terms can we talk about 'good' changes in goals?

In effect, we are asked either to specify a set of super-goals in terms of which alternative goals are evaluated, or to choose among alternatives *now* in terms of the unknown set of values we will have at some future time (or the distribution over time of that unknown set of future values). The former alternative moves us back to the original situation of a fixed set of values – now called 'super-goals' – and hardly seems an important step in the direction of inventing procedures for discovering new goals. The latter alternative seems fundamental enough, but it violates severely our sense of temporal order. To say that we make decisions now in terms of goals that will only be knowable later is nonsensical – as long as we accept the basic framework of the theory of choice and its presumptions of pre-existent goals.

I do not know in detail what is required, but I think it will be substantial. As we challenge the dogma of pre-existent goals, we will be forced to re-examine some of our most precious prejudices: the strictures against imitation, coercion, and rationalization. Each of those honorable prohibitions depends on the view of man and human choice imposed on us by conventional theories of choice.

260   Decision-making under ambiguity

Imitation is not necessarily a sign of moral weakness. It is a prediction. It is a prediction that if we duplicate the behavior or attitudes of someone else, the chances of our discovering attractive new goals for ourselves are relatively high. In order for imitation to be normatively attractive we need a better theory of who should be imitated. Such a theory seems to be eminently feasible. For example, what are the conditions for effectiveness of a rule that you should imitate another person whose values are in a close neighborhood of yours? How do the chances of discovering interesting goals through imitation change as the number of other people exhibiting the behavior to be imitated increases?

Coercion is not necessarily an assault on individual autonomy. It can be a device for stimulating individuality. We recognize this when we talk about parents and children (at least sometimes). What has always been difficult with coercion is the possibility for perversion that it involves, not its obvious capability for stimulating change. What we require is a theory of the circumstances under which entry into a coercive system produces behavior that leads to the discovery of interesting goals. We are all familiar with the tactic. We use it in imposing deadlines, entering contracts, making commitments. What are the conditions for its effective use? In particular, what are the conditions for coercion in social systems?

Rationalization is not necessarily a way of evading morality. It can be a test for the feasibility of a goal change. When deciding among alternative actions for which we have no good reason, it may be sensible to develop some definition of how 'near' to intelligence alternative 'unintelligent' actions lie. Effective rationalization permits this kind of incremental approach to changes in values. To use it effectively, however, we require a better idea of the kinds of metrics that might be possible in measuring value distances. At the same time, rationalization is the major procedure for integrating newly discovered goals into an existing structure of values. It provides the organization of complexity without which complexity itself becomes indistinguishable from randomness.

There are dangers in imitation, coercion, and rationalization. The risks are too familiar to elaborate. We should, indeed, be able to develop better techniques. Whatever those techniques may be, however, they will almost certainly undermine the superstructure of biases erected on purpose, consistency, and rationality. They will involve some way of thinking about action now as occurring in terms of a set of unknown future values.

Play and Reason

A second requirement for a technology of foolishness is some strategy for suspending rational imperatives toward consistency. Even if we know which of several foolish things we want to do, we still need a mechanism for allowing us to do it. How do we escape the logic of our reason?

Here, I think, we are closer to understanding what we need. It is playfulness. Playfulness is the deliberate, temporary relaxation of rules in order to explore the possibilities of alternative rules. When we are playful, we challenge the necessity of consistency. In effect, we announce – in advance – our rejection of the usual objections to behavior that does not fit the standard model of intelligence.

Playfulness allows experimentation. At the same time, it acknowledges reason. It accepts an obligation that at some point either the playful behavior will be stopped or it will be integrated into the structure of intelligence in some way that makes sense. The suspension of the rules is temporary.

The idea of play may suggest three things that are, in my mind, quite erroneous in the present context. First, play may be seen as a kind of Mardi Gras for reason, a release of emotional tensions of virtue. Although it is possible that play performs some such function, that is not the function with which I am concerned. Second, play may be seen as part of some mystical balance of spiritual principles: Fire and water, hot and cold, weak and strong. The intention here is much narrower than a general mystique of balance. Third, play may be seen as an antithesis of intelligence, so that the emphasis on the importance of play becomes a support for simple self-indulgence. My present intent is to propose play as an instrument of intelligence, not a substitute.

Playfulness is a natural outgrowth of our standard view of reason. A strict insistence on purpose, consistency, and rationality limits our ability to find new purposes. Play relaxes that insistence to allow us to act 'unintelligently' or 'irrationally', or 'foolishly' to explore alternative ideas of possible purposes and alternative concepts of behavioral consistency. And it does this while maintaining our basic commitment to the necessity of intelligence.

Although play and reason are in this way functional complements, they are often behavioral competitors. They are alternative styles and alternative orientations to the same situation. There is no guarantee that the styles will be equally well-developed. There is no guarantee that all individuals, all organizations, or all societies will be equally adept in both styles. There is no guarantee that all cultures will be equally encouraging to both.

Our design problem is either to specify the best mix of styles or, failing that, to assure that most people and most organizations most of the time use an alternation of strategies rather than perseverate in either one. It is a difficult problem. The optimization problem looks extremely difficult on the face of it, and the learning situations that will produce alternation in behavior appear to be somewhat less common than those that produce perseveration.

262 Decision-making under ambiguity

Consider, for example, the difficulty of sustaining playfulness as a style within contemporary American society. Individuals who are good at consistent rationality are rewarded early and heavily. We define it as intelligence, and the educational rewards of society are associated strongly with it. Social norms press in the same direction, particularly for men. Many of the demands of modern organizational life reinforce the same abilities and style preferences.

The result is that many of the most influential, best-educated, and best-placed citizens have experienced a powerful overlearning with respect to rationality. They are exceptionally good at maintaining consistent pictures of themselves, of relating action to purposes. They are exceptionally poor at a playful attitude toward their own beliefs, toward the logic of consistency, or toward the way they see things as being connected in the world. The dictates of manliness, forcefulness, independence, and intelligence are intolerant of playful urges if they arise. The playful urges that arise are weak ones.

The picture is probably overdrawn, but not, I believe, the implications. For societies, for organizations, and for individuals, reason and intelligence have had the unnecessary consequence of inhibiting the development of purpose into more complicated forms of consistency. In order to move away from that position, we need to find some ways of helping individuals and organizations to experiment with doing things for which they have no good reason, to be playful with their conception of themselves. It is a facility that requires more careful attention than I can give it, but I would suggest five things as a small beginning:

1 We can treat *goals as hypotheses*. Conventional decision theory allows us to entertain doubts about almost everything except the thing about which we frequently have the greatest doubt – our objectives. Suppose we define the decision process as a time for the sequential testing of hypotheses about goals. If we can experiment with alternative goals, we stand some chance of discovering complicated and interesting combinations of good values that none of us previously imagined.

2 We can treat *intuition as real*. I do not know what intuition is, or even if it is any one thing. Perhaps it is simply an excuse for doing something we cannot justify in terms of present values or for refusing to follow the logic of our own beliefs. Perhaps it is an inexplicable way of consulting that part of our intelligence that is not organized in a way anticipated by standard theories of choice. In either case, intuition permits us to see some possible actions that are outside our present scheme for justifying behavior.

3 We can treat *hypocrisy as a transition*. Hypocrisy is an inconsistency between expressed values and behavior. Negative attitudes

about hypocrisy stem from two major things. The first is a general onus against inconsistency. The second is a sentiment against combining the pleasures of vice with the appearance of virtue. Apparently, that is an unfair way of allowing evil to escape temporal punishment. Whatever the merits of such a position as ethics, it seems to me distinctly inhibiting toward change. A bad man with good intentions may be a man experimenting with the possibility of becoming good. Somehow it seems to me more sensible to encourage the experimentation than to insult it.

4 We can treat *memory as an enemy*. The rules of consistency and rationality require a technology of memory. For most purposes, good memories make good choices. But the ability to forget, or overlook, is also useful. If I do not know what I did yesterday or what other people in the organization are doing today, I can act within the system of reason and still do things that are foolish.

5 We can treat *experience as a theory*. Learning can be viewed as a series of conclusions based on concepts of action and consequences that we have invented. Experience can be changed retrospectively. By changing our interpretive concepts now, we modify what we learned earlier. Thus, we expose the possibility of experimenting with alternative histories. The usual strictures against 'self-deception' in experience need occasionally to be tempered with an awareness of the extent to which all experience is an interpretation subject to conscious revision. Personal histories, and national histories, need to be rewritten rather continuously as a base for the retrospective learning of new self-conceptions.

Each of these procedures represents a way in which we temporarily suspend the operation of the system of reasoned intelligence. They are playful. They make greatest sense in situations in which there has been an overlearning of virtues of conventional rationality. They are possibly dangerous applications of powerful devices more familiar to the study of behavioral pathology than to the investigation of human development. But they offer a few techniques for introducing change within current concepts of choice.

The argument extends easily to the problems of social organization. If we knew more about the normative theory of acting before you think, we could say more intelligent things about the functions of management and leadership when organizations or societies do not know what they are doing. Consider, for example, the following general implications.

First, we need to re-examine the functions of management decision. One of the primary ways in which the goals of an organization are developed is by interpreting the decisions it makes, and one feature of good managerial decisions is that they lead to the development of more interesting value-premises for the organization. As a result, decisions

264   Decision-making under ambiguity

should not be seen as flowing directly or strictly from a pre-existent set of objectives. Managers who make decisions might well view that function somewhat less as a process of deduction or a process of political negotiation, and somewhat more as a process of gently upsetting preconceptions of what the organization is doing.

Second, we need a modified view of planning. Planning in organizations has many virtues, but a plan can often be more effective as an interpretation of past decisions than as a program for future ones. It can be used as a part of the efforts of the organization to develop a new consistent theory of itself that incorporates the mix of recent actions into a moderately comprehensive structure of goals. Procedures for interpreting the meaning of most past events are familiar to the memoirs of retired generals, prime ministers, business leaders, and movie stars. They suffer from the company they keep. In an organization that wants to continue to develop new objectives, a manager needs to be relatively tolerant of the idea that he will discover the meaning of yesterday's action in the experiences and interpretations of today.

Third, we need to reconsider evaluation. As nearly as I can determine, there is nothing in a formal theory of evaluation that requires that the criterion function for evaluation be specified in advance. In particular, the evaluation of social experiments need not be in terms of the degree to which they have fulfilled our *a priori* expectations. Rather we can examine what they did in terms of what we now believe to be important. The prior specification of criteria and the prior specification of evaluational procedures that depend on such criteria are common presumptions in contemporary social policy-making. They are presumptions that inhibit the serendipitous discovery of new criteria. Experience should be used explicitly as an occasion for evaluating our values as well as our actions.

Fourth, we need a reconsideration of social accountability. Individual preferences and social action need to be consistent in some way. But the process of pursuing consistency is one in which both the preferences and the actions change over time. Imagination in social policy formation involves systematically adapting to and influencing preferences. It would be unfortunate if our theories of social action encouraged leaders to ignore their responsibilities for anticipating public preferences through action and for providing social experiences that modify individual expectations.

Fifth, we need to accept playfulness in social organizations. The design of organizations should attend to the problems of maintaining both playfulness and reason as aspects of intelligent choice. Since much of the literature on social design is concerned with strengthening the rationality of decision, managers are likely to overlook the importance of play. This is partly a matter of making the individuals within an organization more playful by encouraging the attitudes and skills of inconsistency. It is also a a matter of making organizational structure and organizational procedure more playful. Organizations can be playful even when the participants in them are not. The managerial devices for maintaining consistency can be varied. We encourage organizational play by permitting (and insisting on) some temporary relief from control, coordination, and communication.

Intelligence and Foolishness

Contemporary theories of decision-making and the technology of reason have considerably strengthened our capabilities for effective social action. The conversion of the simple ideas of choice into an extensive technology is a major achievement. It is, however, an achievement that has reinforced some biases in the underlying models of choice in individuals and groups. In particular, it has reinforced the uncritical acceptance of a static interpretation of human goals.

There is little magic in the world, and foolishness in people and organizations is one of the many things that fail to produce miracles. Under certain conditions, it is one of several ways in which some of the problems of our current theories of intelligence can be overcome. It may be a good way. It preserves the virtues of consistency while stimulating change. If we had a good technology of foolishness, it might (in combination with the technology of reason) help in a small way to develop the unusual combinations of attitudes and behaviors that describe the interesting people, interesting organizations, and interesting societies of the world.

Part III
Implementing the Decision

[13]

Strategic Management Journal, Vol. 8, 1–14 (1987)

IDENTIFYING AND APPRAISING HOW MANAGERS INSTALL STRATEGY[1]

PAUL C. NUTT

Graduate Program in Hospital and Health Services Administration and Faculty of Management and Human Resources, The Ohio State University, Columbus, Ohio, U.S.A.

Cases were profiled to identify tactics used by strategic managers to implement strategy and to determine which tactic was the most effective in promoting adoption. Analysis revealed that four archetype tactics were used almost exclusively. An 'interventionist' approach had the best results but was used in only one case in five. 'Persuasion' and 'participation' were next most effective tactics, and 'edicts' the least effective. The implications of these findings for strategic management practice and the needs for further research are discussed.

INTRODUCTION

According to Ansoff (1965), strategic planning takes place in an integrated system with steps that range from formulation to implementation. Strategy emerges after going through several levels of activity such as strategic options (e.g. new markets); project development (e.g. new products, service, operations, and/or policies); and programming (budgeting and scheduling). This cascaded set of activities begins with the setting of intentions, gradually considering more specific issues to arrive at a specific action, such as a merger or a new service, which requires implementation. Strategic planning involves the identification and selection of what Glueck (1980) calls the 'strategic management elements', determining organizational intentions and selecting priority strategic options, and the 'strategic management process' in which analysis, choice, implementation and evaluation are carried out. Strategic planning is used to create and prioritize strategic options, and project planning devises

specific actions which allow the organization to realize its targeted priorities (Nutt, 1984).

Schendel and Hofer (1979) define strategic implementation in terms of control, ensuring that priority strategic options shape action-taking, and setting in place specific projects. Thus, a key aspect of strategic implementation concerns taking action and measuring performance which stems from this action-taking. The purpose of this paper is to explore the tactics managers use to install this type of plan. Schendel and Hofer (1979) call this set of activities strategic implementation 'narrowly defined'. The research was carried out to identify and describe the approaches that managers use when they go about this type of implementation.

Implementation takes place through managerial action-taking (Simon. 1982). Beyond acknowledging the pivotal role of the manager, little else about implementation seems generally accepted. The widely reported incidence of plan failure (e.g. Schultz and Slevin, 1975) and the needs articulated by managers (Campbell, Daft and Hulin, 1982) suggest that a careful examination of implementation practice is a priority. Two questions can be posed. The first concerns how implementation is carried out by strategic

[1] An earlier version of this paper was presented at the IFORS-TIMS International Conference in Lausanne. Switzerland. July 11-15. 1982.

0143-2095/87/010001-14$07.00

Received 3 February 1984
Revised 8 July 1985

2   *P. C. Nutt*

managers. The second considers the relative effectiveness of these implementation tactics.

A multiple case study approach with testable hypotheses, like that called for by Harrigan (1983), was used. Sixty-eight case studies of strategic planning were examined to discover and explore the merits of implementation tactics used by managers. The cases include a variety of projects used to plan services, internal operations, or policies (e.g. wages and benefits) which help to carry out the strategy formulated by service organizations. Each case in the data base was profiled to identify implementation practices. The outcome of the implementation attempt and key intervening variables were also collected to make a commentary on the effectiveness of the implementation tactics and the influence of context. The cases were categorized according to explanatory variables to make a post-hoc assessment of the effect of these variables.

Like most important questions that must be broadly framed, some rigor has been sacrificed for relevance. The importance of the topic was thought to justify a clear look at the phenomenon as it is *practiced*, using a combination of descriptive and quantitative tools (e.g. Miller and Friesen, 1982).

RESEARCH DESIGN

This paper is a significant departure from the typical study because it attempts to identify and classify patterns of practice used in implementation and measure the merits of these implementation practices. The approach used to identify implementation practice, the independent variable in this study, is discussed in this section of the paper and the measurement of intervening and dependent variables and analysis approach in the next.

Identifying implementation practice

The controlled experiment and the case study bracket approaches which can be used to study implementation. To make inferences about causation, the controlled experiment is limited to the exploration of a few narrowly defined factors. This type of study often has students role-playing managers to determine how various tactics are related to an outcome, such as satisfaction (e.g.

Alavi and Henderson, 1981). This approach has several limitations. First, an effective response, such as satisfaction, may have little to do with an organization's adoption decision. Second, practice and the behavior observed in a laboratory often has little relationship. The laboratory study must be carried out in a narrow context, often with substantial deviations from field conditions, making it difficult to generalize the findings.

Implementation researchers make a strong case for the study of real, rather than simulated, situations, sacrificing some measurement rigor to make direct observations (e.g. Beyer and Trice, 1982). As Schendel and Hofer (1979) point out, executives confronted with the need to direct and manage an organization must have invested considerable time and effort in developing ways to carry out implementation, making the practitioner a crucial source of information. A variety of techniques can be used to surface this information, including: mailed survey (e.g. Duncan, 1974), participant observations (e.g. Mann and Likert, 1952), in-depth single case analysis (e.g. Williams and Evans, 1972), structured and unstructured interview (e.g. Weiss, 1980, 1981), secondary analysis of records and pronouncements (Huff, in press), and critical event identification (Mintzberg and Waters, 1982). These approaches have provided rich descriptions of practice, which are often illuminating, but say little about what may have caused an outcome, such as failure or success.

This research uses a multiple case study approach. Multiple case studies overcome many of the single case study limitations while preserving some strengths of a laboratory study. Realistic measures of success, such as outcome, can be used. Salient features of practice are captured which allow the researcher to identify practice variations. These practice variations become the independent variables in the study, which can be related to success measures. However, care must be taken so that case types are reliably grouped (Yin, 1981).

Selection of projects

Strategic planning projects in 68 different organizations were studied to identify implementation tactics. Organizations that provided clinical education for students served as the data base. The CEO, COO, or CFO in each organization was contacted and asked to participate in a study of strategic planning effectiveness by allowing one of their projects to be profiled. All of the organizations agreed to participate. The contact person was asked to name two executives who were the most familiar with the planning effort for in-depth interviewing, including, if possible, the executive who was administratively responsible for the project.

The contact person was asked to select a plan that had strategic importance to the organization. No other guidelines for selection were offered. Although some biases may have been introduced by allowing the contact person to screen the plan, this approach helped to insure that the participants would be cooperative throughout the interviews. When several options were offered, one was selected that added diversity to the data base, both in terms of type and outcome, such as failures. The plans included mergers; physical plant expansions; major equipment purchases; management information systems; marketing programs; the development of services, such as burn care programs and open heart surgery; product pricing; financial planning; regional center development; organizational restructuring; data processing; facility relocations; and major space renovations.

Each of the participating organizations was involved in some form of service delivery. The participating organizations included hospitals, and other non-profit or third-sector organizations, such as charities and professional societies, and governmental agencies. The generalizability of the study's findings may be limited to these organizations. The organizations were widely dispersed across the United States and Canada, suggesting that a broad range of strategic implementation practice was represented. The cases in this study, like similar studies reported in the literature (e.g. Mintzberg and Waters, 1982), do not represent a random sample. A positive bias may be present because organizations that participate voluntarily are likely to share information about practices and ideas they believe to be high quality.

Profiling implementation tactics

Multiple interviews were used to minimize memory distortion and memory failure, the two most common errors in reconstructing events

(Mintzberg, Raisinghani and Theoret, 1976). Separate interviews with key executives were conducted by the author, asking each interviewee to spell out the sequence of planning steps taken. These initial interviews lasted between 1 and 2 hours. A written summary of these steps was prepared by the author. The summary was presented to each executive to verify that it captured the process as they recalled it. The steps were modified until they were acceptable.

The steps listed by the executives were compared, and differences identified. An additional interview was used to reconcile differences. The executives were asked to modify the list of steps until a consensus emerged. When differences persisted, others involved in the project were also interviewed. This, along with sources such as reports and records, were used to determine which version of events seemed to be the most plausible. If the disagreement persisted after a review of this information, the case would be discarded. A case was retained for the classification phase of the study if two tests were met: agreement on process steps and sufficient detail to understand what was done. All of the cases met these tests.

Data collection and reduction averaged 20 hours per case. The data were compiled over a period of 5 years. The summary of steps described the entire planning process. This study focuses on the steps which pertained to implementation.

Classifying the tactics

An implementation tactic was called unique when distinct steps were used. To identify unique tactics, a one-page summary of the implementation steps was prepared for each case. These summaries were sorted by the author, placing each case in a pile that used similar steps until a set of groupings emerged that seemed mutually exclusive. After sorting, a code number was placed on the back of each case summary and the sorting process repeated. Cases with an ambiguous classification were carefully reviewed, attempting to create a new category or to match it with an existing one.

This process was repeated a year later without reference to the first sort to get an indication of intra-rater reliability. These classifications matched perfectly. A second rater was asked to sort the summaries to get an indication of inter-

4   P. C. Nutt

rater reliability. The classification agreement between raters was quite high (over 90 percent) suggesting that the distinct categories had been identified.

Implementation tactics discovered

Four distinct implementation tactics, some with subclassifications and others representing hybrid forms of two or more of the distinct types, emerged from the analysis. Sixty-two or 91 percent of the cases were classified as one of four distinct types called intervention, participation,

persuasion, and edict. Table 1 summarizes these tactics and how they differ. The remaining six cases (9 percent of the total) used a hybrid approach, such as switching or merging the four basic tactics. There were too few hybrid cases to permit analysis so they were deleted from the study.

Intervention implementation

The intervention tactic was observed in 21 percent of the cases (Table 1). Implementation activities began when a manager was delegated the

Table 1. Salient differences in tactics used for strategic implementation

Tactic	Frequency of occurrence	Key features	A summary of key steps[a]
Intervention implementation	21%	1. A manager is delegated authority to control a planning process 2. Groups used to offer advice which manager can veto	1. *New norms used to identify performance problems in system(s) that the strategy is to change* 2. *New norms justified* 3. *Illustrate how performance can be improved* 4. *Formulate plan[b]* 5. *Show how plan improves performance*
Participation implementation	15%	1. Group can specify plan features, within prestated constraints 2. Staff assigned to support the planning group	1. Manager stipulates strategic needs and opportunities 2. *Form planning group by selecting stakeholders* 3. *Delegate planning to the group and state intentions (objectives and constraints)* 4. *Formulate plan[b]* 5. *Cooptation of key people*
Persuasion implementation	48%	1. Demonstrations of value 2. An expert manages the planning process	1. Manager stipulates strategic needs and opportunities 2. *Authorize an expert to develop ideas responsive to the strategy.* 3. Formulate plan[b] 4. *Expert uses persuasion to sell manager on plan's value as a response to a strategic priority*
Edict implementation	16%	1. The manager and staff share process management 2. Manager uses position power to implement the plan	1. Sponsor stipulates strategic needs and opportunities 2. Formulate plan[b] 3. *Manager issues a directive which calls for plan adoption*

[a] Steps in italics were found to differentiate the implementation tactics.
[b] Several additional steps were taken to develop the plan.

authority to make changes required by a priority strategic option. Next, the manager created a need for change in the minds of key people by renorming the system(s) to be changed. For example, a new norm could be applied to unit cost performance by showing how a comparable organization had been able to get better results. (These new norms were, on occasion, bogus, using anecdotal information and making ad-hoc comparisons, such as comparing costs in full service and small community hospitals. However, in most of the cases the comparisons were legitimate and suggested a real opportunity to make positive change.) These steps were taken to demonstrate that the current performance level was inadequate. This demonstration was followed by the identification of plausible causes of the performance deficiencies. Illustrations of how current practices could be improved were often used to make this point. These suggestions defined options that the planning process had to consider. All planning activities were regulated by the manager, making it clear to all participants who had control. Committees were sometimes used as a sounding board, offering a commentary on ideas as they evolved. After a plan had been devised, the manager demonstrated how action called for by the plan overcomes performance deficiencies, terminating formal project planning activities.

Participation implementation

In participation implementation a manager initiated planning by stipulating strategic needs and an arena of action, specified by a priority strategic option, and delegated project development to a group. The group members were carefully selected so that key points of view and information would be represented. As a result, planning groups were often made up of two types of people: individuals that had either vested interests or the knowledge to offer ideas.

Under the participation tactic both the manager, who initiated planning, and a planning group share responsibility for guiding the process. The planning group made suggestions and decisions, aided by staff who provided the information requested by the group. If the group had the authority to make *decisions* about the features of the plan, the implementation tactic was termed participative. The group leader could

not have veto power. As long as constraints were adhered to, it was understood that the plan proposed by the group would be adopted. The participation tactic was observed in 15 percent of the cases (Table 1).

Persuasion implementation

In persuasion implementation a manager implicitly or explicitly delegates the development of ideas consistent with priority strategic directions to technical staff or consultants. When this delegation was explicit the manager assigned project development to an expert. An implicit delegation occurred when an expert approached the manager and garnered the authority to develop an idea which appeared to aid in the realization of priority strategic aims. The expert used the sponsor's stipulation of priority strategic directions, carried out planning, and then attempted to 'sell' the resulting plan. The plan's ability to help the manager realize a strategic aim was used by the expert to argue for its adoption. The manager became actively involved only at this point, weighing the imperatives to act. Managers often required extensive documentation of benefits before acting, which forced the expert to carry out several evaluations. Note that an expert could be a consultant or an organizational staff; however, only internal staff experts were observed in this study. Persuasion implementation was observed in 48 percent of the cases, making it the most commonly used implementation tactic (Table 1).

Implementation by edict

Managers used an edict when directives for plan adoption were issued. The use of power was the dominant theme in these cases. The manager announced the plan and prescribed the expected behavior using a memorandum, formal presentation, or on-the-job instruction. For example, to introduce a new fringe benefit policy as part of a strategic plan, a manager prepared a memo which listed benefits and co-pay requirements and sent it to all employees.

Edicts were observed when a manager attempted to show that his/her pet idea provided a way to deal with priority directions called for in the strategic plan. Managers with a vested interest often used power tactics. Edicts were also used when the plan had special significance or high visibility in contributing to a priority strategic direction. Building programs and other costly undertakings often conjured up sufficient importance to entice the use of an edict. This tactic was used in 16 percent of the cases (Table 1).

Assessing the implementation tactics

Three types of data were collected from the interviews, in addition to that used to identify implementation tactics. The participating managers were asked to indicate the organization's view of the plan, to identify values for the intervening variables, and to describe plan characteristics. These data were used to specify values for the intervening variables and the dependent variables used to test the merits of each implementation tactic.

The same precautions were taken to verify these estimates as were used in isolating implementation tactics. The estimates were compared and differences discussed, if observed. If differences remained after discussions, the case would be discarded.

Measures of plan merit

Two measures were used to determine the value of the plan: a rating of perceived quality and whether the plan was used. The quality rating was made using an anchored rating scale, with five anchor points, as shown below:

5 = Outstanding, important contribution
4 = Adequate, met our needs
3 = Disappointing, some problems remain
2 = Poor, many problems remain
1 = Unacceptable, plan should be rejected

The managers were asked to compare the plan with others being used by the organization. This approach gives a comparative rating if one assumes that most experienced managers have seen a variety of plans drawn in response to a strategy, both good and bad. Differences in the ratings were discussed and reconciled, following the estimate–discuss–estimate format (Gustafson *et al.*, 1973). The average rating which resulted from this discussion was used in the analysis (Nutt, 1977).

Status was measured objectively, determining whether or not the plan has been adopted by the organization. An implementation success can be defined in various ways (Beyer and Trice, 1982). The strongest test determines if a plan has been institutionalized, as opposed to being used symbolically or conceptually. For instance, a manager can use a plan to enlighten the organization about possibilities (a conceptual use) or to discredit an existing practice (a symbolic use). Neither approach institutionalizes the plan. In this research implementation success was defined as whether or not the plan was put to use by the organization.

Intervening variables

The interviewees were asked to provide data which indicated how the plan was viewed by the organization. The managers indicated which of several descriptions, shown in Table 2, best characterized the project. The EDE format was used to improve the reliability of the classifications. As before the first step had each interviewee fill out the survey. Discrepancies were discussed and reconciled. Disagreements did not occur often and, when they did, discussion produced a mutually agreeable classification.

Planning initially thought to be particularly important in realizing a strategic aim may receive more attention. This attention could have had a greater influence on adoption prospects than the implementation tactics that were applied. This suggests that 'plan importance' should be measured and treated as a potential causal factor. Similarly, the resources available to the project planning process and time constraints imposed by higher-ups, or by circumstances, can have biasing effects, calling for tactics thought to be timely if not ideal. Finally, projects such as building programs associated with creating a new product or service may be viewed as more important than modifying an internal operation, such as data processing. Building programs may call for more managerial attention, which may tend to make success a *fait accompli*. If found to be important, the intervening variables provide a way to qualify the value of implementation tactics. For example, some implementation tactics may be superior when used under conditions of time pressure or low budgets. If the intervening variables are not important, the findings can

Table 2. Planning case profile

Contextual factors	Rating or frequency
Type of strategic response:	
Change in internal operation	20.3%
New internal operation	15.2%
A modification in a service	45.7%
A new service	18.6%
Perceived importance[a]	
Critical, organizational survival at stake	6.2%
Very important, key power centers wanted good results	18.8%
Important, typical or our plans	51.6%
Somewhat important, a routine effort	21.9%
A mistake, plan not needed	0
Support staff skill[a]	
Always performs well	59.3%
Manager told staff would do well	31.2%
No knowledge of staff person's past work	9.4%
Past performance has been poor	0
Time pressure[a]	
Absent	3.1%
Low	16.6%
Moderate	35.9%
High	28.1%
Very high	17.2%
Resources available[a]	
Far above the typical plan	15.9%
Above the typical plan	20.6%
Similar to the typical plan	42.6%
Below the typical plan	15.9%
Far below the typical plan	4.7%
Outcome	
Plan quality[a]	
(rating by managers on scale of 1 = poor and 5 = outstanding)	3.7
Plan status	
Adopted	69.7%
Rejected	23.9%
Shelved, adoption uncertain	6.1%

[a] Perceptions of participating executives

be generalized across comparable projects and environments.

The intervening variables also provide a profile of the data base, as shown in Table 2. Seventy percent of the projects involved the modification of an existing strategy. Most organizations were found to adopt an incremental change in existing practices in response to the strategic directions that were set by the organization. Thirty percent called for innovation, or a radical change in their strategy. Service development accounted for 64 percent of the projects, with the rest concerned

with internal operations. Seventy-eight percent of the strategic plans were perceived to be important to critical. Most (90 percent) sponsors saw the staff support as competent. Time pressure and resources made available to the process seemed normally distributed, with moderate pressure and resources describing the typical plan in the data base (Table 2).

The distribution of the outcome ratings is also shown in Table 2. The average rating was 3.7, suggesting that the typical plan in this study was judged to fall just below 'meeting needs'. Seventy

8   P. C. Nutt

percent of the plans were adopted, 24 percent rejected, and 6 percent shelved.

Analysis approach

The key independent variable in the study was 'implementation tactic'. The dependent variables were the plan's quality rating and status. The intervening variables of project type, perceived plan importance, support staff skill, time pressure, and resources available to planning were included in an attempt to control for the effect of factors external to implementation.

Multivariate techniques were used to determine if the implementation approach, and if the intervening variables, influence the quality ratings and success rates. The anchored rating scale for the quality rating creates interval scale properties in this dependent variable which permits the use of parametric statistics. The adoption factor has but two levels: success and failure. However, Nerlove and Press (1973) find that parametric techniques, such as regression and ANOVA, can be used on a dichotomous dependent variable if the proportion of cases that fall into the two categories have less than an 80/20 split. The adoption rate of 69 percent falls well within this requirement.

Regression techniques were used, so the results of the analyses of the two dependent variables can be contrasted. The independent variables were treated as factors with multiple levels in the analysis. Logit and discriminant analysis are inappropriate because they require the independent variables to be measured on an interval scale. The key independent variable in this study (implementation approach) and several of the intervening variables are categorical, invalidating this type of analysis. Non-parametric ANOVAs using the Kriskal–Wallis chi-square approximations were used to validate the significance levels found in the parametric tests. If similar, the assumptions made in the analysis can be verified.

DISCUSSION OF RESULTS

A series of one-way fixed-effects ANOVAs were run with implementation approach, project type, importance, resources used, skill level of support staff, or time constraints as the independent

variable and with quality rating or status as the dependent variable. Both parametric and non-parametric tests were applied, with nearly identical results. In these analyses only the implementation approach variable proved to be significant ($p \leq 0.05$). This suggests that implementation tactics had an important role in promoting plan success, which merits careful interpretation.

Implementation tactics

A Duncan multiple range test (DMRT), shown in Table 3, was carried out with 'implementation tactic' as the independent variable using first quality rating and then status as the dependent variable. The Duncan test is one of several that can be applied to make *a posteriori* tests of differences among the classification categories of an independent variable. The Duncan test was selected because it uses a level of significance comparable to making comparisons of category pairs using a t-statistic. The Tukey, Scheffe, and Newman–Keuls procedures are viewed as overly conservative for this type of test (Winer, 1971).

The Duncan test compares the implementation tactics two at a time using the equivalent of a t-test to determine if these categories differ for values of a dependent variable (success rates or quality rating). All tests in the DMRT are made

Table 3. Quality and status of plans and implementation tactics

Implementation tactic	N	Rating[a]	Category[b]
Intervention	13	4.3	1
Persuasion	30	3.8	2
Participation	9	3.3	2
Edict	10	3.0	3

Tactic	N	Percent adopted	Category[b]
Intervention	13	100	1
Participation	9	78	2
Persuasion	29	74	2
Edict	10	40	3

[a] Rating scale anchor points: 5 = outstanding, important contribution, to 1 = unacceptable, plan should be rejected.
[b] Duncan multiple range test ($p \leq 0.05$).

using an 0.05 level of significance. A code is used to signify categories (implementation tactics) that have performance differences, as shown in Table 3. For both dependent variables, significant differences were observed. Furthermore, the best-to-worst ordering of the implementation tactic using the DMRT was the same for each dependent variable. Special credence can be given to these findings because conclusions from distinct measures of effectiveness were found to agree (Fisher, 1979).

The intervention tactic had 100 percent adoption rate and a rating of 4.3, making it the most successful tactic. Using the anchor points on the rating scale to interpret the quality rating, the typical plan fell just below making an 'important contribution'. *All* of the plans using the intervention tactic were adopted.

The success of the intervention tactic can be attributed to an executive's ability to make things happen, when they *manage* a planning process to realize their strategic aims. In contrast, merely applying power (using edicts) was found to have a high risk of failure. Edicts had a 40 percent adoption rate. These plans were termed 'disappointing' (3.0) and had the lowest rating among the implementation tactics. This clear-cut distinction between using power and applying the interventionist tools of demonstration and justification seems to illustrate one dimension of the successful strategic manager.

The prospects of a successful strategic implementation using participation and persuasion tactics were found to be similar, using the DMRT. Plans implemented using participation tactics were rated just above 'disappointing' (3.3) and those implemented using the persuasion tactics just below 'meet our needs' (3.8). The participation implemented plans had a 78 percent adoption rate and persuasion implemented projects a 74 percent adoption rate.

The similarity in success rates for the participation and persuasion implementation tactics is surprising. The leverage of cooptation and the disadvantages implicit in a sales approach make participation seem more likely to gain plan adoption. Apparently the staff expert could marshal and use rationale which demonstrated plan value just as effectively as the cooptation inherent in the participation approach. Perhaps more extensive participation involving all of the affected parties would have been more successful.

Conditions of use

A statistical interaction depicts how well each implementation tactic works under various environmental conditions and pressures. The implementation approach variable was paired with each of the intervening variables, one at a time, to explore how the implementation tactics are influenced by staff skill level, time pressure, resources, importance, and project type. The interactions, which determine conditions of use, were marginally significant ($p \leq 0.10$), but the difficulty of data collection justifies an interpretation. The resource factor had no effect in these analyses.

The support staff skill level and implementation approach interaction is shown on Table 4. To conduct this analysis, only the 'performs well' and 'told performs well' (see Table 2) categories of the skill factor were used, so there would be sufficient data to permit analysis. The skill factor was analyzed with these two categories along with the implementation approach factor using a two-way fixed effects ANOVA. The analysis found that the redefined skill factor's main effect was significant but the interaction was not. When the manager had previously *observe* the support staff's past performance both adoption rates and quality ratings increased. These data suggest a preference for support staff with which the manager has had successful past experiences. Managers in this study were reluctant to adopt a staff-advocated plan when they have no personal knowledge of the staff person's prior performance (Table 2).

To determine the effect of perceived time pressure data comparable categories of the time pressure factor were combined so there would be sufficient data to permit analysis. The low and moderate, and the high and very high, categories in Table 2 were merged into new categories called 'low' and 'high', respectively. (There were no projects in the time pressure absent category so this category could be ignored in the analysis.) The time pressure factor with these two categories and the implementation factor were analyzed using a two-way fixed-effects ANOVA format. This analysis found a significant interaction between time pressure and implementation tactics. The effects of time pressure were different for each of the implementation tactics, as shown in Table 5.

10   *P. C. Nutt*

Table 4. Implementation tactics and perceived staff skill

| | | Staff performance verified by | |
		Recommendations	Observations
Tactics	Persuasion	66%[a] / 3.75[b] ($N = 12$[c])	75% / 3.88 ($N = 16$)
	Intervention	100% / 4.0 ($N = 3$)	100% / 4.5 ($N = 8$)
	Participation	75% / 2.75 ($N = 4$)	80% / 3.8 ($N = 5$)
	Edict	25% / 3.0 ($N = 4$)	50% / 3.0 ($N = 6$)

[a] Adoption rate.
[b] Plan quality rating.
[c] Number of projects.
Tactics ($p \leqslant 0.05$).
Skill ($p \leqslant 0.05$).
Skill–tactics interaction (N.S.).

Table 5. Implementation tactics and time pressure

| | | Time pressure | |
		Low	High
Tactics	Persuasion	78.8% / 4.0 ($N = 19$)	59.6% / 3.6 ($N = 10$)
	Intervention	100% / 4.0 ($N = 5$)	100% / 4.42 ($N = 17$)
	Participation	67% / 2.3 ($N = 3$)	83.5% / 3.87 ($N = 6$)
	Edict	25% / 3.2 ($N = 5$)	40% / 2.8 ($N = 5$)

Tactic ($p \leqslant 0.05$).
Time pressure (N.S.).
Tactic–pressure interaction ($p \leqslant 0.10$).

Adoption rates declined when experts attempted to sell a plan under conditions of high time pressure. Nearly 80 percent of the plans were adopted when pressure was low and less than 60 percent when pressure was high. When managers used edicts, or delegated planning to a task force, the reverse occurred. The adoption rates increased under conditions of high time pressure when the participation and edict tactics were used. Apparently a manager's delegation or unilateral action, coupled with time pressure, enhances adoption prospects. Organizational experts may not be seen as legitimate advocates of a plan when time pressure is present.

The differences in plan quality ratings (Table 5) generally agree with those for adoption rates. When the expert develops implementation rationale under conditions of high pressure the plan's rating declines. The ratings increased when the intervention and participation tactics were used. Edicts improved adoption prospects but resulted in a lower rating for plans implemented in this manner.

Again due to small cell sizes, it would be impossible to judge the effect of perceived importance without merging the categories shown in Table 2. New categories were created called moderate, made up of the 'important' and 'somewhat important' categories in Table 2; and high, made up of the 'critical' and 'very important' categories. (There were no projects in the plan 'not needed' category, see Table 2.) A two-way fixed-effects ANOVA was carried out with implementation approach and the redefined importance factor as the independent variables. An interaction was observed ($p \leqslant 0.10$). As shown in Table 6, the importance findings parallel those of time pressure. Persuasion implementation was more successful under conditions of moderate compared to high project importance. Manager-dominated tactics (edict and intervention) and participation were more successful when a plan was thought to have high importance.

Type of change provides a final qualification to the merits of implementation tactics. Plans were grouped first as dealing with either an

Table 6. Implementation tactics and perceived importance

		Perceived/Importance	
		High	Moderate
Tactics	Persuasion	50% / 3.4 (N = 7)	79% / 4.0 (N = 23)
	Intervention	100% / 4.5 (N = 2)	100% / 4.2 (N = 11)
	Participation	100% / 4.0 (N = 1)	85.7% / 3.75 (N = 7)
	Edict	66% / 4.0 (N = 6)	0% / 1.5 (N = 4)

Tactic ($p \leqslant 0.05$).
Importance (N.S.).
Tactic–importance interaction ($p \leqslant 0.10$).

internal operation or a service, and then as a modification of an existing strategy or a new strategy. The ANOVA had either type of change or history as factors coupled with implementation approach. An interaction between implementation approach and type of change was observed ($p \leqslant 0.05$). Persuasion was less successful in implementing internal operations, compared to implementing services (Table 7). The reverse was true for edicts. Edicts were twice as successful for internal operations as compared to services. Perhaps the diversity of stakeholders makes edicts

less likely to work for strategic plans, such as services, that have external implications (e.g. a burn center in a hospital) and more likely to be successful when the plan is to be used internally (e.g. a MIS). The quality ratings in Table 7 generally support these findings.

The history factor and implementation approach also had an interaction. Strategic plans that modify an existing internal operation or service were compared to those that create a new plan. Plans implemented by persuasion and intervention tactics had nearly identical adoption

Table 7. Implementation and type of strategy of response

		Type of plan	
		Internal operation	Product or service
Tactics	Persuasion	55.7% / 3.7 (N = 9)	80% / 4.0 (N = 19)
	Intervention	100% / 3.9 (N = 5)	100% / 4.5 (N = 7)
	Participation	100% / 4.0 (N = 1)	73% / 3.0 (N = 7)
	Edict	52% / 3.15 (N = 6)	25% / 2.75 (N = 4)

Tactics ($p \leqslant 0.05$).
Application (N.S.).
Tactics–application interaction ($p \leqslant 0.05$).

		Plan's history	
		Modification	New practice
Tactics	Persuasion	73% / 3.83 (N = 18)	76.3% / 4.0 (N = 10)
	Intervention	100% / 4.35 (N = 9)	100% / 3.8 (N = 3)
	Participation	60% / 3.17 (N = 6)	100% / 3.0 (N = 2)
	Edict	60% / 3.4 (N = 5)	20% / 2.6 (N = 5)

Tactics ($p \leqslant 0.05$).
History (N.S.).
Tactic–history interaction ($p \leqslant 0.10$).

rates when applied to a new strategy or modifications of an existing strategy. Differences were observed for the participation and edict tactics. Participation improved the prospects of adopting a new plan; edicts lowered them. Edicts did much better when used to modify an existing plan. Quality ratings had less dramatic differences but generally support the findings for status. Apparently edicts should be avoided when a new strategy is required. In contrast, participation was found to be particularly valuable to aid in the implementation of a new strategy.

CONCLUSIONS

In their assessment of the status of strategic management, Schendel and Hofer (1979) conclude that the linkage of strategic and operational management needs attention. This study identified and evaluated principles that managers use to link strategic intention-setting and action-taking, called strategic implementation. Implementation approaches called intervention, participation, persuasion, and edict were found to describe over 90 percent of the tactics used by strategic managers. These tactics were used to organize and focus implementation tools such as structural change, incentives, budgeting, rewards and sanctions, leader selection, and delegation.

The behavior of managers in implementing strategic aims was found to be related to various forms of delegation. Delegation to staff occurs when a plan had less importance in carrying out a strategic aim. The findings also suggest that strategic responses call for a modification of existing practices twice as often as the creation of new practices. In dealing with strategic issues, organizations appear to stress the conventional. Whether or not the plan is rooted in traditional practice, the strategic manager's active participation was found to significantly improve its adoption prospects. However, in nearly half of the cases studied strategic managers failed to act in this way.

The superiority of the intervention tactic and its infrequent use suggests that strategic managers should become more involved with managing a process used to realize strategic aims. When a manager took charge and created an environment where plans that help to realize a strategy could

be justified and understood implementation was *always* successful. Future research should examine the steps of the intervention process as practiced by managers and the steps called for by organizational development (OD) theorists to be applied by an OD specialist (e.g. Lewin, 1947; Dalton, 1970). In this research all interventionists were *managers* whose commitment to the organization could not be questioned. A comparison of these results to the performance of OD consultants, brought in to make a change called for by a strategy, could be instructive.

The human relations movement appears to have created another set of ideas which, as they are practiced, give those affected by a strategic direction a role in forming specific plans (e.g. Delbecq and Van de Ven, 1971). The cooptation of important power centers is thought to be the key to implementation success. This benefit of participation requires qualification. Wherever *key* people are not involved implementation can be problematic. Representing power centers can help, but the power of cooptation dramatically declines for those not directly involved in developmental activities. For example, in several of the cases the scope of cooptation was narrow, with representatives of a large group of stakeholders involved, or the role of the group was limited to, for example, reviewing and commenting on the plan as it evolved. Much of the power of cooptation is lost when participation is limited in these ways. Full participation was not observed in any of the cases studied; perhaps because full participation can be difficult or even impossible when stakeholders are large in number and diffuse. For example, strategies which affect large numbers of people, such as prison or airport sitings, can never hope to involve all those affected. Nevertheless the power of cooptation seems to be limited to the people who participate. Participation should be more carefully defined in future research to account for the participant's role and degree of involvement to sort out the influence of these factors.

Persuasion implementation in which *experts* attempt to persuade a manager to put expert-derived strategic recommendations into practice was far more successful than conventional wisdom would suggest (Churchman, 1975). However, the persuasion tactic had better results when time pressure was low and the perceived importance of the plan was moderate, not high. Furthermore, experts without a successful track record, verified by past work *for* the strategic manager, had more difficulty selling a plan, and perhaps because there was an *a priori* expectation that the plan would lack quality. The plan's scale seems to mitigate the effectiveness of persuasion. Important plans have several people with important stakes riding on the outcome. A manager may allow persuasion implementation for small-scale (low importance and time pressure) plans and avoid this form of implementation for large-scale plans. The mutual understanding dictum of Churchman (Churchman and Schainblatt, 1965) may have significance only for large-scale plans where a manager's reputation can be dramatically affected by the outcome of a highly visible plan. Other plans may be considered 'throw away', and deemed acceptable for the expert to manage.

Future research should consider how consultants perform in the role of an expert. The failure of the cases to capture consultants in the expert role stems from the difficulty in collecting this type of data. Consultants play a vital role in many organizations but their activities and the benefits they create are shrouded in secrecy. More study of consultants and their persuasion tactics seems essential.

The 'edict' tactic treated strategic implementation as an exercise in power where the manager issues a directive, drawing on one or more of the bases of power at his/her disposal (French and Raven, 1959). This tactic was ineffective, leading to low adoption rates and poor quality ratings. Edicts seem to be quite ineffective. Further research should consider conditions under which power can enhance the performance of each of the implementation tactics.

Two final issues should be considered in future research: the contingency use of implementation tactics and the 'managerial pragmatism' measure. All forms of implementation had some degree of success. Because some ways to manage strategic planning for implementation purposes are more costly and less timely than others, future research should determine situations where each implementation tactic can be effective, creating a contingency model.

A key measure used in this research was one of pragmatism: which plans were accepted by the organization and how they were viewed after an implementation attempt. A more powerful measure of plan merit is needed to extend and

qualify the findings of this study. For instance, comparing a plan's cost–benefit with managers' and stakeholders' perceptions of quality and with adoption rates could be instructive. Such a measure would permit the researcher to determine which (if any) of the strategic implementation tactics can overcome resistance to plans that seem desirable (e.g. have a good benefit–cost ratio). It is also important to determine what causes these biases and whether they are accentuated by environmental conditions (e.g. time pressure).

REFERENCES

Alavi, M. and J. C. Henderson. 'An evolutionary strategy for implementing a decision support system', *Management Science*, 27(11), 1981, pp. 1309–1323.

Ansoff, H. I. *Corporate Strategy: An Analytical Approach to Business Policy For Growth and Expansion.* McGraw-Hill, New York, 1965.

Beyer, J. M. and H. M. Trice. 'The utilization process: a conceptual framework and synthesis of empirical findings', *Administrative Science Quarterly*, 27(4/5), 1982, pp. 591–622.

Campbell, J. P., R. L. Daft and C. L. Hulin. *What To Study: Generating and Developing Research Questions.* Sage Publications, London, 1982.

Churchman, C. W. 'Theories of implementation'. In R. L. Schultz and D. P. Slevin (eds), *Implementing Operations Research/Management Science.* Elsevier, New York, 1975.

Churchman, C. W. and A. H. Schainblatt. 'The researcher and the manager: a dialectic of implementation', *Management Science*, 11(4), 1965, pp. B69–B87.

Coch, L. and J. R. P. French. Jr. 'Overcoming resistance to change', *Human Relations*, 1, 1948, pp. 512–532.

Daft, R. L. 'Learning the craft of organizational research', *Academy of Management Review*, 8(4), 1983, pp. 539–546.

Dalton, G. W. 'Influence and organizational change'. In G. W. Dalton, P. Lawrence and L. Greiner (eds), *Organizational Change and Development*, Irwin, Homewood, IL, 1970.

Delbecq, A. and A. Van de Ven. 'A group process model for problem identification and program planning', *Journal of Applied Behavioral Science*, 7(4), 1971, pp. 466–492.

Duncan, W. J. 'The researcher and the manager: a comparative view of the need for multiple understanding', *Management Science*, 20, 1974, pp. 1157–1163.

Fisher, G. W. 'Utility models for multiple objective decisions: do they actually represent human judgment', *Decision Sciences*, 10, 1979, pp. 451–479.

14   *P. C. Nutt*

French, J. and B. Raven. 'The bases of social power'. In D. Cartwright (ed.), *Studies in Social Power*. Institute for Social Research, Ann Arbor, MI, 1959.

Glueck, W. F. *Business Policy and Strategic Management*. McGraw-Hill, New York, 1980.

Gustafson, D. H., R. Shukla, A. Delbecq and G. Wallster. 'A comparative study in subjective likelihood estimates made by individuals, interacting groups, Delphi groups and numeral groups', *Organizational Behavior and Human Performance*, **9**, 1973, pp. 280–291.

Harrigan, K. R. 'Research methodologies for contingency approaches to business strategy', *Academy of Management Review*, **8**(3), 1983, pp. 398–405.

Huff, A. S. 'A rhetorical examination of strategic change'. In L. R. Pondy, P. Frost, G. Morgan and T. Dandredge (eds), *Organizational Symbolism*, in press.

Lewin, K. 'Group decisions and social change'. In J. E. Maccoby, T. W. Newcomb and E. Harley (eds), *Readings in Social Psychology*. Holt, Rinehart, and Winston, New York, 1947.

Mann, F. and R. Likert. 'The need for research on the communication of research results', *Human Organization*, **11**, 1952, pp. 15–20.

Miller, D. and P. Friesen. 'Structural change and performance: quantum   versus piecemeal–incremental approaches', *Academy of Management Journal*, **24**(4), 1982, pp. 855–866.

Mintzberg, H. and J. A. Waters. 'Tracking strategy in an entrepreneurial firm', *Academy of Management Journal*, **25**(3), 1982, pp. 465–499.

Mintzberg, H., D. Raisinghani and A. Theoret. 'The structure of unstructured decision processes', *Administrative Science Quarterly*, **21**(2), 1976, pp. 246–275.

Nerlove, M. and S. J. Press. *Univariate and Multivariate Loglinear and Logistic Models*, Santa Monica, California: Rand Technical Paper, R-1306-EDA/ NIH, 1973.

Nutt, P. C. 'An experimental comparison of the effectiveness of three planning methods', *Management Science*, **23**(4), 1977, pp. 499–511.

Nutt, P. C. 'Stage based and process reconstruction paradigms for planning research', Academy of Management National Meeting, August 12–15, 1983, Dallas, Texas.

Nutt, P. C. *Planning Methods*. Wiley, New York, 1984.

Nutt, P. C. 'A strategic planning network for nonprofit organizations', *Strategic Management Journal*, **5**, 1984, pp. 57–75.

Schein, E. H. 'The mechanisms of change'. In W. Bennis, E. Schein, G. Stelle and A. Berlow (eds), *Interpersonal Dynamics*. Dorsey Press, Homewood, IL, 1964.

Schendel, D. and C. Hofer (eds) *Strategic Management: A New View of Business Policy and Planning*, Little, Brown, Boston, MA, 1979.

Schultz, R. L. and P. O. Slevin. *Implementing Operations Research/Management Science*, Elsevier, New York, 1975.

Simon, M. A. *Understanding Human Action*. Sun Press, Albany, NW, 1982.

Weiss, C. H. 'Knowledge creep and decision accretion', *Knowledge Creation, Diffusion, Utilization*, **1**, 1980, pp. 381–404.

Weiss, C. 'Use of social science research in organizations: the constrained repertoire theory'. In H. Stein (ed), *Organization and Human Services*, Temple University Press, Philadelphia, PA, 1981.

Williams, W. and T. W. Evans. *Evaluating Social Action Programs: Theory Practice, and Politics*. Seminar Press, New York, 1972.

Winer, B. J. *Statistical Principles in Experimental Design*, McGraw-Hill, New York, 1971.

Yin, R. K. 'The case study crisis: some answers', *Administrative Science Quarterly*, **26**(1), 1981, pp. 58–65.

[14]

Academy of Management Review 1981, Vol. 6, No. 4, 577-587

The Escalation of Commitment
To a Course of Action

BARRY M. STAW
University of California - Berkeley

There are many instances in which individuals can become locked into a costly course of action. Because it is often possible for persons who have suffered a setback to recoup their losses through an even greater commitment of resources to the same course of action, a cycle of escalating commitment can be produced. In this paper, I review recent research on the escalation of commitment and try to integrate its complex and often conflicting determinants.

Many of the most difficult decisions an individual must make are choices not about what to do in an isolated instance but about the fate of an entire course of action. This is especially true when the decision is whether to cease a questionable line of behavior or to commit more effort and resources into making that course of action pay off. Do individuals in such cases cut their losses or escalate their commitment to the course of action? Consider the following examples:

1. An individual has spent three years working on an advanced degree in a field with minimal job prospects (e.g., in the humanities or social sciences). The individual chooses to invest more time and effort to finish the degree rather than switching to an entirely new field of study. Having obtained the degree, the individual is faced with the options of unemployment, working under dissatisfying conditions such as part-time or temporary status, or starting anew in a completely unrelated field.

2. An individual purchased a stock at $50 a share, but the price has gone down to $20. Still convinced about the merit of the stock, he buys more shares at this lower price. Soon the price declines further and the individual is again faced with the decision to buy more, hold what he already has, or sell out entirely (case taken from personal experience).

3. A city spends a large amount of money to improve its sewer and drainage system. The proj-

ect is the largest public works project in the nation and involves digging 131 miles of tunnel shafts, reservoirs, and pumping stations. The excavation is only 10 percent completed and is useless until it is totally finished. The project will take the next 20 years to complete and will cost $11 billion. Unfortunately, the deeper the tunnels go, the more money they cost, and the greater are the questions about the wisdom of the entire venture. ["Money down the drain," 1979]

4. A company overestimates its capability to build an airplane brake that will meet certain technical specifications at a given cost. Because it wins the government contract, the company is forced to invest greater and greater effort into meeting the contract terms. As a result of increasing pressure to meet specifications and deadlines, records and tests of the brake are misrepresented to government officials. Corporate careers and company credibility are increasingly staked to the airbrake contract, although many in the firm know the brake will not work effectively. At the conclusion of the construction period, the government test pilot flies the plane; it skids off the runway and narrowly misses injuring the pilot. [Vandiver, 1972]

5. At an early stage of the U.S. involvement in the Vietnam War, George Ball, then Undersecretary of State, wrote the following in a memo to President Johnson: "The decision you face now is crucial. Once large numbers of U.S. troops are committed to direct combat, they will begin to take heavy casualties in a war they are ill equipped to fight in a noncooperative if not

downright hostile countryside. Once we suffer
large casualties, we will have started a well-
nigh irreversible process. Our involvement will
be so great that we cannot—without national
humiliation—stop short of achieving our complete objectives. Of the two possibilities, I think
humiliation would be more likely than the
achievement of our objectives—even after we
have paid terrible costs." [Sheehan & Kenworthy, 1971, memo dated July 1, 1965]

As evidenced in the above examples, many of the
most injurious personal decisions and most glaring
policy disasters can come in the shape of sequential
and escalating commitments. Judging by popular
press accounts and the observation of everyday
events, it appears that individuals may have a tendency to become locked in to a course of action,
throwing good money after bad or committing new
resources to a losing course of action. The critical
question from an analytical point of view is
whether these everyday examples denote a syn-
drome of decisional errors or are just a post hoc
reconstruction of events. That is, do decisions
about commitment to a course of action inherently
lead individuals to errors of escalation or are we, as
observers, simply labeling a subset of decisions
whose outcomes turned out to be negative?

The Fallible Decision Maker

In the psychological literature, there have been
two primary ways of explaining decisional errors.
One is to point to individual limitations in information processing [Ross, 1977; Slovic, Fishhoff, &
Lichtenstein, 1977; Tversky & Kahneman, 1974].
Individuals are limited in their ability and desire to
search for alternatives and input information,
recall information from memory, and to compare
alternatives on multiple criteria. Because of the
limitations to individual ability at each phase of
cognitive information processing, the end-product
of individual decisions may optimize neither personal utility nor collective welfare. A second way to
explain decisional errors is to attribute a breakdown in rationality to interpersonal elements such
as social power or group dynamics. Pfeffer [1977]
has, for example, outlined how and when power
considerations are likely to outweigh more rational
aspects of organizational decision making, and Janis
[1972] has noted many problems in the decision

making of policy groups. Cohesive groups may,
according to Janis, suppress dissent, censor information, create illusions of invulnerability, and stereotype enemies. Any of these by-products of social
interaction may, of course, hinder rational decision
making and lead individuals or groups to decisional
errors.

Although the limitations to rationality posed by
the group dynamics and information processing
literatures can be relevant to commitment decisions, they do not seem to capture the central element of the commitment dilemma. A salient feature of the preceding case examples is that a *series* of
decisions is associated with a course of action
rather than an isolated choice. The consequences of
any single decision therefore can have implications
about the utility of previous choices as well as
determine future events or outcomes. This means
that sunk costs may not be sunk psychologically
but may enter into future decisions.

Under traditional models of economic rationality
[e.g., Edwards, 1954; Vroom, 1964], resources
should be allocated and decisions entered into when
future benefits are greater than future costs.
Losses or costs that may have been experienced in
the past but that are not expected to recur should
not (at least from a normative perspective) enter
into decision calculations. However, individuals
may be motivated to rectify past losses as well as to
seek future gain. One source of this motivation
may be a desire on the part of individuals to appear
rational in their decision making. The literature on
self-justification processes [e.g., Aronson, 1976;
Festinger, 1957] supports this proposition and at
least some of the tendency to escalate commitment
may be explained by self-justification motives.

Research on the
Escalation of Commitment

Self-Justification in Commitment Decisions

The largest and most systematic source of data
on the justification of behavior is provided by the
social psychological literature on forced compliance
(see Wicklund & Brehm [1976] for an excellent
review). Typically, in forced compliance studies an
individual is induced to perform an unpleasant or
dissatisfying act when no compensating external

rewards are present. It is generally predicted that individuals will bias their attitudes on the experimental task in a positive direction so as to justify their previous behavior [Festinger & Carlsmith, 1959; Pallak, Sogin, & Van Zante, 1974; Weick, 1964]. Such biasing of attitudes is most likely to occur when individuals feel personally responsible for negative consequences [Cooper, 1971] and when these consequences are difficult to undo [Brehm & Cohen, 1961; Staw, 1974].

In a series of research studies, my associates and I [Staw, 1976; Staw & Fox, 1977; Staw & Ross, 1978] also used a self-justification framework in investigating whether decision makers can become over committed to a course of action. However, the assumption underlying these studies was that individuals may go beyond the passive distortion of adverse consequences in an effort to rationalize a behavioral error. By committing new and additional resources, an individual who has suffered a setback could attempt to "turn the situation around" or to demonstrate the ultimate rationality of his or her original course of action.

In the first empirical test of an escalation effect [Staw, 1976], I used a simulated business case in which an administrator could recoup losses through the commitment of resources. While acting in the role of a corporate financial officer, business school students were asked to allocate research and development funds to one of two operating divisions of a company. Subjects were then given the results of their initial decisions and asked to make a second allocation of R&D funds. In this study, some participants also were assigned to a condition under which they did not make the initial allocation decision themselves, but were told that it was made earlier by another financial officer of the firm. The results of the experiment showed: (1) that subjects allocated more money to the declining rather than improving division, (2) that subjects allocated more money to the initially chosen division when they, rather than another financial officer, were responsible for the initial decision, and (3) there was a significant interaction such that subjects allocated more money under responsibility for negative consequences than would be expected by the two main effects acting alone. These findings supported the prediction that administrators may seek to justify an ineffective course of action by escalating their

commitment of resources to it.

In a follow-up study [Staw & Fox, 1977], subjects were again assigned to both high- and low-responsibility conditions in the same type of experimental simulation. In this study, however, all subjects were run under a negative-consequences condition that persisted over three time periods. Time was extended to see if the effects of high personal responsibility would persist or whether commitment could be built up over time even though a decision maker may not have been responsible for the original course of action (e.g., the Nixon administration became committed to the Vietnam War although it did not initiate it).

The results of this second study were more complex and difficult to interpret than those of 'the previous one. Although the effect of personal responsibility was replicated when we simply considered Time 1 data, there was a significant decline in commitment over time for high-responsibility subjects, while low-responsibility subjects maintained or slightly increased their commitment. In explaining these results, we noted that commitment did not diminish as one might expect when individuals are given negative feedback or "punishment" over repeated trials. For example, when high commitment was followed by continued negative consequences, commitment was generally decreased, but when low commitment was followed by negative consequences, commitment was generally increased. Thus, it appeared from the data that individuals were actively attempting to probe and learn from the system over time.

The results of these two studies, when considered together, did not provide evidence for a totally self-justifying administrator. The replicated effect of personal responsibility demonstrated that self-justification may motivate the commitment of resources to a course of action. However, when choosing to commit resources, subjects did not appear to persist unswervingly in the face of continued negative results or to ignore information about the possibility of future returns. These inconsistencies led to a third study [Staw & Ross, 1978] designed specifically to find out how individuals process information following negative versus positive feedback.

In this third study, previous success/failure and causal information about a setback were both experimentally varied. Results showed that subjects invested more resources in a course of action when information pointed to an exogenous rather than endogenous cause of a setback, and this tendency was most pronounced when subjects had been given a previous failure rather than a success. The exogenous cause in this experiment was one that was both external to the program in which subjects invested and was unlikely to persist, whereas the endogenous cause was a problem central to the program and likely to persist. These results can be interpreted as showing that individuals will reduce their commitment to a course of action where prospects for future gain are bleak, but that they will continue to invest large amounts of resources when provided an external cause of failure and some hope of recouping their losses. Unfortunately, individuals may selectively filter information so as to maintain their commitment to a policy or course of action [Caldwell & O'Reilly, 1980; Lord, Ross, & Lepper, 1979]. One only has to recall the public statements of policy makers during the Vietnam War to appreciate the tendency to *find* exogenous and nonrecurring sources of setbacks (e.g., monsoon rains, equipment failures, and lead time for training allies).

External vs. Internal Justification

Although research on commitment has emphasized the role of justification, these studies have chiefly tapped what could be labeled an *internal justification* process. When justification is considered primarily as an intra-individual process, individuals are posited to attend to events and to act in ways to protect their own self-images [Aronson, 1968, 1976]. But within most social settings, justification may also be directed externally. When faced with an external threat or evaluation, individuals may be motivated to prove to others that they were not wrong in an earlier decision and the force for such *external justification* could well be stronger than the protection of self-esteem.

Fox and I recently conducted an empirical demonstration of the effect of external justification [1979]. We hypothesized that administrators who are vulnerable to job loss or who implement a policy they know will be unpopular would be especially motivated to protect themselves against failure. In

such cases where there is strong need for external justification, an administrator would most likely attempt to save a policy failure by enlarging the commitment of resources. To test this idea, we conducted a simulation in which business students were asked to play the role of administrators under various conditions of job insecurity and policy resistance. The effect of these manipulations on resource allocation decisions confirmed the hypothesis. When a course of action led to negative results, the administrators who were both insecure in their jobs and who faced stiff policy resistance were most likely to escalate their commitment of resources and become locked in to the losing course of action.

Norms for Consistency

In addition to the internal and external forms of justification, norms for consistency in action may be another major source of commitment. A lay theory may exist in our society, or at least within many organizational settings, that administrators who are consistent in their actions are better leaders than those who switch from one line of behavior to another. The possibility that there exists a shared norm for consistency in behavior is suggested by recent commentary in the popular press on the nature of leadership.

> In a sense, Carter seems at last to have experienced "his Bay of Pigs," the kind of crisis that historians tell us bares the true stuff of presidents, forcing them to search out the bedrock of their own convictions, to urge the nation toward the same conclusions, to make decisions that, if waffled later, could produce national trauma and personal political eclipse . . . . Leadership involves total belief and commitment. [Sidey, 1978]

> Carter has exacerbated many of the difficulties he has faced. His most damaging weakness in his first two years has been a frequent indecisiveness . . . . ["The State of Jimmy Carter," 1979]

> A President must, plainly, show himself to be a man made confident by the courage of his own clear convictions . . . . The American people find it easy to forgive a leader's great mistakes, but not long meanderings. [Hughes, 1978]

Evidence for a preference or norm for consistency is also seen in the results of a national political survey. In a Gallup Poll on President Carter's popularity after his first year in office [Gallup, 1978], respondents who were dissatisfied with the president were asked why they felt this way. "Indecisiveness" was the second-most-frequent response given by the public and the only response that could be coded as a general pattern of behavior (the others were related to specific issues of the economy, foreign policy, campaign promises, etc.).

These survey and anecdotal data point to the possibility of an implicit theory of leadership [Calder, 1977; Pfeffer, 1977b] according to which effective administrators are fully committed to and steadfast in a course of action. In order to test for the existence of such a lay theory, Ross and I conducted an experiment on the reactions of individuals to selected forms of administrative behavior [Staw & Ross, 1980]. Subjects included practicing managers, undergraduates in business, and undergraduates in a psychology course. Each subject was asked to study a case description of an administrator's behavior. Manipulated in these case descriptions was consistency vs. experimentation in the administrator's course of action as well as the ultimate success or failure of the administrator's efforts. In the consistency conditions, the administrator was portrayed as sticking to a single course of action through a series of negative results. In the experimenting conditions, the administrator was portrayed as trying one course of action and, when positive results did not appear, moving to a second and finally third alternative (as an administrator might behave within Campbell's [1969] "experimenting society"). Ultimate success or failure of the administrator's actions was manipulated after two sets of negative results had been received by either the consistent or experimenting administrator.

Results showed that administrators were rated highest when they followed a consistent course of action and were ultimately successful. There was also a significant interaction of consistency and success such that the consistent-successful administrator was rated more highly than would be predicted by the two main effects of these variables. This interaction supported a predicted "hero effect" for the administrator who remained committed through two apparent failures of a course of action, *only to succeed in the end*. Finally, the effect of consis-

tency on ratings of the administrator was shown to vary by subject group, being strongest among practicing administrators, next strong among business students, and weakest among psychology undergraduates. These results suggest not only that consistency in action is perceived to be part of effective leadership, but that this perception may be acquired through socialization in business and governmental roles.

Toward a Theoretical Model

From this review of the research conducted to date, it should be apparent that commitment is a complex process, subject to multiple and sometimes conflicting processes. Therefore, it may be helpful to consolidate in a single theoretical model the shape of the forces affecting commitment decisions, specifying their direction as well as possible effect. Such a model is presented in Figure 1.

The figure depicts four major determinants of commitment to a course of action: motivation to justify previous decisions, norms for consistency, probability of future outcomes, and value of future outcomes. Commitment research has concentrated on the first two of these determinants, and the latter are obviously the two accepted determinants of economic and behavioral decision making. It should be apparent from the foregoing review that commitment research has focused on the processes that may lead to departures from rational decision making, and that such "nonrational" forces can often conflict or interact with traditional elements of rationality. After reviewing the major antecedents of commitment, I will address some of the complexities and interactive features of the commitment process.

In Figure 1, motivation to justify decisions can be seen as a function of responsibility for negative consequences as well as both internal and external demands for competence. As depicted in the model, responsibility for negative consequences leads to a motivation to justify previous decisions, if there is a need to demonstrate competence to oneself or others. As already noted, the traditional literature on dissonance and self-justification considers only the desire of individuals to be correct or accurate in decision making for reasons of self-esteem, but the need to demonstrate competence to external

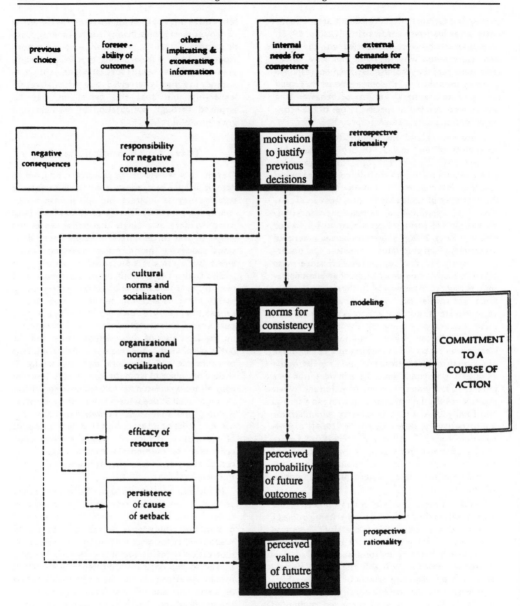

Figure 1
A Model of the Commitment Process

parties may also be a potent force. Our operational-
izations of job insecurity and policy resistance [Fox
& Staw, 1979] can be interpreted conceptually as
manipulations of a need to externally demonstrate
competence. However, although much research
assumes a need for self-justification, few studies
have actually manipulated internal competence
needs. Certainly, Aronson [1968, 1976] speaks of
self-esteem as influencing justification effects, but
it is not yet clear whether a devaluation of self-
esteem would lessen or intensify the need to demonstrate competence to oneself and there are no
empirical results that clarify this issue. Therefore,
at present, it must simply be posited that most
individuals possess sufficient internal as well as
external competence needs for negative consequences to evoke justification effects. Such predictions may be culture bound, but emphases on individual rationality and competence are so strong in
Western societies that they are likely to foster con-
comitant needs for rationalizing one's actions
[Wicklund & Brehm, 1976]. Likewise, because
norms for rationality are so dominant in business and governmental organizations [Thompson,
1967], decision makers in these settings may also
find it necessary to justify their actions to constituents within and outside the organization. In sum, it
is ironic that both internal and external needs to
demonstrate competence can lead to justification,
because justification is exactly what may detract
from the rational or competent decision making
that both individuals and organizations seek to
achieve [Staw, 1980].

Figure 1 shows that there are three determinants
of responsibility for negative consequences. There
is evidence from the forced compliance literature
that previous choice [Collins & Hoyt, 1972; Linder,
Cooper, & Jones, 1967] and foreseeability of
outcomes [Brehm & Jones, 1970; Cooper, 1971;
Goethals, Cooper, & Naficy, 1979] are antecedents of
perceived responsibility. However, as is noted in
the figure, there may be other implicating or exon-
erating information of relevance to the individual,
since a person may be accused of error or may
accept blame even when he or she did not actively
participate in a questionable decision [Caldwell &
O'Reilly, in press.]. Although not every one of
these antecedents of responsibility has been tested
in a commitment context, the overall effect of per-

sonal responsibility on commitment has been replicated several times [Fox, 1981; Staw, 1976; Staw &
Fox, 1977].

Prospective vs. Retrospective Rationality

As illustrated in Figure 1, forces for justification
can lead to a form of "retrospective rationality."
The individual, when motivated by a need to justify, seeks to appear competent in *previous* as opposed
to *future* actions [Staw, 1980]. In contrast, SEU
(subjective expected utility) models of behavior
posit that the individual is prospectively rational,
seeking to maximize future utility. What adds to
the complexity of decision making is the fact that
both forces may operate in commitment decisions.

As determinants of prospective rationality, some
set of perceived probabilities and values should
affect resource allocation decisions. Already within
commitment situations, we have validated the
effects of the efficacy of resources [Staw & Fox,
1977] and the causal persistence of a setback [Staw
& Ross, 1978]. However, it is possible that individual perceptions of the likelihood and value of various outcomes are also influenced by nonobjective
factors. Conlon and Wolf [1980], for example,
found that individuals who use a calculating decision strategy are just as likely to escalate their
commitment as noncalculators. Also, as shown in a
recent experiment by Fox [1981], individuals make
more use of information that exonerates them for
an earlier error than information that is implicating. Thus, it can be expected that motivation to
justify decisions will affect the search for and storage of information by individuals. Likewise, having
been responsible for negative consequences may
make the achievement of future outcomes all the
more important. The value of future returns may
intensify if they are needed to cover past losses.
Hence, Figure 1 shows the interplay between some
of the antecedents of justification and perceived
probability and value of outcomes—the accepted
elements of rational behavior. Because of these
interactions (denoted by dotted lines), it is not
always clear whether behavior can be labeled as
strictly prospectively or retrospectively oriented.

In addition to the confluence of retrospective and
prospective rationality, there is probably a third
force of major importance to commitment deci-

sions. Individuals can become committed to a course of action simply because they believe consistency in action is an appropriate form of behavior [Staw & Ross, 1980]. Individuals sometimes model their own behavior on those they see as successful within organizations and society in general. These effects may be time dependent [Gergen, 1976], inasmuch as high-level administrators model their behavior on leadership stereotypes that exist in the culture at a given time in history. These effects can also be noncognitive, since behavior may be modeled without a direct calculation of costs and benefits [Bandura, 1971]. Thus, the effect of norms for consistency is shown in Figure 1 as being determined by the cultural and organizational norms surrounding individuals and the effect of such norms is posited to lead directly to increases in commitment to a course of action. Obviously, norms could also be integrated into an SEU or expectancy model of decision making [Fishbein & Ajzen, 1975] and viewed as one element of a prospectively rational decision to commit resources. Likewise, norms for consistency can be viewed as an outgrowth of individual needs for cognitive consistency [Festinger, 1957] or socialization for consistency within the general society. The possible effect of justification on norms for consistency is depicted by a dotted line in Figure 1, as is the possible effect of norms on the perceived probability for future outcomes.

In summary, Figure 1 shows commitment to be a complex process dependent on forces for retrospective rationality, prospective rationality, and behavioral modeling. I have emphasized that commitment decisions are different from simple isolated choices, and for that reason, I believe constructs other than SEU can explain much of the commitment process. The crucial feature of commitment decisions is that an entire series of outcomes is determined by a given choice, the consequences of any single decision having implications for past as well as future events. Thus, commitment decisions may be determined as much by a desire to rectify past outcomes as to attain future ones. In addition, because the decisions are associated with each other, norms for consistency in action may override SEU or economic considerations. Most of the antecedents we have explored must of course be viewed as very tentative determinants of commit-

ment. At present, many of the proposed relationships are based as much on theoretical deduction as empirical evidence, and this is especially true for the interactive effects in Figure 1. Existing data have so far identified only simple antecedents of commitment, but the model proposes that commitment is a complex product based on multiple and conflicting processes.

An Assessment of The Commitment Process

This article began with a series of examples and an inquiry into whether commitment situations can inherently lead individuals into errors of escalation. The examples were tilted in the direction of an escalation of commitment and in each case the escalation seemed to lead to further problems or losses. Obviously, it is also possible that escalation of commitment can bring a turnaround of results and positive as well as negative consequences. But this is not the point. The crucial issue is whether there is a tendency to escalate commitment above and beyond what would be warranted by the "objective" facts of the situation. From our research, the answer to this question must be a qualified Yes.

If a decision maker were to escalate commitment only when the facts warranted it, there should be no effects of justification or norms for consistency on commitment. The only variables of relevance to "objective" commitment decisions would be factors influencing the probability and value of future outcomes. However, knowledgeable observers of a commitment situation do not generally reach the same decisions as do actors who have experienced losses. In addition, there may be a simple preference on the part of individuals for consistency in behavior even when it is not warranted by the facts of a commitment situation. Thus, motivation to justify and norms for consistency may each contribute to a general tendency to escalate. If future prospects are especially bleak, and if this information is salient to the individual, escalation tendencies may be outweighed by these more pressing elements of the situation. Nonetheless, I believe research has identified some contributing elements to the commonly observed phenomenon of escalating commitment.

Many researchers may object to the inclusion of "nonrational" elements in a decision framework and prefer to think of commitment strictly as a function of probabilities and valences in an expectancy theory sense [Edwards, 1954; Vroom, 1964]. Of course, it is even possible to collapse all the antecedents of commitment into factors influencing perceived probabilities and valences and finally into an SEU calculation. However, this would neither reduce the number of variables with which we must deal nor improve our understanding. It would simply constitute a semantic transformation of retrospective and normative factors into a purely prospective framework. As examples of this reasoning, factors such as personal responsibility for losses as well as political vulnerability could be reinterpreted as an increase in the value of future returns if a turnaround were to be reached, thus explaining additional commitment to a previously chosen course of action. I do not object to these interpretations, and they may well be validated empirically. However, the usefulness of constructs such as justification and norms for consistency is that they make salient *to the researcher* variables that not only can explain escalation situations, but that would not be emphasized by research posed from other theoretical perspectives.

Implications

If we accept the conclusion that there is a tendency to escalate on the part of individuals, what are its implications? Perhaps the most likely victims of an escalation tendency will be behaviors that are perceptually associated as parts of a single course of action. In such sequences of behavior, both justification and consistency influences have been found to override more objective elements of the situation. Prime candidates for escalation therefore include resource allocation or investment decisions that are identified by an entering and exit value, life choices that are linked together with the label of a career, and policy decisions for which administrators are held accountable by others in an organization or by the general public. In these situations, one must be especially wary of escalation tenden-

cies and perhaps take counteractions to restore balance to decision making.

In counterbalancing an escalation tendency, the variables outlined in Figure 1 may again be of use. For example, individuals should seek and follow the advice of outsiders who can assess the relevant issues of a decision situation without being responsible for previous losses or subject to internal or external needs to justify past actions. Likewise, organizations that have experienced losses from a given investment or course of action should rotate or change those in charge of allocating resources. One applied instance of such a counterbalancing strategy was recently uncovered by Lewicki [1980]. In a comparative case study, procedures were examined in two banks for coping with the problem of delinquent loans. The more financially aggressive bank, which had issued loans with greater risk, utilized separate departments for lending and "workout," the latter department being in charge of efforts to recover the bank's investment from problem accounts. In contrast, the more conservative bank, which had fewer delinquent loans, had developed no formal procedure for separating responsibility for lending and workout, the original loan officer being charged with all phases of the loan relationship.

As a final note, this review should help us recognize how difficult it will be to achieve what Campbell [1969] has described as an "experimenting society." Our research has shown that administrators sometimes become trapped in a course of action by external demands for success [Fox & Staw, 1979], and administrative experimentation is often viewed as an inappropriate form of leadership behavior [Staw & Ross, 1980]. Thus, it may be important to revamp performance evaluation systems facing administrators so that the motivation for action will shift from the defense of past actions to attainment of future gain (e.g., from a retrospective to a prospective basis). It may also be necessary to retrain administrators and resocialize students entering governmental and business organizations about the merits of experimentation versus consistency. In each of these ways, the actions of decision makers can perhaps be directed away from the tendency to escalate.

REFERENCES

Aronson, E. Dissonance theory: Progress and problems. In R. Abelson, E. Aronson, W. McGuire, T. Newcomb, M. Rosenberg, & P. Tannenbaum (Eds.), *Theories of cognitive consistency.* Chicago: Rand McNally, 1968.

Aronson, E. *The social animal.* San Francisco: Freeman, 1976.

Bandura, A. *Psychological modeling: Conflicting theories.* Chicago: Aldine-Atherton, 1971.

Brehm, J.W.; & Cohen, A.E. *Explorations is cognitive dissonance.* New York: Wiley, 1962.

Brehm, J.W.; & Jones, R.A. The effect on dissonance of surprise consequences. *Journal of Experimental Social Psychology,* 1970, 6, 420-431.

Calder, B.J. An attribution theory of leadership In B. Staw & G. Salancik (Eds.), *New directions in organizational behavior.* Chicago: St. Clair Press, 1977.

Caldwell, D.F.; & O'Reilly, C.A. Responses to failure: The effects of choice and responsibility on impression management. *Academy of Management Journal,* in press.

Campbell, D.T. Reforms as experiments. *American Psychologist,* 1979, 24, 409-429.

Collins, B.E.; & Hoyt, M.F. Personal responsibility-for-consequences: An integration and extension of the 'forced compliance" literature. *Journal of Experimental Social Psychology,* 1972, 8, 558-593.

Conlon, E.J.; & Wolf, G. The moderating effects of strategy, visibility, and involvement on allocation behavior: An extension of Staw's escalation paradigm. *Organizational Behavior & Human Performance,* 1980, 26, 172-192.

Cooper, J. Personal responsibility and dissonance: The role of foreseen consequences: An integration and extension of the "forced compliance" literature. *Journal of Personality & Social Psychology,* 1971, 18, 354-363.

Edwards, W. The theory of decision making. *Psychological Bulletin,* 1954, 51, 380-417.

Festinger, L. *A theory of cognitive dissonance.* Stanford: Stanford University Press, 1957.

Festinger, L.; & Carlsmith, J.M. Cognitive consequences of forced compliance. *Journal of Abnormal & Social Psychology,* 1959, 58, 203-210.

Fishbein, M.; & Ajzen, I. *Belief, attitude, intention and behavior: An introduction to theory and research.* Reading, Mass., Addison-Wesley, 1975.

Fox, F.V. *Persistence: Effects of commitment and justification processes on efforts to succeed with a course of action.* Doctoral dissertation in progress, University of Illinois, 1981.

Fox, F.; & Staw, B.M. The trapped administrator: The effects of job insecurity and policy resistance upon commitment to a course of action. *Administrative Science Quarterly,* 1979, 24, 449-471.

Gallup, G. *The Gallup opinion index.* Princeton, N.J.: American Institute of Public Opinion, March 1978.

Goethals, G.; Cooper, J.; & Naficy, A. Role of foreseen, foreseeable, and unforeseeable behavior consequences in the arousal of cognitive dissonance. *Journal of Personality & Social Psychology,* 1979, 37, 1179-1185.

Hughes, E.J. The presidency versus Jimmy Carter. *Fortune.* December 4, 1978, p. 58

Janis, I. *Victims of groupthink.* Boston: Houghton-Mifflin, 1972.

Lewicki, R.J. *Bad loan psychology: Entrapment and commitment in financial lending.* Working paper 80-25, Graduate School of Business Administration, Duke University, 1980.

Linder, E.D.; Cooper, J.; & Jones, E.E. Decision freedom as a determinant of the role of incentive magnitude in attitude change. *Journal of Personality & Social Psychology,* 1967, 6, 245-254.

Lord, C.; Ross, L.; & Lepper, M. Biased assimilation and attitude polarization: The effects of prior theories on subsequently considered evidence. *Journal of Personality & Social Psychology,* 1979, 37, 2098-2109.

Money down the drain. *Time,* June 25, 1979, p. 26.

Pallak, M.S.; Sogin, S.R.; & Van Zante, A. Bad decisions: Effects of volition, locus of causality, and negative consequences on attitude change. *Journal of Personality & Social Psychology,* 1972, 30, 217-227.

Pfeffer, J. The ambiguity of leadership. *Academy of Management Review.* 1977, 2, 104-112. (a)

Pfeffer, J. Power and resource allocation in organizations. In B. Staw & G. Salancik (Eds.), *New directions in organizational behavior.* Chicago: St. Clair Press, 1977. (b)

Read, W. Upward communication in industrial hierarchies. *Human Relations,* 1902, 15, 3-1o.

Ross, L. The intuitive psychologist and his shortcomings: Distortions in the attribution process. In L. Berkowitz (Ed.),

Advances in experimental social psychology (Vol. 10). New York: Academic Press, 1977.

Sheehan, N.; & Kenworthy, E.W. *Pentagon papers*. New York: Bantam Books, 1971.

Sidey, H. The crux of leadership. *Time*, December 11, 1978, p. 44.

Slovic, P.; Fischhoff, B.; & Lichtenstein, S. Behavioral decision theory. *Annual Review of Psychology*, 1977, *28*, 1-39.

The state of Jimmy Carter. *Time*, February 5, 1979, p. 11.

Staw, B.M. Attitudinal and behavioral consequences of changing a major organizational reward: A natural field experiment. *Journal of Personality & Social Psychology*, 1974, *29*, 742-751.

Staw, B.M. Knee-deep in the big muddy: A study of escalating commitment to a chosen course of action. *Organizational Behavior & Human Performance*, 1976, *16*, 27-44.

Staw, B.M. Rationality and justification in organizational life. In B. Staw & L. Cummings (Eds.), *Research in organizational behavior* (Vol. 2). Greenwich, Conn.: JAI Press, 1980.

Staw, B.M.; & Fox, F. Escalation: Some determinants of commitment to a previously chosen course of action. *Human Rela-tions*, 1977, *30*, 431-450.

Staw, B.M.; & Ross, J. Commitment to a policy decision: A multitheoretical perspective. *Administrative Science Quarterly*, 1978, *23*, 40-64.

Staw, B.M.; & Ross, J. Commitment in an experimenting society: An experiment on the attribution of leadership from administrative scenarios. *Journal of Applied Psychology*, 1980, *65*, 249-260.

Tversky, A.; & Kahneman, D. Judgment under uncertainty: Heuristics and biases. *Science*, 1974, *185*, 1124-1131.

Vandiver, K. Why should my conscience bother me? In A. Heilbroner (Ed.), *In the name of profit*. Garden City, N.Y.: Doubleday, 1972.

Vroom, V. *Work and motivation*. New York: Wiley, 1964.

Weick, K.E. Reduction of cognitive dissonance through task enhancement and effort expenditure. *Journal of Abnormal & Social Psychology*, 1964, *68*, 533-539.

White, R.W. Motivation reconsidered: The concept of competence. *Psychological Review*, 1959, *66*, 297-334.

Wicklund, R.; & Brehm, J. *Perspectives on cognitive dissonance*. Hillsdale, N.J.: Lawrence Erlbaum Association, 1976.

Barry M. Staw is a Professor in the School of Business Administration and the Institute of Industrial Relations, University of California, Berkeley.

Received 7/11/80

587

Part IV
Power in Decision Making

[15]

The American
Political Science Review

VOL. LXIII   SEPTEMBER, 1969   NO. 3

CONCEPTUAL MODELS AND THE CUBAN MISSILE CRISIS*

GRAHAM T. ALLISON
Harvard University

The Cuban missile crisis is a seminal event. For thirteen days of October 1962, there was a higher probability that more human lives would end suddenly than ever before in history. Had the worst occurred, the death of 100 million Americans, over 100 million Russians, and millions of Europeans as well would make previous natural calamities and inhumanities appear insignificant. Given the probability of disaster—which President Kennedy estimated as "between 1 out of 3 and even"—our escape seems awesome.[1] This event symbolizes a central, if only partially thinkable, fact about our existence. That such consequences could follow from the choices and actions of national governments obliges students of government as well as participants in governance to think hard about these problems.

Improved understanding of this crisis depends in part on more information and more probing analyses of available evidence. To contribute to these efforts is part of the purpose of this study. But here the missile crisis serves primarily as grist for a more general investigation.

This study proceeds from the premise that marked improvement in our understanding of such events depends critically on more self-consciousness about what observers bring to the analysis. What each analyst sees and judges to be important is a function not only of the evidence about what happened but also of the "conceptual lenses" through which he looks at the evidence. The principal purpose of this essay is to explore some of the fundamental assumptions and categories employed by analysts in thinking about problems of governmental behavior, especially in foreign and military affairs.

The general argument can be summarized in three propositions:

1. Analysts think about problems of foreign and military policy in terms of largely implicit conceptual models that have significant consequences for the content of their thought.[2]

Though the present product of foreign policy analysis is neither systematic nor powerful, if one carefully examines explanations produced by analysts, a number of fundamental similarities emerge. Explanations produced by particular analysts display quite regular, predictable features. This predictability suggests a substructure. These regularities reflect an analyst's assumptions about the character of puzzles, the categories in which problems should be considered, the types of evidence that are relevant, and the determinants of occurrences. The first proposition is that clusters of such related assumptions constitute basic frames of reference or conceptual models in terms of which analysts

* A longer version of this paper was presented at the Annual Meeting of the American Political Science Association, September, 1968 (reproduced by the Rand Corporation, P-3919). The paper is part of a larger study, scheduled for publication in 1969 under the title *Bureaucracy and Policy: Conceptual Models and the Cuban Missile Crisis.* For support in various stages of this work I am indebted to the Institute of Politics in the John F. Kennedy School of Government and the Center for International Affairs, both at Harvard University, the Rand Corporation, and the Council on Foreign Relations. For critical stimulation and advice I am especially grateful to Richard E. Neustadt, Thomas C. Schelling, Andrew W. Marshall, and Elisabeth K. Allison.

[1] Theodore Sorensen, *Kennedy* (New York, 1965), p. 705.

[2] In attempting to understand problems of foreign affairs, analysts engage in a number of related, but logically separable enterprises: (a) description, (b) explanation, (c) prediction, (d) evaluation, and (e) recommendation. This essay focuses primarily on explanation (and by implication, prediction).

both ask and answer the questions: What happened? Why did the event happen? What will happen?[3] Such assumptions are central to the activities of explanation and prediction, for in attempting to explain a particular event, the analyst cannot simply describe the full state of the world leading up to that event. The logic of explanation requires that he single out the relevant, important determinants of the occurrence.[4] Moreover, as the logic of prediction underscores, the analyst must summarize the various determinants as they bear on the event in question. Conceptual models both fix the mesh of the nets that the analyst drags through the material in order to explain a particular action or decision and direct him to cast his net in select ponds, at certain depths, in order to catch the fish he is after.

2. Most analysts explain (and predict) the behavior of national governments in terms of various forms of one basic conceptual model, here entitled the Rational Policy Model (Model I).[5]

In terms of this conceptual model, analysts attempt to understand happenings as the more or less purposive acts of unified national governments. For these analysts, the point of an explanation is to show how the nation or government

[3] In arguing that explanations proceed in terms of implicit conceptual models, this essay makes no claim that foreign policy analysts have developed any satisfactory, empirically tested theory. In this essay, the use of the term "model" without qualifiers should be read "conceptual scheme."

[4] For the purpose of this argument we shall accept Carl G. Hempel's characterization of the logic of explanation: an explanation "answers the question, 'Why did the explanadum-phenomenon occur?' by showing that the phenomenon resulted from particular circumstances, specified in C_1, C_2, ... C_k, in accordance with laws L_1, L_2, ... L_r. By pointing this out, the argument shows that, given the particular circumstances and the laws in question, the occurrence of the phenomenon was to be *expected*; and it is in this sense that the explanation enables us to understand why the phenomenon occurred." *Aspects of Scientific Explanation* (New York, 1965), p. 337. While various patterns of explanation can be distinguished, viz., Ernest Nagel, *The Structure of Science: Problems in the Logic of Scientific Explanation*, New York, 1961), satisfactory scientific explanations exhibit this basic logic. Consequently prediction is the converse of explanation.

[5] Earlier drafts of this argument have aroused heated arguments concerning proper names for these models. To choose names from ordinary language is to court confusion, as well as familiarity. Perhaps it is best to think of these models as I, II, and III.

could have chosen the action in question, given the strategic problem that it faced. For example, in confronting the problem posed by the Soviet installation of missiles in Cuba, rational policy model analysts attempt to show how this was a reasonable act from the point of view of the Soviet Union, given Soviet strategic objectives.

3. Two "alternative" conceptual models, here labeled an Organizational Process Model (Model II) and a Bureaucratic Politics Model (Model III) provide a base for improved explanation and prediction.

Although the standard frame of reference has proved useful for many purposes, there is powerful evidence that it must be supplemented, if not supplanted, by frames of reference which focus upon the large organizations and political actors involved in the policy process. Model I's implication that important events have important causes, i.e., that monoliths perform large actions for big reasons, must be balanced by an appreciation of the facts (a) that monoliths are black boxes covering various gears and levers in a highly differentiated decision-making structure, and (b) that large acts are the consequences of innumerable and often conflicting smaller actions by individuals at various levels of bureaucratic organizations in the service of a variety of only partially compatible conceptions of national goals, organizational goals, and political objectives. Recent developments in the field of organization theory provide the foundation for the second model. According to this organizational process model, what Model I categorizes as "acts" and "choices" are instead *outputs* of large organizations functioning according to certain regular patterns of behavior. Faced with the problem of Soviet missiles in Cuba, a Model II analyst identifies the relevant organizations and displays the patterns of organizational behavior from which this action emerged. The third model focuses on the internal politics of a government. Happenings in foreign affairs are understood, according to the bureaucratic politics model, neither as choices nor as outputs. Instead, what happens is categorized as *outcomes* of various overlapping bargaining games among players arranged hierarchically in the national government. In confronting the problem posed by Soviet missiles in Cuba, a Model III analyst displays the perceptions, motivations, positions, power, and maneuvers of principal players from which the outcome emerged.[6]

[6] In strict terms, the "outcomes" which these three models attempt to explain are essentially actions of national governments, i.e., the sum of activities of all individuals employed by a government relevant to an issue. These models focus not on a state of affairs, i.e., a full description of the

A central metaphor illuminates differences among these models. Foreign policy has often been compared to moves, sequences of moves, and games of chess. If one were limited to observations on a screen upon which moves in the chess game were projected without information as to how the pieces came to be moved, he would assume—as Model I does—that an individual chess player was moving the pieces with reference to plans and maneuvers toward the goal of winning the game. But a pattern of moves can be imagined that would lead the serious observer, after watching several games, to consider the hypothesis that the chess player was not a single individual but rather a loose alliance of semi-independent organizations, each of which moved its set of pieces according to standard operating procedures. For example, movement of separate sets of pieces might proceed in turn, each according to a routine, the king's rook, bishop, and their pawns repeatedly attacking the opponent according to a fixed plan. Furthermore, it is conceivable that the pattern of play would suggest to an observer that a number of distinct players, with distinct objectives but shared power over the pieces, were determining the moves as the resultant of collegial bargaining. For example, the black rook's move might contribute to the loss of a black knight with no comparable gain for the black team, but with the black rook becoming the principal guardian of the "palace" on that side of the board.

The space available does not permit full de-

velopment and support of such a general argument.[7] Rather, the sections that follow simply sketch each conceptual model, articulate it as an analytic paradigm, and apply it to produce an explanation. But each model is applied to the same event: the U.S. blockade of Cuba during the missile crisis. These "alternative explanations" of the same happening illustrate differences among the models—*at work*.[8] A crisis decision, by a small group of men in the context of ultimate threat, this is a case of the rational policy model *par excellence*. The dimensions and factors that Models II and III uncover in this case are therefore particularly suggestive. The concluding section of this paper suggests how the three models may be related and how they can be extended to generate predictions.

RATIONAL POLICY MODEL ILLUSTRATED

Where is the pinch of the puzzle raised by the *New York Times* over Soviet deployment of an antiballistic missile system?[9] The question, as the *Times* states it, concerns the Soviet Union's objective in allocating such large sums of money for this weapon system while at the same time seeming to pursue a policy of increasing détente. In former President Johnson's words, "the paradox is that this [Soviet deployment of an antiballistic missile system] should be happening at a time when there is abundant evidence that our mutual antagonism is beginning to ease."[10] This question troubles people primarily because Soviet antiballistic missile deployment, and evidence of Soviet actions towards détente, when juxtaposed in our implicit model, produce a question. With reference to what objective could the Soviet government have rationally chosen the simultaneous pursuit of these two courses of actions? This question arises only when the analyst attempts to structure events as purposive choices of consistent actors.

world, but upon national decision and implementation. This distinction is stated clearly by Harold and Margaret Sprout, "Environmental Factors on the Study of International Politics," in James Rosenau (ed.), *International Politics and Foreign Policy* (Glencoe, Illinois, 1961), p. 116. This restriction excludes explanations offered principally in terms of international systems theories. Nevertheless, this restriction is not severe, since few interesting explanations of occurrences in foreign policy have been produced at that level of analysis. According to David Singer, "The nation state —our primary actor in international relations . . . is clearly the traditional focus among Western students and is the one which dominates all of the texts employed in English-speaking colleges and universities." David Singer, "The Level-of-Analysis Problem in International Relations," Klaus Knorr and Sidney Verba (eds.), *The International System* (Princeton, 1961). Similarly, Richard Brody's review of contemporary trends in the study of international relations finds that "scholars have come increasingly to focus on acts of nations. That is, they all focus on the behavior of nations in some respect. Having an interest in accounting for the behavior of nations in common, the prospects for a common frame of reference are enhanced."

[7] For further development and support of these arguments see the author's larger study, *Bureaucracy and Policy: Conceptual Models and the Cuban Missile Crisis* (forthcoming). In its abbreviated form, the argument must, at some points, appear overly stark. The limits of space have forced the omission of many reservations and refinements.

[8] Each of the three "case snapshots" displays the work of a conceptual model as it is applied to explain the U.S. blockade of Cuba. But these three cuts are primarily exercises in hypothesis generation rather than hypothesis testing. Especially when separated from the larger study, these accounts may be misleading. The sources for these accounts include the full public record plus a large number of interviews with participants in the crisis.

[9] *New York Times*, February 18, 1967.

[10] *Ibid.*

How do analysts attempt to explain the Soviet emplacement of missiles in Cuba? The most widely cited explanation of this occurrence has been produced by two RAND Sovietologists, Arnold Horelick and Myron Rush.[11] They conclude that "the introduction of strategic missiles into Cuba was motivated chiefly by the Soviet leaders' desire to overcome . . . the existing large margin of U.S. strategic superiority."[12] How do they reach this conclusion? In Sherlock Holmes style, they seize several salient characteristics of this action and use these features as criteria against which to test alternative hypotheses about Soviet objectives. For example, the size of the Soviet deployment, and the simultaneous emplacement of more expensive, more visible intermediate range missiles as well as medium range missiles, it is argued, exclude an explanation of the action in terms of Cuban defense—since that objective could have been secured with a much smaller number of medium range missiles alone. Their explanation presents an argument for one objective that permits interpretation of the details of Soviet behavior as a value-maximizing choice.

How do analysts account for the coming of the First World War? According to Hans Morgenthau, "the first World War had its origin exclusively in the fear of a disturbance of the European balance of power.[13] In the period preceding World War I, the Triple Alliance precariously balanced the Triple Entente. If either power combination could gain a decisive advantage in the Balkans, it would achieve a decisive advantage in the balance of power. "It was this fear," Morgenthau asserts, "that motivated Austria in July 1914 to settle its accounts with Serbia once and for all, and that induced Germany to support Austria unconditionally. It was the same fear that brought Russia to the support of Serbia, and France to the support of Russia."[14] How is Morgenthau able to resolve this problem so confidently? By imposing on the data a "rational outline."[15] The value of this method, according to Morgenthau, is that "it provides for rational discipline in action and creates astounding continuity in foreign policy which makes American, British, or Russian for-

eign policy appear as an intelligent, rational continuum . . . regardless of the different motives, preferences, and intellectual and moral qualities of successive statesmen."[16]

Stanley Hoffmann's essay, "Restraints and Choices in American Foreign Policy" concentrates, characteristically, on "deep forces": the international system, ideology, and national character—which constitute restraints, limits, and blinders.[17] Only secondarily does he consider decisions. But when explaining particular occurrences, though emphasizing relevant constraints, he focuses on the choices of nations. American behavior in Southeast Asia is explained as a reasonable choice of "downgrading this particular alliance (SEATO) in favor of direct U.S. involvement," given the constraint: "one is bound by one's commitments; one is committed by one's mistakes."[18] More frequently, Hoffmann uncovers confusion or contradiction in the nation's choice. For example, U.S. policy towards underdeveloped countries is explained as "schizophrenic."[19] The method employed by Hoffmann in producing these explanations as rational (or irrational) decisions, he terms "imaginative reconstruction."[20]

Deterrence is the cardinal problem of the contemporary strategic literature. Thomas Schelling's *Strategy of Conflict* formulates a number of propositions focused upon the dynamics of deterrence in the nuclear age. One of the major propositions concerns the stability of the balance of terror: in a situation of mutual deterrence, the probability of nuclear war is reduced not by the "balance" (the sheer equality of the situation) but rather by the *stability* of the balance, i.e., the fact that neither opponent in striking first can destroy the other's ability to strike back.[21] How does Schelling support this proposition? Confidence in the contention stems not from an inductive canvass of a large number of previous cases, but rather from two calculations. In a situation of "balance" but vulnerability, there are values for which a rational opponent could choose to strike first, e.g., to destroy enemy capabilities to retaliate. In a

[11] Arnold Horelick and Myron Rush, *Strategic Power and Soviet Foreign Policy* (Chicago, 1965). Based on A. Horelick, "The Cuban Missile Crisis: An Analysis of Soviet Calculations and Behavior," *World Politics* (April, 1964).

[12] Horelick and Rush, *Strategic Power and Soviet Foreign Policy*, p. 154.

[13] Hans Morgenthau, *Politics Among Nations* (3rd ed.; New York, 1960), p. 191.

[14] *Ibid.*, p. 192.

[15] *Ibid.*, p. 5.

[16] *Ibid.*, pp. 5–6.

[17] Stanley Hoffmann, *Daedalus* (Fall, 1962); reprinted in *The State of War* (New York, 1965).

[18] *Ibid.*, p. 171.

[19] *Ibid.*, p. 189.

[20] Following Robert MacIver; see Stanley Hoffmann, *Contemporary Theory in International Relations* (Englewood Cliffs, 1960), pp. 178–179.

[21] Thomas Schelling, *The Strategy of Conflict*, (New York, 1960), p. 232. This proposition was formulated earlier by A. Wohlstetter, "The Delicate Balance of Terror," *Foreign Affairs* (January, 1959).

"stable balance" where no matter who strikes first, each has an assured capability to retaliate with unacceptable damage, no rational agent could choose such a course of action (since that choice is effectively equivalent to choosing mutual homicide). Whereas most contemporary strategic thinking is driven *implicitly* by the motor upon which this calculation depends, Schelling explicitly recognizes that strategic theory does assume a model. The foundation of a theory of strategy is, he asserts: "the assumption of rational behavior—not just of intelligent behavior, but of behavior motivated by conscious calculation of advantages, calculation that in turn is based on an explicit and internally consistent value system."[22]

What is striking about these examples from the literature of foreign policy and international relations are the similarities among analysts of various styles when they are called upon to produce explanations. Each assumes that what must be explained is an action, i.e., the realization of some purpose or intention. Each assumes that the actor is the national government. Each assumes that the action is chosen as a calculated response to a strategic problem. For each, explanation consists of showing what goal the government was pursuing in committing the act and how this action was a reasonable choice, given the nation's objectives. This set of assumptions characterizes the rational policy model. The assertion that Model I is the standard frame of reference implies no denial of highly visible differences among the interests of Sovietologists, diplomatic historians, international relations theorists, and strategists. Indeed, in most respects, differences among the work of Hans Morgenthau, Stanley Hoffmann, and Thomas Schelling could not be more pointed. Appreciation of the extent to which each relies predominantly on Model I, however, reveals basic similarities among Morgenthau's method of "rational reenactment," Hoffmann's "imaginative reconstruction," and Schelling's "vicarious problem solving;" family resemblances among Morgenthau's "rational statesman," Hoffmann's "roulette player " and Schelling's "game theorist."[23]

Most contemporary analysts (as well as laymen) proceed predominantly—albeit most often implicitly—in terms of this model when attempting to explain happenings in foreign affairs. Indeed, that occurrences in foreign affairs are the *acts* of *nations* seems so fundamental to thinking about such problems that this underlying model has rarely been recognized: to explain an occurrence in foreign policy simply means to show how the government could have rationally chosen that action.[24] These brief examples illustrate five uses of the model. To prove that most analysts think largely in terms of the rational policy model is not possible. In this limited space it is not even possible to illustrate the range of employment of the framework. Rather, my purpose is to convey to the reader a grasp of the model and a challenge: let the reader examine the literature with which he is most familiar and make his judgment.

The general characterization can be sharpened by articulating the rational policy model as an "analytic paradigm" in the technical sense developed by Robert K. Merton for sociological analyses.[25] Systematic statement of basic assumptions, concepts, and propositions employed by Model I analysts highlights the distinctive thrust of this style of analysis. To articulate a largely implicit framework is of necessity to caricature. But caricature can be instructive.

RATIONAL POLICY PARADIGM

I. Basic Unit of Analysis: Policy as National Choice

Happenings in foreign affairs are conceived as actions chosen by the nation or national

[22] Schelling, *op. cit.*, p. 4.

[23] See Morgenthau, *op. cit.*, p. 5; Hoffmann, *Contemporary Theory*, pp. 178–179; Hoffmann, "Roulette in the Cellar," *The State of War*; Schelling, *op. cit.*

[24] The larger study examines several exceptions to this generalization. Sidney Verba's excellent essay "Assumptions of Rationality and Non-Rationality in Models of the International System" is less an exception than it is an approach to a somewhat different problem. Verba focuses upon models of rationality and irrationality of *individual* statesmen: in Knorr and Verba, *The International System*.

[25] Robert K. Merton, *Social Theory and Social Structures* (Revised and Enlarged Edition; New York, 1957), pp. 12–16. Considerably weaker than a satisfactory theoretical model, paradigms nevertheless represent a short step in that direction from looser, implicit conceptual models. Neither the concepts nor the relations among the variables are sufficiently specified to yield propositions deductively. "Paradigmatic Analysis" nevertheless has considerable promise for clarifying and codifying styles of analysis in political science. Each of the paradigms stated here can be represented rigorously in mathematical terms. For example, Model I lends itself to mathematical formulation along the lines of Herbert Simon's "Behavioral Theory of Rationality," *Models of Man* (New York, 1957). But this does not solve the most difficult problem of "measurement and estimation."

government.[26] Governments select the action that will maximize strategic goals and objectives. These "solutions" to strategic problems are the fundamental categories in terms of which the analyst perceives what is to be explained.

II. Organizing Concepts

A. *National Actor*. The nation or government, conceived as a rational, unitary decision-maker, is the agent. This actor has one set of specified goals (the equivalent of a consistent utility function), one set of perceived options, and a single estimate of the consequences that follow from each alternative.

B. *The Problem*. Action is chosen in response to the strategic problem which the nation faces. Threats and opportunities arising in the "international strategic market place" move the nation to act.

C. *Static Selection*. The sum of activity of representatives of the government relevant to a problem constitutes what the nation has chosen as its "solution." Thus the action is conceived as a steady-state choice among alternative outcomes (rather than, for example, a large number of partial choices in a dynamic stream).

D. *Action as Rational Choice*. The components include:

1. *Goals and Objectives*. National security and national interests are the principal categories in which strategic goals are conceived. Nations seek security and a range of further objectives. (Analysts rarely translate strategic goals and objectives into an explicit utility function; nevertheless, analysts do focus on major goals and objectives and trade off side effects in an intuitive fashion.)

2. *Options*. Various courses of action relevant to a strategic problem provide the spectrum of options.

3. *Consequences*. Enactment of each alternative course of action will produce a series of

---

[26] Though a variant of this model could easily be stochastic, this paradigm is stated in non-probabilistic terms. In contemporary strategy, a stochastic version of this model is sometimes used for predictions; but it is almost impossible to find an explanation of an occurrence in foreign affairs that is consistently probabilistic.

Analogies between Model I and the concept of explanation developed by R. G. Collingwood, William Dray, and other "revisionists" among philosophers concerned with the critical philosophy of history are not accidental. For a summary of the "revisionist position" see Maurice Mandelbaum, "Historical Explanation: The Problem of Covering Laws," *History and Theory* (1960).

consequences. The relevant consequences constitute benefits and costs in terms of strategic goals and objectives.

4. *Choice*. Rational choice is value-maximizing. The rational agent selects the alternative whose consequences rank highest in terms of his goals and objectives.

III. Dominant Inference Pattern

This paradigm leads analysts to rely on the following pattern of inference: if a nation performed a particular action, that nation must have had ends towards which the action constituted an optimal means. The rational policy model's explanatory power stems from this inference pattern. Puzzlement is relieved by revealing the purposive pattern within which the occurrence can be located as a value-maximizing means.

IV. General Propositions

The disgrace of political science is the infrequency with which propositions of any generality are formulated and tested. "Paradigmatic analysis" argues for explicitness about the terms in which analysis proceeds, and seriousness about the logic of explanation. Simply to illustrate the kind of propositions on which analysts who employ this model rely, the formulation includes several.

The basic assumption of value-maximizing behavior produces propositions central to most explanations. The general principle can be formulated as follows: the likelihood of any particular action results from a combination of the nation's (1) relevant values and objectives, (2) perceived alternative courses of action, (3) estimates of various sets of consequences (which will follow from each alternative), and (4) net valuation of each set of consequences. This yields two propositions.

A. An increase in the cost of an alternative, i.e., a reduction in the value of the set of consequences which will follow from that action, or a reduction in the probability of attaining fixed consequences, reduces the likelihood of that alternative being chosen.

B. A decrease in the costs of an alternative, i.e., an increase in the value of the set of consequences which will follow from that alternative, or an increase in the probability of attaining fixed consequences, increases the likelihood of that action being chosen.[27]

---

[27] This model is an analogue of the theory of the rational entrepreneur which has been developed extensively in economic theories of the firm and the consumer. These two propositions specify the "substitution effect." Refinement of this model and

V. Specific Propositions

A. *Deterrence*. The likelihood of any particular attack results from the factors specified in the general proposition. Combined with factual assertions, this general proposition yields the propositions of the sub-theory of deterrence.

(1) A stable nuclear balance reduces the likelihood of nuclear attack. This proposition is derived from the general proposition plus the asserted fact that a second-strike capability affects the potential attacker's calculations by increasing the likelihood and the costs of one particular set of consequences which might follow from attack—namely, retaliation.

(2) A stable nuclear balance increases the probability of limited war. This proposition is derived from the general proposition plus the asserted fact that though increasing the costs of a nuclear exchange, a stable nuclear balance nevertheless produces a more significant reduction in the probability that such consequences would be chosen in response to a limited war. Thus this set of consequences weighs less heavily in the calculus.

B. *Soviet Force Posture*. The Soviet Union chooses its force posture (i.e., its weapons and their deployment) as a value-maximizing means of implementing Soviet strategic objectives and military doctrine. A proposition of this sort underlies Secretary of Defense Laird's inference from the fact of 200 SS-9s (large intercontinental missiles) to the assertion that, "the Soviets are going for a first-strike capability, and there's no question about it."[28]

VARIANTS OF THE RATIONAL POLICY MODEL

This paradigm exhibits the characteristics of the most refined version of the rational model. The modern literature of strategy employs a model of this sort. Problems and pressures in the "international strategic marketplace" yield probabilities of occurrence. The international actor, which could be any national actor, is simply a value-maximizing mechanism for getting from the strategic problem to the logical solution. But the explanations and predictions produced by most analysts of foreign affairs depend primarily on variants of this "pure" model. The point of each is the same: to place the action within a value-maximizing framework, given certain constraints. Nevertheless, it may be helpful to identify several variants, each of which might be exhibited similarly as a paradigm. The first focuses upon the national actor

specification of additional general propositions by translating from the economic theory is straightforward.

[28] *New York Times*, March 22, 1969.

and his choice in a particular situation, leading analysts to further constrain the goals, alternatives, and consequences considered. Thus, (1) national propensities or personality traits reflected in an "operational code," (2) concern with certain objectives, or (3) special principles of action, narrow the "goals" or "alternatives" or "consequences" of the paradigm. For example, the Soviet deployment of ABMs is sometimes explained by reference to the Soviet's "defense-mindedness." Or a particular Soviet action is explained as an instance of a special rule of action in the Bolshevik operational code.[29] A second, related, cluster of variants focuses on the individual leader or leadership group as the actor whose preference function is maximized and whose personal (or group) characteristics are allowed to modify the alternatives, consequences, and rules of choice. Explanations of the U.S. involvement in Vietnam as a natural consequence of the Kennedy-Johnson Administration's axioms of foreign policy rely on this variant. A third, more complex variant of the basic model recognizes the existence of several actors within a government, for example, Hawks and Doves or military and civilians, but attempts to explain (or predict) an occurrence by reference to the objectives of the victorious actor. Thus, for example, some revisionist histories of the Cold War recognize the forces of light and the forces of darkness within the U.S. government, but explain American actions as a result of goals and perceptions of the victorious forces of darkness.

Each of these forms of the basic paradigm constitutes a formalization of what analysts typically rely upon implicitly. In the transition from implicit conceptual model to explicit paradigm much of the richness of the best employments of this model has been lost. But the purpose in raising loose, implicit conceptual models to an explicit level is to reveal the basic logic of analysts' activity. Perhaps some of the remaining artificiality that surrounds the statement of the paradigm can be erased by noting a number of the standard additions and modifications employed by analysts who proceed *predominantly* within the rational policy model. First, in the course of a document, analysts shift from one variant of the basic model to another, occasionally appropriating in an *ad hoc* fashion aspects of a situation which are logically incompatible with the basic model. Second, in the course of explaining a number of occurrences, analysts sometimes pause over a particular event about which they have a great deal of information and unfold it in such detail that an impression of

[29] See Nathan Leites, *A Study of Bolshevism* (Glencoe, Illinois, 1953).

randomness is created. Third, having employed other assumptions and categories in deriving an explanation or prediction, analysts will present their product in a neat, convincing rational policy model package. (This accommodation is a favorite of members of the intelligence community whose association with the details of a process is considerable, but who feel that by putting an occurrence in a larger rational framework, it will be more comprehensible to their audience.) Fourth, in attempting to offer an explanation— particularly in cases where a prediction derived from the basic model has failed—the notion of a "mistake" is invoked. Thus, the failure in the prediction of a "missile gap" is written off as a Soviet mistake in not taking advantage of their opportunity. Both these and other modifications permit Model I analysts considerably more variety than the paradigm might suggest. But such accommodations are essentially appendages to the basic logic of these analyses.

THE U.S. BLOCKADE OF CUBA: A FIRST CUT[30]

The U.S. response to the Soviet Union's emplacement of missiles in Cuba must be understood in strategic terms as simple value-maximizing escalation. American nuclear superiority could be counted on to paralyze Soviet nuclear power; Soviet transgression of the nuclear threshold in response to an American use of lower levels of violence would be wildly irrational since it would mean virtual destruction of the Soviet Communist system and Russian nation. American local superiority was overwhelming: it could be initiated at a low level while threatening with high credibility an ascending sequence of steps short of the nuclear threshold. All that was required was for the United States to bring to bear its strategic and local superiority in such a way that American determination to see the missiles removed would be demonstrated, while at the same time allowing Moscow time and room to retreat without humiliation. The naval blockade—euphemistically named a "quarantine" in order to circumvent the niceties of international law—did just that.

The U.S. government's selection of the blockade followed this logic. Apprised of the presence of Soviet missiles in Cuba, the President assembled an Executive Committee (ExCom) of the

[30] As stated in the introduction, this "case snapshot" presents, without editorial commentary, a Model I analyst's explanation of the U.S. blockade. The purpose is to illustrate a strong, characteristic rational policy model account. This account is (roughly) consistent with prevailing explanations of these events.

National Security Council and directed them to "set aside all other tasks to make a prompt and intense survey of the dangers and all possible courses of action."[31] This group functioned as "fifteen individuals on our own, representing the President and not different departments."[32] As one of the participants recalls, "The remarkable aspect of those meetings was a sense of complete equality."[33] Most of the time during the week that followed was spent canvassing all the possible tracks and weighing the arguments for and against each. Six major categories of action were considered.

1. Do nothing. U.S. vulnerability to Soviet missiles was no new thing. Since the U.S. already lived under the gun of missiles based in Russia, a Soviet capability to strike from Cuba too made little real difference. The real danger stemmed from the possibility of U.S. over-reaction. The U.S. should announce the Soviet action in a calm, casual manner thereby deflating whatever political capital Khrushchev hoped to make of the missiles.

This argument fails on two counts. First, it grossly underestimates the military importance of the Soviet move. Not only would the Soviet Union's missile capability be doubled and the U.S. early warning system outflanked. The Soviet Union would have an opportunity to reverse the strategic balance by further installations, and indeed, in the longer run, to invest in cheaper, shorter-range rather than more expensive longer-range missiles. Second, the political importance of this move was undeniable. The Soviet Union's act challenged the American President's most solemn warning. If the U.S. failed to respond, no American commitment would be credible.

2. Diplomatic pressures. Several forms were considered: an appeal to the U.N. or O.A.S. for an inspection team, a secret approach to Khrushchev, and a direct approach to Khrushchev, perhaps at a summit meeting. The United States would demand that the missiles be removed, but the final settlement might include neutralization of Cuba, U.S. withdrawal from the Guantanamo base, and withdrawal of U.S. Jupiter missiles from Turkey or Italy.

Each form of the diplomatic approach had its own drawbacks. To arraign the Soviet Union before the U.N. Security Council held little promise since the Russians could veto any proposed action. While the diplomats argued, the missiles would become operational. To send a secret emissary to Khrushchev demanding that

[31] Theodore Sorensen, *op. cit.*, p. 675.

[32] *Ibid.*, p. 679.

[33] *Ibid.*, p. 679.

the missiles be withdrawn would be to pose untenable alternatives. On the one hand, this would invite Khrushchev to seize the diplomatic initiative, perhaps committing himself to strategic retaliation in response to an attack on Cuba. On the other hand, this would tender an ultimatum that no great power could accept. To confront Khrushchev at a summit would guarantee demands for U.S. concessions, and the analogy between U.S. missiles in Turkey and Russian missiles in Cuba could not be erased.

But why not trade U.S. Jupiters in Turkey and Italy, which the President had previously ordered withdrawn, for the missiles in Cuba? The U.S. had chosen to withdraw these missiles in order to replace them with superior, less vulnerable Mediterranean Polaris submarines. But the middle of the crisis was no time for concessions. The offer of such a deal might suggest to the Soviets that the West would yield and thus tempt them to demand more. It would certainly confirm European suspicions about American willingness to sacrifice European interests when the chips were down. Finally, the basic issue should be kept clear. As the President stated in reply to Bertrand Russell, "I think your attention might well be directed to the burglars rather than to those who have caught the burglars."[34]

3. A secret approach to Castro. The crisis provided an opportunity to separate Cuba and Soviet Communism by offering Castro the alternatives, "split or fall." But Soviet troops transported, constructed, guarded, and controlled the missiles. Their removal would thus depend on a Soviet decision.

4. Invasion. The United States could take this occasion not only to remove the missiles but also to rid itself of Castro. A Navy exercise had long been scheduled in which Marines, ferried from Florida in naval vessels, would liberate the imaginary island of Vieques.[35] Why not simply shift the point of disembarkment? (The Pentagon's foresight in planning this operation would be an appropriate antidote to the CIA's Bay of Pigs!)

Preparations were made for an invasion, but as a last resort. American troops would be forced to confront 20,000 Soviets in the first Cold War case of direct contact between the troops of the super powers. Such brinksmanship courted nuclear disaster, practically guaranteeing an equivalent Soviet move against Berlin.

5. Surgical air strike. The missile sites should

be removed by a clean, swift conventional attack. This was the effective counter-action which the attempted deception deserved. A surgical strike would remove the missiles and thus eliminate both the danger that the missiles might become operational and the fear that the Soviets would discover the American discovery and act first.

The initial attractiveness of this alternative was dulled by several difficulties. First, could the strike really be "surgical"? The Air Force could not guarantee destruction of all the missiles.[36] Some might be fired during the attack; some might not have been identified. In order to assure destruction of Soviet and Cuban means of retaliating, what was required was not a surgical but rather a massive attack—of at least 500 sorties. Second, a surprise air attack would of course kill Russians at the missile sites. Pressures on the Soviet Union to retaliate would be so strong that an attack on Berlin or Turkey was highly probable. Third, the key problem with this program was that of advance warning. Could the President of the United States, with his memory of Pearl Harbor and his vision of future U.S. responsibility, order a "Pearl Harbor in reverse"? For 175 years, unannounced Sunday morning attacks had been an anathema to our tradition.[37]

6. Blockade. Indirect military action in the form of a blockade became more attractive as the ExCom dissected the other alternatives. An embargo on military shipments to Cuba enforced by a naval blockade was not without flaws, however. Could the U.S. blockade Cuba without inviting Soviet reprisal in Berlin? The likely solution to joint blockades would be the lifting of both blockades, restoring the new *status quo*, and allowing the Soviets additional time to complete the missiles. Second, the possible consequences of the blockade resembled the drawbacks which disqualified the air strike. If Soviet ships did not stop, the United States would be forced to fire the first shot, inviting retaliation. Third, a blockade would deny the traditional freedom of the seas demanded by several of our close allies and might be held illegal, in violation of the U.N. Charter and international law, unless the United States could obtain a two-thirds vote in the O.A.S. Finally, how

---

[34] Elie Abel, *The Missile Crisis* (New York, 1966), p. 144.

[35] *Ibid.*, p. 102.

[36] Sorensen, *op. cit.*, p. 684.

[37] *Ibid.*, p. 685. Though this was the formulation of the argument, the facts are not strictly accurate. Our tradition against surprise attack was rather younger than 175 years. For example President Theodore Roosevelt applauded Japan's attack on Russia in 1904.

698   THE AMERICAN POLITICAL SCIENCE REVIEW   VOL. 63

could a blockade be related to the problem, namely, some 75 missiles on the island of Cuba, approaching operational readiness daily? A blockade offered the Soviets a spectrum of delaying tactics with which to buy time to complete the missile installations. Was a *fait accompli* not required?

In spite of these enormous difficulties the blockade had comparative advantages: (1) It was a middle course between inaction and attack, aggressive enough to communicate firmness of intention, but nevertheless not so precipitous as a strike. (2) It placed on Khrushchev the burden of choice concerning the next step. He could avoid a direct military clash by keeping his ships away. His was the last clear chance. (3) No possible military confrontation could be more acceptable to the U.S. than a naval engagement in the Caribbean. (4) This move permitted the U.S., by flexing its conventional muscle, to exploit the threat of subsequent non-nuclear steps in each of which the U.S. would have significant superiority.

Particular arguments about advantages and disadvantages were powerful. The explanation of the American choice of the blockade lies in a more general principle, however. As President Kennedy stated in drawing the moral of the crisis:

> Above all, while defending our own vital interests, nuclear powers must avert those confrontations which bring an adversary to a choice of either a humiliating retreat or a nuclear war. To adopt that kind of course in the nuclear age would be evidence only of the bankruptcy of our policy—of a collective death wish for the world.[38]

The blockade was the United States' only real option.

MODEL II: ORGANIZATIONAL PROCESS

For some purposes, governmental behavior can be usefully summarized as action chosen by a unitary, rational decisionmaker: centrally controlled, completely informed, and value maximizing. But this simplification must not be allowed to conceal the fact that a "government" consists of a conglomerate of semi-feudal, loosely allied organizations, each with a substantial life of its own. Government leaders do sit formally, and to some extent in fact, on top of this conglomerate. But governments perceive problems through organizational sensors. Governments define alternatives and estimate consequences as organizations process information. Governments act as these organizations enact routines. Government behavior can therefore be

[38] *New York Times*, June, 1963.

understood according to a second conceptual model, less as deliberate choices of leaders and more as *outputs* of large organizations functioning according to standard patterns of behavior.

To be responsive to a broad spectrum of problems, governments consist of large organizations among which primary responsibility for particular areas is divided. Each organization attends to a special set of problems and acts in quasi-independence on these problems. But few important problems fall exclusively within the domain of a single organization. Thus government behavior relevant to any important problem reflects the independent output of several organizations, partially coordinated by government leaders. Government leaders can substantially disturb, but not substantially control, the behavior of these organizations.

To perform complex routines, the behavior of large numbers of individuals must be coordinated. Coordination requires standard operating procedures: rules according to which things are done. Assured capability for reliable performance of action that depends upon the behavior of hundreds of persons requires established "programs." Indeed, if the eleven members of a football team are to perform adequately on any particular down, each player must not "do what he thinks needs to be done" or "do what the quarterback tells him to do." Rather, each player must perform the maneuvers specified by a previously established play which the quarterback has simply called in this situation.

At any given time, a government consists of *existing* organizations, each with a *fixed* set of standard operating procedures and programs. The behavior of these organizations—and consequently of the government—relevant to an issue in any particular instance is, therefore, determined primarily by routines established in these organizations prior to that instance. But organizations do change. Learning occurs gradually, over time. Dramatic organizational change occurs in response to major crises. Both learning and change are influenced by existing organizational capabilities.

Borrowed from studies of organizations, these loosely formulated propositions amount simply to *tendencies*. Each must be hedged by modifiers like "other things being equal" and "under certain conditions." In particular instances, tendencies hold—more or less. In specific situations, the relevant question is: more or less? But this is as it should be. For, on the one hand, "organizations" are no more homogeneous a class than "solids." When scientists tried to generalize about "solids," they achieved similar results. Solids tend to expand when heated, but some do and some don't. More adequate categorization of the various elements now lumped under the rubric "organizations" is thus required. On the other hand, the behavior of particular organizations seems considerably more complex than the behavior of solids. Additional information about a particular organization is required for further specification of the tendency statements. In spite of these two caveats, the characterization of government action as organizational output differs distinctly from Model I. Attempts to understand problems of foreign affairs in terms of this frame of reference should produce quite different explanations.[39]

ORGANIZATIONAL PROCESS PARADIGM[40]

I. Basic Unit of Analysis: Policy as Organizational Output

The happenings of international politics are, in three critical senses, outputs of organizational processes. First, the actual occurrences are organizational outputs. For example, Chinese entry into the Korean War—that is, the fact that Chinese soldiers were firing at U.N. soldiers south of the Yalu in 1950—is an organizational action: the action of men who are soldiers in platoons which are in companies, which in turn are in armies, responding as privates to lieutenants who are responsible to captains and so on

[39] The influence of organizational studies upon the present literature of foreign affairs is minimal. Specialists in international politics are not students of organization theory. Organization theory has only recently begun to study organizations as decisionmakers and has not yet produced behavioral studies of national security organizations from a decision-making perspective. It seems unlikely, however, that these gaps will remain unfilled much longer. Considerable progress has been made in the study of the business firm as an organization. Scholars have begun applying these insights to government organizations, and interest in an organizational perspective is spreading among institutions and individuals concerned with actual government operations. The "decisionmaking" approach represented by Richard Snyder, R. Bruck, and B. Sapin, *Foreign Policy Decision-Making* (Glencoe, Illinois, 1962), incorporates a number of insights from organization theory.

[40] The formulation of this paradigm is indebted both to the orientation and insights of Herbert Simon and to the behavioral model of the firm stated by Richard Cyert and James March, *A Behavioral Theory of the Firm* (Englewood Cliffs, 1963). Here, however, one is forced to grapple with the less routine, less quantified functions of the less differentiated elements in government organizations.

to the commander, moving into Korea, advancing against enemy troops, and firing according to fixed routines of the Chinese Army. Government leaders' decisions trigger organizational routines. Government leaders can trim the edges of this output and exercise some choice in combining outputs. But the mass of behavior is determined by previously established procedures. Second, existing organizational routines for employing present physical capabilities constitute the effective options open to government leaders confronted with any problem. Only the existence of men, equipped and trained as armies and capable of being transported to North Korea, made entry into the Korean War a live option for the Chinese leaders. The fact that fixed programs (equipment, men, and routines which exist at the particular time) exhaust the range of buttons that leaders can push is not always perceived by these leaders. But in every case it is critical for an understanding of what is actually done. Third, organizational outputs structure the situation within the narrow constraints of which leaders must contribute their "decision" concerning an issue. Outputs raise the problem, provide the information, and make the initial moves that color the face of the issue that is turned to the leaders. As Theodore Sorensen has observed: "Presidents rarely, if ever, make decisions—particularly in foreign affairs —in the sense of writing their conclusions on a clean slate . . . The basic decisions, which confine their choices, have all too often been previously made."[41] If one understands the structure of the situation and the face of the issue— which are determined by the organizational outputs—the formal choice of the leaders is frequently anti-climactic.

II. Organizing Concepts

A. *Organizational Actors.* The actor is not a monolithic "nation" or "government" but rather a constellation of loosely allied organizations on top of which government leaders sit. This constellation acts only as component organizations perform routines.[42]

B. *Factored Problems and Fractionated Power.* Surveillance of the multiple facets of for-

[41] Theodore Sorensen, "You Get to Walk to Work," *New York Times Magazine,* March 19, 1967.

[42] Organizations are not monolithic. The proper level of disaggregation depends upon the objectives of a piece of analysis. This paradigm is formulated with reference to the major organizations that constitute the U.S. government. Generalization to the major components of each department and agency should be relatively straightforward.

700   THE AMERICAN POLITICAL SCIENCE REVIEW   VOL. 63

eign affairs requires that problems be cut up and parcelled out to various organizations. To avoid paralysis, primary power must accompany primary responsibility. But if organizations are permitted to do anything, a large part of what they do will be determined within the organization. Thus each organization perceives problems, processes information, and performs a range of actions in quasi-independence (within broad guidelines of national policy). Factored problems and fractionated power are two edges of the same sword. Factoring permits more specialized attention to particular facets of problems than would be possible if government leaders tried to cope with these problems by themselves. But this additional attention must be paid for in the coin of discretion for *what* an organization attends to, and *how* organizational responses are programmed.

C. *Parochial Priorities, Perceptions, and Issues.* Primary responsibility for a narrow set of problems encourages organizational parochialism. These tendencies are enhanced by a number of additional factors: (1) selective information available to the organization, (2) recruitment of personnel into the organization, (3) tenure of individuals in the organization, (4) small group pressures within the organization, and (5) distribution of rewards by the organization. Clients (e.g., interest groups), government allies (e.g., Congressional committees), and extra-national counterparts (e.g., the British Ministry of Defense for the Department of Defense, ISA, or the British Foreign Office for the Department of State, EUR) galvanize this parochialism. Thus organizations develop relatively stable propensities concerning operational priorities, perceptions, and issues.

D. *Action as Organizational Output.* The preeminent feature of organizational activity is its programmed character: the extent to which behavior in any particular case is an enactment of preestablished routines. In producing outputs, the activity of each organization is characterized by:

1. *Goals: Constraints Defining Acceptable Performance.* The operational goals of an organization are seldom revealed by formal mandates. Rather, each organization's operational goals emerge as a set of constraints defining acceptable performance. Central among these constraints is organizational health, defined usually in terms of bodies assigned and dollars appropriated. The set of constraints emerges from a mix of expectations and demands of other organizations in the government, statutory authority, demands from citizens and special interest groups, and bargaining within the organization. These constraints represent a quasi-resolution of

conflict—the constraints are relatively stable, so there is some resolution. But conflict among alternative goals is always latent; hence, it is a quasi-resolution. Typically, the constraints are formulated as imperatives to avoid roughly specified discomforts and disasters.[43]

2. *Sequential Attention to Goals.* The existence of conflict among operational constraints is resolved by the device of sequential attention. As a problem arises, the subunits of the organization most concerned with that problem deal with it in terms of the constraints they take to be most important. When the next problem arises, another cluster of subunits deals with it, focusing on a different set of constraints.

3. *Standard Operating Procedures.* Organizations perform their "higher" functions, such as attending to problem areas, monitoring information, and preparing relevant responses for likely contingencies, by doing "lower" tasks, for example, preparing budgets, producing reports, and developing hardware. Reliable performance of these tasks requires standard operating procedures (hereafter SOPs). Since procedures are "standard" they do not change quickly or easily. Without these standard procedures, it would not be possible to perform certain concerted tasks. But because of standard procedures, organizational behavior in particular instances often appears unduly formalized, sluggish, or inappropriate.

4. *Programs and Repertoires.* Organizations must be capable of performing actions in which the behavior of large numbers of individuals is carefully coordinated. Assured performance requires clusters of rehearsed SOPs for producing specific actions, e.g., fighting enemy units or answering an embassy's cable. Each cluster comprises a "program" (in the terms both of drama and computers) which the organization has available for dealing with a situation. The list of programs relevant to a type of activity, e.g., fighting, constitutes an organizational repertoire. The number of programs in a repertoire is always quite limited. When properly triggered, organizations execute programs; programs cannot be substantially changed in a particular situation. The more complex the action and the greater the number of individuals involved, the more important are programs and repertoires as determinants of organizational behavior.

5. *Uncertainty Avoidance.* Organizations do not attempt to estimate the probability distribution of future occurrences. Rather, organizations

[43] The stability of these constraints is dependent on such factors as rules for promotion and reward, budgeting and accounting procedures, and mundane operating procedures.

avoid uncertainty. By arranging a *negotiated environment*, organizations regularize the reactions of other actors with whom they have to deal. The primary environment, relations with other organizations that comprise the government, is stabilized by such arrangements as agreed budgetary splits, accepted areas of responsibility, and established conventional practices. The secondary environment, relations with the international world, is stabilized between allies by the establishment of contracts (alliances) and "club relations" (U.S. State and U.K. Foreign Office or U.S. Treasury and U.K. Treasury). Between enemies, contracts and accepted conventional practices perform a similar function, for example, the rules of the "precarious status quo" which President Kennedy referred to in the missile crisis. Where the international environment cannot be negotiated, organizations deal with remaining uncertainties by establishing a set of *standard scenarios* that constitute the contingencies for which they prepare. For example, the standard scenario for Tactical Air Command of the U.S. Air Force involves combat with enemy aircraft. Planes are designed and pilots trained to meet this problem. That these preparations are less relevant to more probable contingencies, e.g., provision of close-in ground support in limited wars like Vietnam, has had little impact on the scenario.

6. *Problem-directed Search*. Where situations cannot be construed as standard, organizations engage in search. The style of search and the solution are largely determined by existing routines. Organizational search for alternative courses of action is problem-oriented: it focuses on the atypical discomfort that must be avoided. It is simple-minded: the neighborhood of the symptom is searched first; then, the neighborhood of the current alternative. Patterns of search reveal biases which in turn reflect such factors as specialized training or experience and patterns of communication.

7. *Organizational Learning and Change*. The parameters of organizational behavior mostly persist. In response to non-standard problems, organizations search and routines evolve, assimilating new situations. Thus learning and change follow in large part from existing procedures. But marked changes in organizations do sometimes occur. Conditions in which dramatic changes are more likely include: (1) Periods of budgetary feast. Typically, organizations devour budgetary feasts by purchasing additional items on the existing shopping list. Nevertheless, if committed to change, leaders who control the budget can use extra funds to effect changes. (2) Periods of prolonged budgetary famine. Though a single year's famine typically

results in few changes in organizational structure but a loss of effectiveness in performing some programs, prolonged famine forces major retrenchment. (3) Dramatic performance failures. Dramatic change occurs (mostly) in response to major disasters. Confronted with an undeniable failure of procedures and repertoires, authorities outside the organization demand change, existing personnel are less resistant to change, and critical members of the organization are replaced by individuals committed to change.

E. *Central Coordination and Control*. Action requires decentralization of responsibility and power. But problems lap over the jurisdictions of several organizations. Thus the necessity for decentralization runs headlong into the requirement for coordination. (Advocates of one horn or the other of this dilemma—responsive action entails decentralized power vs. coordinated action requires central control—account for a considerable part of the persistent demand for government reorganization.) Both the necessity for coordination and the centrality of foreign policy to national welfare guarantee the involvement of government leaders in the procedures of the organizations among which problems are divided and power shared. Each organization's propensities and routines can be disturbed by government leaders' intervention. Central direction and persistent control of organizational activity, however, is not possible. The relation among organizations, and between organizations and the government leaders depends critically on a number of structural variables including: (1) the nature of the job, (2) the measures and information available to government leaders, (3) the system of rewards and punishments for organizational members, and (4) the procedures by which human and material resources get committed. For example, to the extent that rewards and punishments for the members of an organization are distributed by higher authorities, these authorities can exercise some control by specifying criteria in terms of which organizational output is to be evaluated. These criteria become constraints within which organizational activity proceeds. But constraint is a crude instrument of control.

Intervention by government leaders does sometimes change the activity of an organization in an intended direction. But instances are fewer than might be expected. As Franklin Roosevelt, the master manipulator of government organizations, remarked:

The Treasury is so large and far-flung and ingrained in its practices that I find it is almost impossible to get the action and results I want. . . .

But the Treasury is not to be compared with the State Department. You should go through the experience of trying to get any changes in the thinking, policy, and action of the career diplomats and then you'd know what a real problem was. But the Treasury and the State Department put together are nothing compared with the Na-a-vy . . . To change anything in the Na-a-vy is like punching a feather bed. You punch it with your right and you punch it with your left until you are finally exhausted, and then you find the damn bed just as it was before you started punching.[44]

John Kennedy's experience seems to have been similar: "The State Department," he asserted, "is a bowl full of jelly."[45] And lest the McNamara revolution in the Defense Department seem too striking a counter-example, the Navy's recent rejection of McNamara's major intervention in Naval weapons procurement, the F-111B, should be studied as an antidote.

F. *Decisions of Government Leaders.* Organizational persistence does not exclude shifts in governmental behavior. For government leaders sit atop the conglomerate of organizations. Many important issues of governmental action require that these leaders decide what organizations will play out which programs where. Thus stability in the parochialisms and SOPs of individual organizations is consistent with some important shifts in the behavior of governments. The range of these shifts is defined by existing organizational programs.

III. *Dominant Inference Pattern*

If a nation performs an action of this type today, its organizational components must yesterday have been performing (or have had established routines for performing) an action only marginally different from this action. At any specific point in time, a government consists of an established conglomerate of organizations, each with existing goals, programs, and repertoires. The characteristics of a government's action in any instance follows from those established routines, and from the choice of government leaders —on the basis of information and estimates provided by existing routines—among existing programs. The best explanation of an organization's behavior at t is $t - 1$; the prediction of $t + 1$ is t. Model II's explanatory power is achieved by uncovering the organizational routines and repertoires that produced the outputs that comprise the puzzling occurrence.

[44] Marriner Eccles, *Beckoning Frontiers* (New York, 1951), p. 336.

[45] Arthur Schlesinger, *A Thousand Days* (Boston, 1965), p. 406.

IV. *General Propositions*

A number of general propositions have been stated above. In order to illustrate clearly the type of proposition employed by Model II analysts, this section formulates several more precisely.

A. *Organizational Action.* Activity according to SOPs and programs does not constitute far-sighted, flexible adaptation to "the issue" (as it is conceived by the analyst). Detail and nuance of actions by organizations are determined predominantly by organizational routines, not government leaders' directions.

1. SOPs constitute routines for dealing with *standard* situations. Routines allow large numbers of ordinary individuals to deal with numerous instances, day after day, without considerable thought, by responding to basic stimuli. But this regularized capability for adequate performance is purchased at the price of standardization. If the SOPs are appropriate, average performance, i.e., performance averaged over the range of cases, is better than it would be if each instance were approached individually (given fixed talent, timing, and resource constraints). But specific instances, particularly critical instances that typically do not have "standard" characteristics, are often handled sluggishly or inappropriately.

2. A program, i.e., a complex action chosen from a short list of programs in a repertoire, is rarely tailored to the specific situation in which it is executed. Rather, the program is (at best) the most appropriate of the programs in a previously developed repertoire.

3. Since repertoires are developed by parochial organizations for standard scenarios defined by that organization, programs available for dealing with a particular situation are often ill-suited.

B. *Limited Flexibility and Incremental Change.* Major lines of organizational action are straight, i.e., behavior at one time is marginally different from that behavior at $t - 1$. Simpleminded predictions work best: Behavior at $t + 1$ will be marginally different from behavior at the present time.

1. Organizational budgets change incrementally—both with respect to totals and with respect to intra-organizational splits. Though organizations could divide the money available each year by carving up the pie anew (in the light of changes in objectives or environment), in practice, organizations take last year's budget as a base and adjust incrementally. Predictions that require large budgetary shifts in a single year between organizations or between units within an organization should be hedged.

2. Once undertaken, an organizational in-

vestment is not dropped at the point where "objective" costs outweigh benefits. Organizational stakes in adopted projects carry them quite beyond the loss point.

C. *Administrative Feasibility.* Adequate explanation, analysis, and prediction must include administrative feasibility as a major dimension. A considerable gap separates what leaders choose (or might rationally have chosen) and what organizations implement.

1. Organizations are blunt instruments. Projects that require several organizations to act with high degrees of precision and coordination are not likely to succeed.

2. Projects that demand that existing organizational units depart from their accustomed functions and perform previously unprogrammed tasks are rarely accomplished in their designed form.

3. Government leaders can expect that each organization will do its "part" in terms of what the organization knows how to do.

4. Government leaders can expect incomplete and distorted information from each organization concerning its part of the problem.

5. Where an assigned piece of a problem is contrary to the existing goals of an organization, resistance to implementation of that piece will be encountered.

V. *Specific Propositions.*

1. *Deterrence.* The probability of nuclear attack is less sensitive to balance and imbalance, or stability and instability (as these concepts are employed by Model I strategists) than it is to a number of organizational factors. Except for the special case in which the Soviet Union acquires a credible capability to destroy the U.S. with a disarming blow, U.S. superiority or inferiority affects the probability of a nuclear attack less than do a number of organizational factors.

First, if a nuclear attack occurs, it will result from organizational activity: the firing of rockets by members of a missile group. The enemy's *control system*, i.e., physical mechanisms and standard procedures which determine who can launch rockets when, is critical. Second, the enemy's programs for bringing his strategic forces to *alert status* determine probabilities of accidental firing and momentum. At the outbreak of World War I, if the Russian Tsar had understood the organizational processes which his order of full mobilization triggered, he would have realized that he had chosen war. Third, organizational repertoires fix the range of effective choice open to enemy leaders. The menu available to Tsar Nicholas in 1914 has two entrees: full mobilization and no mobilization. Partial mobilization was not an organizational option.

Fourth, since organizational routines set the chessboard, the training and deployment of troops and nuclear weapons is crucial. Given that the outbreak of hostilities in Berlin is more probable than most scenarios for nuclear war, facts about deployment, training, and tactical nuclear equipment of Soviet troops stationed in East Germany—which will influence the face of the issue seen by Soviet leaders at the outbreak of hostilities and the manner in which choice is implemented—are as critical as the question of "balance."

2. *Soviet Force Posture.* Soviet force posture, i.e., the fact that certain weapons rather than others are procured and deployed, is determined by organizational factors such as the goals and procedures of existing military services and the goals and processes of research and design labs, within budgetary constraints that emerge from the government leader's choices. The frailty of the Soviet Air Force within the Soviet military establishment seems to have been a crucial element in the Soviet failure to acquire a large bomber force in the 1950s (thereby faulting American intelligence predictions of a "bomber gap"). The fact that missiles were controlled until 1960 in the Soviet Union by the Soviet Ground Forces, whose goals and procedures reflected no interest in an intercontinental mission, was not irrelevant to the slow Soviet buildup of ICBMs (thereby faulting U.S. intelligence predictions of a "missile gap"). These organizational factors (Soviet Ground Forces' control of missiles and that service's fixation with European scenarios) make the Soviet deployment of so many MRBMs that European targets could be destroyed three times over, more understandable. Recent weapon developments, e.g., the testing of a Fractional Orbital Bombardment System (FOBS) and multiple warheads for the SS-9, very likely reflect the activity and interests of a cluster of Soviet research and development organizations, rather than a decision by Soviet leaders to acquire a first strike weapon system. Careful attention to the organizational components of the Soviet military establishment (Strategic Rocket Forces, Navy, Air Force, Ground Forces, and National Air Defense), the missions and weapons systems to which each component is wedded (an independent weapon system assists survival as an independent service), and existing budgetary splits (which probably are relatively stable in the Soviet Union as they tend to be everywhere) offer potential improvements in medium and longer term predictions.

THE U.S. BLOCKADE OF CUBA: A SECOND CUT

Organizational Intelligence. At 7:00 P.M. on

October 22, 1962, President Kennedy disclosed the American discovery of the presence of Soviet strategic missiles in Cuba, declared a "strict quarantine on all offensive military equipment under shipment to Cuba," and demanded that "Chairman Khrushchev halt and eliminate this clandestine, reckless, and provocative threat to world peace."[46] This decision was reached at the pinnacle of the U.S. Government after a critical week of deliberation. What initiated that precious week were photographs of Soviet missile sites in Cuba taken on October 14. These pictures might not have been taken until a week later. In that case, the President speculated, "I don't think probably we would have chosen as prudently as we finally did."[47] U.S. leaders might have received this information three weeks earlier—if a U-2 had flown over San Cristobal in the last week of September.[48] What determined the context in which American leaders came to choose the blockade was the discovery of missiles on October 14.

There has been considerable debate over alleged American "intelligence failures" in the Cuban missile crisis.[49] But what both critics and defenders have neglected is the fact that the discovery took place on October 14, rather than three weeks earlier or a week later, as a consequence of the established routines and procedures of the organizations which constitute the U.S. intelligence community. These organizations were neither more nor less successful than they had been the previous month or were to be in the months to follow.[50]

The notorious "September estimate," approved by the United States Intelligence Board (USIB) on September 19, concluded that the Soviet Union would not introduce offensive missiles into Cuba.[51] No U-2 flight was directed over the western end of Cuba (after September 5) before

October 4.[52] No U-2 flew over the western end of Cuba until the flight that discovered the Soviet missiles on October 14.[53] Can these "failures" be accounted for in organizational terms?

On September 19 when USIB met to consider the question of Cuba, the "system" contained the following information: (1) shipping intelligence had noted the arrival in Cuba of two large-hatch Soviet lumber ships, which were riding high in the water; (2) refugee reports of countless sightings of missiles, but also a report that Castro's private pilot, after a night of drinking in Havana, had boasted: "We will fight to the death and perhaps we can win because we have everything, including atomic weapons"; (3) a sighting by a CIA agent of the rear profile of a strategic missile; (4) U-2 photos produced by flights of August 29, September 5 and 17 showing the construction of a number of SAM sites and other defensive missiles.[54] Not all of this information was on the desk of the estimators, however. Shipping intelligence experts noted the fact that large-hatch ships were riding high in the water and spelled out the inference: the ships must be carrying "space consuming" cargo.[55] These facts were carefully included in the catalogue of intelligence concerning shipping. For experts sensitive to the Soviets' shortage of ships, however, these facts carried no special signal. The refugee report of Castro's private pilot's remark had been received at Opa Locka, Florida, along with vast reams of inaccurate reports generated by the refugee community. This report and a thousand others had to be checked and compared before being sent to Washington. The two weeks required for initial processing could have been shortened by a large increase in resources, but the yield of this source was already quite marginal. The CIA agent's sighting of the rear profile of a strategic missile had oc-

[46] U.S. Department of State, *Bulletin*, XLVII, pp. 715–720.

[47] Schlesinger, *op. cit.*, p. 803.

[48] Theodore Sorensen, *Kennedy*, p. 675.

[49] See U.S. Congress, Senate, Committee on Armed Services, Preparedness Investigation Subcommittee, *Interim Report on Cuban Military Build-up*, 88th Congress, 1st Session, 1963, p. 2; Hanson Baldwin, "Growing Risks of Bureaucratic Intelligence," *The Reporter* (August 15, 1963), 48–50; Roberta Wohlstetter, "Cuba and Pearl Harbor," *Foreign Affairs* (July, 1965), 706.

[50] U.S. Congress, House of Representatives, Committee on Appropriations, Subcommittee on Department of Defense Appropriations, *Hearings*, 88th Congress, 1st Session, 1963, 25 ff.

[51] R. Hilsman, *To Move a Nation* (New York, 1967), pp. 172–173.

[52] Department of Defense Appropriations, *Hearings*, p. 67.

[53] *Ibid.*, pp. 66–67.

[54] For (1) Hilsman, *op. cit.*, p. 186; (2) Abel, *op. cit.*, p. 24; (3) Department of Defense Appropriations, *Hearings*, p. 64; Abel, *op. cit.*, p. 24; (4) Department of Defense Appropriations, *Hearings*, pp. 1–30.

[55] The facts here are not entirely clear. This assertion is based on information from (1) "Department of Defense Briefing by the Honorable R. S. McNamara, Secretary of Defense, State Department Auditorium, 5:00 p.m., February 6, 1963." A verbatim transcript of a presentation actually made by General Carroll's assistant, John Hughes; and (2) Hilsman's statement, *op. cit.*, p. 186. But see R. Wohlstetter's interpretation, "Cuba and Pearl Harbor," 700.

curred on September 12; transmission time from agent sighting to arrival in Washington typically took 9 to 12 days. Shortening this transmission time would impose severe cost in terms of danger to sub-agents, agents, and communication networks.

On the information available, the intelligence chiefs who predicted that the Soviet Union would not introduce offensive missiles into Cuba made a reasonable and defensible judgment.[56] Moreover, in the light of the fact that these organizations were gathering intelligence not only about Cuba but about potential occurrences in all parts of the world, the informational base available to the estimators involved nothing out of the ordinary. Nor, from an organizational perspective, is there anything startling about the gradual accumulation of evidence that led to the formulation of the hypothesis that the Soviets were installing missiles in Cuba and the decision on October 4 to direct a special flight over western Cuba.

The ten-day delay between that decision and the flight is another organizational story.[57] At the October 4 meeting, the Defense Department took the opportunity to raise an issue important to its concerns. Given the increased danger that a U-2 would be downed, it would be better if the pilot were an officer in uniform rather than a CIA agent. Thus the Air Force should assume responsibility for U-2 flights over Cuba. To the contrary, the CIA argued that this was an intelligence operation and thus within the CIA's jurisdiction. Moreover, CIA U-2's had been modified in certain ways which gave them advantages over Air Force U-2's in averting Soviet SAM's. Five days passed while the State Department pressed for less risky alternatives such as drones and the Air Force (in Department of Defense guise) and CIA engaged in territorial disputes. On October 9 a flight plan over San Cristobal was approved by COMOR, but to the CIA's dismay, Air Force pilots rather than CIA agents would take charge of the mission. At this point details become sketchy, but several members of the intelligence community have speculated that an Air Force pilot in an Air Force U-2 attempted a high altitude overflight on October 9 that "flamed out", i.e., lost power, and thus had to descend in order to restart its engine. A second round between Air Force and CIA followed, as a result of

which Air Force pilots were trained to fly CIA U-2's. A successful overflight took place on October 14.

This ten-day delay constitutes some form of "failure." In the face of well-founded suspicions concerning offensive Soviet missiles in Cuba that posed a critical threat to the United States' most vital interest, squabbling between organizations whose job it is to produce this information seems entirely inappropriate. But for each of these organizations, the question involved the issue: *"Whose job was it to be?"* Moreover, the issue was not simply, which organization would control U-2 flights over Cuba, but rather the broader issue of ownership of U-2 intelligence activities—a very long standing territorial dispute. Thus though this delay was in one sense a "failure," it was also a nearly inevitable consequence of two facts: many jobs do not fall neatly into precisely defined organizational jurisdictions; and vigorous organizations are imperialistic.

Organizational Options. Deliberations of leaders in ExCom meetings produced broad outlines of alternatives. Details of these alternatives and blueprints for their implementation had to be specified by the organizations that would perform these tasks. These organizational outputs answered the question: What, specifically, *could* be done?

Discussion in the ExCom quickly narrowed the live options to two: an air strike and a blockade. The choice of the blockade instead of the air strike turned on two points: (1) the argument from morality and tradition that the United States could not perpetrate a "Pearl Harbor in reverse"; (2) the belief that a "surgical" air strike was impossible.[58] Whether the United States *might* strike first was a question not of capability but of morality. Whether the United States *could* perform the surgical strike was a factual question concerning capabilities. The majority of the members of the ExCom, including the President, initially preferred the air strike.[59] What effectively foreclosed this option, however, was the fact that the air strike they wanted could not be chosen with high confidence of success.[60] After having tentatively chosen the course of prudence—given that the surgical air strike was not an option—Kennedy reconsidered. On Sunday morning, October 21, he called the Air Force experts to a special meeting in his living quarters where he probed once more for the option of a *"surgical"* air strike.[61] General

[56] See Hilsman, *op. cit.*, pp. 172–174.

[57] Abel, *op. cit.*, pp. 26 ff; Weintal and Bartlett, *Facing the Brink* (New York, 1967), pp. 62 ff; *Cuban Military Build-up;* J. Daniel and J. Hubbell, *Strike in the West* (New York, 1963), pp. 15 ff.

[58] Schlesinger, *op. cit.*, p. 804.

[59] Sorensen, *Kennedy*, p. 684.

[60] *Ibid.*, pp. 684 ff.

[61] *Ibid.*, pp. 694–697.

Walter C. Sweeny, Commander of Tactical Air Forces, asserted again that the Air Force could guarantee no higher than ninety percent effectiveness in a surgical air strike.[62] That "fact" was false.

The air strike alternative provides a classic case of military estimates. One of the alternatives outlined by the ExCom was named "air strike." Specification of the details of this alternative was delegated to the Air Force. Starting from an existing plan for massive U.S. military action against Cuba (prepared for contingencies like a response to a Soviet Berlin grab), Air Force estimators produced an attack to guarantee success.[63] This plan called for extensive bombardment of all missile sites, storage depots, airports, and, in deference to the Navy, the artillery batteries opposite the naval base at Guantanamo.[64] Members of the ExCom repeatedly expressed bewilderment at military estimates of the number of sorties required, likely casualties, and collateral damage. But the "surgical" air strike that the political leaders had in mind was never carefully examined during the first week of the crisis. Rather, this option was simply excluded on the grounds that since the Soviet MRBM's in Cuba were classified "mobile" in U.S. manuals, extensive bombing was required. During the second week of the crisis, careful examination revealed that the missiles were mobile, in the sense that small houses are mobile: that is, they could be moved and reassembled in 6 days. After the missiles were reclassified "movable" and detailed plans for surgical air strikes specified, this action was added to the list of live options for the end of the second week.

Organizational Implementation. Ex-Com members separated several types of blockade: offensive weapons only, all armaments, and all strategic goods including POL (petroleum, oil, and lubricants). But the *"details"* of the operation were left to the Navy. Before the President announced the blockade on Monday evening, the first stage of the Navy's blueprint was in motion, and a problem loomed on the horizon.[65] The Navy had a detailed plan for the blockade. The President had several less precise but equally determined notions concerning what should be done, when, and how. For the Navy the issue was one of effective implementation of the Navy's blockade—without the meddling and interference of political leaders. For the President, the problem was to pace and manage

events in such a way that the Soviet leaders would have time to see, think, and blink.

A careful reading of available sources uncovers an instructive incident. On Tuesday the British Ambassador, Ormsby-Gore, after having attended a briefing on the details of the blockade, suggested to the President that the plan for intercepting Soviet ships far out of reach of Cuban jets did not facilitate Khrushchev's hard decision.[66] Why not make the interception much closer to Cuba and thus give the Russian leader more time? According to the public account and the recollection of a number of individuals involved, Kennedy "agreed immediately, called McNamara, and over emotional Navy protest, issued the appropriate instructions."[67] As Sorensen records, "in a sharp clash with the Navy, he made certain his will prevailed."[68] The Navy's plan for the blockade was thus changed by drawing the blockade much closer to Cuba.

A serious organizational orientation makes one suspicious of this account. More careful examination of the available evidence confirms these suspicions, though alternative accounts must be somewhat speculative. According to the public chronology, a quarantine drawn close to Cuba became effective on Wednesday morning, the first Soviet ship was contacted on Thursday morning, and the first boarding of a ship occurred on Friday. According to the statement by the Department of Defense, boarding of the *Marcula* by a party from the *John R. Pierce* "took place at 7:50 A.M., E.D.T., 180 miles northeast of Nassau."[69] The *Marcula* had been trailed since about 10:30 the previous evening.[70] Simple calculations suggest that the *Pierce* must have been stationed along the Navy's original arc which extended 500 miles out to sea from Cape Magsi, Cuba's eastern most tip.[71] The blockade line was *not* moved as the President ordered, and the accounts report.

What happened is not entirely clear. One can be certain, however, that Soviet ships passed through the line along which American destroyers had posted themselves before the official "first contact" with the Soviet ship. On October 26 a Soviet tanker arrived in Havana and was honored by a dockside rally for "running the blockade." Photographs of this vessel show the name *Vinnitsa* on the side of the vessel in

[62] *Ibid.,* p. 697 ; Abel. *op. cit.,* pp. 100–101.
[63] Sorensen, *Kennedy,* p. 669.
[64] Hilsman, *op. cit.,* p. 204.
[65] See Abel, *op. cit.,* pp. 97 ff.

[66] Schlesinger, *op. cit.,* p. 818.
[67] *Ibid.*
[68] Sorensen, *Kennedy.* p. 710.
[69] *New York Times,* October 27, 1962.
[70] Abel, *op. cit.,* p. 171.
[71] For the location of the original arc see Abel, *op. cit.,* p. 141.

Cyrillic letters.[72] But according to the official U.S. position, the first tanker to pass through the blockade was the *Bucharest*, which was hailed by the Navy on the morning of October 25. Again simple mathematical calculation excludes the possibility that the *Bucharest* and the *Vinnitsa* were the same ship. It seems probable that the Navy's resistance to the President's order that the blockade be drawn in closer to Cuba forced him to allow one or several Soviet ships to pass through the blockade after it was officially operative.[73]

This attempt to leash the Navy's blockade had a price. On Wednesday morning, October 24, what the President had been awaiting occurred. The 18 dry cargo ships heading towards the quarantine stopped dead in the water. This was the occasion of Dean Rusk's remark, "We are eyeball to eyeball and I think the other fellow just blinked."[74] But the Navy had another interpretation. The ships had simply stopped to pick up Soviet submarine escorts. The President became quite concerned lest the Navy—already riled because of Presidential meddling in its affairs—blunder into an incident. Sensing the President's fears, McNamara became suspicious of the Navy's procedures and routines for making the first interception. Calling on the Chief of Naval Operations in the Navy's inner sanctum, the Navy Flag Plot, McNamara put his questions harshly.[75] Who would make the first interception? Were Russian-speaking officers on board? How would submarines be dealt with? At one point McNamara asked Anderson what he would do if a Soviet ship's captain refused to answer questions about his cargo. Picking up the Manual of Navy Regulations the Navy man waved it in McNamara's face and shouted, "It's all in there." To which McNamara replied, "I don't give a damn what John Paul Jones would have done; I want to know what you are going to do, now."[76] The encounter ended on Anderson's remark: "Now, Mr. Secretary, if you and your Deputy will go back to your office the Navy will run the blockade."[77]

MODEL III: BUREAUCRATIC POLITICS

The leaders who sit on top of organizations

[72] *Facts on File*, Vol. XXII, 1962, p. 376, published by Facts on File, Inc., New York, yearly.

[73] This hypothesis would account for the mystery surrounding Kennedy's explosion at the leak of the stopping of the *Bucharest*. See Hilsman, *op. cit.*, p. 45.

[74] Abel, *op. cit.*, p. 153.

[75] See *ibid.*, pp. 154 ff.

[76] *Ibid.*, p. 156.

[77] *Ibid.*

are not a monolithic group. Rather, each is, in his own right, a player in a central, competitive game. The name of the game is bureaucratic politics: bargaining along regularized channels among players positioned hierarchically within the government. Government behavior can thus be understood according to a third conceptual model not as organizational outputs, but as outcomes of bargaining games. In contrast with Model I, the bureaucratic politics model sees no unitary actor but rather many actors as players, who focus not on a single strategic issue but on many diverse intra-national problems as well, in terms of no consistent set of strategic objectives but rather according to various conceptions of national, organizational, and personal goals, making government decisions not by rational choice but by the pulling and hauling that is politics.

The apparatus of each national government constitutes a complex arena for the intra-national game. Political leaders at the top of this apparatus plus the men who occupy positions on top of the critical organizations form the circle of central players. Ascendancy to this circle assures some independent standing. The necessary decentralization of decisions required for action on the broad range of foreign policy problems guarantees that each player has considerable discretion. Thus power is shared.

The nature of problems of foreign policy permits fundamental disagreement among reasonable men concerning what ought to be done. Analyses yield conflicting recommendations. Separate responsibilities laid on the shoulders of individual personalities encourage differences in perceptions and priorities. But the issues are of first order importance. What the nation does really matters. A wrong choice could mean irreparable damage. Thus responsible men are obliged to fight for what they are convinced is right.

Men share power. Men differ concerning what must be done. The differences matter. This milieu necessitates that policy be resolved by politics. What the nation does is sometimes the result of the triumph of one group over others. More often, however, different groups pulling in different directions yield a resultant distinct from what anyone intended. What moves the chess pieces is not simply the reasons which support a course of action, nor the routines of organizations which enact an alternative, but the power and skill of proponents and opponents of the action in question.

This characterization captures the thrust of the bureaucratic politics orientation. If problems of foreign policy arose as discreet issues, and decisions were determined one game at a time, this account would suffice. But most "issues," e.g., Vietnam or the proliferation of nuclear weapons, emerge piecemeal, over time, one lump in one context, a second in another. Hundreds of issues compete for players' attention every day. Each player is forced to fix upon his issues for that day, fight them on their own terms, and rush on to the next. Thus the character of emerging issues and the pace at which the game is played converge to yield government "decisions" and "actions" as collages. Choices by one player, outcomes of minor games, outcomes of central games, and "foul-ups"—these pieces, when stuck to the same canvas, constitute government behavior relevant to an issue.

The concept of national security policy as political outcome contradicts both public imagery and academic orthodoxy. Issues vital to national security, it is said, are too important to be settled by political games. They must be "above" politics. To accuse someone of "playing politics with national security" is a most serious charge. What public conviction demands, the academic penchant for intellectual elegance reinforces. Internal politics is messy; moreover, according to prevailing doctrine, politicking lacks intellectual content. As such, it constitutes gossip for journalists rather than a subject for serious investigation. Occasional memoirs, anecdotes in historical accounts, and several detailed case studies to the contrary, most of the literature of foreign policy avoids bureaucratic politics. The gap between academic literature and the experience of participants in government is nowhere wider than at this point.

BUREAUCRATIC POLITICS PARADIGM[78]

I. Basic Unit of Analysis: Policy as Political Outcome

The decisions and actions of governments are essentially intra-national political outcomes:

[78] This paradigm relies upon the small group of analysts who have begun to fill the gap. My primary source is the model implicit in the work of Richard E. Neustadt, though his concentration on presidential action has been generalized to a concern with policy as the outcome of political bargaining among a number of independent players, the President amounting to no more than a "superpower" among many lesser but considerable powers. As Warner Schilling argues, the substantive problems are of such inordinate difficulty that uncertainties and differences with regard to goals, alternatives, and consequences are inevitable. This necessitates what Roger Hilsman describes as the process of conflict and consensus building. The techniques employed in this process often resemble those used in legislative assemblies, though

outcomes in the sense that what happens is not chosen as a solution to a problem but rather results from compromise, coalition, competition, and confusion among government officials who see different faces of an issue; political in the sense that the activity from which the outcomes emerge is best characterized as bargaining. Following Wittgenstein's use of the concept of a "game," national behavior in international affairs can be conceived as outcomes of intricate and subtle, simultaneous, overlapping games among players located in positions, the hierarchical arrangement of which constitutes the government.[79] These games proceed neither at random nor at leisure. Regular channels structure the game. Deadlines force issues to the attention of busy players. The moves in the chess game are thus to be explained in terms of the bargaining among players with separate and unequal power over particular pieces and with separable objectives in distinguishable subgames.

II. Organizing Concepts

A. *Players in Positions.* The actor is neither a unitary nation, nor a conglomerate of organizations, but rather a number of individual play-

Samuel Huntington's characterization of the process as "legislative" overemphasizes the equality of participants as opposed to the hierarchy which structures the game. Moreover, whereas for Huntington, foreign policy (in contrast to military policy) is set by the executive, this paradigm maintains that the activities which he describes as legislative are characteristic of the process by which foreign policy is made.

[79] The theatrical metaphor of stage, roles, and actors is more common than this metaphor of games, positions, and players. Nevertheless, the rigidity connotated by the concept of "role" both in the theatrical sense of actors reciting fixed lines and in the sociological sense of fixed responses to specified social situations makes the concept of games, positions, and players more useful for this analysis of active participants in the determination of national policy. Objections to the terminology on the grounds that "game" connotes non-serious play overlook the concept's application to most serious problems both in Wittgenstein's philosophy and in contemporary game theory. Game theory typically treats more precisely structured games, but Wittgenstein's examination of the "language game" wherein men use words to communicate is quite analogous to this analysis of the less specified game of bureaucratic politics. See Ludwig Wittgenstein, *Philosophical Investigations,* and Thomas Schelling, "What is Game Theory?" in James Charlesworth, *Contemporary Political Analysis.*

ers. Groups of these players constitute the agent for particular government decisions and actions. Players are men in jobs.

Individuals become players in the national security policy game by occupying a critical position in an administration. For example, in the U.S. government the players include "Chiefs": the President, Secretaries of State, Defense, and Treasury, Director of the CIA, Joint Chiefs of Staff, and, since 1961, the Special Assistant for National Security Affairs;[80] "Staffers": the immediate staff of each Chief; "Indians": the political appointees and permanent government officials within each of the departments and agencies; and "*Ad Hoc* Players": actors in the wider government game (especially "Congressional Influentials"), members of the press, spokesmen for important interest groups (especially the "bipartisan foreign policy establishment" in and out of Congress), and surrogates for each of these groups. Other members of the Congress, press, interest groups, and public form concentric circles around the central arena —circles which demarcate the permissive limits within which the game is played.

Positions define what players both may and must do. The advantages and handicaps with which each player can enter and play in various games stems from his position. So does a cluster of obligations for the performance of certain tasks. The two sides of this coin are illustrated by the position of the modern Secretary of State. First, in form and usually in fact, he is the primary repository of political judgment on the political-military issues that are the stuff of contemporary foreign policy; consequently, he is a senior personal advisor to the President. Second, he is the colleague of the President's other senior advisers on the problems of foreign policy, the Secretaries of Defense and Treasury, and the Special Assistant for National Security Affairs. Third, he is the ranking U.S. diplomat for serious negotiation. Fourth, he serves as an Administration voice to Congress, the country, and the world. Finally, he is "Mr. State Department" or "Mr. Foreign Office," "leader of

officials, spokesman for their causes, guardian of their interests, judge of their disputes, superintendent of their work, master of their careers."[81] But he is not first one, and then the other. All of these obligations are his simultaneously. His performance in one affects his credit and power in the others. The perspective stemming from the daily work which he must oversee—the cable traffic by which his department maintains relations with other foreign offices—conflicts with the President's requirement that he serve as a generalist and coordinator of contrasting perspectives. The necessity that he be close to the President restricts the extent to which, and the force with which, he can front for his department. When he defers to the Secretary of Defense rather than fighting for his department's position—as he often must—he strains the loyalty of his officialdom. The Secretary's resolution of these conflicts depends not only upon the position, but also upon the player who occupies the position.

For players are also people. Men's metabolisms differ. The core of the bureaucratic politics mix is personality. How each man manages to stand the heat in his kitchen, each player's basic operating style, and the complementarity or contradiction among personalities and styles in the inner circles are irreducible pieces of the policy blend. Moreover, each person comes to his position with baggage in tow, including sensitivities to certain issues, commitments to various programs, and personal standing and debts with groups in the society.

B. *Parochial Priorities, Perceptions and Issues.* Answers to the questions: "What is the issue?" and "What must be done?" are colored by the position from which the questions are considered. For the factors which encourage organizational parochialism also influence the players who occupy positions on top of (or within) these organizations. To motivate members of his organization, a player must be sensitive to the organization's orientation. The games into which the player can enter and the advantages with which he plays enhance these pressures. Thus propensities of perception stemming from position permit reliable prediction about a player's stances in many cases. But these propensities are filtered through the baggage which players bring to positions. Sensitivity to both the pressures and the baggage is thus required for many predictions.

[80] Inclusion of the President's Special Assistant for National Security Affairs in the tier of "Chiefs" rather than among the "Staffers" involves a debatable choice. In fact he is both super-staffer and near-chief. His position has no statutory authority. He is especially dependent upon good relations with the President and the Secretaries of Defense and State. Nevertheless, he stands astride a genuine action-channel. The decision to include this position among the Chiefs reflects my judgment that the Bundy function is becoming institutionalized.

[81] Richard E. Neustadt, Testimony, United States Senate, Committee on Government Operations, Subcommittee on National Security Staffing, *Administration of National Security*, March 26, 1963, pp. 82–83.

C. *Interests, Stakes, and Power.* Games are played to determine outcomes. But outcomes advance and impede each player's conception of the national interest, specific programs to which he is committed, the welfare of his friends, and his personal interests. These overlapping interests constitute the stakes for which games are played. Each player's ability to play successfully depends upon his power. Power, i.e., effective influence on policy outcomes, is an elusive blend of at least three elements: bargaining advantages (drawn from formal authority and obligations, institutional backing, constituents, expertise, and status), skill and will in using bargaining advantages, and other players' perceptions of the first two ingredients. Power wisely invested yields an enhanced reputation for effectiveness. Unsuccessful investment depletes both the stock of capital and the reputation. Thus each player must pick the issues on which he can play with a reasonable probability of success. But no player's power is sufficient to guarantee satisfactory outcomes. Each player's needs and fears run to many other players. What ensues is the most intricate and subtle of games known to man.

D. *The Problem and the Problems.* "Solutions" to strategic problems are not derived by detached analysts focusing coolly on *the* problem. Instead, deadlines and events raise issues in games, and demand decisions of busy players in contexts that influence the face the issue wears. The problems for the players are both narrower and broader than *the* strategic problem. For each player focuses not on the total strategic problem but rather on the decision that must be made now. But each decision has critical consequences not only for the strategic problem but for each player's organizational, reputational, and personal stakes. Thus the gap between the problems the player was solving and the problem upon which the analyst focuses is often very wide.

E. *Action-Channels.* Bargaining games do not proceed randomly. Action-channels, i.e., regularized ways of producing action concerning types of issues, structure the game by pre-selecting the major players, determining their points of entrance into the game, and distributing particular advantages and disadvantages for each game. Most critically, channels determine "who's got the action," that is, which department's Indians actually do whatever is chosen. Weapon procurement decisions are made within the annual budgeting process; embassies' demands for action cables are answered according to routines of consultation and clearance from State to Defense and White House; requests for instructions from military groups (concerning assistance all the time, concerning operations during war) are composed by the military in consultation with the Office of the Secretary of Defense, State, and White House; crisis responses are debated among White House, State, Defense, CIA, and Ad Hoc players; major political speeches, especially by the President but also by other Chiefs, are cleared through established channels.

F. *Action as Politics.* Government decisions are made and government actions emerge neither as the calculated choice of a unified group, nor as a formal summary of leaders' preferences. Rather the context of shared power but separate judgments concerning important choices, determines that politics is the mechanism of choice. Note the *environment* in which the game is played: inordinate uncertainty about what must be done, the necessity that something be done, and crucial consequences of whatever is done. These features force responsible men to become active players. The *pace of the game*—hundreds of issues, numerous games, and multiple channels—compels players to fight to "get other's attention," to make them "see the facts," to assure that they "take the time to think seriously about the broader issue." The *structure of the game*—power shared by individuals with separate responsibilities—validates each player's feeling that "others don't see my problem," and "others must be persuaded to look at the issue from a less parochial perspective." The *rules of the game*—he who hesitates loses his chance to play at that point, and he who is uncertain about his recommendation is overpowered by others who are sure—pressures players to come down on one side of a 51–49 issue and play. The *rewards of the game*—effectiveness, i.e., impact on outcomes, as the immediate measure of performance—encourages hard play. Thus, most players come to fight to "make the government do what is right." The strategies and tactics employed are quite similar to those formalized by theorists of international relations.

G. *Streams of Outcomes.* Important government decisions or actions emerge as collages composed of individual acts, outcomes of minor and major games, and foul-ups. Outcomes which could never have been chosen by an actor and would never have emerged from bargaining in a single game over the issue are fabricated piece by piece. Understanding of the outcome requires that it be disaggregated.

III. *Dominant Inference Pattern*

If a nation performed an action, that action was the *outcome* of bargaining among individuals and groups within the government. That outcome included *results* achieved by groups committed to a decision or action, *resultants* which emerged from bargaining among groups with quite different positions and *foul-ups.* Model III's explanatory power is achieved by revealing the pulling and hauling of various players, with different perceptions and priorities, focusing on separate problems, which yielded the outcomes that constitute the action in question.

IV. *General Propositions*

1. *Action and Intention.* Action does not presuppose intention. The sum of behavior of representatives of a government relevant to an issue was rarely intended by any individual or group. Rather separate individuals with different intentions contributed pieces which compose an outcome distinct from what anyone would have chosen.

2. *Where you stand depends on where you sit.*[82] Horizontally, the diverse demands upon each player shape his priorities, perceptions, and issues. For large classes of issues, e.g., budgets and procurement decisions, the stance of a particular player can be predicted with high reliability from information concerning his seat. In the notorious B-36 controversy, no one was surprised by Admiral Radford's testimony that "the B-36 under any theory of war, is a bad gamble with national security," as opposed to Air Force Secretary Symington's claim that "a B-36 with an A-bomb can destroy distant objectives which might require ground armies years to take."[83]

3. *Chiefs and Indians.* The aphorism "where you stand depends on where you sit" has vertical as well as horizontal application. Vertically, the demands upon the President, Chiefs, Staffers, and Indians are quite distinct.

The foreign policy issues with which the President can deal are limited primarily by his crowded schedule: the necessity of dealing first with what comes next. His problem is to probe the special face worn by issues that come to his attention, to preserve his leeway until time has clarified the uncertainties, and to assess the relevant risks.

Foreign policy Chiefs deal most often with the hottest issue *de jour,* though they can get the attention of the President and other members of the government for other issues which they judge important. What they cannot guarantee is that "the President will pay the price" or that "the others will get on board." They

must build a coalition of the relevant powers that be. They must "give the President confidence" in the right course of action.

Most problems are framed, alternatives specified, and proposals pushed, however, by Indians. Indians fight with Indians of other departments; for example, struggles between International Security Affairs of the Department of Defense and Political-Military of the State Department are a microcosm of the action at higher levels. But the Indian's major problem is how to get the *attention* of Chiefs, how to get an issue decided, how to get the government "to do what is right."

In policy making then, the issue looking *down* is options: how to preserve my leeway until time clarifies uncertainties. The issue looking *sideways* is commitment: how to get others committed to my coalition. The issue looking *upwards* is confidence: how to give the boss confidence in doing what must be done. To paraphrase one of Neustadt's assertions which can be applied down the length of the ladder, the essence of a responsible official's task is to induce others to see that what needs to be done is what their own appraisal of their own responsibilities requires them to do in their own interests.

V. *Specific Propositions*

1. *Deterrence.* The probability of nuclear attack depends primarily on the probability of attack emerging as an outcome of the bureaucratic politics of the attacking government. First, which players can decide to launch an attack? Whether the effective power over action is controlled by an individual, a minor game, or the central game is critical. Second, though Model I's confidence in nuclear deterrence stems from an assertion that, in the end, governments will not commit suicide, Model III recalls historical precedents. Admiral Yamamoto, who designed the Japanese attack on Pearl Harbor, estimated accurately: "In the first six months to a year of war against the U.S. and England I will run wild, and I will show you an uninterrupted succession of victories; I must also tell you that, should the war be prolonged for two or three years, I have no confidence in our ultimate victory."[84] But Japan attacked. Thus, three questions might be considered. One: could any member of the government solve his problem by attack? What patterns of bargaining could yield attack as an outcome? The major difference between a stable balance of terror and a questionable balance may simply be that in the first case most members of the government

[82] This aphorism was stated first, I think, by Don K. Price.

[83] Paul Y. Hammond, "Super Carriers and B-36 Bombers," in Harold Stein (ed.), *American Civil-Military Decisions* (Birmingham, 1963).

[84] Roberta Wohlstetter, *Pearl Harbor* (Stanford, 1962), p. 350.

appreciate fully the consequences of attack and are thus on guard against the emergence of this outcome. Two: what stream of outcomes might lead to an attack? At what point in that stream is the potential attacker's politics? If members of the U.S. government had been sensitive to the stream of decisions from which the Japanese attack on Pearl Harbor emerged, they would have been aware of a considerable probability of that attack. Three: how might miscalculation and confusion generate foul-ups that yield attack as an outcome? For example, in a crisis or after the beginning of conventional war, what happens to the information available to, and the effective power of, members of the central game.

THE U.S. BLOCKADE OF CUBA: A THIRD CUT

The Politics of Discovery. A series of overlapping bargaining games determined both the *date* of the discovery of the Soviet missiles and the *impact* of this discovery on the Administration. An explanation of the politics of the discovery is consequently a considerable piece of the explanation of the U.S. blockade.

Cuba was the Kennedy Administration's "political Achilles' heel."[85] The months preceding the crisis were also months before the Congressional elections, and the Republican Senatorial and Congressional Campaign Committee had announced that Cuba would be "the dominant issue of the 1962 campaign."[86] What the administration billed as a "more positive and indirect approach of isolating Castro from developing, democratic Latin America," Senators Keating, Goldwater, Capehart, Thurmond, and others attacked as a "do-nothing" policy.[87] In statements on the floor of the House and Senate, campaign speeches across the country, and interviews and articles carried by national news media, Cuba—particularly the Soviet program of increased arms aid—served as a stick for stirring the domestic political scene.[88]

These attacks drew blood. Prudence demanded a vigorous reaction. The President decided to meet the issue head-on. The Administration mounted a forceful campaign of denial designed to discredit critics' claims. The President himself manned the front line of this offensive, though almost all Administration officials participated. In his news conference on August 19, President Kennedy attacked as "irresponsible" calls for an invasion of Cuba, stressing rather "the totality of our obligations" and promising to "watch what happens in Cuba with

[85] Sorensen, *Kennedy*, p. 670.
[86] *Ibid.*
[87] *Ibid.*, pp. 670ff.
[88] *New York Times*, August, September, 1962.

the closest attention."[89] On September 4, he issued a strong statement denying any provocative Soviet action in Cuba.[90] On September 13 he lashed out at "loose talk" calling for an invasion of Cuba.[91] The day before the flight of the U-2 which discovered the missiles, he campaigned in Capehart's Indiana against those "self-appointed generals and admirals who want to send someone else's sons to war."[92]

On Sunday, October 14, just as a U-2 was taking the first pictures of Soviet missiles, McGeorge Bundy was asserting:

I *know* that there is no present evidence, and I think that there is no present likelihood that the Cuban government and the Soviet government would, in combination, attempt to install a major offensive capability.[93]

In this campaign to puncture the critics' charges, the Administration discovered that the public needed positive slogans. Thus, Kennedy fell into a tenuous semantic distinction between "offensive" and "defensive" weapons. This distinction originated in his September 4 statement that there was no evidence of "offensive ground to ground missiles" and warned "were it to be otherwise, the gravest issues would arise."[94] His September 13 statement turned on this distinction between "defensive" and "offensive" weapons and announced a firm commitment to action if the Soviet Union attempted to introduce the latter into Cuba.[95] Congressional committees elicited from administration officials testimony which read this distinction and the President's commitment into the *Congressional Record.*[96]

What the President least wanted to hear, the CIA was most hesitant to say plainly. On August 22 John McCone met privately with the President and voiced suspicions that the Soviets were preparing to introduce offensive missiles into Cuba.[97] Kennedy heard this as what it was: the suspicion of a hawk. McCone left

[89] *New York Times*, August 20, 1962.
[90] *New York Times*, September 5, 1962.
[91] *New York Times*, September 14, 1962.
[92] *New York Times*, October 14, 1962.
[93] Cited by Abel, *op. cit.*, p. 13.
[94] *New York Times*, September 5, 1962.
[95] *New York Times*, September 14, 1962.
[96] Senate Foreign Relations Committee; Senate Armed Services Committee; House Committee on Appropriation; House Select Committee on Export Control.
[97] Abel, *op. cit.*, pp. 17–18. According to McCone, he told Kennedy, "The only construction I can put on the material going into Cuba is that the Russians are preparing to introduce offensive missiles." See also Weintal and Bartlett, *op. cit.*, pp. 60–61.

Washington for a month's honeymoon on the Riviera. Fretting at Cap Ferrat, he bombarded his deputy, General Marshall Carter, with telegrams, but Carter, knowing that McCone had informed the President of his suspicions and received a cold reception, was reluctant to distribute these telegrams outside the CIA.[98] On September 9 a U-2 "on loan" to the Chinese Nationalists was downed over mainland China.[99] The Committee on Overhead Reconnaissance (COMOR) convened on September 10 with a sense of urgency.[100] Loss of another U-2 might incite world opinion to demand cancellation of U-2 flights. The President's campaign against those who asserted that the Soviets were acting provocatively in Cuba had begun. To risk downing a U-2 over Cuba was to risk chopping off the limb on which the President was sitting. That meeting decided to shy away from the western end of Cuba (where SAMs were becoming operational) and modify the flight pattern of the U-2s in order to reduce the probability that a U-2 would be lost.[101] USIB's unanimous approval of the September estimate reflects similar sensitivities. On September 13 the President had asserted that there were no Soviet offensive missiles in Cuba and committed his Administration to act if offensive missiles were discovered. Before Congressional committees, Administration officials were denying that there was any evidence whatever of offensive missiles in Cuba. The implications of a National Intelligence estimate which concluded that the Soviets were introducing offensive missiles into Cuba were not lost on the men who constituted America's highest intelligence assembly.

The October 4 COMOR decision to direct a flight over the western end of Cuba in effect "overturned" the September estimate, but without officially raising that issue. The decision represented McCone's victory for which he had lobbied with the President before the September 10 decision, in telegrams before the September 19 estimate, and in person after his return to Washington. Though the politics of the intelligence community is closely guarded, several pieces of the story can be told.[102] By September 27, Colonel Wright and others in DIA believed that the Soviet Union was placing missiles in the

San Cristobal area.[103] This area was marked suspicious by the CIA on September 29 and certified top priority on October 3. By October 4 McCone had the evidence required to raise the issue officially. The members of COMOR heard McCone's argument, but were reluctant to make the hard decision he demanded. The significant probability that a U-2 would be downed made overflight of western Cuba a matter of real concern.[104]

The Politics of Issues. The U-2 photographs presented incontrovertible evidence of Soviet offensive missiles in Cuba. This revelation fell upon politicized players in a complex context. As one high official recalled, Khrushchev had caught us "with our pants down." What each of the central participants saw, and what each did to cover both his own and the Administration's nakedness, created the spectrum of issues and answers.

At approximately 9:00 A.M., Tuesday morning, October 16, McGeorge Bundy went to the President's living quarters with the message: "Mr. President, there is now hard photographic evidence that the Russians have offensive missiles in Cuba."[105] Much has been made of Kennedy's "expression of surprise,"[106] but "surprise" fails to capture the character of his initial reaction. Rather, it was one of startled anger, most adequately conveyed by the exclamation: "He can't do that to *me!*"[107] In terms of the President's attention and priorities at that moment, Khrushchev had chosen the most unhelpful act of all. Kennedy had staked his full Presidential authority on the assertion that the Soviets would not place offensive weapons in Cuba. Moreover, Khrushchev had assured the President through the most direct and personal channels that he was aware of the President's domestic political problem and that nothing would be done to exacerbate this problem. The Chairman had *lied* to the President. Kennedy's initial reaction entailed action. The missiles must be removed.[108] The alternatives of "doing nothing" or "taking a diplomatic approach" could not have been less relevant to *his* problem.

These two tracks—doing nothing and taking

[98] Abel, *op. cit.*, p. 23.

[99] *New York Times,* September 10, 1962.

[100] See Abel, *op. cit.*, pp. 25–26; and Hilsman, *op. cit.*, p. 174.

[101] Department of Defense Appropriation, *Hearings,* 69.

[102] A basic, but somewhat contradictory, account of parts of this story emerges in the Department of Defense Appropriations, *Hearings,* 1–70.

[103] Department of Defense Appropriations, *Hearings,* 71.

[104] The details of the 10 days between the October 4 decision and the October 14 flight must be held in abeyance.

[105] Abel, *op. cit.*, p. 44.

[106] *Ibid.*, pp. 44ff.

[107] See Richard Neustadt, "Afterword," *Presidential Power* (New York, 1964).

[108] Sorensen, *Kennedy,* p. 676; Schlesinger, *op. cit.*, p. 801.

a diplomatic approach—were the solutions advocated by two of his principal advisors. For Secretary of Defense McNamara, the missiles raised the spectre of nuclear war. He first framed the issue as a straightforward strategic problem. To understand the issue, one had to grasp two obvious but difficult points. First, the missiles represented an inevitable occurrence: narrowing of the missile gap. It simply happened sooner rather than later. Second, the United States could accept this occurrence since its consequences were minor: "seven-to-one missile 'superiority,' one-to-one missile 'equality,' one-to-seven missile 'inferiority'—the three postures are identical." McNamara's statement of this argument at the first meeting of the ExCom was summed up in the phrase, "a missile is a missile."[109] "It makes no great difference," he maintained, "whether you are killed by a missile from the Soviet Union or Cuba."[110] The implication was clear. The United States should not initiate a crisis with the Soviet Union, risking a significant probability of nuclear war over an occurrence which had such small strategic implications.

The perceptions of McGeorge Bundy, the President's Assistant for National Security Affairs, are the most difficult of all to reconstruct. There is no question that he initially argued for a diplomatic track.[111] But was Bundy laboring under his acknowledged burden of responsibility in Cuba I? Or was he playing the role of devil's advocate in order to make the President probe his own initial reaction and consider other options?

The President's brother, Robert Kennedy, saw most clearly the political wall against which Khrushchev had backed the President. But he, like McNamara, saw the prospect of nuclear doom. Was Khrushchev going to force the President to an insane act? At the first meeting of the ExCom, he scribbled a note, "Now I know how Tojo felt when he was planning Pearl Harbor."[112] From the outset he searched for an alternative that would prevent the air strike.

The initial reaction of Theodore Sorensen, the President's Special Counsel and "alter ego," fell somewhere between that of the President and his brother. Like the President, Sorensen felt the poignancy of betrayal. If the President had been the architect of the policy which the missiles punctured, Sorensen was the draftsman. Khrushchev's deceitful move demanded a strong counter-move. But like Robert Kennedy, Sorensen feared lest the shock and disgrace lead to disaster.

To the Joint Chiefs of Staff the issue was clear. *Now* was the time to do the job for which they had prepared contingency plans. Cuba I had been badly done; Cuba II would not be. The missiles provided the *occasion* to deal with the issue: cleansing the Western Hemisphere of Castro's Communism. As the President recalled on the day the crisis ended, "An invasion would have been a mistake—a wrong use of our power. But the military are mad. They wanted to do this. It's lucky for us that we have McNamara over there."[113]

McCone's perceptions flowed from his confirmed prediction. As the Cassandra of the incident, he argued forcefully that the Soviets had installed the missiles in a daring political probe which the United States must meet with force. The time for an air strike was now.[114]

The Politics of Choice. The process by which the blockade emerged is a story of the most subtle and intricate probing, pulling, and hauling; leading, guiding, and spurring. Reconstruction of this process can only be tentative. Initially the President and most of his advisers wanted the clean, surgical air strike. On the first day of the crisis, when informing Stevenson of the missiles, the President mentioned only two alternatives: "I suppose the alternatives are to go in by air and wipe them out, or to take other steps to render them inoperable."[115] At the end of the week a sizeable minority still favored an air strike. As Robert Kennedy recalled: "The fourteen people involved were very significant. . . . If six of them had been President of the U.S., I think that the world might have been blown up."[116] What prevented the air strike was a fortuitous coincidence of a number of factors—the absence of any one of which might have permitted that option to prevail.

First, McNamara's vision of holocaust set him firmly against the air strike. His initial attempt to frame the issue in strategic terms struck Kennedy as particularly inappropriate. Once McNamara realized that the name of the game was a strong response, however, he and his deputy Gilpatric chose the blockade as a fallback. When the Secretary of Defense—whose department had the action, whose reputation in the Cabinet was unequaled, in whom the President demonstrated full confidence—marshalled

[109] Hilsman, *op. cit.*, p. 195.
[110] *Ibid.*
[111] Weintal and Bartlett, *op. cit.*, p. 67; Abel, *op. cit.*, p. 53.
[112] Schlesinger, *op. cit.*, p. 803.

[113] *Ibid.*, p. 831.
[114] Abel, *op. cit.*, p. 186.
[115] *Ibid.*, p. 49.
[116] Interview, quoted by Ronald Steel, *New York Review of Books*, March 13, 1969, p. 22.

the arguments for the blockade and refused to be moved, the blockade became a formidable alternative.

Second, Robert Kennedy—the President's closest confidant—was unwilling to see his brother become a "Tojo." His arguments against the air strike on moral grounds struck a chord in the President. Moreover, once his brother had stated these arguments so forcefully, the President could not have chosen his initially preferred course without, in effect, agreeing to become what RFK had condemned.

The President learned of the missiles on Tuesday morning. On Wednesday morning, in order to mask our discovery from the Russians, the President flew to Connecticut to keep a campaign commitment, leaving RFK as the unofficial chairman of the group. By the time the President returned on Wednesday evening, a critical third piece had been added to the picture. McNamara had presented his argument for the blockade. Robert Kennedy and Sorensen had joined McNamara. A powerful coalition of the advisers in whom the President had the greatest confidence, and with whom his style was most compatible, had emerged.

Fourth, the coalition that had formed behind the President's initial preference gave him reason to pause. *Who* supported the air strike—the Chiefs, McCone, Rusk, Nitze, and Acheson—as much as *how* they supported it, counted. Fifth, a piece of inaccurate information, which no one probed, permitted the blockade advocates to fuel (potential) uncertainties in the President's mind. When the President returned to Washington Wednesday evening, RFK and Sorensen met him at the airport. Sorensen gave the President a four-page memorandum outlining the areas of agreement and disagreement. The strongest argument was that the air strike simply could not be surgical.[117] After a day of prodding and questioning, the Air Force had asserted that it could not guarantee the success of a surgical air strike limited to the missiles alone.

Thursday evening, the President convened the ExCom at the White House. He declared his tentative choice of the blockade and directed that preparations be made to put it into effect by Monday morning.[118] Though he raised a question about the possibility of a surgical air strike subsequently, he seems to have accepted the experts' opinion that this was no live option.[119] (Acceptance of this estimate suggests that he may have learned the lesson of the Bay of Pigs—"Never rely on experts"—less well than

he supposed.)[120] But this information was incorrect. That no one probed this estimate during the first week of the crisis poses an interesting question for further investigation.

A coalition, including the President, thus emerged from the President's initial decision that something had to be done; McNamara, Robert Kennedy, and Sorensen's resistance to the air strike; incompatibility between the President and the air strike advocates; and an inaccurate piece of information.[121]

CONCLUSION

This essay has obviously bitten off more than it has chewed. For further developments and synthesis of these arguments the reader is referred to the larger study.[122] In spite of the limits of space, however, it would be inappropriate to stop without spelling out several implications of the argument and addressing the question of relations among the models and extensions of them to activity beyond explanation.

At a minimum, the intended implications of the argument presented here are four. First, formulation of alternative frames of reference and demonstration that different analysts, relying predominantly on different models, produce quite different explanations should encourage the analyst's self-consciousness about the nets he employs. The effect of these "spectacles" in sensitizing him to particular aspects of what is going on—framing the puzzle in one way rather than another, encouraging him to examine the problem in terms of certain categories rather than others, directing him to particular kinds of evidence, and relieving puzzlement by one procedure rather than another—must be recognized and explored.

Second, the argument implies a position on the problem of "the state of the art." While accepting the commonplace characterization of the present condition of foreign policy analysis—personalistic, non-cumulative, and sometimes insightful—this essay rejects both the counsel of despair's justification of this condition as a consequence of the character of the enterprise, and the "new frontiersmen's" demand for *a priori* theorizing on the frontiers and *ad hoc* appropriation of "new techniques."[123] What is re-

[117] Sorensen, *Kennedy*, p. 686.
[118] *Ibid.*, p. 691.
[119] *Ibid.*, pp. 691–692.

[120] Schlesinger, *op. cit.*, p. 296.
[121] Space will not permit an account of the path from this coalition to the formal government decision on Saturday and action on Monday.
[122] *Bureaucracy and Policy* (forthcoming, 1969).
[123] Thus my position is quite distinct from both poles in the recent "great debate" about international relations. While many "traditionalists" of the sort Kaplan attacks adopt the first posture and

quired as a first step is non-casual examination of the present product: inspection of existing explanations, articulation of the conceptual models employed in producing them, formulation of the propositions relied upon, specification of the logic of the various intellectual enterprises, and reflection on the questions being asked. Though it is difficult to overemphasize the need for more systematic processing of more data, these preliminary matters of formulating questions with clarity and sensitivity to categories and assumptions so that fruitful acquisition of large quantities of data is possible are still a major hurdle in considering most important problems.

Third, the preliminary, partial paradigms presented here provide a basis for serious reexamination of many problems of foreign and military policy. Model II and Model III cuts at problems typically treated in Model I terms can permit significant improvements in explanation and prediction.[124] Full Model II and III analyses require large amounts of information. But even in cases where the information base is severely limited, improvements are possible. Consider the problem of predicting Soviet strategic forces. In the mid-1950s, Model I style calculations led to predictions that the Soviets would rapidly deploy large numbers of long-range bombers. From a Model II perspective, both the frailty of the Air Force within the Soviet military establishment and the budgetary implications of such a buildup, would have led analysts to hedge this prediction. Moreover, Model II would have pointed to a sure, visible indicator of such a buildup: noisy struggles among the Services over major budgetary shifts. In the late 1950s and early 1960s, Model I calculations led to the prediction of immediate, massive Soviet deployment of ICBMs. Again, a Model II cut would have reduced this number because, in the earlier period, strategic rockets were controlled by the Soviet Ground Forces rather than an independent Service, and in the later period, this would have necessitated massive shifts in budgetary

---

many "scientists" of the sort attacked by Bull adopt the second, this third posture is relatively neutral with respect to whatever is in substantive dispute. See Hedly Bull, "International Theory: The Case for a Classical Approach," *World Politics* (April, 1966); and Morton Kaplan, "The New Great Debate: Traditionalism vs. Science in International Relations," *World Politics* (October, 1966).

[124] A number of problems are now being examined in these terms both in the Bureaucracy Study Group on Bureaucracy and Policy of the Institute of Politics at Harvard University and at the Rand Corporation.

splits. Today, Model I considerations lead many analysts both to recommend that an agreement not to deploy ABMs be a major American objective in upcoming strategic negotiations with the USSR, and to predict success. From a Model II vantage point, the existence of an ongoing Soviet ABM program, the strength of the organization (National Air Defense) that controls ABMs, and the fact that an agreement to stop ABM deployment would force the virtual dismantling of this organization, make a viable agreement of this sort much less likely. A Model III cut suggests that (a) there must be significant differences among perceptions and priorities of Soviet leaders over strategic negotiations, (b) any agreement will affect some players' power bases, and (c) agreements that do not require extensive cuts in the sources of some major players' power will prove easier to negotiate and more viable.

Fourth, the present formulation of paradigms is simply an initial step. As such it leaves a long list of critical questions unanswered. Given any action, an imaginative analyst should always be able to construct some rationale for the government's choice. By imposing, and relaxing, constraints on the parameters of rational choice (as in variants of Model I) analysts can construct a large number of accounts of any act as a rational choice. But does a statement of reasons why a rational actor would choose an action constitute an explanation of the *occurrence* of that action? How can Model I analysis be forced to make more systematic contributions to the question of the determinants of occurrences? Model II's explanation of *t* in terms of *t - 1* is explanation. The world is contiguous. But governments sometimes make sharp departures. Can an organizational process model be modified to suggest where change is likely? Attention to organizational change should afford greater understanding of why particular programs and SOPs are maintained by identifiable types of organizations and also how a manager can improve organizational performance. Model III tells a fascinating "story." But its complexity is enormous, the information requirements are often overwhelming, and many of the details of the bargaining may be superfluous. How can such a model be made parsimonious? The three models are obviously not exclusive alternatives. Indeed, the paradigms highlight the partial emphasis of the framework—what each emphasizes and what it leaves out. Each concentrates on one class of variables, in effect, relegating other important factors to a *ceteris paribus* clause. Model I concentrates on "market factors:" pressures and incentives created by the "international strategic marketplace." Models II and III focus on the internal mechanism of the government that chooses in this environment. But can these relations be more fully specified? Adequate synthesis would require a typology of decisions and actions, some of which are more amenable to treatment in terms of one model and some to another. Government behavior is but one cluster of factors relevant to occurrences in foreign affairs. Most students of foreign policy adopt this focus (at least when explaining and predicting). Nevertheless, the dimensions of the chess board, the character of the pieces, and the rules of the game—factors considered by international systems theorists—constitute the context in which the pieces are moved. Can the major variables in the full function of determinants of foreign policy outcomes be identified?

Both the outline of a partial, *ad hoc* working synthesis of the models, and a sketch of their uses in activities other than explanation can be suggested by generating predictions in terms of each. Strategic surrender is an important problem of international relations and diplomatic history. War termination is a new, developing area of the strategic literature. Both of these interests lead scholars to address a central question: *Why* do nations surrender *when?* Whether implicit in explanations or more explicit in analysis, diplomatic historians and strategists rely upon propositions which can be turned forward to produce predictions. Thus at the risk of being timely—and in error—the present situation (August, 1968) offers an interesting test case: Why will North Vietnam surrender when?[125]

In a nutshell, analysis according to Model I asserts: nations quit when costs outweigh the benefits. North Vietnam will surrender when she realizes "that continued fighting can only generate additional costs without hope of compensating gains, this expectation being largely the consequence of the previous application of force by the dominant side."[126] U.S. actions can increase or decrease Hanoi's strategic costs. Bombing North Vietnam increases the pain and thus increases the probability of surrender. This proposition and prediction are not without meaning. That—"other things being equal"—nations are more likely to surrender when the

---

[125] In response to several readers' recommendations, what follows is reproduced *verbatim* from the paper delivered at the September, 1968 Association meetings (Rand P-3919). The discussion is heavily indebted to Ernest R. May.

[126] Richard Snyder, *Deterrence and Defense* (Princeton, 1961), p. 11. For a more general presentation of this position see Paul Kecskemeti, *Strategic Surrender* (New York, 1964).

strategic cost-benefit balance is negative, is true. Nations rarely surrender when they are winning. The proposition specifies a range within which nations surrender. But over this broad range, the relevant question is: why do nations surrender?

Models II and III focus upon the government machine through which this fact about the international strategic marketplace must be filtered to produce a surrender. These analysts are considerably less sanguine about the possibility of surrender *at the point* that the cost-benefit calculus turns negative. Never in history (i.e., in none of the five cases I have examined) have nations surrendered at that point. Surrender occurs sometime thereafter. *When* depends on process of organizations and politics of players within these governments—as they are affected by the opposing government. Moreover, the effects of the victorious power's action upon the surrendering nation cannot be adequately summarized as increasing or decreasing strategic costs. Imposing additional costs by bombing a nation may increase the probability of surrender. But it also may reduce it. An appreciation of the impact of the acts of one nation upon another thus requires some understanding of the machine which is being influenced. For more precise prediction, Models II and III require considerably more information about the organizations and politics of North Vietnam than is publicly available. On the basis of the limited public information, however, these models can be suggestive.

Model II examines two sub-problems. First, to have lost is not sufficient. The government must know that the strategic cost-benefit calculus is negative. But neither the categories, nor the indicators, of strategic costs and benefits are clear. And the sources of information about both are organizations whose parochial priorities and perceptions do not facilitate accurate information or estimation. Military evaluation of military performance, military estimates of factors like "enemy morale," and military predictions concerning when "the tide will turn" or "the corner will have been turned" are typically distorted. In cases of highly decentralized guerrilla operations, like Vietnam, these problems are exacerbated. Thus strategic costs will be underestimated. Only highly *visible* costs can have direct impact on leaders without being filtered through organizational channels. Second, since organizations define the details of options and execute actions, surrender (and negotiation) is likely to entail considerable bungling in the early stages. No organization can define options or prepare programs for this treasonous act. Thus, early overtures will be uncoordinated with the acts of other organizations, e.g., the fighting forces, creating contradictory "signals" to the victor.

Model III suggests that surrender will not come at the point that strategic costs outweigh benefits, but that it will not wait until the leadership group concludes that the war is lost. Rather the problem is better understood in terms of four additional propositions. First, strong advocates of the war effort, whose careers are closely identified with the war, rarely come to the conclusion that costs outweigh benefits. Second, quite often from the outset of a war, a number of members of the government (particularly those whose responsibilities sensitize them to problems other than war, e.g., economic planners or intelligence experts) are convinced that the war effort is futile. Third, surrender is likely to come as the result of a political shift that enhances the effective power of the latter group (and adds swing members to it). Fourth, the course of the war, particularly actions of the victor, can influence the advantages and disadvantages of players in the loser's government. Thus, North Vietnam will surrender not when its leaders have a change of heart, but when Hanoi has a change of leaders (or a change of effective power within the central circle). How U.S. bombing (or pause), threats, promises, or action in the South affect the game in Hanoi is subtle but nonetheless crucial.

That these three models could be applied to the surrender of governments other than North Vietnam should be obvious. But that exercise is left for the reader.

[16]

INFORMATION CONTROL AS A
POWER RESOURCE*

ANDREW M. PETTIGREW

Abstract This study uses a variety of methods—reactive and unobtrusive—to operationalize the filtering of information during an innovative decision process by a gatekeeper. Specific data are presented on gatekeeping *within* the focal organization and also *between* the focal organization and other organizations in its organization set. Theoretically, the paper explores the increased possibilities for filtering information under the uncertain conditions of an innovative decision. Power is discussed both in terms of the resources which form the base of an actor's power and also the tactics of resource use. The focus on decision making as a political process provides an emphasis lacking in current organizational studies.

EVERY organization has a system of communications. The communications serve in the formulation and implementation of organizational goals; they also help to meet the organization's demand for the co-ordination of its diverse activities. Organizational purposes may also be facilitated through adequate informational links with the organization's environment. Communication systems are also carriers of power. This paper focuses on the issue of differential access to the flow of communications during a decision making process. Information access and control is seen as a power resource. This process of control is demonstrated by reference to the structural position of the technical gatekeeper.

Theory and Previous Research

A link between decision making, influence and communications flow is implied in the early literature on mass media and opinion leaders. The Katz and Lazarsfeld (1955) version of this 'two-step' flow of communications argues that the mass media have influence through informal leaders who have high exposure to the mass media and who in turn make their interpersonal influence felt on their close associates. This has also been the general argument in the related body of literature on the diffusion of innovation. The diffusion studies (Menzel and Katz, 1956; Rogers, 1962) argue that innovations take place because the mass media supply ideas to opinion leaders, who then rely on face-to-face contact as the mechanism of diffusion. The problem with this two-step theory of communication, as Janowitz (1970: 59) so perceptively remarks, is that it 'is neither precise enough

* I am grateful to my former colleagues at Yale University, Professors Chris Argyris, Douglas T. Hall, Edward E. Lawler, Benjamin Schneider, and Robert S. Sobel, for their helpful comments on earlier drafts of this paper.

Managerial Decision Making

ANDREW M. PETTIGREW

in its conceptualization of opinion leaders nor detailed enough in its accumulation of empirical materials'.

The latter of these criticisms has been somewhat nullified by the research activities on organizational communications of Thomas J. Allen. In a series of publications Allen (1965; 1966; 1969) and Allen and Cohen (1969) explore the determinants of the flow of technical information in a variety of research and development laboratories. In these studies Allen is able to identify what he calls 'technological gatekeepers' and show that they have a critical role to play in both the transfer of technology between and among organizations. While Allen's discussion of the role of formal structure, informal relations and spatial arrangements as determinants of communication patterns is often novel and illuminating, at no point does he attempt theoretically to relate his ideas to the power and status systems of the organizations he studies. Most importantly, he makes no explicit reference to the potential role of information control as a power resource. This has a major consequence for some of the prescriptive statements he makes about the role of technical gatekeepers in solving problems of organizational boundary impedance. For example, Allen (1966) argues 'these technical gatekeepers allow the effective entry of information into the organization and also abet its dissemination within the organization. Management must locate and utilize the talents of these individuals.' And again (1969: 18), 'the best way to maintain the project team abreast of outside developments lies in understanding and making proper use of existing information systems. This involves the use of technological gatekeepers for project support.' There is an implied assumption in both of these statements that the gatekeepers will use their position for the general good, though it is never made clear whether this involves just the research and development group or the organization as a whole. An alternative empirical possibility is that the gatekeeper may use the advantages of his position to either increase his own power and status or thwart the aggrandizements of others. This view of the structuring of communication flow is somewhat different from the discussion offered by Allen, where the channelling of communications is seen as a technical problem, a matter of arranging the most efficient system for sharing relevant information. As Barber, a political scientist, argues (1966: 65), 'around and beneath the technical considerations another set of meanings, involving the interplay of communications and power, is to be found. Insofar as knowledge is power, communication systems are power systems'.

Power and the Flow of Organizational Information

A power relation is a causal relation between the preferences of an actor regarding an outcome and the outcome itself. Power involves the ability of an actor to produce outcomes consonant with his perceived interests. The basic units of analysis are not individual persons or groups, but actors operating from one or more structural positions within a specific social system. The emphasis on structural position and specificity of system is critical. The resources which form the base of an actor's power are assumed to be differentially located by structural position, and in this sense the transferability of power across system boundaries is regarded as problematic. Power resources must not only be possessed by an actor, they must also be controlled by him. Bannester (1969: 386) makes this point succinctly, 'it is immaterial who owns the gun and is licensed to carry it; the question is, who has his finger on the trigger?' Control, however, may not be enough; there is also the issue of the skillful *use* of resources. The most effective strategy may not always be to pull the trigger.

From this viewpoint, the analysis of organizational power requires some attempt to map out the distribution and use of resources and the ability of actors to produce outcomes consonant with their own or their system's goals. Several authors have mentioned the control over information as a power resource. Mechanic (1962) has argued within organizations dependency can be generated with others by controlling access to the resources of information, persons and instrumentalities. Burns and Stalker (1961) assert that information may become an instrument for advancing, attacking, or defending status. Using the prison as a setting, McCleery (1960) is able to demonstrate how the formal system of authority relations may be considerably modified by the location and control of communication channels. Because all reports had to pass through the custodial hierarchy, this group was able to subvert the industrial and reform goals represented by the Prison Professional Services and Industry programs. The head of the custodial hierarchy, the prison captain, for the same reasons was able to exert considerable control over decisions made by his immediate superior, the warden.

The most comprehensive discussion of the structural impediments to the flow of organizational information is that offered by Harold Wilensky (1967). To Wilensky, hierarchy, specialization, and centralization are the major sources of the distortion and blockage of intelligence. There is also the specific issue of aggrandizement. 'Insofar as the problem of control—co-ordinating specialists, getting work done, securing compliance—is solved by rewards of status, power, and promotion, the problem of obtaining accurate, critical intelligence is intensified. For information is a resource that symbolizes status, enhances authority and shapes careers' Wilensky, (1967: 42).

The Focus of the Present Research

An important part of Easton's (1965) model of the political system is his analysis of the through-put of demands. Following Easton (1965: 38) a demand 'is an expression of an opinion that an authoritative allocation with regard to a particular subject matter should or should not be made by those responsible for doing so'. The process of decision making is viewed as a set of interactions through which demands are processed into outputs. A major assumption is that demands do not flow randomly through a system—they have a directional force towards the locus of power in the organization. Gatekeepers, those who sit at the junction of a number of communication channels, are in a position to regulate the flow of demands and potentially control decisional outcomes. Easton suggests that gate-keepers may not only open and close communication channels, they may also collect, combine and reformulate information; unfortunately he does not supply data demonstrating such a process.

The aim of the present research is to operationalize the often mentioned but rarely researched phenomenon of the self-interested filtering of information during a decision process by a gatekeeper. Specific data will be presented on gatekeeping *within* the focal organization and also *between* the focal organization and other organizations in its organization set. The concern will be to show that decisional outcomes reflect the interests that are communicated most effectively on the administrative level at which decisions are made. The assumption will be that the communication structure is the administrative apparatus of the system of power.

Research Setting and Methods

The study reported on was conducted in a large manufacturing organization in Scotland. For the purpose of this article the organization is called Brian Michaels.* The overall interest of the project was to explore over time, both nationally (in Britain) and in Michaels' the changing patterns of status and power between systems analysts and programmers. The original study, Pettigrew (1970), also reported on the consequences of these changes in status and power for those groups' decision making behaviour.

In the period 1957–1968, Brian Michaels made four computer purchase decisions. From 1967–1968 the writer studied the last of these decisions. Figure 1 illustrates which individuals and groups were involved in the fourth decision.

As Figure 1 suggest the ultimate decision making body in Michaels was the board of directors. In the sense of the term used by Easton (1965), they were the authorities. The Management Services group, headed by Jim Kenny and with two subordinate departments of systems analysts and programmers acted as information gatherers and advisors to the board. It was their task to recommend, with appro-priate arguments, which of the six computer manufacturers should be awarded the contract for the initial hardware and system, estimated initially to be worth £1·5 million but ultimately £3·5 million.

As it turned out, the decision process within the Management Services group developed into a competitive struggle for power between Kenny and his systems manager, Reilly, and between Reilly and the programming manager, Turner. While the details and causes of the conflict cannot be explored here, (the issues are explored more fully in Pettigrew (1970; 1972)) it is significant to note that within three months of the onset of the decision, Kenny, Reilly, and Turner had each

---

* All company and personal names quoted are pseudonyms.

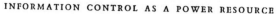

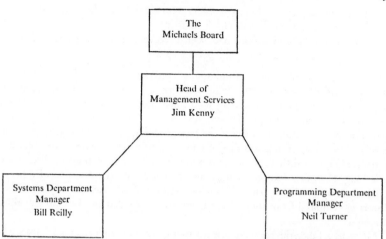

FIG. 1.   1. Mitchell   2. Wilson Electric   3. American Electronics
4. NTL   5. STC   6. BCD.

identified with a particular manufacturer: Kenny with Mitchell, Reilly with
Wilson Electric, and Turner with STC. Much of the remainder of the decision
process involved attempts by the three managers to mobilize power for the
various demands they were making. In terms of our earlier conceptualization,
they sought to use the differential advantages of their resource base in order to
control the decisional outcome and satisfy their own demands.

In what follows the aim is to show that Kenny possessed a major strategic
advantage in the power conflicts because of his placement as a gatekeeper along
two communication channels. Firstly, the channel between his technical subordinates and the Michaels' board; and secondly, between the computer manufacturers
and the Michaels' board. By sitting at the junction of the communications channels
between his subordinates, the manufacturers and the board, Kenny was able to
exert biases in favour of his own demands and at the same time feed the board
negative information about the demands of his opponents.

The Pre-Decision Situation

Because of the speed with which Kenny came out into the open with a demand
that Mitchell be given the contract, together with his hypothesized gating of
information to support this demand, it was thought useful to collect data to find
out if Kenny was predisposed to Mitchell before the decision process began.

Interviews were conducted with three groups of people:

(i) Systems analysts and programmers who had worked in Michaels during
    the previous computer decision (made in 1964) and who had now left.

192   ANDREW M. PETTIGREW

(ii) Systems analysts and programmers who worked on the 1964 decision and were still employed in Michaels in 1966.

(iii) Computer salesmen who had been involved in the 1964 decision and/or interacted with Kenny in the period 1964–1966.

There are a number of methodological problems associated with historical interviews of this sort. Firstly, there is the issue of sampling. It is not always easy to trace and interview people who have moved on to other jobs. This is particularly so with groups like systems analysts and programmers who have been operating in a seller's market for labour and appear to be highly transient. A related validity constraint is that of choosing informants whose status was such as to have equipped them with the requisite kind of information the interviewer is seeking. Historical interviews must also contend with the problem of differentially accurate recall emanating from uncertainty about the past or interviewee distortion acquired from the frame of reference provided by their present social situation.

All these validity threats were present to a greater of lesser degree in this study. While it was possible to counter some of them by using primary sources only— (i.e. eyewitnesses) and by checking interviews internally (do they contain internal contradictions?) and externally (do they go against facts established from other sources?) it was decided to deal with the validity threats in the manner suggested by Campbell and Fiske (1959) and Webb *et al.* (1966). Documentary materials were used as an additional data source. In this way it was possible to test the hypothesis of Kenny's special relationship with Mitchell by developing four different but overlapping unobtrusive measures to add to the interview data.

Kenny gave me access to all his correspondence to and from the computer manufacturers prior to the decision. This effectively meant 1964–1966 inclusive for everybody except Mitchell. Since Kenny did not become involved with Mitchell until late 1964, the Mitchell correspondence is mainly for 1965 and 1966 only. The cut-off point between the pre-decision and decision phase is August, 1966. That was the month Michaels chose to formally write for quotations from the six manufacturers. As Webb *et al.* (1966) note, there are problems with the analysis of documentary sources. These relate particularly to the dual sources of bias emanating from selective deposit and selective survival. However, because in this case, the sources examined were not too old, it is doubtful if selective deposit and survival were real validity threats. Kenny's willingness to allow the inspection of his correspondence before he could remove any threatening items also helped to prevent bias.

The Analysis of Documents During the Decision Process

In order to demonstrate Kenny's hypothesized biasing of information, an analysis was made of all correspondence between the computer manufacturers and Kenny during the decision process. Kenny also made available all the memos and reports he sent to the directors. These were content analyzed according to a pattern suggested by Budd *et al.* (1967). Statements were coded into positive, negative, and neutral categories. A positive statement would be 'Mitchell have never let us down'; a neutral one, a descriptive statement like 'the Wilson Electric input machine was tested last week'. The inter-coder reliability score was computed from a formula given by North *et al.* (1963: 45).

$$\text{Reliability} = \frac{2(C_{1,2})}{C_1 + C_2} = \frac{\text{No. of category assignments on which all coders agree}}{\text{Sum of all category assignments by all coders}}$$

A single re-analysis of the documents by a 'naive' coder produced an inter-coder reliability score of $\cdot 87$. This would suggest that the coding procedures, and therefore the data can be looked at with some confidence.

The Results

The Pre-Decision Situation

Kenny's predisposition to Mitchell seemed apparent enough from the history interviews. There was first of all people's awareness that Kenny had come to power by pushing Mitchell in the 1964 computer decision. The STC salesman recalled:

There was a big power struggle between Kenny and Ramsbottom [Kenny's predecessor]. Kenny won it by doing a switch on Ramsbottom. The fact that STC came out of it badly was just unfortunate.

Another computer salesman said:

Mitchell got the recommendation because Jim [Kenny] saw this as a way of reversing Ramsbottom's recommendation. The board were led to think that Ramsbottom hadn't done a thorough job and he was asked to resign. The decision was used by Jim to oust Ramsbottom.

Neil Turner, the Programming Manager, was equally emphatic:

Jim realized unless he got in on computers, he was a dead duck!

Bill Reilly remarked of the 1964 decision:

It all boiled down to Jim's relationship with the people at the top of Mitchell. He was on personal name contacts with them.

This is certainly the impression given by an analysis of Kenny's correspondence. In a letter to a senior Mitchell director after the Mitchell 350 (the computer bought in 1964) had been installed, Kenny said:

We are today taking over officially the Mitchell 350 from your installation people and I am very happy to tell you that everything has gone better than our expectations . . . I hope that this is a forerunner of a long and fruitful association between our companies in the data processing field.

16th December 1964

By January 1965 Kenny was negotiating with the Vice Chairman of Brian Michaels to open a new Mitchell office in Edinburgh. Kenny took the liberty of writing a draft of a speech that the Vice Chairman might make on that occasion. He said, in effect, of himself:

We have every reason to believe our people have chosen well in deciding on the Mitchell 350. All the signs to date suggest to us that Mitchell are living up to their promises which is not very common practice amongst suppliers today.

As soon as the decision process for the fourth computer started, Kenny's staff felt sure he would push for Mitchell:

We all knew Jim would go for Mitchell, the only doubt was how strong it would be. In fact Mitchell weren't short-listed, he insisted on them.

Jim had a host of reasons for going Mitchell. It's back to the problem of him not having done a data processing job. He had no reason, apart from political, for going Mitchell.

From the moment the job was first mooted there is no doubt Jim was all for Mitchell.

If the researcher is trying to argue that an individual's special relationship with a computer supplier later had a crucial impact on the demand generating process of a decision, he must also be in a position to compare that special relationship with the individual's contact with other suppliers. Relationships can only be special in a relative sense. An analysis was made of all correspondence to and from Kenny and the computer manufacturers prior to the decision. These data not only offered a chance to look for patterns in Kenny's relationship with all six manufacturers, they also enabled multiple unobtrusive measures to be developed to counteract the reactive interview material and aid the process of validation through convergence.

The crudest way to compare the manufacturers is to add up the total correspondence to and from Kenny across all the manufacturers and then work out the percentage of this total accounted for by each manufacturer. Table 1 shows that even though there are only 2 years of correspondence to and from Mitchell as against 3 years from the other manufacturers, Mitchell's correspondence accounts for the largest percentage of the total.

Since the two operating computers in Michaels in the period 1965–1966 were purchased from Mitchell and NTL it is to be expected their files would be the largest. It is noteworthy that Wilson Electric and STC the two manufacturers pushed by Kenny's subordinates and rejected by Kenny during the 1967–1968 computer decision occupied respectively positions 4 and 5.

A further way of looking at the correspondence between Kenny and the manufacturers is in terms of its *reciprocity*. With Kenny as the maiden and the computer manufacturers as his suitors it is possible to calculate the nature and extent of the reciprocity in the relationship by looking at the ratio of correspondence in, to correspondence out.

Table 2 sets out the passion ratios. One might assume the higher the ratio of correspondence out to in, the more equal is the strength of desire between maiden

Table 1

*Percentage of Correspondence by Manufacturer To and From
Kenny and Manufacturers: Before Decision*

	Number	%
Mitchell	55	28·4
NTL	54	27·8
American Electronics	34	17·5
Wilson Electric	21	10·8
STC	20	10·3
BCD	10	5·2

and suitor. The lower the ratio the greater is the strength of desire of the suitor as compared with the maiden's response. Table 2 illustrates that STC was a suitor that, relatively speaking, made many advances but received few responses in return. Surprisingly, Mitchell are placed third. During the decision process a different pattern emerged.

Both these unobtrusive measures offer rather crude indications of special relationship. Few maidens are so undiscriminating as to receive all classes of men. For the present analysis it would be of value to know not only the frequency and reciprocity of communications but also which class of men Kenny corresponded with, manufacturer by manufacturer. Table 3 is extremely revealing in this respect.

Kenny's correspondence to and from the manufacturers was split by source into three groups, salesmen, area managers, and directors. A percentage for each group, for each manufacturer was then computed.

Table 2

Passion Ratio: Kenny and Manufacturers 1964–1966

	Correspondence 1964–1966		Passion Ratio
Wilson Electric	In	11	1:1·1
	Out	10	
NTL	In	31	1:1·3
	Out	23	
Mitchell	In	35	1:1·7
	Out	20	
American Electronics	In	23	1:2·1
	Out	11	
BCD	In	7	1:2·3
	Out	3	
STC	In	14	1:2·3
	Out	6	

Table 3

Percentage Correspondence Between Kenny and Manufacturers and Vice Versa: Before Decision

	Salesmen	Managers	Directors
Mitchell	20%	47·3%	32·7%
NTL	77·8%	18·5%	3·7%
American Electronics	58·8%	41·2%	0
Wilson Electric	66·7%	28·6%	4·7%
STC	100%	0	0
BCD	70%	30%	0

Mitchell is clearly the odd manufacturer. On the salesman line STC are the highest with 100 per cent and Mitchell the lowest with 20 per cent. The other manufacturers are all very much higher than Mitchell; their percentage figures range from 58·81 per cent American Electronics to 77·8 per cent NTL. Moving to the area manager line the position is reversed. Mitchell are highest with 47·3 per cent of the total contacts at this level and STC lowest with none. The other manufacturers range from 41·2 per cent, American Electronics to 18·5 per cent NTL. The most significant finding on Table 3 concerns the directors. 32·7 per cent of all correspondence Kenny had with Mitchell between 1965 and 1966 was at the director level. Three of the other manufacturers never contacted Kenny at the board level. Only Wilson Electric with 4·7 per cent and NTL with 3·7 per cent approached Kenny at the highest level.

The final unobtrusive measure of special relationship involved calculating an invitation acceptancy rate. People in Kenny's position who, as part of their job, are expected to keep in touch with the outside world are pursued by that world. Kenny was repeatedly invited out to golfing and social occasions as well as to equipment demonstrations as one manufacturer after another released its latest piece of electronic gadgetry. A count was made by manufacturer to and from Kenny of the total amount of correspondence on golfing, social, and equipment demonstration invitations. A percentage of invitational correspondence against

Table 4

Kenny's Invitation Acceptancy Rate: By Manufacturer 1964–1966

	Invitations as % of Total Correspondence	Actual Invitations	Acceptancy Rate
Mitchell	36·4	8	87·5%
Wilson Electric	19·0	1	100·0%
STC	20·0	4	25·0%
NTL	29·6	5	20·0%
American Electronics	35·3	5	Nil
BCD	50·0	4	Data unclear

total correspondence by manufacturer was then calculated. A count of actual invitations was made and finally Kenny's acceptance rate. Table 4 sets out these statistics.

Mitchell show the highest percentage but one of invitational correspondence, the highest number of invitations and the highest acceptancy rate. The latter conclusion must be qualified by the 100 per cent acceptance rate for Wilson Electric. However 7 out of 8 acceptancy represents a more reliable indicator of special relationship than 1 out of 1.

In summary the following conclusions may be drawn from the measures of Kenny's special relationship with Mitchell.

1. The Mitchell file in Kenny's office contained more correspondence than any other manufacturer.
2. Kenny had little contact with the Mitchell sales people. Most of the correspondence with other manufacturers was at this level. In consequence Kenny had more contact at the area manager lever with Mitchell than with any other supplier. Most significantly, 32·7 per cent of Kenny's contact with Mitchell was at the director level. He had practically no written contact with the directors of other suppliers.
3. Kenny received more and accepted more invitations from Mitchell than he did from any other manufacturer.

Kenny was quite willing to acknowledge his special relationship with Mitchell:

The present Mitchell machine is my baby. I was responsible for choosing it even though I did this on the basis of a hunch.

As far as I'm concerned I do have a special relationship with Mitchell but it's not an irrational one as far as the company is concerned.

Having established Kenny's predisposition to Mitchell in the years before the 1967–68 decision, the issue becomes one of demonstrating how Kenny used his control over the information flow during the decision process to satisfy his own demands and weaken those of others.

The Technical Gatekeeper

Earlier, it was suggested that Kenny had the potential to be a gatekeeper along two communication channels. Firstly, the channel between his technical subordinates and the Michaels board and secondly between the computer manufacturers and the Michaels board. However, Kenny could only be an effective gatekeeper by preventing both his two technical subordinates and the computer manufacturers from by-passing him and communicating directly with the Michaels board. This he was very successful at doing.

Between January 1967 and April 1968 there were 12 meetings with board members in connection with the proposed new computer system. Kenny attended them all. Reilly was present at one and Turner at two. Neither Reilly nor Turner attended meetings when Brewster, the Managing Director and key figure on the board, was present. In the same period Reilly and Turner sent only one technical report each to the board.

The manufacturers had similar problems in gaining access to the Michaels board. The STC salesman remarked:

We didn't contact any of the directors. Kenny made it apparent he didn't like it. There was no good contacting them anyway unless you had something very specific they were likely to be interested in.

The Wilson Electric salesman admitted he had trouble even contacting Kenny never mind gaining access to the directors:

I never dealt with Michaels above the Bill Reilly level with the exception of a few contacts with Kenny. It was very much an arms length contact, we never got close to Kenny. Looking back now our whole relations were thoroughly unhealthy because they were so much at arms length.

The Mitchell Sales Director later commented on the naivety of the Wilson Electric sales strategy:

Wilson Electric were mistaken in their sales approach . . . . They had to focus on Reilly because Kenny had clearly indicated he wasn't interested . . . . It wasn't possible for Wilson Electric to go above Kenny to the directors because they would merely refer the salesman back to Kenny.

In fact, this is exactly what the Michaels board did in March and April 1968 when STC wrote to them directly for the first time. Brewster merely sent the STC letter down to Kenny and invited him to draft a suitable reply.

Since the computer manufacturers did not contact the Michaels board directly but operated through Kenny, an important piece of data would be the relative level of correspondence between Kenny and the various manufacturers. Table 5 shows that about 35 per cent of the total correspondence Kenny received and sent during the decision process was with Mitchell:

Table 5

Percentage Correspondence by Manufacturer, To and From Kenny and Manufacturers: During Decision

	Number	%
Mitchell	29	35·4
NTL	22	26·8
STC	15	18·3
Wilson Electric	9	11·0
American Electronics	6	7·3
BCD	1	1·2

The high percentage with NTL (26·8 per cent) does not adequately reflect the part they played in the decision process. NTL along with BCD and American Electronics were eliminated fairly early in the tendering process. Much of the 26·8 per cent for NTL is related to the NTL 200 purchased and installed in 1962 and not

INFORMATION CONTROL AS A POWER RESOURCE 199

Table 6

Passion Ratio: Kenny and Relevant Manufacturers
1964–1966 Compared with 1967–1968

	Correspondence 1964–1966		Passion Ratio	Correspondence 1967–1968		Passion Ratio
Mitchell	In	35	1:1·7	In	19	1:1·9
	Out	20		Out	10	
Wilson Electric	In	11	1:1·1	In	7	1:3·5
	Out	10		Out	2	
STC	In	14	1:2·3	In	13	1:6·5
	Out	6		Out	2	

about their involvement in the 1967–1968 purchase decision. It is noticeable that STC and Wilson Electric, the two manufacturers supported by Turner and Reilly, accounted for 29.3 per cent of the total correspondence received and sent in Kenny's file. A look at the nature of the reciprocity in this correspondence puts this 29·3 per cent into perspective.

Table 6 shows that Kenny received more and sent more letters to Mitchell before and during the decision process than he did with the other two manufacturers principally involved in the 1967–1968 decision. The table also illustrates that the STC and Wilson Electric passion ratios changed considerably from the pre-decision to the decision process situation. During the decision process STC and Wilson Electric were strong, if somewhat frustrated suitors. At both time periods the Mitchell-Kenny relationship was more reciprocal. Clearly, they were 'going steady'!

Table 7 replicates the earlier noted tendency for Kenny to receive and send letters to the upper reaches of Mitchell and to correspond with lower level people in the other manufacturers.

On the salesman line the figures for the other manufacturers are 100 per cent, 100 per cent, 83·3 per cent, 73·3 per cent, and 59·1 per cent. Only 17·2 per cent of

Table 7

Percentage of Correspondence Between Kenny and Manufacturers and
Vice Versa: During Decision

	Salesmen	Managers	Directors
Mitchell	17·2%	75·9%	6·9%
NTL	59·1%	31·8%	9·1%
American Electronics	83·3%	16·7%	0
Wilson Electric	100·0%	0	0
STC	73·3%	26·7%	0
BCD	100·0%	0	0

the correspondence Kenny had with Mitchell during the decision process was at the salesman level. The relative positions of the manufacturers were completely reversed on the manager line. The percentages this time are 0, 0, 16·7 per cent, 26·7 per cent, 31·8 per cent, and 75·9 per cent for Mitchell. The director axis shows that Kenny and his friends on the Mitchell board had by this time discontinued a great deal of their early contacts. The reason for this is straightforward; the two Mitchell directors Kenny knew well left the country to take up other appointments. In any case, presumably Mitchell now felt sufficiently sure of Kenny's support not to need regular contacts with him at that level.

While the Kenny-manufacturer relationship is an important one, a key factor in the decision process is likely to be the inputs Kenny receives from the manufacturers and his subordinates *and* how he translates these into outputs for receipt by the Michaels board. An analysis was made of all available memos and technical reports sent by Kenny to the board during the decision process. This correspondence was analysed by abstracting the number of occasions Kenny mentioned the *name* of each manufacturer. Table 8 shows the results.

Kenny mentioned Mitchell's name to the board twice as many times as he did any other manufacturer. Mitchell made up 48·4 per cent of the total, STC were next with 24·2 per cent, and thence down to BCD with 3·2 per cent. It is noticeable that Wilson Electric, the manufacturer pushed hardest by Reilly and his systems analysts for much of 1967 made up only 6·4 per cent of the total.

More significant than Table 8 as an indicator of self interested biasing is the data presented in Table 9. The statements in Kenny's memos and technical reports were content analysed into positive negative and neutral categories. Percentages were calculated for each category by manufacturer and the results presented in Table 9. The inter-coder reliability score for the data was ·87.

Again the data show the strength of Kenny's demand for Mitchell and his corresponding negative feelings towards the other computer suppliers. 71·4 per cent of the statements made by Kenny to the board about Mitchell were positive, only 8·2 per cent negative, and 20·4 per cent neutral. The positive percentages for three of the other manufacturers were 0, 9·9 per cent, and 14·3 per cent STC were slightly higher with 20 per cent positive and Wilson Electric substantially higher

Table 8

Percentage of Occasions Kenny Mentions Manufacturers Name in Communications with Michaels' Board: During Decision

	Number	%
Mitchell	30	48·4
STC	15	24·2
NTL	7	11·4
Wilson Electric	4	6·4
American Electronics	4	6·4
BCD	2	3·2

Table 9

Communications Between Kenny and Michaels' Board
Re: All Manufacturers: During Decision

	Positive Statements	Negative Statements	Neutral Statements
Mitchell	71·4%	8·2%	20·4%
NTL	9·9%	63·6%	26·5%
American Electronics	14·3%	71·4%	14·3%
Wilson Electric	43·0%	23·5%	23·5%
STC	20·0%	52·0%	28·0%
BCD	0	100·0%	0

at 43 per cent. The high positive and relatively low negative (23·5 per cent) percentages for Wilson Electric must be qualified by two factors. Firstly, Kenny made only 7 statements to the board about Wilson Electric and all of these were made in one memo in January 1967. Kenny never mentioned Wilson Electric to the board in the period January–August 1967 when Reilly and his systems team were putting in strong demands for that supplier.

The other main finding from Table 9 is the consistently high level of negative comments fed to the board in discussing the other manufacturers. For BCD the percentage is 100, American Electronics, NTL, STC, and Wilson Electric follow at 71·4 per cent, 63·6 per cent, 52·0 per cent, and 23·5 per cent respectively.

The final piece of evidence illustrating Kenny's effective use of his gatekeeping role combines a positive and negative statement analysis with a time series analysis. Of the six manufacturers originally under consideration, only Mitchell and STC were under review from the management services department throughout the whole period of the decision process. The positive and negative statements were coded into three time periods for Mitchell and STC in the hope of illustrating any affective trend that Kenny may have communicated to the board about those two manufacturers. Time period 1 was December 1966 till August 1967, time period 2 was from September 1967 until December 1967, and time period 3 was January to March 1968.

Again the data are clear. Table 10 shows that over the three time periods the percentage of positive statements made by Kenny to the board concerning

Table 10

Communications Between Kenny and Michaels' Board
Re: Mitchell and STC: At Three Time Periods: During Decision

	Time Period 1		Time Period 2		Time Period 3	
	Positive Statements	Negative Statements	Positive Statements	Negative Statements	Positive Statements	Negative Statements
Mitchell	60%	20%	73·3%	6·7%	75%	4·2%
STC	50%	33·3%	12·5%	50·0%	0	100·0%

Mitchell, increased from 60 per cent to 73·3 per cent to 75 per cent. Meanwhile, the negative statements declined correspondingly from 20 per cent to 6·7 per cent to 4·2 per cent. Exactly the opposite trend occurred when Kenny was reporting his attitudes to STC. The positive statements declined from 50 per cent to 12·5 per cent to 0, while the negative statements increased from 33·3 per cent to 50 per cent to 100 per cent (The differences between the two sets of figures within each manufacturer are accounted for by neutral statements.)

Discussion

The above analysis has put forward a view of decision making as a political process in which outcomes are a function of the balancing of various power vectors. The processing of demands and the generation of support are the principle components of the general political structure through which power is wielded. The final decisional outcome will evolve out of the processes of power mobilization attempted by each party in support of its demand.

Demands are generated and processed in the context of social structures where individuals are differentially located and have by implication access to varying amounts of the resources which are the bases of power. A demand is only politically feasible if sufficient power can be mobilized and committed to it. This involves not only the possession and control of system relevant resources but also their effective use. The successful use of power is a matter of skills rather than just possession.

This paper has focussed on the possession, control, and use of one power resource—namely, control over information flow during a largescale capital investment decision. Data were presented demonstrating the strategic advantages of the structural position of the technical gatekeeper. Control over information was a critical resource used by Kenny for mobilizing power. By sitting at the junction of the communication channels between his subordinates, the manufacturers and board, Kenny was able to exert biases in favour of his own demands and at the same time feed the board negative information about the demands of his opponents.

In two experiments Cyert and March (1963) recognize the existence of biasing in decision making but argue it will be controlled by counter-biasing. 'For the bulk of our subjects in both experiments, the idea that estimates communicated from other individuals should be taken at face value (or that their own estimates would be so taken) was not really viewed as reasonable. For every bias, there was bias discount'. (1963: 77). This rather cavalier statement was qualified in two ways. Firstly, the population studied must be 'an organization of individuals having about the same intelligence' (1963: 77). Secondly, the decision must be 'of the relatively frequent type . . . involved in determining price and output' (1963: 77).

The latter constraint has been challenged in a study of managerial biasing by Lowe and Shaw (1968) who note that the Cyert and March findings were 'based on an experiment which unrealistically reduced the time lags' between decisions

(1968: 314). Lowe and Shaw's own data demonstrated that sales budgeting fore-casts were accepted even though suspected of inaccuracy.

The situation surrounding an innovative decision of the type studied here, especially where there was disparity in the technical competance of the involved parties, would also seem to operate against any automatic process of counter-biasing. It might be argued that in the technical specialist-executive interface, where the information passed is likely to be complex, uncertain and, in the area of computer technology, rapidly changing, the possibility for managers either to identify bias, or deal with it by counter-biasing, is likely to be that much more difficult. March and Simon (1958: 166) imply this when they discuss uncertainty absorption: 'The more complex the data that are perceived and the less adequate the organizational language, the closer to the source of information will the uncertainty absorption take place'. Downs (1967) has also noted a relationship between distortion and uncertainty. He argues that under uncertainty conditions the range of values a set of variables may assume cannot be reduced below a significant size. The greater the uncertainty the wider this range, and the more latitude officials have in emphasizing one part of it without being proved wrong.

The focus of this paper has been on the strategic advantages of control over information flow in a competitive decision making process. While the data presented are the first published, quantitative, time based material illustrating such a process, it would be naive to suggest that the structuring of information in this way is sufficient to have one's demands met. An analysis of power relations cannot stop with highlighting the communication structure; placement in the communications structure needs to be linked to other forms of political access.

In the wider study of which this paper forms a part (Pettigrew, 1970; 1972) it was shown that Kenny was able to reinforce his position in the communications structure with a wider range of movement and wider access to personal contacts than that enjoyed by his subordinates. He was able to control the face-to-face interactions of his subordinates and the computer salesmen. He virtually dominated face-to-face interactions with the Michaels board. There was also the important variable of Kenny's *assessed stature*. His control over information flow in the decision process, his more extensive role-set, his easier access to the locus of power in Michaels must be considered in relationship to what key board members thought of him. His ability to negotiate and persuade in face-to-face interactions rested on his assessed stature with the Michaels board. Finally, there is the important issue of the tactics of resource use. The mobilization of power involves not only the possession and control of system relevant resources, but also their skillful use. Further research using these variables would provide an emphasis woefully lacking in current organizational studies.

Bibliography

ALLEN, THOMAS J. 1965. Problem Solving Strategies in Parallel Research and Development Projects. Working paper, *Massachusetts Institute of Technology, Sloan School of Management, Paper No. 126-65*.

204 ANDREW M. PETTIGREW

ALLEN, THOMAS J. 1966. Managing the Flow of Scientific and Technological information. *Doctoral Dissertation, Massachusetts Institute of Technology.*

ALLEN, THOMAS J. 1969. Meeting the Technical Information Needs of Research and Development Projects. Working paper, *Massachusetts Institute of Technology, Sloan School of Management, Paper No. 431–69.*

ALLEN, THOMAS J. and COHEN, STEPHEN I. 1969. Information flow in research and development laboratories. *Administrative Science Quarterly*, 14(1): 12–19.

BANNESTER, E. MICHAEL 1969. Socio-dynamics: An integrating theorem of power, authority, interinfluence and love. *American Sociological Review*, 34(3): 374–393.

BARBER, JAMES D. 1966. *Power in Committees: An Experiment in the Governmental Process.* Chicago: Rand McNally.

BURNS, TOM. and STALKER, G. M. 1961. *The Management of Innovation.* London: Tavistock.

CAMPBELL, D. T. and D. W. FISKE 1959. Convergent and discriminant validation by the multitrait-multimethod matrix. *Psychological Bulletin*, 56: 81–105.

CYERT, RICHARD M. and MARCH, J. G. 1963. *A Behavioural Theory of the Firm.* Englewood Cliffs, New Jersey: Prentice-Hall.

DOWNS, ANTHONY 1967. *Inside Bureaucracy.* Boston: Little, Brown.

EASTON, DAVID 1965. *A Systems Analysis of Political Life.* New York: Wiley.

JANOWITZ, MORRIS 1970. *Political Conflict.* Chicago: Quadrangle.

KATZ, ELIHU and LAZARSFELD, PAUL F. 1955. *Personal Influence: The Part Played by People in the Flow of Mass Communications.* Glencoe, Illinois: Free Press.

LOWE, E. A. and SHAW, R. W. 1968. An analysis of managerial biasing: Evidence from a company's budgeting process. *Journal of Management Studies*, 5(3): 304–315.

McCLEERY, RICHARD 1960. Communication patterns as bases of systems of authority and power. In *Theoretical Studies in the Social Organization of the Prison.* New York: SSRC Pamphlet.

MARCH J. G. and SIMON, H. A. 1958. *Organizations.* New York: Wiley.

MECHANIC, DAVID 1962. Sources of power of lower participants in complex organizations. *Administrative Science Quarterly*, 7: 349–364.

MENZEL, M. and KATZ, E. 1956. Social relations and innovation in the medical profession: The epidemiology of a new drug. *Public Opinion Quarterly* 19: 337–352.

NORTH, ROBERT C., HOLSTI, O. R., ZANINOVICH, M. G., and ZINNES, D. A. 1963. *Content Analysis: A Handbook with Applications for the Study of International Crisis.* Chicago: Northwestern University Press.

PETTIGREW, ANDREW M. 1970. A Behavioural Analysis of an Innovative Decision. *Doctoral Dissertation, University of Manchester.*

PETTIGREW, ANDREW M. 1972. *The Politics of Organisational Decision Making.* London, Tavistock, forthcoming.

ROGERS, E. M. 1962. *Diffusion of Innovations.* New York: Free Press.

WEBB, E. J., CAMPBELL, D. T., SCHWARTZ, R. D., and SECHREST, L. 1966. *Unobtrusive Measures: Non Reactive Research in the Social Sciences.*

WILENSKY, HAROLD L. 1967. *Organizational Intelligence.* New York: Basic Books.

Biographical Note: ANDREW MARSHALL PETTIGREW, born 1944, Corby, England. University of Liverpool B.A., 1965. Dip. Industrial Administration 1967. University of Manchester: Ph.D. 1970. Research Associate, Manchester Business School, 1966–1968. Visiting Lecturer, Yale University, Department of Administrative Sciences 1969–1971. Lecturer in Organisational Behaviour, London Graduate School of Business Studies from 1971.

[17]

D. J. Hickson, C. R. Hinings, C. A. Lee, R. E. Schneck,
and J. M. Pennings

A Strategic Contingencies'
Theory of Intraorganizational Power

A strategic contingencies' theory of intraorganizational power is presented in which it is hypothesized that organizations, being systems of interdependent subunits, have a power distribution with its sources in the division of labor. The focus is shifted from the vertical-personalized concept of power in the literature to subunits as the units of analysis. The theory relates the power of a subunit to its coping with uncertainty, substitutability, and centrality, through the control of strategic contingencies for other dependent activities, the control resulting from a combination of these variables. Possible measures for these variables are suggested.

Typically, research designs have treated power as the independent variable. Power has been used in community studies to explain decisions on community programs, on resource allocation, and on voting behavior: in small groups it has been used to explain decision making; and it has been used in studies of work organizations to explain morale and alienation. But within work organizations, power itself has not been explained. This paper sets forth a theoretical explanation of power as the dependent variable with the aim of developing empirically testable hypotheses that will explain differential power among subunits in complex work organizations.[1]

The problems of studying power are well known from the cogent reviews by March (1955, 1966) and Wrong (1968). These problems led March (1966: 70) to ask if power was just a term used to mask our ignorance, and to conclude pessimistically that the power of the concept of power "depends on the kind of system we are confronting."

Part of March's (1966) pessimism can be attributed to the problems inherent in community studies. When the unit of analysis is the community, the governmental, political, economic, recreational, and other units which make up the community do not necessarily interact and may even be oriented outside the supposed boundaries of the community. However, the subunits of a work organization are mutually related in the interdependent activities of a single identifiable social system. The perspective of the present paper is due in particular to the encouraging studies of subunits by Lawrence and Lorsch (1967a, 1967b), and begins with their (1967a: 3) definition of an organization as "a system of interrelated behaviors of people who are performing a task that has been differentiated into several distinct subsystems."

Previous studies of power in work organizations have tended to focus on the individual and to neglect subunit or departmental power. This neglect led Perrow (1970: 84) to state: "Part of the problem, I suspect, stems from the persistent attempt to define power in terms of individuals and as a social-psychological phenomenon. . . . Even sociological studies tend to measure

[1] This research was carried out at the Organizational Behavior Research Unit, Faculty of Business Administration and Commerce, University of Alberta, with the support of Canada Council Grants numbers 67-0253 and 69-0714.

216

power by asking about an individual. . . . I am not at all clear about the matter, but I think the term takes on different meanings when the unit, or power-holder, is a *formal group* in an *open system* with *multiple goals,* and the system is assumed to reflect a political-domination model of organization, rather than only a cooperative model. . . . The fact that after a cursory search I can find only a single study that asks survey questions regarding the power of functional *groups* strikes me as odd. Have we conceptualized power in such a way as to exclude this well-known phenomenon?"

The concept of power used here follows Emerson (1962) and takes power as a property of the social relationship, not of the actor. Since the context of the relationship is a formal organization, this approach moves away from an overpersonalized conceptualization and operationalization of power toward structural sources. Such an approach has been taken only briefly by Dubin (1963) in his discussion of power, and incidentally by Lawrence and Lorsch (1967b) when reporting power data. Most research has focused on the vertical superior-subordinate relationship, as in a multitude of leadership studies. This approach is exemplified by the extensive work of Tannenbaum (1968) and his colleagues, in which the distribution of perceived power was displayed on control graphs. The focus was on the vertical differentiation of perceived power, that is the exercise of power by managers who by changing their behavior could vary the distribution and the total amount of perceived power.

By contrast, when organizations are conceived as interdepartmental systems, the division of labor becomes the ultimate source of intraorganizational power, and power is explained by variables that are elements of each subunit's task, its functioning, and its links with the activities of other subunits. Insofar as this approach differs from previous studies by treating power as the dependent variable, by taking subunits of work organizations as the subjects of analysis, and by attempting a multivariate explanation, it may avoid some of the previous pitfalls.

ELEMENTS OF A THEORY

Thompson (1967: 13) took from Cyert and March (1963) a viewpoint which he hailed as a newer tradition: "A newer tradition enables us to conceive of the organization as an open system, indeterminate and faced with uncertainty, but subject to criteria of rationality and hence needing certainty . . . we suggest that organizations cope with uncertainty by creating certain parts specifically to deal with it, specializing other parts in operating under conditions of certainty, or near certainty."

Thus organizations are conceived of as interdepartmental systems in which a major task element is coping with uncertainty. The task is divided and allotted to the subsystems, the division of labor creating an interdependency among them. Imbalance of this reciprocal interdependence (Thompson, 1967) among the parts gives rise to power relations. The essence of an organization is limitation of the autonomy of all its members or parts, since all are subject to power from the others; for subunits, unlike individuals, are not free to make a decision to participate, as March and Simon (1958) put it, nor to decide whether or not to come together in political relationships. They must. They exist to do so. Crozier (1964: 47) stressed in his discussion of power "the necessity for the members of the different groups to live together; the fact that each group's privileges depend to quite a large extent on the existence of other group's privileges." The groups use differential power to function within the system rather than to destroy it.

If dependency in a social relation is the reverse of power (Emerson, 1962), then the crucial unanswered question in organizations is: what factors function to vary dependency, and so to vary power? Emerson (1962: 32) proposed that "the dependence of actor A upon actor B is (1) directly proportional to A's motivational investment in goals mediated by B, and (2) inversely proportional to the availability of those goals to A outside of the A-B relation." In organizations, subunit B will have more power than other subunits to the extent that (1) B has the capacity to fulfill the requirements of the other subunits and (2) B monopolizes this ability. If a central problem facing modern organizations is uncertainty, then B's power in the organization will be partially determined by the extent to which B copes with uncertainties for other subunits, and by the extent to which B's coping activities are available elsewhere.

Thus, intraorganizational dependency can be associated with two contributing variables: (1) the degree to which a subunit copes with uncertainty for other subunits, and (2) the extent to which a subunit's coping activities are substitutable. But if coping with uncertainty, and substitutability, are to be in some way related to power, there is a necessary assumption of some degree of task interconnection among subunits. By definition, organization requires a minimum link. Therefore, a third variable, centrality, refers to the varying degree above such a minimum with which the activities of a subunit are linked with those of other subunits.

Before these three variables can be combined in a theory of power, it is necessary to examine their definition and possible operationalization, and to define power in this context.

Power

Hinings *et al.* (1967: 62) compared power to concepts such as bureaucracy or alienation or social class, which are difficult to understand because they tend to be treated as "large-scale unitary concepts." Their many meanings need disentangling. With the concept of power, this has not yet been accomplished (Cartwright, 1965), but two conceptualizations are commonly employed: (1) power as coercion, and (2) power as determination of behavior.

Power as coercive force was a comparatively early conceptualization among sociologists (Weber, 1947; Bierstedt, 1950). Later, Blau (1964) emphasized the imposition of will despite resistance.

However, coercion is only one among the several bases of power listed by French and Raven (1959) and applied across organizations by Etzioni (1961); that is, coercion is a means of power, but is not an adequate definition of power. If the direction of dependence in a relationship is determined by an imbalance of power bases, power itself has to be defined separately from these bases. Adopting Dahl's (1957) concept of power, as many others have done (March, 1955; Bennis *et al.*, 1958; Emerson, 1962; Harsanyi, 1962; Van Doorn, 1962; Dahlstrom, 1966; Wrong, 1968; Tannenbaum, 1968; Luhmann, 1969), power is defined as the determination of the behavior of one social unit by another.

If power is the determination of A's behavior by B, irrespective of whether one, any, or all the types of bases are involved, then authority will here be regarded as that part of power which is legitimate or normatively expected by some selection of role definers. Authority may be either more or less than power. For subunits it might be represented by the formally specified range of activities they are officially required to undertake and, therefore, to decide upon.

Discrepancies between authority and power may reflect time lag. Perrow (1970) explored the discrepancy between respondent's perceptions of power and of what power should be. Perhaps views on a preferred power distribution precede changes in the exercise of power, which in turn precede changes in expectations of power, that is in its legitimate authority content. Perhaps today's authority hierarchy is partly a fossilized impression of yesterday's power ranking. However this may be, it is certainly desirable to include in any research not only data on perceived power and on preferred power, but also on positional power, or authority, and on participation, or exercised power (Clark [ed.], 1968).

Kaplan (1964) succinctly described three dimensions of power. The weight of power is defined in terms of the degree to which B affects the probability of A behaving in a certain way, that is, determination of behavior in the sense adopted here. The other dimensions are domain and scope. Domain is the number of A's, persons or collectivities, whose behavior is determined; scope is the range of behaviors of each A that are determined. For subunit power within an organization, domain might be the number of other subunits affected by the issues, scope the range of decision issues affected, and weight the degree to which a given subunit affects the decision process on the issues. In published research such distinctions are rarely made. Power consists of the sweeping undifferentiated perceptions of respondents when asked to rank individuals or classes of persons, such as supervisors, on influence. Yet at the same time the complexity of power in organizations is recognized. If it is taken for granted that, say, marketing has most to do with sales matters, that accounting has most to do with finance matters, supervisors with supervisory matters, and so on, then the validity of forcing respondents to generalize single opinions across an unstated range of possibilities is questionable.

To avoid these generalized opinions, data collected over a range of decision topics or issues are desirable. Such issues should in principle include all recognized problem areas in the organization, in each of which more than one subunit is involved. Examples might be marketing strategies, obtaining equipment, personnel training, and capital budgeting.

Some suggested subvariables and indicators of power and of the independent variables are summarized in Table 1. These are

TABLE 1.   VARIABLES AND OPERATIONALIZ-
          ABLE SUBVARIABLES

Power (weight, domain, scope)
Positional power (authority)
Participation power
Perceived power
Preferred power

Uncertainty
Variability of organizational inputs
Feedback on subunit performance;
   Speed
   Specificity
Structuring of subunit activities

Coping with uncertainty, classified as:
By prevention (forestalling uncertainty)
By information (forecasting)
By absorption (action after the event)

Substitutability
Availability of alternatives
Replaceability of personnel

Centrality
Pervasiveness of workflows
Immediacy of workflows

intended to include both individual perceptions of power in the form of questionnaire responses and data of a somewhat less subjective kind on participation in decision processes and on formal position in the organization.

It is now possible to examine coping with uncertainty, substitutability and centrality.

Uncertainty and Coping with Uncertainty

Uncertainty may be defined as a lack of information about future events, so that alternatives and their outcomes are unpredictable. Organizations deal with environmentally derived uncertainties in the sources and composition of inputs, with uncertainties in the processing of throughputs, and again with environmental uncertainties in the disposal of outputs. They must have means to deal with these uncertainties for adequate task performance. Such ability is here called coping.

In his study of the French tobacco manufacturing industry, Crozier (1964: 164) suggested that power is related to "the kind of uncertainty upon which depends the life of the organization." March and Simon (1958) had earlier made the same point, and Perrow (1961) had discussed the shifting domination of different groups in organizations following the shifting uncertainties of resources and the routinization of skills. From studies of industrial firms, Perrow (1970) tentatively thought that power might be due to uncertainty absorption, as March and Simon (1958) call it. Lawrence and Lorsch (1967b) found that marketing had more influence than production in both container-manufacturing and food-processing firms, apparently because of its involvement in (uncertain) innovation and with customers.

Crozier (1964) proposed a strategic model of organizations as systems in which groups strive for power, but his discussion did not clarify how uncertainty could relate positively to power. Uncertainty itself does not give power: coping gives power. If organizations allocate to their various subunits task areas that vary in uncertainty, then those subunits that cope most effectively with the most uncertainty should have most power within the organization, since coping by a subunit reduces the impact of uncertainty on other activities in the organization, a shock absorber function. Coping may be by prevention, for example, a subunit prevents sales fluctuations by securing firm orders; or by information, for example, a subunit forecasts sales fluctuations; or by absorption, for example, a drop in sales is swiftly countered by novel selling methods (Table 1). By coping, the subunit provides pseudo certainty for the other subunits by controlling what are otherwise contingencies for other activities. This coping confers power through the dependencies created.

Thus organizations do not necessarily aim to avoid uncertainty nor to reduce its absolute level, as Cyert and March (1963) appear to have assumed, but to cope with it. If a subunit can cope, the level of uncertainty encountered can be increased by moving into fresh sectors of the environment, attempting fresh outputs, or utilizing fresh technologies.

Operationally, raw uncertainty and coping will be difficult to disentangle, though theoretically the distinctions are clear. For all units, uncertainty is in the raw situation which would exist without the activities of the other relevant subunits, for example, the uncertainty that would face production units if the sales subunit were not there to forecast and/or to obtain a smooth flow of orders. Uncertainty might be indicated by the variability of those inputs to the organization which are taken by the subunit. For instance, a production subunit may face variability in raw materials and engineering may face variability in equipment performance. Lawrence and Lorsch (1967a) attempted categorizations of this kind. In addition, they (1967a: 14) gave a lead with "the time span of definitive feedback from the environment." This time span might be treated as a secondary indicator of uncertainty, making the assumption that the less the feedback to a subunit on the results of what it is doing, and the less specific the feedback, the more likely the subunit is to be working in a vague, unknown, unpredictable task area. Both speed and specificity of feedback are suggested variables in Table 1.

Furthermore, the copious literature on bureaucratic or mechanistic structures versus more organic and less defined structures could be taken to imply that routinized or highly structured subunits, for example, as conceptualized and measured by Pugh *et al.* (1968), will have stable homogeneous activities and be less likely to face uncertainty. This assumption would require empirical testing before structuring of activities could be used as an indicator of uncertainty, but it is tentatively included in Table 1.

In principle, coping with uncertainty might be directly measured by the difference between the uncertainty of those inputs taken by a subunit and the certainty with which it performs its activities nonetheless. This would indicate the degree of shock absorption.

The relation of coping with uncertainty to power can be expressed by the following hypothesis:

Hypothesis 1. The more a subunit copes with uncertainty, the greater its power within the organization.

The hypothesis is in a form which ignores any effects of centrality and substitutability.

Substitutability

Concepts relating to the availability of alternatives pervade the literature on power. In economics theory the degree of competition is taken as a measure of the extent to which alternatives are available from other organizations, it being implied that the power of an organization over other organizations and customers is a function of the amount of competition present. The same point was the second part of Emerson's (1962) power-dependency scheme in social relations, and the second requirement or determinant in Blau's (1964) model of a power relationship.

Yet only Mechanic (1962) and Dubin (1957, 1963) have discussed such concepts as explanations of organizational power. Mechanic's (1962: 358) hypothesis 4 stated: "Other factors remaining constant, a person difficult to replace will have greater power than a person easily replaceable." Dubin (1957) stressed the very similar notion of exclusiveness, which as developed later (Dubin, 1963: 21), means that: "For any given level of functional importance in an organization, the power residing in a functionary is inversely proportional to the number of other functionaries in the organization capable of performing the function." Supporting this empirically, Lipset *et al.* (1956) suggested that oligarchy may occur in trade unions because of the official's monopoly of political and negotiating skills.

The concept being used is represented here by the term substitutability, which can, for subunits, be defined as the ability of the organization to obtain alternative performance for the activities of a subunit, and can be stated as a hypothesis for predicting the power of a subunit as follows:

Hypothesis 2. The lower the substitutability of the activities of a subunit, the greater its power within the organization.

Thus a purchasing department would have its power reduced if all of its activities could be done by hired materials agents, as would a personnel department if it were partially substituted by selection consultants or by line managers finding their staff themselves. Similarly, a department may hold on to power by retaining information the release of which would enable others to do what it does.

The obvious problem in operationalization is establishing that alternative means of performing activities exist, and if they do, whether they could feasibly be used. Even if agents or consultants exist locally, or if corporation headquarters could provide services, would it really be practicable for the organization to dispense with its own subunit? Much easier to obtain are data on replaceability of subunit personnel such as length of training required for new recruits and ease of hiring, which can be regarded as secondary indicators of the substitutability of a subunit, as indicated in Table 1.

Centrality

Given a view of organizations as systems of interdependent roles and activities, then the centrality of a subunit is the degree to which its activities are interlinked into the system. By definition, no subunit of an organization can score zero centrality. With-

out a minimum of centrality, coping with uncertainty and substitutability cannot affect power; above the minimum, additional increments of centrality further differentiate subunit power. It is the degree to which the subunit is an interdependent component, as Thompson (1967: 54) put it, distinguishing between pooled, sequential, and reciprocal interdependence patterns. Blau and Scott (1962) made an analogous distinction between parallel and interdependent specialization. Woodward (1965: 126) also introduced a concept of this kind into her discussion of the critical function in each of unit, large batch and mass, and process production: "there seemed to be one function that was central and critical in that it had the greatest effect on success and survival."

Within the overall concept of centrality, there are inconsistencies which indicate that more than one constitutive concept is being used. At the present stage of conceptualization their identification must be very tentative. First, there is the idea that the activities of a subunit are central if they are connected with many other activities in the organization. This workflow pervasiveness may be defined as the degree to which the workflows of a subunit connect with the workflows of other subunits. It describes the extent of task interactions between subunits, and for all subunits in an organization it would be operationalized as the flowchart of a complete systems analysis. For example, the integrative subsystems studied by Lawrence and Lorsch (1967a: 30), "whose members had the function of integrating the sales-research and the production-research subsystems" and which had structural and cultural characteristics intermediate between them, were presumably high on workflow pervasiveness because everything they did connected with the workflows of these several other subsystems. Research subsystems, however, may have been low on this variable if they led work only to a single integrative, or production subsystem.

Secondly, the activities of a subunit are central if they are essential in the sense that their cessation would quickly and substantially impede the primary workflow of the organization. This workflow immediacy is defined as the speed and severity with which the workflows of a subunit affect the final outputs of the organization. Zald (1962) and Clark (1956) used a similar idea when they explained differential power among institution staff and education faculty by the close relation of their activities to organization goals.

The pervasiveness and immediacy of the workflows of a subunit are not necessarily closely related, and may empirically show a low correlation. A finance department may well have pervasive connections with all other subunits through the budgeting system, but if its activities ceased it would be some time before the effects were felt in, say, the production output of a factory; a production department controlling a stage midway in the sequence of an automated process, however, could have high workflow immediacy though not high pervasiveness.

The two main centrality hypotheses can therefore be stated as follows:

Hypothesis 3a. The higher the pervasiveness of the workflows of a subunit, the greater its power within the organization.

Hypothesis 3b. The higher the immediacy of the workflows of a subunit, the greater its power within the organization.

CONTROL OF CONTINGENCIES

Hypotheses relating power to coping with uncertainty, substitutability, and the subvariables of centrality have been stated in a simple single-variable form. Yet it follows from the view of subunits as interdependent parts of organizational systems that the hypotheses in this form are misleading. While each hypothesis may be empirically upheld, it is also hypothesized that this cannot be so without some values of both the other main independent variables. For example, when a marketing department copes with a volatile market by forecasting and by switching sales staff around to ensure stable orders, it acquires power only because the forecast and the orders are linked to the workflow of production, which depends on them. But even then power would be limited by the availability of a successful local marketing agency which could be hired by the organization, and the fact that

salesmen were low skilled and easily replaceable.

To explain this interrelationship, the concept of control of contingencies is introduced. It represents organizational interdependence; subunits control contingencies for one another's activities and draw power from the dependencies thereby created. As a hypothesis:

Hypothesis 4. The more contingencies are controlled by a subunit, the greater its power within the organization.

A contingency is a requirement of the activities of one subunit which is affected by the activities of another subunit. What makes such a contingency strategic, in the sense that it is related to power, can be deduced from the preceding hypotheses. The independent variables are each necessary but not sufficient conditions for control of strategic contingencies, but together they determine the variation in interdependence between subunits. Thus contingencies controlled by a subunit as a consequence of its coping with uncertainty do not become strategic, that is, affect power, in the organization without some (unknown) values of substitutability and centrality. A strategic contingencies theory of power is therefore proposed and is illustrated by the diagram in Figure 1.

In terms of exchange theory, as developed by Blau (1964), subunits can be seen to be exchanging control of strategic contingencies one for the other under the normative regulation of an encompassing social system, and acquiring power in the system through the exchange. The research task is to elucidate what combinations of values of the independent variables summarized in hypotheses 1-3 allow hypothesis 4 to hold. Ultimately and ideally the aim would be to discover not merely the weightings of each in the total effect upon power, but how these variables should be operationally interrelated to obtain the best predictions. More of one and less of another may leave the resulting power unchanged. Suppose an engineering subunit has power because it quickly absorbs uncertainty by repairing breakdowns which interfere with the different workflows for each of several organization outputs. It is moderately central and non-

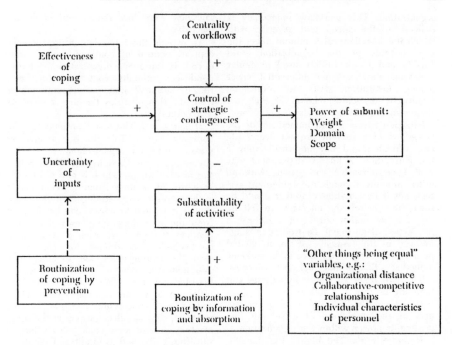

————→ Direct relationship with power; ------- indirect relationship with power; ....
relationship with power other than by control of contingencies.

FIGURE 1.   THE STRATEGIC CONTINGENCIES THEORY AND ROUTINIZATION

substitutable. A change in organization policy bringing in a new technology with a
single workflow leading to a single output
would raise engineering's centrality, since
a single breakdown would immediately stop
everything, but simultaneously the uncertainty might be reduced by a maintenance
program which all but eliminates the possibility of such an occurrence.

Though three main factors are hypothesized, which must change if power is to
change, it is not assumed that all subunits
will act in accord with the theory to increase
their power. This has to be demonstrated.
There is the obvious possibility of a cumulative reaction in which a subunit's power
is used to preserve or increase the uncertainty it can cope with, or its centrality, or
to prevent substitution, thereby increasing

its power, and so on. Nor is it argued that
power or authority are intentionally allocated in terms of the theory, although the
theory is open to such an inference.

Routinization

Most studies that refer to uncertainty contrast is with routinization, the prior prescrip-
tion of recurrent task activities. Crozier
(1964) held that the power of the maintenance personnel in the tobacco plants was
due to all other tasks being routinized. A
relative decline in the power of general
medical personnel in hospitals during this
century is thought to be due to the routinization of some tasks, which previously presented uncertainties which could be coped
with only by a physician, and the transfer

of these tasks to relatively routinized subunits, such as inoculation programs, mass X-ray facilities, and so on (Perrow, 1965; Gordon and Becker, 1964). Crozier (1964: 165) crystallized the presumed effects of routinization; "But the expert's success is constantly self-defeating. The rationalization process gives him power, but the end results of rationalization curtail his power. As soon as a field is well covered, as soon as the first intuitions and innovations can be translated into rules and programs, the expert's power disappears."

The strategic contingencies' theory as developed in Figure 1 clarifies this. It suggests that research has been hampered by a confusion of two kinds of routinization, both of which are negatively related to power but in different ways. Routinization may be (*a*) of coping by prevention, which prevents the occurrence of uncertainty; and (*b*) of coping by information or absorption which define how the uncertainty which does occur shall be coped with.

Preventive routinization reduces or removes the uncertainty itself, for example, planned maintenance, which maintenance in Crozier's (1964) tobacco factories would have resisted; inoculation or X-ray programs; and long-term supply contracts, so that the sales staff no longer have to contend with unstable demand. Such routinization removes the opportunity for power, and it is this which is self-defeating (Crozier, 1964: 165) if the expert takes his techniques to a point when they begin not only to cope but to routinely diminish the uncertainty coped with. Thus reducing the uncertainty is not the same as reducing the impact of uncertainty. According to the hypothesis, a sales department which transmits steady orders despite a volatile market has high power; a sales department which reduces the uncertainty itself by long-term tied contracts has low power.

Routinization of coping by information and absorption is embodied in job descriptions and task instructions prescribing how to obtain information and to respond to uncertainty. For maintenance personnel, it lays down how to repair the machine; for physicians, it lays down a standard procedure for examining patients and sequences of reme-

dies for each diagnosis. How does this affect power, since it does not eliminate the uncertainty itself, as preventive routinization does? What it does is increase substitutability. The means of coping become more visible and possible substitutes more obvious, even if those substitutes are unskilled personnel from another subunit who can follow a standard procedure but could not have acquired the previously unexpressed skills.

There is probably some link between the two kinds of routinization. Once preventive routinization is accomplished, other coping routinization more easily follows, as indeed it follows any reduction of uncertainty.

STUDIES OF SUBUNIT POWER

Testing of Hypotheses on Earlier Work

The utility of the strategic contingencies theory should be tested on published work, but it is difficult to do this adequately, since most studies stress only one possibility. For example, Crozier (1964) and Thompson (1967) stressed uncertainty, Dubin (1963) stressed exclusiveness of function, and Woodward (1965) spoke of the critical function.

The difficulty is also due to the lack of data. For example, among several studies in which inferences about environmental uncertainty are drawn, only Lawrence and Lorsch (1967b) presented data. They combine executive's questionnaire responses on departmental clarity of job requirements, time span of definitive feedback on departmental success in performance, and uncertainty of cause and effect in the department's functional area.

Lawrence and Lorsch (1967b: 127) found that in two food-processing organizations, research was most influential, then marketing, excluding the field selling unit, and then production. However, influence, or perceived power as it is called here, was rated on the single issue of product innovation and not across a range of issues as suggested earlier in this paper; validity therefore rests on the assumption of equal potential involvement of each function in this one issue. Would research still be most influential if the issues included equipment purchase, or capital budgeting, or personnel training? Even so, on influence over product innovation, an uncertainty hypothesis could be said to fit neatly, since the subunits were ordered on perceived uncertainty of sub-environment exactly as they were on influence.

But uncertainty alone would not explain power in the other firms studied. Although in six plastics firms, coordinating sections or integrating units were perceived as having more influence than functional subunits because "integration itself was the most problematic job" (Lawrence and Lorsch 1967b: 62), it was also a central job in terms of workflow pervasiveness.

Furthermore, in two container manufacturing organizations, although the market subenvironment was seen as the least uncertain, the sales subunit was perceived as the most influential (Lawrence and Lorsch 1967b: 111). An explanation must be sought in the contingencies that the sales subunit controls for production and for research. In this industry, outputs must fit varying customer requirements for containers. Scheduling for production departments and design problems for research departments are therefore completely subject to the contingencies of orders brought in by the sales department. Sales has not only the opportunity to cope with such uncertainty as may exist over customer requirements, it is highly central; for its activities connect it directly to both the other departments—workflow pervasiveness—and if it ceased work production of containers would stop—workflow immediacy. The effects of centrality are probably bolstered by nonsubstitutability, since the sales subunit develops a necessary particularized knowledge of customer requirements. Production and research are, therefore, comparatively powerless in face of the strategic contingencies controlled by the sales subunit.

In short, only a sensitive balancing of all three factors can explain the patterns of contingencies from which power strategically flows.

This is plain also in Crozier's (1964) insightful study of small French tobacco-manufacturing plants. Crozier (1964: 109) had the impression that the maintenance engineers were powerful because "machine stoppages are the only major happenings that

cannot be predicted"; therefore the engineers had (Crozier, 1964: 154) "control over the last source of uncertainty remaining in a completely routinized organizational system." But this is not enough for power. Had it been possible to contract maintenance work to consulting engineers, for example, then programs of preventive maintenance might have been introduced, and preventive routinization would have removed much of the uncertainty. However, it is likely that union agreements ensured that the plant engineers were nonsubstitutable. In addition, in these small organizations without specialist control and service departments, the maintenance section's work linked it to all production subunits, that is, to almost every other subunit in the plant. So workflow pervasiveness was high, as was workflow immediacy, since cessation of maintenance activities would quickly have stopped tobacco outputs. The control of strategic contingencies which gave power to the engineers has to be explained on all counts and not by uncertainty alone.

Crozier's (1964) study is a warning against the facile inference that a power distribution fitting the strategic contingencies theory is necessarily efficient, or rational, or functional for an organization; for the power of the engineers to thwart the introduction of programmed maintenance was presumably neither efficient, rational, nor functional.

A challenge to the analysis made is presented by Goldner's (1970) description of a case where there was programmed maintenance and yet the maintenance section held power over production. Goldner (1970) attributed the power of the maintenance subunit to knowing how to install and operate such programs, to coping with breakdowns as in the Crozier (1964) cases, and to knowing how to cope with a critical problem of parts supplies. The strategic contingencies theory accords with his interpretation so long as knowing how to install a program takes effect as coping with uncertainty and not yet as preventive routinization which stops breakdowns. This is where an unknown time element enters to allow for changes in the variables specified and in any associated variables not yet defined. For a time, knowing the answer to an uncertainty does confer power, but the analyses of routinization derived from the theory, as shown in Figure 1, suggests that if this becomes successful preventive routinization, it takes a negative effect upon power. The net result for power in Goldner's (1970) case would then be from the interplay of the opposed effects of activities some of which are preventively routinized, thus decreasing power, and some of which continue to be nonroutine, thus increasing power.

On the other hand, Goldner's (1970) description of the powerful industrial relations subunit in the same plant clearly supports the strategic contingencies theory by showing that coping with uncertainty, centrality, and substitutability had the effect predicted here. The industrial relations subunit exploited uncertainty over the supply and cost of personnel, which arose from possible strikes and pay increases, by (Goldner, 1970: 104) "use of the union as an outside threat." It coped effectively by its nonroutinized knowledge of union officials and of contract interpretation; and its activities were centrally linked to those of other subunits by the necessity for uniform practice on wages and employment. Industrial relations staff developed nonsubstitutable interpersonal and bargaining skills.

There are no means of assessing whether the univariate stress on uncertainty in the handful of other relevant studies is justified. Perrow (1970) explained the greater perceived power of sales as against production, finance, and research, in most of 12 industrial firms, by the concept of uncertainty absorption (March and Simon, 1958). Sales was strategic with respect to the environment. Is the one case where it came second to production the only case where it was also substitutable? Or not central?

White (1961) and Landsberger (1961) both suggested that power shifts over periods of time to follow the locus of uncertainty. Both studied engineering factories. From the histories of three firms, Landsberger (1961) deduced that when money was scarce and uncertain, accounting was powerful; when raw materials were short, purchasing was powerful; and, conversely, when demand was insatiable sales were

weakened. In the Tennessee Valley Authority, a nonmanufacturing organization, Selznick (1949) attributed the eventual power of the agricultural relations department to its ability to cope with the uncertain environmental threat represented by the Farm Bureau.

Yet while these earlier studies emphasized uncertainty in one way or another, others called attention to substitutability and probably also to centrality. Again the implication is that contingencies are not strategically controlled without some combination of all three basic variables. For example, the engineers described by Strauss (1962, 1964) appeared to have more power than purchasing agents because the latter were substitutable, that is, the engineers can set specifications for what was to be bought even though the purchasing agents considered this their own responsibility. Thompson (1956: 300) attributed variations in perceived power within and between two U.S. Air Force wings to the changing "technical requirements of operations," which may have indicated changing centralities and substitutabilities.

In the absence of data, consideration of further different kinds of organization must remain pure speculation, for example, the power of surgical units in hospitals, the power of buyers in stores, the power of science faculties in universities.

Other Variables Affecting Power

In order that it can be testable, the strategic contingencies theory errs on the side of simplicity. Any theory must start with a finite number of variables and presume continual development by their alteration or deletion, or by the addition of new variables. As stated, the theory uses only those variables hypothesized to affect power by their contribution to the control of contingencies exercised by a subunit. Other possible explanations of power are not considered. This in itself is an assumption of the greater explanatory force of the theory. Blalock (1961: 8) put the problem clearly: "The dilemma of the scientist is to select models that are at the same time simple enough to permit him to think with the aid of the model but also sufficiently realistic that the simplifications required do not lead to predictions that are highly inaccurate."

In recognition of this, Figure 1 includes several "other things being equal" variables as they are called, that may affect power, but are assumed to do so in other ways than by control of contingencies. One such range of possible relevant variables is qualities of interdepartmental relationships, such as competitiveness versus collaborativeness (Dutton and Walton, 1966). Does the power exercised relate to the style of the relationship through which the power runs? Another possibility is pinpointed by Stymne (1968: 88): "A unit's influence has its roots partly in its strategical importance to the company and partly in nonfunctional circumstances such as tradition, or control over someone in top management through, for example, family relationship." The tradition is the status which may accrue to a particular function because chief executives have typically reached the top through it. Many case studies highlight the personal links of subunits with top personnel (Dalton, 1959; Gouldner, 1955). The notion might be entitled the organizational distance of the subunit, a variant of social distance.

Finally, but perhaps most important, individual differences must be accepted, that is, differences in the intelligence, skills, ages, sexes, or personality factors such as dominance, assertiveness, and risk-taking propensity, of personnel in the various subunits.

CONCLUSION

The concept of work organizations as interdepartmental systems leads to a strategic contingencies theory explaining differential subunit power by dependence on contingencies ensuing from varying combinations of coping with uncertainty, substitutability, and centrality. It should be stressed that the theory is not in any sense static. As the goals, outputs, technologies, and markets of organizations change so, for each subunit, the values of the independent variables change, and patterns of power change.

Many problems are unresolved. For example, does the theory implicitly assume perfect knowledge by each subunit of the contingencies inherent for it in the activities of the others? Does a workflow of information affect power differently to a workflow of things? But with the encouragement of the improved analysis given of the few existing studies, data can be collected and analyzed, hopefully in ways which will afford a direct test.

David J. Hickson is Ralph Yablon professor of behavioural studies, organizational analysis research unit, University of Bradford Management Centre, England; Christopher R. Hinings is a senior lecturer in sociology, industrial administration research unit, University of Aston-in-Birmingham, England; Charles A. Lee and Rodney E. Schneck are professors in the faculty of business administration and commerce, University of Alberta, Canada; and Johannes M. Pennings is an instructor and doctoral student at the institute for social research, University of Michigan.

REFERENCES

Bennis, Warren G., N. Berkowitz, M. Affinito, and M. Malone
　1958　"Authority, power and the ability to influence." Human Relations, 11: 143–156.
Bierstedt, Robert
　1950　"An analysis of social power." American Sociological Review, 15: 730–736.
Blalock, Hubert M.
　1961　Causal Inferences in Nonexperimental Research. Chapel Hill: University of North Carolina Press.
Blau, Peter
　1964　Exchange and Power in Social Life. New York: Wiley.
Blau, Peter, and W. Richard Scott
　1962　Formal Organizations: A Comparative Approach. London: Routledge and Kegan Paul.
Cartwright, Darwin
　1965　"Influence, leadership, control." In James G. March (ed.), Handbook of Organizations: 1–47. Chicago: Rand McNally.
Clark, Burton R.
　1956　"Organizational adaptation and precarious values: a case study." American Sociological Review, 21: 327–336.
Clark, Terry N. (ed.)
　1968　Community Structure and Decision-Making: Comparative Analyses. San Francisco: Chandler.

Crozier, Michel
1964 The Bureaucratic Phenomenon. London: Tavistock.
Cyert, Richard M., and James G. March
1963 A Behavioral Theory of the Firm. Englewood Cliffs, N.J.: Prentice-Hall.
Dahl, Robert A.
1957 "The concept of power." Behavioral Science, 2: 201–215.
Dahlstrom, E.
1966 "Exchange, influence, and power." Acta Sociologica, 9: 237–284.
Dalton, Melville
1959 Men Who Manage. New York: Wiley.
Dubin, Robert
1957 "Power and union-management relations." Administrative Science Quarterly, 2: 60–81.
1963 "Power, function, and organization." Pacific Sociological Review, 6: 16–24.
Dutton, John M., and Richard E. Walton
1966 "Interdepartmental conflict and cooperation: two contrasting studies." Human Organization, 25: 207–220.
Emerson, R. E.
1962 "Power-dependence relations." American Sociological Review, 27: 31–41.
Etzioni, Amitai
1961 A Comparative Analysis of Complex Organizations. New York: Free Press.
French, John R. P., and Bertram Raven
1959 "The bases of social power." In D. Cartwright (ed.), Studies in Social Power: 150–167. Ann Arbor: University of Michigan.
Goldner, Fred H.
1970 "The division of labor: process and power." In Mayer N. Zald (ed.), Power in Organizations: 97–143. Nashville: Vanderbilt University Press.
Gordon, Gerald, and Selwyn Becker
1964 "Changes in medical practice bring shifts in the patterns of power." The Modern Hospital (February): 89–91, 154–156.
Gouldner, Alvin W.
1955 Wildcat Strike. London: Routledge.
Harsanyi, John C.
1962 "Measurement of social power, opportunity costs, and the theory of two-person bargaining games." Behavioral Science, 7: 67–80.
Hinings, Christopher R., Derek S. Pugh, David J. Hickson, and Christopher Turner
1967 "An approach to the study of bureaucracy." Sociology, 1: 61–72.
Kaplan, Abraham
1964 "Power in perspective." In Robert L.

Kahn and Elise Boulding (eds.), Power and Conflict in Organizations: 11–32. London: Tavistock.
Landsberger, Henry A.
1961 "The horizontal dimension in bureaucracy." Administrative Science Quarterly, 6: 299–332.
Lawrence, Paul R., and Jay W. Lorsch
1967a "Differentiation and integration in complex organizations." Administrative Science Quarterly, 12: 1–47.
1967b Organization and Environment. Cambridge: Division of Research, Graduate School of Business Administration, Harvard University.
Lipset, Seymour M., Martin A. Trow, and James A. Coleman
1956 Union Democracy. Glencoe, Ill.: Free Press.
Luhmann, Niklaus
1969 "Klassische theorie der macht." Zeitschrift fur Politik, 16: 149–170.
March, James G.
1955 "An introduction to the theory and measurement of influence." American Political Science Review, 49: 431–450.
1966 "The power of power." In David Easton (ed.), Varieties of Political Theory: 39–70. Englewood Cliffs. N.J.: Prentice-Hall.
March, James G., and Herbert A. Simon
1958 Organizations. New York: Wiley.
Mechanic, David
1962 "Sources of power of lower participants in complex organizations." Administrative Science Quarterly, 7: 349–364.
Perrow, Charles
1961 "The analysis of goals in complex organizations." American Sociological Review, 26: 854–866.
1965 "Hospitals: technology, structure, and goals." In James G. March (ed.), Handbook of Organizations: 910–971. Chicago: Rand McNally.
1970 "Departmental power and perspectives in industrial firms." In Mayer N. Zald (ed.), Power in Organizations: 59–89. Nashville: Vanderbilt University Press.
Pugh, Derek S., David J. Hickson, Christopher R. Hinings, and Christopher Turner
1968 "Dimensions of organization structure." Administrative Science Quarterly, 13: 65–105.
Selznick, Philip
1949 T.V.A. and the Grass Roots. Berkeley: University of California Press.

Strauss, George
  1962 "Tactics of lateral relationship: the
         purchasing agent." Administrative
         Science Quarterly, 7: 161–186.
  1964 "Work-flow frictions, interfunctional
         rivalry, and professionalism." Human
         Organization, 23: 137–150.
Stymne, Bengt
  1968 "Interdepartmental communication
         and intraorganizational strain." Acta
         Sociologica, 11: 82–100.
Tannenbaum, Arnold S.
  1968 Control in Organizations. New York:
         McGraw-Hill.
Thompson, James D.
  1956 "Authority and power in 'identical'
         organizations." American Journal of
         Sociology, 62: 290–301.
  1967 Organizations in Action. New York:
         McGraw-Hill.
Van Doorn, Jaques A. A.
  1962 "Sociology and the problem of power."
         Sociologica Neerlandica, 1: 3–47.

Weber, Max
  1947 The Theory of Social and Economic
         Organization. Glencoe, Ill.: Free
         Press.
White, Harrison
  1961 "Management conflict and sociometric
         structure." American Journal of So-
         ciology, 67: 185–199.
Woodward, Joan
  1965 Industrial Organization: Theory and
         Practice. London: Oxford University
         Press.
Wrong, Dennis H.
  1968 "Some problems in defining social
         power." American Journal of Sociol-
         ogy, 73, 673–681.
Zald, Mayer N.
  1962 "Organizational control structures in
         five correctional institutions." Ameri-
         can Journal of Sociology, 68: 335–
         345.

[18]

Radical Revisions: Power, Discipline and Organizations

Stewart R. Clegg

Abstract

Stewart R. Clegg
Department of
Sociology, University
of New England,
Armidale, Australia

Typically, organization theorists have defined 'power' against 'authority' around the axis of 'legitimacy'. Power, thus regarded, is a 'capacity' grounded outside the authoritative structure of the organization. Organizations have typically been regarded as coherent and homogenous entities in which these capacities occur. Against these views, organizations are defined here as comprising locales, cross-cut by arenas, in which agencies, powers, networks and interests are constituted. Power is not a thing but a process constituted within struggles. Power is always embedded within rules: these cannot provide for their own interpretation independently of those agencies whose interpretations instantiate, signify or imply them. Specific disciplinary practices within organization studies prescribe these interpretations, but it is argued, they can provide no general theory of the organization.

Introduction

The area of study known as 'Power in Organizations' is one which is well developed in contemporary organization theory (Hickson et al. 1971; Hinings et al. 1974; Pfeffer 1981). Within a contingency perspective, power is usually premised on the resource dependencies which are seen to derive 'from the division of labour that occurs as task specialization is implemented in organizations' (Pfeffer 1981: x). Power is no less central to critical perspectives on organizations. In the work of writers such as Braverman (1974) and Clegg and Dunkerley (1980) power is also linked to the division of labour.

In contingency perspectives, the division of labour is seen as the causal mechanism which produces power, whereas in the neo-Marxian literature the division of labour is regarded as an outcome of power processes, seen in a historical perspective, rather than as its ahistorical cause. Each of these perspectives tends to be somewhat one-sided. Moreover, both can benefit from some incorporation of aspects of the other's way of conceptualizing organizations. However, to develop these into a coherent theoretical framework it is necessary to develop lines of enquiry which neither perspective opens up sufficiently.

Organization Studies
1989, 10/1: 097–115
© 1989 EGOS
0170–8406/89
0010–0005 $1.00

With contingency theory, the paper will argue that strategic position is concequential, although it will conceptualize how it is so in a distinctly different way. Against some strands developed in contingency theory, namely the 'strategic contingencies' model (Hickson et al. 1971) it will be proposed that power is not to be seen as emanating from a given division of labour. Additionally, the tendency to derive *a priori* lists of resource bases will be resisted: almost any phenomenon can be a resource in the appropriate context. The trick resides in constructing the context in which those resources one seeks to employ acquire a privileged status.

In concert with Marxian theory, the centrality of economic domination and relations of production will be stressed. Other central 'relations' will also be stressed. Of equivalent importance to the relations of production are relations of meaning. The person is not only one who sells their labour power and thus alienates their 'species-being' but also one who constitutes, and is constituted by, a moral universe of meaning. A consequence of this is that the embodiment implicit to Marx's 'species-being' becomes explicit. The person is one who is gendered, who has ethnicity, who is a national or non-national subject, and so on. The person is irremediably social. Sociality necessarily pervades organizations and should not evade their conceptualization. In order to arrive at this sociological conception of organizations (and hence renew claims to territory under assault from the sociologically primitive proponents of 'Organization Theory') some conceptual ground requires an initial staking-out. The claim to be mapped concerns the conceptualization of power in organization analysis.

Power: Legitimacy and Authority

Power in organizations must concern the hierarchical structure of offices and their relation to each other, in the classical Weberian sense. Implicitly, this may be considered to be a concern with 'legitimate power'. However, in addition to this perspective, the organization literature has also highlighted what Thompson (1956: 290) termed 'illegitimate power'. In Weberian syntax one might think of this as a perturbation from and within the 'structure of dominancy' (Weber 1978): the formal, legitimated authority structure of hierarchical power. Such perturbations need not necessarily represent a challenge to this structure but may instead be purely local struggles for autonomy and control, which pose no threat to the 'structure' *per se*. On the other hand, on empirically rare occasions they might be such a challenge.

It was the dichotomy of the concepts of 'power' and 'authority' around the axis of legitimacy which became constitutive of the 'contingencies' and 'resource dependence' problematic of power in organizations. Stages in the development of this have been traced elsewhere (Clegg 1977). Subsequently, in this tradition, a great deal of the discussion of the concept of power has been reserved for exercises of discretion by organization members which are not sanctioned by their position in the formal structure. Such exercises are premised on an illegitimate or informal use of resource control, access to which is given by the member's place in the organizational division of labour.

Nowhere is this tendency in the literature developed to a more refined pitch than in Mintzberg's (1983) 'System of Politics'. It can be encapsulated in the phrase 'insiders are not always . . . obedient' (Mintzberg 1983: 171). In Mintzberg's 'systemic' view of organizational life, politics is explicitly defined against the 'Systems' of 'Authority', 'Ideology' and 'Expertise'. Note, before proceeding further, that by creating a 'System of Politics' we can effectively evacuate its key concept, 'power', from the constitution of ideology, authority and expertise. In fact, the 'System of Politics' becomes the residual system which makes the other formal systems work in informal practice:

'Distilled to its essence, therefore, politics refers to individual or group behaviour that is informal, ostensibly parochial, typically divisive, and above all, in the technical sense, illegitimate — sanctioned neither by formal authority, accepted ideology, nor certified expertise' [though it may exploit any one of those]. (Mintzberg 1983: 172, emphasis removed)

The political nature of the 'structure of dominancy' or 'Systems' of 'Authority', 'Ideology' and 'Expertise', themselves being structurally sedimented phenomena which are saturated and imbued with power, is not a perspective which is sharply observed in much of the organization literature (a point made at length elsewhere: Clegg 1975, 1977, 1979; Clegg and Dunkerley 1980), despite claims to the contrary (Donaldson 1985).

A concern with the exercise of power from within a given structure of dominancy is not the same thing as a concern with mechanisms of dominance, strategies of power and regimes of control. The central concern of organization theories of power has been with a restricted conception of 'politics' premised on discretionary control of strategic contingencies of resource dependencies. Regarded in this way, power is a 'capacity' premised on resource control. It is also tautological. How is power to be recognized independently of resource dependency? It is resource dependency of x upon y which is the function of y's power. Equally, it is y's independence which is the function of x's dependence upon y, given the previous x–y relationship. The cause of power is resource dependency. At the same time, its consequence, of resource dependency is equivalent to its cause. Hence notions of cause and consequence are meaningless in such formulae. Part of the problem is the pervasive tendency to think of power as something, rather than as a property of relations. The consequence of this is that the relationship becomes confused with causal mechanisms and their product. The mechanisms are worthy of investigation in their own right.

Mechanisms of Power: Disciplinary Practices of Surveillance

Mintzberg's (1983) stress on 'obedience' is central to an analysis of the product of power in organizations, an insight shared by major precursors such as Weber (1978) and Etzioni (1961). Moreover, it is a focus which has received historical endorsement not only through the corpus of Weberian research (Matheson 1987) but also through recent and related work on the origins of disciplined obedience in monastic organizations (Kieser 1987; Assad 1987). A central theme of the latter research stresses the connection between discipline and organizational virtue. In contemporary and secular terms the latter may be conceptualized as the organizational achievement of that good order which displays the inward appreciation and enactment of one's duty as a member. Recently, the mechanisms of this organizational achievement have come to be termed 'disciplinary practices'.

The concept of 'disciplinary practice' derives from Foucault (1976) but is implicit in Weber (1978). It is meant to depict those micro-techniques of power which inscribe and normalize not only individuals but also collective, organized bodies. For instance, any comparative application of performance data or other forms of surveillance would capture the sense of this. Surveillance, whether personal, technical, bureaucratic or legal, is the central issue. Its types may range through forms of, for instance, supervision, routinization, formalization, mechanization and legislation which seek to effect increasing control of employees' behaviour, dispositions and embodiment, precisely because they are organization members. At the current outer limits of such surveillance the following would be relevant examples:

'Do employers have any business testing workers or job applicants for AIDS? Can supervisors listen to a telephone operator's phone calls? Should they be allowed to program computers to flash subliminal messages to influence employee behaviour? . . . If lie detector tests are considered unreliable in criminal trials, can their results be used as the basis for hiring or firing employees? Can a company dismiss a worker because supervisors don't approve of whom he or she is dating? Should managers have access to their underlings' medical records? . . . (H)ow private is an office or a locker or a desk — or an employee's car parked in an employer's car space?' (Schachter 1987: 11)

These examples represent the extension of direct personal supervisory control into notions of individual space which previously was private. However, surveillance is not simply about such direct control. It may range from cultural practices of moral endorsement, enablement and suasion, to more formalized technical knowledge. At one particular level of application, these can include the use of new technologies such as computer monitoring of keyboard output and efficiency or low cost drug-testing systems (Schachter 1987: 11). At another more general level, one may be dealing with the development of disciplines of knowledge shaped almost wholly by the 'disciplinary gaze' of surveillance, as Foucault (1976) suggests was the case of much nineteenth century social science, particularly branches of social welfare, statistics and administration. Organizationally, the twentieth century development of the personnel function under the 'human relations' guidance of Mayo (1975) may be seen to have had a similar tutelary role with respect to organizationally dependent members (see Clegg 1979; Ray 1986). Through such mechanisms, individuals or bodies collectively, as well as abstract properties of goods and services, may be discriminated and categorized through diverse tactics of ratiocination, localized tactics which 'in their specificity of time, place, aims and objectives reinforce and borrow from each other to form an overall anonymous strategy of discipline' (Girdwood 1987: 22). At the more general level of discipline, this will form organizations into discursive locales of competing calculations. Each disciplinary practice, in its applications, will calculate organizational rationality from distinct auspices of power and knowledge. From such potentially discursive babel, any formally efficient organization will normally attempt to construct the architectonic of some overall strategic practices of discipline. Such practices will not be simply constraining: they do not only punish and forbid — more especially, they endorse and enable obedient wills and constitute organizationally approved forms of creativity and productivity through a process both transitive (via authoritative externalities such as rules, superiors, etc.) and intransitive (via the acquisition of organizationally proper conduct by the member).

The transitive element in the production of disciplined obedience has long been the central focus of organization theory, as evidenced in the classical concern with the formal structure of organization taken as a literal representation of what the organization's 'real' structure is. Doubtless, such representations do have a limited heuristic value when used by researchers. However, in practice, authoritative structures rarely if ever conform to their depiction in the organizational programme. The reasons for this are many: things change imperceptibly over time in ways which are not captured by a static idealization; organizational membership changes and so particularly competent 'power-players' may make more of a position than a less competent predecessor, and so on. However, there is a more fundamental reason than these conjunctural events as to the inadequacy of these depictions of the formal structure of the organization. Recalcitrance is implicit in the intransitive processes which constitute organizational disciplinary practices in an hierarchical field.

Any superordinate member of a complex organization will be just one relay in a complex flow of authority up, down and across organization hierarchies. Ideally, in any rationalistic view by organization elites, planners and seemingly many theorists, such relays should be without resistance, offering no impedance whatsoever, no 'problem of obedience'. Rarely, if ever, will it be the case that this is so, as organization researchers have long known (Coch and French 1948).

Resistance, to continue the metaphor, will tend to be pervasive. Authorities, to use the term as a plural noun, will rarely if ever be resistance-free and passive relays. An explanation for this is available through appreciation of the relationship between organization and agency.

Organization and Agency

Central to this relationship is the realization that although the incorporation of agencies within organizations is normally secured on the basis of contract, such contracts are rarely the reciprocal, conflict free and equal exchanges axiomized in 'transaction cost theory' (Williamson 1981). Such axioms are profoundly unrealistic and, indeed, ill conceived. One aspect of contracts, the resources that empower employees (e.g., the acquisition of firm specific skills and knowledge; collective organization; ownership of physical assets) are stressed as being against the resources that empower employers, notably, ownership of the means and product of production, the support of the state and the legal system, and managerial perogative within organizations, as Neimark and Tinker (1987) have stressed. The overall lack of realism and the subsequent ill-conception of organization reality in the 'transaction's' framework is a result of concept construction which excludes and elides a central axiom of the radical perspective: that organization means control.

Such control is never total, of course: indeed, in some formulations it is the contradictions inherent in the evolution of regimes of control which explain its development (Clegg and Dunkerley 1980). Control can never be totally secured, in part because of agency. It will be open to erosion and undercutting by the active, embodied agency of those people who are its object: the labour power of the organization. To consider these people as 'labour power' as well as, or in opposition to considering them as 'members', immediately invites reflection on them not only as Durkheimian dwellers in an idealized moral community but also as labourers toiling to preserve their 'species-being', resisting alienation, in Marx's metaphor. It is not only in Marx's view of the active embodied person resisting the wasting of their creative powers that we find the locus of agency against organization. It is also implicit in Durkheim's community. What is taken to be sacred and what is taken to be profane depends entirely on relations of meaning. Such relations of meaning are as resistant to total control as are relations of production. This much has been implicit ever since Saussure's (1974) post-Durkheimian de-coupling of any necessary relationship between the signified and the sign. Resistance to any attempt which seeks to freeze meaning in any specific regulation of it will always be intrinsic to the nature of language as a moral community. In terms of Durkheim's heirs to the study of the moral order, ethnomethodology, indexicality may be shown to be present in even the most mundane utterance (Garfinkel 1967).

The implications for organizations of this double focus on the relations of meaning and the relations of production are evident. Organization encounters agency in at least two prototypical forms: the person as an agent of signification and the person as an agent of production. Both meaning and body, fused in the person, are capacities for resisting the encroachment of organization control on the discursive play of individuals as well as on their capacities to work. Consequently, employers face at least two sources of resistance by virtue of their employees having both discursive and bodily capacities that require some disciplining if some control is to be acheived.

The central institution which rational employers will use to try and govern both relations of meaning and relations of production will be the contractual relation. In sociology, such contractual relations have been broadly conceived in terms of the non-contractual elements of trust and power vested by employers, as well as in terms of the discretion and autonomy gained by employees (Fox 1974). The impact of contractual relations are not only experienced by employees at the point of initial sale of their labour power. It is evident that contracting organizations frame the assumptions which structure not only labour's purchase but also its deployment, as Fox (1974) elaborates. This deployment is subject to contest as well as control, in terms of the variable conditions of autonomy and subordination which can be negotiated within the framework of the contract and its everyday constitution in the work routines of the organization. These will vary with the degrees of control people have. Organizations are staffed by people who may be differentiated in terms of their variable control of methods of production, as well as through dichotomous categories of ownership and non-ownership of means of production. Inscribed in the former are the technical relations of production, embedded in diverse occupational identities, while the latter constitutes the key social relations of capitalist modernity: those of production, of property, of ownership and control (Clegg and Dunkerley 1980; Clegg, Boreham and Dow 1986). Through this variable control, variable interests are established, specified in terms of the 'rules of the game'.

Interests are seen at their most general in various models of capitalist production and reproduction such as those presented by Harvey (1982). Whether or not such conception of interests are available as resources which people in organizations will use will depend upon how they represent what they take to be reality. Central to this will be struggles for the 'hearts and minds' of employees by competing representations constituted through agencies such as political parties, the various organs of the state, popular discourse in the media, those of employers' federations or trade unions. In as much as these depict the arena of organizational life in terms of the leitmotif of 'class', they will be attuned to the *general* conditions of economic domination and subordination in organizations as Carchedi (1987: 100) identifies them. General conditions will be at their most pervasive as they impact upon the employment contract and its whole *acôutrement* of tacit conditions and informal 'effort bargains' (Baldamus 1961). Not only are these located at the point of production as Burawoy (1985) demonstrates, but they are also evident in their reproduction in the movements of the broader political economy which contextualized them (Clegg, Boreham and Dow 1986). General conditions of economic domination are also overlain in particular cases by forms of domination endured by *specific* groups of people (Carchedi 1987). Such discrimination is organized on the basis of salient aspects of social identity.

People are not only labour power nor even merely signifiers of meaning.

Necessarily they are subjects of both and are subjected to both, signified as labour power and as the embodiment of differential and related social identities. Available identities are premised on the salience of issues such as ethnicity, gender, age and phenomena which find expression in culture, distinct and hierarchized 'styles of life' (Weber 1978) which display elaborated 'positional goods' (Hirsch 1978) and 'cultural capital' (Bourdieu 1984). These form relational complexes which function as major limits on the discretion of organization action, of whom may do what, how, where, when and in which ways to whatever objects or agencies, as customarily and sometimes legally specific identities are prescribed or proscribed for certain forms of practice. Embodied identities will only be salient in as much as they are socially recognized and organizationally consequent. Other forms of embodiment, for instance, hair colour, size, or physiognymy may be salient aspects of either individual corporeality or organizational cognition but are less generally and strategically so, except in particular circumstances. One thinks, for instance, of the armed forces and of civil stipulations in the police and fire service on a certain weight, height, or even the presence of facial hair — only beards or clean shaven faces are allowed in the British Navy. Moustaches are proscribed. Other instances might be found in more informal organization definitions of 'front stage' actors (Goffman 1959), such as news readers or receptionists. However, few forms of embodiment achieve the generality of age, gender, sexuality, ethnicity and religiosity as practices for stratifying organization members: this is evidenced by their being the precise target of various anti-discrimination laws.

From the person's point of view, it is the employer/employee relationship which is central, as it is this which is constitutive of the context in which other forms of organized social relations come into consideration, (not least those incorporated in the form and actions of unions and the labour movement and in the state and its definitions of citizenship). It is through the ownership/non-ownership issue, as well as through the variable control of methods of production which is vested in people defined in terms of both the formal and informal requirements of organization context as differentially skilled actors, that other forms of identity may achieve organizational expression.

Organizations may be not only hierarchically authoritative structures of class domination but will also be structures of patriarchal domination, ethnic domination and so on. Clearly such matters are contingent: most existing organizations may be structures of gender, ethnic and class dominancy, but not all organizations necessarily are. Both 'meritocracy' and 'socialist organization' may be possible, in principle. A given structure of authority or class domination may be filled without regard to other forms of discrimination or one may seek to abolish it (Carchedi 1987). However, the empirical limits of such an alternative have to be conceptualized (Clegg and Higgins 1987).

Although the vast majority of organizations are structured around an hierarchical calibration and relation of diverse social identities, it is all too easy to argue that this is in some way functional for the reproduction of the central principle of organization. Thus, for example, some neo-Marxists (e.g. Clegg and Dunkerley 1980) propose that gender and class structuration are necessarily reproductive of capitalist control of organizational means of production. The argument is one of 'divide and rule'. However, one could as plausibly counter with an equally general and functional argument, which is as 'pro' capitalist as the other is 'anti'; that equality is best advanced by the embrace of that efficiency and rationality which serves to reduce all identities to those of the market, thus purging particularisms through the universal calculus of unfettered market signals. Neither argument is satisfactory, precisely because of the *general* character of each of them and their reliance on a concept of an expressive principle.

Organizations should not be conceptualized as the phenomenal expression of some essential inner principle such as economic exploitation or rationality. Organizations are better seen as loci of decision and action (Hindess 1987). They do things as a consequence of decisions to act in certain ways by certain other agents. Organizations also do things that are not a consequence of a decision to act in that way, if only because decisions are shaped by struggles around competing substantive objectives — what I call diverse modes of rationality. One cannot explain the politics of all organizations in terms of general theories of their rationality. Organizational action is an indeterminate outcome of substantive struggles between different agencies: between people who deploy different resources; people whose organizational identities will be shaped by the way in which disciplinary practices work through and on them, even in their use of such techniques; people who seek to control and decide the nature of organizational action. Consequently, the interests of actors in organizations and the decisions that they make are necessarily contingent on various forms of organization calculation. Thus, organizational action cannot be the expression of some essential inner principle: claims to such principle as prime movers necessarily neglect the actual complex and contingent conditions under which organizational action occurs.

One can no more explain the politics of all organizations in terms of general theories of labour exploitation that one can in terms of their rationality. For one thing, too much which hinges on other aspects of identity than those of membership or exploitation is left unconsidered in so many such theories. In specific organizational contexts the general conditions of economic domination may not necessarily be the most apparent focus of such resistance or struggle. More specific loci of domination may be organizationally salient; after all, divisions of labour are embodied, gendered, departmentalized, hierarchized, spatially separated, and so on. All of these actualities may give rise to stuggle and resistance, power and consent. However, it is not only issues of identity which limit the salience of such general theories. Another important point must be the realization that in many complex organizations the politics of control and discipline are unlikely to be oriented solely towards people. In most manufacturing firms in the U.S.A., according to some recent estimates (Jelinek 1987), direct costs to labour are unlikely to be more than about 10 percent of costs. Consequently, control is less oriented to the direct labour process but to the issues of product quality, equipment utilization, inventory and markets. General resource dependency perspectives may well be of more explanatory use in such contexts.

Contingency reigns, albeit with a hegemonic personal cast; that is, one can say with a degree of empirical exactness (Heath 1981) that it is apparent, as far as people in organizations are concerned that certain male identities constituted in socially and economically privileged contexts will be routinely more strategically contingent for organizational decision-making, access and success in hierarchically arranged careers. Equally, feminist scholarship (see Martin's 1980 literature review) indicates that female identity should in the aggregate, if not in individual cases, routinely be regarded as a strategic handicap. Note that this is not to say that either class or gender will necessarily function this way: simply, that in the past, sociological observation suggests that it is probable that it will. What is of most interest here, of course, is identifying which national state, legal and organizational characteristics and practices will produce systematic variation in stratifying outcomes constructed in terms of such key markers of identity, as well as studying the organization cultures in which they find particular types of expression.

Organizations and Strategic Agency

Implicit in the view being developed here is a conception of organizations as locales in which negotiation, contestation and struggle between organizationally divided and linked agencies is a routine occurrence. Divisions of labour are to be regarded as both an object and outcome of struggle. All divisions of labour within any employing organization are necessarily constituted within the context of various contracts of employment. Hence the employment relationship, that of economic domination and subordination, is necessarily an organizational fundamental. It is the underlying sediment through which other organization practices are stratified. Often these will overlap with it in quite complex ways.

The sociological consequences of this view of organizations are evident. Divisions of labour, along with their remuneration, as central aspects of the employment contract and effort bargain, will become foci of politics. In these politics, agencies interested in maximizing their strategicality must attempt to transform their point of connection with some other agency or agencies into a 'necessary nodal point': this would be a channel through which traffic between them occurs on terms which privilege the putative strategic agency. Otherwise, strategic inclinations will be unconsummated. From these observations follow the central points of strategic contingency theory.

To achieve strategic agency requires subordinating the discretion of other agencies: at best, from the strategist's point of view, such other agencies will become merely authoritative relays, extensions of strategic agency (Law 1986:

16). Whatever interests such relay agencies would have would be entirely those they are represented as having by the strategically subordinating agency. A totally disciplined army squad in the field of battle, obediently subject to higher authority and its commands, would be the prime example of this evacuation from agency of interests other than those authoritatively attributed to them. The actual agents, in this case the army squad, remain literally non-actors in this process: their only action allowed is to obey unquestioningly. They become agents without interests other than obedience to others' commands. In this respect the army, as Weber was well aware, represents only the most condensed and concentrated form of much 'normal' organizational power and discipline, at least along the transitive dimension. Intransitively, it is expedient if one's military discipline also is buttressed by moral authority, such as, for instance, a religious vocation: soldiers of God, as Anthony (1976) suggests, historically have been the highest expression of obedient organization membership: commerce as a moral crusade would be, perhaps, the ultimate cultural evangelist's dream.

The articulation of interests by strategic agencies is thus the medium and outcome of unique positioning over the discretion of others positioning in the organization field. It has to be reproduced for existing structures of power to be reproduced. Indeed, its reproduction is power; its transformation effective resistance to it. It should be evident that such reproductions are always already structured: never flat, one dimensional topographies. Topography in this instance will always be the result of previous and current contest. In organizational life such field structure has to be reproduced by strategic agencies or it will be open to transformation.

Agency may be evident in any circuit in a network of practices. Typically, but not necessarily, these circuits will be human: but they may be departmental or inanimate. With the latter in mind one might think of examples such as the undoubted agency exercised by the complex, highly coupled computer decision-making systems introduced by the Securities Industry Automation Corporation to Wall Street trading. Some analysts regard these as a contributory factor in the October 19, 1987 stock market crash on Wall Street (Sanger 1987). It is not far fetched under such circumstances to suggest that agencies need not necessarily be human.

One consequence of the position taken here is that organizational locales will more likely be loci of multivalent powers than monadic sites of total control: contested terrains rather than total institutions. Barnes (1986: 184) puts it thus:

'To retain discretion over a large number of routines requires delegation. But for the maximum retained discretion over any particular routine the requirement is that authority be delegated but not power.'

The theoretically most powerful delegation of authority depends upon the delegated agent acting as one who is 'obedient'. Other than this, there is no way that the delegated routines will be directed without discretion. 'Obedience' cannot be guaranteed, despite the search for a secular equivalent to divinely inspired obeisance, if only because of the complexity and contingency of agency, as a nexus of calculation. Discretion need not entail dissent: it may be organizationally creative, productive, reproductive. None the less, to increase the power of a delegating agency does mean authorizing delegated others and delegated authorities cannot be guaranteed to be loci of wholly predictable and controlled agency, other than if they are dutiful servants. Thus the problematic of 'power in organizations' centres not on the legitimacy or otherwise of subordinates, capacities, as in the conventional view, but on the myriad practices which *incapacitate* authorities from becoming powers by restricting action to that which is 'obedient', not only prohibitively but also creatively, productively. Ineluctably, 'ideology', 'expertise' and 'authority', whether 'Systems' or not, are implicated in these practices.

It has been argued thus far that authority is an *a postiori* concept to that of power. The enlargement of an agency's power, except in the unlikely event of omnipotence, must be organizationally achieved through delegation. Delegation implies that discretion attaches to delegates.

Important implications flow from the relationship between power and discretion. Power will always be inscribed within contextual 'rules of the game' which both enable and constrain action (Clegg 1975). These rules may be taken to be the underlying rationale of those calculations which agencies routinely make in organizational contexts. Action can only ever be designated as such-and-such an action by reference to rules which identify it as such. Such rules can never be free of surplus or ambiguous meaning: they are always indexical to the context of interpreters and interpretation. Where there are rules there must be indexicality, as has been demonstrated by texts as diverse as Wittgenstein (1968), Garfinkel (1967), Clegg (1975) and Barnes (1986). Rules can never provide for their own interpretation. Issues of interpretation are always implicated in the processes whereby agencies instantiate and signify rules. 'Ruling' is an activity. It is accomplished by some agency as a constitutive sense-making process whereby meaning is fixed. Both rules and games necessarily tend to the subject of contested interpretation, with some players having not only play-moves but also the refereeing of these as power resources. Consequently, where rules are invoked there must be discretion. Thus, it is not only embodiment, labour power, which is the source of resistance. It is not only the gap between the capacity to labour and its realization in which power and the organization of control is implicated; it is also inherent in the regulation of meaning.

Here we confront the central paradox of power: the power of an agency is increased in principle by that agency delegating authority; the delegation of authority can only proceed by rules; rules necessarily entail discretion and discretion potentially empowers delegates. From this arises the tacit and taken for granted basis of organizationally negotiated order, and on occasion, its fragility and instability, as has been so well observed by Strauss (1978).

Power is implicated in authority and constituted by rules; the interpretation of rules must be disciplined, must be regulated, if new powers are not to be produced and existing powers transformed. In fact, given the inherent indexicality of rule use, things will never be wholly stable; they will usually exhibit tolerances to stress, strain and strife in rule constitution whose limits can only ever be known for sure in their ill-disciplined breach of regulation. By definition, wholly effective discipline admits no breach, no 'disobedience', total rule-boundedness.

None of this is far from Weber (1978) or for that matter Foucault (1976), despite protestations to the contrary: see Foucault (1981). What is surprising, is that aspects of Weber on 'discipline' (which in themselves echo Durkheim's (1964) stress on 'moral regulation') were not developed in the concern of the sociology of organizations with power. Nor were they adequately addressed by the past decade of 'radical', 'critical' organization theory, marred as it was by a certain essentialism which generated a somewhat doctrinaire theoretical incapacity. Put another way, this was a capacity to resist the indexicality of rule use through the presumed unindexical domination of capital. Elements in a critique of these positions have been developed elsewhere (Clegg and Higgins 1987). In these earlier positions, as is now evident, power becomes epiphenomenal (Clegg 1987).

Power is not a thing. As Hindess (1982) has so cogently argued it should not be thought of as an unexercised capacity. It is instead 'a matter of the successful deployment of resources and of means of action in the context of particular conditions of struggle' (Hindess 1982: 509), when the criteria of success, in terms of reproduction and transformation of states of affairs, will themselves be contested. Crucial to these processes will be the degree to which 'struggle' is constrained by agencies working according to legitimated interpretations of rules. In organizational terms this is not simply a question of 'who' is resisted as it is usually posed. Struggles may typically endure beyond actors in organizations, particularly where the struggle is over the identity and conditions and rights of membership (e.g., nationalist struggles; sectarian struggles; class struggles). What is struggled against is a particular legitimated interpretation of rules as a given, specific regime of disciplinary practices. Power is expressed in and through disciplinary practices and in and through struggles against or in resistance to such practices.

Resistance to discipline is irremediable. Not because of 'human nature', 'capitalism' or any other putatively essentialist category. It is irremediable because of the power/rule constitution as a nexus of meaning and interpretation which, because of indexicality, is always open to being re-fixed. This is what couples power/knowledge in Foucault's (1976) formulation, because, at its most pervasive, power positions the subject, through disciplinary practices which constitute the potentialities, incapacities and correlates of specific forms of the person, within the purview of disciplines: of medicine, organizations, psychology, etc.

Hitherto in this argument organizations have been characterized as being composed of locales. While locales may be circumscribed by spatial considerations — the shopfloor, the boardroom, the Council Chamber, the head office, etc. — arenas are institutional assemblies. For instance, as Weber (1978) identifies them, the key institutional arenas for the modern capitalist organization are the labour market, the capital market, the commodities market and the labour process. Struggles within these arenas, in diverse locales, will constitute the agencies, authorities, powers, network and interests characteristic of the everyday life of the organizations in question. The boundaries of the organization are thus an effect of struggle and cannot be specified *a priori*.

Such contingency may sound chaotic. It is not. What is at issue is not a descriptive point but a theoretical caution. Of course, most organizations most of the time are not scenes of pure chaos and struggle. As Mintzberg (1983) puts it, they are characterized by 'obedience'. Such obedience rarely, if ever, will empirically equate with total control. The achievement of obedience will be a variable effect of discipline.

Disciplinary Practices and Disciplinary Matrix

Discipline enters the picture being created here not only through 'disciplinary practices' but also through the 'disciplinary matrix' (Kuhn 1970) within which an organization is represented. Different disciplinary matrices will typically align with organizationally distinct disciplinary practices. Hence, representations of organizations are irredeemably reflexive. Some organizationally distinct disciplinary practices will have a central role to play in the representation of particular organization arena by specific disciplinary matrices. The most evident example of this in recent times has been the centrality of Taylorism/scientific management and work study (disciplinary practice) to post-Braverman labour process debate (disciplinary matrix). Certain texts, such as Braverman (1974), can be said to be windows which attract the gaze from certain disciplinary matrices onto certain disciplinary practices within the organization. Whereas the disciplinary matrix is an assembly of almost infinite possibilities in the abstract probabilities of its bricolage, it rarely is conceived so randomly. Certain well-trained possibilities typically prevail through the practices of normalcy (Kuhn 1970).

The possibilities of disciplinary practice in the organization are altogether more circumscribed, because more local (Gouldner 1957, 1958). While nothing, in principle, limits the discursive forms through which the window may be opened and the gaze focussed on organizational action, the arenas in question are much more contingent. Within such arenas, agents are subject to considerable discursive discipline and limitation. While disciplinary matrices are by no means spheres of free subjectivity (what could be?) they do not share the same restriction of scope that organizational disciplinary practices have. (It should be noted in passing that the possibilities of the former will themselves frequently be limited by the latter — 'this department is focussed on macro-questions'; 'we focus on actors around here', etc.). Disciplinary practices in organizations are localized instantiations, significations and implications of rules and knowledges whose applicability requires interlock with the tacit knowledge of local custom and precedent. Their tap root must reach into the discursive and practical community of local membership and its characteristic 'vocabulary of motives' (Mills 1940) as well as claim sustenance from more general forms of knowledge. Frequently, as institutionalists such as Meyer and Rowan (1977) argue, such disciplinary practices typically display a certain cultural isomorphism, a suggestion quite consistent with Foucault's (1976) research into forms of discipline and surveillance. The pervasiveness of certain forms of discipline may thus be as much cultural as ecological.

Organizational locales are thus sites of diverse disciplinary practice, through which flows organizational traffic via more or less tightly controlled conduits (where control is via the rule boundedness of disciplined practice) into networks precariously reproduced/transformed by those agents struggling to be strategic powers and authorities. Those who do not struggle, who are indifferent, have little efficacy: however, this should be seen not as a taken-for-granted datum but as something which is itself to be explained. From not only what blindness, what ignorance, what blinkers, but more especially what concepts, what knowledge does this indifference, this obedience, derive?

Organizations are thus, above all, locales of politics. This is not to say that necessarily they will be evidenced by a highly articulate or developed sense of 'politicking' within the organization context. Calm surfaces with barely a political ripple disturbing them, just as much as scenes of heroic struggle to the political death are something to be explained, not something to be taken for granted.

Conclusions

As suggestions for analysis of power in organizations, the following are proposed: that research should not simply study just positions but also practices; discretion and not just legitimacy should be conceptualized as the key to understanding power and authority; power is not simply a thing vested in a specific person or agency but a field of force constitutive of organization as a specific alignment of locales, agency, conduits, etc. It is more adequately conceptualized as a set of strategic practices reproducing or transforming a complex ensemble of relations. Its effect, a given structure, should not be confused with a cause.

The paper has argued against a genre of organization analysis which incorporates divergent and antagonistic traditions. These are functionalism and Marxism. What makes them a genre is their common narrative technique of representing organizations as totalities necessarily structured by some essential feature (of goal-orientation or exploitation). Against such essentialist views has been stressed the importance of considering other bases of identity than simply membership or ownership/non-ownership. With Weber, one would stress the fundamental importance not only of differential ownership of means but also methods of production (see Clegg and Dunkerley 1980; Clegg et al. 1986), as well as the centrality of the organizational embededness of those identities which are constituted in civil society, find expression in organizations and are institutionally modulated and regulated by the state. Organizations are composed of competing calculations and modes of rationality rather than being expressive of rationality *per se*. Relations of meaning, as well as relations of production are central to the structure and functioning of organizations, the government of which is expressed through daily 'effort bargains' and struggles over contractual relations which seek to 'fix' these other relations.

Certain consequences flow from the analysis. The reversal of the traditional relationship between authority and power as concepts, for instance: the importance of power as a concept for thinking relationally; the improbability of using this relational concept in anything other than a predictively 'dispositional' way: that is, that certain tendencies would be disposed to occur given our knowledge of organization relationships. Far too many contingencies can enter into the picture to provide a general theory of organizations. For instance, not only does one have to consider the unforeseen external agencies who enter the field of action, or whose powers effect those already there but also the competency of agencies in the struggle.

What the paper does is to provide some concepts with which various studies may be constructed, and certain 'family resemblances' manifested between them. Rather than build another theory, it is proposed that middle level conceptual refinement and empirical application may be a more useful strategy for contemporary organization studies in their approach to the theory of power; approaches whose parameters, although somewhat circumscribed, are perhaps not as superseded as erstwhile radical critics once might have thought.

Note

* I would like to acknowledge helpful comments received from the *O.S.* referees, Mats Alvesson and Hugh Willmott, from my colleagues Ellie Vasta and Alan Black, as well as suggestions from Richard Hall. Ellie, in particular, was a most insightful and helpful critic. The responses of colleagues at the 'Critical Perspectives on Organization Theories' ISA-RC17 Conference, 19–21 July 1987, held at Wassenaar, The Netherlands, deserve an acknowledgement in the gestation of the ideas, as do those of participants at a seminar held at Universiti Brunei Darussallam, including David Richards and Roy Johnson. Peter Blunt of Adelaide University was in at the birth and the maturation of the paper, but neither he nor any of the other people who helped me should be held responsible for the final product.

References

Anthony, P. D.
1976   *The ideology of work*. London: Tavis-
       tock.

Assad, T.
1987   'On ritual and discipline in medieval
       Christian monasteries'. *Economy and
       Society* 16/2: 159–203.

Baldamus, W.
1961   *Efficiency and effort*. London: Tavistock.

Barnes, B.
1986   'On authority and its relationship to power' in *Power, action and belief: a new sociology of knowledge?* J. Law (ed.), Sociological Review Monograph 32, 190–195. London: Routledge and Kegan Paul.

Bourdieu, P.
1984   *Distinction: a social critique of the judgement of taste*. London: Routledge and Kegan Paul.

Braverman, H.
1974   *Labour and monopoly capital: the degradation of work in the twentieth century*. New York: Monthly Review Press.

Burawoy, M.
1985   *The politics of production*. London: Verso.

Carchedi, G.
1987   *Class analysis and social research*. Oxford: Blackwell.

Clegg, S.
1975   *Power, rule and domination: a critical and empirical understanding of power in sociological theory and organizational life*. London: Routledge and Kegan Paul.

Clegg, S.
1977   'Power, organization theory, Marx and critique' in *Critical issues in organizations*. S. Clegg and D. Dunkerley (eds), 21–40. London: Routledge and Kegan Paul.

Clegg, S.
1979   *The theory of power and organization*. London: Routledge and Kegan Paul.

Clegg, S.
1987   'The power of language, the language of power'. *Organization Studies* 8/1: 60–70.

Clegg, S., P. Boreham, and G. Dow
1986   *Class, politics and the economy*. London: Routledge and Kegan Paul.

Clegg, S., and D. Dunkerley
1980   *Organization, class and control*. London: Routledge and Kegan Paul.

Clegg, S., and W. Higgins
1987   'Against the current: sociology, socialism and organizations'. *Organization Studies* 8/3: 201–221.

Coch, L., and J. R. P. French, jnr.
1948   'Overcoming resistance to change'. *Human Relations* 1: 512–532.

Crozier, M.
1964   *The bureaucratic phenomenon*. London: Tavistock.

Donaldson, L.
1985   *In defence of organization sociology: a response to the critics*. Cambridge: Cambridge University Press.

Durkheim, E.
1964   *The division of labour*. New York: Free Press.

Etzioni, A.
1961   *A comparative analysis of complex organizations*. New York: The Free Press of Glencoe.

Foucault, M.
1981   'Questions of Method: an interview with Michel Foucault'. *I & C* 8: 1–14.

Foucault, M.
1976   *Discipline and punish*. Harmondsworth: Penguin.

Fox, A.
1974   *Beyond contract: work, power and trust relation*. London: Faber and Faber.

Jelinek, M.
1987   'Review of "New technology as organizational innovation", edited by J. M. Pennings and A. Buitendam, Cambridge, MA: Belkinger'. *Academy of Management Executive* (August): 259–261.

Garfinkel, H.
1967   *Studies in ethnomethodology*. Englewood Cliffs, NJ.: Prentice Hall.

Girdwood, J.
1987 *On reading Foucault, genealogy and
       power-knowledge.* Honours paper,
       Department of Sociology, University
       of New England.

Goffman, E.
1959 *The presentation of self in everyday
       life.* New York: Doubleday Anchor.

Gouldner, A. W.
1957 'Cosmopolitans and locals: towards an
       analysis of latent social roles - I'.
       Administrative Science Quarterly 2:
       281-306.

Gouldner, A. W.
1958 'Cosmopolitans and locals: towards an
       analysis of latent social roles - II',
       Administrative Science Quarterly 2:
       444-480.

Habermas, J.
1976 *Legitimation crisis.* London: Heine-
       mann.

Harvey, D.
1982 *The Limits of capital.* Oxford:
       Blackwell

Heath, A.
1981 *Social mobility.* Glasgow: Fontana

Hickson, D. J., C. R. Hinings, C. A. Lee, R.
E. Schneck, and J. M. Pennings
1971 ·A strategic contingencies theory of
       intra-organizational power', *Adminis-
       trative Science Quarterly* 16: 216-229.

Hindess, B.
1982 ·Power, interests and the outcomes of
       struggles', *Sociology* 16, 4: 498-511.

Hindess, B.
1987 ·Rationality and the characterization
       of modern society' in *Max Weber,
       rationality and modernity.* S. Whims-
       ter and S. Lash (eds), 137-153. Lon-
       don, Allen and Unwin.

Hinings, C. R., D. J. Hickson, J. M. Pennings, and R. E. Schneck
1974 'Structural conditions of intra-
       organizational power'. *Administrative
       Science Quarterly* 9/1: 22-44.

Hirsch, F. R.
1978 *The social limits to growth.* London:
       Routledge and Kegan Paul.

Kieser, A.
1987 'From asceticism to administration of
       wealth: Medieval monasteries and the
       pitfalls of rationalization'. *Organ-
       ization Studies* 8/2: 103–124.

Kuhn, T. S.
1970 *The structure of scientific revolutions*
       (2nd ed.). Chicago: University of
       Chicago Press.

Law, J.
1986 'Editor's introduction: power/know-
       ledge and the dissolution of the socio-
       logy of knowledge' in *Power, action
       and belief: a new sociology of know-
       ledge?* J. Law (ed.). Sociological
       Review Monograph 32, 1–19. London:
       Routledge and Kegan Paul.

Martin, P. Y.
1980 'Women, labour markets and em-
       ploying organizations; a critical per-
       spective', in *The international year-
       book of organization studies.* D.
       Dunkerley and G. Salaman (eds),
       128–150. London, Routledge and
       Kegan Paul.

Matheson, C.
1987 'Weber and the classification of forms
       of legitimacy'. *British Journal of
       Sociology* XXXVIII/2: 199–215.

Mayo, E.
1975 *The social problems of an industrial
       civilization.* London: Routledge and
       Kegan Paul.

Meyer, J., and B. Rowan
1977 'Institutionalized organizations: for-
       mal structure as myth and ceremony'.
       American Journal of Sociology 83:
       340–363.

Mills, C. W.
1940 'Situated actions and vocabularies of
       motive'. *American Sociological Re-
       view* V: 904–913.

Mintzberg, H.
1983 *Power in and around organizations*, Englewood Cliffs, N.J.: Prentice Hall.

Neimark, M., and T. Tinker
1987 'Identity and non-identity thinking: a dialectical critique of the transaction cost theory of the modern corporation'. Mimeo.

Pfeffer, J.
1981 *Power in organizations*. Boston: Pitman.

Ray, C.
1986 *Social innovation at work: the humanization of workers in twentieth century America*, Ph.D., University of California, Santa Cruz.

Sanger, D. E.
1987 'High tech as villain: on Wall Street, computer programs came to replace individual judgement'. *The International Herald Tribune*, Singapore, December 16, 1–6.

Saussure F. de
1974 *Course in general linguistics*. London: Fontana.

Schachter, J.
1987 'In the US, privacy has become a public affair'. *Sydney Morning Herald*, December 29, 11.

Strauss, A.
1978 *Negotiations: varieties, contexts, processes, and social order*. London: Jossey-Bass.

Thompson, J. D.
1956 'Authority and power in identical organizations'. *American Journal of Sociology* LXII: 290–301.

Weber, M.
1978 *Economy and society: an outline of interpretative sociology*, 2 vols. G. Roth and C. Wittich (eds.). Berkeley: University of California Press.

Williamson, O. E.
1981 'Transaction cost economies: the governance of contractual relations'. *Journal of Law and Economics*: 233–261.

Wilson, H. T.
1983 'Technocracy and late capitalist society: reflections on the problem of rationality and social organization' in *The state, class and the recession*. S. Clegg, G. Dow and P. Boreham (eds.), 152–238. London: Croom Helm.

Wittgenstein, L.
1968 *Philosophical investigations*. Translated by G. E. M. Anscombe. Oxford: Blackwell.

[19]

Journal of Management Studies, **20**, 2, 1983

IMPLANTED DECISION-MAKING: AMERICAN OWNED FIRMS IN BRITAIN [1]

Geoffrey R. Mallory, Richard J. Butler, David Cray,
David J. Hickson and David C. Wilson

Organizational Analysis Research Unit, University of Bradford Management Centre

ABSTRACT

DECISION-MAKING processes are compared in American and British subsidiaries in Britain to investigate how far processual characteristics as distinct from structural features, may be implanted in subsidiaries abroad. Managements in the British owned subsidiaries tend to route their biggest decisions through the formalities of standing committees in conformity with customary procedures, taking a comparatively long time to do so. Managements in the American owned subsidiaries tend to rely on informally assembled working groups which help to arrive at a decision comparatively rapidly through a process which does not ostensibly follow any recognized procedure. The British mode is formal within a non-formalized customary pattern, the American mode informal within a formalized frame.

IMPLANTING PROCESSUAL CHARACTERISTICS

CONVERSATIONS between those who contend with the practical and theoretical obstacles of cross-national comparative research sometimes refer wistfully to an ideal study in which the organizations to be compared are perfectly matched. One ideal is where in comparing, for instance, firms in Japan, the United States, and other countries there would be an exact correspondence of Japanese firms in Japan and Japanese owned subsidiaries in the United States with American firms in the United States and American owned subsidiaries in Japan, and so on. In successive analyzes the apparent effects of national location, and of ownership, could then be controlled and anything due to elements in the national ways of life be more clearly exposed.

Pending such ideals, published research consists of piecemeal accumulation of results from samples each of which contributes only one piece to the picture. But even piecemeal accumulation during the 1970's did begin to put that picture together: '. . . there is gradually increasing understanding, and Child's (1981) review at the end of the decade does not have the despair that Roberts (1970) felt "on looking at an elephant" (as she put it) at the beginning of the decade' (Hickson and McMillan, 1981, p. 187).

Address for reprints: G. R. Mallory, Organizational Analysis Research Unit, University of Bradford Management Centre, Emm Lane, Bradford BD9 4JL.

Managerial Decision Making

GEOFFREY R. MALLORY, ET AL.

The research reported here offers one such piece, the results of a comparison of American owned subsidiaries and British owned subsidiaries *all* with British managers and located in Britain. This has the advantage of controlling for any effects of national location, raising the question whether firms adjacent territorially can differ just because some of them are owned from the territory of another nation. Can the managements of multi-national corporations project national characteristics, which in this case would be 'Americanisms', across the oceans to their subsidiaries?

Since *prima facie* the answer is 'yes' for structural specialization and formalization, for obviously headquarters can require the setting up of specialist departments (*e.g.* insist on a marketing department being established by the subsidiary where there was none before) or conformity to corporation rules (*e.g.* monthly financial returns by the subsidiary in a standard form), what then if the question is asked of processes? This paper examines how far a multi-national's management can project characteristics in the processes of making decisions *even* though those making the decisions are of a *different* nationality, in this case British managers in American-owned subsidiaries where no American manager is personally present. Do the British managements in the subsidiaries tend towards decision-making processes with American characteristics?

Negandhi (1979) showed that the subsidiaries abroad of American multinationals, even if located in culturally different and economically 'developing' societies, do take over all the more formal paraphernalia of modern management normal to the parent corporation. They have comprehensive planning procedures, formalized budgetary controls, effective personnel and training functions *etc.*, whereas similar locally owned firms do not. He compared American owned subsidiaries with locally owned firms in South American and Asia.

In Africa, Ajiboye's (1980) comparison of two locally owned firms with a French subsidiary and a British subsidiary in Nigeria is suggestive in the same direction, but for hierarchical relationships. The two locally owned firms differed from the French and British owned subsidiaries in their employees' responses to questions on hierarchical influence, as plotted on a Tannenbaum (1968) control graph, but even more significantly the French and British owned subsidiaries differed from each other, the British being the less hierarchical. These owning corporations seemed able to stamp their own imprint on the managements of their overseas subsidiaries.

In both the Negandhi (1979) and Ajiboye (1980) studies the means used by the owning corporations appeared to be the export of expatriate top managers to the subsidiaries. Although this may be effective for management systems and the approach taken to subordinates, the national norms of behaviour in which arise the decision-making processes examined in this paper could be resistant to influences from foreign headquarters even when expatriates bring their own customary approach with them. Preliminary impressions of research by Kidd and Teramoto (1981) indicate that although expatriate Japanese managers bring to their European subsidiaries typical Japanese practices such as the widely participative *ringi* decision-making process and the *ringi sho* document which all involved managers sign to signify their assent, such practices do not include nor transfer to their European colleagues (in the particular instance of the *ringi sho* this is virtually impossible by it being in Japanese script). In the same way, the prolonged *nemawashi* process of informal, indeed casual, discussion which precedes the drawing up of the *ringi sho* rarely includes European colleagues who do not have time for it, neither literally nor temperamentally. Thus although the European managers appreciate what they find to be a more communicative organizational climate, despite the normative barriers, their own ways are little affected by the Japanese practices even though their senior colleagues are Japanese.

Given this resistance to the adoption of foreign ways when they are introduced by the presence in person of foreign nationals, the question is whether the decision-making processes of managements in far off subsidiaries show characteristics representing the ways of their foreign owners even when there are no expatriates among them? How influential in this respect are multi-national corporations at, so to speak, one remove?

The importance of local conditioning is evidenced by Kelly and Worthley (1981) who show that Japanese-American managers in Hawaii are more like the Caucasian-American managers with whom they interact, and whose national outlook they share, than they are like Japanese managers in Japan. The implication is that it is difficult to implant characteristics from afar to managements of another nationality. Whilst it is commonplace for multinationals to introduce prescribed information and control systems, it is less likely that they are able to shape the processes by which major decisions are arrived at within their subordinate élites.

CASES COMPARED

The twenty cases of decision-making processes compared in this paper took place over various periods ranging from months to years during the ten years 1969–1979 in two American subsidiaries in Britain with wholly British managements (there were no American expatriates among them at any time), and two British owned subsidiaries in Britain. The selection of American owned subsidiaries parallels that made by Jamieson (1980a; 1980b) who argues that:

> The majority of studies which have attempted to investigate the effect of socio-cultural factors on business behaviour have tended to compare indigenous firms operating in country A with indigenous firms operating in country B. The design of this study is different in that all firms are located in one country, England. I would argue that in two distinct ways

this is a more rigorous test of hypotheses about the effect of culture on business organizations. In the first place the operating environment of the firms is held constant and this is of vital importance. Secondly, if if can be shown that American firms, despite operating in England and employing English nationals, still exhibited the effects of American culture upon their structure and operation, then it can be safely assumed that cultural variables are relevant in the explanation of business behaviour (Jamieson, 1980a, p. 219).

Whilst agreeing with Jamieson's (1980a) point that such a sample can show how far 'culture' can be implanted abroad, it has to be recognized that the case of American firms in Britain is a less rigorous test than he here makes out, for despite fascinating American/British differences the two nations share an Anglo-Saxon cultural heritage that could make the implanting of American characteristics more likely than implanting, for example, from Japanese multi-nationals. This qualification will be referred to again in the interpretation of the result.

This paper also takes the same point of comparison for decision-making processes in the American owned subsidiaries as Jamieson (1980b) took for his comparison of structural, ideological, and organizational climate features, namely British owned subsidiaries. Any differences which may be attributable to American influence are exposed by comparing ten decision-making processes in the two American subsidiaries with ten processes in the two British subsidiaries.

For those who are concerned with cross-national research, this kind of comparison of subsidiaries within the one country might be exploited more than it has been so far. Whilst its interpretation must differ from those of country by country studies, where it is appropriate to research aims it brings the advantage of completely avoiding the costs in travel and time and coordination which those studies incur.

The comparison originated when it was noticed that a sample of thirty diverse organizations in Britain studied for an extensive project over 150 cases on the making of strategic decisions (Butler *et al.*, 1979/80; Butler *et al.*, 1982; Wilson, 1982) included two American subsidiaries. Since there is little or no empirical cross-national comparison of such processes this aroused immediate curiosity. The two most similar British subsidiaries in the same sample were compared. The results of the comparison were of sufficient interest to lead to the writing of this paper. However, an analysis of twenty cases of decision-making in only two pairs of organizations taken from a set chosen primarily for other purposes is strictly limited. This paper is bound by these limits, and its claims to validity rests primarily not on the sampling but on the correspondence of results with the implications of published research. It fulfils these implications in an area previously not directly investigated: decision-making processes.

The Firms

The four firms from which the twenty cases of decision-making are taken are denoted as US–H, US–J, UK–A, UK–M.

Firm US–H is a wholly owned subsidiary of a major U.S. food and chemical corporation. Its principal manufactures are chemicals and paint which it markets together with other agency products through a large and well established distribution network. The company was essentially a family business from its founding in the early 1900's until it went public in the mid-60's, since when it has continually and successfully added to its product range, eventually being taken over by the U.S. corporation in the early 1970's.

Firm US–J is a wholly owned subsidiary of a U.S. engineering group. It specializes in the manufacture of precision tools and also markets a variety of agency products. The company in its present form grew from an initial association of a subsidiary of the U.S. parent with a well established engineering group in the immediate post-war period. Two years later both were combined as a wholly owned subsidiary. It has a U.K. board of directors who are working executives of the company and it is this group, particularly the chairman, who are responsible for dealings with the parent group.

Firm UK–A is a wholly owned subsidiary of a major U.K. engineering group: it manufactures a standard range of construction engineering equipment. The company has gone through many stages of growth and mutation since its foundation in the late 19th century, particularly in the late 1960's when its existing organizational form and pattern of ownership was set, changing from being independent to a wholly owned subsidiary. Manufacturing is at two sites with the company's headquarters located at the major one. Group Head Office is in London.

Firm UK–M is a wholly owned subsidiary of a U.K. textile and engineering group, specializing in the manufacture of friction products which it markets on a worldwide basis to both manufacturer and *via* its own distribution network to replacement customers. The firm's task is difficult to characterize as the product requires an unusual amalgam of both chemical and engineering technologies. The production unit and Head Office function are located on the same site, which also houses the owning group's worldwide headquarters. There is a product division form of organization so that between the board of directors of UK–M and the holding group board, a divisional board is interposed, providing a complex pattern of interlocking directorates. The company began operations in the late 19th century and moved into its present product line in the 1920's; its current organizational form was the result of a succession of amalgamations and reorganizations in the late 1960's.

All four firms have a distinct corporate identity, marketing products under their own name. All had similarly functionally differentiated top manage-

Table I. Four American owned and British owned subsidiaries

	American owned		British owned	
Firm:	US–H	US–J	UK–A	UK–M
Ownership:	Wholly owned	Wholly owned	Wholly owned	Wholly owned
Owning group:	Chemical and food group	Engineering group	Engineering group	Engineering and textile group
Technology/ product:	Large batch chemicals and paint	Large batch precision small tools and their components	Small batch building contractors' equipment	Large batch automotive components (non-metal)
Size: (employees):	350	700	2000	2000

ments, the chief executives' spans of control ranging between six and eight. Table I lists some of their more obvious features, in addition to nationality of ownership, by which differences in decision-making might be explained. The factor on which there is a substantial disparity is size, the British being the larger. This makes some results difficult to interpret, where possible effects of size cannot be distinguished from those of nationality of ownership. This is referred to in the discussion of results.

But the firms themselves are not the primary unit of analysis. This is the decision-making process, of which there are five *per* firm. All but one fall into four categories of decision topics, product decisions, plant/equipment decisions, domain (marketing) decisions, and planning decisions, as shown in table II. There are new product and plant/equipment decisions in all four firms, and marketing and planning decisions in three out of four. This reflects the tendency for given kinds of organization to be preoccupied with certain categories of decision as reported by Hickson *et al.* (1982) in their analysis of the full sample of 150 cases in thirty organizations from which these twenty cases are drawn. Manufacturing firms are typically mostly concerned with product, plant, and marketing issues.

Data Collection

Data on twenty decision-making processes were collected by lengthy interviews with senior executives who had been centrally involved. The firms were first approached by letter, and the chief executives interviewed both to obtain background information on the history, products, and structure of the firm and to obtain a list of decisions defined by the management as major which had been taken within the recent memory of senior managers. The chief executive nominated as many such decisions as could be readily recalled, and from these a selection of five was made to include as far as possible one in each category of topic concerned with inputs, outputs, core technology, personnel and reorganization. Since the research dealt only with

Table II. Twenty decision cases

Firm:	American owned		British owned	
Decision Topic Category:	US–H	US–J	UK–A	UK–M
Products:	1. Extend product range 2. Become agents for German company's products	1. New product	1. New product	1. New product
Plant/equipment:	3. Expand production capacity (rent additional factory)	2. Expand production capacity (new building and plant) 3. Expand data processing facility	2. Expand production capacity (new building and plant) 3. Purchase new lathes	2. New plant 3. Computerize inventory control
Domain (marketing):	4. Stay out of a market 5. Direct sales to retail outlets	4. Create marketing specialism	4. Standardize company name	
Planning:		5. Business plan	5. Production plan	4. Business plan
Personnel:				5. Staff re-grading, using consultants

actual processes within recall the coverage was uneven, as table II shows, for if no reorganization case could be recalled, for example, no attempt was made to strain memory into the distant past to find or 'invent' one. The chief executive nominated one or more key informants from among his colleagues to discuss each decision. The twenty cases discussed in this paper were derived from interviews with from one to three informants *per* case, usually two, ranging from function heads through directors to managing director and chairman: the separate accounts were consolidated into a single process description of each case.

Each interview began with an historical description of the decision-making process from the time the matter was first raised until the decision, positive or negative, was reached. This was followed by a series of standard questions to which responses were either open-ended only or open-ended together with a rating on a short scale.

PROCESS FEATURES COMPARED

A set of concepts of strategic decision-making processes formulated by Astley *et al.* (1982) were used to guide the larger empirical project referred to earlier. From among these concepts, American/British differences were looked for in those listed in table III. It is not implied that the eight listed describe all aspects of decision-making, but they do represent aspects all through the process, from its initiation proactively or reactively, through the horizon of vision and the number of alternatives considered, to the amount and formality of interaction, the level at which the authorized decision was taken, and how long the process went on. It was these eight which carried the strongest presumptions of American/British differences.

These presumptions are succinctly put by McMillan *et al.* (1973, p. 157):

> Predominant American values of rugged individualism, a frontier spirit, a revolutionary character conducive to change and mobility, and a preference for pluralistic authority patterns are all part of a normative cultural mosaic. The much longer history of British society, its traditions and its stability, give it a legacy of normatively legitimized adherence to established institutions and behavioural patterns.

Jamieson (1980a) sees the American values as more fully in keeping with the interests generated by capitalism, so that the greater managerial dedication to all that is implied by 'scientific management' which Inkson *et al.* (1970) found reflected in their empirical results is to be expected.

Hence the 'Impressions of a Visiting Professor' put forward by Dubin (1970) have a ring of truth about them when they accord with these basic societal differences, even though Jamieson (1980a) is inclined to be dismissive about 'impressions'. Impressions are impressive when they accord with so much else, and they have a depth of understanding that is often

Table III. Decision-making process features

Concept	Definition	Operational variables
Proactivity:	The extent to which the process is an initiative.	Six point scale from No Initiative (decision predefined) through Constrained Initiative to Opportunistic Initiative (unexpected event triggers decision beyond any previous ideas).
Horizon:	The extent to which the process generates future resource commitment.	The period for which process participants looked ahead.
Scan:	The extent to which the process surveys available choices.	The number of alternatives considered (doing nothing being counted where it was a viable alternative).
Interaction volume:	The extent to which the process generates interaction among its participants.	Five point rating from None to A Very Great Deal.
Interaction formality:	The extent to which interaction generated in the process is predefined.	The number of working groups, special committees, and standing committees used (a committee being a body formally established, in the case of a special committee for the particular issue being processed).
Standardization:	The extent to which the process follows pre-existing routines.	The number of unwritten or written procedures followed.
Centrality:	The extent to which the process occurs at the summit of the hierarchy.	The level in the hierarchy at which a decision was authorized.
Duration:	The temporal extent of the overall process.	a Gestation time: the period in months from the first mention of an issue to the time identifiable action took place on a specific topic.
		b Process time: the period in months from the time of first action towards decision on a topic to the time the decision is authorized (*i.e.* approved choice is made).

missing from survey-type comparisons. So when Dubin (1970) suggests, as did Granick (1962) before him, that American managers are willing to try something out despite risks, whereas their British counterparts demand that proposals for innovation be proved before they are applied, this does create a presumption that decision processes in American owned firms are more likely to be initiated proactively rather than to be reactive, to go ahead on a shorter view (*i.e.*. time horizon) of possible consequences with less concern for the farflung future, and to scan more alternative possibilities. These features, proactivity, horizon, and scan are the first, second, and third concepts in table III.

Dubin (1970) makes much of the personal trust in subordinates that British management style emphasizes, a trust which requires reciprocal conformity from those subordinates, in contrast to the openness of American management style. This latter might well stimulate a greater interaction volume (table III) since more is open to discussion, and Jamieson (1980a, p. 226) did find 'more meetings of managers' in American owned subsidiaries. In contrast, British style interaction may not only be less but may have more formality (table III) about it, for Jamieson (1980a) found American owned firms comparatively informal in personal relationships. If that is so in American firms it is an intriguing combination with American bureaucratic formalization (pointed to by Inkson *et al.* (1970), McMillan *et al.* (1973), and to a lesser degree by Jamieson (1980b). It leads to a presumption that American-influenced managerial decision-making processes will combine informal interaction with formalized standard procedures (table III: Standardization).

All comparative statements are relative, and although Clark (1979) finds British management more decentralized than equivalent French management, and Budde *et al.* (1982) find some tendency in the same direction on some decisions only in a comparison with West German managements, Jamieson (1980a) suggests that American owned firms are even further decentralized. So their decision processes should culminate at a lower authority level (table III) than do those in British owned firms.

Eggars (1977) asserts that American managers like to get a move on. Comparing them with their French counterparts, he writes:

> An American will probably lose his typical enthusiasm for a project before a Frenchman gets over his typical reservations (Eggars, 1977, p. 137).

This caricature may be overdone just for effect, but it fits well with Jamieson's (1980a) finding that managers in American owned subsidiaries rated forcefulness relatively highly as a characteristic, and with the tendency for his data to support Child and McMillan's (1972) finding that American managers not only work longer than British managers but use leisure time as an 'extension of work' into which work related activities intrude. This pattern of characteristics implies that American-influenced managements may take decisions faster, *i.e.* the duration (table III) of major decision-making processes will be shorter.

In summary, on variables representing the concepts of decision-making process in table III, American influenced subsidiary firms might be anticipated to show greater proactivity, interaction volume, standardization, and scan, and British subsidiaries not so influenced might be anticipated to show longer horizon and greater interaction formality, centrality, and duration. The twenty processes dealing with the decision topics listed in table II are now compared, ten in each pair of subsidiaries. The comparison is on the operational variables in table III, these being taken from those devised by Butler *et al.* (1982) for the larger project.

RESULTS

The differences between decision-making processes in the American owned and British owned subsidiaries are not extensive. It would be surprising if they were. Even comparing firms located in the United States and in Britain, Inkson *et al.* (1970, p. 363) suspected there were ... 'more differences among managers and organizations within both U.S. and G.B. cultures than between these cultures'; and comparing subsidiaries located in Britain, as this paper does, Jamieson (1980a, 1980b) reported few differences.

Across the twenty decision-making processes, the U.S/U.K. proactivity, horizon, scan, interaction volume, and centrality are much the same. There is nothing to suggest that the decisions in the U.S. owned firms were more often launched proactively; nor that the decision-makers in the British owned firms looked further ahead since in both sets of decision processes the horizon averaged about six years (ranging from the very short term to many years); nor that American influence encourages a wider scan of alternatives for in both sets of processes two, three, or four possibilities were usually considered, such as investment in equipment *versus* product rationalization *versus* buying in supplies as alternative ways of circumventing bottlenecks in future plans (table II, US–J5) or several company image names (table II, UK–A4). Thus American ownership did not appear to spur British managements into the more risk-taking mode of proactive, short term, alternative scanning decision-making that Dubin's (1970) impressions suggest.

Likewise, all the decisions in both pairs of subsidiaries were reported as having stimulated comparably busy interaction, a to-ing and fro-ing which rated similarly on a scale of interaction volume. The sheer amount of interaction did not differ.

Finally, centrality of authorization of the decision, either to go ahead or more rarely not to do so (table II, US–H4), was at similar levels. In both pairs of subsidiaries, some decisions were authorized by the chief executive alone (such as the new product decisions in US–J and UK–M: table II), some by the top governing body (such as direct sales to retail outlets decision in US–H), some by that body but subject to ratification by headquarters (such as UK–A's new company name and US–J's data processing expansion). The American owned subsidiaries were not noticeably more decentralized in this respect, despite the anticipation that they were likely to be so.

So on these aspects of process there is no hint of any difference which might be due to American influence. It is in the kinds of interaction and routines that differences stand out, and in the time it takes to take a decision. These differences are apparent in overall comparisons across all the decision topics in table II, and even more clearly if decision topic is controlled for by comparing across only the new product/extend product range topics or expand production/new plant topics that are common to all four subsidiaries (table II: topics 1 and 3, US–H, and topics 1 and 2, US–J, UK–A, UK–M).

Interaction formality (table IV) is indicated by the use of management working groups, special committees, or standing committees during a decision-making process. The working group is informal in origin and composition, and temporary, arising in the course of the particular decision process. For example, senior managers may get together several times although no one sets terms of reference, or agenda, or plans the meeting. Special committees, frequently called task forces or project teams, are formally constituted to accomplish a certain task, but they too are finite. Standing committees are positioned well within the formal institutional framework, being both formally constituted and of infinite life. They meet at regular intervals, with agenda and minutes, and have a comparatively static membership: examples are Management Meetings, Finance Committees, and Boards of Directors.

Table IV compares the decision processes in these terms. The contrast is plain to see. The processes in UK–A and UK–M have all the standing committees and all but two of the special committees. Those in US–H and US–J have all but one of the working groups. The contrast is especially clear if like decision topics only are compared, the four new product cases (all topic 1) and the new plant cases US–H3, US–J2, UK–A2, and UK–M2.

It is tempting to conclude that American influence breaks down the formality of decision-making in British management. The social customs of British society which require a time and a place for everything, including predictable meetings of predictable composition for predictable purposes, give way to informally gathered working groups. Indeed, this is a likely and tenable interpretation, but it has to be held alongside an alternative interpretation that gives primacy to size. As the British owned subsidiaries are larger it can also be argued that interaction has to be more formally pre-planned and regulated to avoid confusion. Probably the influences of American ownership and of size are both operative, but if so and both are working in the same direction their effects cannot be separated in this sample of decision-making processes.

Table IV. American/British differences in decision-making

Firm	Decision topic	Interaction formality — Number of:			Standardization — Any procedures:		Duration — Number of months:	
		Working Groups	Special Committees	Standing Committees	Unwritten	Written	Gestation	Process
US-H	1. Extend product range	1	0	0	0	0	0	5
	2. Become agents for German company's product	0	1	0	0	0	0	10
	3. Expand production capacity	1	0	0	0	0	0	1
	4. Stay out of a market	1	0	0	0	0	96	18
	5. Direct sales to retailers	1	0	0	0	0	180	3
US-J	1. New product	1	0	0	0	0	0	2
	2. Expand production capacity	1	0	0	0	1	0	3
	3. Expand data processing facility	1	0	0	0	0	0	12
	4. Create marketing specialism	1	0	0	0	0	0	12
	5. Business plan	0	1	0	0	1	0	8
UK-A	1. New product	0	1	2	1	0	6	6
	2. Expand production capacity	0	1	3	0	1	0	30
	3. Purchase new lathes	0	1	1	1	0	0	18
	4. Standardize brand name	0	1	0	0	0	1	6
	5. Production plan	0	0	2	1	0	12	1
UK-M	1. New product	0	0	1	1	0	0	27
	2. New plant	0	1	1	0	1	72	24
	3. Computerize inventory control	1	1	2	1	0	22	18
	4. Business plan	0	0	2	1	0	0	2
	5. Staff re-grading, using consultants	0	0	2	0	0	0	11

However, it is possible that within the four firms there is some apparent size effect in the opposite direction, favouring formal committees in the American owned pair and in some degree offsetting any direct size effect in the British owned pair, since the parent corporations of the American pair are somewhat larger.

Other evidence also helps to sustain the interpretation that American ownership is a strong influence. Even though the sizes of the subsidiaries differ their top management echelons do not. It is these echelons whose members generate and take part in the processes of deciding what they regard as major matters, and it is these processes that are the subject of comparison here. It was mentioned earlier that in both pairs of subsidiaries the numbers at the top reporting direct to the chief executive and making up his span of control were similar, as were the functions they represented. Thus UK–A and UK–M did not have greater numbers of immediate participants to coordinate through their standing committees than did US–J and US–H.

Standardization, the second variable in table IV, indicates whether any part or parts of a decision-making process followed a standard procedure, that is a recognized routine existing prior to the particular topic arising and applying also to other decision processes. It can be seen that only two procedures were reported in the processes in US–H and US–J, whereas eight out of the ten processes in UK–A and UK–M followed procedures. Of these eight, most were unwritten rather than bureaucratized: one did follow a written procedure predominantly, but another did so in part only and the others followed what were termed unwritten procedures.

Among the instances of written procedures, US–J5, the business plan decision, had to conform to a procedure imposed by the American owning corporation, a procedure conspicuous in the stack of estimates and supporting data in a standard form which the chief executive heaved from his desk drawer. The other three instances of written procedures all apply to new plant/expand production capacity decisions, and suggest a tendency for this type of decision to be governed by written procedures, whatever the firm. In any firm the renewal or expansion of plant and equipment is likely to be a recurrent topic so that written procedures are evolved for it. Here the topic could be a factor as well as the U.K. bias. But that bias is much the most distinctive in *un*written procedures. They are referred to by the managers in the British owned subsidiaries alone.

These unwritten procedures are the tacit taken-for-granteds such as that this kind of matter is always looked at first by Department X before ever it gets to Committee Y, but of course it must always be considered by Committee Y before anyone can take it on further—yet nowhere is all this written down. Everyone is supposed to know. After all, how else could it be done?

So the decision processes in the American owned subsidiaries were not encrusted with formalized rules to the extent anticipated; it was the British owned subsidiaries which mostly followed procedures, but these were unwritten customary ones. Taken together with the possibility that the British tend to make more use of formal committees, this implies that decision-making in the British owned subsidiaries was more institutionalized in general, following comparatively unvarying custom and practice both in meetings and in the sequence of things to be done and who must be involved, which was sufficiently known and accepted as not to require formalized documentation.

Recalling that the processes in US–H and US–J used working groups whereas those in UK–A and UK–M used special and standing committees, it can be suggested that in UK–A and UK–M the authority over a decision was formally institutionalized into the process by these committees. Special committees (task forces *etc.*) reported to standing committees directly or through managers who reported their results, the function of the standing committee then being collectively to legitimate action. In contrast, the working groups in the American owned subsidiaries did no more than collect and pool information and make recommendations.

But does traditional formal institutionalization slow things down? Table IV compares the duration of the twenty processes, in months, being the period from the first remembered inception of the topic, however casually introduced, to the authorization of a decision, whether to go ahead with implementation or to abandon the idea. The table follows Butler *et al.* (1982) in splitting duration into gestation time and process time. Gestation time is any period from the first inception of an issue (*e.g.* when someone said something about it, or information came in indicating a coming problem), during which nothing is done towards arriving at a decision, but awareness builds up towards the process time. A case does not necessarily have a discernable gestation period (see table IV). Process time follows, being the time period in which an issue becomes a recognized topic for decision, from the first step in the process of moving to a decision (*e.g.* an arranged discussion, or the appearance of the matter on an agenda) to approved choice (*i.e.* authorized decision). For example, the feasibility of bypassing wholesalers and selling direct to retailers had been informally discussed in US–H (topic 5) among various members of management, who came and left, for a gestation period of no less than fifteen years before eventually a working party initiated a rapid process period which led to the decision.

It can be been in table IV that in UK–A and UK–M the process periods far exceed those in US–H and US–J, indeed they are twice as long (mean 14·3 months against 7·4 months). This is very stark when the equivalent topics are compared. In US–H and US–J, new products are decided upon in 5 months and 2 months respectively as against the 6 months and 27 months it took to arrive at decisions in UK–A and UK–M (table IV: topic 1 in each case). New plant decisions also were far faster in US–H and US–J at 1 month and 3 months (table IV: topics 3 and 2) as against 30 months and 24 months in UK–A and UK–M (table IV: topic 2 in each case).

Moreover, gestation periods occur more often in the British owned subsidiaries. Although there are two exceptionally prolonged gestation periods in US–H4 and 5, both were due to the specific difficulties in overcoming or circumventing strong external opposed interests. The decision to stay out of a certain market was reaffirmed despite persistent American head office pressure to go in, and the decision to bypass wholesalers had to await it becoming possible to ignore them and their long connections with US–H. These two decisions are the exceptions. Far more often there are no gestation periods in the American owned subsidiaries, and they not only go right ahead with a decision process once the matter is raised but they then despatch it twice as fast, as Eggars (1977) surely believed they would.

The British owned subsidiaries more often contemplate the matter for months or years before moving in on it, and then take much longer to arrive at a decision. The unmodified institutionalization of their decision-making does seem to slow them down. Everyone knows anecdotes about committee procrastination, and these have never been summed up better than in the couplets published by Downs (1967, p. 160):

Committees of twenty
Deliberate plenty.

Committees of ten
Act now and then.

But most jobs get done
by committees of one.

The comparison in table IV suggests that this is true much more of the formalities of standing and special committees, especially the former, than it is of working groups.

It is interesting to wonder how far the gestation period serves for the British the same integrative function as their *nemawashi* phase serves for the Japanese. Does it enable fears to fade away, resistance to remove itself, communication to counsel understanding? Both societies are homogeneous with immemorial traditions and so may have aspects in common in their decision-making. Perhaps so, but if so then in the British case the gestation period does not speed up the action afterwards as the Japanese is believed to do. Is it more likely to reflect hesitancy, the reluctance to embark upon change noticed by Dubin (1970)?

As has already been said, the influences of American ownership and of organization size cannot be separated in the available sample. Samples of manufacturing subsidiaries of approximately the same sizes would be required for this. Among the thirty organizations of the larger study from which the subsidiaries examined here are drawn, there are four that are British owned and similar in size to the two American owned subsidiaries, and at first sight they give hopes of such a controlled comparison. Unfortunately, they are different in their outputs from the American owned subsidiaries, being a road transport firm, an insurance company, an industrial research association, and a brewery, and different in ownership status, three being independent firms and not subsidiaries. Thus the most controlled comparison available is the one made in this paper in which products and ownership statuses are similar, even though sizes are not. The interpretation that the differences found are due more to the influence from afar of corporation headquarters than to size is encouraged not only by their congruence with the implications of published research but by a lack of correlation between features of decision processes and organization size in the larger study.

SOME COMMENTS

This paper does not conclude with a section headed 'conclusions' for the small scale of the comparison leaves it with clues rather than conclusions.

There are clues to American ownership from afar having little or no influence on the way that decisions arise, the planning horizon, the range of possibilities that are looked at, the straight amount of interaction (as distinct from it forms) that is engaged in, and the level in the hierarchy at which the decision is ultimately authorized. In the terminology of tables III and IV, the ten decision-making processes in the two American owned subsidiaries differ hardly at all from the ten in the two British owned subsidiaries in their proactivity, horizon, scan, interaction volume, and centrality. Differences are less widespread than inferences from existing literature suggested.

But when it comes to the form and length of interaction, the ways in which the processes are typically arranged and conducted between those involved, differences are sharp enough to prompt further research. These are the differences in *interaction formality, procedural standardization,* and *process duration.*

In brief, the clues hint that British managements in British owned subsidiaries are prone to route their biggest decisions through the formalities of standing committees in conformity with pre-existing customary procedures and taking a comparatively long time to do so, often presaged by a prolonged gestation before anything at all is deliberately done. That is, high interaction formality, procedural standardization (unwritten), and duration.

Whereas British managements in American owned subsidiaries tend to rely on informally assembled working groups which help to arrive at a decision comparatively rapidly through a process which does not ostensibly follow any recognized procedure. That is, lower interaction formality, procedural standardization, and duration.

These results add to those of Jamieson (1980a, 1980b) on the informality and openness of personal relationships and managerial meetings, and begin to fill in a possible picture of process characteristics alongside what has often been reported on American/British structural differences. As with the probable process differences, these structural differences are not radical, but they do consistently show American organizations to have more formalized documentation than their British equivalents (*e.g.* Inkson *et al.*, 1970; Jamieson, 1980b; Richardson, 1956). This is commonly argued to be functionally equivalent to British traditionalism in effecting coordination and control, because the American ethnic miscellany requires more deliberate measures to hold it together whereas until very recent years those who had over centuries past contributed to the British mix had merged their differences into long evolved common traditions.

Overall, then, the American mode of making major decisions could be characterized as informal within a formalized frame, the British mode as formal within a non-formalized customary pattern.

Seen like this, the British mode is the more comprehensive in what it covers. No one in the firm, not the managing director nor the chairman, escapes control by custom. All must accept and conform. However, the formalization examined in the literature on bureaucratization (*e.g.* Blau, 1974; Hage, 1981; Hall, 1977; Pugh and Hickson, 1976) is of rules and procedures that govern lower echelons, including middle and senior managers, but do not, if the results in this paper are to be believed, govern the decision-making of the topmost élites themselves. They and their working groups pursue decisions untrammelled.

The argument has now ventured beyond the confines of this paper's coverage, subsidiaries in Britain, to expose the inference that the distinctive characteristics of decision-making in the American owned subsidiaries are indeed American (for they do plausibly accord with the other published research referred to) and that they will be found in the decision-making of American managements in the United States. This, of course, can only be confirmed by a processual study of U.S. firms in the U.S.A. Further, a fully controlled test of differences between subsidiaries would require a comparison of U.S. and U.K. subsidiaries both in a third country, as Jamieson (1980a) points out in assessing his data.

Nevertheless, it appears that multinational corporations can reach beyond the horizon to affect some at least of the interpersonal elements of decision-making processes. In the subsidiaries investigated in this paper they did so even without using their own expatriates, and without any special training of the local managers who only visited the owning corporation very briefly once in years, if ever. The American voice on the phone, the American stamp on the envelope, the telex print-out, the form to be completed, were sufficient. Possibly plus one other factor. Both the American owned subsidiaries had forceful chief executives, a judgment shared by the researchers who met them as well as conveyed by their managerial colleagues. They were men with a capacity to push things along if they wished to. It cannot be determined whether individuals with this characteristic were accidental in these positions, or developed it in response to what they perceived as the style looked for by the firm's owners, or were accurately selected for it. But selection of local managers in their own management image is obviously one means of control available to multinationals.

Of course, any effects brought about by the multinationals in these cases were in the most receptive setting, subsidiaries within the broad Anglo-Saxon English speaking culture, whatever the differences between the two societies. Given this, and that the distinctiveness of the American owned subsidiaries whilst important and interesting was far from total, then it is safer to assume that multinationals can affect only limited features of processes, particularly in societies with more contrasting cultures. Even expatriate representatives on the spot then face greater linguistic and normative barriers.

If process is relatively resistant, what about the decisions themselves? This paper has been wholly concerned with the ways in which decisions are made rather than with what the decisions are. However, it ends by turning to the question of the multinational's influence on what is decided.

Cray (1981) in an extensive study of American multinationals in Europe found that national preferences of the managements of the subsidiaries 'operate within a framework of structure, coordination, communication and control dictated by the American parent'. In the subsidiaries compared in this paper, US–H and US–J, they too worked within broad parameters set by headquarters. Their chief executives said so, and in US–H it was focused in the annual 'end of March panic' when their results for the first quarter of their year became available and remedial action to redress budget imbalances had to be taken as these became exposed to the eyes across the Atlantic. But the American parent attended primarily to budget parameters rather than getting involved in multifarious matters.

Was this borne out by the influence the American parents exerted on the ten major decisions in US–H and US–J? Their specific influence on each decision was commented on by those subject to it, the informants in the subsidiaries, and rated by them on a five-point influence scale (from 'a little influence' to 'a very great deal') which served to focus their perceptions. In both subsidiaries, multinational headquarters was seen as exerting its greatest influence on decisions which committed money, namely those on plant and equipment or the business plan (table II: US–H3; US–J2, 3, 5), and its least influence on those concerning products and marketing (table II: US–H1, 2, 4, 5; US–J1, 4). This supports the view that American multinationals do not enter into operating decisions, even those regarded as major, but rely primarily on financial controls.

Thus both in decisions and in decision-making the multinational permits wide scope to its subsidiary managements. It sets ultimate limits to decisions but within these grants considerable freedom, and it affects some aspects of decision-making but probably most are typically indigenous. But whereas its effects on decisions are deliberate and known to managers in headquarters and subsidiaries alike, its probable effects on decision-making have gone unseen.

NOTES

[1] This research was supported financially by the British Social Science Research Council and the University of Bradford Management Centre.

REFERENCES

AJIBOYE, GBENGA Y. (1980). *Control in Nigerian Organizations: Hierarchy and Functional Differentiation*. Master of Business Administration Dissertation. University of Bradford.

ASTLEY, W. GRAHAM, AXELSSON, RUNO, BUTLER, RICHARD J., HICKSON, DAVID J. and WILSON, DAVID C. (1982). 'Complexity and cleavage: dual explanations of strategic decision-making.' *Journal of Management Studies*, **19**, 4, 357–75.

BLAU, PETER M. (1974). *On the Nature of Organizations*. New York: Wiley.

BUDDE, ANDREAS, CHILD, JOHN, FRANCIS, ARTHUR and KIESER, ALFRED. (1982). 'Corporate goals, managerial objectives, and organizational structures in British and West German companies'. *Organizational Studies*, **3**, 1.

BUTLER, RICHARD J., ASTLEY, W. GRAHAM, HICKSON, DAVID J., MALLORY, GEOFFREY R. and WILSON, DAVID C. (1979/80). 'Strategic decision-making: concepts of content and process'. *International Studies of Management and Organization*, **IX**, 4, 5–32.

BUTLER, RICHARD J., ASTLEY, W. GRAHAM, CRAY, DAVID, HICKSON, DAVID J., MALLORY, GEOFFREY R. and WILSON, DAVID C. (1982). 'Strategic decision-making: a large scale study'. (forthcoming).

CHILD, JOHN (1981). 'Culture, contingency and capitalism in the cross-national study of organizations'. In Cummings, L. L. and Staw, B. M. (Eds.), *Research in Organizational Behavior*, Vol. 3. Greenwich, Conn: JAI Press.

CHILD, JOHN and MACMILLAN, BRENDA (1972). 'Managerial leisure in British and American contexts'. *Journal of Management Studies*, **9**, 2, 182–193.

CLARK, PETER (1979). 'Cultural context as a determinant of organizational rationality: a comparison of the tobacco industries in Britain and France'. In Lammers, C. J. and Hickson, D. J. (Eds.), *Organizations Alike and Unlike*. London: Routledge and Kegan Paul.

CRAY, DAVID (1981). 'Control in multinational corporations'. Paper presented at the meetings of the American Sociological Association, 1980: to appear in Bacharach, S. B. (Ed.), *Yearbook of Organizational Sociology*.

DOWNS, ANTONY (1967). *Inside Bureaucracy*. Boston: Little Brown.

DUBIN, ROBERT (1970). 'Management in Britain: impressions of a visiting professor'. *Journal of Management Studies*, **7**, 2, 183–198.

EGGARS, E. RUSSELL (1977). 'How to do business with a frenchman'. In Weinshall, T. D. (Ed.), *Culture and Management*. Harmondsworth: Penguin.

GRANICK, DAVID (1962). *The European Executive*. London: Weidenfeld and Nicolson.

HAGE, JERALD (1981). *Theories of Organizations: Form, Process and Transformation*. New York: Wiley.

HALL, RICHARD, H. (1977). *Organizations: Structure and Process.* (2nd edition). Englewood Cliffs, N.J.: Prentice-Hall.

HICKSON, DAVID J. and McMILLAN, CHARLES J. (1981). *Organization and Nation: The Aston Programme IV.* Farnborough: Gower.

HICKSON, DAVID J., BUTLER, RICHARD, J., CRAY, DAVID, MALLORY, GEOFFREY R. and WILSON, DAVID C. (1982). 'Decisional differences in decision-making: subject and process'. (forthcoming).

INKSON, J. H. K., SCHWITTER, J. P., PHEYSEY, D. C. and HICKSON, D. J. (1970). 'A comparison of organizational structure and managerial roles: Ohio, U.S.A. and Midlands, England'. *Journal of Management Studies,* **7,** 3, 347–363.

JAMIESON, IAN (1980a). Capitalism and culture: a comparative analysis of British and American manufacturing organizations'. *Sociology,* **14,** 2, 217–246.

JAMIESON, IAN (1980b). *Capitalism and Culture: A Comparative Analysis of British and American Manufacturing Organizations.* Farnborough: Gower.

KELLEY, LANE and WORTHLEY, REGINALD (1981). 'The role of culture in comparative management: a cross-cultural perspective'. *Academy of Management Journal,* **24,** 1, 164–73.

KIDD, JOHN B. and TERAMOTO, YOSHIYA (1981). 'Japanese production subsidiaries in the United Kingdom: a study of managerial decision-making'. *Working Paper,* No. 203, University of Aston Management Centre.

McMILLAN, C. J., HICKSON, D. J., HININGS, C. R. and SCHNECK, R. E. (1973). 'The structure of work organizations across societies'. *Journal of Academy of Management,* **16,** 4, 555–69.

NEGANDHI, ANANT R. (1979). 'Convergence in organizational practices: an empirical study of industrial enterprises in developing countries'. In Lammers, C. J. and Hickson, D. J. (Eds.), *Organizations Alike and Unlike,* London: Routledge and Kegan Paul.

PUGH, DEREK S. and HICKSON, DAVID J. (1976). *Organizational Structure in its Context: The Aston Programme I.* Farnborough and New York: Saxon House and D. C. Heath.

RICHARDSON, S. A. (1956). 'Organizational contrasts in British and American ships'. *Administrative Science Quarterly,* **1,** 3, 189–207.

ROBERTS, KARLENE (1970). 'On looking at an elephant: an evaluation of cross-cultural research related to organizations'. *Psychological Bulletin,* **74,** 5, 327–50.

TANNENBAUM, ARNOLD, S. (1968). *Control in Organizations.* New York: McGraw-Hill.

WILSON, DAVID C. (1982). 'Electricity and resistance: a case study of innovation and politics. *Organization Studies,* **3,** 2.

Name Index